THE THEORY AND PRACTICE OF

PARTNERSHIP TAXATION

By

Darryll K. Jones

Associate Dean and Associate Professor of Law
University of Pittsburgh School of Law

AMERICAN CASEBOOK SERIES®

THOMSON

WEST

Mat #40306233

American Casebook Series and West Group are trademarks registered in the U.S. Patent and Trademark Office.

© 2005 West, a Thomson business
     610 Opperman Drive
     P.O. Box 64526
     St. Paul, MN 55164–0526
     1–800–328–9352

Printed in the United States of America

ISBN 0–314–15624–0

TEXT IS PRINTED ON 10% POST
CONSUMER RECYCLED PAPER

Acknowledgment

"Praise God from whom all blessings flow"

Thanks to David H. Kirk (Pitt Law, 2005) and Omar S. Mir (Pitt Law, 2005) for their helpful review and comments on earlier drafts.

*

A Note to Students and Teachers

I wrote this book because I realized that most of my partnership tax students completed the course without having read significant portions of the Subchapter K regulations. I will admit that I too "successfully" completed partnership tax without having read significant portions of the Subchapter K regulations. I read and closely studied all the assigned code and regulations, the author summaries, and the cases and rulings. I completed all the casebook problems and performed fairly well on a difficult exam. But I didn't read and re-read large sections of the Subchapter K regulations. Authors generally assign very selective portions to save time, even while including lots of secondary material in the casebook the reading of which takes up time. I also read only a relative few of the numerous and helpful examples in the regulations (there are nearly 60 examples in Regulation 1.704–1(b)(5) alone!). There was simply too much casebook material and not enough time to read everything. Like many students, I improvised. I "learned the casebook."

Existing partnership casebooks and treatises contain wonderfully detailed explanations of Subchapter K. For my students, at least, the casebook or treatise invariably became an obstacle or a crutch. The casebooks are so well written that students, short on time as they often are, could actually gain a sufficient understanding merely be reading the author's summary. This is a good testament to the skill and knowledge of partnership tax authors and experts. But after they "successfully" completed partnership tax, many students expressed a nagging sense of doubt regarding whether they really understood the fundamentals (nevermind the mechanics for a moment) of Subchapter K. I attribute this to the fact that existing casebooks are indeed so well written that students are discouraged, unintentionally, from reading most of the Subchapter K regulations. I may be engaging in what psychologists refer to as transference— projecting my feelings onto students. But I have found at least the following to be undeniable: If time-pressed students are faced with the choice of reading tax regulations and detailed examples, or an author's summary and less detailed examples, they will chose the latter.

The pedagogy of any tax course seeks at least two outcomes. One outcome is that students learn an existing scheme of taxation, whether the course involves individual, partnership, corporate, or estate and gift taxation. This outcome can no doubt be achieved by use of casebooks and the like. The second outcome, though, is that students learn the theory, language and syntax of the tax jurisprudence so that they can teach themselves, clients, judges, and legislators new schemes of taxation as the need arises. The second outcome also provides students with the tools to fix or intelligently apply existing schemes as opportunities arise in their lives as tax professionals. The second outcome, it seems to me, can only be achieved by deciphering the statute and regulations for oneself. That skill takes practice and is only delayed by helpful summaries, regardless of how accurate or clearly written.

It just so happens that using a pedagogical method that focuses almost exclusively on primary sources—the code and regulations— achieves both outcomes. The prevailing *de facto* pedagogical method that many students adopt—reading casebook summaries and examples— achieves only the first outcome. And if students forsake the code and regulations because of time concerns, the *de facto* pedagogical method actually prevents achievement of the second and more important outcome. For these reasons, this book strives to preclude the *de facto* learning method. Subjects are divided into Lessons and each Lesson contains a [hopefully] brief discussion of theory only. Rarely do the Lessons provide a restatement of statutory or regulatory mechanics, or provide examples of how the mechanics should be applied to a particular transaction. Two subjects—the introduction of capital accounting, and disproportionate distributions—are just so unfamiliar and time consuming that detailed explanations and examples are unavoidable. Nevertheless, this book relies on the detail and examples in the code and regulations to teach the mechanics. Practice problems are taken directly from examples in the regulations (except when the regulations do not provide examples) so that students can do two things at once—read as many examples as possible and apply learned concepts to new situations. Those new situations are created by merely changing a fact or two in examples and asking students to reconstruct the outcome. Hence, students must read the examples to complete the problems.

This book and its process may be a bit more difficult and anxious for students during the first week or two of the course than it would be if students were provided with traditional author summaries and step by step examples. But once students realize that they can actually master a detailed regulation or a complicated example by themselves, they will lose their anxiety and learn more. In any event, because each Lesson strives for brevity, students will have more time to read more of the Subchapter K regulations and examples. That's my theory and I'm sticking to it.

A final word on methodology: Students should read the summaries for each Lesson in the table of contents. Then, each Lesson cites to primary references—code and regulations and sometimes administrative materials (e.g., Revenue Rulings and Procedures)—that students must read and re-read. It is alright, and probably preferable for most students, to read the theoretical discussion before reading the assigned code and regulations. In practice, you will no doubt be oriented to an issue before diving into statutory and regulatory detail. The theoretical discussion is designed to orient students to the academic issue at hand.

Lessons also contain citations to secondary and case references that are very helpful but need not be read. Indeed, students should rarely read secondary references, as they will be sufficiently referred to in the brief theoretical discussion. Students should certainly read primary materials two or three times before devoting scarce time to secondary sources. That may sound strange, but the goal is to obtain a broad and detailed understanding of Subchapter K, proper. The goal is not to spend precious time on nuance or judicial gloss as you would and should when you graduate and actually practice partnership taxation. A broad and detailed understanding of the Code and regulations will (1) make the nuances obvious now or in your practice, and (2) provoke and allow you to recognize and research the unanswered questions when you actually practice partnership tax law. Practice is for the purpose of learning nuance (and making a living). Spending time on nuance at this point will merely delay or prevent a broad and detailed understanding. You will know a bit of trivia, really, but the big picture may elude you.

I may yet be proven wrong regarding my pedagogical philosophy. All I know for sure is that I came to appreciate the complex beauty of partnership tax only after I thought to discard my own crutches and read the Subchapter K provisions for myself. I welcome comments from students and teachers as well.

DARRYLL K. JONES

Pittsburgh, Pennsylvania
November, 2004

*

Table of Contents

Lesson 1 examines the tax cost factors that influence business owners' choice of entity decisions. Students will read and understand the "check the box regulations," ponder the meaning of an "entity" for tax purposes and then read and critique an actual choice of entity analysis. Students also consider the use of partnerships for improper purposes and are introduced to the partnership anti-abuse regulations insofar as those regulations relate to the question whether an alleged partnership should be recognized for tax purposes.

Lesson 2 examines the tax reporting requirements pertaining to partnerships. Students are introduced to the "entity" and "aggregate" approaches to partnership taxation. Students will complete an actual Form 1065, and Schedule K–1. The main goal of this exercise is to gain an overview of partnership taxation by use of the Form 1065 and Schedule K–1 instructions. Students will learn that partnership items are characterized at the partnership level under an entity approach and that elections must be made at the partnership level as well. Students are introduced to "hot assets" via IRC 724, which mandates partner level characterization of certain gains and losses realized by the partnership.

Lesson 3 examines the special audit procedures applicable to most partnerships. The aggregate theory of taxation interferes with proper administration and therefore audit and litigation procedures are based on the entity theory of partnership taxation. Students will understand the importance of the "tax matters partner," as well as the consistency and notice requirements applicable to partners and the IRS.

Lesson 4 begins the introduction of the single most important concept regarding partnership taxation—that regarding the proper maintenance of partnership capital accounts. Students will be introduced to the basic capital accounting rules pertaining to all phases of a partnership's life— contribution, operation, distribution, revaluation, liquidations, and terminations. It is most imperative that students have a firm grasp of the basic rules before proceeding. Finally, students will learn terminology applicable to tax/book balance sheet, including the meaning of "book gain or loss".

Lesson 5 considers the methods by which individuals obtain partnership interests directly from the partnership (as opposed to a purchase from an existing partner). Students will understand how fundamental rules of income taxation—sale or exchange, basis, amount realized and recognition, and transferred basis—apply to partnership formations and contributions to ongoing partnerships. Students will also analyze the treatment of liability assumption and discharge in conjunction with a purchase of partnership interests directly from the partnership.

Lesson 6 considers the tax consequences when a service provider receives an interest in partnership capital as compensation. Tax/book accounts as they might have appeared in *McDougal v. Commissioner* are utilized to demonstrate how fundamental income tax principles contained in IRC 61 and 1001 are implicated when a "service partner" receives a capital interest. Students will understand that a partnership may recognize gain or loss upon the transfer of capital as compensation and how a single transaction is deconstructed to determine tax consequences to all parties.

Lesson 7 considers how service partners are taxed upon the receipt of a partnership "profit interest" as compensation for services. The Lesson summarizes the largely unexpected, yet fundamentally sound conclusion in *Diamond v. Commissioner*. *Diamond* concludes, on rather unique facts, that the receipt of a profit interest constitutes taxable income. The IRS' subsequent reversal of *Diamond* begins with *Campbell v. Commissioner* and was completed with the issuance of Revenue Procedures 93–27 and 2001–43, both of which are reprinted in this lesson.

Lesson 8 begins the discussion of a fundamental goal of Subchapter K. It demonstrates how a partner's outside basis is used as an accounting method designed to ensure that income and deductions are taxed at least once but only once. The maintenance of each partner's outside basis takes into account previously taxed income and deductions in a manner designed to ensure single taxation. The effect of current and liquidating distributions on outside basis is shown to be consistent with this goal. Students will understand the interplay between the recognition of gain or loss from distributions and the goal of ensuring that income and deductions are taxed once and only once.

Lesson 9 continues the discussion regarding the overall purpose of basis in Subchapter K. It demonstrates that the partnership's aggregate basis in held assets should equal the partners' aggregate outside basis if income and deductions are to be taxed at least once but only once. The Lesson shows, however, that because of the basis rules applicable to property distributions, a partnership's aggregate inside basis may be greater or less than partners' aggregate outside basis, allowing for deferral of taxation. Students will learn that IRC 754 allows optional adjustments to inside basis to correct this deferral. Students consider the planning opportunities and pitfalls of a 754 election.

Lesson 10 lays a necessary foundation for proper understanding of the rules regarding the determination of partners' distributive shares. It uses *Orrisch v. Commissioner* and Revenue Ruling 99–43 to demonstrate the tax planning opportunities that IRC 704(b) and accompanying regulations are designed to limit. The case and the ruling preview the concepts of "economic effect" and "substantiality." Those concepts form the backbone of the 704(b) regulations. Students will identify the factors that raise a suspicion that partnership allocations should not be respected.

Lesson 11 begins the consideration of the detailed safe harbor rules regulating the manner in which partners may divide the tax liabilities arising from partnership operations amongst themselves. The Lesson begins by relating the perceived harms in *Orrisch* and Revenue Ruling 99–43 to the regulatory detail in Regulation 1.704–1(b). Students will review an actual partnership agreement which demonstrates how the economic effect test is articulated in actual practice. Students will understand the primary and alternate rules of economic effect, the importance of qualified income offset (QIO) provisions. They will also understand that the concept of "substantiality" as it relates to tax deferral or character conversion.

Lesson 12 contains an in-depth study of the meaning of "partner's interest in the partnership," a vague concept that applies primarily as a result of insufficient tax planning or purposeful tax avoidance. Students will understand that PIP is based on the unique facts and circumstances of each case, though there are at least three generic rules that apply, respectively, when allocations lack economic effect, violate the deficit reduction rule pertaining to the alternate economic effect test, or lack substantiality. There are two "optional reading" cases reprinted in this Lesson.

Lesson 13 relates the holdings of *Crane v. Commissioner* and *Commissioner v. Tufts* to the problem of dividing deductions generated by nonrecourse borrowing amongst partners. The lesson demonstrates the economic illogic of allowing deductions to persons who, as an economic matter, do not also possess the burdens and risks of property ownership. Because *Crane* and *Tufts* nevertheless mandates deductions be claimed by nominal owners, Regulations 1.704–2 assigns nonrecourse deductions to partners under the assumption that partners will eventually take on the burdens and risks of property ownership. Students will learn a new vocabulary in this lesson, including "partnership minimum gain," "nonrecourse deductions," and "minimum gain chargeback." They will review a partnership agreement to see how that new vocabulary is utilized in actual practice.

Lesson 14 considers the application of assignment of income principles in the partnership context. It reminds students of fundamental lessons taught by *Lucas v. Earl, Helvering v. Horst,* and *Helvering v. Eubanks.* The fundamental lessons of those cases are contained in the rule that pre-contribution gains and losses from property must be taxed to the partner who owned the property when those gains and losses accrued. Students will easily recognize the concept and then will learn how the concept is applied via the "traditional," "curative" and "remedial" allocation methods. This lesson will provide opportunity to further understand the capital accounting rules, the distinctions between tax and book accounting, and reverse 704(c) allocations that result when partnerships "book-up" capital accounts. Students will also consider the allocation of recapture gain.

Lesson 15 returns again to *Crane v. Commissioner* and *Commissioner v. Tufts.* It demonstrates how the fundamental assumption of those cases is applied in the partnership setting. The assumption is that partners get basis credit for borrowed money because they will eventually repay the money using after-tax income. Partners therefore get basis credit for recourse liabilities in accordance with their deficit reduction obligation. Partners get basis credit for nonrecourse liabilities in accordance with the manner in which profits are allocated. Both methods of giving basis credit for liabilities are based on an estimation of which partner will actually pay the liability.

Lesson 16 considers the tax consequences upon the sale of a partnership interest. It shows how the aggregate theory of partnership tax is applied to characterize gains and losses under IRC 751(a) and 741. Students will understand that a sale of a single item of property (the partnership interest) is treated a sale of several properties (the partner's proportionate share of each asset held by the partnership). The Lesson will also return to the notion that basis is a means to assure income and deductions are taxed once and only once. Students will see that upon purchase of a partnership interest, a buyer may subsequently be over- or under-taxed depending on the nature of the assets held by the partnership. IRC 754, and in some instances 732(d), allow an adjustment to the buying partner's share of inside basis to prevent over- or under-taxation.

Lesson 17 considers the question whether partners can logically engage in sales or exchanges with their own partnerships. The question arises primarily if the partnership is viewed as an aggregate rather than an entity. IRC 707 resolves the issue by treating the partnership as an entity with regard to transactions with partners if the partner is performing services not within the scope of her reasonable obligations as a partner, or if the partnership is treating the partner as though she were an unrelated employee or service provider with a fixed right to payment regardless of partnership income.

Lesson 18 considers the manner in which payments made to a retiring partner or a deceased partner's estate are taxed. IRC 736 essentially performs a traffic directing purpose whereby liquidating payments are treated as distributions, distributive shares, or guaranteed payments. Once payments are classified under IRC 736(a) or (b), they are taxed under previously learned Subchapter K rules.

Lesson 19 considers the Subchapter K rules that determine a partnership's taxable year. Students will understand that a partnership taxable year is determined by reference to the taxable years of the primary partners—as determined by ownership interests—and in a manner that precludes manipulation for tax deferral purposes. In addition, Lesson 18 considers the methods by which partnerships are considered terminated for federal tax purposes and the rather limited but important consequences of "technical terminations." Finally, students will consider the issues relating to the closing of a partnership's taxable year with respect to a deceased partner.

Lesson 20 is the first of five lessons (Lessons 20–24) that deal with abuses and anti-abuse provisions. Students will become painfully aware that much of the volume and complexity in Subchapter K results from Congressional efforts to curb tax avoidance. The at-risk and passive activity rules demonstrate how abuses and anti-abuses can escalate in never-ending battle between tax avoiders and tax collectors.

All lessons from this point primarily involve the application of previously learned individual and partnership tax provisions to new transactional contexts. Lesson 19 deals with taxpayer efforts to accelerate deductions or defer income. Because an allocation of income to one partner reduces taxable income to others, an allocation can be used to generate the equivalent of a deduction for the partnership when a deduction would otherwise be denied under IRC 263. The contribution and distribution rules provide opportunity for tax avoidance, as for example, when a sale or exchange is treated instead as a contribution followed by a distribution. In the latter instance, the nonrecognition rules of Subchapter K allows for deferral. IRC 707(a)(2) attempts to apply objective rules to determine whether a transaction is a contribution or a sale. Once the determination is made, familiar rules of IRC 1001, 162, and 263 are applied to a sale, and 721, 731, and 732 are applied to a contribution and distribution.

Lesson 22 concerns a second previously popular abuse known as "mixing bowl transactions." Previously learned Subchapter K rules pertaining to contributions and distributions of property allow for assignment or deferral with regard to built-in gains and losses. IRC 704(c)(1)(b) and 737 are designed to accelerate gains and losses to avoid improper taxation or deferral. Students will recall that Subchapter K's goal is to impose the same tax liability on partners as would be imposed on similar transactions outside of the partnership setting. As a result, exchanges that would not be taxed if undertaken in a non-partner status (like-kind exchanges) are exempted from IRC 704(c)(1)(B).

Lesson 23 continues the review and application of familiar individual and partnership tax principles to new transactions. The Lesson demonstrates Subchapter K's arguably inordinate concern with conversion of income opportunities (particularly when the gap between capital and ordinary rates is small). This Lesson probably provides more opportunity to learn the interrelationship of partnership and individual tax provisions than any other. Students will get a more in-depth concern for "hot assets" and will likely conclude that any benefits resulting from disproportionate distributions (when a partnership holds hot assets) are not worth the transactional and administrative costs.

Lesson 24 considers the problems and abuses that arise from changes in a partner's partnership interest during the taxable year. Students will understand the "proration" and "interim closing of the books" method by which allocations are made with respect to partners' varying interest in the partnership. Students will also understand the Congressional response to "retroactive allocations."

Lesson 25 considers the tax consequences when partnerships convert to or from different entities ("partnership to partnership conversions, or conversions to and from sole proprietorships) or reorganize (mergers or division). Students will determine the consequences of conversions and reorganizations by applying previously learned Subchapter K concepts to new transactions. In particular, students will apply capital accounting rules, distribution rules, liability allocation rules and 704(c) rules to determine tax consequences upon conversion, mergers, and divisions. This Lesson relies heavily on revenue rulings because Subchapter K contains very little explicit guidance with regard to conversions and reorganizations. For example, Revenue Ruling 2004–43 applies many of the previously learned Subchapter K rules in articulating the concept of "new" 704(c) gain.

Lesson 26 uses tiered partnerships to complete the review of Subchapter K fundamentals. Perceptive students will recognize that the review actually began in Lesson 21—students actually completed the course after Lesson 20—and continues through this Lesson. Indeed, there have been very few, if any, new principles introduced after Lesson 20. Instead, old principles have been applied and adapted to new, frequently encountered situations. This is the essence of legal practice. The issues discussed in this lesson might therefore have been interspersed in various other lessons. It is helpful to a complete understanding, though, to recognize that there are a relative few principles to understand in partnership taxation, and those principles provide reasonable solutions to varied circumstances that seem unfamiliar at first. Tiered partnerships are considered separately, in part to reinforce to students that they really can and (if they have put forth some effort) do understand Subchapter K.

Table of Cases

The principal cases are in bold type. Cases cited or discussed in the text are roman type. References are to pages. Cases cited in principal cases and within other quoted materials are not included.

*

THE THEORY AND PRACTICE OF

PARTNERSHIP TAXATION

*

Lesson 1

CHOICE OF ENTITY

Primary References: IRC 761(a), (b); 7701(a)(2), (3)(a)–(b)
Treas. Reg. 301.7701–1,–2,–3, (check the box regulations)
Treas. Reg. 1.701–2(a)–(d) Examples 1–4, 1.701–2(e)–(f) Examples 1–2 (anti-abuse regulations), 1.701–2(i)

Case References: **Brown Group, Inc. v. Commissioner, 77 F.3d 217 (1996)**
ASA Investerings Partnership v. Commissioner, 201 F.3d 505 (D.C. Cir. 2000)

Theory

Most every business tax text begins with a rather obligatory discussion of the tax considerations informing an owner's decision regarding whether to conduct business as a sole proprietor, a partnership or LLC, an S corporation or a C corporation. The discussions are too brief and disconnected from the myriad provisions of the tax code that should inform an owner's choice of entity. In most business tax books, including this one, brevity is necessary because there usually is not even enough space (or time) to cover the entity specific tax rules to which the book and its associated course is devoted. Ideally, though, choice of entity ought to be considered in a stand-alone course that is last in a sequence of business and tax courses. A business tax student might study business organizations, agency and partnership, federal income tax, corporate tax, mergers and acquisitions (corporate tax, part II), partnership tax, S corporations, and only then undertake a thorough study of business planning in a stand-alone course. But we do not live in an ideal world. The following discussion is not intended to analyze the substantive tax considerations informing choice of entity. The task, as with entity planning in general, is merely to identify relevant tax considerations. As already implied, substantive tax results are analyzed in separate courses devoted to different entities.

1

One tax oriented choice of entity method is to compare the tax costs and opportunities of each available entity option. In general, there are three types of costs: (1) entry costs refer to the potential taxes imposed when assets are transferred to a new business, or when an entity converts from one form to another, (2) operating costs refer to the tax costs pertaining to the business' income, gain, loss and deductions, and (3) exit costs refer to the taxation of liquidations or reorganizations. In most instances there is no tax cost when a business begins, except for a person who becomes an owner as a result of the performance of services (see Lesson 6, regarding service partners). There may also be tax costs when an entity converts from one form to another. *See* Treas. Reg. 301.7701–3(g)(1) (2004).

Operating costs most often refer to how income is taxed and losses are claimed. For example, in a C corporation, income will be subject to "double taxation," while in pass thru form income will be subject to single taxation. In C corporation, owners cannot themselves deduct losses directly, but S corporation and partnership owners allow losses to pass through to the owners (hence, the phrase "pass-thru" entity). This is an especially relevant consideration for start-ups, which might suffer a few years of losses before becoming profitable. C corporations are also subject to tax on the increase in asset values, while pass thru entities are not. See IRC 311(b). Prior to the Jobs Growth and Tax Relief and Reconciliation Act of 2003, C corporations nevertheless offered some opportunity for tax advantaged accumulations since rates were lower on the first $75,000 earned by corporations than they were on like amounts earned by individuals. This is no longer true, though, as discussed in the following article. A C corporation might still result in lower tax costs for owners who want to reinvest any amount in excess of $75,000 back into the business. In any event, different tax rates should be considered when making predictions regarding operating costs.

Exit costs refer to taxes that might apply upon liquidation or acquisition of the entity or of an owner's individual interest. Generally, liquidations of partnerships result in less tax than liquidations of corporations since partnerships are not subject to an entity tax on appreciated assets. In general, a corporation's distribution of appreciated asset will result in taxable gain to the corporation. On the other hand, sales of corporate stock are taxed at advantageous capital gains rates. In many instances, sales of partnership interests will be taxed at higher ordinary rates. The amount realized from the sale of a partnership interest is allocated to the underlying partnership assets that comprise the partnership interest. Corporate reorganizations can also be structured with more predictable nonrecognition effects than partnership reorganizations, though with the 2001 amendment to the IRC 708 regulations the distinction may no longer be as significant. In most instances, partnership reorganizations can be accomplished without recognition of gain, though there is a much less voluminous body of case law and rulings to guide the process.

Tax opportunities refer to specific advantages that may arise from the use of one entity rather than another. Partnerships, for example, allow owners to divide tax liabilities and compensate for risks in many different ways via "special allocations" and preferential distributions. S Corporations cannot make special allocations. Corporations allow owners who are not also employees to avoid employment taxes and historically have granted more advantageous treatment of employee benefits, such as health care premiums and the like. Corporations also allow profit to be withdrawn at the lower capital gains rate, while pass thru entities do not. Of course this advantage is often eliminated by the entity level tax on C Corporations.

The foregoing discussion, and indeed the application of the "check-the-box" regulations, assume that an actual business entity exists for tax purposes. But not every joint undertaking creates a business entity. Read regulation 301.7701–1(a)(2) closely. The first sentence summarizes, with deceptive simplicity, the basic requirements pertaining to the existence of a business entity for tax purposes. Two or more participants must (1) carry on a trade or business, financial operation, or venture, and (2) divide the profits from the trade, business, financial operation or venture. The regulation also states that it is not sufficient that two or more persons share expenses, or co-own property from which income is derived. These two basic requirements have mushroomed into a mountain of case law that attempts to distinguish a host of non-business relationships from those that actually create an entity for tax purposes. The ultimate question in all cases is whether the participants actually intended to associate together in a profit-seeking activity and divide the profits among themselves. The cases are far too legion to elevate one or the other by inclusion in this lesson. A review of one of the major partnership tax treatises,[1] however, indicates that the problem of distinguishing business entities from other relationships arises in the following contexts: (1) hobby groups, i.e., a group of people who pool resources to pursue a shared, non-profit making activity, (2) expense sharing arrangements, for example when two lawyers share office space and administrative employees but do not otherwise integrate their practices, (3) employee profit sharing arrangements whereby an employer compensates an employee by reference to a profit percentage, (4) pay-out arrangements involving the sale of a business, the price for which is contingent upon the future profits of the business, (5) debtor/creditor arrangements that give the lender so many rights (for example, extensive veto or management participation rights) that she may be something more than a creditor, and (6) lease arrangements in which the lessor participates to such an extent in the operation of the property that he might more accurately be treated as a partner.

---

1. William S. McKee, William F. Nelson, Robert L. Whitmire, FEDERAL TAXATION OF PARTNERSHIPS AND PARTNERS, ¶ 3.02 (1997 with 2003 supplement). This source provides a comprehensive, annotated discussion of the many cases in which the question of entity existence is litigated.

More recently, the existence of an entity for tax purposes has arisen in the context of tax shelter transactions. The Service has frequently challenged the very existence of an entity when the participants appear only to be seeking tax benefits (rather than after-tax profit) by use of an alleged entity. These efforts have resulted in a great deal of time and energy being devoted to the basis question, "what is a business entity?" They prove that the question is not merely prefatory or academic.

Usually, the issue arises when taxpayers engage in what seem like unnecessarily complex transactions but which result in a tax benefit. Most such cases are difficult to conceptualize at first. The following discussion summarizes one such complex transaction. Readers should not concern themselves with the substance of Subpart F or the detailed complexity, but rather on whether the described partnership should have been recognized as a business entity.

In *Brown Group, Inc. v. Commissioner,* a 100% U.S. corporate parent of a controlled foreign corporation ("CFC") avoided tax on "Subpart F income" by forming a partnership. The CFC held an 88% interest in the partnership. The CFC served as purchasing broker for its parent corporation prior to the partnership's formation; the partnership took over that function using the same persons the CFC had previously used. By use of the partnership, however, the CFC and its affiliated entities were able to pay those persons more compensation (and thereby expect better performance). If the CFC itself had earned commissions as buying agent, the commissions would have been immediately taxable to the U.S. shareholder as "subpart F income." This is because the CFC would have been purchasing foreign goods for, or on behalf of a related party (the controlling parent corporation), a fact that would trigger subpart F income and immediate taxation. If the purchases were made neither for nor on behalf of a related party, the commissions would not have been subpart F income. The partnership in which the CFC held an 88% interest was not a related party (under prior law) to the CFC or the parent corporation, even though the CFC was its majority owner. The partnership thereby earned income as a buying agent for the U.S. parent corporation (just as the CFC would have done directly) and passed that income to the CFC, free of its subpart F income taint. Hence, by interposing a partnership between itself and buyers, the CFC avoided being cast as the purchaser of goods on behalf of a related party. In this manner, the U.S. parent corporation successfully avoided tax on income otherwise immediately taxable.

One theory the Service somewhat implicitly asserted was that the partnership should not be recognized as a business entity because it had no business purpose. This argument may have been factually correct, but it had no statutory or regulatory support at the time. The anti-abuse regulations were not yet in effect, though the court might have applied judicial doctrines, such as the sham transaction principle or the lack of business purpose. As the Court noted, however, the Service might have been successful had the partnership anti-abuse regulations been promulgated sooner. Regulation 1.701–2 recognizes the legitimacy of considering tax costs in choice of entity decisions but also incorporates, as a first principle, the basic requirement that to be recognized for tax purposes, a partnership must be formed for a "substantial business purpose." An entity that runs afoul of the anti-abuse regulations may be disregarded under Regulation 1.701–2(e). That is, a partnership without a substantial business purpose may not be an entity at all!

Practice:

1. How might *Brown Group, Inc.* have been decided under the anti-abuse regulations? Are there any facts in the summary above that might support an argument that the partnership should have been recognized as an entity even if the anti-abuse regulations were in effect at the time?

2. Read Regulation 301.7701–1(a)(2) again. Does the regulation leave you with a sense of confidence that you can distinguish between an entity and a joint undertaking that does not give rise to entity status? Consider the following questions based on passages from the regulation:

> If two or more persons jointly construct a ditch merely to drain surface water from their properties, they have not created a separate entity for federal tax purposes.

a. Why would these facts not create an entity?

> Similarly, mere co-ownership of property that is maintained, kept in repair, and rented or leased does not constitute a separate entity for federal tax purposes. For example, if an individual owner, or tenants in common, of farm property lease it to a farmer for a cash rental or a share of the crops, they do not necessarily create a separate entity for federal tax purposes.

b. Why doesn't the preceding arrangement necessarily create an entity? Aren't the co-owners jointly exploiting property for profit?

3. What facts would you look for in discovery if you were litigating for or against the assertion of entity status?

4. Read Treasury Regulation 1.701–2(d), Example 3 again. If the parties intentionally adopted partnership form to take advantage of the higher foreign tax credit, why is the partnership nevertheless respected as an entity?

5. Read Treasury Regulation 1.701–2(f), Examples 1 and 2 again. What general principle of law can be derived from those examples?

6. For purposes of this practice question, recall that the installment sale rule, 14A.453–1(c)(3)(i), states that in an installment sale where the maximum selling price cannot be determined but the period over which payments are made is known, seller's basis is recovered in equal amounts over the period of time payments are to be made. If seller's basis is $100 and payments, the amounts of which will vary, are required over five years, seller recovers $20 basis per year. Any payment in excess of amortized basis is income in the year received. For example, payment of $30 in year 1 would result in $10 income to seller.

Suppose *A* expects to realize $2,400,000 in capital gains and wishes to avoid the tax liability by generating a loss from another transaction. A forms a partnership with a foreign entity not subject to U.S. tax, supplying the partnership with $1,000,000 and inducing the partner to supply $9,0000,000. The partnership pays $10,000,000 for property eligible for installment sale treatment under § 453, and, as the ink is drying on the purchase documents, sells the property, for $5,000,000 in cash and a variable payment, five-year debt instrument. The cash payment produces a gain of $3,000,000 ($5,000,000 minus $2,000,000 basis allocable to the first year), 90% of which goes to the nontaxable foreign entity. Then ownership adjustments are made so that *A* owns 90% of the partnership. In year 2 the instrument is sold for $5,000,000, yielding a tax loss of $3,000,000 ($5,000,000 minus $8,000,000, the basis in the instrument), 90% of which is allocable to *A*. *A* has generated a tax loss of $2,400,000 ($2,700,000 loss in Year 2, offset by $300,000 gain in Year 1), with no material change in his financial position-other than receipt of the valuable tax loss.

Will this strategy work? What does Treas. Reg. 1.701–2(e) have to say about this strategy? *See* ASA Investerings Partnership v. Commissioner, 201 F.3d 505 (D.C. Cir. 2000) (from which the facts of this question are derived).

This Lesson ends with an article that exemplifies choice of entity planning considerations. The article responds to a change in the tax law, which is usually an appropriate time to reconsider a client's previous choice of entity. Read the article leisurely, certainly not as you should read the code and regulation assignments in this book (read those carefully!). The purpose at this point is not to "know" or memorize any particular substantive conclusion but merely to introduce one choice of entity determination methodology and analysis.[1.5] After reading the article, consider the following questions:

Practice:

1. In light of the analysis contained in the article set out below, would you recommend C corporation or partnership status for a small to medium business? Is the triple split a feasible strategy? As a general matter, what are the risks attendant to an "aggressive tax strategy?" Have the authors neglected to consider any relevant tax cost or opportunity?

CHOICE OF ENTITY PLANNING AFTER JGTTRA: BRAINSTORMING THE TRIPLE SPLIT

Darryll K. Jones* and David Kirk**
Journal of Business Entities, March, at 18 (2004).

Introduction

A small business owner's choice of entity decision was rather presumptive so long as C corporation income was taxed at corporate rates

---

1.5 Indeed, two more tax acts have been enacted since the article was written and they change choice of entity analysis. See e.g. Burgess Raby and William Raby, Tax

Savings Through Multiple Small Corporations, 105 Tax Notes 555 (2004).

* Associate Dean and Associate Professor of Law, University of Pittsburgh School of when earned and then again at ordinary individual rates when distributed.[2] Assume, for example, that a small business generated $250,000 gross income. Prior to the Jobs and Growth Tax Relief Reconciliation Act of 2003 (JGTRRA)[3], a C corporation owner would have paid $127,208.50 in income taxes, leaving $122,791.50.[4] Pass thru owners would have paid only $93,011.07 leaving $156,988.13.[5] The C corporation owner could achieve *de facto* pass thru treatment by paying the entity's profit to herself as compensation.[6] A C corporation owner with predictable income flows could actually fare better than a pass-thru owner if it is assumed that both owners use some of the entity's profit for business expansion. For example, suppose both owners want to devote the first $75,000 to business operations or expansion. The pass thru owner will be taxed on the entire $250,000,[7] while the C corporation owner will be taxed only on $175,000 though the first $75,000 will be taxed to the corporation. Business planners familiar with the "income splitting" technique will nevertheless recognize the beneficial affect.[8] The undistributed $75,000 was taxed at lower rates if left in corporate solution than it would have been if distributed and then reinvested. Thus, the pass thru owner would still pay $93,011.07 even though she intended to leave $75,000 in the entity's coffers. The C corporation owner would pay only $78,141.50, leaving her with nearly $15,000 more for operation, expansion or savings.[9]

Both the zeroing out and the income splitting strategy assume that a significant portion of C corporation income will be paid as compensation to an owner/employee and thereafter taxed at the individual graduated rates. Several of the provisions in JGTRRA provide an incentive to rethink or brainstorm the methods by which C corporations achieve *de facto* pass thru or income splitting. In particular, the treatment of dividends as net capital gains and the reduction of the maximum capital gains rate to 15% makes dividends preferable to compensation, at least

Law. JD 1986, University of Florida College of Law, LLM (Tax) 1994.

** Certified Public Accountant & Certified Financial Planner. Second year student at the University of Pittsburgh School of Law, Pittsburgh PA.

2. See IRC § 11 (2004), IRC § 1, 61 (2002). Prior to the Jobs and Growth Tax Relief and Reconciliation Act of 2003, dividends were taxable to shareholders as ordinary income.

3. Pub. L. No. 108–27, 117 Stat. 752 (codified in scattered sections of 26 U.S.C.).

4. The tax under IRC § 11 would have been $80,750 and the tax on dividends of $169,250 would have been $46,458.50.

5. IRC § 1(a), 1401 (2002). We use the married filing jointly status throughout. The pass thru owner would pay income and self-employment tax.

6. IRC § 162(a)(1) (2002).

7. See IRC § 702, 1366 (2002).

8. For a thorough discussion of "income splitting" see, John W. Lee, *A Populist Political Perspective of the Business Tax Entities Universe: "Hey the Stars Might Lie But the Numbers Never Do."*, Tex. L. Rev. 885 (2000). The author concludes that most small businesses were better off even before JGTRRA if they electing C corporation status and taking advantage of the "inside shelter" provided by the lower corporate rates on the first $75,000.

9. The corporate tax would have been only $13,750 on the $75,000. IRC § 11 (2002). By contrast, the individual rate on the first $75,000 would have been $15,656. IRC § 1(a) (2002). The shareholder owner would still get the benefits of the 15% and 28% progressive rates on the remaining $175,000, bringing her total tax (after adding in employment tax) to $78,141.

with regard to the shareholder level tax.[10] Compensation remains preferable if the corporation cannot replace the compensation deduction with another deduction that does not trigger an ordinary tax on the shareholder, particularly if the corporation would otherwise be taxed at the 34% rate or higher. It makes no sense to pay 34% or higher at the corporate level to obtain income taxed at 15% at the shareholder level. For example, if our post-JGTRRA C corporation owner posited above has no other deductions, her total tax liability will be $106,137 if she does not zero out through a compensation deduction, but only $84,671.50 if she does. After JGTRRA, the opportunity to pay only 15% on all, or nearly all income, is real enough that the business owner ought to devote more attention to the C corporation than was previously considered necessary.

What prompted our reconsideration of the choice of entity analysis were the commonly heard statements that pass thru treatment is still presumptively preferable to C corporation treatment even though dividends are now taxed at much lower rates than compensation. While the statement has intuitive appeal, we suspected that it was prematurely made and wanted to analytically confirm or deny our suspicion. We posited that a business owner should chose the C corporation if it were possible to (1) zero out, or nearly zero out, corporate level income without total reliance on compensation, (2) generate deductions that require no immediate cash outlay—i.e., leveraged deductions, and (3) pay out immediate earnings as dividends taxed as net capital gain. Ideally, entity profits should be split three ways. Using a moderate income entity—one earning $250,000 per year—we decided that an amount of profit not to exceed the amount taxable at no more than 15% should be retained in corporate solution, a like amount should be paid as compensation to the principle owner and the remaining amount should be distributed as a dividend. By doing so, the owner might limit her tax on all income to no more than 15%. We then set out to analyze the likely consequences of each step in the triple split. We found that while it is possible that the strategy can generate significant reduction in tax costs, thus making the C corporation election preferable, it also creates a significant risk of higher long term tax cost primarily because appreciated assets are likely to generate corporate level taxable income. We conclude that while the triple split seems more than feasible as a theoretical matter, we are nevertheless left with uncomfortable risks. We hope that readers find sufficient flaws in our analysis that justify a more optimistic assessment.

A Preview of Risks

The basic problem is that to achieve the lower 15% rate, the C corporation owner must find other ways to avoid corporate level tax at the 34% rate or higher because JGTTRA leaves compensation taxable at the higher individual rates. Two provisions in JGTRRA provide possible solutions. JGTRRA's provisions relating to IRC 179 expensing and the

---

10. *See* IRC § 1(h) (2004).

increased bonus depreciation deduction can, in most circumstances and possibly without a present cash outlay, substitute for the compensation deduction.[11] Another method would be to divide compensation among close family members, but paying no single family member more than the amount taxable at 15% or 25%.[12] There are risks with any tax plan, particularly those adopted in a volatile political environment, so after providing some detail on what we refer to as the "triple split," we end the article with some risk assessments and potential solutions.

A few risks arise, however, from the imperative to zero out corporate income without using compensation. First, the Internal Revenue Service ("the Service") will likely scrutinize an ostensible dividend to see whether it is actually compensation taxable at the mostly higher rates and subject to employment taxes.[15] We think the payment of compensation, even though taxed at only 15%, will make a successful challenge less likely, though not altogether unlikely. There are sufficient labor data[16] and enough caselaw from the S corporation arena by which to support a reasonable prediction with regard to whatever level of compensation is selected.[17] Second, the use of leveraged depreciation deductions will generate appreciated assets that may increase long term tax costs. JGTRRA does not change the treatment of appreciated assets. C corporations remain taxable on the disposition of appreciated assets and if a zeroing out strategy requires the use of accelerated depreciation deductions, there may result significant exit costs.[18] A midstream S election is one possible way to avoid this problem but there is still the matter of the 10 year holding period necessary to avoid the built in gains tax.[19] Another possible solution involves the use of rental expenses rather than depreciation to zero out corporate income. This solution, though, might

---

11. IRC § 168(k)(4), 179(b)(1) (2004). Professor Calvin H. Johnson calculates that leveraged assets eligible for the new 50% bonus depreciation actually result in a cash subsidy for the highest income corporate taxpayers equal to 17 cents on every dollar used to purchase the asset. Calvin H. Johnson, *Depreciation Policy During Carnival: The New 50 Percent Bonus Depreciation*, 100 TAX NOTES 713 (2003). It follows that smaller income corporate taxpayers will receive a subsidy as well, though not as great.

12. The first $56,800 is taxed at rates below 15%. The 25% rate tops out $114,650. *See* IRC § 1(a).

15. The issue has previously arisen with regard to S corporation owners who sought to lessen their tax liability by characterizing as dividends what should more accurately have been viewed as compensation subject to employment taxation. *See* Michael P. Walters and Daryl Burckel, *Establishing Reasonable of Compensation Cases in Difficult IRS Attacks*, 8 AKRON TAX J. 147 (1991).

16. For example, the United States Department of Labor, Bureau of Labor Statistics reports that the nationwide mean annual salary for all occupations is $35,560. United States Department of Labor, Bureau of Labor Statistics, *Occupational Employment Statistics*, available at http://stats.bls.gov/oes/2002/oes_nat.htm (last visited, January 20, 2003) (hereinafter, *"Occupational Employment Statistics"*). On the other hand, the nationwide mean annual salary for managerial positions nationwide ranges from about $38,000 for hotel managers to about $135,000 for chief executives.

17. *See, e.g.,* Yeagle Drywall Co. v. Commissioner, 2003–1 USTC ¶ 50,141 (3rd Cir. 2002). For a somewhat dated, but still helpful discussion of the "inadequate compensation" cases with regard to S corporations see.

18. IRC § 311(b), 336 (2004).

19. IRC § 1374 (2004) (imposing a corporate level tax on S corporations upon the distribution of assets, the gain from which accrued while the entity was a C corporation, but only if the assets are disposed of within the ten year period beginning on the 1st day of the taxable year in which its S election takes affect).

require significant transaction costs. Finally, the risk of trapped losses relating to the use of C corporation seems to be one that simply requires a more realistic crystal ball regarding the entity's expected cash flow. Entrepreneurs always expect to make a fortune, yet most businesses fail. Carrybacks and carryovers ameliorate the risk somewhat but the strategy may still be unsuitable for the highly risk averse. Probably the only solution to this problem relates to the observation that the triple split strategy is least suitable for risky start-ups, and most suitable for small and middle income businesses with an established or at least highly predictable profit flow. Before delving into the specifics, though, this article very briefly discusses the check the box regulations.[20] The purpose is not to summarize again the all too familiar detail of the regulations[21] but merely to make the point that there are no ethical implications raised when taxpayers alter business structures solely in response to favorable or unfavorable tax changes. Such is precisely the case as a result of JGTRRA. Because the tax cost of salaries at the owner/individual level are now higher than the costs of dividends, it makes sense to re-evaluate the traditional method of obtaining *de facto* pass thru or income splitting treatment in the corporate form. After that, we briefly discuss JGTRRA's impact on the conventional wisdom relating to choice of entity, and then fill in the detail with regard to the triple split.

Basic Check the Box Planning

When the Internal Revenue Service (the Service) enacted the "check the box" regulations it essentially imposed a truce in what had been a long fought battle over business owners' right to actively determine for themselves the tax regime applicable to their business activities.[22] Before check the box, the Service adhered instead to a lottery approach of sorts, assuming that legitimate taxpayers decide on an appropriate business model without explicitly factoring in tax costs, and that the tax consequences would follow naturally rather than by taxpayer predestination.[23] Quite naturally, rational taxpayers spent time and money structuring business vehicles that sought business objectives with the least amount of tax cost. An owner whose business structure included limited liability, centralized management, perpetual existence and free transferability of interest presumptively incurred the generally higher tax costs associated

---

20. Treas. Reg. 301.7701–1, 301.7701–2, 301.7701–3, 301.7701–4 (2003).

21. *See* George K. Yin, *The Taxation of Private Business Enterprises: Some Policy Considerations Stimulated By The "Check-the-Box" Regulations,* 51 S.M.U. L. Rev. 125 (1997).

22. *See* Thomas M. Hayes, *Checkmate, The Treasury Finally Surrenders: The Check the Box Treasury Regulations and Their Effect on Entity Classification,* 54 Wash. & Lee L. Rev. 1147 (1997).

23. George K. Yin, *supra* note 13 at 130 (In general, the tax system does not permit taxpayers to elect the rules applicable to them. Rather, the system generally attempts to impose tax rules that follow and are consistent with some economic characteristic of the taxpayer or the taxpayer's activities. It is unclear why the check-the-box regulations should deviate from this usual approach).

with Subchapter C.[24] To obtain the lesser costs traditionally thought to apply to Subchapter K, an owner had to give up two or more of those included factors. Check the box implicitly concedes that tax costs are real business expenses that should, like any other cost, legitimately be taken into account in business planning. The regulations therefore merged previously separate planning considerations—business and tax. Hence, there can be no official or theoretical objection when advisors suggest changes in business structures as a result of tax law changes. It is entirely legitimate that business structures be adopted or modified in a manner that achieves a taxpayer's intended tax objective.

Under the check the box regulations, a sole proprietor can determine that her business endeavors should be viewed as self generated wealth—taxed to the owner in the same manner as wages, for example—or wealth created by a separate entity and taxed to that entity.[25] Pass-thru treatment is a compromise between these two approaches. Pass thru treatment imposes tax liability directly on the owner without regard to whether the entity makes distributions to that owner, but the liability is calculated by reference to the entity's existence.[26] Thus, capital gain realized by the entity creates a personal liability to the owner for a capital gains tax even if the gain would have been ordinary if the entity's existence were disregarded and even if the gain is not distributed to the owner. At one time, pass thru treatment was unavailable to sole proprietors. A single owner could not logically conduct business as a partnership. The enactment of Subchapter S and the recognition of single member limited liability companies (LLCs), however, allows for pass-thru treatment for sole proprietors. Multiple owners of a single business can elect to be taxed under Subchapter C, K, or S but they cannot elect for the income be taxed to their individual selves without pass-thru treatment.[27] Thus, check the box allows all owners to explicitly determine for themselves the tax costs applicable to their business form.

Prior to the enactment of Subchapter S, single and multiple owners who sought limited liability were obliged to incur the potentially higher tax costs of Subchapter C. Some view the liability protection afforded by state incorporation as redundant and that opinion ought to be factored into the choice of entity analysis.[28] Small business owners, whether conducting business as a C corporation or otherwise, already obtain limited liability from the private market or as a matter of specific statutory law. Those private and public liability protections are rarely voided, so resort to the liability protection afforded by state incorpo-

24. *See* Morrissey v. Commissioner, 296 U.S. 344 (1935); U.S. v. Kintner, 216 F.2d 418 (9th Cir. 1954); Treas. Reg. 301–7701–1 through 11 (1993) (the old entity classification regulations).

25. Treas. Reg. 301.7701–2(c)(2) (2004). A sole proprietorship will be disregarded if the owner does not elect to be taxed as a corporation. Treas. Reg. 301.7701–3(b)(1)(ii) (2004).

26. IRC 702, 1366 (2004).

27. Treas. Reg. 301.7701–3(b)(1)(i), (c)(1) (2004).

28. John Lee, *supra* note 7, at 897–98 (making the case that C corporation limited liability is a myth).

ration is a rare event indeed. For example, the market demands liability protection for most risks by imposing, in one way or another, a requirement to purchase liability insurance. State workers' compensation and even bankruptcy laws are forms of statutory liability protection. These types of liability protection are probably superior to C corporation liability protection because in most instances they cannot be waived nor forfeited based on a fact finder's equitable sensitivities. In contrast, C corporation liability protection must often be waived as well-informed lenders or vendors require that small business owners provide personal guarantees to borrow money or purchase goods on credit. If nothing else, though, the C corporation liability protection provides C corporation owners a measure of psychological protection that is apparently worth the extra potential tax costs. Liability protections previously obtained only at the higher tax costs of Subchapter C can now also be obtained under the presumptively lower tax costs applicable to Subchapters K and S, though such liability remains a redundancy and even a myth to some observers.

Conventional Wisdom

The foregoing discussion seems only to buttress conventional wisdom. If C corporation liability protection is redundant, at best, and a plain waste of money at worst, then conventional wisdom correctly considers pass thru treatment as presumptively best for small business. Conventional wisdom, though, is premised upon several assumptions relating to the taxation of corporations and shareholders that are either incorrect or exist only in the very small minority of instances. Conventional wisdom would always apply if inside corporate rates were equivalent to the outside individual rates applicable to C corporation owners and pass thru owners. But prior to JGTRRA, the inside rates applicable to corporate profits were lower on the first $75,000 than the rates applicable to the first $75,000 taxable to pass thru owners. After JGTRRA, the outside rates are actually lower on the first $75,000 than the inside rates[29] Still, the inside rates are lower than the outside rates on the second $75,000 and as a result a tax savings can be achieved by splitting the first $150,000, leaving $75,000 in corporate solution and distributing the next $75,000 as compensation. Second, conventional wisdom assumes that outside rates on C corporation owners are always equivalent to the outside rates on pass thru owners. This assumption was generally, though not always true prior to JGTRRA. As a result of JGTRRA, outside rates on C corporation owners are equivalent to or greater than outside rates on pass thru owners only if C corporation owners' so chose. Because C corporation owners may take wealth from their business entities in the form of compensation or as a return of

---

29. *Compare* IRC § 1 and § 11 (2002). Prior to JGTRRA, only the first $36,900 was taxed at 15%, with the remaining $38,100 taxed at 28%. By comparison, the first $50,000 of corporate income was (and is) taxed at 15%, with the remaining $25,000 taxed at only 25%. After JGTRRA, the outside tax on the first $75,000 is lower than the inside corporate tax on the same amount (the inside corporate tax on $75,000 is $13,750, while the outside tax is only $12,370).

capital, they can choose between the higher ordinary rates or the significantly lower capital gains rate. A final assumption is that small business owners generally prefer immediate personal consumption over business reinvestment. That assumption is irrational even in the absence of statistics indicating that small business owners need and prefer reinvestment, at least during the business' initial period of existence. It is more logical to assume that business owners start small and dream big. Conventional wisdom, then, is presumptively correct only if one assumes nonexistent or irrational facts.

The data support the disconnect between reality and conventional wisdom. Professor John Lee's recent pioneering work challenging the notion that pass thru entities are presumptively best demonstrated the fallacies of conventional wisdom even before the changes enacted by JGTRRA.[30] Lee showed that most small businesses are owned by the wealthiest taxpayers, the vast majority of whom pay taxes at the highest individual marginal and effective rates.[31] He further demonstrated that because the overwhelming majority of C corporations had income taxed at 34% or below, their owners paid fewer taxes overall on income earned through a C corporation than they would have paid if the income had been earned through a pass-thru entity.[32] From this, he concluded that Subchapter C does not, in fact, impose an additional tax cost on business owners. To the contrary, Lee concluded that Subchapter C provides a subsidy for C corporation owners and that the subsidy is unavailable for owners of pass-thru entities.[33] Only with regard to the highest income C corporations—those taxed at a 35% on all their income—does conventional wisdom hold true.

Significantly, Lee conducted his study when the highest individual rates were 39.6% and dividends were taxed at those same ordinary individual rates. His conclusions were correctly premised on the assumption that small business owners zeroed out income at the corporate level, or maintained corporate income at levels below the 35% rate, by distributing enough profits to owners in the form of compensation and fringe benefits. While most fringe benefits were (and are) non-taxable to recipients, compensation was taxed at the individual rates that were generally higher then the rates applicable to the corporation on the same amounts of income. Hence, high income owners whose C corporations earned moderate amounts of income were better off, from a tax standpoint, having earned income in corporate rather than pass thru form. Those owners could pay a portion of their corporate profits to themselves as compensation and leave the rest to be taxed at corporate rates lower than would apply to individuals with the same amount of income. Thus, C corporation owners enjoyed a competitive business advantage over pass thru owners. C corporation owners who were unconcerned with business expansion could simply pay out all profits as compensation and thereby place themselves in the same position as pass thru owners.

30. John W. Lee, *supra* note 7.

31. *Id.* at 908, n. 141, 983.

32. *Id.* at 903–922.

33. *Id.* at 922.

The Triple Split

With these premises in mind, we thought that JGTRRA could allow a C corporation owner to achieve the best of all worlds—sheltering income at the lower corporate rates (compared to the rates on income above $75,000), and receiving income for personal consumption at the equally low capital gains rates. Instead of dividing corporate profits between retention in corporate solution and compensation, a C corporation owner should retain some profit in corporate solution, pay some as taxable compensation and nontaxable employee benefits, and distribute the rest as dividends taxable at the low corporate rates. This strategy is not available to pass-thru owners[37] and for this reason C corporations might actually be better.

Assume, for example, a post-JGTRRA moderate income business owner with $250,000 taxable income before taking a deduction for owner/employee compensation. A pass thru owner will pay $81,540.47 in income and employment taxes after JGTRRA. If she reinvests $75,000 in the business for expansion or savings, she will have $93,459 for personal living expenses. A C corporation owner could retain $50,000 in corporate solution, pay $56,800 in compensation, and distribute $143,200 in dividends (hence, the term "triple split"). Note that by this strategy none of the income is taxed at more than 15%. The total income and employment tax due from the C corporation owner would be $45,490.40. If she contributed $25,000 back to the corporation, she would be left with $129,509.60 for personal living expenses. This is $36,050.60 more for the C corporation owner who can either live higher on the hog than the pass thru owner or expand her business at a faster rate than the pass thru owner.

The foregoing analysis assumes that the C corporation owner can find at least $143,200 in deductions other than the deduction for compensation paid to herself. The search for substitute deductions should not be difficult, at least not in the short run. First, the triple split calls for payment of compensation up to the 15% rate ($56,800). Doing so creates two other important effects. First, the payment of some compensation, even if less than what might have been paid before JGTRRA, makes a successful challenge to an unreasonably low salary less likely.[38] More importantly for purposes of zeroing out, the payment of compensation allows the corporation to pay deductible, but non-taxable fringe benefits and deferred compensation to the owner/employee. Assuming conservatively that deductible but non-taxable fringe benefits and deferred compensation are set at twice the amount of non-deferred compensation (i.e., $113,600) means that our hypothetical owner needs only

---

37. Nor is this strategy available to personal holding companies, whose income is taxed at a flat 35%. IRC § 11(b)(2).

38. *But See* IRC § 1366(e) (2004); Treas. Reg. 1.1366–3 (2004), both of which allow the service to re-characterize ostensible dividends as compensation. The analysis that has applied for so long under these provisions will most likely be applied in the post JGTRRA world as S and C corporation owners recognize the significant advantages of taking profit as dividends rather than compensation. *See also, infra* note 14.

another $29,600 in other deductions to zero out C corporation income completely.

As has already been noted, JGTRRA expands upon some already very generous depreciation deductions. The increased 179 expensing election,[39] which is available in addition to the new 50% bonus depreciation,[40] provides ample opportunities to zero out income without sole reliance on owner compensation. If the properties to which the 179 election and bonus depreciation are applied are financed, particularly via nonrecourse facilities, the C corporation can take the interest deduction as well and will be even better off.[41] Theoretically, at least, these opportunities seem entirely sufficient to zero out the remaining C Corporation income without depriving the owner of immediate use of the income.

Caveat Emptor

As implied earlier, and as with all cases indeed, there is no such thing as a foolproof plan. With rewards there come risks, and the triple split presents no exception to the rule. First, the Service may mount an inadequate compensation salary challenge, alleging that a portion of the dividends received under a triple split are actually wages subject to employment tax and taxable at the probably higher individual rates. If successful, this would increase the aggregate tax paid because the additional deduction to the corporation against 15% corporate income would be more than offset by the 35% tax (or higher, if phase-outs apply) at the individual rates and would increase the employment tax. The payment of $56,800 in compensation, though, ought to make it more difficult to mount a successful challenge. Such a salary may be low for a principle employee, but we might safely assume that it will rarely be "unreasonably low," given that median salary in the United States is approximately $35,000.[42] A less aggressive strategy for those who want to more confidently avoid the inadequate compensation issue would be to pay compensation up to the amount taxable at 25% ($114,650). In any event, reasonable compensation analysis traditionally involves a computation of all value provided, and the $56,800 amount should logically be supplemented by nontaxable fringe benefits and deferred compensation.[43] Finally, the Service has been most successful with regard to inadequate compensation disputes when a principle owner pays him-or herself nothing or very close to nothing.

---

39. JGTTRA increases the limitation on the expense election to $100,000 but only for 2003, 2004, 2005. IRC § 179(b)(1).

40. IRC § 168(k)(4)(B). The 50% bonus depreciation applies only for property acquired and place in service after May 2003 and before January 2005.

41. *See* Calvin H. Johnson, *supra* note 10. The typically high income owners of small business may have greater access to recourse and nonrecourse financing than other taxpayers. In addition, nonrecourse financing will, in most cases be of greater tax utility to C corporation owners than to pass-thru owners since non-recourse financing will generally not support deductions for pass thru owners. *See* IRC § 465 (2004) (pertaining to the at-risk limitation on deductions).

42. *See supra* note 15.

43. *See e.g.* Treas. Reg. 53.4958–4(b)(1)(ii) (2004) (relating to the determination of reasonable compensation for officers of tax exempt organizations).

A second, more important problem relates to the anti-General Utilities provisions that apply to C corporations but not to partnerships and newly formed S corporations. The triple split relies on deductions using either borrowed funds or existing cash at the corporate level. It is not feasible if, using the example above, the $143,200 is needed to pay a dividend to the owner and also generate $143,200 in deductions to bring corporate taxable income down to $50,000. The $143,200 in cash from the current year's operations simply cannot be used to satisfy both objectives. Reliance on leveraged 179 expensing and depreciation deductions to zero out corporate income will generate assets with a basis significantly less than their fair market value, the disposition of which will create corporate level ordinary income. To make matters even worse, in future years the corporation will have taxable income greater than cash flow because nondeductible loan payments must be made with after-tax funds. In effect, cost recovery and other debt financed deductions will not eliminate corporate income but merely defer it for later taxation. Additional borrowing will be necessary if the corporate taxpayer intends on minimizing future taxable income at the corporate level. This year-over-year borrowings will severely hamper the corporation's long term viability. Eventually and inevitably, the piper will have to be paid.[44]

We considered three possible solutions to the debt-financed inside appreciation problem described above. The unyielding criteria, though, is that any solution must achieve the goal of providing as much 15% taxable income to the owners as possible. The first solution would be to simply pay more salary and benefits and rely less on leveraged deductions. Since the triple split assumes that the 15% rate has already been achieved by the principal owner, the additional compensation should be paid to a family member—preferably a child living in the home—and certainly the amount should less than $56,800.[45] Of course, the family member needs to perform enough services so as to avoid re-characterization of the salary as a constructive dividend to the principal owner.[46] Such a finding would leave the income taxed at no more than 15%, but it would deprive the corporation of a deduction. So long as the family member is performing adequate services these issues should be manageable. The drawback to this approach is that it will increase employment

44. The triple split idea is based solely on the timing of deductions and income. The success of the idea is a result of the present value of the tax benefits received in the current year(s) over the tax cost in the future year when the loan is paid off and no additional timing deductions are available. A simple present value spreadsheet should be able to determine the viability of the idea in individualized situations.

45. The payment of salary should not be to the owner/employee's spouse because the salary of the spouse will be included 'on top' of the first spouse's salary. The owner/employee would have already taken ad-

vantage of the lower marginal rates on the joint return. In addition, the salary to the spouse would be subject to full employment taxes, whereas the owner/employee would have the FICA portion (12.4%) end at 87,-000.

46. Gift Tax is outside the scope of this article, however, the payment of an unsubstantiated salary to a family member may constitute a taxable gift under Chapter 12 if it is deemed excessive and recharacterized as a dividend to the owner. The owner, after having received a dividend, may be deemed to have transferred that amount to the family member.

taxes, but probably not to an extent that outweighs the benefit from the overall strategy. Income sharing between family members is often undertaken in the pass thru context. In many cases, it is prudent financial and estate planning to transfer business ownership to family members. Children and other family owners may be limited partners or S corporation shareholders. The spreading of the ownership across the low end of the individual graduated rates is therefore a strategy often undertaken by planners even in the absence of tax cost considerations. The results are similar to that of C corporation salary payments without the employment tax bite.

Another possible, but perhaps more risky solution to anti-General Utilities problem is to plan for an S election to be made once depreciation deductions lose their utility for non-tax reasons or the owner begins actively planning an exit. Once the S election is made, the ten year holding period begins and the owner can avoid the corporate level tax by holding the assets long term.[47] The risk, of course, is that the depreciable assets will not be held for one reason or another. An owner might minimize this risk by relying more on family member compensation to zero out corporate income.[48] This, of course, creates a significant and unavoidable disadvantage of the triple split strategy—the imperative to minimize or defer cost recovery deductions.[49] Pass-thru entities can take full advantage of the deductions without later incurring an entity level tax. Still, the long-term deferral of the anti-General Utilities tax for long periods may prove beneficial even if the tax ultimately becomes due. And in any event, the problem of appreciated assets existed pre-JGTRRA and yet many taxpayers nonetheless utilized the income splitting device.[50] This indicates that while a business planning advisor might and should strenuously emphasize the problem, taxpayers may still opt for the more immediate advantages despite the long term disadvantages.

The third potential solution involves a shareholder's purchase of new property, plant and equipment outside of the corporation, coupled with an arms-length rental to the corporation.[51] The shareholder would use the current year's dividends or salary plus borrowed funds to purchase, for example, a new building and then rent the building to the corporation.[52] The rental expense would generate an ordinary deduction

47. IRC § 1374(d)(7) (2004).

48. The ability to pay salaries to zero out income is limited by the amount of free cash flow available to the S Corporation. At some point though, the corporation's taxable income will be greater than free cash flow because prior year's loan principal payments will require cash but not provide a current year deduction.

49. Minimizing cost recovery deductions may not avoid the presence of appreciated assets in any event, since the basis of property must be adjusted for the depreciation "allowable." IRC § 1016(a)(2)(B) (2004).

50. John W. Lee *supra* note 7.

51. This is different than 'Sale–Lease-back' transactions because the new P,P & E is purchased from unrelated 3rd parties and placed into service for the first time by the shareholder.

52. The idea is most effective when borrowed money is used to purchase non-depreciating property. In this case, non-depreciating property is defined as property that retains a market value after its tax useful life has expired. The best example is real estate. The corporate rental payments would pay off the borrowed funds over time. At the end of the transaction, the idea transferred, for example, a building to the shareholder with little capital outlay on the under Section 162. The amount of rental income to the shareholder/lessor should exceed the depreciation deduction so the shareholder's depreciation deduction is not suspended.[53] The corporation would annually pay out its cash from operations in a manner that would accomplish similar objectives as zeroing by salary, but without the employment tax. By keeping appreciating assets outside the corporation, the owner might successfully avoid the nearly inevitable corporate level tax, as well as the problem of taxable income exceeding cash flow.

Finally, business tax planning can never be conducted in a vacuum. Politics is the great wildcard that must be considered. Most of JGTRRA's provisions relating to the triple split are either explicitly temporary or subject to calls for repeal.[54] One might assume that if the present Executive or Legislative branch administrations do not survive the next general election, the rules will revert back to pre-JGTRRA days. In such cases, though, a small C corporation owner might not lose all that much since the income split will presumably be available to achieve *de facto* pass thru taxation.

Conclusion

Choice of entity analysis traditionally involved asking "why shouldn't the taxpayer elect pass-thru treatment?" The different tax consequences pertaining to C corporations and pass-thru entities were thought to be so stark as to make pass-thru the overwhelmingly presumptive choice. Zeroing out income rendered the choices between C corporation and pass thru roughly equivalent, while the income splitting strategy actually made C corporations preferable for small and middle income taxpayers. The income split allowed the first $75,000 of C corporation income to be taxed at lower rates than would apply if earned by a pass thru owner. The remaining income would be taxed at the owner's individual progressive rate. JGTRRA, however, raises the possibility, risky though it may be, that all income earned via a C corporation can be taxed at no more than a 15% rate. By splitting income three ways—retaining the first $50,000 in corporate solution, paying no more than $56,800 as compensation to any single employee, and distributing the remainder as dividends—the C corporation owner can achieve a 15% rate not available to pass thru owners. There are certain risks, as with any tax strategy, but the triple split is feasible enough that perhaps the choice of entity question should be "why shouldn't this business owner elect C corporation treatment?"

---

part of the shareholder. If the building would have been purchased on the inside of corporate solution, the distribution of the building would be subject to corporate level tax and possibly dividend treatment to the shareholder.

53. The loss will not be disallowed as a related party transaction under loss § 267

or as a passive activity loss under § 469. As long as the transaction is arms-length and the rental amount is at fair market value, there is minimal risk of adjustment by the Service.

54. The reductions in individual rates, for example, are set to sunset in 2010.

Lesson 2

PARTNERSHIP TAX REPORTING REQUIREMENTS

Primary References: IRC 701, 702, 703, 724
Treas. Reg. 1.701–1, 1.702–1, 1.703–1

Secondary References: IRS Form 1065, Schedule K–1,
Instructions to Form 1065 and Schedule K–1

Case References: United States v. Basye, 410 U.S. 441 (1973)
Demirjian v. Commissioner, 457 F.2d 1 (3rd Cir. 1972)

Theory

The partnership tax reporting and audit procedures (audit procedures are considered in Lesson 3) provide the first opportunity to consider the tax nature of partnerships. As you study partnership tax you will frequently encounter the words, "conduit," "entity" and "aggregate." None of these words are entirely accurate or inaccurate when applied to the partnership. The partnership firm is, all at once, a conduit, an entity and a mere aggregate of its owners. The first word, "conduit" refers to the taxation of income earned by a partnership directly to the partners in their individual capacities. The primary manifestation of a partnership's nature as a conduit is that income earned by a partnership is immediately taxable, but only to the individual partners under IRC 701. On the other hand, the tax characteristics of income, gain, loss, and deductions, (character, holding period, etc.) are determined as if the partnership is a separate entity under IRC 702(b), except when IRC 724 applies. The Supreme Court described the overall scheme more than thirty years ago in *United States v. Basye*. Note, too, the Court's remark in footnote 8 regarding the terms "conduit" and "entity."

Section 703 of the Internal Revenue Code of 1954, insofar as pertinent here, prescribes that "the taxable income of a partnership shall be computed in the same manner as in the case of an individual." 26 U. S. C. § 703 (a). Thus, while the partnership itself pays no taxes, 26 U. S. C. § 701, it must report the income it generates and such income must be calculated in largely the same manner as an individual computes his personal income. For this purpose, then, the partnership is regarded as an independently recognizable entity apart from the aggregate of its partners. Once its income is ascertained and reported, its existence may be disregarded since each partner must pay a tax on a portion of the total income as if the partnership were merely an agent or conduit through which the income passed.[8]

IRC 724 is an anti-conversion provision that is intended to prevent the use of partnerships to convert ordinary into capital gain, or capital losses into ordinary losses. When IRC 724 is inapplicable, the tax characteristics of the partners (e.g., whether the partner is a dealer, or the length of time a partner has held a partnership interest before receipt of income traced to a capital asset held long term by the partnership) are ignored and the partnership's characteristics determine the type of income taxable to each partner. This is an example of how the entity theory determines tax consequences. When IRC 724 applies, the aggregate theory determines tax consequences.

The term "aggregate" is somewhat, though not precisely synonymous with the word "conduit" in that it conveys that a transaction involving the partnership is analyzed as though the partnership did not exist. For example, when a partner sells her partnership interest she might be viewed in the same manner as a stockholder who sells stock. Under the entity approach, the thing sold, (i.e., the stock) is viewed as a capital asset notwithstanding that it may ultimately represent ownership of capital and non-capital assets (such as land and inventory, respectively). But the partnership rules treat the sale of the partnership interest as a sale of the partner's separate interest in each asset held by the partnership, some of which would have generated ordinary income if actually sold directly by the partner. You might surmise that application of the aggregate approach in such circumstances sometimes requires complicated calculations. The sale of partnership interests is considered more fully in Lesson 16.

---

8. There has been a great deal of discussion in the briefs and in the lower court opinions with respect to whether a partnership is to be viewed as an "entity" or as a "conduit." We find ourselves in agreement with the Solicitor General's remark during oral argument when he suggested that "it seems odd that we should still be discussing such things in 1972." The legislative history indicates, and the commentators agree, that partnerships are entities for purposes of calculating and filing informational returns but that they are conduits through which the taxpaying obligation passes to the individual partners in accord with their distributive shares. See, e. g., H. R. Rep. No. 1337, 83d Cong., 2d Sess., 65–66 (1954); S. Rep. No. 1622, 83d Cong., 2d Sess., 89–90 (1954); 6 J. Mertens, Law of Federal Income Taxation § 35.01 (1968); S. Surrey & W. Warren, Federal Income Taxation 1115–1116 (1960); Jackson, Johnson, Surrey, Tenen & Warren, The Internal Revenue Code of 1954: Partnerships, 54 Col. L. Rev. 1183 (1954).

Procedurally, the code rather clearly adopts an entity approach. Income earned by the partnership must be reported by the partnership, just as if the partnership were an actual taxpayer.[1] Certain items must be separately listed because those items will be combined with each partner's non-partnership income, deductions and credits and therefore will be taxed differently depending on each partner's separate tax characteristics. Except in a few instances, if there is an optional tax treatment that depends upon an election, the election must be made by the partnership. IRC 703(b). The partnership's election, or lack thereof, will bind the partners. *Demirjian v. Commissioner* provides an oft-cited example. In that case, a partnership's building was involuntarily condemned and the partnership received condemnation proceeds from the municipal authority. Under IRC 1033, an owner of property can defer recognition of gain realized on an involuntary conversion, but only by affirmative election and then only to the extent the proceeds are used to acquire similar property. The partners used the condemnation proceeds to purchase replacement property but the partnership, itself, did not purchase the replacement property nor make the election required by IRC 1033(a)(2)(A). Since the building was actually owned by the partnership, the condemnation proceeds were subject to nonrecognition at the partnership's election. The partnership's failure to elect resulted in reportable income at the partnership level, and taxable income to the partners, despite their efforts to elect individually.

Practice

1. This practice problem involves the preparation of a partnership's tax return and one or more accompanying Schedules K–1. Tax attorneys are generally only secondarily involved in actual tax reporting. Tax accountants are primarily responsible for reporting because they will most likely be involved in maintaining partnership books and records. Tax counsel is more likely to be involved in preparing the partnership or operating agreement and in planning or defending transactions.

The problem's greatest usefulness is in providing a broad overview of partnership taxation. The time spent on this problem is well worth it because the problem is designed to contribute to a broad theoretical discussion of partnership tax and to introduce the big issues. These issues include the treatment of nonrecourse liabilities, transactions between partners and their own partnerships, allocations, contributions and distributions of property, guaranteed payments, unrealized receivables and inventory items, the partnership taxable year, and partnership terminations. Each of those topics (and more) is taken up in separate lessons. For now, professors may use the instructions as a guide for providing an early semester overview, and students should refer back to

---

1. Note that IRC 761(a) and Regulation 1.761–2 allows certain joint owners to elect out of Subchapter K. In general, the election is available when the owners maintain a certain degree of separateness with regard to the property from which income is derived.

the instructions later in the course to remind themselves of the big picture (which is sometimes missed due to all the detail in Subchapter K).

1. Prepare the ABC partnership's Form 1065 and B's schedule K–1. Use the Forms 1065 and Schedule K–1 included in Appendix 2. On Form 1065, do not complete Schedules L, M–1, or M–2. Refer to the instructions as you prepare the return, particularly pages 9–10, 19–22, and the line by line instructions for Form 1065. The instructions provide a broad overview of partnership taxation in general. Include citations to relevant code and regulation provisions for separate entry of items of income, gain, loss and deduction. Read, but do not complete Schedule B, L, M–1 and M–2.

ABC, LLC sells landscaping equipment. A and B are individuals; Before becoming a member of ABC, B sold widgets for a living. ABC is not a dealer in widgets. B contributed his entire widget inventory (adjusted basis = $61,000, FMV = $90,000) to ABC upon becoming a member. C is a closely held corporation owned by C1. A is the tax matters partner.

The operating agreement states that all partners have contributed equal amounts of capital and that all income, gain, loss, deduction and credit will be shared divided amongst the members, except as otherwise required by law. The limited liability corporation has always elected to be taxed as a partnership. In the taxable year, ABC has the following items:

Gross Receipts from landscape equipment:	$577,000
Gain from one time sale of widgets sold three years after contribution:	$ 29,000
Dividends from a domestic corporation	$ 20,000
Short Term Capital Gain	$ 24,000
Long Term Capital Gain	$ 500
Cost of Goods sold (do not complete Sch. A)	($180,000)
Depreciation:	($35,000)

Expenses:

Rent	($14,000)
Salaries	($45,000)
Guaranteed Payments	($33,000)
Short Term Capital Loss	($13,000)
Long Term Capital Loss	($1,000)
Charitable contribution:	($12,000)

In addition, ABC purchased capital equipment for $35,000. The equipment is subject to the optional 179 expense deduction. Partner A makes the 179 election on her individual return, but partners B and C do not. The first year, straight line depreciation on the equipment (not taken into account above) is $2,500.

Lesson 3

PARTNERSHIP TAX AUDIT PROCEDURES

Primary References: IRC 6221–6229, 6230(b), (e)–(f), 6231(a)–(b), 6233
Treas. Regs. 301.6221–1, 301.6222(a)–1, –2, 301.6222(b)–2, 301.6223(a)–2, 301.6223(e)–1, 301.6224(a)–1, 301.6224(c)–1, –2, –3, 301.6226(f)–1, 301.6231(a)(3)–1, 301.6231(a)(7)–2

Theory

A practical but important consequence of the conduit or aggregate nature of partnerships (as opposed to a partnership's entity treatment) is that enforcement mechanisms are much more difficult to apply. Under an aggregate approach, each partner is treated as a separate taxpayer and the IRS must pursue appropriate remedies arising from partnership operations one partner at a time. The practical difficulties arising from having to chase down or respond to individual partners, as further described in the following excerpt, led to the enactment of the Partnership Tax Audit Procedures in IRC 6221–6235. The Partnership Tax Audit Procedures eliminate, or at least reduce those difficulties by applying an entity approach to partnerships for purposes of audit and enforcement. That is, a partnership is treated as a single taxpayer for auditing and litigation purposes. The IRS therefore need only pursue "one" party—the partnership—with regard to improper or erroneous tax positions. In effect, an IRS challenge to any individual partner's tax treatment of a partnership item must be effectuated via a challenge against the partnership. Likewise, the IRS can treat individual refund requests at the partnership level. If certain due process procedures are followed, the outcome of an IRS challenge to a partnership item or its deposition of a refund request will be binding on all partners.

24

TEFRA'S NEW PARTNERSHIP AUDITING PROCEDURES: WAS THE SMALL PARTNER LEFT OUT?

Jay Rosen

38 Tax L. Rev. 479, 480–83 (1983).

History of Pre–TEFRA Procedures

Tax shelters have become big business in the United States. From the hue and cry of Congress, the Treasury, and commentators, one might conclude that tax shelters have replaced baseball as our national pastime. They are an ever growing drain on tax revenues and a sign of an increasing reluctance of taxpayers to accept a self assessment system of taxation.

Partnerships, most particularly limited partnerships, are ideal vehicles for tax shelter investments. Generally, a tax shelter provides loss deductions or credits to investors that do not represent economic losses or expenses. A partnership is a means by which many investors can join in a tax shelter investment but take the losses or credits generated by the investment in their separate returns. The Code treats partnerships, in general, as aggregates of their partners. Partnerships pay no federal income taxes. The income, losses, deductions, and credits of a partnership flow directly to its partners with the tax character left unchanged. A limited partner can enjoy this tax treatment while remaining aloof from the management of the investments that generate the sheltering losses or credits, a position much desired by the typical tax shelter investor who wishes to avoid taxes expeditiously without diverting his time and energies away from his principal business or professional activities.

Until TEFRA, the Code provided no efficient means to audit many tax shelters organized as partnerships. Partnership items were audited only in the partners' returns. The increasing size of tax shelter partnerships had made this task especially formidable. While the number of partnerships doing business in the United States increased by 16.3 percent from 1966 through 1975, the number of partnerships with more than 500 members increased 76.4 percent, and the average number of partners per partnership rose by 52.6 percent during that period. One promoter put together 35 partnerships with 55,000 partners, the average partnership having 1,500 partners and the largest having 7,500 partners. The tax deficiencies resulting from an adjustment to the gross income, deductions, or credits of a partnership with 7,500 partners could be assessed and collected only by proceedings against at least 7,500 persons.

Partnerships have also become more complex. Often tax shelter partnerships are composed of corporations, trusts, and other partnerships as well as individuals. Because trusts and partnerships are generally treated as flow through entities, their use in a tax shelter adds layers between the partnership that generate tax benefits and the taxpayers who ultimately claim the benefits.

Pre–TEFRA administrative procedures ill equipped the Service to enforce substantive limitations on the tax benefits claimed by tax shelter partnerships. Although the Code requires partnerships to file information returns, it did not, until 1978, impose penalties for failure to file these returns. Reporting by partnerships was therefore sporadic and often contained incomplete, inaccurate, or out of date information on the partnership and the partners. Incorrect reporting of the names and addresses of partners made it difficult for the Service to locate partners. In many cases, field agents spent months searching for the partners of a particular shelter. Multi-tiered partnerships and wide geographical dispersion of partners exacerbated the problem. If an inquiry began with a middle tier partner, the agents had to trace both up and down the structure to determine the identities of the partners. The dispersion of partners often required that several Service district offices handle a single case. Each office examined the partners of a particular shelter only within its geographical area.

These problems led many tax shelter promoters and investors to believe it was unlikely that their schemes would be audited. In the President's 1978 Tax Program, the Treasury complained that "highly creative and ingenious tax positions which are often taken by a tax shelter limited partnership and which are questionable under the law go unchallenged because of the necessity to audit separately each and every member of the partnership within the requisite limitation periods."

The Service's problems, however, went beyond the task of locating partners. In an effort to have consistent treatment of the partners of large partnerships, the Service often requested that most partners waive the statute of limitations on assessments and consent to the holding of their cases in suspense while test cases proceeded through litigation. The requested waivers, if signed, kept the partners' taxable years open for all issues, a consequence that caused some partners to refuse to sign. To preserve its claims, the Service was forced to send notices of deficiency to all nonconsenting partners. In proceedings affecting one partnership item, some partners might waive the statute of limitations to await the results of a test case, others might refuse the waiver and receive notices of deficiency, and still others might escape liability because they were not located before the statute of limitations expired.

The right of each partner to separately litigate a partnership issue further complicated the matter. A partner who received a notice of deficiency had the option to petition the Tax Court for review or pay the asserted deficiency and contest the Service's position in a district court or the Claims Court through a refund suit. Therefore, even if the Service initiated a successful audit, each partner could choose the judicial forum in which the Service's action with respect to him would be reviewed.

Tax shelter audits and litigation, as pursued under the pre-TEFRA procedures, seriously threatened the administration of the tax system and caused a huge backlog in the Tax Court. Ten percent of the cases pending in the Tax Court in 1979 involved partnership issues, and the Service was then carrying approximately 100,000 cases in suspense.

To remedy this quagmire, the Treasury, in 1978, proposed the forerunner of TEFRA's partnership auditing procedures. Congress then declined to make such a radical departure from the existing procedures. The Revenue Act of 1978 instead made two less significant changes. First, to spur prompt and proper reporting of partnership items and the identity of partners, Congress provided civil and criminal penalties for failing to file and late filing of partnership returns. Second, in order to give the Service additional time to locate partners of large, complex tax shelters, Congress extended the statute of limitations for assessing tax on partnership items of some partnerships to four years from the filing date of the partnership return. The House Ways and Means Committee suggested that the Treasury combat the multi-tier problem by regulations that would require reporting of the identities of persons who owned partnership interests indirectly through partnerships or trusts.

The Treasury and the Tax Section of the American Bar Association concluded that the 1978 amendments failed to correct the Service's administrative problems. Both continued to advocate proposals similar to those proposed by the Treasury in 1978. In TEFRA, Congress finally enacted the Treasury's proposals.

Broadly put, the Partnership Tax Audit Procedures requires the IRS to proceed against the partnership and provide written notice to the "tax matters partner" (TMP) and all "notice partners" whenever it challenges any partner's treatment of a partnership item, provided the partner has reported that item in a manner consistent with the partnership's reporting of the item. The requirements also apply if the partner reports an item in a manner inconsistent with the source partnership but also notifies the IRS of the inconsistent treatment. In the latter instance, however, the IRS may treat the item as a "nonpartnership item" and deal with the particular partner individually rather than by way of partnership proceedings.

The TMP is the primary liaison between the IRS and partnerships, though all other "notice" partners are entitled to notice and all partners (even non-notice partners) may participate in negotiations and litigation over which the TMP has primary managerial authority. The procedures implement rules that seek consistent outcomes amongst all partners. To that end, for example, the rules eliminate the opportunity for forum shopping by vesting exclusive jurisdiction in the Tax Court, or if no petition is filed in the Tax Court, in the first other court in which a petition has been filed. To combat the problem of unknown partners, the rules require the partnership to notify the Service of names and addresses of all partners and extend the statute of limitations with respect to all unknown partners.

Small partnerships—those with no more than 10 partners or members (as owners of LLC's are referred to) are not covered by the procedures, though they may elect to apply the procedures. Large partnerships are subject to streamlined procedures but those procedures are not covered here. Finally, the Partnership Tax Audit Procedures allow for both entity level refund actions (aka "administrative adjustments") as well as procedures by which individual partners may request refunds.

There are plenty more details but a broad understanding is sufficient for pedagogical purposes. The questions below help isolate some of the major details.

Practice:

1. In Example 2, Regulation 301.6222(a)–1(c), what effect will C's inconsistent reporting treatment have on his or the IRS' procedural entitlements and requirements?

2. Assume that in Example 5, Regulation 301.6222(a)–(2), the correct result is that partners C, D, E, and F, must report $25,000 as their share of income from Partnership B. The facts indicate however that Partnership B reported E's share as $20,000. Why is it that E is nevertheless treated as complying with the consistency requirement when she reported her share as $25,000?

3. Read Example 1, Regulation 301.6223(e)–1(b)(2) again. What result if ABC had more than 100 partners and A holds a less than 1% interest? What can A do to change this result?

4. What are the consequences of the IRS's failure to provide timely notice to a partner to whom notice is due?

5. What result in Regulation 301.6224(c)–1(b)(2) (example) if C had filed a statement not to be bound by the any agreement entered into by the Tax Matters Partner of Partnership J?

6. What if, in Regulation 301.6224(c)–1(b)(2) (example) if C filed the same statement as B, but Partnership J's Tax Matters Partner entered into the agreement along with Partnership P's Tax Matter's Partner?

7. What if, in Regulation 301.6224(c)–3(d), Example 1, the Service settled with Partner X for $15,000. What is the amount of settlement the Service would be obligated to offer to partner Y?

8. Prove the following summary of the Partnership Tax Audit Procedures by citing to relevant authorities:

> When adjusting a partnership item, the IRS must provide notice of the beginning of an administrative proceeding to all notice partners. No earlier than four months after doing so, it may mail a notice of final partnership administrative adjustment to the tax matters partner. The TMP has 90 days in which to file a petition for review. All other notice partners have 60 days after the 90 day period applicable to the TMP in which to initiate an independent action if the TMP has not filed a petition. The IRS cannot make an assessment with regard to a final partnership administrative adjustment until after 150 days from the mailing of the FPAA to the TMP, or a decision from a timely filed court decision becomes final (whichever is latest). In general, the IRS has 3 years from the date a partnership return is due or filed to assessing a tax on any partner with regard to a partnership item.

Lesson 4

INTRODUCTION TO CAPITAL ACCOUNTING

Primary References: **Treas. Reg. 1.704–1(b)(2)(iv)(a)–(d)(2),(e)–(f), (h), (i), (l), (q)**

Theory

Accounting can be defined as "the system of recording and summarizing business and financial transactions and analyzing, verifying, and reporting the results." In large part, the study of partnership tax is really nothing more than combining tax principles with financial accounting. Only rarely does partnership tax involve the study of new substantive tax principles—gross income is no different whether the taxpayer is a partnership or an individual, definitions pertaining to capital gains and losses are the same, recapture provisions apply just as they might to an individual, and the list goes on. To be sure, a few fundamental tax principles are altered when applied in the partnership arena. A primary example is the assignment of income doctrine. We will see that Subchapter K tolerates a certain amount of income assignment. But most fundamental tax principles encountered in the initial tax course apply as well to the study of partnership tax.

The initial demand made by Subchapter K is that partnerships keep track of—account for—financial and business transactions so that the each partner's tax liability can be verified from year to year, and tax burdens and benefits are "accurately" assigned to those whose economic participation generates those burdens and benefits. In the corporate world, there are literally reams of statutes, rules, and forms that standardize corporate accounting. Partnership accounting, on the other hand, is accomplished largely by tradition and expediency rather than in accordance with state or federal regulation and mandate. There simply isn't the large body of regulatory material or disclosure mandates with regard to partnership accounting. There are nevertheless certain baseline approaches with which readers should be familiar, since those approaches have been incorporated into Subchapter K. In turn, the

Subchapter K partnership accounting rules have taken on the role of a "uniform law" of sorts with regard to partnership accounting. The only difference, though, is that partnership tax accounting is not for the purpose of informing creditors and potential investors, but solely for properly assigning tax burdens and benefits to partners.

The regulations cited as primary references above introduce the "uniform law" by which the preferred partnership tax accounting method is articulated. In Lesson 11, readers learn that a partnership need not utilize the particular method, but failing to do so will deprive the partners of the ability to predict whether their tax conclusions—i.e., their allocations—will be "respected." If an allocation is not respected, the partners may find themselves with an unexpected tax liability or denied an anticipated tax benefit, as the Service can comb through the partnership books and itself decide how tax burdens and benefits are divided amongst the individual partners based on an elusive and uncertain concept revolving around each "partner's interest in the partnership." Well advised partnerships therefore adhere to the Subchapter K tax accounting rules. In this Lesson, readers are introduced to those "safe harbor" rules that, if followed, provide predictability with regard to each partner's tax outcome. It is assumed throughout the remainder of this text that partners seek to comply with the capital accounting rules stated in the regulations.

Consider the "tax/book" balance sheet on the next page. It is referred to as such because it contains columns by which to record tax (adjusted basis) and capital account (book) information. Do not be concerned at this point about the two "tax" columns. We take those up in subsequent lessons. This particular tax/book balance sheet shows a partnership in which A has contributed $50, B has contributed equipment worth $150, but subject to a liability of $100. Note that the $100 liability is subtracted from B's capital account balance and is instead listed adjacent to the word "liabilities." The balance sheet records information pertaining to the partnership as an entity as well as the partners as separate individuals. The partnership information is shown on the left hand side, while the partners' information is shown on the right hand side. A little algebra (don't panic!) helps explain the goal. The aggregate book values of the assets shown on the left hand side should always equal the sum of the liabilities and equity (book values) on the right side. Thus, assets = liabilities + partners' capital. Compare, Treas. Reg. 1.704–1(b)(2)(iv)(q). An addition or subtraction on one side must be accompanied by a corresponding entry on the other. This is a basic rule of equations. As a matter of tax principles, the total tax basis on the partnership side should also equal the total tax basis on the partners' side. Sometimes, the two tax columns will not be equal because of limitations imposed by the tax code in pursuit of a fundamental tax goal, such as preventing a partner from converting ordinary income to capital gain. The inequality, as will be seen in Lessons 8 and 16 (relating to the IRC 754 election), suggests the need for an adjustment.

Assets			Liabilities and Partners' Capital Liabilities: 100 Capital		
	Tax	Book		Tax	Book
Land		50	A		50
Equipment		150 200	B		50 200

Sometimes, the columns will have different labels, though the meaning is the same:

Assets			Liabilities and Partners' Capital Liabilities: 100 Capital		
	AB	Capital		AB	Capital
Land		50	A		50
Equipment		150 200	B		50 200

A further variation occurs when a third column on both sides of the balance sheet, entitled "Fair Market Value" (or some variation of that title) is inserted to the right of the Book (or Capital) column. The Book (or Capital) column is merely a "snapshot" rather than a moving picture. It shows value as of a certain date and is sometimes referred to as "historical cost." Partnerships might therefore include a third "Fair Market Value" column to show actual value as of a later date. A final observation concerns terminology. Oftentimes, the two columns—tax and book/capital—will be referred to as "tax basis" and "book basis" (or "basis per books"). "Tax basis" is solely a tax concept, while "book basis" refers to a figure derived by applying the tax accounting rules introduced in this lesson.

Partners own undivided interests in their partnership's capital. That is, a partner has equity in the partnership. To keep track of that equity, each partner is assigned a "capital account" that designates her relative ownership of the firm. The partners' capital accounts are in the far right column of the partnership's tax/book balance sheet. A capital account represents a partner's share of the partnership's total capital. The regulations govern how partner capital accounts must be maintained if the partners want to achieve predictability with regard to the positions they take on their individual tax returns. Note that the regulations are silent with regard to the partnership's capital account.

As implied above, capital account values are not necessarily synonymous with fair market values. The partnership's assets may have appreciated or depreciated over time, and yet the assets remain listed on their books at their historical cost. In the examples above, partners A and B each own 50% of the partnership's total capital. If the land has appreciated to $100, A and B actually would be entitled to $75 each upon liquidation (after payment of the liability), not $50, assuming the partnership agreement calls for an equal sharing of appreciation. If the land had decreased in value to $25, each partner would be entitled to $37.50, not $50, upon liquidation.

The figure in the capital account is determined by the basic rules in Treasury Regulation 1.704–1(b)(2)(iv)(b). A partner's capital account is increased by the amount of money she contributes to the partnership, the fair market value of property (decreased by the amount of liabilities attached to the contributed property), and "allocations" to the partner of income and gain. Partnership liabilities do not increase capital accounts. Instead, the amount of the liability is listed directly above the column for each partners' capital adjacent to the word, "liabilities."

A little more explanation is in order regarding the meaning of the term "allocation". Suppose a two person equal partnership earns $100. That income will taxed to the partners, whether distributed or not, in accordance with a respected (i.e., not successfully challenged by the IRS) allocation scheme. The allocation scheme is simply the manner in which the taxpayers decide to divide the income for reporting purposes only. Allocations need not be consistent with distributions and is certainly not synonymous with that term. If the partnership agreement states that all items of income, gain, loss and deduction are to be allocated equally, each partner will have an allocation of $50 and their capital accounts will be increased by that amount. If the partnership agreement allocated income 80% to A and 20% to B, A's capital account would increase by $80, and B's by $20. We will study allocations in great detail in Lessons 10 through 14.

A partner's capital account must also decrease under the basic rules. Capital accounts must be decreased by cash distributions and the fair market value of distributed property (minus any liability to which the property is subject), allocations of expenses that are neither deductible to the partnership nor subject to capitalization, and allocations of deductible losses (such as depreciation) and expenses. Remember that additions and subtractions to capital accounts on one side are matched by additions and subtractions, respectively on the other. For example, if a two person, 50–50 partnership earns $100 in the taxable year, but has depreciation of $200, the partnership's capital accounts will show an aggregate decrease of $100 (a new asset—"cash"—will show a book basis of $100, and the depreciation will decrease the book basis of the asset on which depreciation is taken), and each partner's capital account will be increased by $50, and then decreased by $100. There will be a bottom line decrease of $50 in each partner's capital account, equal to the overall $100 loss for the partnership. If a partner receives a distribution of $100, her capital account must be decreased by that amount, as will the partnership's capital account showing the value of cash.

The basic capital accounting rules apply at all times—beginning of the partnership, operation of the partnership and termination of the partnership. Test your understanding by configuring the partners' capital accounts for the following events:

Practice

1. Read the first sentence of Example 1(i), Treasury Regulation 1.704–1(b)(5). What are the capital account balances for each partner after the cash contributions? Construct the tax/book balance sheet, leaving tax columns blank.

2. If the partnership agreement in Example 1, Treasury Regulation 1.704–1(b)(5) states that all depreciation deductions will be allocated equally and the partnership has a $20,000 depreciation deduction in year one, what will be the capital account balances at the end of year 1? What if the agreement states that depreciation deductions will be allocated 60% to A and 40% to B?

3. Read the first sentence of Example 1(ix), Treasury Regulation 1.704–1(b)(5). What effect does A's contribution of her promissory note have on her capital account?

4. Read Example 18(i), Treasury Regulation 1.704–1(b)(5).

   a. Show the partnership's tax/book balance sheet after the partnership purchases the tangible personal property? (leave the tax columns blank)

   b. Show the tax/book balance sheet as it would appear if, in year three, the partnership earns $400,000, has a depreciation deduction of $200,000, and distributes $200,000 to each of its partners? (leave the tax columns blank)

   c. Show the tax/book balance sheet as it would appear if, in year four, the partnership sold the property for $300,000 (ignore any recapture implications and leave tax columns blank), distributed all of its cash to the partners and terminated.

Note that in question 4c. the partnership will have "book gain" equal to the difference between the amount realized (which must include any amount of liability relief under general tax principles) and the book basis (in this case 0) when it sells the property. Book gains (and losses) must be allocated to each partner's capital account in accordance with the allocation scheme stated in the partnership or LLC agreement. If an asset sells for less than its book basis, the partnership suffers a "book loss" and the loss must be allocated to each partner's capital account. The partnership will also have a tax gain or loss depending on the partnership's tax basis in the property, and those tax gains and losses will likewise be allocated to each partner's tax account. When tax basis equals book basis, book gains and losses will equal tax gains and losses. When the tax and book basis differ, book gains and tax gains will also differ. When we study allocations, we will learn that it is possible and common to have differing book and tax gains and losses from a single transaction. For now, remember that for every transaction a partnership will have both a book gain/loss and a tax gain/loss and the two types of results need not be the same.

A common circumstance where partners have a book gain/loss different from tax gains/losses is when the partners decide to revalue the partnership's property. Remember, capital accounts merely show the value of assets as of a certain date and that value will change over time. Over time, the value should either increase or decrease. Decreases that are accounted for by a deduction (such as a depreciation) will be reflected in the partners' capital accounts under the general rule requiring that additions and subtractions on one side be similarly reflected on the other. Economic appreciation or depreciation will not be automatically reflected. In certain circumstances, partners may wish to revalue the partnership's properties to reflect fair market value as of the date of revaluation. Restating the books essentially means that for book purposes only, the partnership treats each asset as if it were sold and allocates the book gain or loss to the partners' book (i.e., capital) accounts in accordance with the allocation method stated in their partnership agreement. This process is referred to as "booking up" (note the term's erroneous assumption that capital accounts are never revalued to reflect economic depreciation). In such instances, the tax gain/loss will always be zero since a revaluation is merely a paper transaction. At this point, you will not completely understand the meaning of Regulation 1.704–1(b)(2)(iv)(f)(1)–(4) (relating to how the book gain must be allocated if the partners want to ensure all allocations after a "booking-up" will be respected). For now, you should know that Regulation 1.704–1(b)(2)(iv)(f)(1)(5) limits the circumstances in which revaluations may occur.

Another circumstance that will trigger book gain/loss in the absence of tax gain/loss is the distribution of property from the partnership to a partner. We will consider the complete consequences in a later chapter, but note that Regulation 1.704–1(b)(2)(iv)(e) requires the partnership to treat a distribution as though there was a book sale of the property (amount realized equal to fair market value), generating book gain or loss. The book gain or loss must be allocated amongst the partners in accordance with the partnership agreement prior to the distribution—i.e., capital accounts must be increased or decreased as if the property had been sold. The distribution then results in a decrease to the recipient partner's capital account by an amount equal to the property's booked-up (or down) fair market value.

One final point should be made with regard to maintenance of capital accounts. The rules in Regulation 1.704–1(b)(2)(iv) should be consulted with regard to all partnership transactions or accounting changes. They will eventually become intuitive but they will never lend themselves to memorization.

Practice:

1. What are the partners' capital account balances after the following transaction:

> A, B, C, and D each have capital account balances of $1000, as shown below. The partnership agreement allocates all gains and losses equally. The partnership owns property with a tax and book basis of $200. The property is distributed to D when it has a value of $600.

Capital Accounts

A	B	C	D
1000	**1000**	**1000**	**1000**

2. Show the partnership's tax/book balance sheet if, instead of distributing the property, the partnership decides to restate capital accounts to show the property's present value.

3. How much does each partner receive if instead of distributing the property or restating capital accounts, the partnership sells the property for $600 and liquidates. Assume that the partnership had $3,800 cash on hand immediately prior to the liquidation.

Lesson 5

CAPITALIZING THE PARTNERSHIP

Primary References: IRC 709, 721, 722, 723, 731(a), 733, 752(a)–(c), 1223(1)–(2)
Treas. Reg. 1.721–1(a), 1.722–1. 1.723–1, 1.351–1(c)

Case References: **Cottage Savings Association v. Commissioner, 499 U.S. 554 (1991); Philadelphia Park Amusement Co. v. United States, 126 F. Supp. 184 (1954)**

Secondary References: IRC 61(a)(3), 1001, 1016, 453B(a), 1245(b)(3)
Treas. Reg. 1.752–1, 1.1001–1(a), 1.1001–2(a)(1), (a)(4)(iv)

Theory

When a person acquires a partnership interest from a partnership, in exchange for cash or property she and the partnership might be viewed as engaging in a sale or exchange. She is transferring value for value. When the purchase is made with money, there is no immediate tax effect except that the previously taxed (or exempted) income is embodied in the property acquired. The previously taxed income constitutes basis and, in effect, represents a credit against future income resulting from the subsequent disposition of the property received. What happens when a person acquires property by transferring other property? We know three things from which to answer this question. From *Cottage Savings Association* we know that an exchange of property is taxable if the properties are "materially different," though we may not always know what "materially different" means. We know from Treasury Regulation 1.1001–2 that the satisfaction of an obligation with appreciated or depreciated property results in a realized gain or loss, respectively. We also know from *Philadelphia Park* that the basis in property received in a taxable exchange is equal to its fair market value

36

on the date of the exchange. This makes sense because the wealth embodied in the property received has been fully taxed after the exchange.

From these principals, it follows that when taxpayer A transfers appreciated or depreciated property in exchange for materially different property—such as a partnership interest—she realizes gain or loss that must be recognized under traditional tax principles. What effect might that immediate recognition have on the formation of partnerships? We might expect that people would be discouraged from pooling their resources for business purposes. Economist might refer to the immediate tax as an "entry cost" or "entry barrier." One rationale sometimes offered for not requiring immediate recognition relates to the idea of "continuity of interest." We might say that the taxpayer has not really "cashed in" on the appreciation in the property given up, but has merely changed the form of, and continued her prior investment. But actually, there has been a realization event. The taxpayer has done more than simply continue her interest in similar property. The exchange of property for a partnership interest is more akin to (1) the sale of property for cash by a partner, followed by (2) a purchase of an undivided interest in the other assets held or to be held by the partnership, and (3) a repurchase of the first property by the partnership. Thus, the taxpayer should pay tax after step one and the partnership should take a cost basis in the asset. The only problem is, although a contribution to a partnership is substantially identical to the three steps described above, it is procedurally different. The taxpayer who exchanges property for property has a liquidity problem and sometimes illiquidity justifiably postpones taxation.

In the partnership context, the imperative to encourage efficient pooling of income is another, more important reason to postpone taxation. Whenever the Code affirmatively postpones the recognition of gains and losses derived from dealings in property, it preserves the appreciation or depreciation for later taxation by assigning a transferred basis and a "tacked" holding period to the property received. The goal is to preserve the *status quo ante*. The pattern holds true with regard to partnerships.

In many instances, individuals may own and contribute to a partnership property that is encumbered by a liability. We know from *Crane v. Commissioner,* and Treasury Regulation 1.1001–2, that a sale or disposition of encumbered property results in an amount realized not less than the discharged liability. We also know that the basis in property includes the amount borrowed to purchase that property. The IRC 721 nonrecognition rule, however, overrides the fundamental tax rule with regard to gain recognition, including gain caused by the assumption of a liability. Hence, the liability discharge resulting from the exchange of encumbered property for a partnership interest will not cause a taxable event for the transferor partner, except when the liability discharge cannot be preserved for later taxation. The transferor partner's basis in the property received, however, should be reduced to the extent the transferor partner is no longer expected to pay the liability. That is, the amount of potential gain in the property received should be increased by the liability discharged.

Under state law, general partners are jointly and severally liable for partnership liabilities. When encumbered property is contributed by one partner to a partnership the logical result is that the partner is relieved of a liability to the extent the other partners become obligated. It is as if the transferring partner received partial payment for the contributed property. Regulation 1.722–1 treats the liability discharge as a recovery of capital that results in a decrease in the transferor's "outside" basis (i.e., the basis assigned to the intangible property—the partnership interests—received). The partners who are now obligated to pay a portion of the debt are treated as if they paid an additional amount for their partnership interest, and their "outside" basis gets an increase.

Regulation 1.722–1 makes reference to IRC 752 which is more thoroughly considered in Lesson 15. A short summary is appropriate here though. IRC 752(a) treats an increase in a partner's share of partnership liabilities as a contribution of cash, to which 721 will apply. In effect, the partner who now has an increased liability is treated as though she has made an additional purchase and should therefore get a basis equal to the purchase price. IRC 752(b) treats a decrease in liabilities as a distribution of cash—a recovery of capital under Regulation 1.722–1. To the extent the distribution of cash exceeds unrecovered capital it must logically be treated as gain. That gain should be taxable immediately because it represents a "cashing in" of investment appreciation. Treas. Reg. 1.722–1, Example 2 demonstrates that if the deemed distribution of cash exceeds the transferor partner's outside basis, the transferor partner will take a basis of zero in the partnership interest and must recognize gain to the extent of the excess.

Practice

1. Read the first three sentences of Example 13(i), Regulation 1.704–1(b)(5). What is the partnership's amount realized, gain recognized, basis and holding period in the properties it receives? What are each partner's amount realized, gain recognized, basis and holding period upon the receipt of their partnership interest?

2. Construct the tax/book balance sheet (showing each partner's and the partnership's tax and book accounts) immediately after the contributions of property in Example 13(i), Regulation 1.704–1(b)(5).

3. Read Example 1, Regulation 1.722–1. If there were two other individuals, B and C, each of whom had contributed $16,000, what would their outside bases be after A's contribution? Construct the tax/book balance sheet.

4. Read Example 2, Regulation 1.722–1. Assume there are two other partners, B and C, who each hold a 40% interest. Speculate on how the result would change if A were obligated to reimburse B and C for any amount of the mortgage for which either of them were to be held liable?

5. Suppose three individuals and a corporation desire to form a partnership to construct and operate an office building. The corporation is a construction company that provides services as a general contractor for various construction projects. The partnership agreement states that the three individuals will contribute adjacent parcel's of land (each individual's land has a basis of $100,000 and a fair market value of $300,000) to the partnership and the corporation will serve as general contractor for the construction of the building. Under normal circumstances, the corporation would charge $300,000 as general contractor. Under the terms of the partnership agreement the corporation will supervise construction of the building (i.e., serve as general contractor) and waive its fee in exchange for a one-fourth interest in the partnership. Will any of the partners recognize gain on the formation of the partnership?

Lesson 6

PARTNERSHIP CAPITAL INTEREST FOR SERVICES

Primary Reference: IRC 83(a)–(c)(1)–(2), (h), 721
Treas. Reg. 1.83–1(a)(1), 1.704–1(b)–1(b)(2)(iv)(f), 1.721–1(b)(1)–(2), 1.722–1, Prop. Treas. Reg. 1.721–1(b)(1)

Case Reference: McDougal v. Commissioner, 62 T.C. 720 (1974)

Secondary References: IRC 61(a)(1), 162(a)(1), 212, 263
Treas. Reg. 1.61–2(d)(1)–(2), Treas. Reg. 1.1001–2(c), Example 8

Theory

Suppose two people join together to form a partnership. Partner A contributes $100,000 working capital while the Partner B agrees to lend her expertise, but no initial capital. If the partnership agreement provides that partners shall have an equal interest in the capital and profits of the firm, will there be a taxable event? To answer that question we need to deconstruct the transaction. The partnership's total capital is $100,000, because no value is assigned to B's "human capital." B is $50,000 wealthier because she obtained a half interest in the partnership's capital in exchange for future services. To prove this, ask yourself how much B could sell her interest for immediately after the partnership is formed.

As a matter of economic substance, the transaction is very similar to a transaction in which the capital partner paid the expertise partner $50,000 for her services and then each partner contributed $50,000 to a joint venture. If that is the proper view of the transaction, the expert partner should have taxable income immediately prior to the formation of the partnership and the capital partner might have an ordinary and necessary business expense or an amortizable start-up cost. That, in-

40

deed, is precisely the result when a "service partner" is granted a capital interest in exchange for her past or future services.

When the partnership's only capital is cash the outcome is easily demonstrated. It is not terribly more difficult when the partnership's capital is appreciated or depreciated property. It may be a bookkeeping nightmare for a partnership with vast property holdings, but the solution is derived from a single fundamental tax rule: the satisfaction of an obligation with appreciated or depreciated property results in gain or loss to the extent of the appreciation or depreciation. In *McDougal v. Commissioner,* the McDougal's owned a thoroughbred horse for which they paid $10,000. They began to race the horse and take depreciation deductions. McClanahan worked for the McDougal's as a skilled horse trainer. In exchange for his services, McClanahan was granted a one half interest in the horse. IRC 61(a)(1) and Regulation 1.61–2 clearly show that McClanahan had gross income when he received his one half interest in the horse. The McDougals and McClanahan earned income together by racing and putting the horse out to stud. By doing so, the horse owners created an entity—a partnership. The Tax Court, relying on the fundamental principle discussed above, deconstructed the single transaction and then determined the tax consequences based upon the deconstructed parts:

> When, on formation of a joint venture, a party contributing appreciated assets satisfies an obligation by granting his obligee a capital interest in the venture, he is deemed to have transferred to the obligee an undivided interest in the assets contributed, equal in value to the amount of the obligation so satisfied. He and the obligee are deemed thereafter and in concert to have contributed those assets to the joint venture. The contributing obligor will recognize gain on the transaction to the extent that the value of the undivided interest which he is deemed to have transferred exceeds his basis therein. The obligee is considered to have realized an amount equal to the fair market value of the interest which he receives in the venture and will recognize income depending upon the character of the obligation satisfied. The joint venture's basis in the assets will be determined under section 723.

The court went on to explain that any deduction arising from the payment of compensation must be taken by the party for whose benefit the services are preformed. Thus, if the transfer occurred prior to the formation of the partnership, whatever deduction authorized would be taken by the individual transferors. If the transfer was made after the formation of the partnership and the services were performed for the partnership, the partnership would report the deduction and allocate it amongst the partners in accordance with the partnership agreement. Once it is understood that the receipt of a capital interest for services actually represents three transactions—a sale of property, a payment of compensation, and a contribution to a partnership—it becomes easy to determine the taxable outcomes by simply applying fundamental concepts to the deconstructed parts.

If the McDougals had a basis of $6000 in the horse, and the horse was worth $60,000 when the one half interest was transferred to McClanahan, the McDougals would have $27,000 in recognizable gain (a sale of property with a basis of $3,000 for its fair market value of $30,000) and would have paid compensation of $30,000 (the fair market value of the transferred interest in the horse) resulting in a deduction or capitalization of that amount. McClanahan would have taxable compensation income of $30,000 and a tax cost basis in the one half horse equal to that amount. These consequences occur before the partnership is formed. Upon the deemed contribution of the property to the new partnership, the partnership takes a split basis in the horse equal to the McDougal's $3000 and the McClanahan's $30,000 (i.e., treat the one-half interests in the horse as separate properties). The McDougals have an outside basis of $3000, McClanahan has an outside basis of $30,000 and each partner has a capital account balance of $30,000.

McDougal involved the transfer of partnership capital as compensation for past services. What should be the effect of a capital transfer made in exchange for future services? *North American Oil v. Burnett* and *Commissioner v. Glenshaw Glass* tell us that income occurs when a taxpayer exercises "dominion" over wealth. The mere possibility that income will have to be returned does not prevent immediate recognition. Under IRC 83(a), however, a service provider whose compensation is subject to a "substantial risk of forfeiture" will not have income until the risk lapses. The requirement to perform future services is designated as a substantial risk of forfeiture under IRC 83(c) and indeed the regulations state that the property does not actually transfer until the risk lapses. If McClanahan received his partnership interest in exchange for future services, when then would he have income and when would he become a partner? Proposed Regulation 1.721–1(b) appears to confirm that IRC 83 applies (but remember, its only a proposed regulation). And if IRC 83 applies, Treas. Reg. 1.83–1(a)(1) suggests that the service provider is not the owner of transferred property (i.e., the partnership interest) until the risk lapses. Thus, any amounts received by the service provider are treated as additional compensation until the partnership interest vests. How might partners avoid this theoretical problem? See IRC 83(b).

Practice

1. Construct the tax book balance sheet for the McDougal—McClanahan partnership using the values stated in the summary above. Assume both partners are unmarried individuals.

2. *McDougal* concerned the tax consequences upon the formation of a partnership. Regulation 1.721–1(b) applies more broadly to both formations and to admissions of a new partner to an ongoing partnership. If you methodically apply the steps set out in McDougal, you will be able to determine the tax consequences when an existing partnership transfers a capital interest to a service partner. Try to do so with the following hypothetical:

Suppose Partnership AB's tax/book balance sheet appears as follows:

				Liabilities and Partners' Capital **Liabilities:**		
Assets				**Capital**		
	Tax	Book			Tax	Book
Land	10,000	10,000	A		10,000	10,000
Equipment	10,000	10,000	B		10,000	10,000
	20,000	20,000			20,000	20,000

Partner A and B share all income, gain, loss and deductions equally. If Partnership AB admits C as an equal one third capital partner in exchange for services to the partnership what are the tax consequences to all parties, assuming the land and the equipment are each worth $60,000 when C is admitted? Construct the tax book accounts after the transaction.

Theory–Revaluation redux

In the last problem above, note that the book basis of each property is far less than its fair market value as of the date C was admitted. This will normally be the case as assets will have increased (or decreased) in value between the date they are contributed and the date a new partner is admitted. Suppose again that Partnership AB's tax/book balance sheet appeared as follows immediately after formation:

				Liabilities and Partners' Capital **Liabilities:**		
Assets				**Capital**		
	Tax	Book			Tax	Book
Land	10,000	10,000	A		10,000	10,000
Equipment	10,000	10,000	B		10,000	10,000
	20,000	20,000			20,000	20,000

Three years later, the land is worth 60,000 the equipment is worth 60,000 and the Partnership wants to admit another partner who will have an equal capital interest. If the third partner is going to contribute cash, she might be tempted to contribute 10,000. This makes no sense, though, because the partnership is worth 120,000 before admission of the new partner, not 20,000. To have an equal capital interest, the new partner should actually contribute 60,000. If the new partner contributes 60,000 and nothing else occurs, it may appear that the new partner owns the majority of the capital and that too is inconsistent with the economic deal.

To avoid distorting their true economic deal (i.e., all partners shall have an equal one third ownership of partnership capital), the partnership should "restate" the capital accounts. Read Treas. Reg. 1.704–

1(b)(2)(iv)(f) carefully again. The process of restating (i.e., "booking up") capital accounts allows a second review of the difference between book gain and tax gain. In short, book gain or loss refers to the difference between the present value realized and the historical "book value" shown on the books. Tax gain or loss refers to the difference between the amount realized, in an actual sale or disposition, and the partnership's tax basis in the asset sold. If you keep in mind the distinction between book and tax accounting throughout the course, you will gain a better understanding.

Restating the books essentially means that for book purposes only (i.e., for purposes of the book columns), the partnership treats the asset as if they were sold and allocates the book gain to the partners' capital accounts in accordance with the partnership agreement. Since there has not been an actual sale or disposition, there is never a tax gain when the balance sheets are restated. In this instance, there would be a book gain of 50 because the land is now worth 60 and book basis is 10. The same result would apply to the equipment and the book values for both assets would be increased to 60. The 50 book gain on each asset would be allocated equally to the present partners' capital accounts and they would each have 60 in their capital accounts. There would be no changes to the tax accounts because there has not been an actual tax event.

At this point, the partnership can more accurately determine the value of the new partner's one third interest. The new partner could simply contribute 60 if she wanted to be an equal capital partner. If the new partner did not have sufficient capital (and the existing partners were willing) she might be granted a one third interest in existing capital in exchange for past or future services. In that case, the analysis specified in *McDougal* would be applied by reference to the capital accounts. Here are the deconstructed steps (which take place after the restatement described in the previous paragraph):

(1) The partnership would be treated as if it transferred a one third interest in each of its assets in satisfaction of a $40,000 obligation. One third of each asset's basis would be subtracted from one third of each asset's fair market value, resulting in a tax gain of $16,666.67 per asset ($33,333.34 total gain). The basis of the two thirds interest in property not deemed sold would be $6,667.67 each. One third of each asset's book basis ($20,000) would be subtracted from one third of each asset's fair market value ($20,000) resulting in no book gain or loss. Remember for every actual transaction there is both tax and book gain or loss.

(2) The tax gain or loss on the deemed one third sale would be allocated to the partners and reflected in their outside bases, both of which would be increased by $16,666.67 to $26,666.67 (we study outside basis in detail in Lesson 8). Since there is zero book gain (book amount realized is 20,000 and book basis is 20,000) on the sale of a one third interest, there is no change to either partner's capital accounts. Each partner's capital account remains at $60,000.

(3) Next, the partnership would be treated as if it transferred $40,000 worth of capital (20,000 from each asset) to the new partner as compensation for services—the new partner reports $40,000 as taxable compensation income and takes a $20,000 tax cost basis in his one third interest in each asset. The partnership would be entitled to a tax and book deduction equal to the value of the capital ($40,000).

(4) The allocated tax deduction would decrease each partner's outside basis to $6,666.67 ($26,667.67 minus $20,000). The allocated book loss would decrease each partner's capital account to $40,000 ($60,000 minus $20,000). Note that the total outside basis ($13,-335.34, which is $6,667.67 per partner) equals the total of the partnership's "inside" basis in the two thirds property not deemed sold ($13,335.34, which is $6,667.67 per partner). Likewise, outside book accounts equal inside book accounts ($40,000 each).

(5) Finally, the new partner would contribute his one third interest in each asset back to the partnership. His outside basis would be $40,000 ($20,000 per asset) and his capital account balance would be $40,000 ($20,000 per asset). Note that the partnership's inside basis would now equal $6,667.67 in two thirds of each asset, and $20,000 in one third of each asset. The two third and one third interest in each asset would be carried on the books as separate assets. The capital accounts would show the following after all is said and done:

				Liabilities and Partners' Capital **Liabilities:**		
Assets				**Capital**		
	Tax	Book			Tax	Book
2/3 Land	6,667	40,000	A		6,667	40,000
1/3 Land	20,000	20,000	B		6,667	40,000
2/3 Equip	6,667	40,000	C		40,000	40,000
					53,334	120,000
1/3 Equip	20,000	20,000				
	53,334	120,000				

Practice

Suppose Partnership AB's tax/book balance sheet appears as follows before the admission of partner C:

				Liabilities and Partners' Capital **Liabilities:**		
Assets				**Capital**		
	Tax	Book			Tax	Book
Cash	60	60	A		40	40
Land	20	20	B		40	40

1. Assume the land is now worth 60 and the partnership wants to admit C, as an equal one third partner in recognition of her past three years of loyal service to the partnership. What are the tax consequences to all parties? Show the resulting tax book balance sheet.

2. Read IRC 83(a)–(c) and Treasury Regulation 1.83–1(a) again. What result if C in question 1 above is admitted as a partner on the condition that she perform management services for the partnership over the next three years and if she does not complete three years service, her interest reverts back to A and B? When does C become a partner and how are allocations to her during the first three years treated?

Lesson 7

PARTNERSHIP PROFIT INTEREST
FOR SERVICES

Primary References: IRC 721
Treas. Reg. 1.721–1(b)(1)

Case References: Diamond v. Commissioner, 492 F.2d 286
(1974)
Campbell v. Commissioner, 943 F.2d 815
(1991)
Rev. Proc. 93–27, 1993–2 C.B. 343 (reprinted below)
Rev. Proc. 2001–43, 2001–43 C.B. 191 (reprinted below)

Secondary References: IRC 61(a)(1), 83(a)–(c), (h)

Theory

In Lessons 5 and 6, we saw that nonrecognition treatment is not applicable unless the receipt of a partnership interest is in exchange for property. Property can be tangible or intangible but does not include human labor. Thus, Regulation 1.721–1(b)(1) states that when a partner obtains a capital interest in partnership money or property in exchange for services, a compensatory event occurs. The recipient partner must report the income and the payor (either the partnership or one or more partner) may be entitled to a deduction. Deconstructed, the transaction is treated as though the payor transferred money or property to the recipient, and the recipient then contributed the property to the partnership in a 721 transaction. If appreciated or depreciated property is transferred, the payor will have a realization event. As we have seen, the service partner ultimately receives an outside basis and capital account with a balance equal to the amount previously taxed to her as compensation. The increase in the Service partner's capital account confirms that the Service partner has received tangible property.

Suppose, however, that the economic deal between the parties states that the recipient will not receive a credit to her capital account.

47

Remember, capital account balances represent each partner's relative ownership of partnership assets. An individual who receives a share of capital in exchange for services is therefore being compensated by other partners who, by contrast, are relinquishing a share of their own capital. If a partner renders services and ends up with a zero capital account balance, has she still received compensation? That is, the parties agree that in exchange for services, the recipient will receive, say, 20% of all future profits (i.e., a "profit share"). Should this transaction be treated as a compensatory event requiring immediate recognition? If so, how much income does the recipient partner have?

In *Diamond v. Commissioner,* Sol Diamond agreed to arrange a $1.1 million dollar loan for Phil Kargman's purchase of a building. In exchange, Kargman agreed that Diamond would receive 60% of the profits from their joint operation of the building. The joint venture agreement stated that Kargman would provide all the cash needed beyond the loan amount for the purchase of the building, and that proceeds of any sale of the building would be distributed to Kargman to the extent of his cash contribution. Any sale proceeds beyond Kargman's repayment right (i.e., any profit) would be divided equally. Kargman eventually contributed $78,000 in addition to the loan proceeds to the joint venture. Note, that if the parties adhered to the basic capital accounting rules, the partnership balance sheet would have looked like this when the partnership was formed (do you understand why?):

Assets			Liabilities and Partners' Capital		
			Liabilities:		$1,100,000
			Capital		
	Tax	**AB**		**Tax**	**Book**
Building	1.178	1.178	Kargman	1.178	78,000
			Diamond	0	0

The balance sheet visually confirms what Treas. Reg. 1.721–1(b)(1) implicitly suggests. Since Kargman has retained his right to be repaid his contributed money or property, there has been no shift of capital. If the partnership immediately liquidated, only Kargman would be entitled to liquidation proceeds. There has not been an explicit shift of capital from Kargman to Diamond in exchange for Diamond's services. We know, however, that IRC 61(a)(1) taxes compensation no matter the form in which paid. Look at the sentence containing the second parenthetical in Regulation 1.721–1(b)(1). Commentators and even the *Diamond* court suggested that the parenthetical language could reasonably be interpreted as confirmation that the nonrecognition rule of IRC 721 applies if there is no capital shift to a service partner. If so, what are we to make of IRC 61(a)(1), and can Treasury actually legislate such a change?

Remember, Congress grants nonrecognition in IRC 721 only upon the contribution of *property*. Here, Diamond contributed services and receives something of value in return—the right to share in future profit. One of the goals of partnership tax, though, is to impose no more or less tax on joint profit-seekers than would be imposed if the profit-seekers acted individually. Individuals are not taxed on the value of their human capital—i.e, their skill, training and education—until they receive actual payment for the use of their human capital. This observation is not entirely satisfactory because when a service partner obtains the right to future profits in exchange for her human capital, she has indeed received payment. The right can be pledged or transferred, particularly if the future profits are predictable. An individual cannot pledge or transfer the right to her services (something about involuntary servitude renders the pledge or transfer illusory). There is a stronger case for taxing a service partner upon the receipt of a profit interest than there is for taxing an individual immediately after she completes a course of study that increases her earning potential. The service partner actually receives transferable "property" for her human capital and is more appropriately taxed.

Tax law, though, oftentimes defers taxation upon a realization event when administrative or valuation concerns make it difficult to apply fundamental rules. One argument that successfully carried the day prior to *Diamond* was that the actual value of the profit interest was too speculative and therefore should not be taxed upon receipt. In *Diamond,* however, Sol Diamond sold his partnership interest less than one month later for $40,000. The court viewed the sale price as conclusive evidence of its value on the date received, thereby eliminating the objection that the interest was too speculative to include in income. Thus, Sol Diamond had ordinary income upon receipt of the interest. The court adhered to this conclusion despite noting the possible administrative burdens that follow:

> There must be wide variation in the degree to which a profit-share created in favor of a partner who has or will render service has determinable market value at the moment of creation. Surely in many if not the typical situations it will have only speculative value, if any. In the present case, taxpayer's services had all been rendered, and the prospect of earnings from the real estate under Kargman's management was evidently very good. The profit-share had determinable market value. If the present decision be sound, then the question will always arise, whenever a profit-share is created or augmented, whether it has a market value capable of determination. Will the existence of this question be unduly burdensome on those who choose to do business under the partnership form? Each partner determines his income tax by taking into account his distributive share of the taxable income of the partnership. Taxpayer's position here is that he was entitled to defer income taxation on the compensation for his services except as partnership earnings were realized. If a partner is taxed on the determinable market value of a profit-share at the time it is created in his favor, and is also taxed on his full share of earnings as realized, there will arguably be double taxation, avoidable by permitting him to amortize the value which was originally treated as income. Does the absence of a recognized

procedure for amortization militate against the treatment of the creation of the profit-share as income? Do the disadvantages of treating the creation of the profit-share as income in those instances where it has a determinable market value at that time outweigh the desirability of imposing a tax at the time the taxpayer has received an interest with determinable market value as compensation for services? We think, of course, that the resolution of these practical questions makes clearly desirable the promulgation of appropriate regulations, to achieve a degree of certainty. But in the absence of regulation, we think it sound policy to defer to the expertise of the Commissioner and the Judges of the Tax Court, and to sustain their decision that the receipt of a profit-share with determinable market value is income.

Diamond caused quite a stir amongst tax practitioners who had previously advised clients that profit interests were never taxable. The Tax Court reaffirmed its *Diamond* reasoning nearly 20 years later when it decided in *Campbell v. Commissioner* that the receipt of a profit interest for services was immediately taxable under IRC 61(a). Significantly, the taxpayer in *Campbell* did not immediately sell the interest, suggesting that the holding in *Diamond* applied in all instances and that valuation was another issue altogether. On appeal, the government surprisingly conceded error, arguing that receipt of a profit interest was not a taxable event but that taxation occurred for other reasons. The Eighth Circuit, however, refused to accept the concession, though it reversed the Tax Court's because it found that the taxpayer's compensation was "without fair market value at the time he received [it] and should not have been included in his income for the years in issue." It is difficult to know what the Eighth Circuit intended to convey since it (1) rejected the government's concession of error, but (2) held that a profit interest that cannot be easily valued is not income upon receipt. It is nevertheless helpful to consider how the court distinguished the receipt of a capital interest (taxable under Regulation 1.721–1(b)(1)) and the receipt of a profit interest (taxable under *Diamond*, but subject to deferral if not capable of valuation):

> Section 721 codified the rule that a partner who contributes property to a partnership recognizes no income. And, regulation 1.721–1(b)(1) simply clarified that the nonrecognition principles no longer apply when the right to return of that capital asset is given up by transferring it to another partner. At that time, the property has been disposed of and gain or loss, if realized, must be recognized. As a corollary, section 1.721–1(b)(1) outlines the tax treatment of the partner who receives that capital interest. A substantial distinction, however, exists between a service partner who receives a capital interest and one who receives a profits interest. When one receives a capital interest in exchange for services performed, a shift in capital occurs between the service provider and the individual partners. The same is not true when a service partner receives a profits interest. In the latter situation, prior contributions of capital are not trans-

ferred from existing partners' capital accounts to the service provider's capital account. Receipt of a profits interest does not create the same concerns because no transfer of capital assets is involved. That is, the receipt of a profits interest never affects the nonrecognition principles of section 721. Thus, some justification exists for treating service partners who receive profits interests differently than those who receive capital interests.

Because *Campbell* did not clearly distinguish or overrule *Diamond,* taxpayers and tax advisors remained uncertain. The Service finally gave in to the hue and cry for "relief" by issuing Revenue Procedure 93–27 and then later Revenue Procedure 2001–43, both of which are brief enough to be reprinted in full.

REVENUE PROCEDURE 93–27
1993–2 C.B. 343

SEC. 1. PURPOSE

This revenue procedure provides guidance on the treatment of the receipt of a partnership profits interest for services provided to or for the benefit of the partnership.

SEC. 2. DEFINITIONS

The following definitions apply for purposes of this revenue procedure.

.01 A capital interest is an interest that would give the holder a share of the proceeds if the partnership's assets were sold at fair market value and then the proceeds were distributed in a complete liquidation of the partnership. This determination generally is made at the time of receipt of the partnership interest.

.02 A profits interest is a partnership interest other than a capital interest.

SEC. 3. BACKGROUND

Under section 1.721–1(b)(1) of the Income Tax Regulations, the receipt of a partnership capital interest for services provided to or for the benefit of the partnership is taxable as compensation. On the other hand, the issue of whether the receipt of a partnership profits interest for services is taxable has been the subject of litigation. Most recently, in *Campbell v. Commissioner,* 943 F.2d 815 (8th Cir. 1991), the Eighth Circuit in dictum suggested that the taxpayer's receipt of a partnership profits interest received for services was not taxable, but decided the case on valuation. Other courts have determined that in certain circumstances the receipt of a partnership profits interest for services is a taxable event under section 83 of the Internal Revenue Code. *See, e.g., Campbell v. Commissioner,* T.C.M. 1990–162, *rev'd,* 943 F.2d 815 (8th Cir. 1991); *St. John v. United States,* No. 82–1134 (C.D. Ill. Nov. 16, 1983). The courts have also found that typically the profits interest received has speculative or no determinable value at the time of receipt. *See* Campbell, 943 F.2d at 823; St. John. In *Diamond v. Commissioner*, 56 T.C. 530 (1971), *aff'd*, 492 F.2d 286 (7th Cir. 1974), however, the court assumed that the interest received by the taxpayer was a partnership profits interest and found the value of the interest was readily determinable. In that case, the interest was sold soon after receipt.

SEC. 4. APPLICATION

.01 Other than as provided below, if a person receives a profits interest for the provision of services to or for the benefit of a partnership in a partner capacity or in anticipation of being a partner, the Internal Revenue Service will not treat the receipt of such an interest as a taxable event for the partner or the partnership.

.02 This revenue procedure does not apply:

(1) If the profits interest relates to a substantially certain and predictable stream of income from partnership assets, such as income from high-quality debt securities or a high-quality net lease;

(2) If within two years of receipt, the partner disposes of the profits interest; or

(3) If the profits interest is a limited partnership interest in a "publicly traded partnership" within the meaning of section 7704(b) of the Internal Revenue Code.

Another issue that arises with respect to profit interests concerns timing. If the interest is conditioned upon the future performance of services and may be forfeited if those services are not performed, at what point should the determination regarding the service providers' receipt of a capital or profit interest be made? For example if the service provider is to perform services for two years in exchange for a percentage of the profits accruing to the partnership during that two year period, but payable only at the end of the second year, will she receive an interest in capital upon vesting? Logically, it would seem so since during the two year period profits would have accrued to the partnership (increasing existing capital accounts). Upon vesting, those profits would be transferred and distributed to the service partner (thereby resulting in a capital shift).

Most partnerships avoided this problem by requiring the service partner to make an immediate 83(b) election. Since the value of that received would normally be too speculative to value, the service partner would report no income (citing Campbell) and because she would be deemed to be a partner on the date of the 83(b) election, the later vesting would not result in taxable income. The cost, of course, to the partnership is that it is entitled to an IRC 162 deduction for salaries equal to the fair market value of the compensation. Since the compensation had no value, neither could the deduction. This strategy seemed effective but in the absence of statutory or regulatory guidance, there remained some degree of uncomfortable uncertainty. Revenue Procedure 2001–43 is intended to resolve the uncertainty by simply treating all service partners receiving profit interests as having made an 83(b) election provided the service partner is actually treated as a partner from the date the interest is granted.

REVENUE PROCEDURE 2001–43

2001–2 C.B. 191

SECTION 1. PURPOSE

This revenue procedure clarifies Rev. Proc. 93–27, 1993–2 C.B. 343, by providing guidance on the treatment of the grant of a partnership profits interest that is substantially nonvested for the provision of services to or for the benefit of the partnership.

SECTION 2. BACKGROUND

Rev. Proc. 93–27 provides that (except as otherwise provided in section 4.02 of the revenue procedure), if a person receives a profits interest for the provision of services to or for the benefit of a partnership in a partner capacity or in anticipation of being a partner, the Internal Revenue Service will not treat the receipt of the interest as a taxable event for the partner or the partnership. For this purpose, section 2.02 of Rev. Proc. 93–27 defines a profits interest as a partnership interest other than a capital interest. Section 2.01 of Rev. Proc. 93–27 defines a capital interest as an interest that would give the holder a share of the proceeds if the partnership's assets were sold at fair market value and then the proceeds were distributed in a complete liquidation of the partnership. Section 2.01 of Rev. Proc. 93–27 provides that the determination as to whether an interest is a capital interest generally is made at the time of receipt of the partnership interest.

SECTION 3. SCOPE

This revenue procedure clarifies Rev. Proc. 93–27 by providing that the determination under Rev. Proc. 93–27 of whether an interest granted to a service provider is a profits interest is, under the circumstances described below, tested at the time the interest is granted, even if, at that time, the interest is substantially nonvested (within the meaning of § 1.83–3(b) of the Income Tax Regulations). Accordingly, where a partnership grants a profits interest to a service provider in a transaction meeting the requirements of this revenue procedure and Rev. Proc. 93–27, the Internal Revenue Service will not treat the grant of the interest or the event that causes the interest to become substantially vested (within the meaning of § 1.83–3(b) of the Income Tax Regulations) as a taxable event for the partner or the partnership. Taxpayers to which this revenue procedure applies need not file an election under section 83(b) of the Code.

SECTION 4. APPLICATION

This revenue procedure clarifies that, for purposes of Rev. Proc. 93–27, where a partnership grants an interest in the partnership that is substantially nonvested to a service provider, the service provider will be treated as receiving the interest on the date of its grant, provided that:

.01 The partnership and the service provider treat the service provider as the owner of the partnership interest from the date of its grant and the service provider takes into account the distributive share of partnership income, gain, loss, deduction, and credit associated with that interest in computing the service provider's income tax liability for the entire period during which the service provider has the interest;

.02 Upon the grant of the interest or at the time that the interest becomes substantially vested, neither the partnership nor any of the partners deducts any amount (as wages, compensation, or otherwise) for the fair market value of the interest; and

.03 All other conditions of Rev. Proc. 93–27 are satisfied.

Practice

1.   Revenue Procedures 93–27 and 2001–43 have essentially put the matter to rest, however much untidily. A recent private letter ruling considered the application of the procedures in the context of a corporation's profit sharing plan. The facts are reprinted below. Analyze the tax results to participants in the plan.

Facts:

Real Corporation (Real) develops, acquires, manages, operates, and owns a diverse portfolio of real property. Corporation is the sole general partner of Limited, a limited partnership. Corporation also owns a limited partnership interest in Limited. Limited is an operating partnership that owns a diverse portfolio of real property.

Real currently has an incentive compensation arrangement that provides certain key executives of Real, Limited, and Real's affiliates with restricted stock grants. Real proposes to supplement this arrangement with interests in Plan B, under which participating executives will receive interests in Limited. These interests will generally be identical to common limited partnership interests of Limited, but will be subject to vesting and forfeiture, and will not have redemption rights. Participating executives will make a capital contribution of $100 and will receive an initial capital account of $100. Participants will thereafter be entitled to receive 1% of Limited' profits and losses. Over the past five years, Limited's profits have average about $2,000,000 per year. In connection with the issuance of Plan B units, Limited will revalue its assets and adjust its existing partners' capital accounts.

What are the tax consequences to executives who participate in Plan B. Assume that common limited partnership interests of the type Plan B interests are modeled after are sold at private offerings for significantly more than $100, though the exact price depends on market factors on the date of sale. What requirements must be met to ensure the Service does not seek to immediately tax the value of the profit interest? What other facts do you need to know to give a reasonably conclusive opinion?

2.   Does the IRS' concession with regard to profit interest cost the government any revenue? Consider again the second requirement in section 4.02, Rev. Proc. 2001–02 before answering.

3.   Are profit interests tax shelters for the wealthy? Since service partners who receive profit interest are taxed when profits are earned by the partnership isn't this issue purely academic?

4.   The following hypothetical is a modified version of one found in American Law Institute, Federal Income Tax Project: Subchapter K–Proposals of The American Law Institute on The Taxation of Partners, 146 (1984):

> Stewart Rod is so prominent and popular an entertainer at the moment that any show he participates in is virtually guaranteed to earn profits equal to at least 300% of the cost to put on the show. Rod usually charges $2,000,000 per show when he performs for others. In this instance, however, Rod agrees to contribute his services for a period of ten weeks without cost, to a partnership comprised of him and King Don, an entertainment promoter. King Don will contribute $1,000,000 and the partnership will use the cash to produce a show staring Rod. Rod and Don will be equal partners but Don will have the right to a return of his capital before Rod gets any distribution.

What are the tax consequences to Rod upon the formation of the partnership?

Lesson 8

PARTNERS' OUTSIDE BASIS

Primary References: IRC   704(d),   705,   722,   731(a)–(c)(1),
732(a)–(d), 733, 742, 751(c)–(d)
Treas. Reg. 1.704–1(d), 1.705–1(a), 1.731–
1, 1.732–1(a)–(c)

Secondary References: 1.704–1(b)(2)(iv)(e)

Theory

Basis is the fundamental mechanism by which our tax system
accounts for previously taxed accessions to wealth. Basis assures that
income is taxed only once. Assume for example a taxpayer earns $40,000
salary in year one. We know that she has an accession to wealth and
(assuming a flat 15% rate), she will pay $6000. Her after tax income is
$34,000. Now suppose she purchases property for $34,000. Forty thousand dollars of previously taxed wealth (i.e., $34,000) is now embodied in
property. The taxpayer is no wealthier than before. If she sells the
property later for $40,000, the taxpayer will have $40,000 in cash. She
will not be $40,000 richer, but only $6,000 richer. Her accession to
wealth will be $6,000 and she will pay $900 in taxes. To ensure that our
system taxes accessions to wealth—i.e., net rather than gross income—
we need a method by which to keep track of previously taxed wealth.
Basis is that method. Thus, the owner of property purchased with
previously taxed wealth has a basis equal to the after tax value of that
wealth. In this case, the owner has a basis equal to the after tax value of
$40,000, or $34,000. Over the course of two transactions (the receipt of
salary and the sale of the property), the taxpayer's wealth increased by
$46,000 and she should have paid $6900—$6,000 on the receipt of salary
and $900 on the sale of property.

In this Lesson, we consider the rules that ensure that income and
expenses earned or paid via a partnership are taxed or deducted once
and only once. If you keep this goal in mind, the calculations will make
more sense. Keep in mind, also, that the rules discussed in this section
apply only to the partners' outside bases. The regulations under IRC 704

(considered in Lessons 4, and 10 through 14) control the maintenance of partners' capital accounts.

a. Effect of allocated income and gain on partners' outside basis

A partner's basis in her partnership interest is calculated so as to keep track of previously taxed income. In this manner, a partner (just as any other property owner) is not taxed twice on the same wealth. We have already seen that the contribution of property to a partnership is a nontaxable event and that a partner takes an exchanged basis in the partnership interest obtained thereby. The assignment of an exchanged basis is typical whenever the code defers recognition. Like-kind exchanges, which you may have studied in an initial tax course, are but one example of how basis ensures that income is taxed only once, but at least once. Basis changes, though, as taxpayers invest or recover previously taxed income embodied in the property to which the basis is assigned.

Suppose each partner in a two person partnership have outside bases of zero and that the partnership earns $500 in year one. Under IRC 702 the income is taxed immediately to the partners. They will then own property (the partnership interest) that embodies previously taxed, unrecovered capital. Accordingly, they will be entitled to increase their aggregate bases by that amount ($500). IRC 705 determines each partner's "outside basis" in this manner and thus keeps track of income previously taxed and unrecovered. A partner's outside basis, for example, is increased by her distributive share of income. It may be easier to understand the results by looking at the tax book balance sheet and a summary of the partner's individual tax liabilities at the end of year one during which the partnership earned $500:

Assets			Liabilities and Partners' Capital Liabilities: Capital		
	Tax	Book		Tax	Book
Cash	500	500	A	250	250
			B	250	250

A's gross income: $250
B's gross income: $250

Note that each partner's outside basis equals the amount of their respective gross incomes from the partnership.

IRC 731(a) works in conjunction with IRC 705 to ensure that accessions to wealth via the partnership are not double taxed. When distributions are made at a later date, there is no tax unless a distribution of cash exceeds the partner's outside basis. A distribution of cash will only exceed a partner's outside basis if the amount thereof has not previously been taxed to the recipient partner. Hence, there is no double tax to the recipient since only the distributed cash in excess of previously taxed income is taxed. In effect, the distribution is treated as a recovery of capital embodied in basis. A partner's outside basis is therefore decreased upon each distribution of cash so that she receives only a single credit for each previously taxed dollar (i.e., each dollar of basis). If a partner receives a distribution of cash that exceeds her outside basis, she is taxed on the excess but only because she has not previously been taxed on that amount. Take a look at the partnership's tax/book accounts, and the partner's taxable income assuming a distribution of $250 to each partner.

Assets			Liabilities and Partners' Capital Liabilities: Capital		
	Tax	Book		Tax	Book
Cash	0	0	A	0	0
			B	0	0

A's gross income: $0
B's gross income: $0

The $250 distributions had already been taxed to each partner once, as represented by the year one increase in their outside basis to $250. Thus, upon actual hands-on receipt of the money (i.e., the recovery of capital), the partners will not be taxed again. Note, too, that the distribution did not exceed outside basis.

b.   Effect of allocations of exempt income on outside basis

In addition to keeping track of previously taxed income, basis also tracks previous accessions to wealth that are specifically exempted from tax. For example, wealth received by a decedent's beneficiary is specifically exempted from taxation so the beneficiary receives a fair market value basis under IRC 1014. The wealth is not previously taxed, but to preserve the exemption the code provides a basis equal to fair market value. The same process works via partnerships. If the partnership earns tax exempt income, no partner will pay taxes on the income—i.e., the income will be reported by the partners as tax exempt. But if partners do not get basis credit for the income, it will be taxed when distributed. Suppose for example a two person partnership earns $200 in tax exempt income and $200 in ordinary income. In year one, each partner will report $100 income and their outside basis will be increased by $100. If, in year two, the partnership distributes $200 to each partner, the partners will each report $100 of taxable income (the amount by which the distribution of cash exceeds the outside basis). In the aggregate, they will have paid taxes on $200, when $100 per partner should have been exempted. To prevent this result, IRC 705(a)(1)(B) mandates a basis increase for a partnership's tax exempt income. The effect is to ensure that the Congressionally granted tax exemption flows through to the partners. The results can be seen in the partnership tax book accounts:

Assets			Liabilities and Partners' Capital Liabilities: Capital		
	Tax	Book		Tax	Book
Cash	400	400	A	200	200
			B	200	200

A's gross income: $100
B's gross income: $100

Note that the partners have outside bases that indicate a future credit of $200 against taxable income, but have reported only $100. This is proper because the other $100 is specifically exempted from tax. The extra $100 basis means that the partnership can distribute $200 to each partner without the partners incurring a tax liability (they have already paid tax on $100 and the other $100 is exempt from taxation). If the partners' outside bases were not increased by the non-taxable $100, a distribution of $200 to each partner would trigger a tax (because $200 exceeds $100 by $100). The exempt nature of the interest income would have been stripped during distribution.

c. Effect of allocated deductions and loss on partners' outside basis

Clearly, outside basis keeps track of taxpayer's unrecovered, previously taxed (or exempted) capital. The recovery, or deductible consumption of capital supports a one time charge against taxable income. Thus, a distribution of cash is, as we have seen, a nontaxable recovery of capital but only to the extent of the capital not yet recovered (i.e., the adjusted basis). A loss deduction is allowable to the extent invested capital is consumed in a profit-seeking (or tax favored) manner—i.e., a deduction represents a permanent loss of capital for which a tax concession is granted. Basis is therefore equal to the amount of capital invested and not recovered or consumed (deducted). It follows that basis should be decreased as capital is recovered or consumed. If not, a property owner will be allowed to deduct the same dollar twice. For this reason, IRC 705(a)(2) mandates a decrease in a partner's outside basis upon a distribution of cash (a recovery of capital) or an allocation of deductions (a permanent loss of capital) to the partner.

IRC 705(a)(2)(B) further exemplifies the notion that each invested dollar supports one, and only one, dollar of deduction. Suppose, for example, a two person partnership earns $200 and makes a $200 charitable contribution in year one. The partnership may not deduct the contribution in calculating its taxable income (IRC 703(a)(2)(3)), nor is the amount properly capitalized, so the partnership will report $200 income on Form 1065. Nevertheless, the $200 charitable contribution is passed through and reported by the partners and claimed by each partner. It is as if the partners earned $200 and then "consumed" the capital in a transaction generating a deduction. They should record that deduction by decreasing their outside basis by that amount since basis is an account of unrecovered, unconsumed capital and here $100 has in fact been consumed in a deductible manner. If the partners' outside basis is not adjusted downward, they will get to claim the deduction twice. In year one, they will report $100 and deduct the $100 charitable contribution leaving no taxable income. Both partners should have zero outside bases. This result is ensured, though, only if the charitable contribution allocation causes a decrease in the partners' outside bases (even though the deduction was unavailable to the partnership). Thus, IRC 705(a)(2)(B) mandates a decrease in the partner's outside basis in year one equal to the non-deductible, non-capitalized amount. Take a look at tax/book balance sheet without accounting for the charitable contribution as compared to the tax book balance sheet properly accounting for the charitable contribution:

(1) Year 1, income of $200, charitable contribution of $200 (without reduction for the charitable contribution):

			Liabilities and Partners' Capital		
			Liabilities:		
Assets			**Capital**		
	Tax	Book		Tax	Book
Cash	0	0	A	100	100
			B	100	100

A's taxable income: $0 ($100 income less $100 charitable contribution deduction)
B's taxable income: $0 ($100 income less $100 charitable contribution deduction)

Note that the partners have no taxable income for the year, but they have a $100 basis (i.e., a future credit [mis]representing previously taxed, unrecovered and unconsumed capital). Note also that the books are off balance—assets do not equal liabilities plus capital—an indication that something is amiss. The correct representation is as follows:

(1) Year 1, income of $200, charitable contribution of $200.

			Liabilities and Partners' Capital		
			Liabilities:		
Assets			**Capital**		
	Tax	Book		Tax	Book
Cash	0	0	A	0	0
			B	0	0

A's taxable income: $0 ($100 income, $100 deduction)
B's taxable income: $0 ($100 income, $100 deduction)

In this instance, outside basis shows that all capital has been previously recovered or consumed and there is no previously taxed income embodied in either partner's property interest.

d. Effect of proportionate distributions of property on partner's outside basis

A distribution of property implicates three consequences. First, the recipient partner may receive a return of capital (to the extent of the partner's outside basis immediately before the distribution). Second, the recipient partner may receive value in excess of her invested capital as represented by her outside basis (to the extent the property's value exceeds outside basis). In theory, the value in excess of basis represents an accession to wealth and triggers recognition under fundamental tax principles. Third, or perhaps merely another way of viewing the second consequence, there may be unrealized gain or loss inherent in the property distributed (i.e., the partnership's inside basis in the property distributed may be different from the property's fair market value).

One of the economic goals of subchapter K is to make joint profit-seeking no more taxable than is individual profit-seeking. Think about this for a minute. A sole proprietor would not be taxed when the business is started, nor would she be taxed upon the withdrawal of assets from the business. The proprietor would have the same basis in withdrawn property as she had when it was used in business. If a sole proprietor sold her assets at some later date and received cash in excess of basis, she would have to recognize gain. This result is analogous to the result when a partnership distributes cash in excess of basis. Likewise, the rules regarding the distribution of property from a partnership are constructed, with one significant exception, so that when a partner withdraws property from the partnership there is no immediate tax effect. But to the extent the partner has recovered capital, her outside basis should be reduced and assigned to the distributed property. These two imperatives—not taxing the partner upon a withdrawal of property, but accounting for the recovery of capital—requires that the distributed property's basis to the recipient partner, plus that of the remaining partnership interest still held, equal the partner's unrecovered outside basis immediately before the distribution.

Thus, unrecovered capital previously embodied in the partner's outside basis is essentially divided and embodied in two (or more) separate properties—the partnership interest and the distributed property. As a practical matter, this means that the combined bases of the partnership interest and the distributed property can never exceed the partner's outside basis, immediately before a distribution less any cash distributed. This outcome, that the combined adjusted basis of the distributed properties and the partner's outside basis equal the outside basis immediately prior to the distribution, less cash, is easy enough to achieve when there is a current distribution of one piece of property. Under IRC 731 and 732(a), the partner simply reduces her basis by the amount of cash (if any) distributed, the distributed property takes the lesser of the partnership's basis in the property immediately before the distribution or the reduced outside basis, and finally the partner's outside basis is reduced by the basis assigned to the property.

In a liquidating distribution consisting solely of cash, "hot assets" or a combination of both, a recipient partner is allowed to recognize loss. Hot assets include unrealized receivables and inventory items and are so called because transactions involving those assets may trigger less favorable tax consequences, such as immediate recognition of ordinary income (considered in Lesson 23) than transactions involving other assets. This is because under IRC 732(c), a partner's basis in hot assets can never exceed the partnership's basis in those assets immediately prior to the distribution. Other assets may end up with a higher basis in the hands of the recipient partner. *See* Treas. Reg. 1.732–1(b), Example. Hot assets, however, will always take a basis in the hands of the recipient partner equal to their basis in the partnership's hands or the partner's outside basis, whichever is less. This rule is stated in an almost indecipherable language in IRC 732(c)(1)(A). The goal is to preserve the exact amount of ordinary gain or loss the partner would have recognized if the partnership had sold the hot assets prior to the distribution.

If a partnership makes a liquidating distribution of $10,000 cash and inventory with an inside basis of $10,000 to a partner with an outside basis of $25,000, the first $10,000 of outside basis will be consumed by the cash and the recipient will take a $10,000 basis in the inventory. IRC 732(c)(1)(A) does not authorize a stepped up basis for inventory in order that the basis in distributed properties after the distribution equal the outside basis immediately prior to the distribution. Instead, any remaining outside basis can only be allocated to other distributed assets. Because there are no other assets in the example, and the partner no longer holds an interest in the partnership (to which the remaining $5000 unrecovered capital could otherwise be assigned), $5000 of his capital is lost forever. IRC 731(a)(2) allows a loss deduction in this instance.

With a theoretical understanding tentatively in hand, we can turn to the method by which IRC 732 and 733 determine outside basis upon the distribution of property. Note that the determination of outside basis necessarily requires the calculation of the distributed properties' basis to the recipient partner. Unfortunately, IRC 732 is a rather poor articulation of the process. Important points to remember: if there is a distribution of multiple properties, the combined bases of all the properties, plus the outside basis in the partnership must equal either (1) the outside basis immediately prior to the distribution reduced by any cash simultaneously distributed or (2) the outside basis plus any recognized loss, and (3) the basis of distributed "hot assets" to a partner can never be more than the partnership's basis in the assets immediately prior to the distribution. In all circumstances, basis is assigned first to distributed hot assets, if any. A 1997 House Committee Report provides general guidance:

Under the provision, basis is allocated first to the extent of each distributed property's adjusted basis to the partnership. Any remaining basis adjustment, if an increase, is allocated among properties with unrealized appreciation in proportion to their respective amounts of unrealized appreciation (to the extent of each property's appreciation), and then in proportion to their respective fair market values. For example, assume that a partnership with two assets, A and B, distributes them both in liquidation to a partner whose basis in its interest is 55. Neither asset consists of inventory or unrealized receivables. Asset A has a basis to the partnership of 5 and a fair market value of 40, and asset B has a basis to the partnership of 10 and a fair market value of 10. Under the provision, basis is first allocated to asset A in the amount of 5 and to asset B in the amount of 10 (their adjusted bases to the partnership). The remaining basis adjustment is an increase totaling 40 (the partner's 55 basis minus the partnership's total basis in distributed assets of 15). Basis is then allocated to asset A in the amount of 35, its unrealized appreciation, with no allocation to asset B attributable to unrealized appreciation because its fair market value equals the partnership's adjusted basis. The remaining basis adjustment of 5 is allocated in the ratio of the assets' fair market values, i.e., 4 to asset A (for a total basis of 44) and 1 to asset B (for a total basis of 11).

If the remaining basis adjustment is a decrease, it is allocated among properties with unrealized depreciation in proportion to their respective amounts of unrealized depreciation (and then in proportion to their respective adjusted bases (taking into account the adjustments already made)). A remaining basis adjustment that is a decrease arises under the provision when the partnership's total adjusted basis in the distributed properties exceeds the amount of the partner's basis in its partnership interest, and the latter amount is the basis to be allocated among the distributed properties. For example, assume that a partnership with two assets, C and D, distributes them both in liquidation to a partner whose basis in its partnership interest is 20. Neither asset consists of inventory or unrealized receivables. Asset C has a basis to the partnership of 15 and a fair market value of 15, and asset D has a basis to the partnership of 15 and a fair market value of 5. Under the provision, basis is first allocated to the extent of the partnership's basis in each distributed property, or 15 to each distributed property, for a total of 30. Because the partner's basis in its interest is only 20, a downward adjustment of 10 (30 minus 20) is required. The entire amount of the 10 downward adjustment is allocated to the property D, reducing its basis to 5. Thus, the basis of property C is 15 in the hands of the distributee partner, and the basis of property D is 5 in the hands of the distributee partner.

IRC 732(c) provides two formulas for assigning basis to all the distributed properties owned by the partner after a distribution. One formula applies when the partner's outside basis is less than the combined bases of the distributed properties to the partnership, and another applies when the outside basis is greater than the combined bases to the partnership of the distributed properties. The second formula, however, will only be necessary when property is distributed to a retiring partner. In a current distribution, the outside basis in excess of the combined basis of distributed property simply becomes the basis of the partnership interest. In liquidating distributions, the excess basis cannot be the basis in the partnership interest because the partner no longer holds such an interest.

High basis is always good. In the grand scheme of taxing income from property, probably the only thing better than high basis is complete tax exemption. A high basis results in less gain recognition on the sale of property, or higher depreciation deductions from the business use of property. And high basis is even better if it can be generated with "other peoples' money" (OPM). We will study the intersection of basis and OPM in Lesson 15, regarding the allocation of liabilities amongst partners. For now, take note of Treasury Regulation 1.704–1(d)(4), Example 2. In that example C increases her basis using OPM and thereby accelerates a $4000 loss deduction. The last part of this Lesson 8 deals with the effect of low outside basis on individual partners. Read IRC 704(d), particularly the second sentence. The simple rule is that a partner can deduct allocated losses only to the extent the losses do not exceed outside basis. What does the second sentence mean when it says that any excess loss can only be taken when the excess is "repaid" to the partnership?

In general, deductions are personal to each taxpayer. A deduction means that a taxpayer has consumed her own capital in a tax favored manner (e.g., in the pursuit of profit). One taxpayer's financial expenditure cannot generate a deduction for someone else. Even a deduction generated by borrowed money fits this theory because it is assumed that the borrower will eventually pay the loan. When a partner is allocated a loss deduction that exceeds the amount of her capital invested in the partnership (i.e., exceeds her outside basis), she is essentially borrowing from the other partners (or a nonpartner in the case of lender financing) because the expense giving rise to the deduction had to have been paid by someone. When the expense was generated by another partner's capital, (as for example, when one partner has contributed most of the capital but losses are disproportionately allocated to another partner), the loss-claiming partner is essentially borrowing capital from the other partner. The deduction assumes a financial expenditure but since the partner has not invested any of her own capital, she must have "borrowed" it from somewhere. Since there is usually a personal relationship between partners, the law does not assume that the loan will eventually be repaid the way we can assume with an outside lender. Therefore, the "borrowing" partner does not get the benefit of the deduction until the amount is actually repaid and it can then be conclusively said that the deduction represents a personal financial outlay by that partner.

Practice

1. Read Example 1, Regulation 1.704–1(d)(4). What would A's outside basis be if in 1957 the partnership earned $50,000 and distributed $10,000 to A? Assume income is allocated equally to A and B.

2. What would A's basis be in 1958 if the partnership lost $10,000 and, in addition, made a $5,000 charitable contribution to an animal rescue organization? How much of A's allocated loss could she deduct? Assume all items are allocated equally.

3. Read Example 3, Regulation 1.704–1(d)(4). What would C's deductible losses be in 1956 if the partnership had $15,000 income and $21,000 in losses consisting of: $7,000 in short term capital losses, $3,000 in 1231 losses, and $10,000 ordinary and necessary business expenses? Assume C is allocated one third of all partnership items.

4. Read Example 1, Regulation 1.731–1(a)(2)(ii). What would be the tax consequences to A if her basis was $5000 immediately prior to the distribution?

5. Read Example 2, Regulation 1.731–1(a)(2)(ii). What is B's basis in the distributed real property if the partnership distributed $2,000 cash, real property with a basis of $7,000 and unrealized receivables with a basis of $3,000?

6. Read Example 1, Regulation 1.732–1(a). What would A's basis in the property be if the partnership distributed $6000 cash and the property to A? What would A's outside basis be?

7. What result in Example 2, Regulation 1.732–1(a) if the partnership distributed the property on March 1 and the cash on October 9th? Assume the partnership uses the calendar year as its taxable year.

8. What result in Regulation 1.732–1(b), Example, if the retiring partner had an adjusted basis of $6,000 immediately before the liquidating distribution.

10. Read Example 1, Regulation 1.732–1(c)(4). What result if the inventory had a basis of $150, and asset X had a basis of $100? What is the amount and character of gain if the distributee partner, who is not a dealer with regard to the inventory, sells the inventory for $200 two years later? See IRC 735

11. Read Example 2, Regulation 1.732–1(c)(4). What result if the partnership also distributed inventory with a basis of $150 along with assets X and Y in complete liquidation?

12. Read Example 4, Regulation 1.732–1(c)(4). What result if the partnership also distributed a capital asset with a basis of $1000 to the partnership?

Lesson 9

PARTNERSHIP INSIDE BASIS

Primary References:	IRC 723, 731(a)–(b), 732(a)–(c), 734, 754, 755
	Treas. Reg. 1.723–1, 1.734–1, 1.754–1, 1.755–1(a)(1), (c), 1.701–2(d), Examples 8 and 9
Secondary Reference:	Treas. Reg. 1.704–1(b)(z)(iv)(m)(4), 1.705–2(a)

Theory

You may recall from Lesson 4 that a fundamental precept of partnership tax accounting is that assets equal liabilities plus capital. That is a rule of financial accounting—it relates to the book values on the left and right side of the tax/book balance sheet. A fundamental rule of partnership taxation is that income is taxed once and only once. Outside and inside bases are calibrated to achieve this result. We saw in the last lesson that IRC 705, 731, 732, and 733 work together to prevent double taxation of partnership gains and losses. The goal, as noted in Regulation 1.705–2(a) is "preserve equality between the adjusted basis of a partner's interest in a partnership (outside basis) and such partner's share of the adjusted basis in partnership assets (inside basis)." Those rules, however, do not work perfectly. In some instances, they may cause an inequality between outside and inside basis and that inequality will cause over- or under-taxation. Tax/Book examples allow us to visualize the distortion. In all the examples in this Lesson, assume the capital accounts have been revalued in conjunction with the distribution as allowed by Regulation 1.704–1(b)(iv)(f)(5)(ii). Assume a four person partnership with the follow tax/book balance sheet:

Book 1:

Assets			Liabilities and Partners' Capital Liabilities: Capital		
	Tax	**Book**		**Tax**	**Book**
Cash	20,000	20,000	A	10,000	14,000
Land	6,000	14,000	B	10,000	14,000
Stock	6,000	7,000	C	10,000	14,000
Inventory	8,000	15,000	D	10,000	14,000
	40,000	56,000		40,000	56,000

Note that there is $16,000 in unrealized gain in the partnership (the difference between the partnership tax and book bases). At some point, that gain should be taxed once and only once. If the partnership distributed the land to partner A in a current distribution, A would recognize no gain and the land would have a basis of $6,000 in A's hands. His outside basis would decrease to $4,000. The tax book balance sheet would be adjusted as follows:

Book 2:

Assets			Liabilities and Partners' Capital Liabilities: Capital		
	Tax	**Book**		**Tax**	**Book**
Cash	20,000	20,000	A	4,000	0
Stock	6,000	7,000	B	10,000	14,000
Inventory	8000	15,000	C	10,000	14,000
	34,000	42,000	D	10,000	14,000
				34,000	42,000

Eight thousand of the partnership's $16,000 would eventually be taxed to A, leaving $8,000 taxable to the partnership. If A sold the land at its then fair market value, he would recognize $8,000 gain upon the sale. When the partnership sold its inventory and stock, the partners would collectively report $8,000. Thus, the entire $16,000 would have been taxed once and only once. In this instance, IRC 731, 732, and 733 work perfectly.

Suppose, instead, that A's outside basis was only $4,000 before any distribution (and B, C, and D's bases were $12,000 each). He would still recognize no gain on the distribution of land, but his basis in the land would be only $4,000 under IRC 732(a)(2). The partnership balance sheet after the distribution would appear thusly:

Book 3:

Assets			Liabilities and Partners' Capital Liabilities: Capital		
	Tax	**Book**		**Tax**	**Book**
Cash	20,000	20,000	A	0	0
Stock	6,000	7,000	B	12,000	14,000
Inventory	8,000	15,000	C	12,000	14,000
	34,000	42,000	D	12,000	14,000
				36,000	42,000

Note that the partnership and partner's tax accounts are now off balance. The partnership's inside basis is less than the partners' aggregate outside basis by $2000. When partner A sells the land, he will have $10,000 gain. When the partnership sells the stock and the inventory, it (and therefore the partners) will have $8000 gain. The total gain taxed to the partners will be $18,000, when in fact the untaxed appreciation immediately before the distribution was only $16,000. In this instance, IRC 731, 732, and 733 do not work perfectly because $2,000 will be taxed twice.

Let's go back to the original hypothetical when all the partners had a $10,000 outside basis and $14,000 capital account (Book 1). If, instead of distributing the land, the partnership distributed $14,000 to A, A would recognize $4000 under IRC 731(a) and the partnership balance sheet would look like this:

Book 4:

Assets			Liabilities and Partners' Capital Liabilities: Capital		
	Tax	**Book**		**Tax**	**Book**
Cash	6,000	6,000	A	0	0
Land	6,000	14,000	B	10,000	14,000
Stock	6,000	7,000	C	10,000	14,000
Inventory	8,000	15,000	D	10,000	14,000
	26,000	42,000		30,000	42,000

Here, too, the tax accounts are off-balance and when the partnership sells its land, stock and inventory, it will have $16,000 taxable gain. Since A will have already reported $4,000 taxable gain, the distribution would have caused an increase in taxable income by $4,000.

Since we know that basis represents previously taxed (or exempted) income, we should conclude that the partnership's inside basis in Books

3 and 4 ought to be increased to avoid double taxation. At this point, we understand the proper outcome and it is now simply a matter of deciphering the mechanics.

IRC 754 authorizes an election whereby the partnership may increase it's inside basis and thereby avoid double taxation. Be sure you understand how to make, and the effect of the election. *See* Treas. Reg. 1.754–1. Once an election is made, it will apply to all distributions (and transfers of partnership interests, discussed in a later Lesson) and will not be revocable without the Commissioner's consent. You should be able to intuitively predict the amount of adjustment based on the results in Books 3 and 4. In Book 3, the partnership is potentially overtaxed by $2000 (the difference between the land's inside basis and its basis to Partner A). In Book 4, the partnership is potentially overtaxed by $4000, the amount of gain immediately taxed to partner A. In both instances, the adjustment to the partnership's inside basis equals the amount of income potentially over-taxed. IRC 734(b), which is triggered by a 754 election, brings about these results.

An analysis of the tax/book accounts after a liquidating distribution to a partner whose outside basis (less cash received in the same distribution) exceeds the partnership's basis in distributed properties demonstrates the need for a downward adjustment. Suppose the tax/book balance sheet appeared as follows prior to a distribution and that the partnership distributed the inventory to A in complete liquidation of her interest:

Book 5:

Assets			Liabilities and Partners' Capital Liabilities: Capital		
	Tax	**Book**		**Tax**	**Book**
Cash	20,000	20,000	A	10,000	14,000
Land	6,000	14,000	B	10,000	14,000
Stock	6,000	8,000	C	10,000	14,000
Inventory	8,000	14,000	D	10,000	14,000
	40,000	56,000		40,000	56,000

Under 732(c), A would take an $8000 basis and would recognize a $2000 capital loss. After the distribution, the tax/book balance sheet would appear as follows:

Book 6:

Assets			Liabilities and Partners' Capital Liabilities: Capital			
	Tax	**Book**			**Tax**	**Book**
Cash	20,000	20,000	B		10,000	14,000
Land	6,000	14,000	C		10,000	14,000
Stock	6,000 32,000	8,000 42,000	D		10,000 30,000	14,000 42,000

That the partnership's aggregate inside basis is greater than the partners' aggregate outside basis indicates that something is amiss and an adjustment is appropriate. IRC 734(b)(2) would mandate the appropriate adjustment if an IRC 754 election were in effect. Note, that partnership inside basis will be decreased, if at all, only upon the liquidation of a partner's interest in the partnership (i.e., where the partner is allowed to recognize a loss or where the partner's basis in distributed property is greater than the partnership's inside basis immediately prior to the distribution). A downward adjustment is not possible or appropriate with respect to a current distribution.

The method of allocating adjustments to undistributed property is designed to ensure that the partnership gets an appropriate credit against the same character of gain taxed, or to be taxed, to the partner. Thus, if the partner recognized capital gain or loss as a result of a distribution of cash, the increase will be allocated solely to undistributed capital gain property (thus resulting in less capital gain when the partnership sells or disposes of the undistributed capital gain property). If the partner's basis in distributed property is greater or less than the partnership's basis in the same property immediately prior to the distribution, the adjustment will be allocated to undistributed property of a similar type (ordinary or capital asset) as the distributed property. If the partnership does not have the relevant type of property after the exchange, it may not make an immediate increase but must wait until it acquires such property.

If the partnership has more than one type of property in the class to which increases should be allocated, the increases are divided amongst the properties within the class, first in proportion to the relative percentages of aggregate appreciation amongst the properties (but the amount of increase cannot be greater than actual appreciation in each property) and then in proportion to the relative percentages of the aggregate fair market value of the properties within the class. This is the same formula used in IRC 732(c)(2). The IRC 732(c)(3) formula is used to allocate decreases.

In the absence of a 754 election, partnership income or deduction will be distorted, perhaps until the partnership liquidates. In Book 6, for example, if the partnership does not decrease the inside basis in the land or stock by $2,000, it will recognize only $10,000 upon the sale of those assets. Since A would recognize only $4,000 overall ($6,000 on the sale of the distributed inventory, minus the $2,000 loss on the earlier distribution), the distribution would result in $2,000 of the pre-distribution $16,000 escaping taxation. If the partnership sold all of its assets and liquidated however, (distributing $14,000 cash to each partner) the partners would collectively report $12,000 capital gain rather than $10,000 (the difference between inside tax and book basis). The extra $2,000 would represent the $2,000 previously untaxed. Still, the partners would be better off since a $1.00 exemption today is worth more than $1.00 of taxable income at a future date. Hence, when a 754 election mandates a decrease in inside basis, the partners are better off if the election is not in effect, even though the absence of an election will cause the partners to duplicate losses (at least temporarily). The legitimacy of exploiting this opportunity is considered in question 5 below.

The distortions resulting from the absence of a 754 election were often decried as unnecessary because Congress could simply make the 734 basis adjustments mandatory. In 2004, Congress did just that but only when the distortion is large enough (i.e., greater than $250,000) to make the administrative burden worth the effort. An example from the American Jobs Creation Act of 2004 Committee Report demonstrates when a 734 adjustment is mandatory:

> Assume that A and B each contributed $2.5 million to a newly formed partnership and C contributed $5 million, and that the partnership purchased LMN stock for $3 million and XYZ stock for $7 million. Assume that the value of each stock declined to $1 million. Assume LMN stock is distributed to C in liquidation of its partnership interest. Under present law, the basis of LMN stock in C's hands is $5 million. Under present law, C would recognize a loss of $4 million if the LMN stock were sold for $1 million. Under the provision, there is a substantial basis adjustment because the $2 million increase in the adjusted basis of LMN stock (described in section 734(b)(2)(B)) by $2 million is greater than $250,000.

Practice

1.   Read Example 2, Regulation 1.734–1(b)(1)(ii). Suppose the partnership distributed Property Y to D and the partnership had not made a 754 election. What would D's basis in the property B? How much gain would he recognize if he sold the property immediately after receiving it for its $18,000 value? How much gain or loss would partners E and F recognize if the partnership sold Property X and distributed all the cash equally to E and F in complete liquidation of the partnership? Taken together, are these results appropriate? Why might Congress have decided to make the appropriate basis adjustment optional?

2.   Read Example 2, Regulation 1.734–1(b)(2)(ii). What might the partnership assert in support of its application to revoke its 754 election for the year of the distribution?

3. Read Example 3, Regulation 1.732–1(c)(4). Suppose the partnership still owns inventory—adjusted basis of $50,000 and fair market value of $66,000—and land with an adjusted basis of $30,000 and a fair market value of $32,000. What would be the bases of the two properties if a 754 election were in effect? What would be the basis of the inventory if that was the partnership's only remaining asset?

4. What result in Example(i)–(iii), Regulation 1.755–1(c)(5) if Assets 4 and 5 were distributed to A. Assume Asset 4 has an adjusted basis and fair market value as stated in the example but Asset 5 has an adjusted basis of $20,000 and a fair market value of $75,000. (Ignore 751(b)).

5. What result in question 4 above if Asset 3 were also Ordinary Income property?

6. Read Treas. Reg. 1.701–2(d), Examples 8 and 9. What limits on a partnership's decision to make a 754 election are discernable from the examples?

Lesson 10

SPECIAL ALLOCATIONS

Primary References: Orrisch v. Commissioner, 55 T.C. 395 (1970) (reprinted below); Revenue Ruling 99–43, 1999–2 C.B. 506 (reprinted in part below); Treas. Reg. 1.701–2(a)–(c), (d) Example 5

Secondary References: Lucas v. Earl, 281 U.S. 111 (1930); Helvering v. Horst, 311 U.S. 112 (1940)

Theory

One of the primary reasons why partnerships and LLC's (taxed as partnerships) are viewed as superior to S and C corporations is the ability to divide the tax burden in a manner differently from the relative percentage of capital each partner contributes to the partnership. Theoretically, a partner who has contributed 80% of the capital ought to be responsible for and get the benefit of 80% of the income and deductions, respectively at least until she has recovered her initial investment. Broadly speaking, "special allocations" occur when the tax responsibilities and benefits are divided in a manner that does not correspond with the relative capital contributions. Thus, a partnership agreement might state that the partner who contributed 80% of the capital will be allocated only 50% of the income. A partnership agreement may allocate all items equally between partners but allocate one particular item (e.g., depreciation) to just one partner. Indeed, a partnership agreement can separate out all the various types of income, deductions, and credits and allocate them in an infinite variety of ways.

The problem with the flexibility afforded partnerships is that it lends itself to an undermining of the tax base. Remember, partners separately combine their income from their partnership with income from other sources in determining their annual tax liabilities. The ability to do so creates incentives for each partner to select those items of partnership income that will result in the best individual and aggregate tax outcome. A simple example helps demonstrate this point.

Suppose a two person partnership, each partner contributing exactly 50% of the underlying capital, earned $300 in income and had depreciation deductions of $150. If partner A has $150 in deductible losses from non-partnership activities, and the partnership allocated its tax items equally, partner A's income and deductions would appear as follows:

Gross Income:	$150.00	(partnership income)
Deductions	($150.00)	(non-partnership loss)
	($75.00)	(partnership depreciation)
Taxable Income:	0	

In the hypothetical above, A might generically be referred to as a "zero-bracket taxpayer." A zero bracket taxpayer is one who will pay no tax on all or some of her allocated income. In some instances, a person is a zero bracket taxpayer because of tax concessions that apply to taxpayers individually. For example, in Revenue Ruling 99–43, below, B is a zero bracket taxpayer with respect to income from the discharge of indebtedness. A zero bracket taxpayer can also be an entity wholly exempt from U.S. taxation, such as a charity or foreign person or entity.

Since partner A already had enough non-partnership loss to offset her partnership income, she is in effect a zero bracket taxpayer for the year and does not need the $75.00 depreciation deduction. Suppose partner B had no other income or deductions except those derived via the partnership. Partner B might convince Partner A to amend the partnership agreement so that 100% of the depreciation deductions were to be allocated to B. Without such an amendment, B's taxable income for the year would appear as follows:

Gross Income:	$150.00	(partnership income)
Deductions	($ 75.00)	(partnership depreciation)
Taxable Income:	$75.00	

With the special allocation, B would take the entire depreciation deduction and her tax liability would be reduced to zero. A would not be any worse off because her taxable income would be zero even without her share of the depreciation deduction. Typically, A would agree to the original disproportionate depreciation deduction only in exchange for a later disproportionate allocation of gain from the sale of the depreciated asset. The later disproportionate allocation of gain (referred to as a "chargeback") would equal the amount of the earlier foregone depreciation deduction. Who, if anybody, is harmed by this arrangement? Two other generic factors, besides differential tax rates between partners, make the lure of tax savings from special allocations especially enticing: the use of borrowed money to increase basis and accelerated depreciation both generate deductions before an actual expenditures.

The best known judicial response to "special allocations" is *Orrisch v. Commissioner.* It is one of the bedrock cases in Subchapter K and is therefore reprinted below. There is at least one more generic factor common to tax avoidance allocations in *Orrisch* not identified in this introduction. The case predates present law but its teachings reverberate throughout the IRC 704 regulations. Revenue Ruling 99–43, also reprinted below, provides a more contemporary example of how distributive shares may be manipulated for tax purposes. In reading the case and the rulings, try to identify the "red flags" that suggest the partners are engaging in tax avoidance rather than business planning.

STANLEY C. ORRISCH AND GERTA E. ORRISCH, PETITIONERS v. COMMISSIONER OF INTERNAL REVENUE, RESPONDENT

55 T.C. 395
(1970)

Respondent determined deficiencies in petitioners' income tax for 1966 and 1967 in the respective amounts of $2,814.19 and $3,018.11. The only issue for decision is whether an amendment to a partnership agreement allocating to petitioners the entire amount of the depreciation deduction allowable on two buildings owned by the partnership was made for the principal purpose of avoidance of tax within the meaning of section 704(b).

FINDINGS OF FACT

Stanley C. Orrisch (hereinafter sometimes referred to as Orrisch) and Gerta E. Orrisch were husband and wife until a judgment of divorce was entered by the Superior Court of San Mateo County, Calif., on May 22, 1969. They filed joint Federal income tax returns for 1966 and 1967 with the district director of internal revenue, San Francisco, Calif. At the time they filed their petition, they were legal residents of Burlingame, Calif.

In May of 1963, Domonick J. and Elaine J. Crisafi (hereinafter the Crisafis) and petitioners formed a partnership to purchase and operate two apartment houses, one located at 1255 Taylor Street, San Francisco, and the other at 600 Ansel Road, Burlingame, Calif. The cost of the Taylor Street property was $229,011.08, and of the Ansel Road property was $155,974.90. The purchase of each property was financed principally by a secured loan. Petitioners and the Crisafis initially contributed to the partnership cash in the amounts of $26,500 and $12,500, respectively. During 1964 and 1965 petitioners and the Crisafis each contributed additional cash in the amounts of $8,800. Under the partnership agreement, which was not in writing, they agreed to share equally the profits and losses from the venture.

During each of the years 1963, 1964, and 1965, the partnership suffered losses, attributable in part to the acceleration of depreciation— the deduction was computed on the basis of 150 percent of straight-line depreciation. The amounts of the depreciation deductions, the reported loss for each of the 3 years as reflected in the partnership returns, and the amounts of each partner's share of the losses are as follows:

Year	Depreciation Deducted	Total loss	Each partner's share of the losses—50 percent of the Total loss
1963	$9,886.20	$9,716.14	$4,858.07
1964	21,051.95	17,812.33	8,906.17
1965	19,894.24	18,952.59	9,476.30

Petitioners and the Crisafis respectively reported in their individual income tax returns for these years the partnership losses allocated to them.

Petitioners enjoyed substantial amounts of income from several sources, the principal one being a nautical equipment sales and repair business. In their joint income tax returns for 1963, 1964, and 1965, petitioners reported taxable income in the respective amounts of $10,462.70, $5,898.85, and $50,332, together with taxes thereon in the amounts of $2,320.30, $1,059.80, and $12,834.

The Crisafis were also engaged in other business endeavors, principally an insurance brokerage business. They owned other real property, however, from which they realized losses, attributable largely to substantial depreciation deductions. In their joint income tax returns for 1963, 1964, and 1965, they reported no net taxable income.

Early in 1966, petitioners and the Crisafis orally agreed that, for 1966 and subsequent years, the entire amount of the partnership's depreciation deductions would be specially allocated to petitioners, and that the gain or loss from the partnership's business, computed without regard to any deduction for depreciation, would be divided equally. They further agreed that, in the event the partnership property was sold at a gain, the specially allocated depreciation would be "charged back" to petitioner's capital account and petitioners would pay the tax on the gain attributable thereto.

The operating results of the partnership for 1966 and 1967 as reflected in the partnership returns were as follows:

Year	Depreciation Deducted	Loss(including depreciation)	Gain (or loss) without regard to depreciation
1966	$18,412.00	$19,396.00	($984.00)
1967	17,180.75	16,560.78	619.97

The partnership returns for these years show that, taking into account the special arrangement as to depreciation, losses in the amounts of $18,904 and $16,870.76 were allocated to petitioners for 1966 and 1967, respectively, and petitioners claimed these amounts as deductions in their joint income tax returns for those years. The partnership returns reported distributions to the Crisafis in the form of a $492 loss for 1966 and a $309.98 gain for 1967. The Crisafis' joint income tax returns reflected that they had no net taxable income for either 1966 or 1967.

The net capital contributions, allocations of profits, losses and depreciation, and ending balances of the capital accounts, of the Orrisch–Crisafi partnership from May 1963 through December 31, 1967, were as follows:

	Petitioners'	Crisafis'
Excess of capital contributions over withdrawals during 1963	$26,655.55	$12,655.54
Allocation of 1963 loss	(4,858.07)	(4,858.07)
Balance 12/31/63	21,797.48	7,797.47
Excess of capital contributions over withdrawals during 1964	4,537.50	3,537.50
Allocation of 1964 loss	(8,906.17)	(8,906.16)
Balance 12/31/64	17,428.81	2,428.81
Excess of capital contributions over withdrawals during 1965	4,337.50	5,337.50
Allocation of 1965 loss	(9,476.30)	(9,476.29)
Balance 12/31/65	12,290.01	(1,709.98)
Excess of capital contributions over withdrawals during 1966	2,610.00	6,018.00
Allocation of 1966 loss before depreciation	(492.00)	(492.00)
Allocation of depreciation	(18,412.00)	0
Balance 12/31/66	(4,003.99)	3,816.02
Excess of withdrawals over capital contributions during 1967	(4,312.36)	(3,720.35)
Allocation of 1967 profit before depreciation	309.99	309.98
Allocation of depreciation	(17,180.75)	0
Balance 12/31/67	(25,187.11)	405.65

OPINION

The only issue presented for decision is whether tax effect can be given the agreement between petitioners and the Crisafis that, beginning with 1966, all the partnership's depreciation deductions were to be allocated to petitioners for their use in computing their individual income tax liabilities. In our view, the answer must be in the negative, and the amounts of each of the partners' deductions for the depreciation of partnership property must be determined in accordance with the ratio used generally in computing their distributive shares of the partnership's profits and losses.

Among the important innovations of the 1954 Code are limited provisions for flexibility in arrangements for the sharing of income, losses, and deductions arising from business activities conducted through partnerships. The authority for special allocations of such items appears in section 704(a), which provides that a partner's share of any item of income, gain, loss, deduction, or credit shall be determined by the partnership agreement. That rule is coupled with a limitation in section

704(b), however, which states that a special allocation of an item will be disregarded if its "principal purpose" is the avoidance or evasion of Federal income tax. In case a special allocation is disregarded, the partner's share of the item is to be determined in accordance with the ratio by which the partners divide the general profits or losses of the partnership. Sec. 1.704–1(b)(2), Income Tax Regs.

The report of the Senate Committee on Finance accompanying the bill finally enacted as the 1954 Code (S. Rept. No. 1622, to accompany H.R. 8300 (Pub.L. No. 591), 83d Cong., 2d Sess., p. 379 (1954)) explained the tax-avoidance restriction prescribed by section 704(b) as follows:

> Subsection (b) * * * provides that if the principal purpose of any provision in the partnership agreement dealing with a partner's distributive share of a particular item is to avoid or evade the Federal income tax, the partner's distributive share of that item shall be redetermined in accordance with his distributive share of partnership income or loss described in section 702(a)(9) [i.e., the ratio used by the partners for dividing general profits or losses].
> * * *
>
> Where, however, a provision in a partnership agreement for a special allocation of certain items has substantial economic effect and is not merely a device for reducing the taxes of certain partners without actually affecting their shares of partnership income, then such a provision will be recognized for tax purposes. * * *

This reference to "substantial economic effect" did not appear in the House Ways and Means Committee report (H. Rept. No. 1337, to accompany H.R. 8300 (Pub.L. No. 591), 83d Cong., 2d Sess., p. A223 (1954)) discussing section 704(b), and was apparently added in the Senate Finance Committee to allay fears that special allocations of income or deductions would be denied effect in every case where the allocation resulted in a reduction in the income tax liabilities of one or more of the partners. The statement is an affirmation that special allocations are ordinarily to be recognized if they have business validity apart from their tax consequences. Driscoll, "Tax Problems of Partnerships—Special Allocation of Specific Items," 1958 So. Cal. Tax Inst. 421, 426.

In resolving the question whether the principal purpose of a provision in a partnership agreement is the avoidance or evasion of Federal income tax, all the facts and circumstances in relation to the provision must be taken into account. Section 1.704–1(b)(2), Income Tax Regs., lists the following as relevant circumstances to be considered:

> Whether the partnership or a partner individually has a business purpose for the allocation; whether the allocation has "substantial economic effect", that is, whether the allocation may actually affect the dollar amount of the partners' shares of the total partnership income or loss independently of tax consequences; whether related items of income, gain, loss, deduction, or credit from the same source are subject to the same allocation; whether the allocation was

made without recognition of normal business factors and only after the amount of the specially allocated item could reasonably be estimated; the duration of the allocation; and the overall tax consequences of the allocation. * * *

Applying these standards, we do not think the special allocation of depreciation in the present case can be given effect.

The evidence is persuasive that the special allocation of depreciation was adopted for a tax-avoidance rather than a business purpose. Depreciation was the only item which was adjusted by the parties; both the income from the buildings and the expenses incurred in their operation, maintenance, and repair were allocated to the partners equally. Since the deduction for depreciation does not vary from year to year with the fortunes of the business, the parties obviously knew what the tax effect of the special allocation would be at the time they adopted it. Furthermore, as shown by our Findings, petitioners had large amounts of income which would be offset by the additional deduction for depreciation; the Crisafis, in contrast, had no taxable income from which to subtract the partnership depreciation deductions, and, due to depreciation deductions which they were obtaining with respect to other housing projects, could expect to have no taxable income in the near future. On the other hand, the insulation of the Crisafis from at least part of a potential capital gains tax was an obvious tax advantage. The inference is unmistakably clear that the agreement did not reflect normal business considerations but was designed primarily to minimize the overall tax liabilities of the partners.

Petitioners urge that the special allocation of the depreciation deduction was adopted in order to equalize the capital accounts of the partners, correcting a disparity ($14,000) in the amounts initially contributed to the partnership by them ($26,500) and the Crisafis ($12,500). But the evidence does not support this contention. Under the special allocation agreement, petitioners were to be entitled, in computing their individual income tax liabilities, to deduct the full amount of the depreciation realized on the partnership property. For 1966, as an example, petitioners were allocated a sum ($18,904) equal to the depreciation on the partnership property ($18,412) plus one-half of the net loss computed without regard to depreciation ($492). The other one-half of the net loss was, of course, allocated to the Crisafis. Petitioners' allocation ($18,904) was then applied to reduce their capital account. The depreciation specially allocated to petitioners ($18,412) in 1966 alone exceeded the amount of the disparity in the contributions. Indeed, at the end of 1967, petitioners' capital account showed a deficit of $25,187.11 compared with a positive balance of $405.65 in the Crisafis' account. By the time the partnership's properties are fully depreciated, the amount of the reduction in petitioners' capital account will approximate the remaining basis for the buildings as of the end of 1967. The Crisafis' capital account will be adjusted only for contributions, withdrawals, gain or loss, without regard to depreciation, and similar adjustments for these factors will also be made in petitioners' capital account. Thus, rather than correcting an imbalance in the capital accounts of the partners, the special allocation of depreciation will create a vastly greater imbalance than existed at the end of 1966. In the light of these facts, we find it incredible that equalization of the capital accounts was the objective of the special allocation.[1]

Petitioners rely primarily on the argument that the allocation has "substantial economic effect" in that it is reflected in the capital accounts of the partners. Referring to the material quoted above from the report of the Senate Committee on Finance, they contend that this alone is sufficient to show that the special allocation served a business rather than a tax-avoidance purpose.

According to the regulations, an allocation has economic effect if it "may actually affect the dollar amount of the partners' shares of the total partnership income or loss independently of tax consequences."[2] The agreement in this case provided not only for the allocation of depreciation to petitioners but also for gain on the sale of the partnership property to be "charged back" to them. The charge back would cause the gain, for tax purposes, to be allocated on the books entirely to petitioners to the extent of the special allocation of depreciation, and their capital account would be correspondingly increased. The remainder of the gain, if any, would be shared equally by the partners. If the gain on the sale were to equal or exceed the depreciation specially allocated to petitioners, the increase in their capital account caused by the charge back would exactly equal the depreciation deductions previously allowed to them and the proceeds of the sale of the property would be divided equally. In such circumstances, the only effect of the allocation would be a trade of tax consequences, i.e., the Crisafis would relinquish a current depreciation deduction in exchange for exoneration from all or part of the capital gains tax when the property is sold, and petitioners would enjoy a larger current depreciation deduction but would assume a larger ultimate capital gains tax liability. Quite clearly, if the property is sold at

1. We recognize that petitioners had more money invested in the partnership than the Crisafis and that it is reasonable for the partners to endeavor to equalize their investments since each one was to share equally in the profits and losses. However, we do not think sec. 704(a) permits the partners' prospective tax benefits to be used as the medium for equalizing their investments, and it is apparent that the economic burden of the depreciation (which is reflected by the allowance for depreciation) was not intended to be the medium used. This case is to be distinguished from situations where one partner contributed property and the other cash; in such cases sec. 704(a) may allow a special allocation of income and expenses in order to reflect the tax consequences inherent in the original contributions.

2. This language of sec. 1.704–1(b)(2), Income Tax Regs., listing "substantial economic effect" as one of the factors to be considered in determining the principal purpose of a special allocation, is somewhat similar to the material quoted in the text from S. Rept. No. 1622, to accompany H.R. 8300 (Pub. L. No. 591), 83d Cong., 2d Sess., p. 379 (1954). But the latter is broader. It is an explanation of the "principal purpose" test of sec. 704(b), and contemplates that a special allocation will be given effect only if it has business validity apart from its tax consequences. Driscoll, "Tax Problems of Partnerships—Special Allocation of Specific Items," 1958 So. Cal. U. Tax Inst. 421, 429 fn. 17; Willis, Handbook of Partnership Taxation 141 (1957).

a gain, the special allocation will affect only the tax liabilities of the partners and will have no other economic effect.

To find any economic effect of the special allocation agreement aside from its tax consequences, we must, therefore, look to see who is to bear the economic burden of the depreciation if the buildings should be sold for a sum less than their original cost. There is not one syllable of evidence bearing directly on this crucial point. We have noted, however, that when the buildings are fully depreciated, petitioners' capital account will have a deficit, or there will be a disparity in the capital accounts, approximately equal to the undepreciated basis of the buildings as of the beginning of 1966. Under normal accounting procedures, if the building were sold at a gain less than the amount of such disparity petitioners would either be required to contribute to the partnership a sum equal to the remaining deficit in their capital account after the gain on the sale had been added back or would be entitled to receive a proportionately smaller share of the partnership assets on liquidation. Based on the record as a whole, we do not think the partners ever agreed to such an arrangement. On dissolution, we think the partners contemplated an equal division of the partnership assets which would be adjusted only for disparities in cash contributions or withdrawals. Certainly there is no evidence to show otherwise. That being true, the special allocation does not "actually affect the dollar amount of the partners' share of the total partnership income or loss independently of tax consequences" within the meaning of the regulation referred to above.

Our interpretation of the partnership agreement is supported by an analysis of a somewhat similar agreement, quoted in material part in our Findings, which petitioners made as part of a marital property settlement agreement in 1968. Under this agreement, Orrisch was entitled to deduct all the depreciation for 1968 in computing his income tax liability, and his wife was to deduct none; but on the sale of the property they were to first reimburse Orrisch for "such moneys as he may have advanced," and then divide the balance of the "profits or proceeds" of the sale equally, each party to report one-half of the capital gain or loss on his income tax return. In the 1969 amendment to this agreement the unequal allocation of the depreciation deduction was discontinued, and a provision similar to the partnership "charge back" was added, i.e., while the proceeds of the sale were to be divided equally, only Orrisch's basis was to be reduced by the depreciation allowed for 1968 so that he would pay taxes on a larger portion of the gain realized on the sale. Significantly, in both this agreement and the partnership agreement, as we interpret it, each party's share of the sales proceeds was determined independently from his share of the depreciation deduction.

In the light of all the evidence we have found as an ultimate fact that the "principal purpose" of the special allocation agreement was tax avoidance within the meaning of section 704(b). Accordingly, the deduction for depreciation for 1966 and 1967 must be allocated between the parties in the same manner as other deductions.

REVENUE RULING 99–43

1999–2, C.B. 506.

FACTS

A and *B*, both individuals, formed a general partnership, *PRS. A* and *B* each contributed $1,000 and also agreed that each would be allocated a 50–percent share of all partnership items. The partnership agreement provides that, upon the contribution of additional capital by either partner, *PRS* must revalue the partnership's property and adjust the partners' capital accounts under § 1.704–1(b)(2)(iv)(*f*).

PRS borrowed $8,000 from a bank and used the borrowed and contributed funds to purchase nondepreciable property for $10,000. The loan was nonrecourse to *A* and *B* and was secured only by the property. No principal payments were due for 6 years, and interest was payable semi-annually at a market rate.

After one year, the fair market value of the property fell from $10,000 to $6,000, but the principal amount of the loan remained $8,000. As part of a workout arrangement among the bank, *PRS, A,* and *B,* the bank reduced the principal amount of the loan by $2,000, and *A* contributed an additional $500 to *PRS. A's* capital account was credited with the $500, which *PRS* used to pay currently deductible expenses incurred in connection with the workout. All $500 of the currently deductible workout expenses were allocated to *A. B* made no additional contribution of capital. At the time of the workout, *B* was insolvent within the meaning of § 108(a) of the Internal Revenue Code. *A* and *B* agreed that, after the workout, *A* would have a 60–percent interest and *B* would have a 40–percent interest in the profits and losses of *PRS*.

As a result of the property's decline in value and the workout, *PRS* had two items to allocate between *A* and *B*. First, the agreement to cancel $2,000 of the loan resulted in $2,000 of cancellation of indebtedness income (COD income). Second, *A's* contribution of $500 to *PRS* was an event that required *PRS,* under the partnership agreement, to revalue partnership property and adjust *A's* and *B's* capital accounts. Because of the decline in value of the property, the revaluation resulted in a $4,000 economic loss that must be allocated between *A's* and *B's* capital accounts.

Under the terms of the original partnership agreement, *PRS* would have allocated these items equally between *A* and *B. A* and *B,* however, amend the partnership agreement (in a timely manner) to make two special allocations. First, *PRS* specially allocates the entire $2,000 of COD income to *B,* an insolvent partner. Second, *PRS* specially allocates the book loss from the revaluation $1,000 to *A* and $3,000 to *B*.

While *A* receives a $1,000 allocation of book loss and *B* receives a $3,000 allocation of book loss, neither of these allocations results in a tax loss to either partner. Rather, the allocations result only in adjustments to A's and B's capital accounts. Thus, the cumulative effect of the special allocations is to reduce each partner's capital account to zero immediately following the allocations despite the fact that B is allocated $2,000 of income for tax purposes.

The law, analysis, and holding of Revenue Ruling 99–43 are omitted at this point. It is more useful to deconstruct the whole transaction—and thereby isolate the potential abuse that the 704(b) regulations seek to prevent. You will have an opportunity to analyze the proper result for yourself in Lesson 11. Let's go back and reconstruct the partnership tax/book balance sheet, relying on the basic capital accounting rules studied in Lesson 4.

The opening tax/book balance sheet should appear as follows:

			Liabilities and Partners' Capital		
			Liabilities:		
Assets			**Capital**		
	Tax	**Book**		**Tax**	**Book**
Cash	2,000	2,000	A	1,000	1,000
			B	1,000	1,000
				2,000	2,000

When the partnership borrows $8000 and purchases nondepreciable property, the books appear as follows (do not be concerned with the reason why each party has a 5,000 basis at this point):

			Liabilities and Partners' Capital		
			Liabilities:		8000
Assets			**Capital**		
	Tax	**Book**		**Tax**	**Book**
Prop	10,000	10,000	A	5,000	1,000
			B	5,000	1,000
				10,000	10,000

When Partner A contributes an additional $500, the partnership restates the capital accounts (in this instance capital accounts are "booked-down" to reflect the property's economic depreciation to $6,000—a $4,000 book loss). Additionally, if the $2,000 COD is allocated in accordance with the original agreement (i.e., equally) and the $500 of current expenses are allocated to A, the books would appear as follows (allocate each item, beginning with capital accounts of $1,000 to make sure you understand):

	Liabilities and Partners' Capital				
			Liabilities:		6,000
Assets			**Capital**		
	Tax	**Book**		**Tax**	**Book**
Prop	10,000	6,000	A	5,000	0
			B	5,000	0
				10,000	6,000

The COD income, allocated equally to A and B, would flow through to A and B and each would report $1,000 gross income on their separate tax returns. B however, would pay no taxes since his $1,000 COD income would be exempt from taxation under IRC 108 (because B is insolvent). In effect, B is a zero bracket taxpayer with respect to COD income. If the partnership sold its property, paid its liability and liquidated, each would report an aggregate $5,000 capital loss ($2,000 each on the sale of the property and $3,000 upon liquidation under IRC 731(a)(2)).

When the taxpayers amended the partnership agreement to allocate all of the COD income to B, and three fourths of the book loss to B, the partnership balance sheet appear as follows after the "workout.":

	Liabilities and Partners' Capital				
			Liabilities:		6,000
Assets			**Capital**		
	Tax	**Book**		**Tax**	**Book**
Prop	10,000	6,000	A	4,000	0
			B	6,000	0
				10,000	6,000

Capital accounts are no different but in this instance A will report no partnership income since all the COD income was allocated to B. Because B is insolvent, she will also recognize no gross income. The partners will nevertheless have equal ownership of the partnership's sole asset. If they sold the property for its $6,000 value, paid the liability and liquidated (distributing nothing), A would recognize a $1,000 capital gain and B would recognize a $1,000 capital loss under IRC 731(a)(2).[1] A will have deferred taxes on $1,000 of COD income in exchange for a lower capital loss (i.e., more gain) later. B would be compensated for agreeing to the special allocation by a higher capital loss later. By manipulating the allocation scheme, the partners have effectively reduced their overall taxes. A was made better off at no expense to B.

Practice

1. Should partners be allowed to structure their arrangement in a manner that will achieve the best aggregate tax outcome? What is the

---

1. A's gain would arise from a "deemed distribution" of cash caused by the reduction of her share of liabilities from $3,000 to 0 (i.e., a liability relief of $3,000 on the sale of property with a basis of $2,000, A's remaining basis after allocating the $4,000 loss equally to each partner). You will understand this point better after Lesson 15.

harm and what sort of business justifications might the partners assert in defense of the arrangement? Should they be required to assert a business justification, such as that suggested in *Orrisch at* footnote 1?

2. What is the significance, if any, of the fact that the special allocations were inserted into the partnership agreement in both *Orrisch* and Revenue Ruling 99–43 after the partners became aware of the partnership's income for the year?

3. As noted in *Orrisch,* prior law disallowed allocations made for tax avoidance purposes. From the case and the ruling, prepare a list of facts that might suggest an allocation is made for tax avoidance purposes.

4. Could the partners in *Orrish* or Revenue Ruling 99–43 added anything to their agreements to increase their chances of success?

Lesson 11

SUBSTANTIAL ECONOMIC EFFECT

Primary References: IRC 704(a)–(b), 761(c)
Treas. Reg. 1.704–1(a)–1.704–1(b)(2)(iii)
Treas. Reg. 1.704–1(b)(5), Examples 1(i)–
(ix), 2,3, 8, 16

Case Reference: Orrisch v. Commissioner, 55 T.C. 395
(1970)
Revenue Ruling 99–43, 1999–2 C.B. 506

Secondary Reference: Sample Partnership Agreement (Appendix 1)
Treas. Reg. 1.704–1(b)(2)(iv)

Orrisch and Revenue Ruling 99–43 demonstrate the opportunities that the substantial economic affect test referred to in IRC 704(b)(2) is designed to limit. In *Orrisch*, the special allocation had no "economic effect" most simply because it sole impact was a reduction of aggregate taxes. First, the existence of the chargeback provision (i.e., all gain on the sale of the depreciated asset would be allocated to Orrisch) meant that in exchange for more deductions and less tax liability early, Orrisch would simply recognize more income later. In effect, she simply deferred her proper tax liability, and since the other partner had sufficient outside losses to absorb whatever income was disproportionately allocated to her, Orrisch's deferral cost her nothing. The overall result was simply an aggregate deferral of tax liability.

Second, the special allocation represented an early capital recovery for Orrisch, but Orrisch was nevertheless to be treated as if she previously received none of her capital. Under the agreement, Orrisch would be entitled to one half the proceeds, as if she had previously recovered none of the capital invested in the partnership's asset. To have economic effect, the allocations should have actually reduced Orrisch's claim to liquidation proceeds—it is as if Orrisch previously withdrew capital from the partnership and therefore should not be entitled to withdraw more capital upon liquidation. Since the special allocation did not affect

86

Orrisch's claim to future liquidations, it was meaningful only from a tax reduction standpoint and had no economic effect.

In Revenue Ruling 99–43, the allocations would have dictated each partner's ultimate "take" from the partnership, but that ultimate take was no different than it would have been in the absence of the special allocation. The special allocations' only affect was to reduce the partners' aggregate tax liability because the special allocation reduced partner A's taxes and did not increase partner B's taxes. A reduction in aggregate tax liability, coupled with an identical economic result as would have occurred in the absence of the special allocation is the hallmark of allocations that are based solely on tax reduction goals rather than non-tax, economic considerations. Of course, legitimate business planning considerations may also result in tax reduction. Thus, the goal of IRC 704(b) is to prohibit tax avoidance without interfering with legitimate business planning—a difficult task, to say the least.

Strangely, or perhaps not, one of the best teaching tools by which to understand (or at least picture) the Subchapter K provisions, other than the regulatory examples to which you are directed at the end of this Lesson, is an actual partnership agreement. Having an actual agreement just seems to put the "real" to otherwise sterile and sometimes incomprehensible theory. Appendix 1 contains a rather complex partnership agreement to which you should refer in studying IRC 704 and accompanying regulations. A complex partnership agreement can take up hundreds of pages, not counting appendices, amendments, or schedules. By contrast, the provisions pertaining to tax may take up only a relative few pages, though they may have overriding importance.

IRC 704(a) states a general rule of partnerships. A partnership is essentially a contractual arrangement between individuals. The partners can structure their relationships in whatever manner they want. State laws relating to partnerships express this sort of *laissez faire* attitude. Fundamental tax law, too, strives to be neutral with regard to economic choices. The one tax limitation—one easier stated than applied—is that economic decisions should not be made solely to reduce taxes. Thus, IRC 704(b)(2) means that the partners' agreement as to how they will divide the tax consequences from their partnership will be disregarded if the division is not consistent with the "partner's interest in the partnership." We will study the meaning of this phrase in the next lesson. Suffice it to say for now that the PIP standard is one that should be avoided because of its uncertainty.

IRC 704(b)(2) provides the exclusive method by which to steer clear of the PIP standard. The partnership agreement must state each partner's distributive share and the distributive share must have "substantial economic effect." If stated allocations have substantial economic effect they will be respected—meaning they will not be disregarded—even if the allocations otherwise achieve the partners' tax reduction goals. If the statute were left at the admonition that allocations must have "substantial economic effect" we would have no more guidance than that distributive shares must be based on economic rather than tax reduction goals. The regulations fill in the blanks with great detail. But first, note that 704 is meant to defines each partner's "distributive share." We have seen this phrase before in IRC 702 (requiring that each partner take account separately his distributive share) and in IRC 705 (regarding increases and decreases to each partner's outside basis resulting from each partner's distributive share). Keep the big picture in mind. IRC 704 impacts on each partner's tax liability for the year and her outside basis.

Regulation 1.704–1(b)(2) provides the substance missing from IRC 704(b). In short, it sets forth the general rule—by reference to benefits and burdens—that an allocation must meaningfully affect a partner's bottom line "take", without regard to its tax impact. As a practical matter, the determination is made via a two part test set out in the regulations. First, the allocation must have economic effect—which can be achieved simply by inserting, and then complying with, the proper language in the partnership agreement—and second, the affect must be "substantial," a concept that primarily relates to the deferral, conversion, or complete avoidance of tax liabilities as in Revenue Ruling 99–43. Read Regulation 1.704–1(b)(2)(ii) and compare that with the partnership agreement in appendix 1.

Then read Regulation 1.704–1(b)(2)(iii) and compare it to the facts in *Orrisch* (particularly the chargeback provision) and Revenue Ruling 99–43. Note that Regulation 1.704–1(b)(2)(iii) refers to "shifting" and "transitory" allocations. Which of those labels applies to the allocations in *Orrisch* and which applies to the allocations in Revenue Ruling 99–43?

One provision you may not find in many partnership agreements, or that may apply to fewer than all partners in many partnership agreements relates to the requirement in Regulation 1.704–1(b)(2)(ii)(b)(3). That regulation essentially requires that all partners be obligated to contribute more capital to the partnership to the extent that partner has previously received disproportionate allocations or distributions. Disproportionate allocations and distributions could cause a partner's capital account to have a deficit equal to an amount owing to another partner or an outside creditor. (Do you remember the discussion in Lesson 8 of a partner having to "repay" an amount to the partnership if allocated deductions exceed outside basis?) Note, however, that if all partners are required to contribute more to the partnership in order to compensate other partners or outside creditors, then all partners are essentially general partners. In this day and age, it is more likely that at least some partners will have no obligation to contribute more capital, i.e., they are limited partners. Under the rule stated in Regulation 1.704–1(b)(2)(ii), allocations to limited partners would never have economic effect and therefore would have to be tested under the uncertain PIP standard. It would be burdensome and unpredictable to make special allocations to limited partners, some of whom might contribute most of the capital and therefore expect disproportionate allocations of deductions, for example. The Service promulgated Regulation 1.704–1(b)(2)(ii)(d) in light of this economic reality. That provision provides what is normally referred to as the "alternate economic effect" test. The important thing to remember is that the alternate economic effect test is available only if the partnership agreement contains a "qualified income offset" provision. In effect, when a QIO is triggered it will override stated allocations of income and gain. That is, income and gain must be allocated first to a partner who— because of unexpected distributions or losses—has a deficit that exceeds her deficit reduction obligation. This means a partner may recognize gain even if the partnership has an overall loss for the year. Any income or gain remaining after allocations pursuant to the QIO is allocated in accordance with the partnership agreement.

Practice

1. Will allocations made pursuant to the partnership agreement in Appendix 1 have economic effect? Can you tell whether the economic effect, if any, will be substantial? What else might you want to know?

2. Do the allocations in Revenue Ruling 99–43 (reprinted, in part, in Lesson Ten) have substantial economic effect? If not, are the allocations transitory, shifting or simply in violation of the general rule of substantiality contained in Regulation 1.704–1(b)(iii)(a)? You should attempt to answer by re-reading the substantiality regulations, but you can also download the full ruling to see what the Service concluded.

3. Read Example 1(iii), Regulation 1.704–1(b)(5). How would the result change if the partnership knew that it would be distributing $25,000 in year 2?

4. Read Example 1(vi), Regulation 1.704–1(b)(5). What result if the partnership has already signed an agreement with the buyer by which it will sell the property at a gain of $20,000 early in year 3 and allocate that gain equally to the partners? What if A honestly intends to contribute additional property worth $10,000 to the partnership in year 3?

4. In Example (1)(ix), Regulation 1.704–1(b)(5) if A pays the note off in year 4 will he still be considered as having an obligation to contribute an additional $5000.

5. Read Example 2, Regulation 1.704–1(b)(5). What facts might be relied upon to determine that there is a "strong likelihood" that income or losses for any given year will be a certain amount? What is the logical relevance of the "strong likelihood" standard?

6. Assuming that there is no "strong likelihood" in Example 3, Regulation 1.704–1(b)(5) at the time the allocations become part of the partnership agreement, will the allocations still meet the substantial economic effect test if the partnership makes an astounding discovery in its fifth year, the royalty income from which is ten times the amount of all previous year's losses?

7. What if, in Example 8, Regulation 1.704–1(b)(5) Partner O's net operating loss carryovers will not expire until the end of seven years

from the current year? What if the Partner O did not have any net operating loss carryover?

8.   Read Example 16(ii), Regulation 1.704–1(b)(5). If the partners make no further contributions and the partnership earns no income over its life, what is the total amount of loss than can be allocated to WN over the life of the partnership?

Lesson 12

PARTNER'S INTEREST IN THE PARTNERSHIP

Primary References: IRC 704(b)
Treas. Reg. 1.704–1(b)(3), 1.704–1(b)(5), examples 1(i) and (ii), (iv)–(v), (4)(i), (5), (6), (7), (8), (10), (15)

Case References: **Vecchio v. Commissioner, 103 T.C. 170 (1994) (reprinted below); Estate of Tobias v. Commissioner, T.C. Memo 2001–37 (Feb. 14, 2001) (reprinted below)**

IRC 704(b) provides that if a partnership agreement does not state the manner in which partnership income, gain, loss, deduction, or credit ("partnership items") are allocated, or if stated allocations do not have substantial economic effect, partnership items will be allocated (or reallocated) "in accordance with the partner's interest in the partnership" (PIP). We can anticipate that PIP is a vague and uncertain standard because the statute parenthetically adds that PIP is to be "determined by taking into account all facts and circumstances." The regulations at 1.704–1(b)(3) provide little additional help. It may be useful, though, to ask how the partnership items might be allocated amongst the partners in a world without taxes. The regulation seems to take that approach when it states that "all partners' interests in the partnership are presumed to be equal (determined on a per capita basis)." The statement harkens back to the traditional method of allocating economic items in proportion to the relative amounts of capital contributed by each shareholder in a corporation. A 50% shareholder, for example receives 50% of declared dividends and as an economic matter bears 50% percent of the corporation's tax burden.

The flexibility of partnerships, however, means that the presumption derived from a no tax world will not always apply. The per capita presumption is only the starting point and may be altered by particular facts and circumstances. Hence, the regulation indicates that the PIP standard allows for and even requires the equivalent of special allocations, depending on the interplay of all the facts and circumstances, including four specifically mentioned facts and circumstances. The many examples in the regulations provide three general rules (one of the practice questions below sorts the examples by type and then ask you to discover and articulate those general rules for yourself).

In one instance, however, the regulations provide an explicit special rule. Regulation 1.704–1(b)(3)(iii) is particularly vague, but after reading the examples several times one might derive the following rule: If an allocation does not have substantial economic effect only because the partnership agreement does not impose a deficit reduction obligation, does not contain a qualified income offset (QIO), or contains a QIO but the allocation would result in a deficit greater than that allowed under the alternate economic effect test, deductions and loss must be allocated to partners whose capital accounts can have a further deficit balance (i.e., to those who would be liable for further deficits) or who would suffer an actual loss if the partnership liquidated, and items of partnership income or gain must be allocated to partners with an improper deficit *as if* the partnership agreement contained a QIO (that is, in amounts sufficient to cure any intolerable deficit).

The two cases reprinted below serve two general purposes. *Vecchio* provides a nice wrap-up of the history and background of the substantial economic effect standard, and then demonstrates how PIP is determined in certain cases. It also provides an opportunity to step back and reconsider the forest. *Estate of Tobias* applies the facts and circumstances test to a situation where the partners completely failed to reduce their agreement to writing (a common situation). Unless your professor insists otherwise, you may safely postpone reading the cases and go straight to the practice problems. When you do read the cases, it should not escape your notice that the PIP standard is applied usually as a result of a lack of tax planning. The cases therefore confirm what is implicit throughout Subchapter K–partnership agreements should be carefully drafted to ensure allocations will have substantial economic effect to avoid the cost and uncertainty of the PIP standard! Of course, taxpayers may sometimes draft partnership agreements knowing the allocations will not be substantial but in hopes that the allocations will never be challenged. Is it ethical for tax advisors to assist in this effort?

SAM J. VECCHIO v. COMMISSIONER OF INTERNAL REVENUE

103 T.C. 170
(1994)

Parker, *Judge:* Respondent determined a deficiency in petitioner's Federal income tax for the taxable year 1980 in the amount of $286,693. In an amendment to answer, respondent later asserted an increased deficiency of $349,198.25.

After concessions, the primary issue to be decided is the amount of gain resulting from the sale of real property by Johanna Properties

Partnership that properly is allocable to petitioner and includable in his income in the taxable year 1980. In reaching our decision on the primary issue, we must initially determine how the gain should be allocated among the three partners' interests in the partnership.

[**Editor's Note**: From 1974 through 1978, the partnership agreement allocated 80% of the depreciation deductions from the partnership's primary asset to Equity, one of the partners. All other allocations were made as stated in the opinion. The case involves a disproportionate allocation of the gain to Equity from the sale of the depreciated asset (i.e., a chargeback), in light of the earlier unchallenged special allocation of depreciation deductions]. The petitioner will be allocated more gain if the chargeback is disallowed.

OPINION

This case demonstrates not only the complexity of partnership taxation, but also the careful consideration and analysis that should be applied in determining the tax consequences of partnership transactions. Partnership income or loss, distributions to partners, and gain on the sale of partnership interests are each taxed separately and are each subject to different provisions of the Internal Revenue Code. Generally, allocation of partnership income and loss is subject to the rules of sections 704 and 761(c), and the taxation of distributions to partners is determined by section 731. When there is a sale or exchange of a partnership interest during a taxable year, allocation of partnership income and loss is subject to the rules of sections 706, 708, and 761(c), in addition to section 704, and the gain on the sale or exchange of a partnership interest is determined by section 741.

I. Allocation of Gain From the Sale of the Real Property

In determining his income tax, a partner must take into account his "distributive share" of each item of partnership income, gain, loss, deduction, and credit. Sec. 702(a). Each partner is taxed on his distributive share of the partnership income without regard to whether the amount is actually distributed to him. Sec. 1.702–1(a), Income Tax Regs.; see also *United States v. Basye*, 410 U.S. 441, 453 (1973). A partner's distributive share of partnership income or loss is to be determined by the partnership agreement, provided the allocation has substantial economic effect. Sec. 704(a). If the partnership agreement does not provide as to the partner's distributive share, or if the partnership agreement provides for an allocation that does not have substantial economic effect, then a partner's distributive share is determined by the partner's "interest in the partnership". Sec. 704(b). A partner's interest in the partnership is determined by taking into account all facts and circumstances. *Id.*

A. The Partnership Agreement Allocation

Petitioner argues that the partnership agreement required allocating the first $1,410,232 of the gain to Equity. He contends that section

4.4(b) of the partnership agreement required Equity to bring its capital account balance to zero upon the sale of its interest to him and, therefore, Equity must be allocated more of the gain on the sale of the real property. Section 4.4(b) of the partnership agreement provides as follows:

> Except to the extent guaranteed payments are made, if at any time the Partnership shall suffer a loss as a result of which the capital account of any Partner shall be a negative amount, such loss shall be carried as a charge against his capital account, and his share of subsequent profits of the Partnership shall be applied to restore such deficit in his capital account.

That provision, however, merely permits a partner to continue to receive a share of partnership losses even though the loss creates a negative capital account. The provision requires that "his share of subsequent profits" be applied to restore the deficit; it does not, however, redefine his share of such profits or allocate a greater share of the profits to such partner.

For purposes of allocating partnership income or loss, a partnership agreement includes any modifications made prior to, or at, the time prescribed for filing the partnership return for the taxable year (not including extensions), provided the modifications were agreed to by all the partners, or adopted as otherwise required by the partnership agreement. Sec. 761(c). Where a modification alters the profit-sharing interests of existing partners and does not result in the retroactive allocation of partnership income or losses to a new partner, the courts generally have given effect to the amended provision, provided the allocation has substantial economic effect. See *Smith v. Commissioner*, 331 F.2d 298, 301 (7th Cir. 1964), affg. T.C. Memo. 1962–294; *Foxman v. Commissioner*, 41 T.C. 535, 554 (1964), affd. 352 F.2d 466 (3d Cir. 1965).

Johanna Properties' partnership agreement specifies that after January 1, 1979, the net profits and losses including depreciation of the partnership were to be divided among the partners in the following percentages:

Development Systems	45.%
John Takacs	5.1
Equity	49.0

Prior to January 12, 1979, Takacs withdrew from the partnership, Berzon obtained a 3.5–percent interest in the partnership, and petitioner obtained Development Systems' interest plus an additional 1.6–percent interest. Those events modified the partnership agreement so that in 1980, prior to the sale of the real property and prior to petitioner's purchase of Equity's interest in the partnership, profits and losses were allocated 47.5 percent to petitioner, 49 percent to Equity, and 3.5 percent to Berzon.

Johanna Properties' partnership agreement further provides that profits and losses arising from the disposition of assets were to be taken into account as of the date of disposition. Thus, the gain from the sale of the property was to be taken into account as of the sale date, December 10, 1980.

[A] final judgment of the State court further amended Johanna Properties' partnership agreement. The final judgment, however, does not specify how the gain on any sale of the property should be allocated between Equity and petitioner. There is nothing in any of the pertinent written documents that would alter the profit-sharing percentages explicitly set forth in the partnership agreement.

A modification, however, need not necessarily be written, unless the partnership agreement so requires. Sec. 1.761–1(c), Income Tax Regs. Johanna Properties' partnership agreement does not require a modification to be in writing or prohibit an oral modification. Petitioner testified that Equity agreed that the gain from the sale of the real property would be shared as reported by Johanna Properties on its return.

A portion of the gain Johanna Properties realized on the sale of the property was attributable to the recapture of the depreciation previously deducted from the partnership's basis in the property. Petitioner testified that, because Equity had a negative capital account balance resulting from the disproportionate allocation of depreciation deductions to Equity, all the partners agreed that the gain from the sale of the real property would be allocated first to Equity in an amount necessary to restore its negative capital account to zero. That amount, $1,410,232, was determined as follows:

Beginning year balance	($1,251,898)
Capital contributed during year	30,953
Share of 1980 ordinary loss	(119,287)
Distribution during year	(70,000)
Capital account balance prior to allocation of gain	(1,410,232)

Johanna Properties realized $4,659,832 of gain on the sale of the property, of which $1,986,913 was taxable in 1980. The first $1,410,232 of the realized gain was allocated to Equity. The balance of the realized gain was allocated $3,218,522 to petitioner and $31,078 to Berzon. The $1,986,913 of gain taxable in 1980 was allocated $1,410,232 to Equity, $13,170 to Berzon, and the balance to petitioner.

We found petitioner to be a credible witness as to the partnership's method of allocating the gain and the partners' agreement to such allocation. The allocation will be recognized provided it has substantial economic effect or otherwise satisfies the requirements of section 704.

B. Substantial Economic Effect

Before 1976, section 704(b)(2) provided that a special allocation under a partnership agreement would not be recognized if its principal purpose was to avoid or evade any income tax. Section 1.704–1(b)(2), Income Tax Regs., was promulgated under the prior law and provided several tests to determine tax evasion or avoidance. The regulations'

"substantial economic effect" test became the preeminent test for determining whether the principal purpose was tax evasion or avoidance.
Harris v. Commissioner, 61 T.C. 770, 785 (1974); *Orrisch v. Commissioner*, 55 T.C. 395 (1970). In the Tax Reform Act of 1976, Pub. L. 94–455,
section 213(d), 90 Stat. 1520, 1548, Congress elevated the "substantial
economic effect" test from the regulation to the statute.

Regulations setting forth the requirements for substantial economic
effect were issued on December 31, 1985, and made effective for taxable
years beginning after December 31, 1975. The regulations provide that
the determination of whether an allocation has substantial economic
effect involves a two-part test. Sec. 1.704–1(b)(2)(i), Income Tax Regs.
Under the first part of the test, the allocation must have economic effect.
Sec. 1.704–1(b)(2)(ii), Income Tax Regs. Under the second part, the
economic effect of the allocation must be substantial. Sec. 1.704–
1(b)(2)(iii), Income Tax Regs. For taxable years beginning after December 31, 1975, but before May 1, 1986, an allocation that does not satisfy
the two-part test nonetheless will be respected if the allocation has
substantial economic effect as interpreted under the relevant case law
and the legislative history of section 213(d) of the Tax Reform Act of
1976, Pub. L. 94–455, 90 Stat. 1520, 1548. Sec. 1.704–1(b)(1)(ii), Income
Tax Regs.

1. Economic Effect

In order to have economic effect, the partnership agreement must
satisfy three requirements provided in section 1.704–1(b)(2)(ii)(*b*), Income Tax Regs. An allocation of income, gain, loss, or deduction (or item
thereof) to a partner will have economic effect if, and only if, throughout
the full term of the partnership, the partnership agreement provides
that (1) the partners' capital accounts be kept in accordance with the
regulations, (2) liquidating distributions be made in accordance with
positive capital account balances, and (3) a partner is required to restore
a deficit capital account balance following the liquidation of the partnership or of his interest in the partnership. Sec. 1.704–1(b)(2)(ii)(*b*),
Income Tax Regs. An allocation does not have economic effect if it fails
to satisfy any one of the three parts of the test. In this case, special
allocation of the gain taxable in the year of the sale fails all three parts
of the test.

a. Maintenance of Capital Accounts

The regulations require that each partner's capital account be
increased by his share of partnership gain as computed for book purposes (book gain). Sec. 1.704–1(b)(2)(iv)(*b*), 1.704–1(b)(2)(iv)(*g*), Income
Tax Regs. Johanna Properties realized $4,659,832 of gain on the sale of
the property, of which $1,986,913 was reportable in 1980. The realized
gain was allocated $1,410,232 to Equity, $3,218,522 to petitioner, and
$31,078 to Berzon. The partners' capital account balances were properly
adjusted to reflect that allocation. The partners' capital account balances, however, cannot be further adjusted to reflect the allocation of the
portion of the gain taxable in the year of the sale. Thus, although the

partnership properly elected to report the gain from the sale under the installment sale provisions of section 453, the partners' capital accounts must be adjusted to reflect the entire book gain realized in the year of the sale. The partners' shares of corresponding taxable gain for 1980 are not independently reflected by further adjustments to the partners' capital accounts. This result is further demonstrated by the fact that the capital accounts will not be further adjusted in later years as the deferred gain is recognized. Thus, separate allocation of these tax items cannot satisfy the first requirement of the economic effect test. See sec. 1.704–1(b)(4)(i), Income Tax Regs.

b. Liquidating Distributions

The second requirement of the economic effect test requires that liquidating distributions are required in all cases to be made in accordance with the positive capital account balances of the partners. Johanna Properties' partnership agreement provides that, upon the sale of the real property or liquidation of the partnership, Equity was to receive a return of its investment before distributions could be made to other partners. The partnership agreement does not require that liquidating distributions be in accordance with the partners' positive capital account balances. Therefore, the second requirement of the economic effect test is not satisfied, and the allocations cannot have economic effect.

c. Obligation To Restore Deficit Capital Account

The third part of the economic effect test requires that the partnership agreement require a partner with a deficit capital account balance after the liquidation of his interest in the partnership, determined after taking into account all capital account adjustments for the year, to restore the amount of the deficit. Sec. 1.704–1(b)(2)(ii)(b)(3), Income Tax Regs. Petitioner argues that section 4.4(b) of the partnership agreement requires partners to restore deficit capital account balances. As discussed above, that provision merely permits a partner to continue to receive a share of partnership losses even though the loss creates a negative capital account. The provision requires that such partner's share of subsequent profits be applied to restore the deficit; it does not redefine his share of such profits, allocate a greater share of the profits to such partner, or require a partner to contribute additional funds to the partnership to restore the deficit account. To the contrary, the agreement specifically provides that Equity, the only partner with a deficit capital account balance, is not required to provide additional funds to the partnership.[19]

19. If the partnership agreement had satisfied the first two parts of the test (proper maintenance of capital accounts and liquidation distributions in accordance with capital accounts), but failed the third requirement (obligation to restore deficit capital account balances), the regulations provide an alternative economic effect test. Sec. 1.704–1(b)(2)(ii)(d), Income Tax Regs. Because the partnership agreement did not satisfy the first two parts of the test, the alternative economic effect test is not available. We note, however, that the partnership agreement does not provide for a qualified income offset or otherwise satisfy the requirements of the alternative economic effect test.

2. Economic Effect Equivalence

Allocations made to a partner that do not otherwise satisfy the economic effect test, nevertheless, are deemed to have economic effect, provided that, as of the end of each partnership taxable year, a liquidation of the partnership at the end of such year or at the end of any future year would produce the same economic results to the partners as would occur if all the requirements of the economic effect test had been satisfied, regardless of the economic performance of the partnership. Sec. 1.704–1(b)(2)(ii)(*i*), Income Tax Regs.; see also *Elrod v. Commissioner*, 87 T.C. 1046, 1086 n.23 (1986). Petitioner has not argued and has not demonstrated that the allocation satisfies this economic effect equivalence test.

3. Prior Law

Although the allocation does not satisfy the substantial economic effect test of the regulations, it will be permitted if it has substantial economic effect under the applicable paragraph of the regulation in effect for taxable years beginning before May 1, 1986, the relevant case law, and the relevant legislative history of the Tax Reform Act of 1976. Sec. 1.704–1(b)(1)(ii), Income Tax Regs. Guided by those provisions, the courts developed a "capital accounts analysis" to determine whether an allocation had substantial economic effect. *Ogden v. Commissioner*, 788 F.2d 252, 261 (5th Cir. 1986), affg. 84 T.C. 871 (1985); *Allison v. United States*, 701 F.2d 933, 939 (Fed. Cir. 1983); *Goldfine v. Commissioner*, 80 T.C. 843, 852–853 (1983). That analysis, however, also requires that capital accounts be properly maintained and that liquidating distributions be made in accordance with positive capital account balances. Thus, under the relevant precedent, petitioner has failed to demonstrate that the allocation satisfies the requirements for substantial economic effect.

C. Partners' Interests in the Partnership

If the partnership agreement provides for an allocation that does not have substantial economic effect, then a partner's distributive share is determined by the partner's interest in the partnership. As stated above, special allocation of the gain taxable in the year of the sale cannot affect the capital accounts and, therefore, cannot have economic effect. The taxable gain must be allocated in accordance with the partners' interests in the partnership. A partner's interest in the partnership is determined by taking into account all facts and circumstances. Sec. 704(b). Among the relevant factors to be taken into account in determining the partners' interests in the partnership are (1) the partners' relative contributions to capital, (2) the interests of the respective partners in profits and losses (if different from that in taxable income or loss), (3) their relative interests in cash-flow and other nonliquidating distributions, and (4) their rights to distributions of capital upon liquidation. Sec. 1.704–1(b)(3)(ii), Income Tax Regs.

Section 1.704–1(b)(3)(i), Income Tax Regs., generally defines a partner's interest in the partnership as follows:

References in section 704(b) and this paragraph to a partner's interest in the partnership, or to the partners' interests in the partnership, signify the manner in which the partners have agreed to share the economic benefit or burden (if any) corresponding to the income, gain, loss, deduction, or credit (or item thereof) that is allocated. Except with respect to partnership items that cannot have economic effect (such as nonrecourse deductions of the partnership), this sharing arrangement may or may not correspond to the overall economic arrangement of the partners. * * * Thus, a partner who has a 50 percent overall interest in the partnership may have a 90 percent interest in a particular item of income or deduction. (For example, in the case of an unexpected downward adjustment to the capital account of a partner who does not have a deficit makeup obligation that causes such partner to have a negative capital account, it may be necessary to allocate a disproportionate amount of gross income of the partnership to such partner for such year so as to bring that partner's capital account back up to zero.) The determination of a partner's interest in a partnership shall be made by taking into account all facts and circumstances relating to the economic arrangement of the partners. All partners' interests in the partnership are presumed to be equal (determined on a per capita basis). However, this presumption may be rebutted by the taxpayer or the Internal Revenue Service by establishing facts and circumstances that show that the partners' interests in the partnership are otherwise.

The regulation anticipates that, in situations where prior deductions have created a negative capital account, gain may be allocated in a manner which produces the same results as an allocation that has substantial economic effect. The fundamental principle for requiring that an allocation have economic effect is that the allocation must be consistent with the underlying economic arrangement of the partners. "This means that in the event there is an economic benefit or economic burden that corresponds to an allocation, the partner to whom the allocation is made must receive such economic benefit or bear such economic burden." Sec. 1.704–1(b)(2)(ii)(a), Income Tax Regs.

As of the end of 1979, as a result of the disproportionate allocation of Johanna Properties' operating loss and depreciation deductions, Equity had a negative capital account balance. The remaining partners, petitioner and Berzon, had positive capital account balances. Respondent does not dispute that the allocation of partnership losses from those prior years was properly reflected in the partners' capital accounts.

The partner to whom the item is specially allocated for tax purposes must bear the economic burdens and benefits of that specially allocated item. *Goldfine v. Commissioner*, 80 T.C. at 851. Equity's share of partnership depreciation and losses exceeded its contribution to the partnership, which resulted in a deficit in Equity's capital account of $1,251,898 at the beginning of the year at issue. Petitioner and Berzon had positive capital account balances at the beginning of the year.

Petitioner argues, and we agree, that, because Equity received the benefit of the prior deductions, Equity should bear the economic burden of gain in an amount necessary to bring its capital account to zero. Absent such allocation, the other partnership interests would have to bear part of the economic cost of the special allocation that resulted in the deficit capital account. *Elrod v. Commissioner*, 87 T.C. at 1084; *Ogden v. Commissioner*, 84 T.C. 871, 884 (1985), affd. 788 F.2d 252 (5th Cir. 1986); *Goldfine v. Commissioner, supra* at 852; *Harris v. Commissioner*, 61 T.C. at 786; *Orrisch v. Commissioner*, 55 T.C. at 403–404.

Furthermore, under the partnership agreement, Equity was entitled to the first $766,100 of proceeds from the sale of the partnership real property. Thereafter, additional funds were to be distributed 10 percent to Equity and 90 percent to petitioner and Berzon until Equity had received 49 percent (counting the $766,100), petitioner had received 47.5 percent, and Berzon had received 3.5 percent of the cash distribution. Thereafter all funds were to be distributed 49 percent to Equity, 47.5 percent to petitioner, and 3.5 percent to Berzon. During the operation of the partnership, petitioner and Berzon (or Takacs) bore the risk that a sale of the property would not provide distributable proceeds in excess of Equity's right to the first $766,100 of proceeds. In order for the partners' capital accounts to reflect that right, gain in the year of the sale should have been allocated first to Equity's interest in an amount necessary to bring its capital account to zero ($1,410,232) and then to a positive $766,100. Therefore, the first $2,176,332 of the gain from the sale should be allocated to Equity's interest. Thus the entire $1,986,913 of gain taxable in the year of the sale must be allocated to Equity's interest. This allocation of the gain taxable in the year of the sale of the real property also reflects the risk of economic loss in a later year borne by petitioner and Berzon in the event that the purchaser of the real property should fail to pay an installment due in the later year.

Practice

1.   Did the allocation of depreciation deductions in the years 1974 through 1980 have substantial economic effect?

2.   If the partnership agreement had a QIO and had complied with the alternative economic effect test, how would the gain have been allocated? (Assume that Equity's deficit balance was entirely unexpected.)

ESTATE OF JAMES R. TOBIAS v. COMMISSIONER OR INTERNAL REVENUE, DARWIN R. TOBOAS, SR., AND SHIRLEY I. TOBIAS v. COMMISSIONER OF INTERNAL REVENUE

T.C. Memo 2001–37

WHALEN, JUDGE: These consolidated cases are before the Court to decide the motion for summary judgment filed by the Estate of James R. Tobias and Ms. V. Pauline Tobias, the cross-motion for summary judgment filed by Mr. Darwin R. Tobias, Sr., and Ms. Shirley I. Tobias, and the cross-motion for summary judgment filed by respondent. The principal issues for decision in these cases involve the allocation of income pursuant to section 704 from an animal farm business. All section references in this opinion are to the Internal Revenue Code as in effect during the years in issue, unless specified otherwise. Respondent's determinations have the effect of allocating all of the income from the business for the years 1991 and 1993 to Mr. James R. Tobias and allocating 50 percent of the income from the same business for the years 1990, 1991, and 1993 to Mr. Darwin R. Tobias.

BACKGROUND

The two cases consolidated herein involve petitions filed by or on behalf of two brothers and their wives. The first brother, Mr. James R. Tobias, died on September 8, 1996. In this opinion, he is sometimes referred to as the decedent or James. His wife, Ms. V. Pauline Tobias, was appointed executrix of his estate. She resided in Halifax, Pennsylvania, at the time the instant petition was filed on her behalf. The decedent and his wife filed joint Federal income tax returns for each of the years in issue in their case, 1991 and 1993. In the notice of deficiency issued to them, respondent determined income tax deficiencies of $10,587 and $5,674, respectively.

The second brother, Mr. Darwin R. Tobias, Sr., and his wife, Ms. Shirley I. Tobias, filed joint Federal income tax returns for each of the years in issue in their case, 1990, 1991, and 1993. In the notice of deficiency issued to them, respondent determined income tax deficiencies of $12,371, $9,841, and $6,055, respectively. Darwin and his wife resided in Halifax, Pennsylvania, when the instant petition was filed on their behalf.

Circa 1960, James and Darwin orally agreed to operate an animal farm business as partners, but they never reduced their agreement to writing. Their agreement was general and did not include specific terms regarding how they would operate the business. For example, they never agreed to a specific division of labor. Over the years James spent a disproportionately greater amount of time and effort developing and expanding the business than his brother, Darwin. Each of the brothers had independent means of earning a living, and neither received a salary for his services to the business. It is not clear from the record whether they opened a bank account specifically for the business or whether they used an existing account, but it is clear that both of their signatures were required on checks drawn on the account.

The operation of the animal farm business took place primarily on land owned by James and his wife. Darwin also owned land that was farmed for the benefit of the animal farm business. In 1972, the brothers agreed that the business should pay rent for the use of each brother's personal land by the business. While Darwin often received his land rents, James frequently deferred his land rents until the business had the funds available to pay him.

In addition to using their land for business purposes, each brother occasionally made expenditures for the business with his own funds. Except for the reimbursement of some business expenses and the payment of land rents, neither brother received a distribution from the animal farm business. All profits were reinvested in the business.

In 1986, the brothers' relationship became acrimonious. James evicted Darwin from the business and prohibited him from coming onto the business premises. After his eviction, Darwin did not participate in the business or receive a distribution of any kind from the business. James continued to operate the animal farm business at least through December 31, 1993.

Following James' actions, on October 21, 1986, Darwin sued James in the Court of Common Pleas for Dauphin County, Pennsylvania (hereinafter State court), alleging that the business was an equally owned partnership. Darwin sought dissolution of the partnership and an accounting. See Tobias v. Tobias, No. 4583 (Ct. C.P. Dauphin County, Pa. July 7, 1992). On July 7, 1992, the State court issued its opinion holding that the animal farm business was a partnership under Pennsylvania State law (hereinafter the 1992 State court opinion). The State court found that Darwin had been "wrongfully excluded from the business" and was entitled to dissolution of the partnership and an accounting. In considering the question whether the partnership was an equal partnership, the State court found that James' contributions to the partnership far exceeded Darwin's contributions and that an inequity would be visited on James if the profits of the business were shared equally. The State court ordered that each partner be repaid his capital contributions before the profits of the partnership were divided equally between them. The order of the State court stated as follows:

> AND NOW, this 7 day of JULY, 1992, WE FIND that the business was operated on a partnership basis; the assets of the business are as set forth in this opinion. Plaintiff is entitled to dissolution of the partnership and an accounting. The profits will be shared equally after the partners are repaid their contribution as provided by the act.

The State court entered a second opinion on January 6, 1997, after 16 days of hearings, resolving differences between the brothers over an account of the business that had been filed by James and excepted to by Darwin (hereinafter the 1997 State court opinion). In the 1997 State court opinion, the State court determined that James had made capital contributions to the partnership of $1,001,558.60, that Darwin had made capital contributions to the partnership of $2,320, and that the partnership had $23,311.87 in its bank accounts. The court ordered payment of the outstanding liabilities of the partnership totaling $23,335.47. The court also ordered the sale of partnership equipment at a public auction, with all profits from the sale to be deposited into the partnership bank account. The partnership equipment included various pieces of restaurant equipment, such as a popcorn machine and an ice cream freezer, and various pieces of agricultural or farming equipment, such as a hay rake and a baler. Finally, the State court found that the partnership owned no land but that the value of certain fixtures and improvements to land occupied by the partnership was $144,234.

The State court ordered all partnership assets remaining after payment of partnership liabilities, including cash, to be distributed to James' estate "to repay on a dollar-for-dollar basis to the extent of such assets the contributions to capital made by James R. Tobias." The State court allocated none of the remaining partnership assets to Darwin. It is implicit in the order of the State court that the proceeds from the sale of the equipment would not equal James' disproportionately large capital contributions.

From 1965 until 1992, James treated the animal farm business as a sole proprietorship and reported the entire income from the business on his individual tax returns. After the State court found that the business was a partnership, James caused the partnership to file returns for the years 1990 through 1993. Darwin did not participate in the preparation or filing of the partnership returns. The partnership returns identify James and Darwin as 50–percent partners and allocate 50 percent of each distributive share item of the partnership to each of them. The partnership returns for 1992 and 1993 include Schedules K–1, Partner's Share of Income, Credits, Deductions, etc., which report identical capital accounts for each brother.

James and his wife included 50 percent of the partnership's ordinary income and interest income for 1991 and 1993 in the gross income reported on their joint returns for the years 1991 and 1993. They did not include in their gross income for 1993 any of the long-term capital gain realized by the partnership during 1993. The notice of deficiency issued to them states as follows:

> As it cannot be determined what the allocable share of such partner-ship income is for any of the partners for any of the years, all of the income has been allocated to each partner, thus increasing your taxable income a net $25,208 and $18,089 [sic] for taxable years ending December 31, 1991 and 1993, respectively.

Thus, the notice of deficiency issued to James and his wife has the effect of allocating to James 100 percent of the partnership's ordinary income and interest income for 1991 and 1993 and 50 percent of the partnership's long-term capital gain for 1993. In respondent's answer to the petition that was filed on behalf of James and his wife, respondent asserts that there is an increased deficiency due from James and his wife on the theory that 100 percent of the long-term capital gain realized by the partnership during 1993 should be allocated to James.

Darwin and his wife did not include any partnership income in the gross income reported on their joint returns for the years 1990, 1991, and 1993. The notice of deficiency issued to them states as follows:

As it cannot be determined what the allocable share of such partnership income is for any of the partners for any of the years, all of the income has been allocated to each partner, thus increasing your taxable income a net $37,661, $25,208 and $18,089 [sic] for taxable years ending December 31, 1990, 1991 and 1993, respectively.

Thus, the notice of deficiency issued to Darwin and his wife allocates to Darwin 50 percent of the ordinary income, interest income, and long-term capital gain realized by the partnership for the years 1990, 1991, and 1993.

Discussion

In its motion for summary judgment, the estate takes the position that respondent committed error by increasing James' taxable income by 50 percent of the partnership's income and, thus, by treating him as subject to tax on all of the partnership's income. According to the estate, the State court determined, consistent with Darwin's allegations, "that a 50–50 partnership did exist between James and Darwin with respect to the Lake Tobias Animal Farm." The estate argues that, notwithstanding "Darwin's eviction from active participation in the business", the partnership continued to exist during the years in issue for Federal tax purposes because there was no termination pursuant to section 708. Thus, according to the estate, partnership income for the years in issue must be allocated equally to the partners, "in accordance with their respective partnership interests."

Darwin and his wife oppose the estate's motion for summary judgment. They argue that the partnership terminated in 1986 and that any income from the business after 1986, including the subject income, must be allocated entirely to James. In their cross-motion for summary judgment, they argue that "the facts and circumstances of the case require allocation of all income and expenses to James pursuant to the partners [sic] interest in the partnership test. (Regs. section 1.704–1(b)(1)(I) [sic])." They further argue that liquidation of the partnership, pursuant to the order of the State court, is evidence that James bore the economic benefit and burden of the partnership income. Accordingly, they argue that all of the income from the business should be allocated to James, or in the alternative, that the income should be allocated in accordance with the partners' capital contributions; i.e., 99.98 percent to James and .02 percent to Darwin.

Respondent also opposes the estate's motion for summary judgment and has filed a cross-motion for summary judgment in which respondent, like the estate, takes the position that the partnership income at issue in these cases must be allocated in accordance with the "partner's interest in the partnership", pursuant to section 1.704–1(b)(3)(i), Income Tax Regs. Respondent disagrees, however, with the estate's assertion that the partners each have a 50–percent interest in the partnership, and instead argues that James has a 100–percent interest in the partnership. Thus, respondent contends that all of the income reported by the animal farm business for the years 1990 through 1993 should be allocated to the estate. In support thereof, respondent notes that, "up to 1994, James had contributed almost $1,000,000 more in capital to the partnership than Darwin." Respondent further notes that, "under applicable state law, James is entitled to a liquidation distribution of the amount by which his contributions exceed Darwin's before Darwin is entitled to any distributions." Finally, respondent notes that "the value of the partnership's assets in excess of its liabilities amounted to less than $150,000". Therefore, according to respondent, James bore the entire economic benefit and burden of the partnership income during the years in question and should be allocated all of the partnership income for the years in issue.

In effect, respondent acknowledges that the protective notice of deficiency issued to Darwin and his wife in which respondent adjusts their income for 1990, 1991, and 1993 to include 50 percent of the income of the partnership is inconsistent with respondent's position that all partnership income should be allocated to James. The memorandum in support of respondent's cross-motion for summary judgment states: "If and to the extent the respondent's motion is granted, the respondent will stipulate to a decision reducing Darwin's income accordingly."

The estate makes three arguments in opposition to the cross-motions for summary judgment filed by Darwin and respondent and in support of its position that respondent erred by allocating to James all of the partnership income for the years in issue. First, the estate reiterates its position that the income of the partnership for the years in question must be allocated in accordance with the "partner's interest in the partnership." According to the estate: "The state court expressly found in considering all relevant facts and circumstances that both James and Darwin owned a 50 percent partnership interest in the business." On that basis, the estate contends that the income of the partnership should be allocated to the partners equally.

Second, the estate argues, in the alternative, that such a 50–50 income allocation has substantial economic effect. The estate recognizes that, if a partnership agreement is silent as to how partnership income should be allocated, as is the case here, then income is allocated according to the partners' interests in the partnership and, in that event, the substantial economic effect test of section 704(b)(2) has no application. Nevertheless, the estate is concerned by the statement in Darwin's cross-motion for summary judgment that "no provision exists in the partnership agreement for the restoration of a deficit in a partners [sic] capital account." Because, in the estate's view, the Court could find that a 50–50 allocation does not have substantial economic effect, the estate includes a discussion of the substantial economic effect of such an allocation.

Third, contrary to respondent's position, the estate argues that a "50–50 income allocation is consistent with the requirements of the Internal Revenue Code under all of the undisputed facts and circumstances of this case." In support of this argument, the estate notes that no distributions of income were made by the partnership during any of the years in issue and asserts that the income reported by the partnership during those years did not inure to James' benefit. In this connection, the estate argues that the income reported by the partnership did not increase the asset value of the partnership and any "distribution to James upon liquidation will be minimal." Furthermore, the estate argues that it is improper to use the 1997 State court opinion "with respect to an accounting of ownership of partnership assets under Pennsylvania state law to retrospectively reallocate income for federal income tax purposes for the calendar years 1990 through 1993."

In order to put this issue in context, we recall the following statement from our opinion in Vecchio v. Commissioner, 103 T.C. 170, 185–186 (1994):

> In determining his income tax, a partner must take into account his "distributive share" of each item of partnership income, gain, loss, deduction, and credit. Sec. 702(a). Each partner is taxed on his distributive share of the partnership income without regard to whether the amount is actually distributed to him. Sec. 1.702–1(a), Income Tax Regs.; see also United States v. Basye, 410 U.S. 441, 453, 35 L. Ed. 2d 412, 93 S. Ct. 1080 (1973). A partner's distributive share of partnership income or loss is to be determined by the partnership agreement, provided the allocation has substantial economic effect. Sec. 704(a). If the partnership agreement does not provide as to the partner's distributive share, or if the partnership agreement provides for an allocation that does not have substantial economic effect, then a partner's distributive share is determined by the partner's "interest in the partnership". Sec. 704(b). A partner's interest in the partnership is determined by taking into account all facts and circumstances. Id.

As suggested above, section 704 provides the framework for determining a partner's distributive share of partnership income, gain, loss, deductions, or credits and governs the allocation of such partnership items.

None of the parties to the instant cases claims that there is a partnership agreement under which either partner's distributive share of income, gain, loss, deduction, or credit can be determined, as provided by section 704(a). This is consistent with the fact that James and Darwin did not enter into a written partnership agreement and the fact that their oral agreement was merely an informal, general agreement to operate an animal farm and did not contain any specific terms. Because there is no partnership agreement in these cases, there is no need to address the estate's "alternative" argument that a 50–50 allocation of partnership income has substantial economic effect. See Brooks v. Commissioner, T.C. Memo 1995–400; Mammoth Lakes Project v. Commissioner, T.C. Memo 1991–4. All of the parties to the instant cases take the position that the subject income must be allocated in accordance with each partner's interest in the partnership, as provided by section

704(b)(1). Accordingly, we must determine the interests of James and Darwin in the subject animal farm partnership.

The regulations promulgated under section 704 define the phrase "partner's interest in the partnership" as the "manner in which the partners have agreed to share the economic benefit or burden (if any) corresponding to the income, gain, loss, deduction, or credit (or item thereof) that is allocated." Sec. 1.704–1(b)(3)(i), Income Tax Regs. The regulations also provide that the determination of a partner's interest shall be made by taking into account all facts and circumstances relating to the economic arrangement of the partners. See sec. 1.704–1(b)(3)(i), Income Tax Regs. Specifically, section 1.704–1(b)(3)(ii), Income Tax Regs., provides that the following four factors shall be considered in determining a partner's interest in the partnership: (1) The partners' relative contributions to capital; (2) the partners' interests in economic profits and losses; (3) the partners' interests in cash-flow and other nonliquidating distributions; and (4) the rights of the partners to distributions of capital upon liquidation of the partnership. See Vecchio v. Commissioner, supra at 193; PNRC Ltd. Partnership v. Commissioner, T.C. Memo 1993–335.

The first factor, the partners' relative capital contributions, was discussed in the 1997 State court opinion. The State court found that James' capital contributions totaled $1,001,568.60 and Darwin's contributions totaled $2,320. The parties to the instant cases do not challenge the findings of the State court regarding the capital contributions of each partner. The 1997 State court opinion does not set forth the dates on which James made his contributions, but from our review of the 1992 and 1997 State court opinions, we conclude that a substantial percentage of James' contributions, at least $700,000, was made before the years in issue. According to the 1997 State court opinion, all of Darwin's contributions, in the aggregate amount of $2,320, were made before the years in issue.

The second factor to consider in determining a partner's interest in the partnership is the partner's interest in economic profits and losses. The 1992 State court opinion states that the partners would share the profits of the business after they were repaid their capital contributions.

The third factor to consider in determining a partner's interest in the partnership is the partner's interest in cash-flow and other nonliquidating distributions. Although all of the profits of the business were reinvested in the business, James and Darwin were reimbursed for various business expenses that they personally incurred. However, after his eviction in 1986, Darwin did not personally incur any business expenses because he did not participate in the business. Thus, for the years in issue, Darwin did not have any interest in the cash-flow or other nonliquidating distributions of the business.

The fourth factor to consider in determining a partner's interest in the partnership is the partner's right to distributions of capital upon liquidation of the partnership. This factor requires that we determine how the partnership would have been liquidated in each of the years in issue. This factor is directly related to the capital contributions of each partner. As discussed earlier, the State court determined that James' contributions, $1,001,568.60, substantially exceeded Darwin's contributions, $2,320, and our review of the State court opinions suggests that James had contributed a substantial amount of the total, at least $700,000, before the years in issue.

Furthermore, the partnership returns filed by James report total assets for 1990 through 1993 of $171,769, $164,956, $166,836, and $200,135, respectively. This is corroborated by the 1997 State court opinion, which found that the value of the assets of the partnership was in approximately the same order of magnitude. Thus, the value of partnership assets did not approach the total of James' disproportionately large capital contributions for any of the years in issue. Accordingly, if the partnership had been liquidated at any time during the years in issue, all of the partnership assets would have been distributed to James. It is evident, therefore, that during each of the years in issue James bore the economic benefit of 100 percent of the income realized by the partnership. See sec. 1.704–1(b)(3), Income Tax Regs.

The estate argues that "the state court's determination that James and Darwin each own a 50 percent interest in the partnership is applicable for allocation of income for Federal income tax purposes pursuant to I.R.C. section 704(b)(1)." In our view, the estate disregards the fact that under the State court determination profits would be shared equally only "after the partners are repaid their contribution as provided by the act." In discussing the partners' rights in the partnership, the 1992 State court opinion focuses on the fact that James had made disproportionately greater capital contributions and on the inequity of dividing partnership profits equally before he was repaid. The 1992 State court opinion states the following:

> Under the partnership act above [referring to 15 Pa. Cons. Stat. section 8331] each partner is repaid his contribution whether by way of capital or advances to the partnership property. The court found that James' contribution [sic] far exceeded contributions made by Darwin. Hence it appears that an inequity would be visited on James if the partners share equally in profit, however the provision allowing repayment of advances to the partnership will level the playing field.

> * * *

> After each partner is compensated for his contribution, i.e., capital advancement or property to the partnership distribution of profits on an equal basis would seem equitable. [Tobias v. Tobias, No. 4583 (Ct. C.P. Dauphin County, Pa. July 7, 1992).]

The 1997 State court opinion summarizes Pennsylvania law as "holding that the repayment of capital investments before distribution of any profits is an essential element of every partnerships agreement implied as a term of law." The 1997 State court opinion effects the 1992 State court opinion by determining the partnership's assets and liabilities, and the capital contributions of each partner, and by directing that after payment of the partnership's liabilities, "all other assets of the partnership shall be delivered to the Estate of James R. Tobias to repay on a dollar-for-dollar basis to the extent of such assets the contributions to capital made by James R. Tobias."

We do not interpret the State court opinions as determining that "James and Darwin each own a 50–percent interest in the partnership" during the years in issue. Rather, the State court opinions determined the appropriate distributions to the partners upon the dissolution and liquidation of the partnership, on the basis of State law, the relative capital contributions of the partners, and principles of equity.

It appears that the estate seizes on the statements in the State court opinions that "the profits will be shared equally" and asks this Court to find that each of the partners held a 50–percent interest in the partnership for purposes of section 704(b)(1). In effect, the estate asks us to make that finding without considering the relative capital contributions of the partners or the other factors listed in section 1.704–1(b)(3)(ii), Income Tax Regs.

Although the estate does not discuss the four factors listed in section 1.704–1(b)(3)(ii), Income Tax Regs., the estate argues that a "50–50 income allocation is consistent with the requirements of the Internal Revenue Code under all of the undisputed facts and circumstances of this case." We consider the facts and circumstances the estate relies on.

First, the estate argues that the partnership income for the years in issue did not inure to the benefit of James. According to the estate, this is shown by the fact that the asset value of the partnership was not increased by the amount of income reported by the partnership, and by the fact that any distribution to James upon liquidation of the partnership would be minimal. Second, the estate argues that respondent "is improperly attempting to use a state court decision rendered in 1997 with respect to an accounting * * * to retrospectively reallocate income for federal income tax purposes for the calendar years 1990 through 1993."

Contrary to the estate's argument, the net asset value of the partnership increased each year by the amount of partnership income. In the following schedule, we have computed the net asset value of the partnership using the balance sheets filed with the partnership returns as Schedule L, and we have compared the annual increases in net asset value to the income reported:

	1990	1991	1992	1993
Total assets	$171,769	$164,956	$166,836	$200,135
Total liabilities	57,267	0	1,856	56
Net asset value (NAV)	114,502	164,956	164,980	200,079
Increase in NAV from previous year	n/a	50,454	24	35,099
Total partnership income	75,321	50,416	24	36,175

The above schedule shows a direct correlation between the increase in the net asset value of the partnership for each year and the amount of income reported. Because the State court ordered that all remaining assets of the partnership be distributed to James, we agree with respondent that the income of the partnership for the years in issue inured to James' benefit.

Furthermore, it is not evident that any distribution to James or to his estate upon liquidation of the partnership would be minimal. Under the 1997 State court opinion, after the partnership's liabilities are paid, the estate is to receive various real estate improvements and fixtures valued by the State court at $144,234 and other assets. Moreover, even if the amount of the distribution were "minimal", a partner is subject to tax on his share of partnership income whether or not such income is actually distributed to him. See United States v. Basye, 410 U.S. 441, 453–454, 35 L.Ed.2d 412, 93 S.Ct. 1080 (1973); sec. 1.702–1(a), Income Tax Regs.

We also reject the estate's argument that respondent erred by allocating partnership income for 1990 through 1993 on the basis of the 1997 State court opinion. In these cases, it is necessary to determine the interest of each brother in the partnership for purposes of section 704(b)(1), and the determination must be made by taking into account all of the facts and circumstances relating to the economic arrangement of the partners. See sec. 1.704–1(b)(3)(i), Income Tax Regs. We believe that respondent has correctly reviewed the effect of the 1997 State court opinion and the other facts and circumstances relating to the financial arrangements of the brothers in determining their interests in the partnership.

On the basis of the four factors listed in section 1.704–1(b)(3)(ii), Income Tax Regs., and all the facts and circumstances of these cases, we find that during each of the years in issue James had a 100–percent interest in the partnership income and Darwin had a zero interest in the partnership income. Accordingly, we agree with respondent and Darwin that 100 percent of the income of the partnership during the years in issue should be allocated to James.

Practice

1. Is it logical to conclude that a partnership even existed if one partner has a 100% interest in profits? Re-read Treas. Reg. 301.7701–1(a)(2).

2. The examples in Regulation 1.704–1(b)(5) demonstrate rules regarding the meaning of a "partner's interest in the partnership." Read the examples in a., b., and c., below; try to prepare written articulations of the rules demonstrated in those examples.

    a. Examples 1(i)–(ii), 4(i), and 16(i) demonstrate the same rule.

    b. Examples 1(iv), and 15(ii) demonstrate the same rule.

    c. Examples 5, 6, 7, 8(i), and 10(ii) demonstrate the same rule.

3. If in Example 10(ii), Regulation 1.704–1(b)(5), the partnership earned $100,000 of income from the foreign country and $90,000 domestically, how should the income be allocated?

4. If in Example 16(i), Regulation 1.704–1(b)(5), the partnership suffered an overall loss of $300,000 ($200,000 depreciation and $100,000 ordinary expenses), how should the losses be allocated?

Lesson 13

ALLOCATION OF DEDUCTIONS GENERATED BY NONRECOURSE BORROWING

Primary Reference: Treas. Reg. 1.704–2(a)–(j), (m)(1)(i)–(viii); 1.1001–2(a)(4)(i)

Case Reference: Crane v. Commissioner, 331 U.S. 1 (1947); Commissioner v. Tufts, 461 U.S. 300 (1983)

Theory

The best of all tax worlds—besides tax exemption, perhaps—is getting a tax deduction without an actual economic outlay. When deductions are generated using OPM, allocations of those deductions logically cannot have economic effect unless the person claiming the deduction is personally obligated to repay the loan. If the person claiming the deduction is not personally obligated to repay the loan beyond a requirement to return the property upon default (i.e., the loan is "nonrecourse"), it is the lender who bears the risk of loss relating to the property. The owner can simply transfer the property back to the lender in full satisfaction of the loan. If the property depreciates to a value less than the loan amount, the owner should do so assuming no other considerations except the value of the property as compared to the principal owing on the loan. Hence, it is the lender who should be treated as the real owner of the deduction-generating property, at least to the extent of the outstanding balance on the loan. *Crane*, though, rejected the notion that the lender is the true owner, to whom deductions are properly due, and *Tufts* confirms that upon the sale of property encumbered by a liability for which the property owner is not personally obligated, the owner's amount realized is the amount of the liability plus any cash or other property received. These two holdings set the stage for the use of OPM to increase basis and thereby generate valuable deductions. This Lesson simply applies *Crane* and *Tufts* to partnerships.

112

Regulation 1.704–2(b) begins by recognizing that allocations to partners of deductions generated by nonrecourse loans are essentially illogical from an economic standpoint. Nevertheless, *Crane* requires that those deductions be taken by the nominal property owners—the partners. The regulation therefore sets out to establish a logical approach to something that is ultimately illogical. In short, deductions generated by nonrecourse borrowing may be allocated in any manner that is "consistent" with the allocations of other "significant" items from the encumbered property, the allocations of which have substantial economic effect, provided the partnership agreement contains a "minimum gain chargeback" provision and all other "material" allocations and capital account adjustments have substantial economic effect.

Besides defining the words "consistent" and "significant," and the phrase "minimum gain chargeback," readers will need to understand the following terms and how the terms arise: (1) partnership minimum gain (PMG), (2) nonrecourse deductions (NRD), (3) increase/decrease in partnership minimum gain, (4) partner's share of PMG, (5) nonrecourse liability, (6) partner's share of the decrease in PMG, and (7) minimum gain chargeback. Note that in one respect, allocating NRD's is simply a matter of including the proper language in the partnership agreement, just as partners would insert the proper language to ensure allocations have economic effect. The regulations are fairly clear with regard to these terms and when they apply.

Complying with the mechanical requirements for allocating nonrecourse deductions is essentially a matter of following certain steps. First, determine the amount of PMG for the year. Second, compare the present year's PMG to the prior year's PMG. If there is an increase in PMG, all deductions for the year are NRD's to the extent of the increase—certain "ordering rules" apply in Regulation 1.704–2(j) that identify which deductions are nonrecourse and therefore subject to the consistency requirement. Third, if the PMG for the year exceeds partnership deductions, the excess is treated as PMG in the next year and must be added to any amount of PMG in that next year. Fourth, if there is a decrease in PMG from one year to another, the minimum gain chargeback provision is triggered and operates in the same manner as a QIO, unless one of the exceptions to the chargeback requirement applies. The minimum gain chargeback, as with the QIO, override the general allocation method specified in the partnership or LLC agreement.

It may occur to readers that a rational lender would never loan money on a nonrecourse basis. Why should a lender do such a silly thing? It is probably the case that lenders only do so for their very best and wealthiest customers who have extraordinary access to credit and in hopes that the lender will be used for whatever other financial services the borrower needs. Another circumstance might be that the borrower has valuable property that is virtually guaranteed to appreciate in value while the loan is outstanding. In most other circumstances, particularly those involving small businesses, partnerships will not have the economic clout to demand true nonrecourse financing. Instead, the partnership or one or more partners will be required to personally guarantee the liability. In the latter instance, other partners will remain immune from liability, leaving only the guaranteeing partner or partners subject to personal liability.

Readers can probably predict from the initial paragraph above who gets to claim deductions generated by the guaranteed liability—referred to as "partner nonrecourse liability." If indeed there is a partner who is ultimately responsible for a debt, she is the true economic owner and deductions relating to that property should be allocated to her. Thus, "partner nonrecourse deductions," another new phrase in the regulations, must be allocated solely to the guaranteeing partner, and that partner will be subject to a "partner nonrecourse minimum gain chargeback." In essence, the rules with regard to partner nonrecourse deductions mirror those applicable to nonrecourse deductions. In both cases, it is merely a matter of understanding a new lexicon and going through the accounting troubles necessary to keep track of deductions generated by nonrecourse borrowing. As always, the examples are very helpful in clarifying what first seems like an indecipherable puzzle. Take the time to read them thoroughly.

Practice:

1. Read Example 1 and 3(i), Regulation 1.704–2(m). If LP in example 1, and A in example 3 are not subject to a deficit reduction obligation, why do the allocations of loss to those partners in year three (example 1) and year 2 (example 3(i)) have substantial economic effect?

2. What is the rule by which to determine whether nonrecourse deductions are allocated in a manner that is "reasonably consistent" with allocations that have substantial economic effect of other significant items?

3. What is the authority by which partners in example 1(iv) are not subject to a minimum gain chargeback? What is the effect of a minimum gain chargeback?

4. In Example 1(i), Regulation 1.704–2(m) assume the partnership agreement were amended at the beginning of the partnership's fourth year so that "all items of income, gain, loss, and deductions were to be allocated equally (subject to any special allocations required by IRC 704)." If the partnership has $270,000 in expenses, sells the building for $1,000,000, and pays the liability, how must the income and expenses be allocated in order that they be respected?

5. If a partnership agreement contains a QIO and a minimum gain chargeback and, in one year, Partner A as a $100 decrease in her share of PMG, and Partner B has an unexpected $100 capital account deficit, a minimum gain chargeback applies to partner A and a qualified income offset applies to partner B, which provision—the QIO or the minimum gain chargeback applies first? Assume the partnership has $100 gross income for the year and $100 of deductible expenses.

6. Does the partnership agreement in Appendix 1 contain all the necessary language so that nonrecourse deductions will be respected?

7. Read Example 1(viii), Regulation 1.704–2(m). How would the result change if Partner GP agreed to indemnify Partner LP to the extent of $200,000 of the $800,000 partner nonrecourse debt?

8. What would be the result in Example 1(viii), Regulation 1.704–2(m) if LP's guarantee of the debt expired in year four so that the debt converted to nonrecourse (assume all other facts are as stated in the example)?

9. Rework Example 1(i)–(ii), Regulation 1.704–2(m), assuming that all the facts are the same except that the partnership agreement allocates nonrecourse deductions 70% to LP and 30% to GP and the property is sold for $1,000,000 at the end of year 4.

10. What result in Example 1(v), Regulation 1.704–2(m) if the nonrecourse and recourse loans are of equal priority?

11. What result in Example 1(iv), Regulation 1.704–2(m), if GP contributed the entire $160,000 used to pay down the nonrecourse liability?

Lesson 14

ASSIGNMENT OF INCOME: ALLOCATIONS OF ITEMS FROM BUILT–IN GAIN OR LOSS PROPERTY

Primary References: 704(c)(1)(A), Treas. Reg. 1.704–1(b)(2)(iv)(d), 1.704–1(b)(2)(iv)(f), 1.704–1(b)(2)(iv)(g), 1.704–3(a)–(e)(2), 1.704–1(b)(5), Example 14(i)–(iv), 1.704–1(e)

Case References: Schneer v. Commissioner, 97 T.C. 643 (1991)

Secondary References: Lucas v. Earl, 281 U.S. 111 (1930); Helvering v. Horst, 311 U.S. 112 (1940); Helvering v. Eubank, 311 U.S. 122 (1940) IRC 168(i)(7)(A)–(B)(i), IRC 704(e), 1245(a)(1)–(3); Treas. Reg. 1.1245–1(e)

Theory

Suppose two attorneys who have been practicing separately for a number of years decide to join together in a partnership. We know that if one attorney transfers a contractual right to receive $40,000 in legal fees for services performed while she was a sole practitioner, she will recognize neither gain nor loss upon the receipt of her partnership interest. IRC 721. Under IRC 722, she will take a zero outside basis in her partnership interest and under Treas. Reg. 1.704–1(b)(2)(iv) her capital account will be credited with $40,000. Assume the other attorney contributes $40,000 cash. Her results will be the same except that she will take a $40,000 outside basis in her partnership interest. If the partnership later collects on the contractual right, how should the income be allocated amongst the partners, assuming they agree to allocate all partnership items equally?

The secondary references cited above tell us that income is taxed to its earner. To allow anticipatory assignments of income would be incon-

116

sistent with progressive taxation. On the other hand, we may rightly suspect from our study of special allocations and substantial economic effect that the assignment of income doctrine is subordinated to the idea that individuals should be allowed as much flexibility as possible with respect to their joint economic activities. In reality, neither principle— assignment of income nor flexible allocation of partnership items—is compromised by the other. In our example above, the partnership should be allowed to allocate its earned income in a manner that is dispropor- tionate to any partner's capital contributions, but the income from the accounts receivable is really not partnership income is it? The income is properly attributable not to the partnership's services, but to an individ- ual's services rendered prior to her admission into the partnership and should be taxed accordingly. And indeed, that individual has previously realized the income as evidenced by her increased capital account. So we are not really limiting the partners' ability to specially allocate its own income when we tax a partner's individual income to her, though that income is not recognized until after the underlying property is trans- ferred to the partnership.

When individuals join together income from each of their separate activities in furtherance of the joint venture may logically be deemed earned by them all. In that instance, there is technically no assignment of income. For example, even if a law partnership's income is attribut- able primarily to one well-known partner it cannot be said that her association with less well known attorneys had nothing whatever to do with the income. The condition precedent, of course, is whether one partner's efforts are in furtherance of the joint efforts or are in further- ance of an unrelated purpose. The approach of determining whether income is earned by the partner in her individual capacity (taxable solely to the individual), or the partnership (and thereafter subject to allocation to all partners) was used to justify the taxation of service income earned by one partner to the partnership and therefore all the partners in *Schneer v. Commissioner*, cited above.

If we keep in mind that income from services and property is indeed taxed to the earner or owner, then we know that IRC 704(c) is most properly viewed as merely a restatement of the judicially created "as- signment of income" doctrine in the partnership setting. It might even be redundant as a technical matter. Note, however, that IRC 704(c)(1) applies solely to contributed property, not services. The proper treat- ment of income from services will be determined under judicial doctrines by asking whether a partner was acting in her capacity as such when the services were performed. What facts do you think would be relevant in making this determination? These inquiries are particularly fact specific but center around the expectations of all involved and the similarities between an individual's activities and the goals of the partnership of which the individual is a member.

In any event, the distinction is not full proof and Subchapter K certainly allows some degree of income shifting. For example, suppose the attorney in the initial hypothetical was the firm's "rainmaker" and workhorse. Even if the partnership's income for the entire year were attributable to one partner's services (in a big case, for example), the income would likely be earned by the partnership and therefore subject to allocation amongst the partners, notwithstanding the assignment of income doctrine. *Schneer v. Commissioner.* Should it make a difference if a former sole proprietor, now partner, in an environmental consulting firm has 30 years of experience and special knowledge and the other partners are her two adult children who have only recently completed law school? As we saw in Lesson 10, income shifting is a distinct possibility under Subchapter K. Income shifting opportunities are especially available in family partnerships. Question 9, below, provokes greater exploration of the income shifting possibilities with regard to family partnerships.

The mechanics of IRC 704(c)(1)(A) are really not difficult but you must read the regulations thoroughly (perhaps more so than normally because of the "ceiling rule" discussed below). Remember, the statute merely extends the assignment of income principle to the taxation of income or loss accruing before property is contributed to a partnership, but recognized only after contribution. Suppose instead of a law firm, the partnership referred to above developed and sold real estate and one partner contributed appreciated or depreciated land to the partnership. Upon the subsequent sale or disposition of the property, the appreciation (i.e., the built-in gain) or depreciation (i.e., the built-in loss) as of the date of the contribution should be taxed to the contributing partner because she has previously realized the benefit or burden of that appreciation or depreciation as evidenced by her capital account balance. Thus, allocations of "built-in" gain or loss should be made to the contributing partner. As a side note, when the built-in gain or loss is recognized, it will have no affect on any partner's capital accounts. Regulation 1.704–1(b)(2)(iv)(d)(3). This is because the capital accounts will already reflect the property's appreciated or depreciated value.

The basic IRC 704(c) allocation method is applied easily enough but gets somewhat more complicated by the presence of depreciable property and the "ceiling rule" stated rather obliquely in Regulation 1.704–3(b)(1) (second to the last sentence). IRC 704(c) requires that any recognized tax gain on contributed property, to the extent it does not exceed built in gain, be allocated solely to the contributing partner and that tax depreciation be allocated first to noncontributing partners to the extent of their allocable shares of book depreciation. Allocating depreciation deductions first to noncontributing partners is essentially the same thing as allocating income first to contributing partners. In either event, the contributing partner retains sole responsibility for paying tax on the appreciation. A similar mechanism prevents the shifting of loss from the contributing partner to other partners. IRC 704(c) requires that any recognized tax loss, to the extent such loss does not exceed built-in loss, be allocated to the contributing partner. The loss in excess of the built in loss, is allocated in accordance with the partnership agreement for both tax and book purposes.

When built in gain or loss property (i.e., 704(c) property) is subsequently sold or disposed of in a taxable transaction, the partners' book results will differ from their tax results. For example, a partnership may simultaneously experience a book loss and a tax gain, or a book gain and tax loss, on the sale of property. In the former case, all the partners will have suffered an economic loss, though the contributing partner will nevertheless have taxable income. Still, the contributing partner will pay taxes on an amount of income that is less than her initial accession to wealth (as represented by the credit to her capital account when the property was contributed). The contributing partner will take account of the book loss by reporting less income, but the ceiling rule will prevent the noncontributing partners from taking their economic loss into account by way of a loss deduction. In plain English, the ceiling rule means that a partner may not take a deduction for a real economic loss if the partnership has not recognized sufficient tax losses (measured by the difference between amount realized and tax basis) to allocate such a loss to the partner. Thus, while IRC 704(c) intends to decrease the book/tax disparity with regard to the contributing partner, the ceiling rule prevents the full effectuation of that intent by increasing disparities with regard to the non-contributing partner, and in some cases preventing the proper taxation of previously realized gain to the contributing partner.

When the ceiling rule applies to prevent a noncontributing partner from deducting a loss equal to her economic loss (as represented by an allocation of book loss), the noncontributing partners' capital accounts will be decreased but their outside bases will remain the same (book loss, tax gain). The contributing partner will report gain in an amount less than the previously realized value of her contributed property. The increased disparity is not a mere accounting matter, but results from the denial of a tax deduction to which noncontributing partners are economically due and the deferral of tax on the contributing partner. The result works in the opposite direction when the partnership sells built in loss property for an amount greater than its book value as of the date of contribution but less than its basis (book gain, tax loss). All partners will increase their capital accounts while the contributing partner will report a loss for tax purposes. The ceiling rule will dictate that no partner report a gain for tax purposes. In this instance the distortion of the tax/book accounts is beneficial to the noncontributing partners since they are wealthier but need not recognize their increased wealth for tax purposes.

Likewise, the ceiling rule will limit deductions for depreciation if the partnership's tax depreciation differs from its book depreciation. Tax and book depreciation will differ indeed because IRC 168(i)(7) requires that the partnership calculate depreciation deductions for tax purposes as if the property were still held by the contributing partner. Regulation 1.704–1(b)(2)(iv)(g)(3) requires that the same percentage used to determine tax depreciation be applied to determine book depreciation. Book and tax depreciation are calculated differently, however, if the partnership elects the "remedial method" explained in Regulation 1.704–3(d)(2).

The partnership will therefore have more book depreciation if the property is built-in gain property and less book depreciation if it is built-in loss property. In the former instance, non-contributing partners will be allocated tax depreciation in an amount equal to their book depreciation if there is sufficient tax depreciation to do so. Any and all remaining tax depreciation must be allocated to the contributing partner.

A purist might object to the presence of the ceiling rule. But perhaps because the ceiling rule works to the advantage of some partners and the disadvantage of others, the Regulations do not impose a solution. Rather, the regulations essentially make the ceiling rule optional on a property by property basis. Thus, partners can decide on a property by property basis whether the ceiling rule is to apply, so long as once the decision is made it is applied consistently. Presumably, and consistent with the *laissez faire* approach, the code allows the ultimate choice to be dictated by the partners' differing economic interests. The "traditional method" of allocating items from 704(c) property involves application of the ceiling rule. If the partners decide that they do not want to apply the ceiling rule, they can safely apply one of two other methods. The first is referred to as the "traditional method with curative allocations." This method involves making disparate allocations of book and tax items derived from other partnership property in a manner that eliminates the tax/book disparities caused by the ceiling rule. The second safe harbor method is referred to as the "remedial method" and essentially involves shifting tax items away from non-contributing partners and back to the contributing partner. The traditional method with curative allocations requires that the partnership actually realize other tax items similar to the items otherwise affected by the ceiling rule. The remedial method does not.

There is one other instance, besides the contribution of appreciated or depreciated property to the partnership, when the 704(c) principles apply. Recall that the partners' book accounts will record the historical values of contributed properties, as well as positive and negative allocations. In certain circumstances, the partnership may "book up" or "book down" capital accounts to reflect the current value of the partnership's underlying assets. Treas. Reg. 1.704–1(b)(2)(iv)(f). In such cases, capital accounts are increased or decreased while tax accounts are unaffected— there is book gain or loss but no tax gain or loss. The result will be that tax and book accounts differ just as they would if the property had been contributed with appreciated or depreciated values. When the partnership actually recognizes gain or loss with respect to revalued property, the gains or losses must be allocated to the partners whose capital accounts were adjusted in the same manner as though the properties were contributed to the partnership with bases that differed from their fair market values. Regulation 1.704–3(a)(6) refers to the process of allocating built in gain or loss created by a revaluation as "reverse 704(c) allocations."

In Lesson 2, we learned that partnership items are generally characterized at the partnership level. One exception appears in IRC 724. We also learned in Lessons 11 that partners have wide latitude in allocating items of different character to partners. The substantiality prong of the substantial economic effect test imposes rather permissive limits. The allocation of recapture, though, adheres more closely to the theory that the partnership should be transparent for tax purposes and partners should, to the extent possible, be taxed as though they engaged in the partnership transaction directly and individually. The allocation rules with respect to the allocation of depreciation recapture follow that model. In essence, the partners to whom depreciation was previously allocated will be subject to recapture (i.e., taxed at ordinary income rates) on subsequent gain realized on the sale or exchange of 1245 property to the extent of previous depreciation deductions allocated to them. Regulation 1.1245–1(e) takes into account any curative or remedial allocations in determining the amount of previous depreciation deductions allocated to a partner.

Practice

1. Regulation 1.704–1(b)(2)(iv)(f)(3)–(4) and Regulation 1.704–1(b)(2)(iv)(d)(3) require the inclusion of certain language related to IRC 704(c) in the partnership agreement if allocations with respect to built-in gain or loss property are to have economic effect. Does the partnership agreement in Appendix 1 contain the necessary language?

2. Read Example 1(i), Regulation 1.704–3(b)(2). If A sells her entire interest to C and the partnership sells the property for $12,000, how much tax and book gain would be allocated to Partners B and C? Assume the property was sold on January 1 and that the property was non-depreciable instead of depreciable.

3. Read Example 1(ii), Regulation 1.704–3(b)(2). How much tax and book depreciation would Partners A and B be entitled to if the property had been contributed to the partnership after having been depreciated for 5 years and had five years remaining on the recovery period?

4. What result in question 3 above if the depreciable property had a value of only $3000 when it was contributed to the partnership (assume A also contributed $7000 cash)? What result if the property were sold for $3000 after the first year of depreciation?

5. Read Example 1, Regulation 1.704–3(c)(4). How would curative allocations be made if instead of purchasing inventory for $10,000 the partnership had purchased stock as an investment and had sold the stock for $11,000 at the end of the year?

6. Read Example 2, Regulation 1.704–3(c)(4). What would be the tax and book allocations to each partner if the partnership elected the remedial method instead of the traditional method with curative allocations?

7. Read Example 14(i), Regulation 1.704–1(b)(5). What would be the book and tax allocations if the securities were sold for: (1) $40,000, or (2) $60,000 immediately after SK's admission?

8. Read Example 14(v), Regulation 1.704–1(b)(5). Assuming each partner received one third of the shares and the shares had a basis to the partnership of $20,000, what are the partner's outside bases after the distribution?

9. Read IRC 704(e) and Treas. Reg. 1.704–1(e). What is that statute and regulation trying to accomplish? Is it relevant to either of the two scenarios below, and if so how? If it is not relevant to either scenario, what factors should be considered in analyzing the tax outcomes:

   a. Mother is a 30 year, well respected environmental consultant with special knowledge in her field. As a sole proprietor, she earns about $400,000 on average per year. This year, she formed a partnership with her two children, both of whom recently graduated from college. The partnership agreement allocates three fourths of the partnership income to Mother, and one fourth equally to the two children.

   b. Father has owned and operated a construction business for the past 30 years. He has on hand over $10,000,000 worth of construction and factory equipment. The business earns about $400,000 per year. This year, he formed a partnership with his two children, both of whom recently graduated from college. The first child has a degree in psychology and the second a degree in chemical engineering. The partnership agreement allocates three fourths of the partnership income to Father and one fourth equally to the two children.

10. Read and re-read Examples 1–3, Regulations 1.1245–1(e) and be prepared to lead a class discussion of the principles demonstrated in those examples.

Lesson 15

WHICH PARTNERS GET BASIS CREDIT FOR PARTNERSHIP LIABILITIES?

Primary References: IRC 752
Treas. Reg. 1.752–1 (omit example (g)(2)),–2,–3; 1.722–1, 1.1001–2

Case References: Crane v. Commissioner, 331 U.S. 1 (1947); Commissioner v. Tufts, 461 U.S. 300 (1983); U.S. v. Kirby Lumber, 284 U.S. 1 (1931), Rev. Rul. 88–77

Secondary References: IRC 722, 731(a),

Theory

IRC 752 is based in part on the notion that one person's assumption of another's promise to repay a loan is the economic equivalent of the original promisor's receipt of cash. One well-known theory, articulated in *Kirby Lumber*, is that when the promisor is relieved of the liability, the money that has been or would have been set aside to repay the liability is "freed up" for personal consumption and therefore the promisor has gross income. We also know that *Crane* and *Tufts* operate under the assumption that people pay their debts and therefore are entitled to basis credit in property purchased with borrowed money. IRC 752 simply injects these principles into the partnership context. This means that when a partnership takes ownership of property, and responsibility for the property's accompanying liability, the previous owner experiences the economic equivalent of cash received from the partnership. What are the tax consequences when a partnership distributes cash to a partner? Likewise, when the partnership accepts encumbered property, it is as if all or some of the partners sign agreements to pay off the loan. In effect, all or some of the partners have entered into an arrangement to contribute cash to the partnership at a later date. What are the tax consequences when partners contribute cash to their partnership? Read the examples in Regulation 1.722–1 again to get a general answer to these questions.

The theory of 752 is simple enough to understand. But, as always, complications arise from the application of that theory. The necessary start point is determining which partner should get basis credit for partnership liabilities and how much credit should any particular partner get. The regulations begin by adopting the assumption underlying *Crane* and *Tufts*. The partner with ultimate responsibility to repay the loan gets an increase in her basis equal to the monetary value of that responsibility. That too makes easy sense if we remember that repayment will be made from after tax income and basis is essentially a credit against future tax, representing previously taxed (or specifically exempted) income.

Regulation 1.752–2(b) applies a "doomsday" method by which to determine the extent of each partner's relative responsibility to pay all or part of a partnership liability. The doomsday scenario also serves to determine whether a liability is recourse or nonrecourse. The doomsday scenario assumes that all the partnership's cash and assets, except those pledged as security on a loan for which the lender has no other remedy, are worthless and are sold for an amount realized of zero. Note the doomsday scenario is merely a fictional transaction having no effects on the partner's capital accounts. The only affect is to determine who gets basis credit for partnership liabilities and by how much. In a doomsday transaction, the partnership will suffer a loss equal to its aggregate book basis in all of its assets, including cash, but excluding assets pledged as collateral for a loan for which the creditor has no other remedy. The amount realized on the latter type of property is deemed to be used to pay off the loan and any amount left over is gain to the partnership. The loss from the doomsday transaction must be hypothetically allocated to each partner's capital account in accordance with the partnership agreement. The partnership's stated method of allocation applies here, subject to IRC 704(b) and the 704(b) regulations. A partner's deficit capital account balance—remember, a partner cannot have a deficit unless the partner also has an unlimited deficit reduction obligation or is subject to a QIO—will generally equal the amount of partnership liability for which she is responsible, and therefore the credit to her basis. If no partner has a negative capital account after the doomsday transaction, the liability will be considered "nonrecourse."

The method of allocating liabilities specified in Regulation 1.752–2 is premised on the assumption that one or more partners is legally obligated to repay the liability, notwithstanding the interposition of the partnership between lenders and partners. But we know that in certain seemingly strange circumstances lenders will loan money on a nonrecourse basis. And yet *Tufts* instructs that taxpayers are entitled to basis credit with respect to loans for which they are not personally liable. *Tufts* is admirably based on the assumption that everybody pays their debts even when the law would not force us to do so. Regulation 1.752–3 is based on another assumption related to human nature; humans pay even their unenforceable debts to the extent they have the income from which to do so.

Thus, nonrecourse liabilities are generally credited to each partner's basis in the same manner as profits must and will be allocated to the partners. This means that liabilities are credited to each partner's outside basis in the same manner the partners allocates profits in the partnership agreement. The assignment of nonrecourse liabilities follows this general pattern. Nonrecourse liabilities are credited to each partner's basis in the same manner that profits are validly allocated to each partner. This observation means that you must understand substantial economic effect, nonrecourse deductions and 704(c) allocations because the allocation of profit is impacted by each of those subjects.

Practice:

1. Read Example 1, Regulation 1.752–1(g). What result if two other persons were general partners in the partnership, and B contributed the property to the partnership in exchange for a one-third limited partnership interest, after which he would be required to make no further contributions to the partnership? Incidentally, what is the amount in B's capital account upon contribution of the property?

2. Suppose in Example 1, Regulation 1.752–1(g) (as originally stated), B sells her interest to C for $1,250 cash and C takes B's place in the partnership. What is B's amount realized?

3. What result in Example 1, 1.752–2(f), if the A is a limited partner but that the partnership agreement did not contain a QIO? What are A and B's basis under these new facts? What result if A, as limited partner in a partnership without a QIO, indemnifies B against her obligation to repay the debt?

4. Suppose in Example 3, Regulation 1.752–2(g), partner F does not guarantee the loan but instead pledges her own separate property worth $15,000 as collateral for the loan?

5. Read Example 8, 1.752–2(g), what are each partner's outside bases if profits and losses are allocated 55% to J and 45% to K?

6. Read Example 1, Regulation 1.752–3(c). How would the liability be allocated if instead of purchasing the property, the partnership received the property as a contribution from B when the property had an adjusted basis of $500, a fair market value of $2000 and was encumbered by a $1000 liability?

7. Read Example 3(ii), Regulation 1.752–3(c). What result if the partnership allocated the entire $120 liability to property Y and the partnership allocates the excess nonrecourse liability using the method stated in the example.

8. Read Example 2, Regulation 1.752–2(f) again. Suppose that in the year following the contribution, the partnership incurs a $2,000 loss, allocated equally between the partners. In the next year, the partners amend the partnership agreement so that D becomes a limited partner

with no obligation to cure any capital account deficit. The partnership inserts a qualified income offset provision into the agreement. In that year the partnership has no income, gain, loss, credits or deductions to allocate. What result to C and D?

More Theory:

One issue not previously addressed in this Lesson is the meaning of "liability." We can safely start with the notion that a liability means an obligation to make a payment. But, as explained in the following revenue ruling, not all obligations are "liabilities" under IRC 752. Obligations the payment of which will generate a deduction are not liabilities. This conclusion is derived more from expediency than theory, though theory (taxing only real accessions to wealth) has something to do with it. Excluding obligations, the payment of which would have given rise to a deduction is simply a way of saying that the discharge of the obligation should not result in a taxable accession to wealth (because payment of the liability would have generated an offsetting "negative" accession to wealth, recognized by grant of a deduction). In other words, simply ignoring the obligation saves time and paperwork, and also prevents distortion. The question that follows Rev. Rul. 88–77 shows how that conclusion might be exploited for illegitimate tax gain.

REVENUE RULING 88–77
1988–2 C.B. 128

ISSUE

For purposes of computing the adjusted basis of a partner's interest in a cash basis partnership, are accrued but unpaid expenses and accounts payable "liabilities of a partnership" or "partnership liabilities" within the meaning of section 752 of the Internal Revenue Code?

FACTS

A is a partner in P partnership. P files returns on a calendar year basis and uses the cash receipts and disbursements method of accounting. At the close of the taxable year at issue, P's accrued expenses and accounts payable consisted of $100x$ dollars for interest expense and accounts payable of $200x$ dollars for services received.

LAW AND ANALYSIS

Section 722 of the Code provides that a partner's basis is increased by the amount of money the partner contributes to the partnership.

Section 752(a) of the Code provides that any increase in a partner's share of the liabilities of a partnership, or any increase in a partner's individual liabilities by reason of the assumption by the partner of partnership liabilities, is treated as a contribution of money by the partner to the partnership.

Rev. Rul. 60–345, 1960–2 C.B. 211, holds that, for purposes of section 752 of the Code, the term "liabilities" includes a cash basis partnership's obligations for the payment of outstanding trade accounts, notes, and accrued expenses. The present issue is similar to that arising under section 357(c) of the Code when property and liabilities are contributed to a controlled corporation in exchange for stock. For purposes of determining the basis of the stock received in the exchange under section 358 and any gain that must be recognized on the exchange under section 357(c), section 357(c)(3) provides that the term "liabilities" shall not include obligations the payment of which would give rise to a deduction or that would constitute a guaranteed payment under section 736(a). This rule is subject to an exception found in section 357(c)(3)(B) for liabilities the incurrence of which resulted in the creation of, or an increase in, the basis of any property. Section 357(c)(3) was added by the Revenue Act of 1978.

The legislative history accompanying the amendment to section 704(c) made by the Tax Reform Act of 1984 explicitly rejected the conclusion reached in Revenue Ruling 60–345 in favor of an interpretation of section 752 that is consistent with section 357(c). See H.R. Rep. No. 861, 98th Cong., 2d Sess. 856–857 (1984), 1984–3 (Vol. 2) C.B. 110, 111.

Under P's method of accounting, P's obligations to pay amounts incurred for interest and services are not deductible until paid. For purposes of section 752 of the Code, the terms "liabilities of a partnership" and "partnership liabilities" include an obligation only if and to the extent that incurring the liability creates or increases the basis to the partnership of any of the partnership's assets (including cash attributable to borrowings), gives rise to an immediate deduction to the partnership, or, under section 705(a)(2)(B), currently decreases a partner's basis in the partner's partnership interest. The preceding sentence uses the term "assets" to include capitalized items that are properly allocable to future periods, such as organizational expenses and construction period expenses.

The liabilities incurred by P for interest expense and services do not create or increase the basis of a partnership asset or give rise to a deduction when incurred. Therefore, for purposes of computing A's adjusted basis in P, A may not treat P's accrued expenses and accounts payable as a liability of the partnership.

HOLDING

For purposes of computing the adjusted basis of a partner's interest in a cash basis partnership, accrued but unpaid expenses and accounts payable are not liabilities of a "partnership" or "partnership liabilities" within the meaning of section 752 of the Code.

Practice:

1. Assume cash basis Taxpayer transfers Land with a basis of $10,000 to Partnership B. The Land is subject to an environmental cleanup liability of $10,000. Payment of the environmental liability would generate a deduction but no payment has been made. Thus, the

obligation is not a "liability" under Revenue Ruling 88–77 and taxpayer's outside basis is $10,000. Taxpayer 2 contributes $10,000 for a preferred partnership interest that grants her the right to receive distributions prior to any distributions to Taxpayer 1. Assume the preferential distribution right to Taxpayer 2 renders Taxpayer 1's interest practically worthless. Taxpayer 1 then sells her interest to an accommodation party for a nominal amount and claims a loss approximately equal to the environmental liability. The Partnership later pays the environmental liability (with borrowed money perhaps) and claims a $10,000 loss deduction. Essentially, the parties have generated a deduction for Taxpayer 1 who has made no economic outlay (he exchanged one asset with a basis of $10,000 for $10,000 cash–the relief of liability—and then took a deduction worth $10,000). The parties have also created a duplicate deduction for the partnership. Does this strategy work?

Lesson 16

SALE OF A PARTNERSHIP INTEREST

Primary References: IRC 732(d), 741, 742, 743, 751(a)(c), (d) 752(d), 754, 755
Treas. Reg. 1.704–1(b)(2)(iv)(*l*)–(m), 1.704–1(b)(5) Example 13(iii)–(iv), 1.732–1(d)(1), 1.741–1, 1.742–1, 1.743–1(a)–(g), (j)(4), 1.751–1(a), (c)(1)–(3), (d)(2)–(g), Example 1, 1.755–1(b)(1)–(3)

Secondary References: IRC 1(a)–(e), (h), 1060
Treas. Reg. 1.1001–2

Theory

When the owner of a corporation sells her business via an asset (rather than stock) transfer, she is treated as if she separately sold each of the assets comprising the business. As a result, the owner will realize a mix of ordinary and capital gains and losses. If the owner wants to realize only capital gain or loss, she can simply sell her stock. IRC 741 seems, upon first impression, to provide the same capital gain or loss treatment for the sale of all or some of a partnership interest. But IRC 751(a), which is referenced in IRC 741, imposes an item by item approach similar to that applying under IRC 1060. Simply put, IRC 751 and Treas. Regulation 1.751–1(a) requires the first fruits of the amount realized to be allocated to the partner's share of unrealized receivables and inventory (aka, "hot assets"). IRC 752(d), by the way, reminds us that a discharged liability is to be included in the seller's amount realized. A partner who has basis credit for a portion of partnership liabilities will therefore have an amount realized at least equal to the share of liabilities reflected in her credit. The difference between the amount allocated to the hot assets and the total gain or loss on the overall sale is treated as capital gain or loss. Regulation 1.751–1(g), Example 1 nicely demonstrates how the approach works.

IRC 742 makes the observation that a transferee's basis in the received partnership interest is determined under the old familiar rules applicable to transfers in all sorts of contexts. If the transferee receives the interest by gift, her basis will be determined by IRC 1015, and if by bequest her basis will be determined by IRC 1014. If the transferee purchases her partnership interest, she will presumably have paid a price equal to the interest's full value and her basis will be determined by IRC 1012. Any appreciation attributable to the selling partner's proportionate share of partnership assets will be taxed to the selling shareholder (whose gains and losses will be characterized by referenced to IRC 741 and 751). Likewise, if there were loss assets in the partnership prior to the sale, the selling partner would effectively have realized and recognized her proportionate share of the losses upon the transfer. All of this creates a potential for double taxation or deduction because the partnership's inside basis of assets, a proportionate share of the appreciation or depreciation on which has been appropriately taxed to the selling partner, will not be adjusted to prevent double taxation or deduction.

Assume that A and B form a partnership with each partner contributing $50,000. The partnership buys a building and five years later the building is worth $100,000. (For simplicity's sake, assume no depreciation deductions). The capital accounts should appear as follows:

**Liabilities and Partners' Capital
Liabilities:**

Assets:					Capital:		
	Tax	Book	FMV			Tax	Book
Building	50	50	100	A		50	50
Cash	50	50	50	B		50	50
	100	100	150			100	100

Remember that the partnership and partner capital accounts reflect historical cost—they are essentially a snapshot of the partnership's total value and each partner's relative wealth embodied in the partnership. Capital accounts do not reflect changing values and can only be restated upon the occurrence of certain events specified in Regulation 1.704–1(b)(2)(iv)(f)(5). Thus, A would not sell her interest to C for $50,000 (the stated capital account balance) but for $75,000, the current value of her interest. A will therefore report $25,000 in capital gains (there being no 751 assets). The $25,000 gain is attributable to A's share of previously untaxed appreciation in the building. Only the building's remaining $25,000 appreciation is untaxed. But what happens when the partnership sells the building at its fair market value ($100,000)? The partnership will realize and recognize $50,000, even though $25,000 has already been taxed to A. Logically, the partnership's inside basis should be increased but only with respect to C's share of the asset, since B has not been taxed on her share of the building's appreciation.

If we assume, instead, that the building and cash had a basis and value of $100,000 each when contributed, but the building had a fair market value of $50,000 on the date A sold her interest (for $75,000), A will have reported a $25,000 loss attributable to her share of the building's economic depreciation. If the partnership thereafter sold the building it would realize and recognize a $50,000 loss even though $25,000 of that loss has already been claimed by A. Here, the partnership's inside basis should be decreased by $25,000, but only with regard to C's share of the asset, since B has not yet been allowed a deduction with regard to her share of the building's depreciation. In either event the partnership will list the single asset as though it were two different assets with differing bases. When the asset is sold, the aggregate amount realized will be allocated between the "two" assets in proportion to their relative values, and gain or loss will be allocated in a manner similar to the allocation of 704(c) gain or loss.

In our first hypothetical above, where the building was worth $100,000 when C purchased her interest, C's 50% interest in the building should take a special inside basis of $50,000 and B's 50% interest should take a basis of $25,000. The gain of $50,000 on the later sale would then be allocated $25,000 to B and $25,000 to C. B would therefore report a $25,000 tax gain while C would report neither gain nor loss because she would be entitled to subtract her special basis adjustment of $25,000 from the allocated gain. Both partners' capital accounts would be increased by $25,000.

In the second hypothetical, where the building is worth $50,000 when C purchases her interest, C's 50% interest in the building should take a basis of $25,000 and B's 50% interest should take a basis of $50,000. When the building is sold for $50,000, the loss will be similarly divided so that B will report a $25,000 loss and C will report neither gain nor loss because she would be required to add her special basis adjustment of $25,000 to the allocated loss. Treas. Reg. 1.743–1(j)(3)(i).

The proper results described above are optional, except when the partnership has "substantial built-in loss" immediately after the distribution. Thus, if the partnership's unrealized loss immediately after the distribution exceeds $250,000, the 743 basis adjustments are mandatory.[1] Obviously, Congress considers any distortion of $250,000 or less to be de minimis. In those instances, the appropriate basis adjustment is optional.

If the partnership has made an election under IRC 754, or if IRC 743 is mandatory, it must adjust the inside basis of one or more assets as generally outlined above. If the partnership has an election under IRC 754 in effect for the year of the sale, it must adjust the inside basis of one or more assets as generally outlined above. In short, Regulation 1.743–1(b) requires an increase when income would otherwise be taxed twice and a decrease when a loss would otherwise be claimed twice. The phrase, "previously taxed capital," used in Regulation 1.743–1(b), con-

---

1. The basis adjustment was made mandatory the American Jobs Act of 2004. IRC 743(d) allows an exception for electing "investment partnerships," but only on the condition that the transferee/buying partner not claim the loss already taken into account by the transferor/selling partner.

firms that the goal is to ensure through determination of a proper basis that income is taxed and losses are deducted once and only once. As an overall matter, the buyer will begin with the same share of aggregate basis as the seller, and then increase or decrease that basis to take into account the appreciation or depreciation effectively taxed or deducted by the selling partner.

If the partnership has not made a 754 election, and basis adjustment is not mandatory the buying partner will be over-or under-taxed. The distortion, though, is considered temporary because when the buyer finally disposes of her partnership interest her gain or loss will take into account the previously over-or under-taxed income. *See* Question 1, in Lesson 9. The problem for the over-taxed buyer is that the amount of time between a buyer's purchase of the partnership interest and her liquidation of that interest may be so indefinite as to make the future correction meaningless from an economic standpoint. The real dollar value of the basis adjustment decreases over time. Of course, the under-taxed buyer will not be concerned but the public loses as time goes by in that instance. These observations suggest that the IRC 754 election should be mandatory in all instances. Congress has not taken that step but it has provided a small bit of relief to the overtaxed buyer in IRC 732(d). That provision grants a buying partner the option to treat distributed property as though it were subject to the 743 basis adjustment it would have taken if the partnership had made a 754 election. It applies, though, only to distributions made within 2 years of the buyer's purchase of the partnership interest and therefore provides rather limited relief. And because it is optional, it will hardly ever provide correction when a buying partner is under-taxed (because the buying partner is not likely to elect 732(d) in that instance).

Regulation 1.755–1(b) explains how the basis adjustment should be divided between the partnership's assets when a 754 election is in effect. Note, in particular, that even when a buyer's overall 754 adjustment is zero, the partnership may still have to alter the bases of properties. The reason is that though gains and losses may previously have been taken into account, the buying partner will be allowed, or suffer, a conversion of gains and losses from ordinary to capital (or vice-versa) if proper adjustments are not made. Regulation 1.755–1(b)(2)(ii), Example 2 demonstrates this point quite nicely. The essential point is that the separate adjustments to different classes of property must equal the aggregate basis adjustment determined under Regulation 1.743–1(b). (And math phobics should remember that "A minus negative B" is equivalent to A+B). To further complicate matters, Regulation 1.743–1(b)(3) sets forth a rule that dictates how basis adjustments that are allocated between capital and ordinary income are further allocated to properties within each class. The algebra is not at all difficult once you have worked through the examples for yourself.

Much of the complexity in partnership taxation is caused by domino effects. A change or optional result in one instance necessitates a change in another and so forth. Such is the case with a 743(b) adjustment. An adjustment to a partner's share of the partnership's basis in partnership property will alter the determination of that partner's distributive shares. Cost recovery, for example, will be different for the transferee partner because that partner has more or less cost to recover, relative to other partners. Regulation 1.743–1(j)(4) sets forth methods by which to account for changes to distributive shares resulting from a 743(b) adjustment. If the 743(b) adjustment is positive, the increase is treated as though it is attributable to a new asset, the depreciation from which is allocated solely to the transferee partner. If the adjustment is negative, the decrease reduces the transferee's distributive share of depreciation deductions from that property. If the reduction in any year is greater than the distributive share it is applied against the distributive share of depreciation from other properties, and if there are no other depreciable properties, the partner will recognize ordinary income! The examples in Regulation 1.743–1(j)(4)(ii) show how these rules are implemented.

Another collateral consideration to keep in mind with respect to a 754 election relates to capital accounts. The election will prevent the buying partner from recognizing tax gain or loss if the underlying appreciated or depreciated property is sold for its value on the date the buying partner purchased her interest. Nevertheless, the partnership will have book gain or loss and that loss must be reflected in partner's capital accounts, including the buying partner's account. Treas. Reg. 1.704–1(b)(2)(iv)(m). The buying partner's special inside basis will have no impact on her capital account. Instead, book gains and losses allocated to the partners will be determined as if the basis adjustment had not been made. Be sure you understand how this rule works by reading Example 13 (iii) and (iv), Regulation 1.704–1(b)(5) closely.

Overall, the 754 election requires careful tax planning. Since the 743 (and 734) adjustments are mandatory once a 754 election is made, and IRC 754 elections cannot be revoked simply to avoid a basis decrease, partnerships must seriously consider the likely consequences before making the 754 election.

Practice:

1. Read Example 1, Regulation 1.743–1(d)(3). To which properties would the $7000 basis adjustment be allocated?

2. Read Example 1, Regulation 1.743–1(d)(3). What would be the result if the land had a basis of $900 when contributed by A?

3. Read Example 1(i), Regulation 1.755–1(b)(2)(ii). Assume that Asset 3 is an unrealized receivable and Asset 4 is 4 is inventory.

    a. What is the amount and character of A's gain on the sale of his partnership interest? How would your answer change if Asset 4 had a fair market value of $20,000 and Asset 2 had a fair market value of $100,000? (All other values remain the same).

    b. Show the calculations leading to the conclusion that T's share of the adjusted basis to the partnership of partnership property is $75,000.

c. Assume T sells her interest to S for $130,000, after Asset 2 appreciates in value to $137,000. Calculate T's amount and character of income. What is the 743(b) adjustment with respect to S?

4. Show the calculations and cite the authority for the purchaser's (1) share of adjusted basis to the partnership of partnership property, and (2) her 743(b) adjustment in Examples 1–3, Regulation 1.743–1(j)(3)(ii).

5. Read Example 3(i)–(ii), Regulation 1.743–1(j)(4)(ii)(C), again. Is there anything that T could have done to avoid the recognition of ordinary income?

Lesson 17

TRANSACTIONS BETWEEN PARTNERS AND THEIR PARTNERSHIP

Primary References: IRC 707(a)(1), (b)–(c), 267(c)–(d)
Treas. Reg. 1.707–1, 1.731–1(c)(2)

Case References: **Pratt v. Commissioner, 64 T.C. 203 (1975)** *aff'd in part,* **550 F.2d 1023 (5th Cir. 1977); Rev. Rul. 81–300, 1981–2 C.B. 143, Rev. Rul. 81–301, 1981–2 C.B. 144.**

Secondary References: IRC 61, 162, 263, 1001

If an individual is a partner, can she also be an employee or independent contractor for the partnership? The question vexed courts prior to 1954. On the one hand, an individual cannot be her own employee. But that statement assumes a partnership has no existence separate from the partners and in any event is correct only to the extent of the employee or independent contractor's separate interest in the partnership—if a partnership has no separate existence, the transaction is nevertheless between two or more parties to the extent of the other partners' interests. On the other hand, partnerships are separate and apart from their owners under state law, and therefore it is not illogical to say that a partnership ought to be able to transact business with its partners. The question is not merely academic. If a partnership's payment to a partner is considered compensation, for example, the partnership may be entitled to a deduction under IRC 162 and this deduction will reduce the distributive shares i.e., taxable income to all partners. If a payment is a distribution, it will not have that effect. To prove this point, consider the tax consequences to the partners under the following simple circumstance, assuming (1) the payment is treated as compensation to the partner and alternatively (2) the payment is merely a distribution of partnership profits:

The AB partnership earns $500 in year one and has no other cash on hand. For simplicity, assume A and B each have outside bases of $0. A provided necessary service to the partnership in that year. The partnership paid A $500.00.

If the payment is considered compensation for A's services, it would normally be deductible (unless it is a capital expenditure) and the partnership would have no taxable income. A would have $500 ordinary income, but A and B's distributive share would be zero. A might seek deferral by delaying the actual or constructive receipt of the $500, and if the partnership uses the accrual method it could take the deduction before actual payment (that is, in the absence of IRC 707(c)). If the payment is considered a distribution, the partnership would not be entitled to a deduction, A would report $250 ordinary income and B would report $250 ordinary income and $250 capital gain upon the distribution of $500. In this instance B has a current tax liability but no cash flow. Even so, B may prefer this outcome if she has sufficient losses from outside sources to soak up the $250 distributive share.

Predictably, partners structured their receipt of income from their partnerships in a manner that suited their particular circumstances. The result was a number of cases involving the theoretical argument regarding whether a partnership should be treated as a separate entity or a mere aggregate of which the recipient was one part. The results in various cases were hardly consistent. IRC 707 resolves the issue by treating the partnership as a separate entity, so long as the partner is not acting in her capacity as a partner. If the partner is acting in her capacity as a partner, a compensatory payment is treated either as a distributive share under 704(a) or, to the extent the payment is not contingent on the partnership's fortunes, a "guaranteed payment" under 707(c).

The concept of "guaranteed payment" is meant to resolve a theoretical conundrum. When a partner performs services germane to the partnership's operations (i.e., the partner is acting in her capacity as a partner), her resulting income should logically be viewed as a distributive share. IRC 704 is consistent with that conclusion. But to the extent a partner has a fixed right to receive payment, she is just as logically treated as an employee even though her services performed are germane to partnership operations. IRC 707(a) implements that conclusion. IRC 707(c) agrees with and implements both views. For timing purposes (and all other purposes under the Code except those mentioned in Regulation 1.707–1(c)), a guaranteed payment is treated as a distributive share taxable to the partner when paid or accrued (i.e., when deducted) by the partnership. Hence, a guaranteed payment is taxable to the recipient partner without regard to actual receipt or the partner's outside basis just as would occur under IRC 704. For characterization and deduction purposes, however, a guaranteed payment is treated as compensation for services or the use of property provided by a nonpartner, and therefore taxable as ordinary income to the partner and deductible (subject to IRC 263) by the partnership as would occur under IRC 707(a). Thus, for timing purposes a guaranteed payment is taxed under an aggregate theory; for characterization and deduction purposes a guaranteed payment is taxed under an entity theory.

Sometimes a fixed right to payment will be articulated in a partnership agreement in a manner that is dependent upon a partners distributive share. For example, a partner might be guaranteed a minimal payment with a right to share in income above that minimal payment. In effect, the partner is being treated like an employee to the extent her downside risk is eliminated and an owner to the extent of her right to participate in upside potential. In those cases, the amount of guaranteed payment will vary from year to year. If the partner's distributive share is at least equal to the guaranteed minimal amount, the entire amount is treated as a distributive share for all purposes. If not, the amount by which the minimal amount exceeds the distributive share is treated as a guaranteed payment. Examples 2 and 3 Regulation 1.707–1(c), demonstrate this point, while Example 4 simply shows the consequences of the entity treatment of guaranteed payments.

In other instances, whether a partnership agreement calls for a guaranteed payment will depend on an interpretation of the contractual language in light of the Congressional decision to treat the partnership as a separate entity. For example, a provision in the partnership agreement providing that "Partner A shall receive payment equal to 20% of the partnership's gross income" could be construed as something other than a guaranteed payment since the measure of the payment is made with "regard to income of the partnership." Consider the IRS' resolution of that issue in the following revenue rulings:

REVENUE RULING 81–300
1981–2 C.B. 143

ISSUE

Are the management fees paid to partners under the circumstances described below distributive shares of partnership income or guaranteed payments under section 707(c) of the Internal Revenue Code?

FACTS

The taxpayers are the general partners in a limited partnership formed to purchase, develop and operate a shopping center. The partnership agreement specifies the taxpayers' shares of the profit and loss of the partnership. The general partners have a ten percent interest in each item of partnership income, gain, loss, deduction, or credit. In addition, the partnership agreement provides that the general partners must contribute their time, managerial abilities and best efforts to the partnership and that in return for their managerial services each will receive a fee of five percent of the gross rentals received by the partnership. These amounts will be paid to the general partners in all events.

Pursuant to the partnership agreement, the taxpayers carried out their duties as general partners and provided the management services required in the operation of the shopping centers. The management fee of five percent of gross rentals were reasonable in amount for the services rendered.

LAW AND ANALYSIS

Section 707(a) of the Code provides that if a partner engages in a transaction with a partnership other than in the capacity of a member of such partnership, the transaction shall, except as otherwise provided in this section, be considered as occurring between the partnership and one who is not a partner.

Section 1.707–1(a) of the Income Tax Regulations provides that a partner who engages in a transaction with a partnership other than in the capacity of a partner shall be treated as if the partner were not a member of the partnership with respect to such transaction. The regulation's section further states that such transactions include the rendering of services by the partner to the partnership and that the substance of the transaction will govern rather than its form.

Section 707(c) of the Code provides that to the extent determined without regard to the income of the partnership, payments to a partner for services, termed "guaranteed payments", shall be considered as made to one who is not a member of the partnership, but only for purposes of section 61(a) and, subject to section 263, for purposes of section 162(a).

In *Pratt v. Commissioner,* 64 T.C. 203 (1975), *aff'd in part, rev'd in part,* 550 F.2d 1023 (5th Cir. 1977), under substantially similar facts to those in this case, both the United States Tax Court and the United States Court of Appeals for the Fifth Circuit held that management fees based on a percentage of gross rentals were not payments described in section 707(a) of the Code. The courts found that the terms of the partnership agreement and the actions of the parties indicated that the taxpayers were performing the management services in their capacities as general partners. *Compare* Rev. Rul. 81–301, this page, this Bulletin.

When a determination is made that a partner is performing services in the capacity of a partner, a question arises whether the compensation for the services is a guaranteed payment under section 707(c) of the Code or a distributive share of partnership income under section 704. In *Pratt,* the Tax Court held that the management fees were not guaranteed payments because they were computed as a percentage of gross rental income received by the partnership. The court reasoned that the gross rental income was "income" of the partnerships and, thus, the statutory test for a guaranteed payment, that it be "determined without regard to the income of the partnership", was not satisfied. On appeal, the taxpayer's argument was limited to the section 707(a) issue and the Fifth Circuit found it unnecessary to consider the application of section 707(c).

The legislative history of the Internal Revenue Code of 1954 indicates the intent of Congress to treat partnerships as entities in the case of certain transactions between partners and their partnerships. See S. Rep. No. 1622, 83d Cong., 2d Sess. 92 (1954). The Internal Revenue Code of 1939 and prior Revenue Acts contain no comparable provision and the courts had split on the question of whether a partner could deal with the partnership as an outsider. *Compare Lloyd v. Commissioner,* 15 B.T.A. 82 (1929) and *Wegener v. Commissioner,* 119 F.2d 49 (5th Cir. 1941), *aff'g* 41 B.T.A. 857 (1940), *cert. denied* 314 U.S. 643 (1941). This resulted both in uncertainty and in substantial computational problems when an aggregate theory was applied and the payment to a partner exceeded the partnership income. In such situations, the fixed salary was treated as a withdrawal of capital, taxable to the salaried partner to the extent that the withdrawal was made from the capital of other partners. *See,* for example, Rev. Rul. 55–30, 1955–1 C.B. 430. Terming such treatment as unrealistic and unnecessarily complicated, Congress enacted section 707(a) and (c) of the Code of 1954. Under section 707(a) the partnership is considered an unrelated entity for all purposes. Under section 707(c), the partnership is considered an unrelated entity for purposes of sections 61 and 162 to the extent that it makes a guaranteed payment for services or for the use of capital.

Although a fixed amount is the most obvious form of guaranteed payment, there are situations in which compensation for services is determined by reference to an item of gross income. For example, it is not unusual to compensate a manager of real property by reference to the gross rental income that the property produces. Such compensation arrangements do not give the provider of the service a share in the profits of the enterprise, but are designed to accurately measure the value of the services that are provided.

Thus, in view of the legislative history and the purpose underlying section 707 of the Code, the term "guaranteed payment" should not be limited to fixed amounts. A payment for services determined by reference to an item of gross income will be a guaranteed payment if, on the basis of all of the facts and circumstances, the payment is compensation rather than a share of partnership profits. Relevant facts would include the reasonableness of the payment for the services provided and whether the method used to determine the amount of the payment would have been used to compensate an unrelated party for the services.

It is the position of the Internal Revenue Service that in *Pratt* the management fees were guaranteed payments under section 707(c) of the Code. On the facts presented, the payments were not disguised distributions of partnership net income, but were compensation for services payable without regard to partnership income.

HOLDING

The management fees are guaranteed payments under section 707(c) of the Code. Compare Rev. Rul. 81–301, below, for an example of when section 707(a) of the Code applies to services rendered by a partner not acting in its capacity as a partner.

REVENUE RULING 81–301
1981–2 C.B. 144

ISSUE

Is an allocation based on a percentage of gross income paid to an advisor general partner subject to section 707(a) of the Internal Revenue Code, under the circumstances described below?

FACTS

ABC is a partnership formed in accordance with the Uniform Limited Partnership Act of a state and is registered with the Securities and Exchange Commission as an open-end diversified management company pursuant to the Investment Company Act of 1940, as amended. Under the partnership agreement, *ABC*'s assets must consist only of municipal bonds, certain readily-marketable temporary investments, and cash. The agreement provides for two classes of general partners: (1) "director general partners" (directors) who are individuals and (2) one "adviser general partner" (adviser) that is a corporate investment adviser registered as such in accordance with the Investment Advisers Act of 1940, 15 U.S.C.A., section 80b–5 (1971).

Under the partnership agreement, the directors are compensated and have complete and exclusive control over the management, conduct, and operation of *ABC*'s activities. The directors are authorized to appoint agents and employees to perform duties on behalf of *ABC* and these agents may be, but need not be, general partners. Under the partnership agreement, the adviser has no rights, powers, or authority as a general partner, except that, subject to the supervision of the directors, the adviser is authorized to manage the investment and reinvestment of *ABC*'s assets. The adviser is responsible for payment of any expenses incurred in the performance of its investment advisory duties, including those for office space and facilities, equipment, and any of its personnel used to service and administer *ABC*'s investments. The adviser is not personally liable to the other partners for any losses incurred in the investment and reinvestment of *ABC*'s assets.

The nature of the adviser's services are substantially the same as those it renders as an independent contractor or agent for persons other than *ABC* and, under the agreement, the adviser is not precluded from engaging in such transactions with others.

Each general partner, including the adviser general partner, is required to contribute sufficient cash to *ABC* to acquire at least a one percent interest in the partnership. The agreement requires an allocation of 10 percent of *ABC*'s daily gross income to the adviser. After reduction by the compensation allocable to the directors and the adviser,

ABC's items of income, gain, loss, deduction, and credit are divided according to the percentage interests held by each partner.

The adviser's right to 10 percent of *ABC*'s daily gross income for managing *ABC*'s investment must be approved at least annually by a majority vote of the directors or a majority vote of all the partnership interests. Furthermore, the directors may remove the adviser as investment manager at any time on 60 days written notice to the adviser. The adviser can terminate its investment manager status by giving 60 days written notice to the directors. The agreement provides that the adviser will no longer be a general partner after removal or withdrawal as investment manager, but will continue to participate as a limited partner in the income, gains, losses, deductions, and credits attributable to the percentage interest that it holds.

LAW AND ANALYSIS

Section 61(a)(1) of the Code provides that, except as otherwise provided by law, gross income means all income from whatever source derived, including compensation for services, including fees, commissions, and similar items.

Section 702(a) of the Code provides that in determining the income tax of a partner each partner must take into account separately such partner's distributive share of the partnership's items of income, gain, loss, deduction, or credit.

Section 707(a) of the Code provides that if a partner engages in a transaction with a partnership other than as a member of such partnership, the transaction shall, except as otherwise provided in section 707, be considered as occurring between the partnership and one who is not a partner.

Section 1.707–1(a) of the Income Tax Regulations provides that a partner who engages in a transaction with a partnership other than in the capacity as a partner shall be treated as if not a member of the partnership with respect to such transaction. Such transactions include the rendering of services by the partner to the partnership. In all cases, the substance of the transaction will govern rather than its form.

Section 707(c) of the Code provides that to the extent determined without regard to the income of the partnership, payments to a partner for services shall be considered as made to one who is not a member of the partnership, but only for purposes of section 61(a) and, subject to section 263, for purposes of section 162(a).

Although the adviser is identified in the agreement as an "adviser general partner," the adviser provides similar services to others as part of its regular trade or business, and its management of the investment and reinvestment of *ABC*'s assets is supervised by the directors. Also it can be relieved of its duties and right to compensation at any time (with 60 days notice) by a majority vote of the directors. Further, the adviser pays its own expenses and is not personally liable to the other partners for any losses incurred in the investment and reinvestment of *ABC*'s assets. The services performed by the adviser are, in substance, not performed in the capacity of a general partner, but are performed in the capacity of a person who is not a partner.

The 10 percent daily gross income allocation paid to the adviser is paid to the adviser in its capacity other than as a partner. Therefore, the gross income allocation is not a part of the adviser's distributive share of partnership income under section 702(a) of the Code or a guaranteed payment under section 707(c).

HOLDING

The 10 percent daily gross income allocation paid to the adviser is subject to section 707(a) of the Code and taxable to the adviser under section 61 as compensation for services rendered. The amount paid is deductible by the partnership under section 162, subject to the provisions of section 265.

Compare Rev. Rul. 81–300, for an example of when section 707(c) of the Code applies to services rendered by a partner for a partnership.

There will be opportunities for tax reduction to the extent the code recognizes transactions between partners and their own partnerships. For example, a partner who wishes to recognize a loss without actually disposing of loss property might sell her property to her own partnership. She would thereafter deduct the loss while still owning the property via the partnership buyer. Partners might also convert ordinary income into capital gain by selling, rather than contributing inventory or other non capital assets to the partnership. If ordinary income property were contributed partners would recognize ordinary pass-thru gain on subsequent sale by the partnership. If ordinary income property is purchased from partners who are not dealers the gain to those partners would be capital, rather than ordinary, and upon resale by the partnership there would be no further gain or loss to report. IRC 707(b) addresses both of these attempts by denying loss on sales of property to (or from) a controlled partnership and recharacterizing any gain on the sale of capital gain property to (or from) the partnership if the property is ordinary income property in the hands of the buyer.

Practice:

1. IRC 707(a) applies when a partner is not acting as a partner but is instead dealing with the partnership as though she were a stranger. What facts should be considered in making that threshold determination? Draft an amendment to IRC 707 or 1.707–1 that would define when a partner is acting (or not acting) as a partner.

2. Read Regulation 1.707–1(b)(3). What result if A sells property with an adjusted basis of $1000 to the partnership for $650 and the ABT partnership later sells the property for $800 to Partnership ACAW in which A and AW together own a 33% interest and C, an unrelated person, owns 67%? What result if ABT sells the property to ACAW for $400?

3. Read Example 1, Regulation 1.707–2(c). What would A's income from the partnership be if the $10,000 payment to her were made for her legal services related to the partnership's purchase of land? Is there any strategy the partners might utilize to avoid this result?

4. Read Example 2, Regulation 1.707–2(c). What result if the partnership had a loss of $10,000 for the year?

5. What would be the proper treatment of the payments in Rev. Rul. 81–300 if the partners were not considered to be acting within their role as partners? What would be the proper treatment in Rev. Rul. 81–301 if the partner was considered to be acting within its role as a partner?

6. How is it determined whether a partner is acting as a partner?

Lesson 18

PAYMENTS IN LIQUIDATION OF A RETIRED OR DECEASED PARTNER

Primary References: IRC 736,
Treas. Reg. 1.736–1

Theory

Congress' concern with the proper treatment of payments to retiring partners is primarily administrative and, to a large extent, not as acute as it has been in the past. Prior to 1954, Subchapter K did not regulate the classification of retirement payments. Because partnerships received an immediate deduction (or the equivalent thereof) if payments were classified as distributive shares or guaranteed payments, and retiring partners were subjected to capital gains rates if payments were classified as distributions, the government was sometimes "whipsawed." In controversies with the partnership after a retirement, it might have been successfully argued that the retirement payments were distributive shares or guaranteed payments and therefore properly deductible by the partnership. The conclusion necessarily implies that the income should be taxed at ordinary rates to the retired partner. But in a subsequent controversy with the retired partner, it may have been successfully argued that the payments were distributions (implying that the partnership's earlier successful deduction was improper) and therefore properly taxed under IRC 731 (resulting in deferral or capital gain).

As Regulation 1.736–1(a)(2) suggests, retirement payments may represent compensation for different types of assets calling for different tax results. Initially, payments to retiring partners may represent compensation for the partner's share of the partnership's assets. If the retiring partner had sold her interest to a third party, she would have realized capital gain and ordinary income under IRC 741 and 751. In addition, though, a payment may represent compensation for a partner's share of unrealized receivables. Had the partner remained in the partnership until the receivables were realized, she would have recognized her share of ordinary income and other partners would have taken the equivalent of a deduction in the amount of the recipient's share. Compensation to a retiring partner might also represent a pension and this too would likely have been taxed as ordinary income.

Controversies usually arose because agreements by which retirement payments were made were ambiguous, sometimes intentionally so. The stakes are not so high these days because the marginal ordinary rates are much lower than they were prior to 1954 (sometimes as high as 91% with capital gains rates around 25%). Nevertheless, IRC 736 now requires that agreements state the portion of the retirement payment that is compensation for fixed assets (and goodwill, if the parties want the goodwill payment to be taxed as a distribution) and therefore taxed under the normal distribution rules, subject to IRC 751(b) by virtue of IRC 736(b), and how much of the payment is for other consideration and therefore taxed under IRC 736(a) as ordinary income, and effectively resulting in a deduction to the remaining partners. By this manner, retirement payments are treated as they would be if the partnership did not exist and the retiring partner merely sold her assets. If an IRC 736(b) payment results in an exchange of hot assets, the payment will be taxed under the lovely IRC 751(b) procedures (IRC 751(b) is postponed until Lesson 23), ensuring that all partners recognize their share of ordinary income. Note, in this regard that payment attributed to a general partner's share of unrealized receivables in a service partnership are always treated as a 736(a) payment. IRC 751(b)(2)(B) therefore excludes that payment from consideration under IRC 751(b). The one exception regarding the identity of tax results between retirement payments and sales outside the partnership context, relates to the treatment of a general partner's goodwill in a service partnership. At best, a purchaser of goodwill is normally entitled to deduct the cost of goodwill over a 15 year period under IRC 197. IRC 736(b)(2), though, allows purchasing partners in a service partnership to fully deduct the cost in the year of sale if a selling general partner agrees to treat the sale of her share of goodwill as an IRC 736(a) payment.

Regulations 1.736–1 contain a nice summary of the mechanics, including how to tax payments made over a period of years and how to tax payments that are not fixed in amount. The 736 rules are essentially applied by agreement of the parties. Regulation 1.736–1(b)(2) leaves it to the partners to decide the appropriate value of 736(a) and (b) payments. If the valuation is arrived at in "arm's length" negotiations, they will generally not be challenged. Instead, the regulations assume that the theoretically adverse interests between the parties will ensure the proper valuation. Note that the regulations also assume that retirement payments are always made in cash. This is a reasonable assumption since an ongoing partnership will likely wish to retain fixed assets in the continuing business. However, it is theoretically possible that retirement payments could be made in-kind.

Practice:

1.   Read Example 1, Regulation 1.736–1(b)(7). Assume that in order to reduce the amount of ordinary income that A would have to recognize each year, the agreement terminating A's interest stated that his interest was worth $20,000, but that all other facts remain the same. How would that agreement change the analysis? Could the partners validly agree upon a $20,000 valuation?

2.   Same as question 1, but A will receive an annual percentage of income for the next three years rather than a fixed amount.

3.   In Example 3, Regulation 1.736–1(b)(7), what would the be the result if the partners valued A's interest and goodwill as stated (i.e., $15,000), but did not include a provision in the partnership agreement stating that the retirement payment includes $9000 for goodwill?

Lesson 19

TAXABLE YEAR AND
PARTNERSHIP TERMINATIONS

Primary References: 706(a)–(c); 708(a)–(b)(1); 761(e)
Treas. Reg. 1.706–1(a)–(b)(3)(i), (4), (7),
(8), (c)(1) 1.706–1(c); 1.708–1; 1.704–
1(b)(2)(iv)(l);   1.704–1(b)(5),   Example
13(v)

Secondary References: IRC 444, 7519

Theory

Why might Congress have devoted as much statutory detail to the partnership taxable year as it has in IRC 706? By the end of this course you will have surmised that statutory detail is prompted by perceptive tax planners and taxpayers. The following example demonstrates this phenomenon with regard to partnership taxable years:

A, B, C, and D are all calendar year taxpayers. They form the ABCD partnership and adopted a taxable year ending on January 31. For the first taxable year (Feb. 1, 2003–Jan. 31, 2004), the partnership earns $400,000. If the partnership's taxable year is valid, A, B, C, and D will not have to report and pay taxes on the income until April 15, 2005. That means they can defer taxes on present income anywhere from 15 ½ months (for income realized in January, 2004) to 27 ½ months (for income realized in February 2003)!

IRC 706(a) provided, and still provides that partnership income is reportable by a partner in the partner's taxable year with or within which the partnership's taxable year ends. In this case, then, the partnership income is reportable by the partners in 2004 (the due date for the return for 2004 is April 15, 2005) because the partnership's taxable year ends "within" the partner's taxable year 2004. By contrast, calendar year taxpayers who receive wages get deferral of 3 ½ (on income realized in December) to 16 ½ months (for income realized in January).

Prior to 1954, there were no rules with regard to a partnership's taxable year. The 1954 code required a partnership to adopt the taxable year of all of its "principle partners"—defined as any partner "having an interest of 5 percent or more in partnership profits or capital." If all the principal partners did not have the same taxable year, the partnership could adopt a calendar year. No other taxable year was allowed unless the partnership could show a business purpose. The rules applied, though, only to newly formed partnerships. Existing partnerships were allowed to keep whatever taxable years they previously adopted.

Present law requires a partnership's taxable year to conform to the taxable year of their majority owners. If the majority owners do not have identical taxable years, the partnership must adopt the taxable year of its principal owners. If the principal owners do not have the same taxable year, the partnership must adopt the calendar year or a year specified in the regulations and designed to eliminate to the extent possible the type of deferral discussed in the example above.

IRC 708 establishes a single federal rule for partnership terminations. In its absence, partnerships might be considered terminated, and their taxable years closed, under various circumstances depending on different state laws. Actually, most state statutes are alike with regard to partnership terminations, but IRC 708 eliminates the theoretical possibility that partnerships might be subject to different rules depending on their state of domicile. The rules for partnership terminations are fairly straightforward. Actual terminations, described in Regulation 1.708–1(b)(1) usually do not occur without the partners dividing up the assets. The tax consequences will be determined by applying the distribution rules under IRC 731 through 736. The more potentially surprising results occur in "technical terminations" described in IRC 708(b)(1)(B) and Regulation 1.708–1(b)(2).

Ironically, the statute and regulations seem to work at opposite purposes. Under the statute, a partnership terminates upon the sale or exchange of 50% or more of the capital and profit interests within a twelve month period. Yet regulations 1.708–1(b)(2), and 1.704–1(b)(2)(iv)(l) work together so that the "new" partnership (i.e., the partnership as constituted after the sale of at least 50% of the capital and profit interests) simply carries on with more or less partners (a technical termination can occur when 50% is sold to another existing partner) than were previously in the partnership. Inside and outside bases, and capital accounts remain the same. It is almost as if 708(b)(2) does not exist.

There are, however, at least two significant collateral effects from a technical termination. First, the partnership year closes on the date of the termination. This result, in conjunction with IRC 706(a), may require that a partner report on a single tax return income (or deductions) recognized over a period of more than twelve months. Question 5 below allows you to work through a scenario that demonstrates this "bunching" problem. Second, a technical termination allows the "new" partnership to avoid a prior 754 election made by the "old" partnership. In effect, the old partnership no longer exists so any elections made by the old partnership lapse. The new partnership gets a new opportunity to decide whether to make the 754 election.

The rules with regard to the closing of a partnership's taxable year with respect to a deceased partner can, in limited circumstances, be somewhat harsh. Suppose, for example, that a calendar year partner in a partnership with a taxable year ending on January 31 dies on December 31, 2004. If the partnership taxable year closed with respect to the deceased partner on the date of her death, she would be required to report 23 months of partnership income. On her 2004 return, she would report twelve months of income relating to the prior partnership taxable year that ended on January 31, 2003 and 11 months of partnership income for the period from Feb. 1, 2004 to December 31, 2004 (the 2004 income would have been reported in 2006 if the partner had not died). This is precisely the result under IRC 706(c)(2)(A). The harshness is more apparent than real though because most partnerships will have the same taxable year as their partners as a result of IRC 706(b). Hence, if the partnership above used a calendar year, the partner would report only twelve months of income on her last tax return.

Practice:

1. Read the Example in Regulation 1.706–1(b)(5)(ii). What taxable year would the partnership be required to adopt if the tax exempt partner were actually a taxable corporation with a taxable year ending on July 31?

2. What taxable year would the partnership be required to adopt in question 1 if the taxable corporation owned a 30% capital and profit interest and 15 other calendar year individuals owned capital and profits interests of 2% each? For this question, assume the corporation is a calendar year taxpayer.

3. What taxable year would the partnership be required to adopt if the taxable corporation used a taxable year ending on July 31, owned a 25% capital and profit interest in the partnership and 75 limited partners, all calendar year taxpayers, each owned a 1% capital and profit interest in the partnership? What if there were 35 of the limited partners used a taxable year ending on September 30th and 35 were calendar year taxpayers?

4. What taxable year must a partnership adopt under the following circumstances:

In Partnership ABCDE, Able, Baker, Charlie, Delta, and Echo each own 20% interests. Each partner uses the calendar year. On Jan 1, 2004 Able, Baker and Charlie sell their interests to Foxtrot Corporation. Foxtrot Corporation's taxable year ends on September 30th. On Jan 1, 2005, Foxtrot corporation sells its interest to Golf Corporation, whose taxable year ends on July 31.

5. Assume in the Example in Regulation 1.708–1(b)(4), that A owned a 51% profit and capital interest and B owned a 49% profit and capital interest prior to A's sale of her entire interest to C.

    a. If A used a fiscal year ending on September 30, what taxable year be would the partnership have?

    b. If the partnership had $900,000 income from October 1, 2003 to September 30, 2004, and $700,000 gain from the sale of property on November 13, 2004, how much income would B be required to report on his 2004 tax return, assuming B is a calendar year taxpayer and A had not sold its interest?

    c. Assume the same income as in b. How much income would B have to report in 2004 if A sold her interest on November 23? If A were favorably inclined, what might it do to prevent this result to B?

6. If in the Example in Regulation 1.706–1(a)(2), A received $70,000 on May 30, 2002 and $50,000 on March 2, 2003, when would have to include the payments?

Lesson 20

AT RISK AND PASSIVE ACTIVITY LOSS LIMITATIONS

Primary References:	**IRC 465 (omit 465(c)(4)–(7))**
Case References:	**Crane v. Commissioner, 331 U.S. 1 (1947)**
Secondary References:	**Prop. Treas. Regs. 1.465–1 though 1.465–7; 1.465–9 through 1.465–13; 1.465–22 through 1.465–26; 1.465–38 through 1.465–39; 1.465–41, 1.465–45, 1.465–66 through 1.465–69**

Theory

Nonrecourse financing and accelerated depreciation deductions work together to create a lethal weapon for tax avoiders. When used in a setting that allows the parties themselves to divide tax burdens and benefits, the weapon can be irresistible. Those fortunate enough to be granted nonrecourse credit can use the proceeds to invest in depreciable property via partnerships and take depreciation deductions with very little cash outlay. Though the fortunate borrower may have to repay the loan later—or suffer a chargeback at a much later time by way of higher gain on disposition of the property, most likely subject to ordinary income rates under IRC 1245—the early deduction can be quite valuable considering the time value of money. Of course, many transactions using this technique were economically nonsensical—lousy movies or speculative oil and gas investments—except for the enormous early tax benefits to be derived. It may be assumed, without detailed debate or data, that economically nonsensical transactions are bad for the economy because they divert capital from more useful investments that might motivate expansion, spur capital investment and create jobs. If nothing else, very sensational tax schemes engender resentment amongst taxpayers upon whom our tax system's smooth functioning is dependent.

The 1976 enactment of IRC 465 is viewed by many as Congress' first major offensive against tax shelters. The battle against tax shelter is still being waged and the public, the ultimate victims of tax shelters, is by no means close to victory. Each new year seems to bring word of new shelters that provoke expensive litigation and more convoluted and complex legislative response. IRC 465 is actually easy compared to other anti-abuse provisions. Its basic premise is that an investor should not be granted loss deductions in excess of the amount actually lost! But recall that *Crane* and *Tufts* rest on the proposition that taxpayers pay their bills and because borrowed money will eventually be repaid with after tax money, it is reasonable and administratively convenient to give taxpayers a basis in property (remember, basis represents personal after tax investment in property) not less than the amount borrowed to purchase the property. And depreciation deductions begin from the date property is placed in business service, not when the nominal owner thereof earns equity.

IRC 465 represents a sort of overruling of that logic. It rests on the assumption that a taxpayer may never even pay the nonrecourse loan and therefore should not be allowed deductions based on the assumption that she will. Deductions are allowed only to the extent a taxpayer is actually "at-risk"—that is, only to the extent a taxpayer has put her personal fortune into the deduction-generating trade or business. To the extent a taxpayer does not really accept the risk of loss by investing her own wealth, she should not be granted a deduction from that activity. The person who actually is at risk should get the deduction. *Crane*, of course, rejected the suggestion that the lender should get the deduction as unworkable. IRC 465 does not directly disagree. It simply postpones or denies the deduction to the borrower until the borrower actually incurs the cost of the deduction.

In the tax shelter industry, labels are intentionally deceiving and Congress knows this fact all too well. "Nonrecourse" is a clear signal that there is no risk to the borrower, but "recourse" credit may also be structured so as to eliminate the risk to the borrower. IRC 465(b)(3)–(4) therefore make the at-risk limitations applicable whenever a taxpayer is not really at-risk, regardless of the label applied by the parties. Politics and influence are also a reality in the tax shelter battle and real estate ownership is the stuff of American legend. IRC 465(b)(6) represents a significant nod to politics and influence. Nonrecourse financing with regard to real estate investment is treated like an owner's personal investment provided it is obtained from an independent third party that is likely to enforce repayment. Indeed, the third party may even be a relative, provided the relative imposes and presumably enforces "commercially reasonable terms."

As usual, anti-abuse provisions trigger avoidance followed by anti-avoidance provisions. IRC 465(e) demonstrates this predictable phenomenon. In deciphering IRC 465, start with the knowledge that "basis" and "at risk amounts" are not synonymous. A taxpayer who finances an acquisition entirely with nonrecourse money will have a basis equal to the purchase cost but unless the real property exception applies, her amount at risk will be zero. She can never have a negative basis, but IRC 465(b)(5) suggests that she can have a negative at risk amount. Suppose an investor borrows $100,000 on a recourse basis and invests in depreciable property. In years 1 through 5 she may deduct up to $100,000 in losses because she is personally liable to repay the loan and therefore it seems safe to assume that the cost of the deductions are financed from her personal after-tax wealth. Deductions taken during the first five years will reduce the amount at risk under IRC 465(b)(5). If, in year six, she and the lender convert the loan to nonrecourse (assume no principle payment is due until year 10), the effect would be to retroactively eliminate whatever risk may have justified the prior deductions. IRC 465(b)(5) instructs that those prior deductions must be subtracted from her at risk amount in each year. Since her at risk amount in year six started out as zero, the subtraction of previously allowed losses will result in a negative at-risk amount. She is essentially back in the position of a taxpayer who might not ever pay the amounts that originally generated the deductions. IRC 465(e) snatches back the prior deductions to the extent of the negative at risk amount, by way of recapture. Those recaptured deductions become 465 losses that may be deducted in subsequent years to the extent the taxpayer becomes at risk in those subsequent years.

The Treasury Department has issued several pages of proposed regulations, all directed towards enforcing the basic premise that only one who expends her personal wealth is entitled to a deduction, and then only as the wealth is expended. The regulations were proposed nearly 30 years ago but have yet to be finalized. For the most part, the conclusions drawn in the regulations can be derived from an understanding of underlying theory without ever reading the regulations. Still, the examples in the proposed regulations are fairly comprehensive so students may wish to refer to them as they study IRC 465.

Primary References: IRC 469(a)–(i)(2)
                              Treas. Reg. 1.469–1T(d)(1), 1.469–5T

Theory

SENATE REPORT 99–313; 99th CONGRESS; 2d Session

In general, no limitations are placed on the ability of a taxpayer to use deductions from a particular activity to offset income from other activities. Similarly, most tax credits may be used to offset tax attributable to income from any of the taxpayer's activities.

There are some exceptions to this general rule. For example, deductions for capital losses are limited to the extent that there are not offsetting capital gains. For purposes of the alternative minimum tax applying to individuals, expensed intangible drilling costs may be used to reduce net oil and gas income to zero, but may not offset other income of the taxpayer. Foreign tax credits may be used to reduce tax on foreign source income, but not U.S. source income. Research and development credits may be used by individuals to reduce tax liability attributable to research and development activities, but not taxes attributable to other income of the taxpayer.

In the absence of more broadly applicable limitations on the use of deductions and credits from one activity to reduce tax liability attributable to other activities, taxpayers with substantial sources of positive income are able to eliminate or sharply reduce tax liability by using deductions and credits from other activities, frequently by investing in tax shelters. Tax shelters commonly offer the opportunity to reduce or avoid tax liability with respect to salary or other positive income, by making available deductions and credits, possibly exceeding real economic costs or losses currently borne by the taxpayer, in excess or in advance of income from the shelters.

Reasons for Change

In recent years, it has become increasingly clear that taxpayers are losing faith in the Federal income tax system. This loss of confidence has resulted in large part from the interaction of two of the system's principal features: its high marginal rates (in 1986, 50 per cent for a single individual with taxable income in excess of $88,270), and the opportunities it provides for taxpayers to offset income from one source with tax shelter deductions and credits from another.

The prevalence of tax shelters in recent years—even after the highest marginal rate for individuals was reduced in 1981 from 70 percent to 50 percent—has been well documented. For example, a recent Treasury study revealed that in 1983, out of 260,000 tax returns reporting "total positive income" in excess of $250,000, 11 percent paid taxes equaling 5 percent or less of total positive income, and 21 percent paid taxes equaling 10 percent or less of total positive income. Similarly, in the case of tax returns reporting total positive income in excess of $1 million, 11 percent paid tax equaling less than 5 percent of total positive income, and 19 percent paid tax equaling less than 10 percent of total positive income.

Such patterns give rise to a number of undesirable consequences, even aside from their effect in reducing Federal tax revenues. Extensive shelter activity contributes to public concerns that the tax system is unfair, and to the belief that tax is paid only by the naïve and the unsophisticated. This, in turn, not only undermines compliance, but encourages further expansion of the tax shelter market, in many cases diverting investment capital from productive activities to those principally or exclusively serving tax avoidance goals.

The committee believes that the most important sources of support for the Federal income tax system are the average citizens who simply report their income (typically consisting predominantly of items such as salaries, wages, pensions, interest, and dividends) and pay tax under the general rules. To the extent that these citizens feel that they are bearing a disproportionate burden with regard to the costs of government because of their unwillingness or inability to engage in tax-oriented investment activity, the tax system itself is threatened.

Under these circumstances, the committee believes that decisive action is needed to curb the expansion of tax sheltering and to restore to the tax system the degree of equity that is a necessary precondition to a beneficial and widely desired reduction in rates. So long as tax shelters are permitted to erode the Federal tax base, a low-rate system can provide neither sufficient revenues, nor sufficient progressivity, to satisfy the general public that tax liability bears a fair relationship to the ability to pay. In particular, a provision significantly limiting the use of tax shelter losses is unavoidable if substantial rate reductions are to be provided to high-income taxpayers without disproportionately reducing the share of total liability under the individual income tax that is borne by high-income taxpayers as a group.

The question of how to prevent harmful and excessive tax sheltering is not a simple one. One way to address the problem would be to eliminate substantially all tax preferences in the Internal Revenue Code. For two reasons, however, the committee believes that this course is inappropriate.

First, while the bill reduces or eliminates some tax preference items that the committee believes do not provide social or economic benefits commensurate with their cost, there are many preferences that the committee believes are socially or economically beneficial. This is especially true when such preferences are used primarily to advance the purposes upon which Congress relied in enacting them, rather than to avoid taxation of income from sources unrelated to the preferred activity.

Second, it would be extremely difficult, perhaps impossible, to design a tax system that measures income perfectly. For example, the statutory allowance for depreciation, even under the normative system used under the bill for alternative minimum tax purposes, reflects broad industry averages, as opposed to providing precise item-by-item measurements. Accordingly, taxpayers with assets that depreciate less rapidly than the average, or that appreciate over time (as may be the case with certain real estate), may engage in tax sheltering even under the minimum tax, unless Congress directly addresses the tax shelter problem.

Even to the extent that rules for the accurate measurement of income can theoretically be devised, such rules may involve undue complexity from the perspective of many taxpayers. For example, a system that required all taxpayers to use a theoretically pure accrual method of accounting (e.g., including unrealised appreciation, and allowing only the amount of depreciation actually incurred for each specific asset in each taxable year) would create serious difficulties in both compliance and administration.

However, when the tax system, in order to avoid such complexity, permits simpler rules to be applied (e.g., generally not taxing unrealized gain, and allowing depreciation based on broad industry averages), opportunities for manipulation are created. Taxpayers may structure transactions specifically to take advantage of the situations in which the simpler rules lead to undermeasurement or deferral of income.

The question of what constitutes a tax shelter that should be subject to limitations is closely related to the question of who Congress intends to benefit when it enacts tax preferences. For example, in providing preferential depreciation for real estate or favorable accounting rules for farming, it was not Congress's primary intent to permit outside investors to avoid tax liability with respect to their salaries by investing in limited partnership syndications. Rather, Congress intends to benefit and provide incentives to taxpayers active in the businesses to which the preferences were directed.

In some cases, the availability of tax preferences to nonparticipating investors has even harmed the industries that the preferences were intended to benefit. For example, in the case of farming, credits and favorable deductions have often encouraged investments by wealthy individuals whose principal or only interest in farming is to receive an investment return, largely in the form of tax benefits to offset tax on positive sources of income. Since such investors may not need a positive cash return from farming in order to profit from their investments, they have a substantial competitive advantage in relation to active farmers, who commonly are not in a position to use excess tax benefits to shelter unrelated income. This has significantly contributed to the serious economic difficulties presently being experienced by many active farmers.

The availability of tax benefits to shelter positive sources of income also has harmed the economy generally, by providing a non-economic return on capital for certain investments. This has encouraged a flow of capital away from activities that may provide a higher pre-tax economic return, thus retarding the growth of the sectors of the economy with the greatest potential for expansion.

The committee believes that, in order for tax preferences to function as intended, their benefit must be directed primarily to taxpayers with a substantial and bona fide involvement in the activities to which the preferences relate. The committee also believes that it is appropriate to encourage nonparticipating investors to invest in particular activities, by permitting the use of preferences to reduce the rate of tax on income from those activities; however, such investors should not be permitted to use tax benefits to shelter unrelated income.

There are several reasons why it is appropriate to examine the materiality of a taxpayer's participation in an activity in determining the extent to which such taxpayer should be permitted to use tax benefits from the activity. A taxpayer who materially participates in an activity is more likely than a passive investor to approach the activity with a significant nontax economic profit motive, and to form a sound judgment as to whether the activity has genuine economic significance and value.

A material participation standard identifies an important distinction between different types of taxpayer activities. In general, the more passive investor is seeking a return on capital invested, including returns in the form of reductions in the taxes owed on unrelated income, rather than an ongoing source of livelihood. A material participation standard reduces the importance, for such investors, of the tax-reduction features of an investment, and thus increases the importance of the economic features in an investor's decision about where to invest his funds.

Moreover, the committee believes that restricting the use of losses from business activities in which the taxpayer does not materially participate against other sources of positive income (such as salary and portfolio income) addresses a fundamental aspect of the tax shelter problem. As discussed above, instances in which the tax system applies simple rules at the expense of economic accuracy encourage the structuring of transactions to take advantage of the situations in which such rules give rise to undermeasurement or deferral of income. Such transactions commonly are marketed to investors who do not intend to participate in the transactions, as devices for sheltering unrelated sources of positive income (e.g., salary and portfolio income). Accordingly, by creating a bar against the use of losses from business activities in which the taxpayer does not materially participate to offset positive income sources such as salary and portfolio income, the committee believes that it is possible significantly to reduce the tax shelter problem.

Further, in the case of a nonparticipating investor in a business activity, the committee believes that it is appropriate to treat losses of the activity as not realized by the investor prior to disposition of his interest in the activity. The effort to measure, on an annual basis, real economic losses from passive activities gives rise to distortions, particularly due to the nontaxation of unrealized appreciation and the mismatching of tax deductions and related economic income that may occur, especially where debt financing is used heavily. Only when a taxpayer disposes of his interest in an activity is it possible to determine whether a loss was sustained over the entire time that he held the interest.

The relationship to an activity of an investor who does not materially participate may be little different from the relationship of a shareholder to a corporation. So long as the investor retains an interest in the activity, any reduction in the value of such interest not only may be difficult to measure accurately, but has not been realized by the investor to a greater extent than in the context of a C corporation. In the case of a C corporation, losses and expenses borne by the corporation, and any decline in the value of the corporation's stock, do not give rise to the recognition of any loss on the part of shareholders prior to disposition of their stock.

The distinction that the committee believes should be drawn between activities on the basis of material participation bears no relationship to the question of whether, and to what extent, the taxpayer is at risk with respect to the activities. In general, the fact that a taxpayer has placed a particular amount at risk in an activity does not establish, prior to a disposition of the taxpayer's interest, that the amount invested, or any amount, has as yet been lost. The fact that a taxpayer is potentially liable with respect to future expenses or losses of the activity likewise has no bearing on the question whether any amount has as yet been lost, or otherwise is an appropriate current deduction or credit.

At-risk standards, although important in determining the maximum amount that is subject to being lost, are not a sufficient basis for determining whether or when net losses from an activity should be deductible against other sources of income, or for determining whether an ultimate economic loss has been realized. Congress' goal of making tax preferences available principally to active participants in substantial businesses, rather than to investors seeking to shelter unrelated income, can best be accomplished by examining material participation, as opposed to the financial stake provided by an investor to purchase tax shelter benefits.

In certain situations, however, the committee believes that financial risk or other factors, rather than material participation, should be the relevant standard. A situation in which financial risk is relevant relates to the oil and gas industry, which at present is suffering severe hardship due to the worldwide collapse of oil prices. The committee believes that relief for this industry requires that tax benefits be provided to attract outside investors. Moreover, the committee believes that such relief should be provided only with respect to investors who are willing to accept an unlimited and unprotected financial risk proportionate to their ownership interests in the oil and gas activities. Granting tax shelter benefits to investors in oil and gas activities who did not accept unlimited risk, proportionate to their ownership investments in the activities, would permit the benefit of this special exception to be diverted unduly to the investors, while providing less benefit to oil and gas activities and threatening the integrity of the entire rule limiting the use of nonparticipatory business losses.

A further area in which the material participation standard is not wholly adequate is that of rental activities. Such activities predominantly involve the production of income from capital. For this reason, rental income generally is not now subject to the self-employment taxes, whether or not the activity constitutes a trade or business (sec. 1402(a)(1)). Rental activities generally require less on-going management activity, in proportion to capital invested, than business activities involving the production or sale of goods and services. Thus, for example, an individual who is employed fulltime as a professional could more easily provide all necessary management in his spare time with respect to a rental activity than he could with respect to another type of business activity involving the same capital investment. The extensive use of rental activities for tax shelter purposes under present law, combined with the reduced level of personal involvement necessary to conduct such activities, make clear that the effectiveness of the basic passive loss provision could be seriously compromised if material participation were sufficient to avoid the limitations in the case of rental activities.

A limited measure of relief, however, is believed appropriate in the case of certain moderate-income investors in rental real estate, who otherwise might experience cash flow difficulties with respect to investments that in many cases are designed to provide financial security, rather than to shelter a substantial amount of other income.

Further, additional considerations apply in the case of limited partnerships. In order to maintain limited liability status, a limited partner generally is precluded from materially participating in the business activity of the partnership; in virtually all respects, a limited partner more closely resembles a shareholder in a C corporation than an active business entrepreneur. Moreover, limited partnerships commonly are used as vehicles for marketing tax benefits to investors seeking to shelter unrelated income. In light of the widespread use of limited partnership interests in syndicating tax shelters, the committee believes that losses from limited partnership interests should not be permitted, prior to a taxable disposition, to offset positive income sources such as salary.

Practice:

These questions provoke a broad overview of IRC 704(d), 465, and 469.

A, B, C and D contributed $5,000 each to the ABCD partnership upon formation. The partnership executes a note for $40,000 as payment to Cowpoke in exchange for Cowpoke's herd of cattle. All tax items are to be allocated equally amongst the partners (i.e., liabilities are allocated equally).

1. If, in year one, the partnership has a loss of $20,000, how much may each partner deduct on their individual tax returns? What if partners B and C contributed $10,000 each, partners C and D contributed nothing and losses were nevertheless allocated equally?

2. If, in year two (and taking into account the previous year's losses, and ignoring the alternate scenario), the partnership suffer an additional $20,000 loss, how much can each partner deduct on their individual tax returns if the $40,000 note is nonrecourse? What are their outside bases?

3. How much can each taxpayer deduct on their additional tax return in year three (taking into account previous years) if B contributes $10,000 and C contributes property with an adjusted basis of $5000? Assume in year three that the partnership has an additional $20,000 loss. What if in year three the partnership had a $20,000 gain instead.

4. How much can each partner deduct in year two if the $40,000 note is recourse? What happens if, in year three, the $40,000 recourse note is converted to $40,000 nonrecourse?

5. How much can each partner deduct if the $40,000 note is recourse, and each partner spent about 150 hours during the year

tending to the cattle and other farm operations? Nobody else performed services with respect to the cattle and farm operations. What if the note is nonrecourse?

6. Same as question 5, but what if, Cowhand, a partnership employee spent about 800 hours tending to the cattle and farm operations during the year? What would the partners' outside basis be at the end of the year?

7. What result in question 6 if D was engaged in another passive activity that generated $40,000 of income?

Lesson 21

ABUSE AND ANTI–ABUSE: DISGUISED CAPITAL EXPENDITURES AND SALES

Primary Reference:	**IRC 707(a)(2), 705, 721, 731(a), 733**
	Treas. Reg. 1.707–3,–4,–5 (omit subparagraph (b) and examples 7–9 in subparagraph (f)),–6(a),–8, 1.731–1(c)(3)
Secondary Reference:	**IRC 263, 709 1001**

Allocations, outside basis, and the nonrecognition rules that apply throughout subchapter K provide opportunities to accelerate deductions or otherwise defer income. It is easy to see how deferral works—a contribution of property results in no gain to the contributor who instead transfers the basis in the contributed property to her interest in the partnership. The partnership takes a transferred basis in the property. If the contributing partner wishes to get her equity from the property—as she could have done by selling the property—she may convince the other partners to amend the partnership agreement to provide for a distribution of income in an amount equal to the property's value. The difference as between a contribution followed by a distribution and an outright sale is that in the former instance the partner may not have any taxable gain to report until much later.

Recall the questions from Lesson 17. You should have learned that when a partnership engages in transactions with a partner not in her partner capacity, the partnership must apply the same rules that would apply if the transaction were with a complete stranger. Thus, any payment made with the partner as stranger will either generate a current expense or capital expenditure. In the latter instance, the deduction is allowed only by way of depreciation—in effect, the deduction is allowed over the useful life (or recovery period) of the property and all partners will have more taxable income to report in the payment year. Question 3 in Lesson 17 asked what might the partners have done to try to prevent the delay imposed by IRC 263. IRC 704, 721 and 731

161

suggest a solution. Instead of performing services for the partnership in exchange for payment designated as compensation, partners might simply agree to a higher allocation and distribution of income to the service providing partner. If successful, the strategy would have the effect of decreasing the amount of partnership income taxable to other partners. The partnership would get the economic benefit of a current deduction even though an undisguised purchase of the same service or property would have generated a capital expenditure.

IRC 707(a)(2) is designed to thwart these strategies. The legislative history reprinted below discusses the abuse and the anti-abuse.

H.R. Rep. No. 432 (Pt. 2), 98th Cong., 2d Sess. 1218, 1220 (1984) (H.R. Rep.)

The committee is concerned that partnerships have been used to effectively circumvent the requirement to capitalize certain expenses and other rules and restrictions concerning various expenses by making allocations of income and corresponding distributions in place of direct payments for property or services. The committee believes that these transactions must be expressly prohibited if the integrity of the capitalization requirements of present law is to be preserved. For example, in *Ellison v. Commissioner,* 80 T.C. 391 (1983), the Tax Court rejected use of a similar technique to convert purchase price into the equivalent of a deductible expense and concluded that a retained income interest in the seller of property was in reality a disguised purchase price.

In the case of disguised sales, the committee is concerned that taxpayers have deferred or avoided tax on sales of property (including partnership interests) by characterizing sales as contributions of property (including money) followed (or preceded) by a related partnership distribution. Although Treasury regulations provide that the substance of the transaction should govern, court decisions have allowed tax-free treatment in cases which are economically indistinguishable from sales of property to a partnership or another partner. The committee believes that these transactions should be treated for tax purposes in a manner consistent with their underlying economic substance.

Explanation of Provisions

    a.   Characterization of payments for services or property.—If a partner performs services for, or transfers property to, a partnership, and, in connection therewith, receives a related partnership allocation and distribution, the transaction will be treated as a transaction between the partnership and a person who is not a partner, if under all the facts and circumstances, the transaction is more properly characterized as a payment to a partner acting in his non-partner capacity. In such a case, the amount paid to the partner, in consideration for the property or services will be treated as a payment for services or property provided to the partnership (as the case may be), and, where appropriate, the partnership will be required to capitalize these amounts (or otherwise treat such amounts in a manner consistent with the recharacterization). The partnership will treat the purported allocation to the partner performing services or transferring property to the partnership as a payment to a non-partner in determining the partners' shares of taxable income or loss.

The committee does not intend that this provision will apply in every instance in which a partner acquires an interest in a partnership and also performs services or transfers property to the partnership. In particular, the committee does not intend to repeal the general rule under which gain or loss in not recognized on a contribution of property in return for a partnership interest (sec. 721) or apply this new provision in cases in which a partner receives an allocation (or an increased allocation) for an extended period to reflect his contribution of property or services to the partnership provided the facts and circumstances indicate that the partner is receiving the allocation in his capacity as a partner. However, the committee does intend that the provision apply to allocations which are determined to be related to the performance of services for, or the transfer of property to, the partnership and which, when viewed together with distributions, have the substantive economic effect of direct payments for such property or services under the facts and circumstances of the case.

The bill authorizes the Treasury Department to prescribe such regulations as may be necessary or appropriate to carry out the purposes of the provision. In prescribing these regulations, the Treasury should be mindful that the committee is concerned with transactions that work to avoid capitalization requirements or other rules and restrictions governing direct payments and not with non-abusive allocations that reflect the various economic contributions of the partners. These regulations may apply the provision both to one-time transactions and to continuing arrangements which utilize purported partnership allocations and distributions in place of direct payments. The committee specifically intends that the provision will apply to allocations used to pay partnership organization or syndication fees subject to the general principles above.

These regulations will provide, when appropriate, that the purported partner performing services or transferring property is not a partner at all. Once it is determined that the service performer or property transferor is actually a partner, the committee believes the factors described below should be considered in determining whether the partner is receiving the putative allocation and distribution in his capacity as a partner.

The first, and generally the most important, factor is whether the payment is subject to an appreciable risk as to amount. Partners extract the profits of the partnership with reference to the business success of the venture while third parties generally receive payments which are not subject to this risk. An allocation and distribution provided for a service partner under the partnership agreement which subjects the partner to significant entrepreneurial risk as to both the amount and the fact of payment generally should be recognized as a distributive share and a partnership distribution, while an allocation and distribution provided for a service partner under the partnership agreement which involves limited risk as to amount and payment should generally be treated as a fee under sec. 707(a). For example, allocations that limit a partner's risk may be either "capped" allocations of partnership income (i.e., percentage or fixed dollar amount allocations subject to an annual maximum amount when the parties could reasonably expect the cap to apply in most years) or allocations for a fixed number of years under which the income that will go to the partner is reasonably certain. Similarly, continuing arrangements in which purported allocations and distributions (under a formula or otherwise) are fixed in amount or reasonably determinable under all the facts and circumstances and which arise in connection with services also shield the purported partner from entrepreneurial risk. Although short-lived gross income allocations are particularly suspect in this regard, gross income allocations may, in very limited instances, represent an entrepreneurial return, classifiable as a distributive share under sec. 704. Similarly, while net income allocations generally appear to constitute distributive shares, some net income allocations may be fixed as to amount and probability of payment and if coupled with a distribution or payment from the partnership, should be characterized as fees.

The second factor is whether the partner status of the recipient is transitory. Transitory partner status suggests that a payment is a fee or is in return for property. The fact that the partner status is continuing, however, is of no particular relevance.

The third factor is whether the distribution and allocation that are made to the partner are close in time to the partner's performance of services for or transfers of property to the partnership. In the case of continuing arrangements, the time at which income will be allocated to the partner may be a factor indicating that an allocation is, in fact, a disguised payment. For example, an allocation close in time to the performance of services, or the transfer of property, is more likely to be related to the services or property. Also, when the income subject to allocation arises over an extended period or is remote in time from the services or property contributed by a partner the risk of not receiving payment (the first factor described above) may increase.

The fourth factor is whether, under all the facts and circumstances, it appears that the recipient became a partner primarily to obtain tax benefits for himself or the partnership which would not have been available if he had rendered services to the partnership in a third party capacity. The fact that a partner has significant non-tax motivations in becoming a partner is of no particular relevance.

The fifth factor, which relates to purported allocations/distributions for services, is whether the value of the recipient's interest in general and continuing partnership profits is small in relation to the allocation in question. This is especially significant if the allocation for services is for a limited period of time. The fact that the recipient's interest in general and continuing partnership profits is substantial does not, however, suggest that the purported partnership allocation/distribution arrangement should be recognized.

The sixth factor, which relates to purported allocation/distributions for property, is whether the requirement that capital accounts be respected under section 704(b) ... makes income allocations which are disguised payments for capital economically unfeasible and therefore unlikely to occur. This generally will be the case unless (i) the valuation of the property contributed by the partner to the partnership is below the fair market value of such property (thus improperly understating the amount in such partner's capital account), or (ii) the property is sold by the partner to the partnership at a stated price below the fair market value of such property, or (iii) the capital account will be respected at such a distant point in the future that its present value is small and there is to be no meaningful return on the capital account in the intervening period.

The committee anticipates that the Secretary may describe other factors that are relevant in evaluating whether a purported allocation and distribution should be respected. In applying these various factors, the Treasury and courts should be careful not to be misled by possibly self-serving assertions in the partnership agreement as to the duties of a partner in his partner capacity but should instead seek the substance of the transaction.

In the case of allocations which are only partly determined to be related to the performance of services for, or the transfer of property to, the partnership, the provision will apply to that portion of the allocation which is reasonably determined to be related to the property or services provided to the partnership. Finally, it is anticipated that Treasury regulations will provide for the coordination of this provision with the existing rules of section 707 and other provisions of subchapter K such as section 736. The committee does not intend to create any inference regarding the tax treatment of the transactions described above under existing law.

The principles of this provision can be illustrated by the following examples.

Example 1.—A commercial office building constructed by a partnership is projected to generate gross income of at least $100,000 per year indefinitely. Its architect, whose normal fee for such services is $40,000, contributes cash for a 25–percent interest in the partnership and receives both a 25–percent distributive share of net income for the life of the partnership, and an allocation of $20,000 of partnership gross income for the first two years partnership operations after leaseup. The partnership is expected to have sufficient cash available to distribute $20,000 to the architect in each of the first two years, and the agreement requires such a distribution. The purported gross income allocation and partnership distribution should be treated as a fee under sec. 707(a), rather than as a distributive share. Factors which contribute to this conclusion are (1) the special allocation to the architect is fixed in amount and there is substantial probability that the partnership will have sufficient gross income and cash to satisfy the allocation/distribution; (2) the value of his interest in general and continuing partnership profits is relatively small in relation to the allocation in question; (3) the distribution relating to the allocation is fairly close in time to the rendering of the services; and (4) it is not unreasonable to conclude from all the facts and circumstances that the architect became a partner primarily for tax motivated reasons. If, on the other hand, the agreement allocates to the architect 20 percent of gross income for the first two years following construction of the building a question arises as to how likely it is that the architect will receive substantially more or less than his imputed fee of $40,000. If the building is pre-leased to a high credit tenant under a lease requiring the lessee to pay $100,000 per year of rent, or if there is low vacancy rate in the area for comparable space, it is likely that the architect will receive approximately $20,000 per year for the first two years of operations. Therefore, he assumes limited risk as to the amount or payment of the allocation and, as a consequence, the allocation/distribution should be treated as a disguised fee. If, on the other hand, the project is a "spec building," and the architect assumes significant entrepreneurial risk that the partnership will be unable to lease the building, the special allocation might (even though a gross income allocation), depending on all the facts and circumstances, properly be treated as a distributive share and partnership distribution.

Example 2.—There may be instances in which allocation/distribution arrangements that are contingent in amount may nevertheless be recharacterized as fees. Generally, these situations should arise only when (1) the partner in question normally performs, has previously performed, or is capable of performing similar services for third parties; and (2) the partnership agreement provides for an allocation and distribution to such partner that effectively compensates him in a manner substantially similar to the manner in which the partner's compensation from third parties normally would be computed.

For example, suppose that a partnership is formed to invest in stock. The partnership admits a stock broker as a partner. The broker agrees to effect trades for the partnership without the normal brokerage commission. In exchange for his partnership interest, the broker contributes 51 percent of partnership capital and receives a 51 percent interest in residual partnership profits and losses. In addition, he receives an allocation of gross income that is computed in a manner which approximates his foregone commissions. It is expected that the partnership will have sufficient gross income to make this allocation. The agreement provides that the broker will receive a priority distribution of cash from operations up to the amount of the gross income allocation. In this case, even though the broker/partner's special allocation appears contingent and not substantially fixed as to amount, it is computed by means of a formula like a normal brokerage fee and effectively varies with the value and amount of services rendered rather than with the income of the partnership. Thus, this contingent gross income allocation along with the equivalent priority distribution should be treated as a fee under sec. 707(a), rather than as a distributive share and partnership distribution.

The disguised sale rule renders suspect all contributions of property that are closely followed or preceded by partnership distributions of money or property to the contributor. And yet it is often the case that contributing partners rely on or bargain for immediate returns on their investment in the partnership. A partner who is dependent upon the partnership for her livelihood, or who has other investment options, may seek and be granted a guaranteed payment or a preferred return. Additionally, the partnership may have a policy of making annual cash flow distributions. In other instances, a partner may only be able to contribute encumbered property—when the partnership takes the property the contributing partner effectively receives a distribution of cash in the form of liability relief. IRC 707 makes it somewhat dangerous to engage in otherwise routine and legitimate transactions.

Like most anti-abuse provisions, IRC 707(a)(2) therefore occasions a ripple effect of ameliorative provisions designed to limit unintended results of the anti-abuse provision. Regulations 1.707–4,–5, and–6 seek to prevent the disguised sale rule from discouraging legitimate transactions. The overall theory is that to the extent a transfer of money or other property would have taken place in a tax free world, the disguised sale rule should not apply. The regulations attempt to make that determination by looking for objective factors that prove the transaction is not tax motivated but would have occurred anyway. Rather than providing blanket exceptions for transactions that should not be taxed, the regulations rely on a series of presumptions that apply if certain objective facts are present. The regulations are quite detailed but theoretically simple if it is kept in mind that they merely seek to articulate objective rules by which to distinguish disguised sales from payments that would be made to partners without regard to tax avoidance.

Practice:

1. What result in Example 1, Regulation 1.707–3(f) if the transfer and subsequent distribution is not viewed as part of a sale or exchange and A's outside basis immediately before the transfer was $3,000,000?

2. Read example 3, Regulation 1.707–3(f). What is the logical relevance to the factors listed in 3(iii) and (iv). Why are those factors probative to the ultimate question whether the transaction is a disguised sale?

3. In Example 4, Regulation 1.707–3(f), what is the gain or loss to E, his outside basis and capital account balance, and the partnership's inside basis in parcel 3 after the transaction? To simplify the math, assume E received $350,000 from the sale of Parcel 1 and F received $150,000.

4.   Read Example 1, Regulation 1.707–4(a)(4). Suppose A could have obtained a 10 percent return on his capital from other sources and the partnership was willing to pay a premium. What is the highest percentage return he could receive from the partnership without losing the benefit of the presumption stated in Regulation 1.707–4(a)(ii).

5.   What result in Example 1, Regulation 1.707–4(a)(4) if the payment to A was designated as a guaranteed payment for services?

6.   What result in Example 1, Regulation 1.707–5(f) if the office building had been used in B's failed dental practice and the loan had been taken out to purchase the building? B also owned and used office equipment, and two dental X-ray machines but he did not transfer those assets to the partnership.

7.   What is C's gain, outside basis and capital account balance after the transaction in Example 2, Regulation 1.707–5(f)?

8.   Read Example 5, Regulation 1.707–5(f). What result if the partnership distributed $50,000 to F and the transaction was determined to be a sale or exchange without regard to the liability?

Lesson 22

ABUSE AND ANTI-ABUSE: MIXING BOWL TRANSACTIONS

Primary References: IRC 704(c)(1)–(3), 737
                           Treas. Reg. 1.704–4, 1.737–1, 3

Secondary References: IRC 731, 732, 734, 754, 1031

Theory

In Lesson 14, we learned that taxpayers should not escape tax on realized appreciation upon a contribution of built-in gain property to a partnership. Nor can taxpayers assign losses by contributing loss property to a partnership. The built-in gain or loss should eventually be taxed to or deducted by the contributing partner when the partnership sells the property. If, rather than selling the property, the partnership distributed it to another partner, the contributing partner might nevertheless achieve an assignment since distributions are generally not recognition events for the partnership or partners. The partner receiving the distribution would generally take a carryover basis and upon subsequent sale of the property would recognize the built in gain or loss. This outcome would allow for an additional, unintended nonrecognition opportunity.

IRC 704(c)(2) is designed to prevent the use of distributions to engage in what should otherwise be considered a taxable exchange. The distribution focused on in IRC 704(c)(2) is similar to a taxable exchange because the partner contributing appreciated or depreciated property will eventually receive different property or cash that logically would have been distributed to the partner receiving the 704(c) property. In effect, the partners will have entered into a deferred exchange. The immediate and simple consequence when IRC 704(c)(1)(B) applies is that the contributing partner recognizes gain or loss just as if the property had been sold. The character is determined as if the property had been sold to the distributee. Hence, if IRC 707(b)(2) would have applied had the partnership actually sold the property to the distributee, it will likewise apply to characterize the gain that must be recognized under IRC 707(b)(2).

Recall that basis represents previously taxed (or previously exempted) and unrecovered income invested in property. Because IRC 704(c)(1)(B) forces recognition, there should also be an adjustment to the partner's outside basis and to the partnership's basis in the property with respect to which gain or loss is recognized. IRC 704(c)(1)(B)(iii) confirms the necessity for making basis adjustments. Regulation 1.704–4(e) provides the details. If you keep in mind that the basis adjustments are treated as if they occur prior to the actual distribution, the mechanics will be easy. (1) The contributing partner recognizes gain or loss, (2) the contributing partner's outside basis is increased for gain or decreased for loss, (3) the basis of the property to the partnership is also increased or decreased, (4) the property is distributed, (5) the distributee partner's basis is determined under IRC 732, (6) the partnership makes adjustments to undistributed property if an IRC 754 election is in effect.

Congress expected IRC 737 to work in conjunction with IRC 704(c)(1)(B). One "loophole" thought to exist in IRC 704(c)(1)(B) is that a contributor of 704(c) property may no longer be a partner when the contributed property is distributed. In such cases, the contributing partner will not be taxed on the built-in gain or loss because she will have retired from the partnership prior to the distribution (or sale) of the 704(c) property. IRC 737 contemplates that a contributing partner's exit will have been accompanied by a distribution of property—in effect, the contributing partner can affect an exchange of her 704(c) property for property received in complete liquidation of her interest and under IRC 731 and 732 defer tax on the built-in gain. IRC 737 therefore attacks the assignment of income problem from the opposite side of the transaction. Note that IRC 737 is broader than perhaps it needs to be. Since it is based on the assumption that the contributor of 704(c) property has retired from the partnership prior to sale or distribution of the 704(c) property, it should logically only apply to distributions in liquidation of the contributor's partnership interest. Instead, IRC 737 applies to all distributions within seven years of the contribution of appreciated property.

IRC 704(c)(1) and 737 are both subject to several exceptions all of which apply when a transaction does not shift built in gain or loss. For example, if contributed property is distributed back to the contributor, the provisions will generally not apply. Since the contributing partner's basis in the "previously contributed property" will be limited to the partnership's basis, the built in gain (to the extent it has not already been taxed under the depreciation rules applicable to the property) will be preserved. The provisions will also not apply to deemed distributions under IRC 708(b)(1)(B) (relating to partnership terminations), nor to nonrecognition transactions such as partnership mergers, split-offs, or incorporations (so long as the 704(c) property is never actually distributed to existing partners (other than the contributing partner) as part of the reorganization). The common thread in each of these exceptions is that ownership of, and basis in the 704(c) property remains unchanged so that the built in gain or loss remains taxable to the contributing partner.

Note that IRC 737 does not apply when a partner who has contributed built-in loss property receives a distribution of other property. As a result, it is possible that losses can be duplicated or assigned. For example, assume A contributes $10,000 cash, B contributes stock with an adjusted basis and fair market value of $10,000 and C contributes property worth $15,000 and having an adjusted basis of $10,000. Assume that two years later the stock and property are still worth $10,000 and the partnership distributes $10,000 cash to C in complete liquidation of her interest. C will recognize a $5000 loss under IRC 731(a)(2), but if the partnership has not made an IRC 754 election, it too will recognize a loss on the later sale of property. Fundamentally, the loss should not be allocated to either A or B. C has already claimed the loss and neither A nor B have suffered an economic loss (there is no book loss on the sale of the property). Some partnerships apparently allocated the tax loss, nevertheless, to A and B, resulting in a duplication of loss.[2] The American Jobs Creation Act of 2004 added IRC 704(c)(1)(C) to prevent this duplication. See if you can explain in your own words why it is broadly accurate to conclude that IRC 704(c)(1)(C)(ii) essentially mandates a IRC 734 basis adjustment when property is distributed to a partner who contributed built-in loss property.

One exception, contained in 704(c)(1) but not in IRC 737, involves like-kind exchanges. IRC 704(c)(2) recognizes that if a contributing partner could have exchanged 704(c) property in a tax free, like-kind exchange, she should not be taxed if a like-kind exchange occurs through the use of a partnership. Regulation 1.704–4(d)(4) exemplifies this exception. The same exception would seem applicable to IRC 737, but is curiously absent.

As always, simple solutions beget more problems. Such is the case with IRC 737. Keep in mind that income should be taxed once and only once and that is why basis adjustments are necessary in the partnership context. Adherence to this rule with regard to IRC 737 distributions properties results in what might be described as cascading basis adjustments. Regulation 1.737–1(b)(3), 1.737–1(c)(2), and 1.737–3 together indicate that basis adjustments may arise under IRC 704, 752, and 734 and that those adjustments may or may not affect the bases assigned under IRC 732. Individually, those provisions are not difficult. Taken together, these adjustments can seem incomprehensible. The difficulty in deciphering adjustments in the context of an IRC 737 distribution arises from determining the order in which the many potential adjustments should be made. The goal is simply to prevent double taxation. One method of understanding the ordering of basis adjustments is to "back-

---

2. A and B might be subject to a recapture of sorts on the later liquidation of the partnership but that event might not take place for several years. To see how the recapture would work, determine the re-sults if the partnership allocated the loss to A and B, and in the next year sold the stock (for $10,000) and distributed the proceeds (along with the $10,000 from the sale of the property) in complete liquidation.

date" adjustments to the date of contribution. That is, treat the property as though it had a basis equal to fair market value on the date of contribution. All other basis consequences flow from that treatment.

Simple solutions also begat complex avoidance techniques that, in turn, begat more complex solutions. IRC 737(d) is a primary example. Example 2, Regulation 1.737–2(e) exemplifies the avoidance technique to which IRC 737 is directed. It applies to one single type of silly transaction (other than the tax benefits to be derived) whereby taxpayers use two different entities in an effort to avoid tax on exchanges that do not qualify for nonrecognition under IRC 1031.

Practice:

1.   What is C's basis in the properties distributed in Example 1, Regulation 1.704–4(a)(5)? What is A's outside basis immediately after the distribution?

2.   Why doesn't A get allocated any tax depreciation in Example 2(ii), Regulation 1.704–4(a)(5)?

3.   What would be the result in Example 3, Regulation 1.704–4(a)(5) if the partnership agreement stated that the partnership used the traditional method with curative allocations?

4.   What is the rationale for exempting B from recognizing gain in the example in Regulation 1.704–4(a)(7)? What would be the result if the property had a fair market value of $20,000 immediately prior to the distribution?

5.   Read Example 1, Regulation 1.737–1(e). What is A's basis in property B immediately after the distribution? What result to the partnership if the partnership has a 754 election in effect?

6.   What result in Example 2, Regulation 1.737–1(e) if nonrecourse liabilities were allocated 50% to C, and 25% each to A and B?

7.   What result in Example 2 if Property B had a value of $17,000 when distributed to A? Assume all other facts in the example remain the same.

8.   What result in Example 3, Regulation 1.737–1(e) if the partnership distributed property A1 and C (adjusted basis and fair market value of $10,000) to A in complete liquidation?

9.   What result in Example 1, Regulation 1.737–2(e) if the partnership distributed property A1 and $10,000 to A?

Lesson 23

ABUSE AND ANTI–ABUSE: CONVERSION OF INCOME VIA DISPROPORTIONATE DISTRIBUTIONS

Primary References: IRC 751(b)–(d)
Treas. Reg. 1.751–1(b)–(g), Examples 2–4

Secondary References: IRC 61(a)(3), 1001, 1012
Treas. Reg. 1.61–6, 1.1001–1

Case References: **Cottage Savings Association v. Commissioner, 499 U.S. 554 (1991); Philadelphia Park Amusement Co. v. United States, 126 F. Supp. 184 (1954)**

Theory

Subchapter K recognizes that markets are served when economic actors pool their wealth for profit-seeking purposes. Subchapter K represents Congress' attempt to "bend over backwards" to accommodate pooling efforts. Congress relaxes fundamental rules of recognition and assignment of income to encourage pooling. But there are limits. IRC 704(c)(1)(A), for example, seeks to prevent assignment of income and IRC 751(a) seeks to prevent conversion of income. Those efforts are undercut by the general rule of nonrecognition with respect to distributions. Hence, IRC 704(c)(1)(B) requires gain recognition on distributions of 704(c) property (IRC 737 is a merely a back-up mechanism to 704(c)(1)(A)). This recognition rule results in the same outcome that would occur if 704(c) property were sold. IRC 751(b) is analogous to 704(c)(1)(B) in that it makes certain distribution of "hot assets" analogous to a sale of those assets, or a sale of a partnership interest to which 751 would apply.

Simply put (and that ain't easy), if a partnership makes a distribution the effect of which will allow any partner to avoid recognizing her share of ordinary income, IRC 751(b) recasts the transaction as a sale resulting in ordinary income. That is, if a distribution results in a partner receiving more or less than her share of hot assets, a sale or exchange has occurred and the transaction must be accounted for and reported as such. Theoretically, this is simple enough to understand. As has been noted earlier, though, for every simple solution there is a complex problem. IRC 751(b) is probably the best example of that axiom.

Recasting a distribution as a sale results in domino effects that seem indecipherable at first, but actually only requires the recollection, application and keeping track of fundamental tax rules as they are applied in the partnership setting. First, recall that every property has a basis and to the extent property is divisible, so too is basis. Hence, if a piece of land with a basis of $10,000 is subdivided into ten equal parts, each subdivision will have a $1000 basis. Treas. Reg. 1.61–1. Second, *Cottage Savings* teaches that an exchange of dissimilar properties is a recognition event. Third, IRC 1001(b) tells us that the amount realized is the fair market value of property received. Fourth, *Philadelphia Park* teaches that the transferor's basis in the property received in the exchange is equal to that property's fair market value. Both parties to an exchange realize gain or loss, except when one party exchanges cash for property. If you keep these fundamental principles in mind, and follow them as you would a checklist, IRC 751(b) will not be as difficult as it seems.

The best way to learn the mechanics of IRC 751(b) is to decipher the examples on your own or with a group of other scholars. Your understanding will be far less complete if you simply read somebody else's explanation. For this reason, readers should stop here and read the assigned examples as many times as it takes to come up with their own steps for determining the tax consequences when 751(b) applies. It will probably take the average serious student, who is not tired from studying everything else or from partying, about four close reads. The next page contains an explanation and step by step method for applying IRC 751(b). Remember, though, that it doesn't profit you if you simply follow someone else' map. As a tax professional, you should strive to map out tax provisions yourself. The rewards will be much greater as you learn to do so.

If you understand the four fundamental points discussed and demonstrated in the secondary references, then errors with respect to 751(b) transactions will likely result from simply forgetting to add or subtract when appropriate. Reducing or eliminating these simple errors is a matter of developing and closely following an accurate checklist. To be sure, there is still some legal analysis and planning involved, but analysis and planning cannot be completed until the mechanics are worked out and understood. With that said, the following checklist (which is articulated with more detail than most) is useful:

751(b) ANALYSIS METHODOLOGY

A. Is IRC 751(b) applicable? If a partner receives in a distribution no more or less than her share of hot assets, she will take a basis in those assets determined under IRC 732. That basis will preserve that partner's gain or loss to be recognized upon subsequent sale of the assets. Likewise, the remaining partners' gain or loss will have been preserved (in some cases assuming a 754 election is in effect) in the undistributed hot assets.

    1. Determine the value of the distributee partner's interest in 751 and non-751 ("N751") assets immediately prior to the distribution. The value of a partner's interest in any asset is equal to the amount that would be allocated to the partner if the asset were sold for its fair market value.

    2. Determine the value of the distributee partner's interest in 751 and N751 assets immediately after the distribution.

    3. If the values in step 1 and step 2 are equivalent, IRC 751(b) does not apply to the transaction.

    4. If the value of the distributee partner's 751 assets in step 2 is greater than the value of the distributee partner's 751 assets before the distribution, use method A, below.

    5. If the value of the distributee partner's 751 assets in step 2 is less than the value of the distributee partner's 751 assets before the distribution, use method B, below.

METHOD A. This method applies when the substance of the transaction is that the distributee partner has sold N751 assets for 751 assets. In effect, the distributee partner has received excess 751 assets and other partners have received excess N751 assets. If there are various types of 751 and N751 assets, the partners may designate the properties exchanged in the deemed sale, and conversely the properties received in a distribution subject to IRC 731–736. This is an important planning opportunity because if the partners designate appreciated or depreciated property as sold rather than distributed a recognition event will occur on one or both sides of the deemed sale. If the partners designate neither appreciated nor depreciated property, there will be no recognition event with respect to the designated assets. If all 751 or N751 properties are appreciated or depreciated, there will be a recognition event on at least one side of the transaction with respect to the designated assets. The gain or loss with respect to designated assets is in addition to the gain or loss explicitly mandated by IRC 751(b). Here are the steps to take when the distributee is treated as having sold all or some of her N751 assets.

    1. Pretend that the partnership distributes the distributee partner's original portion of designated N751 assets not actually received. The distribution is hypothetical, but the following consequences are real and must be taken into account for tax purposes:

        a. IRC 731 applies. No gain or loss to distributee, unless cash exceeds basis.

b. IRC 732 applies to determine the basis to the distributee of the N751 assets other than cash.

c. The partnership reduces its aggregate inside basis in N751 assets by the amount of basis attributable to the hypothetical distribution to the partner.

d. No gain or loss to the partnership.

2. The distributee partner sells or exchanges the N751 assets to the partnership for 751 assets designated by the partnership.

a. The distributee partner has gain or loss equal to the difference between her adjusted basis in the N751 assets and the fair market value of 751 assets designated by the partnership. IRC 1001

b. The distributee partner's basis in the 751 assets received in exchange for N751 assets is equal to fair market value. IRC 1012

c. If the designated 751 assets used as consideration is appreciated or depreciated property, the partnership has ordinary gain or loss, respectively. IRC 1001, *Cottage Savings and Loan*

d. The partnership increases its aggregate inside basis in N751 assets by an amount equal to the FMV of N751 assets deemed to have been purchased from distributee partner (i.e., the fair market value of 751 assets designated as consideration in the deemed sale). IRC 1012

3. Subtract the consideration used to purchase the N751 assets from the total actual distributions. The remaining amount is considered as having been distributed in a transaction to which IRC 751(b) is inapplicable.

a. IRC 731–733 applies

b. Make IRC 734(b) adjustment if a 754 election is in effect.

METHOD B: After reading Examples 2 and 3, Regulation 1.751–1(g), you should already know that the basic formula is the same regardless of which type of property–N751 or 751 assets—the distributee partner is treated as selling or exchanging. Here are the steps to analyze that transaction:

1. Pretend that the partnership distributes to the distributee partner the portion of her 751 assets not actually received. The distribution is hypothetical, but the following consequences are real and must be taken into account for tax purposes:

a. IRC 731 applies. No gain or loss to the distributee (because no cash is distributed).

b. IRC 732 applies to determine the basis to the distributee of the 751 assets other than cash.

c. The partnership reduces its aggregate inside basis in 751 assets by the amount of basis attributable to the pretend distribution to the partner.

d. No gain or loss to the partnership on a distribution of property.

2. The distributee partner sells or exchanges the 751 assets to the partnership for N751 assets designated by the partnership.

a. The distributee partner has ordinary gain or loss equal to the difference between her adjusted basis in the 751 assets and the fair market value of N751 assets designated by the partnership. IRC 1001.

b. The distributee partner's basis in the N751 received in exchange for 751 assets is equal to face (if the consideration is cash) or fair market value. IRC 1012.

c. If the designated N751 assets used as consideration are appreciated or depreciated property, the partnership recognizes gain or loss, equal to the appreciation or depreciation (i.e., the difference between the N751's adjusted basis and FMV). IRC 1001, *Cottage Savings and Loan*. If the designated N751 asset is cash, or property that has neither appreciated nor depreciated the partnership will not have gain or loss.

d. The partnership increases its aggregate inside basis in 751 assets by an amount equal to the FMV of 751 assets purchased from distributee partner (i.e., the fair market value N751 assets designated as consideration in the deemed sale). IRC 1012

3. Subtract the consideration used in the deemed purchase of the 751 assets from the total actual distribution. The amount remaining is treated as having been distributed in a transaction to which IRC 751(b) is inapplicable.

a. IRC 731–733 applies

b. Make IRC 734(b) adjustment if a 754 election is in effect.

Practice:

1. Read Example 2, Regulation 1.751–1(g) again. Why aren't the accounts receivables treated as "unrealized receivables"?

2. Assume the partnership in Example 2, Regulation 1.751–1(g) used the cash method of accounting and had not yet collected the accounts receivable. If the inventory's basis was still $21,000 but the value only $24,000, would 751(b) still apply to the distribution?

3. In Example 3, Regulation 1.751–1(g), if the partners had agreed that $7000 of cash in excess of C's share of cash (rather than $7000 of inventory) was received by C in exchange for $7000 depreciable property, how would the results change?

4. Skim, but certainly do not study Examples 5 and 6, Regulation 1.751–1(g) (unless you really are a tax geek!). Note, by the way, that 751(b) applies to operating as well as liquidating distributions. More importantly, though, it should be painfully obvious that disproportionate distributions will generate significant transaction costs for those conscientious enough to seek compliance with IRC 751(b). Since unrealized receivables and inventory are short term assets by definition, it generally should make no sense to make disproportionate distributions while the partnership holds hot assets and thereby provoke the wrath of IRC 751(b). Wouldn't it be better to simply sell the hot assets, allocate gains and losses to each partner and then distribute the cash and remaining assets (disproportionately if desired)? There ought to be a significant and unavoidable imperative to do otherwise. Can you think of any such reasons?

Lesson 24

ABUSE AND ANTI–ABUSE: VARYING INTERESTS AND RETROACTIVE ALLOCATIONS

Primary References: IRC 706(c)–(d)(2)
Treas. Reg. 1.706–1(c)(1)–(2) (omit (2)(i)),
1.704–1(b)(5), Example 13(ii)

Theory

IRC 706(c)(2)(B) and (d)(1) essentially mandate that allocations of partnership items may only be made to partners who were actually partners on the date the deduction generating expense was paid or accrued. If a partnership uses the "interim closing of the books" method allocations will precisely comply with the rule. If a partnership uses the proration method allocations will be made in a manner that approximates compliance with the rule. Both methods are described below.

Since 1956, partners have been required to adjust allocations when one partner sold part or all of her interest to another during the taxable year. There was doubt, however, as to whether the requirement applied when a partner joined a partnership during the year by purchasing her interest directly from the partnership (i.e., by a 721 transaction) rather than from another partner. If she acquired her interest in October via a 721 transaction could she be allocated a deduction that actually arose in June? Aggressive taxpayers took the position that allocations of June losses were permissible since the partnership interest was not obtained by sale, and because 761(c) allows retroactive changes to the partnership agreement.

Under 706(d), though, "retroactive allocations" are now prohibited. The term "retroactive allocation" is actually a bit misleading. It is not that allocations were related back to an earlier date, but that an individual's status as a partner was related back to a date earlier than the actual date she became a partner. By this method, the latter-day partner claimed deductions for expenses that were attributable to periods before she actually owned the property (i.e., before she became a

179

partner). Old IRC 706(c)(2)(B) was thought insufficient to deal with this problem because it arguably required that allocations be made in accordance with partners' "varying interests" only when interests varied as a result of a partner's sale of all or a portion of her interest. Retroactive allocations therefore became widely used, and often litigated, with respect to partners who obtained interests other than by purchase from a partner (e.g., by purchasing an interest directly from the partnership). The legislative history reprinted below provides more detail on how Congress responded to retroactive allocations. The mechanics of making allocations in accordance with partners' varying interest is explained after the legislative history.

TAX REFORM ACT OF 1976

House Report No. 94–658, 94th Congress, 1st Session, 112 (Nov. 12, 1975)

12. Retroactive Allocations of Partnership Income or Loss (sec. 210(c) of the bill and secs. 704(a) and 706(c) of the code)

Present law

Investments in tax shelter limited partnerships are commonly made toward the end of the taxable year. It is also common for the limited partnership to have been formed earlier in the year on a skeletal basis with one general partner and a so-called "dummy" limited partner. In many cases, the limited partnership incurs substantial deductible expenses prior to the year-end entry of the limited partner-investors.

In these tax shelter limited partnerships, the limited partnership usually allocates a full share of the partnership losses for the entire year to those limited partners joining at the close of the year. These are referred to as "retroactive allocations." For example, in the case of a limited partnership owning an apartment house which has been under construction for a substantial part of the year, where construction interest and certain deductible taxes have been paid during that time, such deductions might be retroactively allocated to investors entering the partnership on, say, December 28th of that year.

Present law is not clear whether retroactive allocations are permissible under the Internal Revenue Code. Essentially, there are four partnership Code provisions which have a direct or indirect bearing on this issue—sections 704(a), 761(c), [prior law] 704(b)(2), and [prior law] 706(c)(2)(B).

Section 704(a) provides, in effect, that except as otherwise provided in section 704, the partnership agreement will govern the manner of allocation of "income, gain, loss, deduction, or credit." With respect to a particular taxable year, section 761(c) treats a partnership agreement as consisting of any amendment made up to and including the time for which the partnership's tax return must be filed for such year. It has been argued that sections 704(a) and 761(c), particularly when read together, allow retroactive allocations. On the other hand, it has been argued that sections 704(b)(2) and/or 706(c)(2)(B), discussed below, would prohibit some or all retroactive allocations.

[Old] Section 704(b)(2) prohibits the allocation of items of income, deduction, loss or credit (such as capital gains and depreciation) where the principal purpose of the allocation is the avoidance or evasion of tax. This provision, it has been argued, would prohibit any retroactive allocation having tax avoidance as its principal purpose. The counter-argument to this claim has been that section [old] 704(b)(2) is inapplicable to retroactive allocations of taxable income and loss, since, by its own terms, it only pertains to allocations of particular *items* of income, deduction, loss, or credit [now see Treas. Reg. 1.704–1(b)(2)(vii) which makes IRC 704 applicable to "bottom line" allocations of taxable income and loss as well as particular items].

The main case dealing with the interpretation of section 704(b)(2) with respect to this issue is *Jean V. Kresser,* 54 T.C. 1621 (1970). In *Kresser,* the retroactive allocation involved was disallowed upon the court's findings that the partnership agreement was not amended to provide for the allocation and the allocation of income was, in fact, nothing more than a paper transaction lacking in economic substance. One of the arguments of the Government was that section 704(b)(2) precluded the retroactive allocation. The court dealt with this contention in a footnote (*supra,* at p. 1631), which indicated support for the interpretation of section 704(b)(2) as applying only to allocations of particular items of income, deduction, or credit, and not to allocations of the composite of the partnership's income or loss. However, because of the court's initial findings (i.e., the absence of both an amendment to the partnership agreement and a bona fide reallocation of income), it did not resolve this issue.

[Old] Section 706(c)(2)(B) provides that where a partner disposes of less than his entire interest in a partnership, or his interest is reduced, the partnership taxable year does not close as to such partner, but that his distributive share of partnership income and loss is determined "by taking into account his varying interests in the partnership during the taxable year." While not specifically stated in this provision or the relevant regulations (Reg. § 1.706–1(c)(4)), it is implicit that the transferee of less than the entire interest of the transferor-partner would necessarily be subject to the same rule, i.e., his distributive share of partnership income and loss would be determined by taking into account his varying interests in the partnership during the taxable year. For example, if, on July 1, a person who was not previously a partner, were to acquire from an existing partner a 25 percent interest in a calendar year reporting partnership, which had a loss for the year of $1,000, then, by taking into account his varying interests of zero during the first half of the year and 25 percent during the second half, $125 of the loss would be allocable to the transferee-partner.

As previously stated, [old] section 706(c)(2)(B) also applies where the interest of a partner is reduced. It is unclear whether this provision pertains to the situation where a partner's proportionate interest in the partnership is reduced as the result of the purchase of an interest directly from the partnership. Consequently, it is unclear whether an incoming partner, who purchased his interest directly from the partnership, would be subject to the rule of including partnership income and loss according to his varying interests during the year. Some argue that the varying interests rule of [old] section 706(c)(2)(B) is inapplicable to this situation.

It is further argued that, even if [old] section 706(c)(2)(B) imposed the varying interests rule in the above situation, a timely amendment to the partnership agreement providing for a retroactive allocation of the entire year's losses would, pursuant to sections 704(a) and 761(c), override this provision.

Section 706(c)(2)(A) provides that where a partner retires or sells his entire interest in a partnership, the taxable year of the partnership will close and the partner's distributive share of various income and deduction items will be determined under the income tax regulations. Essentially, the regulations (Reg. § 1.706–1(c)(2)(ii)) provide the alternatives of either an interim closing of the partnership books or the estimation of a partner's distributive share of income and deductions by a proration of such items for the taxable year, based upon the portion of the taxable year that had elapsed prior to the sale or retirement. These alternative methods of computation are not specifically provided, however, with respect to the sale or exchange of, or a reduction in, a partnership interest under section 706(c)(2)(B). In cases to which section 706(c)(2)(B) applies, the only guidance provided is that income and loss allocations should take into account a partner's "varying interests in the partnership during the taxable year."

General reasons for change

Under present law, it is unclear whether section 706(c)(2)(B) requires the inclusion of income and loss according to a partner's varying interests during the year where the partner's interest is acquired directly from the partnership. Even if it were clear that section 706(c)(2)(B) did impose the varying interests rule in this situation, there is the further ambiguity whether a retroactive allocation provided in a partnership agreement would, under the authority of sections 704(a) and 761(c), override any allocation provided under section 706(c)(2)(B). Moreover, even if it were established that section 706(c)(2)(B) was not overridden by a retroactive allocation pursuant to sections 704(a) and 761(c), no clear method is provided in the code or regulations for taking into account the varying interests of the partners during the partnership year.

In essence, the consequence of allowing retroactive allocations is that new partners investing in the partnership towards the close of the taxable year are allowed to deduct expenses which were incurred prior to their entry into the partnership. Some argue that these retroactive allocations are proper because the funds invested by the new partners serve to reimburse the original partners for their expenditures and that, as an economic matter, the new partners have incurred the costs for which they are claiming deductions. However, this argument loses its persuasiveness when the new partner in a partnership situation is compared to that of an investor who directly purchases property which had previously generated tax losses during the taxable year. It is clear that in the latter case the investor would not be entitled to deduct the losses incurred prior to his ownership of the property, notwithstanding the fact that he may, in effect, be reimbursing the seller of the property for losses already incurred.

Explanation of provisions

The bill amends present law (sec. 706(c)(2)(B)) to make it clear that the varying interests rule of this provision is to apply to any partner whose interest in a partnership is reduced, whether by sale, exchange, or otherwise, such as by the admission of a new partner who purchased his interest directly from the partnership. Correspondingly, the provision is to apply to the incoming partner so as to take into account his varying interests during the year. In addition, regulations are to apply the same alternative methods of computing allocations of income and loss to situations falling under section 706(c)(2)(B) as that currently provided with respect to section 706(c)(2)(A) situations (sale or liquidation of an entire interest). These rules will permit a partnership to choose the easier method of prorating items according to the portion of the year for which a partner was a partner or the more precise method of an interim closing of books (as if the year had closed) which, in some instances, will be more advantageous where most of the deductible expenses were paid or incurred upon or subsequent to the entry of the new partners to the partnership.

In addition, the present law provision relating to the effect of a partnership agreement (sec. 704(a)) is amended to provide that it is overridden by any contrary provisions of the partnership provisions (under subchapter K, including section 706(c)(2)(B)). Thus, a partnership agreement, amended (pursuant to section 761(c)) to provide for a retroactive allocation, will not override an allocation required under section 706(c)(2)(B) [now 706(d)(1)].

If A and B are equal partners (each with $4000 outside bases) in a calendar year, cash method partnership that has $3000 in losses for the whole year, they will each report a $1,500 loss on their separate tax returns. But what if A sells one half of her interest in the partnership to C on July 1? A and C would each have 25% interests in the partnership as of July 1, while B's interest would remain 50%. A's varying interest has two effects. First, income and losses prior to the sale that are (or will be) taxed to A should be reflected in A's outside basis in determining gain or loss on the sale of half her interest. Second, allocations of items attributable to the period after July 1 should naturally be adjusted to take into account the changed interests of A and C.

IRC 706(d) does not state exactly how the change in interests should affect allocations. Regulation 1.706–1(c)(2)(ii), however, contemplates two types of allocation methods described succinctly in the following excerpt:

> The proration method involves computing partnership income or loss at the end of the partnership year and allocating the year-end totals ratably over the year according to the partners' percentage interests and the number of days they owned interests in the partnership. *Johnsen v. Commissioner,* 84 T.C. 344, 347 (1985), supplementing 83 T.C. 103 (1984), revd. on another issue 794 F.2d 1157 (6th Cir. 1986); *Moore v. Commissioner* [Dec. 35,477], 70 T.C. 1024, 1035–1036 (1978); *Sartin v. United States* 5 Cl. Ct. 172, 175 (1984). The interim closing of the books method requires a closing of the partnership books as of the date of entry of the new partner and the computation of the various items of partnership income, gain, loss, deduction, and credit as of that date. See *Johnsen v. Commissioner,* 84 T.C. at 347; *Moore v. Commissioner,* 70 T.C. at 1035; *Sartin v. United States,* 5 Cl.Ct. at 175. A taxpayer who elects to use the interim closing of the books method has the additional burden of establishing the date when each partnership item was paid or incurred and what receipts the partnership had during the short period. *Johnsen v. Commissioner,* 84 T.C. at 348, 349–354; *Moore v. Commissioner,* 70 T.C. at 1036; *Sartin v. United States,* 5 Cl. Ct. at 175–176. *Richardson v. Commissioner,* 76 T.C. at 527; see also *Johnsen v. Commissioner,* 84 T.C. at 354. Of the two methods, the interim closing of the books method is the more accurate, but the proration method is simpler to apply. See *Lipke v. Commissioner*, 81 T.C. 689, 699 (1983), affd. without published opinion 751 F.2d 369 (2nd Cir. 1984).

If the AB partnership hypothesized above uses the interim closing of the books method, it will allocate the $3000 loss to those who were partners as of the date the expense was paid or accrued, and in accordance with those partners' relative interests as of that date. Assume for example, the expense giving rise to the $3000 loss can be traced to an expense paid on May 1. A and B would each be allocated $1500, reducing their outside basis to $2500. A's basis in the interest sold to C would therefore be $1,250. If the AB partnership had $3000 gain traceable to May 1, the gain would be allocated to A and B, A's basis would be increased to $5,500 and her basis in the interest sold to C would be $2,750. If A sold one half of her interest to C before the $3000 gain or loss were paid or accrued, her basis would have been $2000. If the partnership earned or lost $3000 on November 1, the gain or loss would be allocated $750 to A, $1500 to B and $750 to C, because those would be the partners (and relative interests) on the date the partnership realized the gain or loss.

If the AB partnership uses the proration method instead, it will divide the $3000 gain or loss by 365 days (regardless of when the gain or loss was actually realized). The partnership will therefore have $8.22

gain or loss per day. The $1500 (rounded up) gain or loss prorated to the first 182 days (assuming 29 days in February) would be allocated to A and B—$750 each in accordance with their 50% interests. A's basis would be adjusted for the allocation of gain or loss immediately prior to the sale to C (and C would take a cost basis under IRC 1012). The $1500 gain or loss prorated to the remaining 183 days would be allocated to A ($750), B ($1500) and C ($750) and their bases would be adjusted accordingly.

The 1976 amendment to IRC 706 was sufficient to clarify that the varying interest rule applied whether an interest was acquired by sale from another partner or directly from the partnership (as when a new partner is admitted to the partnership via a 721 contribution). Nevertheless, manipulations of payment dates by cash method partnerships continued to result in tax avoidance possibilities.

Suppose the AB cash method partnership uses the interim closing of the books method. In year 1 it rents office space for $60,000 ($5,000 per month). On December 15th C contributes capital in exchange for a one third interest in the partnership. The partnership pays the full amount on December 20th. Under the interim closing of the books method, and in light of the partnership's use of the cash method, C would be allocated a deduction of $20,000 (one third of $60,000 rental expense paid after she became a member of the partnership). If the rental had been paid as the property were provided to the partnership, C would have been allocated only $825.00 (one third of the one half month's rent paid after C's admission). The same result would occur if the partnership used the proration method, regardless of whether it was cash or accrual. IRC 709(d), adopted in 1984, forces this result, as explained in the following bit of legislative history:

> **Cash basis partnership.**—With respect to partnerships using the cash method of accounting, the bill provides new rules for the allocation of items among partners when there is a change in partnership interests. First, for specified cash basis items, the bill requires that the item be assigned to each day in the period to which it is attributable. The amounts so assigned are then apportioned among the partners in proportion to their interest in the partnership at the close of each day. These rules (which apply except when regulations otherwise provide) effectively require, for purposes of determining the partners' varying interests in a partnership taxable year, that certain items be allocated under the accrual method. The items to which the provision applies are (1) interest, (2) taxes, (3) payment for services or for the use of property, and (4) any other item of a kind specified in Treasury regulations with respect to which the rule is necessary to avoid retroactive allocations to the partners. For example, if a new partner joins a calendar-year partnership on December 1, and if the partnership on December 31 pays an interest expense which has accrued over the course of the entire year, the partner would be entitled to 1/12 of his otherwise allocable share of deduction for that item. If the expense were attributable

only to the final 6–months of the year, he would receive 1/6 of his otherwise allocable share of that item. The committee intends that the determination of the period to which an expense is attributable will be made in accordance with economic accrual principles.

The bill provides that when application of the economic accrual principles described above would result in allocating an item to periods before or after the current taxable year, those items are to be allocated entirely to the first day of the year in the case of items allocable to prior years and entirely to the last day of the year in the case of items allocable to future periods. This rule does not make any substantive change to the timing of any deduction under present law; rather, it merely describes the treatment of amounts that are currently deductible even though allocable to a past or future year in economic terms. For example, if a cash method partnership failed to pay for services provided to it in year 1 until the middle of year 2, the amount of the year 2 deduction would be allocated to the first day of year 2. Similarly, if the partnership was required to pay property taxes in year 1 for the last half of year 1 and the first half of year 2, the amount allocable to year 2 would be treated as paid on the last day of year 1. Of course, this latter rule will have limited application because of the general limitations on the deductibility of prepaid expenses.

Practice:

1. Read Example 13(ii), Regulation 1.704–1(b)(5). How would the capital accounts appear if the partnership sold the G corporation securities on August 1, and Y sold 50% of her interest on September 1? How would the capital accounts appear if the partnership used the proration method rather than the interim closing of the books method (assuming the sale of Y's 50% interest and the G corporation securities occurred on September 1, and August 1, respectively)?

2. Suppose ABCD each own 25% interests in the ABCD partnership. For the year the partnership has $4000 in gross income and $1200 in deductible expenses. If C sells one half of her interest to E on June 15th how should allocations be made assuming:

(a) the calendar year partnership uses the cash and the interim closing of the books methods; the income occurred from a sale of inventory on June 1, the expense resulted from the purchase of office supplies on October 1.

(b) the calendar year partnership uses the cash and the proration methods; the income occurred from a sale of inventory on June 1, the expense resulted from the purchase of office supplies on October 1.

(c) the calendar year partnership uses the accrual method and the interim closing of the books methods: the income occurred from a sale of inventory on October 1, the expense resulted from the October 1 payment of rent for the period March 1–May 30.

(d) the calendar year partnership uses the cash and interim methods; the income occurred from the sale of inventory on October 1, the expense resulted from the October 1 payment of rent for the period March 1–May 30.

3. Suppose that on January 31, 2005, the ABCE cash method partnership pays $200,000 for rent due for the period July 1, 2004–December 31, 2004. E acquired her 25% interest in the partnership by purchase from D on December 31, 2004. How must the partnership allocate the rental payment. Assume that all partners share equally in profits and losses. Assume also that the partnership's assets include cash, corporate stock and inventory.

4. What if E acquired a 20% interest by contributing property to partnership ABCDE on December 15, 2004 and the $200,000 rental payment was made on December 31, 2004?

Lesson 25

PARTNERSHIP CONVERSIONS, MERGERS AND DIVISIONS

Primary Sources: IRC 708(b)(2)
Treas. Reg. 1.704–1(b)(2)(iv)(l), 1.704–4(c)(4), 1.708–1(c)–(d), 1.737–2(b)(2), 1.752–1(f), (g), Example 2, 301.7701(g)(1)(i)(2)

Case References: Rev. Rul. 84–52, 1984–1 C.B. 157; Rev. Rul. 95–37, 1995–1 C.B. 130; Rev. Rul. 99–5, 1999–1 C.B. 434; Rev. Rul. 99–6, 1999–1 C.B. 432; Rev. Rul. 2004–43, 2004–18, I.R.B. 842 (all revenue rulings are reprinted below)

Secondary Sources: Revised Uniform Partnership Act (RUPA) 905–908

Theory

Business entities sometimes evolve into different legal forms over the period of their existence. The evolutionary process may result from changes in state law, the emergence of new business opportunities, increased or decreased liability exposure or costs, changing priorities amongst joint owners, retirement of one or more joint owners, or many other reasons. In this Lesson, we undertake a broad overview of the tax consequences pertaining to partnership conversions, mergers, and divisions. Partnership conversions are surprisingly simple but only for those who have a broad understanding of Subchapter K. (The accounting mechanics may be complex and burdensome but the tax consequences are theoretically simple). As a general matter, tax consequences are derived by defining the underlying substantive transaction (e.g., a sale of property or a contribution) and applying the basic (e.g. IRC 1001) or Subchapter K (e.g., IRC 721 and 752) rule to the defined transaction. The following four short revenue rulings demonstrate the relative tax simplicity of four common conversions: (1) general to limited partnership, (2) partnership to limited liability company, (3) sole proprietorship to partnership or LLC, and (4) partnership or LLC to sole proprietorship. Partnerships may also convert to C or S corporations but this lesson does not include a discussion of those tax consequences.

REVENUE RULING 84–52
1984–1 C.B. 157.

ISSUE

What are the federal income tax consequences of the conversion of a general partnership interest into a limited partnership interest in the same partnership?

FACTS

In 1975, *X* was formed as a general partnership under the Uniform Partnership Act of state *M*. *X* is engaged in the business of farming. The partners of *X* are *A, B, C,* and *D*. The partners have equal interest in the partnership.

The partners propose to amend the partnership agreement to convert the general partnership into a limited partnership under the Uniform Limited Partnership Act of State *M*, a statute that corresponds in all material respects to the Uniform Limited Partnership Act. Under the certificate of limited partnership, *A* and *B* will be limited partners, and both *C* and *D* will be general partners and limited partners. Each partner's total percent interest in the partnership's profits, losses, and capital will remain the same when the general partnership is converted into a limited partnership. The business of the general partnership will continue to be carried on after the conversion.

LAW AND ANALYSIS

Section 741 of the Internal Revenue Code provides that in the case of a sale or exchange of an interest in a partnership, gain or loss shall be recognized by the transferor partner. Under section 1001 of the Code, if there is a sale or other disposition of property, the entire amount of the gain or loss realized thereunder will be recognized, unless another section of subtitle A provides for nonrecognition.

Under section 721 of the Code, no gain or loss is recognized by a partnership or any of its partners upon the contribution of property to the partnership in exchange for an interest therein. Section 708 of the Code provides that a partnership is considered to be continuing if it is not terminated. A partnership is terminated if (1) no part of any business, financial operation, or venture of the partnership continues to be carried on by any of its partners in a partnership, or (2) within a 12–month period there is a sale or exchange of 50 percent or more of the total interest in partnership capital and profits.

Section 1.708–1(b)(1)(ii) [NOW 1.708–1(b)(2)] of the Income Tax Regulations provides that a contribution of property to a partnership does not constitute a sale or exchange for purposes of section 708 of the Code. Section 722 of the Code generally provides that the basis of an interest in a partnership acquired by a contribution of property equals the transferor partner's adjusted basis in the contributed property.

Section 1223(1) of the Code provides that the holding period of property received in exchange for other property includes the holding period of the property exchanged, if the property received has the same basis (in whole or in part) as the property exchanged.

Under section 731 of the Code, if a partnership distributes money to a partner, then that partner will generally recognize gain only to the extent that the amount of money distributed (or deemed distributed) exceeds the adjusted basis of the partner's interest in the partnership immediately before the distribution. Under section 733 of the Code, if there is a distribution by a partnership to a partner and if there is no liquidation of that partner's interest, then the adjusted basis of that partner's interest in the partnership must be reduced (but not below zero) by the amount of money distributed to the partner.

Section 752(a) of the Code states, in part, that any increase in a partner's share of the partnership's liabilities is considered to be a contribution of money by the partner to the partnership. Section 752(b) of the Code states in part, that any decrease in a partner's share of a partnership's liabilities is considered to be a distribution of money by the partnership to the partner.

Section 1.752–1(e) of the regulations provides rules for determining a partner's share of partnership liabilities with respect to both limited partnerships and general partnerships. Under the facts of this revenue ruling, A, B, C, and D, will remain partners in X after X is converted to a limited partnership. Although the partners have exchanged their interests in the general partnership X for interests in the limited partnership X, under section 721 of the Code, gain or loss will not be recognized by any of the partners of X except as provided in section 731 of the Code.

Holdings

(1) Except as provided below, pursuant to section 721 of the Code, no gain or loss will be recognized by A, B, C, or D under section 741 or section 1001 of the Code as a result of the conversion of a general partnership interest in X into a limited partnership in X.

(2) Because the business of X will continue after the conversion and because, under section 1.708–1(b)(1)(ii) of the regulations, a transaction governed by section 721 of the Code is not treated as a sale or exchange for purposes of section 708 of the Code, X will not be terminated under section 708 of the Code.

(3) If, as a result of the conversion, there is no change in the partners' shares of X's liabilities under section 1.752–1(e) of the regulations, there will be no change to the adjusted basis of any partner's interest in X, and C and D will each have a single adjusted basis with respect to each partner's interest in X (both as limited partner and

general partner) equal to the adjusted basis of each partner's respective general partner interest in X prior to the conversion. *See* Rev. Rul. 84–53, page 159, this Bulletin.

(4) If, as a result of the conversion, there is a change in the partners' shares of X's liabilities under section 1.752–1(e) of the regulations, and such change causes a deemed contribution of money to X by a partner under section 752(a) of the Code, then the adjusted basis of that partner's interest shall, under section 722 of the Code, be increased by the amount of such deemed contribution. If the change in the partners' shares of X's liabilities causes a deemed distribution of money by X to a partner under section 752(b) of the Code, then the basis of that partner's interest shall, under section 733 of the Code, be reduced (but not below zero) by the amount of such deemed distribution, and gain will be recognized by that partner under section 731 of the Code to the extent the deemed distribution exceeds the adjusted basis of that partner's interest in X.

(5) Pursuant to section 1223(1) of the Code, there will be no change to the holding period of any partner's total interest in X.

The holdings contained herein would apply with equal force if the conversion had been of a limited partnership to a general partnership.

REVENUE RULING 95–37

1995–1 C.B. 13.

Issues

(1) Do the federal income tax consequences described in Rev. Rul., 84–52, 1984–1 C.B. 157, apply to the conversion of an interest in a domestic partnership into an interest in a domestic limited liability company (LLC) that is classified as a partnership for federal tax purposes?

(2) Does the taxable year of the converting domestic partnership close with respect to all the partners or with respect to any partner?

(3) Does the resulting domestic LLC need to obtain a new taxpayer identification number?

Law and Analysis

In Rev. Rul. 84–52, a general partnership formed under the Uniform Partnership Act of State M proposed to convert to a limited partnership under the Uniform Limited Partnership Act of State M. Rev. Rul. 84–52 generally holds that (1) under § 721 of the Internal Revenue Code, the conversion will not cause the partners to recognize gain or loss under §§ 741 or 1001, (2) unless its business will not continue after the conversion, the partnership will not terminate under § 708 because the conversion is not treated as a sale or exchange for purposes of § 708, (3) if the partners' shares of partnership liabilities do not change, there will be no change in the adjusted basis of any partner's interest in the partnership, (4) if the partners' shares of partnership liabilities change and cause a deemed contribution of money to the partnership by a partner under § 752(a), then the adjusted basis of such a partner's interest will be increased under § 722 by the amount of the deemed contribution, (5) if the partners' shares of partnership liabilities change and cause a deemed distribution of money by the partnership to a partner under § 752(b), then the basis of such a partner's interest will be reduced under § 733 (but not below zero) by the amount of the deemed distribution, and gain will be recognized by the partner under § 731 to the extent the deemed distribution exceeds the adjusted basis of the partner's interest in the partnership, and (6) under § 1223(1), there will be no change in the holding period of any partner's total interest in the partnership.

The conversion of an interest in a domestic partnership into an interest in a domestic LLC that is classified as a partnership for federal tax purposes is treated as a partnership-to-partnership conversion that is subject to the principles of Rev. Rul. 84–52.

Section 706(c)(1) provides that, except in the case of a termination of a partnership and except as provided in § 706(c)(2), the taxable year of a partnership does not close as the result of the death of a partner, the entry of a new partner, the liquidation of a partner's interest in the partnership, or the sale or exchange of a partner's interest in the partnership.

Section 706(c)(2)(A) provides that the taxable year of a partnership closes with respect to a partner who sells or exchanges the partner's entire interest in a partnership. . . .

In the present case, the conversion of an interest in a domestic partnership into an interest in a domestic LLC that is classified as a partnership for federal tax purposes does not cause a termination under § 708. *See* Rev. Rul. 84–52. Moreover, because each partner in a converting domestic partnership continues to hold an interest in the resulting domestic LLC, the conversion is not a sale, exchange, or liquidation of the converting partner's entire partnership interest for purposes of § 706(c)(2)(A). *See* Rev. Rul. 86–101, 1986–2 C.B. 94 (the taxable year of a partnership does not close with respect to a general partner when the partnership agreement provides that the general partner's interest converts to a limited partnership interest on the general partner's death because the decedent's successor continues to hold an interest in the partnership). Consequently, the conversion does not cause the taxable year of the domestic partnership to close with respect to all the partners or with respect to any partner.

Because the conversion of an interest in a domestic partnership into an interest in a domestic LLC that is classified as a partnership for federal tax purposes does not cause a termination under § 708, the resulting domestic LLC does not need to obtain a new taxpayer identification number.

(1) The federal income tax consequences described in Rev. Rul. 84–52 apply to the conversion of an interest in a domestic partnership into an interest in a domestic LLC that is classified as a partnership for federal tax purposes. The federal tax consequences are the same whether the resulting LLC is formed in the same state or in a different state than the converting domestic partnership.

(2) The taxable year of the converting domestic partnership does not close with respect to all the partners or with respect to any partner.

(3) The resulting domestic LLC does not need to obtain a new taxpayer identification number.

The holdings contained herein would apply in a similar manner if the conversion had been of an interest in a domestic LLC that is classified as a partnership for federal tax purposes into an interest in a domestic partnership. The holdings contained herein apply regardless of the manner in which the conversion is achieved under state law.

This revenue ruling does not address the federal tax consequences of a conversion of an organization that is classified as a corporation into an organization that is classified as a partnership for federal tax purposes. *See, e.g.,* §§ 336 and 337.

REVENUE RULING 99–5

1999–1 C.B. 432

ISSUE

What are the federal income tax consequences when a single member domestic limited liability company (LLC) that is disregarded for federal tax purposes as an entity separate from its owner under § 301.7701–3 of the Procedure and Administration Regulations becomes an entity with more than one owner that is classified as a partnership for federal tax purposes?

FACTS

In each of the following two situations, an LLC is formed and operates in a state which permits an LLC to have a single owner. Each LLC has a single owner, *A*, and is disregarded as an entity separate from its owner for federal tax purposes under § 301.7701–3 . In both situations, the LLC would not be treated as an investment company (within the meaning of § 351) if it were incorporated. All of the assets held by each LLC are capital assets or property described in § 1231 . For the sake of simplicity, it is assumed that neither LLC is liable for any indebtedness, nor are the assets of the LLCs subject to any indebtedness.

Situation 1. B, who is not related to *A*, purchases 50% of *A*'s ownership interest in the LLC for $5,000. *A* does not contribute any portion of the $5,000 to the LLC. *A* and *B* continue to operate the business of the LLC as co-owners of the LLC.

Situation 2. B, who is not related to *A,* contributes $10,000 to the LLC in exchange for a 50% ownership interest in the LLC. The LLC uses all of the contributed cash in its business. *A* and *B* continue to operate the business of the LLC as co-owners of the LLC.

After the sale, in both situations, no entity classification election is made under § 301.7701–3(c) to treat the LLC as an association for federal tax purposes.

LAW AND ANALYSIS

Section 721(a) generally provides that no gain or loss shall be recognized to a partnership or to any of its partners in the case of a contribution of property to the partnership in exchange for an interest in the partnership. Section 722 provides that the basis of an interest in a partnership acquired by a contribution of property, including money, to the partnership shall be the amount of the money and the adjusted basis of the property to the contributing partner at the time of the contribution increased by the amount (if any) of gain recognized under § 721(b) to the contributing partner at such time.

Section 723 provides that the basis of property contributed to a partnership by a partner shall be the adjusted basis of the property to the contributing partner at the time of the contribution increased by the amount (if any) of gain recognized under § 721(b) to the contributing partner at such time. Section 1001(a) provides that the gain or loss from the sale or other disposition of property shall be the difference between the amount realized therefrom and the adjusted basis provided in § 1011 .

Section 1223(1) provides that, in determining the holding period of a taxpayer who receives property in an exchange, there shall be included the period for which the taxpayer held the property exchanged if the property has the same basis in whole or in part in the taxpayer's hands as the property exchanged, and the property exchanged at the time of the exchange was a capital asset or property described in § 1231 .

Section 1223(2) provides that, regardless of how a property is acquired, in determining the holding period of a taxpayer who holds the property, there shall be included the period for which such property was held by any other person if the property has the same basis in whole or in part in the taxpayer's hands as it would have in the hands of such other person.

HOLDING(S)

Situation 1. In this situation, the LLC, which, for federal tax purposes, is disregarded as an entity separate from its owner, is converted to a partnership when the new member, *B,* purchases an interest in the disregarded entity from the owner, *A. B*'s purchase of 50% of *A*'s ownership interest in the LLC is treated as the purchase of a 50% interest in each of the LLC's assets, which are treated as held directly by *A* for federal tax purposes. Immediately thereafter, *A* and *B* are treated as contributing their respective interests in those assets to a partnership in exchange for ownership interests in the partnership.

Under § 1001, *A* recognizes gain or loss from the deemed sale of the 50% interest in each asset of the LLC to *B*.

Under § 721(a), no gain or loss is recognized by *A* or *B* as a result of the conversion of the disregarded entity to a partnership.

Under § 722, *B*'s basis in the partnership interest is equal to $5,000, the amount paid by *B* to *A* for the assets which B is deemed to contribute to the newly-created partnership. *A*'s basis in the partnership interest is equal to *A*'s basis in *A*'s 50% share of the assets of the LLC.

Under § 723, the basis of the property treated as contributed to the partnership by *A* and *B* is the adjusted basis of that property in *A*'s and *B*'s hands immediately after the deemed sale.

Under § 1223(1), *A*'s holding period for the partnership interest received includes *A*'s holding period in the capital assets and property described in § 1231 held by the LLC when it converted from an entity that was disregarded as an entity separate from *A* to a partnership. *B*'s holding period for the partnership interest begins on the day following the date of *B*'s purchase of the LLC interest from *A*. See Rev. Rul. 66–7, 1966–1 C.B. 188, which provides that the holding period of a purchased asset is computed by excluding the date on which the asset is acquired. Under § 1223(2), the partnership's holding period for the assets deemed transferred to it includes *A*'s and *B*'s holding periods for such assets.

Situation 2. In this situation, the LLC is converted from an entity that is disregarded as an entity separate from its owner to a partnership when a new member, *B*, contributes cash to the LLC. *B*'s contribution is treated as a contribution to a partnership in exchange for an ownership interest in the partnership. *A* is treated as contributing all of the assets of the LLC to the partnership in exchange for a partnership interest.

Under § 721(a), no gain or loss is recognized by *A* or *B* as a result of the conversion of the disregarded entity to a partnership.

Under § 722, *B*'s basis in the partnership interest is equal to $10,000, the amount of cash contributed to the partnership. *A*'s basis in the partnership interest is equal to *A*'s basis in the assets of the LLC which *A* was treated as contributing to the newly-created partnership.

Under § 723, the basis of the property contributed to the partnership by *A* is the adjusted basis of that property in *A*'s hands. The basis of the property contributed to the partnership by *B* is $10,000, the amount of cash contributed to the partnership.

Under § 1223(1), *A*'s holding period for the partnership interest received includes *A*'s holding period in the capital and § 1231 assets deemed contributed when the disregarded entity converted to a partnership. *B*'s holding period for the partnership interest begins on the day following the date of *B*'s contribution of money to the LLC. Under

§ 1223(2), the partnership's holding period for the assets transferred to it includes *A*'s holding period.

REVENUE RULING 99–6
1999–1 C.B. 432.

ISSUE

What are the federal income tax consequences if one person purchases all of the ownership interests in a domestic limited liability company (LLC) that is classified as a partnership under § 301.7701–3 of the Procedure and Administration Regulations, causing the LLC's status as a partnership to terminate under § 708(b)(1)(A) of the Internal Revenue Code ?

FACTS

In each of the following situations, an LLC is formed and operates in a state which permits an LLC to have a single owner. Each LLC is classified as a partnership under § 301.7701–3. Neither of the LLCs holds any unrealized receivables or substantially appreciated inventory for purposes of § 751(b). For the sake of simplicity, it is assumed that neither LLC is liable for any indebtedness, nor are the assets of the LLCs subject to any indebtedness.

Situation 1. *A* and *B* are equal partners in *AB*, an LLC. *A* sells *A*'s entire interest in *AB* to *B* for $10,000. After the sale, the business is continued by the LLC, which is owned solely by *B*.

Situation 2. *C* and *D* are equal partners in *CD*, an LLC. *C* and *D* sell their entire interests in *CD* to *E*, an unrelated person, in exchange for $10,000 each. After the sale, the business is continued by the LLC, which is owned solely by *E*.

After the sale, in both situations, no entity classification election is made under § 301.7701–3(c) to treat the LLC as an association for federal tax purposes.

LAW

Section 708(b)(1)(A) and § 1.708–1(b)(1) of the Income Tax Regulations provide that a partnership shall terminate when the operations of the partnership are discontinued and no part of any business, financial operation, or venture of the partnership continues to be carried on by any of its partners in a partnership.

Section 731(a)(1) provides that, in the case of a distribution by a partnership to a partner, gain is not recognized to the partner except to the extent that any money distributed exceeds the adjusted basis of the partner's interest in the partnership immediately before the distribution.

Section 731(a)(2) provides that, in the case of a distribution by a partnership in liquidation of a partner's interest in a partnership where no property other than money, unrealized receivables (as defined in

§ 751(c)), and inventory (as defined in § 751(d)(2)) is distributed to the partner, loss is recognized to the extent of the excess of the adjusted basis of the partner's interest in the partnership over the sum of (A) any money distributed, and (B) the basis to the distributee, as determined under § 732, of any unrealized receivables and inventory.

Section 732(b) provides that the basis of property (other than money) distributed by a partnership to a partner in liquidation of the partner's interest shall be an amount equal to the adjusted basis of the partner's interest in the partnership, reduced by any money distributed in the same transaction.

Section 735(b) provides that, in determining the period for which a partner has held property received in a distribution from a partnership (other than for purposes of § 735(a)(2)), there shall be included the holding period of the partnership, as determined under § 1223, with respect to the property.

Section 741 provides that gain or loss resulting from the sale or exchange of an interest in a partnership shall be recognized by the transferor partner, and that the gain or loss shall be considered as gain or loss from a capital asset, except as provided in § 751 (relating to unrealized receivables and inventory items).

Section 1.741–1(b) provides that § 741 applies to the transferor partner in a two-person partnership when one partner sells a partnership interest to the other partner, and to all the members of a partnership when they sell their interests to one or more persons outside the partnership.

Section 301.7701–2(c)(1) provides that, for federal tax purposes, the term "partnership" means a business entity (as the term is defined in § 301.7701–2(a)) that is not a corporation and that has at least two members.

In *Edwin E. McCauslen v. Commissioner*, 45 T.C. 588 (1966), one partner in an equal, two-person partnership died, and his partnership interest was purchased from his estate by the remaining partner. The purchase caused a termination of the partnership under § 708(b)(1)(A). The Tax Court held that the surviving partner did not purchase the deceased partner's interest in the partnership, but that the surviving partner purchased the partnership assets attributable to the interest. As a result, the surviving partner was not permitted to succeed to the partnership's holding period with respect to these assets.

Rev. Rul. 67–65, 1967–1 C.B. 168, also considered the purchase of a deceased partner's interest by the other partner in a two-person partnership. The Service ruled that, for the purpose of determining the purchaser's holding period in the assets attributable to the deceased partner's interest, the purchaser should treat the transaction as a purchase of the assets attributable to the interest. Accordingly, the purchaser was not permitted to succeed to the partnership's holding period with respect to these assets. *See also* Rev. Rul. 55–68, 1955–1 C.B. 372.

Situation 1. The *AB* partnership terminates under § 708(b)(1)(A) when *B* purchases *A*'s entire interest in *AB*. Accordingly, *A* must treat the transaction as the sale of a partnership interest. Reg. § 1.741–1(b). *A* must report gain or loss, if any, resulting from the sale of *A*'s partnership interest in accordance with § 741.

Under the analysis of *McCauslen* and Rev. Rul. 67–65, for purposes of determining the tax treatment of *B*, the *AB* partnership is deemed to make a liquidating distribution of all of its assets to *A* and *B*, and following this distribution, *B* is treated as acquiring the assets deemed to have been distributed to *A* in liquidation of *A*'s partnership interest.

B's basis in the assets attributable to *A*'s one-half interest in the partnership is $10,000, the purchase price for *A*'s partnership interest. Section 1012. Section 735(b) does not apply with respect to the assets *B* is deemed to have purchased from *A*. Therefore, *B*'s holding period for these assets begins on the day immediately following the date of the sale. See Rev. Rul. 66–7, 1966–1 C.B. 188, which provides that the holding period of an asset is computed by excluding the date on which the asset is acquired.

Upon the termination of *AB*, *B* is considered to receive a distribution of those assets attributable to *B*'s former interest in *AB*. *B* must recognize gain or loss, if any, on the deemed distribution of the assets to the extent required by § 731(a). *B*'s basis in the assets received in the deemed liquidation of *B*'s partnership interest is determined under § 732(b). Under § 735(b), *B*'s holding period for the assets attributable to *B*'s one-half interest in *AB* includes the partnership's holding period for such assets (except for purposes of § 735(a)(2)).

Situation 2. The *CD* partnership terminates under § 708(b)(1)(A) when *E* purchases the entire interests of *C* and *D* in *CD*. *C* and *D* must report gain or loss, if any, resulting from the sale of their partnership interests in accordance with § 741.

For purposes of classifying the acquisition by *E*, the *CD* partnership is deemed to make a liquidating distribution of its assets to *C* and *D*. Immediately following this distribution, *E* is deemed to acquire, by purchase, all of the former partnership's assets. Compare Rev. Rul. 84–111, 1984–2 C.B. 88 (Situation 3), which determines the tax consequences to a corporate transferee of all interests in a partnership in a manner consistent with *McCauslen*, and holds that the transferee's basis in the assets received equals the basis of the partnership interests, allocated among the assets in accordance with § 732(c).

E's basis in the assets is $20,000 under § 1012. *E*'s holding period for the assets begins on the day immediately following the date of sale.

The Tax Code contains voluminous detail with regard to corporate consolidations and divisions ("reorganizations"). By contrast, it is nearly silent with regard to partnership reorganizations. The "special rules" in

IRC 708(b)(2)—regarding the continuation or termination of reorganized partnerships—are the only indication that the Code is aware of reorganizations outside the corporate arena. The Code's silence with regard to partnership reorganizations, however, is consistent with non-tax jurisprudence. The Uniform Partnership Act is also silent with regard to partnership reorganizations. As a result, most mergers and divisions were effectuated via asset transfers. For example, a partnership wishing to merge with another, might distribute its assets to its partners in complete liquidation of their interests. Those liquidated partners would thereafter contribute the assets to the acquiring partnership. Another method involved one partnership contributing all of its assets to an acquiring partnership for a partnership interest in the acquiring partnership. The terminating partnership would distribute the new partnership interest to its partners in complete liquidation of their interests and those partners would promptly become partners in the acquiring partnership.

The Revised Uniform Partnership Act (RUPA)—which has been adopted in more than 30 states as of 2004—explicitly recognizes partnership reorganizations. The main feature of RUPA Article 9 is that title to assets transfer automatically upon completion, approval and (in some states) filing of a written plan of merger by consolidating partnerships. Hence, partnership mergers are now rather simply accomplished under state laws. In most instances there need not even be any actual asset transfers. The execution of the written plan of merger transfers title as a matter of law. Uncertainty remained with regard to the tax consequences because although partnership reorganizations were (and are) akin to corporate reorganizations—i.e., considered mere changes to the form by which business assets were held and exploited—and therefore appropriate for nonrecognition treatment, there were no provisions in the Subchapter K that explicitly recognized the theory of nonrecognition (and carryover basis) with regard to partnership reorganizations. Nonrecognition treatment could nevertheless be obtained by means of carefully planned and coordinated transactions that ensured that no single step in the reorganization plan would result in gain recognition if analyzed separately.

For partnership tax lovers, the merger process is actually fun and challenging since it provides opportunity to test one's understanding of many provisions in Subchapter K. But the process can be unnecessarily expensive for partnerships with lots of varied assets. Regulation 1.708–1(c)–(d) nevertheless follows this dissecting approach under which the consequences of each step are separately analyzed, rather than the corporate approach under which the ultimate result is key (though form is nevertheless important). This actually seems rather curious given the long-standing approach to corporate mergers and the step transaction doctrines, both of which essentially compress several transactions into one and then analyzes the ultimate result. In most cases, though, the results will be nonrecognition and carryover basis under the default rule stated in the recently enacted regulations. The Preamble to the proposed

708(b) regulations, set out below, provides history and background to those regulations:

DEPARTMENT OF THE TREASURY INTERNAL REVENUE SERVICE

Preamble to Proposed Regulations, 65 Federal Register, 1572 (Jan. 11, 2000).

This document proposes to amend sections 708 . . . and 752 of the Income Tax Regulations regarding partnership mergers and divisions.

PARTNERSHIP MERGERS

Background

Section 708(b)(2)(A) provides that in the case of a merger or consolidation of two or more partnerships, the resulting partnership is, for purposes of section 708, considered the continuation of any merging or consolidating partnership whose members own an interest of more than 50 percent in the capital and profits of the resulting partnership. Section 1.708–1(b)(2)(i) of the Income Tax Regulations provides that if the resulting partnership can be considered a continuation of more than one of the merging partnerships, the resulting partnership is the continuation of the partnership that is credited with the contribution of the greatest dollar value of assets to the resulting partnership. If none of the members of the merging partnerships own more than a 50 percent interest in the capital and profits of the resulting partnership, all of the merged partnerships are considered terminated, and a new partnership results. The taxable years of the merging partnerships that are considered terminated are closed under section 706(c).

Although section 708 and the applicable regulations provide which partnership continues when two or more partnerships merge, the statute and regulations do not prescribe a form for the partnership merger. (Often, state merger statutes do not provide a particular form for a partnership merger.) In revenue rulings, however, the IRS has prescribed the form of a partnership merger for Federal income tax purposes.

In Rev. Rul. 68–289 (1968–1 C.B. 314), three existing partnerships (P1, P2, and P3) merged into one partnership with P3 continuing under section 708(b)(2)(A). The revenue ruling holds that P1 and P2, the two terminating partnerships, are treated as having contributed all of their respective assets and liabilities to P3, the resulting partnership, in exchange for a partnership interest in P3. P1 and P2 are considered terminated and the partners of P1 and P2 receive interests in P3 with a basis under section 732(b) in liquidation of P1 and P2 (Assets–Over Form). Rev. Rul. 77–458 (1977–2 C.B. 220), and Rev. Rul. 90–17 (1990–1 C.B. 119), also follow the Assets–Over Form for a partnership merger.

Explanation of Provisions

A. Form of a Partnership Merger

The IRS and Treasury are aware that taxpayers may accomplish a partnership merger by undertaking transactions in accordance with jurisdictional laws that follow a form other than the Assets–Over Form. For example, the terminating partnership could liquidate by distributing its assets and liabilities to its partners who then contribute the assets and liabilities to the resulting partnership (Assets–Up Form). In addition, the partners in the terminating partnership could transfer their terminating partnership interests to the resulting partnership in exchange for resulting partnership interests, and the terminating partnership could liquidate into the resulting partnership (Interest–Over Form).

In the partnership incorporation area, a taxpayer's form generally is respected if the taxpayer actually undertakes, under the relevant jurisdictional law, all the steps of a form that is set forth in one of three situations provided in Rev. Rul. 84–111 (1984–2 C.B. 88). The three situations that Rev. Rul. 84–111 sets forth are the Assets–Over Form, Assets–Up Form, and Interest–Over Form. Rev. Rul. 84–111 explains that, depending on the form chosen to incorporate the partnership, the adjusted basis and holding periods of the various assets received by the corporation and the adjusted basis and holding periods of the stock received by the former partners can vary. Like partnership incorporations, each form of a partnership merger has potentially different tax consequences.

Under the Assets–Up Form, partners could recognize gain under sections 704(c)(1)(2) and 737 (and incur state or local transfer taxes) when the terminating partnership distributes the assets to the partners. However, under the Assets–Over Form, gain under sections 704(c)(1)(B) and 737 is not triggered. See sections 1.704–4(c)(4) and 1.737–2(b). Additionally, under the Assets–Up Form, because the adjusted basis of the assets contributed to the resulting partnership is determined first by reference to section 732 (as a result of the liquidation) and then section 723 (by virtue of the contribution), in certain circumstances, the adjusted basis of the assets contributed may not be the same as the adjusted basis of the assets in the terminating partnership. These circumstances occur if the partners' aggregate adjusted basis of their interests in the terminating partnership does not equal the terminating partnership's adjusted basis in its assets. Under the Assets–Over Form, because the resulting partnership's adjusted basis in the assets it receives is determined solely under section 723, the adjusted basis of the assets in the resulting partnership is the same as the adjusted basis of the assets in the terminating partnership.

The regulations propose to respect the form of a partnership merger for Federal income tax purposes if the partnerships undertake, pursuant to the laws of the applicable jurisdiction, the steps of either the Assets–Over Form or the Assets-Up Form. (This rule applies even if none of the merged partnerships are treated as continuing for Federal income tax purposes.) Generally, when partnerships merge, the assets move from one partnership to another at the entity level, or in other words, like the Assets–Over Form. However, if as part of the merger, the partnership titles the assets in the partners' names, the proposed regulations treat the transaction under the Assets–Up Form. If partnerships use the

Interest–Over Form to accomplish the result of a merger, the partnerships will be treated as following the Assets–Over Form for Federal income tax purposes.

In the context of partnership incorporations, Rev. Rul. 84–111 distinguishes among all three forms of incorporation. However, with respect to the Interest–Over Form, the revenue ruling respects only the transferors' conveyances of partnership interests, while treating the receipt of the partnership interests by the transferee corporation as the receipt of the partnership's assets (i.e., the Assets–Up Form). The theory for this result, based largely on *McCauslen v. Commissioner,* 45 T.C. 588 (1966), is that the transferee corporation can only receive assets since it is not possible, as a sole member, for it to receive and hold interests in a partnership (i.e., a partnership cannot have only one member; so, the entity is never a partnership in the hands of the transferee corporation).

Adherence to the approach followed in Rev. Rul. 84–111 creates problems in the context of partnership mergers that are not present with respect to partnership incorporations. Unlike the corporate rules, the partnership rules impose certain tax results on partners based upon a concept that matches a contributed asset to the partner that contributed the asset. Sections 704(c) and 737 are examples of such rules. The operation of these rules breaks down if the partner is treated as contributing an asset that is different from the asset that the partnership is treated as receiving.

Given that the hybrid treatment of the Interest–Over Form transactions utilized in Rev. Rul. 84–111 is difficult to apply in the context of partnership mergers, another characterization will be applied to such transactions. The Assets–Over Form generally will be preferable for both the IRS and taxpayers. For example, when partnerships merge under the Assets–Over Form, gain under sections 704(c)(1)(B) and 737 is not triggered. Moreover, the basis of the assets in the resulting partnership is the same as the basis of the assets in the terminating partnership, even if the partners' aggregate adjusted basis of their interests in the terminating partnership does not equal the terminating partnership's adjusted basis in its assets.

If partnerships merge under applicable law without implementing a form, the proposed regulations treat the partnerships as following the Assets–Over Form. This approach is consistent with the treatment of partnership to corporation elective conversions under the check-the-box regulations and technical terminations under section 708(b)(1)(B), other formless movements of a partnership's assets.

B. *Adverse Tax Consequences of the Assets–Over Form*

The IRS and Treasury are aware that certain adverse tax consequences may occur for partnerships that merge in a transaction that will be taxed in accordance with the Assets–Over Form. These proposed regulations address some of the adverse tax consequences regarding section 752 liability shifts and buyouts of exiting partners.

1. Section 752 Revisions

If a highly leveraged partnership (the terminating partnership) merges with another partnership (the resulting partnership), all of the partners in the terminating partnership could recognize gain because of section 752 liability shifts. Under the Assets–Over Form, the terminating partnership becomes a momentary partner in the resulting partnership when the terminating partnership contributes its assets and liabilities to the resulting partnership in exchange for interests in the resulting partnership. If the terminating partnership (as a momentary partner in the resulting partnership) is considered to receive a deemed distribution under section 752 (after netting increases and decreases in liabilities under section 1.752–1(f)) that exceeds the terminating partnership's adjusted basis of its interests in the resulting partnership, the terminating partnership would recognize gain under section 731. The terminating partnership's gain then would be allocated to each partner in the terminating partnership under section 704(b). In this situation, a partner in the terminating partnership could recognize gain even though the partner's adjusted basis in its resulting partnership interest or its share of partnership liabilities in the resulting partnership is large enough to avoid the recognition of gain, provided that the decreases in liabilities in the terminating partnership are netted against the increases in liabilities in the resulting partnership.

The proposed regulations clarify that when two or more partnerships merge under the Assets–Over Form, increases or decreases in partnership liabilities associated with the merger are netted by the partners in the terminating partnership and the resulting partnership to determine the effect of the merger under section 752. The IRS and Treasury consider it appropriate to treat the merger as a single transaction for determining the net liability shifts under section 752. Therefore, a partner in the terminating partnership will recognize gain on the contribution under section 731 only if the net section 752 deemed distribution exceeds that partner's adjusted basis of its interest in the resulting partnership.

2. Buyout of a Partner

Another adverse tax consequence may occur when a partner in the terminating partnership does not want to become a partner in the resulting partnership and would like to receive money or property instead of an interest in the resulting partnership. Under the Assets–Over Form, the terminating partnership will not recognize gain or loss under section 721 when it contributes its property to the resulting partnership in exchange for interests in the resulting partnership. However, if, in order to facilitate the buyout of the exiting partner, the resulting partnership transfers money or other consideration to the terminating partnership in addition to the resulting partnership interests, the terminating partnership may be treated as selling part of its property to the resulting partnership under section 707(a)(2)(B). Any gain or loss recognized by the terminating partnership generally would be allocated to all the partners in the terminating partnership even though only the exiting partner would receive the consideration.

The IRS and Treasury believe that, under certain circumstances, when partnerships merge and one partner does not become a partner in the resulting partnership, the receipt of cash or property by that partner should be treated as a sale of that partner's interest in the terminating partnership to the resulting partnership, not a disguised sale of the terminating partnership's assets. Accordingly, the proposed regulations provide that if the merger agreement (or similar document) specifies that the resulting partnership is purchasing the exiting partner's interest in the terminating partnership and the amount paid for the interest, the transaction will be treated as a sale of the exiting partner's interest to the resulting partnership. This treatment will apply even if the resulting partnership sends the consideration to the terminating partnership on behalf of the exiting partner, so long as the designated language is used in the relevant document.

In this situation, the exiting partner is treated as selling a partnership interest in the terminating partnership to the resulting partnership (and the resulting partnership is treated as purchasing the partner's interest in the terminating partnership) immediately prior to the merger. Immediately after the sale, the resulting partnership becomes a momentary partner in the terminating partnership. Consequently, the resulting partnership and ultimately its partners (determined prior to the merger) inherit the exiting partner's capital account in the terminating partnership and any section 704(c) liability of the exiting partner. If the terminating partnership has an election in effect under section 754 (or makes an election under section 754), the resulting partnership will have a special basis adjustment regarding the terminating partnership's property under section 743. The proposed regulations provide that the resulting partnership's basis adjustments under section 743 must be ultimately allocated solely to the partners who were partners in the resulting partnership immediately before the merger; the adjustments do not affect the common basis of the resulting partnership's assets. [**Note:** The final regulations eliminated the requirement of the previous sentence].

C. Merger as Part of a Larger Transaction

The proposed regulations provide that if the merger is part of a larger series of transactions, and the substance of the larger series of transactions is inconsistent with following the form prescribed for the merger, the form may not be respected, and the larger series of transactions may be recast in accordance with their substance. An example illustrating the application of this rule is included in the proposed regulations.

D. Measurement of Dollar Value of Assets

As discussed above, the regulations currently provide that in a merger of partnerships, if the resulting partnership can be considered a continuation of more than one of the merging partnerships, the resulting partnership is the continuation of the partnership that is credited with the contribution of the greatest dollar value of assets to the resulting partnership. Commentators have questioned whether this rule refers to the gross or net value of the assets of a partnership. The proposed regulations provide that the value of assets of a partnership is determined net of the partnership's liabilities.

PARTNERSHIP DIVISIONS

Background

Section 708(b)(2)(B) provides that, in the case of a division of a partnership into two or more partnerships, the resulting partnerships (other than any resulting partnership the members of which had an interest of 50 percent or less in the capital and profits of the prior partnership) are considered a continuation of the prior partnership. Section 1.708–1(b)(2)(ii) provides that any other resulting partnership is not considered a continuation of the prior partnership but is considered a new partnership. If the members of none of the resulting partnerships owned an interest of more than 50 percent in the capital and profits of the prior partnership, the prior partnership is terminated. Where members of a partnership that has been divided do not become members of a resulting partnership that is considered a continuation of the prior partnership, such partner's interest is considered liquidated as of the date of the division.

Section 708(b)(2)(B) and the applicable regulations do not prescribe a particular form for the division involving continuing partnerships. The IRS has not addressed in published guidance how the assets and liabilities of the prior partnership move into the resulting partnerships. Taxpayers generally have followed either the Assets–Over Form or the Assets–Up Form for partnership divisions.

Under the Assets–Over Form, the prior partnership transfers certain assets to a resulting partnership in exchange for interests in the resulting partnership. The prior partnership then immediately distributes the resulting partnership interests to partners who are designated to receive interests in the resulting partnership.

Under the Assets–Up Form, the prior partnership distributes certain assets to some or all of its partners who then contribute the assets to a resulting partnership in exchange for interests in the resulting partnership.

Explanation of Provisions

A.   Form of a Partnership Division

As with partnership mergers, the IRS and Treasury recognize that different tax consequences can arise depending on the form of the partnership division. Because of the potential different tax results that could occur depending on the form followed by the partnership, the regulations propose to respect for Federal income tax purposes the form of a partnership division accomplished under laws of the applicable jurisdiction if the partnership undertakes the steps of either the Assets–Over Form or the Assets–Up Form. Thus, the same forms allowed for partnership mergers will be allowed for partnership divisions.

Generally, an entity cannot be classified as a partnership if it has only one member. This universally has been held to be the case in classifying transactions where interests in a partnership are transferred to a single person, so that the partnership goes out of existence. McCauslen v. Commissioner, 45 T.C. 588 (1966); Rev. Rul. 99–6, 1999–6 I.R.B. 6; Rev. Rul. 67–65, 1967–1 C.B. 168; Rev. Rul. 55–68, 1955–1 C.B. 372. However, in at least one instance involving the contribution of assets by an existing partnership to a newly-formed partnership, regulations have provided that the momentary existence of the new partnership will be respected for Federal income tax purposes. See section 1.708–1(b)(1)(iv). Pursuant to the proposed regulations, under the Assets–Over Form of a partnership division, the prior partnership's momentary ownership of all the interests in a resulting partnership will not prevent the resulting partnership from being classified as a partnership on formation.

The example in current section 1.708–1(b)(2)(ii) indicates that when a partnership is not considered a continuation of the prior partnership under section 708(b)(2)(B) (partnership considered a new partnership under current section 1.708–1(b)(2)(ii)), the new partnership is created under the Assets–Up Form. The regulations propose to modify this result and provide examples illustrating that partnerships can divide and create a new partnership under either the Assets–Over Form or the Assets–Up Form.

Consistent with partnership mergers, if a partnership divides using a form other than the two prescribed, it will be treated as undertaking the Assets–Over Form.

These proposed regulations use four terms to describe the form of a partnership division. Two of these terms, prior partnership and resulting partnership, describe partnerships that exist under the applicable jurisdictional law. The prior partnership is the partnership that exists under the applicable jurisdictional law before the division, and the resulting partnerships are the partnerships that exist under the applicable jurisdictional law after the division. The other two terms, divided partnership and recipient partnership, are Federal tax concepts. A divided partnership is a partnership that is treated, for Federal income tax purposes, as transferring assets in connection with a division, and a recipient partnership is a partnership that is treated, for Federal income tax purposes, as receiving assets in connection with a division. The divided partnership must be a continuation of the prior partnership. Although the divided partnership is considered one continuing partnership for Federal income tax purposes, it may actually be two different partnerships under the applicable jurisdictional law (i.e., the prior partnership and a different resulting partnership that is considered a continuation of the prior partnership for Federal income tax purposes).

Finally, because in a formless division it generally will be unclear which partnership should be treated, for Federal income tax purposes, as transferring assets (i.e, the divided partnership) to another partnership (i.e., the recipient partnership) where more than one partnership is a continuation of the prior partnership, the proposed regulations provide that the continuing resulting partnership with the assets having the greatest fair market value (net of liabilities) will be treated as the divided partnership. This issue also is present where the partnership that, in form, transfers assets is not a continuation of the prior partnership, but more than one of the other resulting partnerships are continuations of the prior partnership. The same rule applies to these situations.

B. Consequences under Sections 704(c)(1) (B) and 737

Gain under sections 704(c)(1)(B) and 737 may be triggered when section 704(c) property or substituted section 704(c) property is distributed to certain partners. These rules often will be implicated in the context of partnership divisions.

Where a division is accomplished in a transaction that is taxed in accordance with the Assets–Over Form, the partnership interest in the recipient partnership will be treated as a section 704(c) asset to the extent that the interest is received by the divided partnership in exchange for section 704(c) property. Section 1.704–4(d)(1). Accordingly, the distribution of the partnership interests in the recipient partnership by the divided partnership generally will trigger section 704(c)(1)(B) where the interests in the recipient partnership are received by a partner of the divided partnership other than the partner who contributed the section 704(c) property to the divided partnership. In addition, section 737 may be triggered if a partner who contributed section 704(c) property to the divided partnership receives an interest in the recipient partnership that is not attributable to the section 704(c) property.

Where a division is accomplished under the Assets–Up Form, assets are distributed directly to the partners who will hold interests in the recipient partnership. The distribution could trigger section 704(c)(1)(B) or 737 depending on the identity of the distributed asset and the distributee partner.

The regulations under section 737 provide an exception for certain partnership divisions. Section 737 does not apply when a transferor partnership transfers all the section 704(c) property contributed by a partner to a second partnership in a section 721 exchange, followed by a distribution of an interest in the transferee partnership in complete liquidation of the interest of the partner that originally contributed the section 704(c) property to the transferor partnership. Section 1.737–2(b)(2). This rule, however, may not apply to many partnership divisions because the original contributing partner often remains a partner in the divided partnership. No similar rule is provided under section 704(c)(1)(B).

In many instances, the application of sections 704(c)(1)(B) and 737 will be appropriate when a partnership divides under either the Assets–

Over Form or the Assets–Up Form. Consider the following example: A, B, C, and D form a partnership. A contributes appreciated property X ($0 basis and $200 value), B contributes property Y ($200 basis and $200 value), and C and D each contribute $200 cash. The partnership subsequently divides into two partnerships using the Assets–Over Form, distributing interests in the recipient partnership in accordance with each partner's pro rata interest in the prior partnership. Property X remains in the prior partnership, and property Y is contributed to the recipient partnership. Under these facts, section 737 could be avoided if an exception were created for the distribution of the recipient partnership interests. If, subsequent to the division, half of property Y is distributed to A, section 737 would not be triggered because property X (the section 704(c) property) is no longer in the same partnership as property Y.

While the IRS and Treasury generally believe that it is appropriate to apply sections 704(c)(1)(B) and 737 in the context of partnership divisions, comments are invited on whether it would be appropriate to expand the exceptions to these sections in certain circumstances relating to divisive transactions.

C. Division as Part of a Larger Transaction

The proposed regulations provide the same rule for partnership divisions that applies to partnership mergers.

As implied in the preamble, a partnership merger or division will trigger tax consequences that are determined by reference to the separate steps by which the reorganization is completed. These tax consequences relate to the application of *Crane* and *Tufts* gain to partnerships (i.e., relief of liabilities) and the assignment of income doctrine that underlies IRC 704(c)(1)(A). The following revenue ruling painstakingly demonstrates how "new" 704(c) gain results from a partnership merger. It is included also because it provides just one example of how Subchapter K provisions are so thoroughly interrelated.

REVENUE RULING 2004–43
2004–18 I.R.B. 842.

ISSUES

(1) Does § 704(c)(1)(B) of the Internal Revenue Code apply to § 704(c) gain or loss that is created in an assets-over partnership merger?

(2) For purposes of § 737(b), does net precontribution gain include § 704(c) gain or loss that is created in an assets-over partnership merger?

FACTS

Situation 1. On January 1, 2004, A contributes Asset 1, with a basis of $200x and a fair market value of $300x to partnership AB in exchange for a 50 percent interest. On the same date, B contributes $300x of cash to AB in exchange for a 50 percent interest. Also on January 1, 2004, C contributes Asset 2, with a basis of $100x and a fair market value of $200x to partnership CD in exchange for a 50 percent interest. D contributes $200x of cash to CD in exchange for a 50 percent interest.

On January 1, 2006, AB and CD undertake an assets-over partnership merger in which AB is the continuing partnership and CD is the terminating partnership. At the time of the merger, AB's only assets are Asset 1, with a fair market value of $900x, and $300x in cash, and CD's only assets are Asset 2, with a fair market value of $600x and $200x in cash. After the merger, the partners have capital and profits interests in AB as follows: A, 30 percent; B, 30 percent; C, 20 percent; and D, 20 percent.

The partnership agreements for AB and CD provide that the partners' capital accounts will be determined and maintained in accordance with § 1.704–1(b)(2)(iv) of the Income Tax Regulations, distributions in liquidation of the partnership (or any partner's interest) will be made in accordance with the partners' positive capital account balances, and any partner with a deficit balance in the partner's capital account following the liquidation of the partner's interest must restore that deficit to the partnership (as set forth in § 1.704–1(b)(2)(ii)(b)(2) and (3)). AB and CD both have provisions in their partnership agreements requiring the revaluation of partnership property upon the entry of a new partner. AB would not be treated as an investment company (within the meaning of § 351) if it were incorporated. Neither partnership holds any unrealized receivables or inventory for purposes of 751. AB and CD do not have a § 754 election in place. Asset 1 and Asset 2 are nondepreciable capital assets.

On January 1, 2012, AB has the same assets that it had after the merger. Each asset has the same value that it had at the time of the merger. On this date, AB distributes Asset 2 to A in liquidation of A's interest in AB.

Situation 2. The facts are the same as in Situation 1, except that on January 1, 2012, Asset 1 has a value of $275x, and AB distributes Asset 1 to C in liquidation of C's interest in AB.

LAW

Under § 704(b) and the regulations thereunder, allocations of a partnership's items of income, gain, loss, deduction, or credit provided for in the partnership agreement will be respected if the allocations have substantial economic effect. Allocations that fail to have substantial economic effect will be reallocated according to the partners' interests in the partnership.

Section 1.704–1(b)(2)(iv)(f) provides that a partnership may, upon the occurrence of certain events (including the contribution of money to the partnership by a new or existing partner), increase or decrease the partners' capital accounts to reflect a revaluation of the partnership property.

Section 1.704–1(b)(2)(iv)(g) provides that, to the extent a partnership's property is reflected on the books of the partnership at a book value that differs from the adjusted tax basis, the substantial economic effect requirements apply to the allocations of book items. Section 704(c) and 1.704–1(b)(4)(i) govern the partners' distributive shares of tax items.

Section 1.704–1(b)(4)(i) provides that if partnership property is, under § 1.704–1(b)(2)(iv)(f), properly reflected in the capital accounts of the partners and on the books of the partnership at a book value that differs from the adjusted tax basis of the property, then depreciation, depletion, amortization, and gain or loss, as computed for book purposes, with respect to the property will be greater or less than the depreciation, depletion, amortization, and gain or loss, as computed for federal tax purposes, with respect to the property. In these cases the capital accounts of the partners are required to be adjusted solely for allocations of the book items to the partners (see § 1.704–1(b)(2)(iv)(g)), and the partners' shares of the corresponding tax items are not independently reflected by further adjustments to the partners' capital accounts. Thus, separate allocations of these tax items cannot have economic effect under § 1.704–1(b)(2)(ii)(b)(1), and the partners' distributive shares of tax items must (unless governed by § 704(c)) be determined in accordance with the partners' interests in the partnership. These tax items must be shared among the partners in a manner that takes account of the variation between the adjusted tax basis of the property and its book value in the same manner as variations between the adjusted tax basis and fair market value of property contributed to the partnership are taken into account in determining the partners' shares of tax items under § 704(c).

Section 704(c)(1)(A) provides that income, gain, loss, and deduction with respect to property contributed to the partnership by a partner shall be shared among the partners so as to take account of the variation between the basis of the property to the partnership and its fair market value at the time of contribution.

Section 1.704–3(a)(2) provides that, except as provided in § 1.704–3(e)(2) and (3), § 704(c) and § 1.704–3 apply on a property-by-property basis.

Section 1.704–3(a)(3)(i) provides that property contributed to a partnership is § 704(c) property if at the time of contribution its book value differs from the contributing partner's adjusted tax basis. For purposes of § 1.704–3, book value is determined as contemplated by § 1.704–1(b). Therefore, book value is equal to fair market value at the time of contribution and is subsequently adjusted for cost recovery and other events that affect the basis of the property.

Section 1.704–3(a)(3)(ii) provides that the built-in gain on § 704(c) property is the excess of the property's book value over the contributing partner's adjusted tax basis upon contribution. The built-in gain is thereafter reduced by decreases in the difference between the property's book value and adjusted tax basis.

Section 1.704–3(a)(6) provides that the principles of § 1.704–3 also apply to "reverse § 704(c) allocations" which result from revaluations of partnership property pursuant to § 1.704–1(b)(2)(iv)(f).

Section 1.704–3(a)(7) provides that, if a contributing partner transfers a partnership interest, built-in gain or loss must be allocated to the transferee partner as it would have been allocated to the transferor partner. If the contributing partner transfers a portion of the partnership interest, the share of built-in gain or loss proportionate to the interest transferred must be allocated to the transferee partner.

Section 704(c)(1)(B) provides that if any property contributed to the partnership by a partner is distributed (directly or indirectly) by the partnership (other than to the contributing partner) within seven years of being contributed: (i) the contributing partner shall be treated as recognizing gain or loss (as the case may be) from the sale of the property in an amount equal to the gain or loss which would have been allocated to the partner under § 704(c)(1)(A) by reason of the variation described in § 704(c)(1)(A) if the property had been sold at its fair market value at the time of the distribution; (ii) the character of the gain or loss shall be determined by reference to the character of the gain or loss which would have resulted if the property had been sold by the partnership to the distributee; and (iii) appropriate adjustments shall be made to the adjusted basis of the contributing partner's interest in the partnership and to the adjusted basis of the property distributed to reflect any gain or loss recognized under § 704(c)(1)(B).

Section 1.704–4(c)(4) provides that § 704(c)(1)(B) and § 1.704–4 do not apply to a transfer by a partnership (transferor partnership) of all of its assets and liabilities to a second partnership (transferee partnership) in an exchange described in § 721, followed by a distribution of the interest in the transferee partnership in liquidation of the transferor partnership as part of the same plan or arrangement. Section 1.704–4(c)(4) also provides that a subsequent distribution of § 704(c) property by the transferee partnership to a partner of the transferee partnership is subject to § 704(c)(1)(B) to the same extent that a distribution by the transferor partnership would have been subject to § 704(c)(1)(B).

Section 1.704–4(d)(2) provides that the transferee of all or a portion of the partnership interest of a contributing partner is treated as the contributing partner for purposes of § 704(c)(1)(B) and § 1.704–4 to the extent of the share of built-in gain or loss allocated to the transferee partner.

Section 708(a) provides that, for purposes of subchapter K, an existing partnership shall be considered as continuing if it is not terminated.

Section 708(b)(2)(A) provides that in the case of the merger or consolidation of two or more partnerships, the resulting partnership shall, for purposes of § 708, be considered the continuation of any merging or consolidating partnership whose members own an interest of more than 50 percent in the capital and profits of the resulting partnership.

Section 1.708–1(c)(3)(i) provides that when two or more partnerships merge or consolidate into one partnership under the applicable jurisdictional law without undertaking a form for the merger or consolidation, or undertake a form for the merger or consolidation that is not described in § 1.708–1(c)(3)(ii), any merged or consolidated partnership that is considered terminated under § 1.708–1(c)(1) is treated as undertaking the assets-over form for federal income tax purposes. Under the assets-over form, the merged or consolidated partnership that is considered terminated under § 1.708–1(c)(1) contributes all of its assets and liabilities to the resulting partnership in exchange for an interest in the resulting partnership, and immediately thereafter, the terminated partnership distributes interests in the resulting partnership to its partners in liquidation of the terminated partnership.

Section 737(a) provides that, in the case of any distribution by a partnership to a partner, the partner shall be treated as recognizing gain in an amount equal to the lesser of (1) the excess (if any) of (A) the fair market value of property (other than money) received in the distribution over (B) the adjusted basis of the partner's interest in the partnership immediately before the distribution reduced (but not below zero) by the amount of money received in the distribution, or (2) the net precontribution gain of the partner. Gain recognized under the preceding sentence shall be in addition to any gain recognized under § 731. The character of the gain shall be determined by reference to the proportionate character of the net precontribution gain.

Section 737(b) provides that for purposes of § 737, the term 'net precontribution gain' means the net gain (if any) which would have been recognized by the distributee partner under § 704(c)(1)(B) if all property which (1) had been contributed to the partnership by the distributee partner within seven years of the distribution, and (2) is held by the partnership immediately before the distribution, had been distributed by the partnership to another partner.

Section 1.737–1(c)(1) provides that the distributee partner's net precontribution gain is the net gain (if any) that would have been recognized by the distributee partner under § 704(c)(1)(B) and § 1.704–4 if all property that had been contributed to the partnership by the distributee partner within seven years of the distribution and is held by the partnership immediately before the distribution had been distributed by the partnership to another partner other than a partner who owns, directly or indirectly, more than 50 percent of the capital or profits interest in the partnership.

Section 1.737–1(c)(2)(iii) provides that the transferee of all or a portion of a contributing partner's partnership interest succeeds to the transferor's net precontribution gain, if any, in an amount proportionate to the interest transferred.

Section 1.737–2(b)(1) provides that § 737 and § 1.737–2 do not apply to a transfer by a partnership (transferor partnership) of all of its assets and liabilities to a second partnership (transferee partnership) in an exchange described in § 721, followed by a distribution of the interest in the transferee partnership in liquidation of the transferor partnership as part of the same plan or arrangement.

Section 1.737–2(b)(3) provides that a subsequent distribution of property by the transferee partnership to a partner of the transferee partnership that was formerly a partner of the transferor partnership is subject to § 737 to the same extent that a distribution from the transferor partnership would have been subject to § 737.

ANALYSIS

Section 1.704–4(c)(4) describes the effect of an assets-over partnership merger on pre-existing § 704(c) gain or loss for purposes of § 704(c)(1)(B). Under § 1.704–4(c)(4), if the transferor partnership in an assets-over merger holds contributed property with § 704(c) gain or loss, the seven year period in § 704(c)(1)(B) does not restart with respect to that gain or loss as a result of the merger. Section 1.704–4(c)(4) does not prevent the creation of new § 704(c) gain or loss when assets are contributed by one partnership to another partnership in an assets-over merger. Section 704(c)(1)(B) applies to this newly created § 704(c) gain or loss if the assets contributed in the merger are distributed to a partner other than the contributing partner (or its successor) within seven years of the merger.

Section 1.737–2(b)(1) and (3) describes the effect of an assets-over partnership merger on net precontribution gain that includes pre-existing § 704(c) gain or loss. Under § 1.737–2(b)(3), if the transferor partnership in an assets-over merger holds contributed property with § 704(c) gain or loss, the seven year period in § 737(b) does not restart with respect to that gain or loss as a result of the merger. Section 1.737–2(b)(3) does not prevent the creation of new § 704(c) gain or loss when assets are contributed by one partnership to another partnership in an assets-over merger. This gain or loss must be considered in determining the amount of net precontribution gain for purposes of § 737 if the continuing partnership distributes other property to the contributing partner (or its successor) within seven years of the merger.

Section 1.704–3(a)(6)(i) provides that the principles of § 1.704–3 apply to reverse § 704(c) allocations. In contrast, the regulations under § 704(c)(1)(B) and § 737 contain no similar rule requiring that the principles of § 704(c)(1)(B) and § 737 apply to reverse § 704(c) allocations. Under those regulations, § 704(c)(1)(B) and § 737 do not apply to reverse § 704(c) allocations.

In both of the situations described above, on the date of the partnership merger, CD contributes cash and Asset 2 to AB in exchange for an interest in AB. Immediately thereafter, CD distributes, in liquidation, interests in AB to C and D. Asset 2 has a basis of $100x and a fair market value of $600x upon contribution. Of the $500x of built in gain in Asset 2, $100x is pre-existing § 704(c) gain attributable to C's contribution of Asset 2 to CD, and $400x is additional § 704(c) gain created as a result of the merger. As the transferees of CD's partnership interest in AB, C and D each succeed to one-half of CD's $400x of § 704(c) gain in Asset 2 (each $200x). Section 1.704–3(a)(7). Thus, C's share of § 704(c) gain is $300x, and D's share of § 704(c) gain is $200x. The entry of CD as a new partner of AB causes partnership AB to revalue its property. When CD enters as a new partner of AB, Asset 1 has a basis of $200x and a fair market value of $900x. Of the $700x of built-in gain in Asset 1, $100x is pre-existing § 704(c) gain attributable to the contribution of Asset 1 by A. The revaluation results in the creation of $600x of reverse § 704(c) gain in Asset 1. This layer of reverse § 704(c) gain is shared equally by A and B ($300x each). Thus, A's share of § 704(c) gain is $400x, and B's share of § 704(c) gain is $300x.

In Situation 1, the distribution of Asset 2 to A occurs more than seven years after the contribution of Asset 2 to CD. Therefore, § 704(c)(1)(B) does not apply to the $100x of pre-existing § 704(c) gain attributable to that contribution. However, the distribution of Asset 2 to A occurs within seven years of the contribution of Asset 2 by CD to AB. The contribution of Asset 2 by CD to AB creates § 704(c) gain of $400x. As the transferees of CD's partnership interest in AB, C and D each succeed to one-half of the $400x of § 704(c) gain created by the merger. Section 1.704–3(a)(7). Section 704(c)(1)(B) applies to that § 704(c) gain, causing C and D each to recognize $200x of gain.

The distribution of Asset 2 to A occurs more than seven years after the contribution of Asset 1 to AB, and A made no subsequent contributions to AB. Therefore, A's net precontribution gain for purposes of § 737(b) at the time of the distribution is zero. AB's $600x of reverse § 704(c) gain in Asset 1, resulting from a revaluation of AB's partnership property at the time of the merger, is not net precontribution gain. Accordingly, A will not recognize gain under § 737 as a result of the distribution of Asset 2.

In Situation 2, § 704(c)(1)(B) does not apply to the distribution by the continuing partnership of Asset 1 to C on January 1, 2012. The distribution of Asset 1 to C occurs more than seven years after the contribution of Asset 1 to AB, and § 704(c)(1)(B) does not apply to the reverse § 704(c) gain in Asset 1 resulting from a revaluation of AB's partnership property at the time of the merger. Accordingly, neither A nor B will recognize gain under § 704(c)(1)(B) as a result of the distribution of Asset 1 to C.

The distribution of Asset 1 to C occurs more than seven years after the contribution of Asset 2 to CD. Therefore, C's net precontribution gain at the time of the distribution does not include C's $100x of pre-existing § 704(c) gain attributable to that contribution. However, the distribution of Asset 1 to C occurs within seven years of the contribution of Asset 2 by CD to AB. The contribution of Asset 2 by CD to AB creates net precontribution gain of $400x. As the transferees of CD's partnership interest in AB, C and D each succeed to one-half of CD's $400x of net precontribution gain in Asset 2. Section 1.737–1(c)(2)(iii). Thus, C's portion of CD's net precontribution gain created by the merger is $200x. The excess of Asset 1's fair market value, $275x, over the adjusted tax basis of C's interest in AB immediately before the distribution, $100x, is $175x, which is less than C's $200x of net precontribution gain. Therefore, C will recognize $175x of capital gain under § 737 as a result of the distribution. Because no property is distributed to D and none of the property treated as contributed by D is distributed to another partner, D recognizes no gain under § 737 or § 704(c)(1)(B).

Holdings

(1) Section 704(c)(1)(B) applies to newly created § 704(c) gain or loss in property contributed by the transferor partnership to the continuing partnership in an assets-over partnership merger, but does not apply to newly created reverse § 704(c) gain or loss resulting from a revaluation of property in the continuing partnership.

(2) For purposes of § 737(b), net precontribution gain includes newly created § 704(c) gain or loss in property contributed by the transferor partnership to the continuing partnership in an assets-over partnership merger, but does not include newly created reverse § 704(c) gain or loss resulting from a revaluation of property in the continuing partnership.

Practice:

1. The following questions pertain to the examples in Regulation 1.708–1(c)(5):

   a. If no other details were provided or available, what "form" should be applied to the merger in Example 1? Describe, in general, the constituent steps of that form and all Subchapter K provisions relevant to each step.

   b. What result in Example 2 if partnership X and Y each contributed assets with a value of $200X to the merged partnership?

   c. If the terminating partnership in Example 3 had unrealized receivables or substantially appreciated inventory prior to the merger, would IRC 751(b) apply?

   d. If IRC 751(b) is inapplicable to Example 3, under what circumstances might A or B recognize gain?

   e. Which of the two merger forms is likely to be the most advantageous to a terminating partnership?

2. Recall the example given in the preamble to Regulation 1.708–1(d):

A, B, C, and D form a partnership. A contributes appreciated property X ($0 basis and $200 value), B contributes property Y ($200 basis and $200 value), and C and D each contribute $200 cash. The partnership subsequently divides into two partnerships using the Assets–Over Form, distributing interests in the recipient partnership in accordance with each partner's pro rata interest in the prior partnership. Property X remains in the prior partnership, and property Y is contributed to the recipient partnership.

Assume that partnership ABCD transferred $200 cash along with property Y in the divisive reorganization. A, B, C, and D are also partners in the recipient partnership. That is, the same partners will remain partners in two separate partnerships. What are the tax consequences to A upon receipt of her recipient partnership interest?

3.   What would be the result in question 2 if only A and B received interests in the recipient partnership in complete liquidation of their interests in ABCD?

4.   What would be the tax consequences in Example 2, Regulation 1.752–1(f), if the merger had been completed using the assets-up form? What if the merger was completed using the assets-over form, but B's basis in the terminating partnership was $335 before the transaction?

5.   Read Example 2, Regulation 1.708–1(d)(5). What results to all parties if immediately prior to the transaction, (1) partner C has an adjusted basis of 80 and D an adjusted basis of 70 and (2) property Y has an adjusted basis of 70 and property Z has an adjusted basis of 100?

6.   Read Example 4, Regulation 1.708–1(d)(5). Which partnership is the "divided" partnership?

7.   In Revenue Ruling 2003–43, what are the analytical and theoretical justifications for concluding that partners A and B do not have "new" 704(c) gain while partners C and D do have "new" 704(c) gain?

Lesson 26

TIERED PARTNERSHIPS

Secondary References: IRC 761(e); Treas. Reg. 1.704–2(k) 1.704–3(a)(9), 1.705–2(a), 1.707–5(e), 1.708–1(b)(2), 1.752–2(i), 1.752–4(a)

Case References: Rev. Rul. 77–311, 1977–2 C.B. 218 (reprinted below)

Theory

The phrase "tiered partnerships" describes a structure involving a partnership, one or more of the partners of which is another partnership. The partnership that owns an interest in another partnership is usually referred to as the "upper tier partnership" ("UTP") and the partnership in which an interest is owned by another partnership is referred to as the "lower tier partnership" ("LTP"). Generally speaking, Subchapter K treats an upper tier partnership just like any other partner. Tax attributes derived from the lower tier partnership are treated as if they were derived directly by the upper tier partnership and allocated or assigned to the UTP's partners. In practice, the ultimate tax effect may seem obscured by the two or more tiers. Usually, an accurate diagram of the partnerships and their partners will remove some of the obscurity and make the appropriate tax outcome obvious (assuming an understanding of the Subchapter K fundamentals). Unfortunately, there is no single rule or section in Subchapter K that explains how Subchapter K rules should be applied to tiered partnerships. In its 1982 study of Subchapter K, the American Law Institute noted:

> It would be ideal if a general rule could be proposed to deal with tiered-partnership problems. Taking account of tiered partnerships in statutory drafting can be difficult, and a general rule would reduce the need for repetitive drafting. However, a single rule will not solve all tiered-partnership problems ... Of course, a court faced with a tiered-partnership problem can—and it is believed, should—interpret the substantive provision at issue so as to best implement a pass-through model; the interpretation should generally have the

217

effect that any partnership that is a partner in a lower-tier partnership is treated as if it carried on its share of the business of the lower-tier partnership directly. However, this interpretative principle cannot easily be embodied in a statutory rule specifically addressed to tiered partnerships.

American Law Institute: FEDERAL INCOME TAX PROJECT SUBCHAPTER K: PROPOSALS OF THE AMERICAN LAW INSTITUTE ON THE TAXATION OF PARTNERS (1984). Subchapter K takes the approach discussed in the ALI study. First, the treatment of tiered partnerships is explained in various provisions and revenue rulings rather than in a single regulation. Second, those provisions generally apply a "look-through" approach to tiered partnerships whereby the upper tier partnership is treated as though it incurred the partnership item directly. Partners of the upper tier are then taxed accordingly with regard to the UTP's items. The ruling below demonstrates the approach and the questions below allow you to apply this approach to some of the common additional situations. The questions require you to apply earlier-learned principles to tiered partnerships. As noted above, the task will be easier if you create an accurate diagram of the tiered structure in each instance. This Lesson, it should be noted, is designed only to make readers aware of special rules relating to tiered partnerships. A thorough study would require a rehash of all or many previous Lessons and that seems inefficient.

REVENUE RULING 77–311

1977–2 C.B. 218.

Advice has been requested whether, under the circumstances described below, the method of allocating a partnership loss is an acceptable method of allocation for purposes of section 706(c)(2)(B) of the Internal Revenue Code of 1954, as amended by the Tax Reform Act of 1976, Pub. L. 94–455, 1976–3 C.B. (Vol. 1) 23.

A, an individual, was the general partner of *X*, a limited partnership formed on January 2, 1976. *Y*, another limited partnership formed on January 2, 1976, was one of the limited partners of *X*. The sole activity of both partnerships is investing in real property (other than mineral property). Under the *X* partnership agreement, the profits and losses were to be shared 10 percent for *A* and 30 percent each for *Y* and the other two limited partners. When *Y* was formed, the general partner of *Y* was *B*, an individual, and the sole limited partner of *Y* was *C*, an individual. Under the *Y* partnership agreement, the profits and losses originally were to be shared 20 percent for *B* and 80 percent for *C*. On December 1, 1976, *D*, an individual, contributed cash to *Y*'s capital and was admitted as a limited partner of *Y*. The *Y* partnership agreement was amended in accordance with the partners' relative investments. *D*'s profits and losses sharing percentage was established at 25 percent and *B*'s and *C*'s percentages were reduced to 15 percent and 60 percent respectively.

For its taxable year ended December 31, 1976, X sustained a loss from its business operations in substantially equal amounts each month. Y's distributive share of X's loss for its taxable year ended December 31, 1976, 1200x dollars, was allocated to Y's partners at year end as follows:

Partner	Profits and Losses Percentage	Distributive Share of Loss
B	15	180x
C	60	720x
D	25	300x
Totals	100 percent	1200x dollars

As shown above, the 1200x dollars loss was retroactively allocated to the partners for the entire year based on their profit and loss sharing percentages on December 31, 1976, even though D was a partner for only 1 month.

Section 702(a) of the Code provides the general rule that in determining a partner's income tax, the partner shall take into account separately such partner's distributive share of partnership items of income, gain, loss, deduction, or credit.

Section 704(d) of the Code, which provides a limitation on the allowance of a partner's distributive share of partnership loss, does not apply with respect to any activity to the extent that section 465 (relating to amounts at risk in certain activities) applies, nor does it apply to any partnership, the principal activity of which (as in the instant case) is investing in real property (other than mineral property).

Section 706(a) of the Code provides, in part, that in computing the taxable income of a partner for a taxable year, the inclusions required by section 702 with respect to a partnership shall be based on the income, gain, loss, deduction, or credit of the partnership for any taxable year of the partnership ending within or with the taxable year of the partner.

The language of section 706(a) of the Code does not mean that Y's distributive share of X's loss was sustained by Y on December 31, 1976. That language merely describes in which taxable year the partnership items shall be included in the taxable income of a partner.

Section 706(c)(2)(B) of the Code provides, in part, that the taxable year of a partnership shall not close (other than at the end of a partnership's taxable year) with respect to a partner whose interest is reduced (whether by entry of a new partner, partial liquidation of a partner's interest, gift, or otherwise), but such partner's distributive share of items described in section 702(a) shall be determined by taking into account such partner's varying interests in the partnership during the taxable year.

The report of the Senate Finance Committee on the Tax Reform Act of 1976, *S. Rep. No. 94–938*, 94th Cong., 2d Sess. 96–97 (1976), 1976–3

C.B. (Vol. 3) 134–135, states, in part, that while not specifically stated in section 706(c)(2)(B) of the Code or the relevant regulations, it is implicit that the transferee of less than the entire interest of the transferor-partner would necessarily be subject to the same rule as the transferor. This means that the transferee-partner's distributive share of partnership income and loss would be determined by taking into account the transferee-partner's varying interests in the partnership during the year. The report also states that in order to deal with the problem of retroactive allocations and clarify the treatment of a partner's interest where the partner acquired the interest directly from the partnership, the committee amendment specifically denies retroactive allocations and provides that the present varying interests rule is to apply to a partner's interest acquired directly from the partnership.

The import of section 706(c)(2)(B) of the Code is that partners whose interests are changed will not be allocated income they have not realized nor losses they have not sustained. This same principle applies even when a partnership (Y in this case) is itself a partner in a second partnership (X in this case). Further, Y's distributive share of any items of income gain, loss, deduction, or credit of X would be considered to be realized or sustained by Y at the same time and in the same manner as such items were realized or sustained by X. Thus, the partners of Y are considered to have sustained that portion of their distributive shares of Y's loss (which consists of X's loss distributed to Y) at the same time and in the same manner that the loss was considered to be sustained by Y.

Accordingly, in the instant case, since the method of computing the partners' distributive shares of Y's partnership loss did not take into account the existing partners' and the new partner's varying interests in Y during the year, the method used is not a proper method for purposes of section 706(c)(2)(B) of the Code.

An acceptable method in the instant case, for purposes of section 706(c)(2)(B) of the Code, is to allocate the partnership's items among the partners based on their differing profit and loss sharing percentages and the periods during the year each partner's differing percentage interests existed. Thus, for example, D would be allocated a distributive share of the partnership loss only for the period (1 month) that D was a partner. In the instant case, the partners would have computed their distributive shares of the $1200x$ dollars loss as follows:

Partner	Profit/Loss Percentages	Months Held	Computations	Distributive Shares of Loss
B	20	11	11/12 x 20/100 x 1200 =	$220x$
	15	1	1/12 x 15/100 x 1200 =	$15x$
C	80	11	11/12 x 80/100 x 1200 =	$880x$
	60	1	1/12 x 60/100 x 1200 =	$60x$
D	25	1	1/12 x 25/100 x 1200 =	$25x$

Total loss $1200x$ dollars

Practice:

1. Read Regulation 1.704–3(a)(9) and determine the tax consequences under the following circumstances:

A and B form partnership AB. Partners allocate all items equally, except as otherwise required under IRC 704. A contributes Asset 1 with an adjusted basis of $40,000 and a fair market value of $100,000. B contributes $100,000. Partnership AB contributes its assets to partnership ABC. C contributes $200,000 to partnership ABC. ABC sells Asset 1 for $150,000.

2. Read Regulations 1.752–2(i) and 1.752–4(a) and determine the tax consequences under the following circumstances:

A and B form AB, a limited partnership in which A is the general partner and B is the limited partner. A and B contributed $5000 each and allocate all items equally. ABC is a general partnership to which AB contributed $10,000 and is an 80% general partner, C contributed $2,000 and is a 20% general partner. ABC borrows $100,000 of recourse debt to purchase Asset 1 for $112,000. None of the limited partners have deficit reduction obligations (though the agreement contains a QIO). How much of the debt is allocated to partnership AB and to partners A, B, and C? How would the consequences differ if B unconditionally agreed to reimburse C if C is required to pay any portion of the liability?

3. Read Regulations 1.708–1(b)(2) and consider the following hypothetical (borrowed from an examples in the ALI study cited earlier at page 519):

A and B are partners in Partnership AB, which is a 70% partner in partnership ABCD. A and B each own 50% of Partnership A and B. If A sells his interest to E on June 1, what result to Partnership AB? What result to Partnership ABCD? What result to both partnerships if alternatively B sells 50% of his interest in AB to E on June 1, 2005 and the remaining 50% to F on July 4, 2006?

*

Appendix 1

JOINT VENTURE AGREEMENT BY AND BETWEEN COLUMBIA JACKSONVILLE HEALTHCARE SYSTEM, INC., JACKSONVILLE HEALTH GROUP, INC., AND UNIVERSITY MEDICAL CENTER, INC.

TABLE OF CONTENTS

JOINT VENTURE AGREEMENT

This Joint Venture Agreement is made and entered into as of March 26, 1996, by and between Columbia Jacksonville Healthcare System, Inc. ("Columbia/Jacksonville"), a Florida corporation, Jacksonville Health Group, Inc. ("JHG"), a Florida not-for-profit corporation, and University Medical Center, Inc. ("UMC"), a Florida not-for-profit corporation (JHG and UMC are hereinafter referred to collectively as "JHG/UMC").

WITNESSETH:

WHEREAS, Columbia/Jacksonville and its affiliates directly or indirectly own all or a controlling interest in Memorial Healthcare Group, Inc. ("MHG"), a Florida corporation, Galen of Florida, Inc. ("GFI"), a Florida corporation, Jacksonville Surgery Center, Ltd. ("JSC"), a Florida limited partnership, Doctors' Specialty Surgery Center of Jacksonville, Ltd. ("DSC"), Memorial Surgicare, Ltd. ("MSC"), a Florida limited partnership, San Pablo Surgery Center, Ltd., a Florida limited partnership ("SPSC"), Surgicare of Orange Park, Ltd. ("SCOP"), a Florida limited partnership, and Westside Surgery Center, Ltd. ("WSC"), a Florida limited partnership; and

WHEREAS, MHG owns and operates Memorial Hospital of Jacksonville and Memorial Specialty Hospital located in Jacksonville, Florida and certain other healthcare facilities and operations in connection therewith (collectively, the "Jacksonville Memorial Facilities"); and

WHEREAS, MHG is a general partner and owns a controlling interest in JSC and DSC, which each own and operate an ambulatory surgery center located in Jacksonville, Florida; and

WHEREAS, Surgicare Corporation, an indirectly wholly owned subsidiary of Columbia/HCA Healthcare Corporation ("Columbia/HCA") and affiliate of Columbia/Jacksonville, is a general partner and owns a controlling interest in MSC, which owns and operates an ambulatory surgery center located in Jacksonville, Florida; and

WHEREAS, MHG is a special limited partner and owns a minority interest in SPSC, which owns and operates San Pablo Surgery Center located in Jacksonville, Florida; and

WHEREAS, GFI owns and operates Orange Park Medical Center located in Orange Park, Florida and certain other healthcare facilities and operations in connection therewith (collectively, the "Orange Park Facilities"); and

WHEREAS, Surgicare of Orange Park, Inc., an indirectly wholly owned subsidiary of Columbia/HCA and affiliate of Columbia/Jacksonville, is a general partner and owns a controlling interest in SCOP, which owns and operates an ambulatory surgery center in Orange Park, Florida; and

WHEREAS, Paragon WSC, Inc., an indirectly wholly owned subsidiary of Columbia/HCA and affiliate of Columbia/Jacksonville, is a general partner and owns a controlling interest in WSC, which owns and operates an ambulatory surgery center in Orange Park, Florida ("WSC", and together with SCOP, the "Orange Park Surgery Centers"); and

(The Jacksonville Memorial Facilities, Jacksonville Surgery Center, Single Day Surgery Center, Memorial Surgery Center, San Pablo Surgery Center, the Orange Park Facilities, and the Orange Park Surgery Centers are sometimes hereinafter referred to collectively as the "Columbia/Jacksonville Related Facilities"); and

WHEREAS, JHG maintains certain rights and reserved powers regarding the governance and operation of UMC and additionally is a recognized support organization acting on behalf of UMC; and

WHEREAS, UMC leases from the City of Jacksonville, Florida and operates University Medical Center located in Jacksonville, Florida, and operates certain other facilities and operations in connection therewith (collectively, the "JHG/UMC Facilities"); and

WHEREAS, JHG is the sole owner of First Coast Enterprises, Inc., a Florida for profit corporation (JHG, UMC and First Coast Enterprises, Inc. are hereinafter referred to collectively as the "JHG/UMC Entities"); and

WHEREAS, the JHG/UMC Entities provide broad access to health care services to residents of First Coast Area, including services to indigent residents, pursuant to the Indigent Care Contract (as hereinafter defined), consistent with the prior operation of University Medical Center by the City of Jacksonville under the name of University Hospital of Jacksonville; and

WHEREAS, the JHG/UMC Entities continue the teaching mission of UMC, which was initiated in 1926 with the establishment at the hospital of Florida's first medical residents program, as evidenced by the Affiliation Agreement (as hereinafter defined) with the University of Florida; and

WHEREAS, the Columbia/Jacksonville Related Facilities and the JHG/UMC Facilities (collectively, the "Facilities") provide healthcare services in Baker, Clay, Duval, Nassau and St. John's Counties of Florida (collectively, the "First Coast Area"); and

WHEREAS, JHG/UMC, after witnessing the formation of several multi-hospital health care provider networks in the First Coast region, has concluded that participation in a geographically disbursed integrated health care delivery system is the best method for assuring the continuation of the JHG/UMC Entities' health care and teaching missions;

WHEREAS, JHG/UMC, after considering a number of affiliation opportunities, has determined that a joint venture with Columbia/Jacksonville presents the best opportunity for the

JHG/UMC Entities to participate in a geographically disbursed integrated health care delivery system; and

WHEREAS, JHG/UMC has determined that their health care and teaching missions will be perpetuated by the formation of a joint venture with the Columbia/Jacksonville; and

WHEREAS, Columbia/HCA Healthcare Corporation, Columbia/Jacksonville, JHG and UMC entered into a letter of intent wherein they expressed their intention to form a joint venture to integrate the provision of healthcare services in the First Coast Area through the Facilities and such other facilities as they or the contemplated joint venture may hereafter acquire.

NOW, THEREFORE, for and in consideration of the mutual promises, covenants and undertakings hereinafter contained, and other good and valuable consideration, the receipt and sufficiency of which are acknowledged, the Columbia/Jacksonville and JHG/UMC agree as follows:

1.   <u>Definitions</u>.

As used herein, the following terms have the following meanings:

1.1.   "<u>Acquiring Joint Venturer</u>" shall have the meaning set forth in <u>Section 1.44</u>.

1.2.   "<u>Act</u>" means the Florida Uniform Partnership Act, as amended from time to time.

1.3.   "<u>Additional Facility</u>" shall have the meaning set forth in <u>Section 1.44</u>.

1.4.   "<u>Additional Joint Venturer</u>" means a Person who is admitted to the Joint Venture pursuant to the terms of <u>Section 12</u>.

1.5.   "<u>Affiliation Agreement</u>" means that certain Affiliation Agreement dated September 2, 1988 by and among JHG, UMC and the University of Florida.

1.6.   "<u>Agreement</u>" means this Joint Venture Agreement, as amended from time to time pursuant to <u>Section 27.14</u>.

1.7.   "<u>Approval of the Governing Board</u>," "<u>Approved by the Governing Board</u>" or similar phrase means approval by the Category A Governors and by the Category B Governors. The Category A Governors and the Category B Governors shall each vote as a block.

1.8.   "<u>Bankruptcy</u>" means, as to any Joint Venturer, the Joint Venturer's taking or acquiescing to the taking of any action seeking relief under, or advantage of, any applicable debtor relief, liquidation, receivership, conservatorship, bankruptcy, moratorium, rearrangement, insolvency, reorganization or similar law affecting the rights or remedies of creditors generally, as in effect from time to time. For the purpose of this definition, the term "acquiescing" shall include, without limitation, the failure to file, within thirty (30) days after its entry, a petition, answer or motion to dismiss, vacate or to discharge any petition, order, judgment or decree providing for any relief under any such law.

1.9.   "Capital Account" means a capital account to be established for each Joint Venturer (or transferee of a Joint Venturer who is not admitted to the Joint Venture as a Joint Venturer, provided that the maintenance of such Capital Account will not constitute the admission of the transferee as a Substituted or Additional Joint Venturer) which shall be (i) credited with a) the amount of Capital Contribution and the initial Gross Market Value of property contributed to the Joint Venture by such Person, b) any Profit allocated to such Person, c) any items in the nature of income and gain which are specially allocated under Sections 5.3 and 5.4 hereof, and d) the amount of any Joint Venture liabilities that are assumed by such Person or that are secured by any Joint Venture property distributed to such Person and (ii) debited with a) the amount of cash and the Gross Market Value (as determined at the time of distribution) of any property distributed to such Person by the Joint Venture, b) any Loss allocated to such Person, c) any items in the nature of expenses and losses that are specially allocated under Sections 5.3 and 5.4, and d) the amount of any liabilities of such Joint Venturer that are assumed by the Joint Venture or that are secured by any property contributed by such Person to the Joint Venture. In the event any Joint Venturer transfers its interest in the Joint Venture in accordance with the terms of this Agreement, the transferee shall succeed to the Capital Account of the transferor Joint Venturer to the extent such Capital Account relates to such transferred interest. In determining the amount of any liability for purposes of this Section 1.10 there shall be taken into account Code section 752(c) and any other applicable provisions of the Code and Regulations.

1.10.   "Capital Contribution" means, as to any Joint Venturer, the amount of cash or the Gross Market Value of all property contributed to the Joint Venture by the Joint Venturer, the initial contribution being set forth opposite such Joint Venturer's name on the attached Exhibit "A" under the heading "Capital Contribution."

1.11.   "Category A Governors" means those members of the Governing Board elected or appointed from time to time by JHG/UMC. The number of Category A Governors shall be five (5).

1.12.   "Category B Governors" means those members of the Governing Board elected or appointed from time to time by Columbia/Jacksonville. The number of Category B Governors shall be five (5).

1.13.   "Code" means the Internal Revenue Code of 1986, as amended from time to time (or any corresponding provisions of succeeding law).

1.14.   "Columbia/HCA" means Columbia/HCA Healthcare Corporation, a Delaware corporation, and any successor in interest.

1.15. "Columbia/HCA Affiliate" means any corporation or other entity which is connected with Columbia/HCA through one or more corporations or other entities linked through a fifty percent (50%) or greater ownership, or any partnership (general or limited) or limited liability company or tiers of partnerships or limited liability companies of which Columbia/HCA Affiliates are the sole general partners or have a fifty percent (50%) or greater general partnership or limited liability company interest therein or which is otherwise Controlled by Columbia/HCA, irrespective of any ownership interest in the Joint Venture.

1.16. "Columbia/Jacksonville Related Entities" means Columbia Jacksonville Healthcare System, Inc., Memorial Healthcare Group, Inc., Galen of Florida, Inc., Jacksonville Surgery Center, Ltd., Doctors' Specialty Surgery Center of Jacksonville, Ltd., Memorial Surgicare, Ltd., San Pablo Surgery Center, Ltd., Surgicare of Orange Park, Ltd., Westside Surgery Center, Ltd., and their respective successors in interest.

1.17. "Control" or "Controlled" means the legal right or practical capability to direct or determine (directly or indirectly) the policies, management or activities of an entity, regardless of whether such right or capability arises out of an ownership interest, a contractual arrangement, or any other relationship. Ownership (directly or indirectly) of fifty percent (50%) or more of the equity or voting interests in an entity shall be conclusively presumed to constitute Control; however, a lesser ownership percentage of equity or voting interests may also constitute Control in appropriate circumstances. For purposes of determining Control, a person or entity shall be treated as owning any interest in a subject entity which, if the interest was stock and the subject entity was a corporation, would be treated as constructively owned by such person or entity under section 1563(e) of the Code.

1.18. "Depreciation" means, for federal income tax purposes, for each Joint Venture fiscal year or other Joint Venture period, an amount equal to the depreciation, amortization or other cost recovery deduction allowable with respect to a Joint Venture asset for such year or other period. If the Joint Venture asset's adjusted basis for federal income tax purposes differs from its Gross Market Value at the beginning of such year or other period, Depreciation shall be an amount which bears the same ratio to such beginning Gross Market Value as the federal income tax depreciation, amortization or other cost recovery deduction for such year or other period bears to such beginning adjusted tax basis. If, however, the federal income tax depreciation, amortization or other cost recovery deduction for such year is zero, Depreciation shall be determined with reference to such beginning Gross Market Value using any reasonable method selected by the Manager.

1.19. "Direct Corporate Chain" means ownership, directly or through a subsidiary, of any of the voting securities of the Person in question.

1.20. "EBDITA" shall be calculated in accordance with Schedule 1.20.

1.21. "Economic Risk of Loss" shall have the meaning set forth in Section 1.752-2 of the Regulations.

–5–

1.22.   "Excess Cash Flow" means Net Cash Flow less a reserve for contingencies Approved by the Governing Board and a reserve for other commitments necessary for future operations approved by the Governing Board.

1.23.   "Expansion Expenditures" shall have the meaning set forth in Section 7.1.

1.24.   "Facilities" means the hospitals (including the Hospitals) and all outpatient surgery and other facilities (including with limitation the Jacksonville Surgery Center, the Single Day Surgery Center and the Orange Park Surgery Centers), clinics, medical office buildings, rural health clinics, community health centers, management service organizations, and other healthcare facilities now owned or hereafter acquired by the Joint Venture or any of the Joint Venturers and located in the First Coast Area, except as provided in Section 1.46.

1.25.   "Final Percentage" shall have the meaning set forth in Section 14.6.

1.26.   "First Coast Area" means the area included within any of the following Florida counties: Baker, Clay, Duval, Nassau and St. John's.

1.27.   "Generally Accepted Accounting Principles" or "GAAP" means those principles of accounting set forth in pronouncements of the Financial Accounting Standards Board and, to the extent not inconsistent therewith, the American Institute of Certified Public Accountants, historically applied on a consistent basis. All financial accounting terms not otherwise defined in this Agreement shall be presumed to have the meaning ascribed to them by GAAP unless the context clearly requires otherwise.

1.28.   "Governing Board" shall have the meaning set forth in Section 10.2(a).

1.29.   "Gross Market Value" means, with respect to any Joint Venture asset, the adjusted basis of such asset for federal income tax purposes, except as follows:

(a) the initial Gross Market Value of any asset contributed by a Joint Venturer to the Joint Venture shall be the gross fair market value of such asset as determined by the contributing Joint Venturer and the Governing Board;

(b) the Gross Market Value of all Joint Venture assets shall be adjusted to equal their respective gross fair market values, as determined by the Manager, as of the following times:

(i) the acquisition of an additional interest in the Joint Venture by any new or existing Joint Venturer in exchange for more than a de minimis capital contribution;

(ii) the distribution by the Joint Venture to a Joint Venturer of more than a de minimis amount of Joint Venture assets as consideration for the disposition of an interest in the Joint Venture; and

(iii) the liquidation of the Joint Venture within the meaning of Section 1.704-1(b)(2)(ii) of the Regulations.

(c) If the Gross Market Value of an asset has been determined or adjusted as provided in this Section 1.29, the Gross Market Value of the respective asset shall thereafter be adjusted by the Depreciation taken into account with respect to the asset for purposes of computing Profit and Loss;

(d) The Gross Market Value of any Joint Venture asset distributed to any Joint Venturer shall be the gross fair market value of the distributed asset, as proposed by the Manager and Approved by the Governing Board, on the date of distribution; and

(e) The Gross Market Value of any Joint Venture assets shall be increased (or decreased) to reflect any adjustments to the adjusted basis of the Joint Venture assets pursuant to Code section 732, Code section 734(b) or Code section 743(b), but only to the extent that such adjustments are taken into account in determining the Joint Venture's Capital Accounts pursuant to Regulations Section 1.704-1 (b)(2)(iv)(m). The Gross Market Value of the Joint Venture's assets shall not, however, be adjusted under this Section 1.29(e) to the extent that the Manager determines that an adjustment pursuant to Section 1.29(b) is necessary or appropriate in connection with a transaction that would otherwise result in an adjustment pursuant to this Section 1.29(e).

1.30.   "Hospitals" means Memorial Hospital of Jacksonville, Memorial Specialty Hospital, Orange Park Medical Center and University Medical Center, together with any other hospitals subsequently acquired by any of the Joint Venturers or by the Joint Venture, but excluding any hospital that is no longer owned by any of the Joint Venturers or the Joint Venture located in the First Coast Area. "Hospital" means any one of the Hospitals.

1.31.   "Indigent Care Contract" means that certain Amended Agreement dated March 25, 1988 by and between UMC and the City of Jacksonville, Florida, as amended.

1.32.   "Interim Management Services Agreement" means the Interim Management Services Agreement among Columbia/Jacksonville and JHG/UMC, a copy of which is attached hereto as Exhibit B, and with respect to any Additional Facility which may hereafter be acquired by any JHG/UMC Entity or any JHG/UMC Affiliate, the interim management agreement among JHG/UMC, such JHG/UMC Entity or JHG/UMC Affiliate, and the Manager with respect thereto.

1.33. "JHG/UMC" means Jacksonville Health Group, Inc. and University Medical Center, Inc., and their respective successors and assigns.

1.34. "JHG/UMC Affiliate" means any corporation or other entity which is connected with JHG or UMC through one or more corporations or other entities linked through fifty percent (50%) or greater ownership, or any partnership (general or limited) or limited liability company or tiers of partnerships or limited liability companies of which a JHG/UMC Affiliate is the sole general partner or has a fifty percent (50%) or greater general partnership or limited liability company interest therein or which is otherwise Controlled by JHG or UMC, irrespective of any ownership interest in the Joint Venture.

1.35. "JHG/UMC Entities" means Jacksonville Health Group, Inc., University Medical Center, Inc. and First Coast Enterprises, Inc., and their respective successors in interest.

1.36. "Joint Venture" means the joint venture formed and continued under this Agreement.

1.37. "Joint Venture Equalizing Payments" shall have the meaning set forth in Section 8.

1.38. "Joint Venture Minimum Gain" means the amount determined in accordance with the principals of Section 1.704-2(d) of the Regulations.

1.39. "Joint Venture Nonrecourse Debt" has the meaning set forth in Section 1.704-2(b)(4) of the Regulations.

1.40. "Joint Venture Nonrecourse Deductions" means any and all items of loss, deduction or expenditure (including any expenditure described in Section 705(a)(2)(B) of the Code) that, in accordance with the principles of Section 1.704-2(i) of the Regulations, are attributable to a Joint Venture Nonrecourse Debt.

1.41. "Joint Venture Stage II Commencement Date" shall have the meaning set forth in Section 18.1.

1.42. "Joint Venture Termination Payments" shall have the meaning set forth in Section 15.8.

1.43. "Joint Venturers" means Columbia/Jacksonville and JHG/UMC, and any Substituted Joint Venturers and Additional Joint Venturers.

1.44. "Sharing Percentage" means

     (a)   With respect to Columbia/Jacksonville (subject to decrease to the extent Columbia/Jacksonville fails to make any capital contribution required under this Agreement, subject to decrease to the extent provided in subsection (c), and subject to increase or decrease pursuant to the last paragraphs of this Section 1.44), seventy-eight percent (78%).

(b)   With respect to JHG/UMC (subject to decrease to the extent JHG/UMC fails to make any capital contribution required under this Agreement, subject to increase to the extent provided in subsection (c), and subject to increase or decrease to the extent provided in the last paragraphs of this Section 1.44), twenty-two percent (22%).

(c)   The parties shall reevaluate their respective Sharing Percentages on the Joint Venture Stage II Commencement Date based on the financial performance of the JHG/UMC Facilities and the Columbia/Jacksonville Related Facilities for the twelve (12) full calendar months immediately preceding the Joint Venture Stage II Commencement Date according to the formula set forth in Schedule 1.44 (the "Lookback Valuation"). In the event the Lookback Valuation determines, based on unaudited financial statements prepared in accordance with the Manager's accounting policies and procedures consistently and commonly applied, but at all times according to GAAP, that the Sharing Percentage of JHG/UMC should be less than twenty-two percent (22%), JHG/UMC may elect i) to terminate this Agreement, or ii) to proceed with the Closing, in which case its Sharing Percentage shall be not less than twenty-two percent (22%). In the event such Lookback Valuation determines that the Sharing Percentage of JHG/UMC should be twenty-two percent (22%) or greater, the Sharing Percentage of JHG/UMC shall be as determined by the Lookback Valuation based on audited financial information prepared in accordance with the Manager's accounting policies and procedures consistently and commonly applied, but at all times according to GAAP, but in no event shall the Sharing Percentage of JHG/UMC be less than twenty-two percent (22%). In the event the Joint Venture Stage II Commencement Date would otherwise occur prior to June 30, 1997, JHG/UMC may elect by written notice to Columbia/Jacksonville to defer the Joint Venture Stage II Commencement Date to June 30, 1997. The parties will provide to one another all financial information necessary to perform the Lookback Valuation promptly, but in no event later than thirty (30) days with respect to unaudited financial information and ninety (90) days with respect to audited financial information after the date on which the Joint Venture Stage II Commencement Date shall be effective. The parties will each bear their own costs associated with the preparation of the audited financial information. In the event that any party is dissatisfied with the Sharing Percentages determined by the Lookback Valuation, such party shall notify the other parties in writing of its dissatisfaction, specify the reasons for its dissatisfaction, propose alternate Sharing Percentages, and provide financial and other information supporting their proposed Sharing Percentages, all within ten (10) days after receipt of the Lookback Valuation. In the event the other parties do not accept such proposed alternate Sharing Percentages within ten (10) days of receipt of such notice or the parties are not otherwise able to mutually agree on the Sharing Percentages, then the Chairman of the Board of JHG, the Chairman of the Board of UMC and the Chairman of the Board of Columbia (together, the "Chairmen") shall promptly meet to negotiate the Sharing Percentages. In the event the Chairmen are unable to agree on Sharing Percentages within ten (10) days, such inability to agree shall be deemed a "Material Dispute" and shall be resolved pursuant to Section 10.7.

Notwithstanding the foregoing, each Joint Venturer's Sharing Percentage will be subject to renegotiation in the event that the Indigent Care Contract, or UMC's responsibility thereunder, is modified in such a manner as to increase or decrease materially the aggregate EBDITA of the JHG/UMC Facilities before Joint Venture Equalizing Payments. Such a renegotiation of each Joint Venturer's Sharing Percentage shall include measurement of the increase or decrease in the EBDITA of the JHG/UMC Facilities.

Further notwithstanding the foregoing, each Joint Venturer's Sharing Percentage will be subject to renegotiation in the event that a) there is a material increase or decrease in the aggregate EBDITA of the Columbia/Jacksonville Related Facilities before Joint Venture Equalizing Payments, b) such material increase or decrease occurs as a result of i) Medicare reimbursement to Memorial Specialty Hospital being modified from cost-reimbursement, ii) payments by Genesis Health, Inc. ("Genesis") to Memorial Hospital of Jacksonville under that certain Shared Services Agreement dated August 21, 1995, and/or iii) Medicare disallowances of cost allocations from Memorial Hospital of Jacksonville to Genesis being imposed, and c) in the event of a material decrease, the affected Columbia/Jacksonville Related Facilities are not able to substantially offset such decrease with changes in their respective operations. Such a renegotiation of each Joint Venturer's Sharing Percentage shall include measurement of the increase or decrease in the aggregate EBDITA of the Columbia/Jacksonville Related Facilities.

Further notwithstanding the foregoing, each Joint Venturer's Sharing Percentage also will be subject to renegotiation for a period of ten (10) years from the date hereof if as a result of modifications to State Formulae which currently regulate payments under the State of Florida's regular Medicaid Disproportionate Share Program or other action by state or federal regulatory agencies there is a reduction equal to or greater than ten percent (10%) of UMC's current reimbursement "match portion" (approximately $14,000,000 for fiscal year 1995) under such program. Renegotiation of each Joint Venturer's Sharing Percentage under this paragraph is inclusive of replacement reimbursement funds (whether from Federal, State, or other sources) and is also inclusive of operational changes which may serve to financially offset the impact of the reduction in reimbursement ("Net Effect"). UMC is required to demonstrate to the Columbia/Jacksonville Related Entities the Net Effect no later than one hundred and twenty (120) days from the close of the fiscal year in which such reduction occurs, and adjustment to the Joint Venturers' Sharing Percentages shall be effective as of the first day of the fiscal year following the year in which such reduction occurs.

In addition to the foregoing, any healthcare facility or other healthcare business located in the First Coast Area which is acquired by a Joint Venturer (an "Acquiring Joint Venturer") after

July 25, 1995 but prior to the Joint Venture Stage II Commencement Date, other than the CareOne and Olsten home healthcare facilities and the Orange Park Surgery Center owned and operated by Surgicare of Orange Park, Ltd. which were acquired after July 25, 1995 but which are already included herein (an "Additional Facility") shall be included in the Joint Venture. Unless the other Joint Venturer (the "Non-Acquiring Joint Venturer") elects to maintain its respective Sharing Percentages, each Joint Venturer's Sharing Percentage shall be adjusted proportionately to reflect the consideration paid by the Acquiring Joint Venturer (the "Purchase Price") for such Additional Facility. Such election must be made at the time such an acquisition is consummated; provided a Joint Venturer shall not be required to make such an election unless it has received all information it may reasonably request in respect thereof. The Non-Acquiring Joint Venturer may prevent its Sharing Percentage from being so reduced by making a cash payment to the Acquiring Joint Venturer equal to (i) the Non-Acquiring Joint Venturer's Sharing Percentage times the Purchase Price, plus (ii) interest thereon at the prime rate, as quoted from time to time by NationsBank of Florida, N.A., plus two (2) percentage points from the date such Additional Facility was acquired by the Acquiring Joint Venturer to but not including the Joint Venture Stage II Commencement Date. The Non-Acquiring Joint Venturer desiring to maintain its Sharing Percentage must make such payment at the Closing. Notwithstanding the foregoing, no such acquisition shall be made a part of the Facilities if the effect of such acquisition would be to reduce the Sharing Percentage of JHG/UMC to less than twenty percent (20%) or, if such acquisition occurs subsequent to the maturity of the Refunding Loan and the Refunding Loan was not fully repaid resulting in a reduction of the JHG/UMC Sharing Percentage, such acquisition shall be not be made a part of the Facilities if the cumulative effect of such acquisition and other acquisitions subsequent to the maturity of the Refunding Loan would be to further reduce the Sharing Percentage of JHG/UMC by more than two (2) percentage points. If as a result of the provisions of the preceding sentence, such proposed Additional Facility is not included in the Joint Venture, the Acquiring Joint Venturer may own and operate such facility without the restrictions imposed under the terms of the covenant not to compete set forth in Section 24.

1.45. "Liquidator" means the Person who liquidates the Joint Venture under Section 14.1 hereof.

1.46. "Manager" means the person or entity managing the JHG/UMC Facilities pursuant to the Interim Management Services Agreement and the Management Services Agreement. Initially, the Manager shall be Columbia/Jacksonville.

1.47. "Management Services Agreement" means the Management Services Agreement among the JHG/UMC Entities and the Manager, a copy of which is attached hereto as Exhibit "C", and, with respect to any healthcare facilities which may hereafter be acquired by the Joint Venture, any JHG/UMC Entity or any JHG/UMC Affiliate, the management services agreements between the Joint Venture. JHG/UMC or such Person, as the case may be, and the Manager with respect thereto.

-11-

1.48. "Material Dispute" means a dispute as to which one Category of Governors has notified in writing the other Category of Governors that a dispute is material.

1.49. "Net Cash Flow" means, for each fiscal year, the net income of the Joint Venture (and not for the respective Joint Venturers), plus depreciation and amortization and debt proceeds less capital expenditures and debt repayments, all as determined in accordance with GAAP.

1.50. "Net Effect" shall have the meaning set forth in Section 1.44.

1.51. "Non-Acquiring Joint Venturer" shall have the meaning set forth in Section 1.44.

1.52. "Nonrecourse Deductions" means any and all items of loss, deduction or expenditures (described in Section 705(a)(2)(B) of the Code), that, in accordance with the principals of Section 1.704-2(c) of the Regulations, are attributable to a Nonrecourse Liability.

1.53. "Nonrecourse Liability" has the meaning set forth in Section 1.752-1(a)(2) of the Regulations.

1.54. "On-Campus Expansion Facilities" shall have the meaning set forth in Section 7.1.

1.55. "Person" means any individual, partnership, corporation, trust or other entity.

1.56. "Profits and Losses" means for each fiscal-year or other period an amount equal to the taxable income or loss of the Joint Venture (and specifically not income or loss for the respective Joint Venturers) for such year or period, determined in accordance with section 703(a) of the Code (for this purpose, all items of income, gain, loss, or deduction required to be stated separately pursuant to section 703(a)(1) of the Code shall be included in taxable income or loss), with the following adjustments:

    (a)   Any income of the Joint Venture that is exempt from federal income tax and not otherwise taken into account in computing Profits or Losses pursuant to this Section 1.56 shall be added to such taxable income or loss;

    (b)   Any expenditures of the Joint Venture described in section 705(a)(2)(B) of the Code or treated as Code section 705(a)(2)(B) expenditures pursuant to Sections 1.704-1(b)(2)(iv)(1) and 1.704-2(j) and (i)(1) of the Regulations and not otherwise taken into account in computing Profits or Losses pursuant to this Section 1.56 shall be subtracted from such taxable income or loss;

    (c)   In the event the Gross Market Value of any Joint Venture asset is adjusted pursuant to Section 1.29 hereof, the amount of such adjustment shall be taken into account as gain or loss from the disposition of such asset for purposes of computing

Profits or Losses, and shall be allocated to each Joint Venturer's Capital Account in accordance with the allocation percentages in effect immediately prior to the event giving rise to such adjustment;

      (d)   Gain or loss resulting from any disposition of property with respect to which gain or loss is recognized for federal income tax purposes shall be computed by reference to the Gross Market. Value of the property disposed of, notwithstanding that the adjusted tax basis of such property differs from its Gross Market Value;

      (e)   In lieu of the depreciation, amortization, and other cost recovery deductions taken into account in computing such taxable income or loss, there shall be taken into account Depreciation for such fiscal year or other period, computed in accordance with Section 1.18 hereof; and

      1.57.   "Purchase Price" shall have the meaning set forth in Section 1.44 hereof.

      1.58.   "Refunding Loan" means the secured loan to be provided to University Medical Center, Inc. by Columbia/HCA or a Columbia/HCA Affiliate as provided in Section 4.3(b).

      1.59.   "Substituted Joint Venturer" means a Person who is admitted to the Joint Venture pursuant to the terms of Section 13,

      1.60.   "Tax Matters General Partner" means Columbia/Jacksonville or any replacement Tax Matters General Partner in the Joint Venture, but excluding any Person who ceased to be the Tax Matters General Partner in the Joint Venture pursuant to this Agreement.

      1.61.   "Total Final EBDITA" shall have the meaning set forth in Section 14.6.

      1.62.   "Treasury Regulations" or "Regulations" means Income Tax Regulations, including Temporary Regulations, promulgated under the Code, as such regulations may be amended from time to time (including corresponding provisions in succeeding regulations).

      1.63.   "UMC Lease" shall mean that certain Amended and Restated Lease Agreement dated December 15, 1987 by and between University Medical Center, Inc. and the Duval County Hospital Authority.

      1.64.   "UMC Tax Exempt Bonds" means Hospital Revenue Bonds, Series 1988, Series 1989, and Series 1992, inclusive.

      1.65.   "Unmatured Expansion Assets" shall have the meaning set forth in Section 7.1.

2.   Formation of Joint Venture

2.1.   Formation. JHG/UMC and Columbia/Jacksonville hereby form a joint venture on the terms and conditions, and for the specific and limited purposes, set forth in this Agreement. Except as otherwise set forth in this Agreement, the Act shall govern the rights and liabilities of the Joint Venturers. Notwithstanding the other provisions hereof, prior to the Joint Venture Stage II Commencement Date:

   (a)   the activities of the Joint Venture shall be limited to (i) the activity of the Governing Board specified in Section 10.2 for the period prior to the Joint Venture Stage II Commencement Date, and (ii) the activities and responsibilities provided for in the Interim Management Services Agreement; and

   (b)   (i) the proceeds of the UMC Tax Exempt Bonds will be used in accordance with the Bond Restrictions; (ii) the JHG/UMC Facilities will be operated and controlled in accordance with the Bond Restrictions; and (iii) the assets of JHG/UMC will remain subject to the lien and security interest, if any, created by or pursuant to the Bond Restrictions.

The term "Bond Restrictions" means applicable bond document restrictions contained in the indentures, security instruments and agreements related to the UMC Tax Exempt Bonds and the limitations on private business use under Sections 103 and 141 through 150 of the Code, applicable provisions of Florida law and applicable state and federal regulations.

2.2.   Name. The Joint Venture shall be conducted under such name as may be Approved by the Governing Board from time to time.

2.3.   Principal Office. The principal office of the Joint Venture shall be located at 3627 University Boulevard, Jacksonville, Florida 32218, or at such other place or places as the Governing Board may from time to time determine.

2.4.   Term. The Joint Venture shall begin on the date hereof (the "Joint Venture Commencement Date") and shall continue until the earlier of (a) the expiration or earlier termination of the UMC Lease (including any renewals and extensions thereof), or (b) the date on which the Joint Venture is dissolved pursuant to Section 13, and thereafter, to the extent provided for by applicable law, until wound up and terminated pursuant to Section 14 hereof.

3.   Purposes and Powers of the Joint Venture: Nature of the Business of the Joint Venture

3.1.   Purposes. The purposes of the Joint Venture are (i) to submit to common management those Facilities which are owned and/or operated by the Joint Venturers, (ii) to own, manage, operate, lease and take any action in connection with operating the Facilities which may hereafter be owned and/or operated by the Joint Venture; (iii) to acquire (through asset acquisition, stock acquisition, lease or otherwise) and develop other property, both real and personal, in connection with providing healthcare related services, including without limitation, general acute care hospitals, specialty care hospitals, surgery centers, nursing homes, rehabilitation centers and agencies, and other similar healthcare facilities and services; (iv) to enter into, from time to time, such financial arrangements as the Governing Board may determine to be necessary, appropriate or advisable (including, without limitation, borrowing money and issuing evidences of indebtedness and securing the same by mortgage, deed of trust, security interest or other encumbrance upon one or more or all of the Joint Venture assets); (v) to sell, assign, lease, exchange or otherwise dispose of, or refinance or additionally finance, one or more or all of the Joint Venture assets; and (vi) generally to engage in such other business and activities and to do any and all other acts and things that the Governing Board deems necessary, appropriate or advisable from time to time in furtherance of the purposes of the Joint Venture as set forth in this Section 3.1. Specifically, the Joint Venture shall be operated and governed in accordance with and in a manner which is reasonably intended to develop, maintain and expand a geographically dispersed spectrum of appropriate healthcare services in a regionally integrated system of healthcare providers capable of assuming responsibility for the health status of defined populations within the First Coast Area, and, with respect to the Facilities, acting through the Governing Board, take those actions set forth in Section 10.

    3.2.   Nature of the Business. The nature of the business of the Joint Venture shall be to own, manage, operate, lease or take any action in connection with the ownership and/or operation of the Facilities, and the delivery of healthcare services. The Governing Board shall use its good faith best efforts and judgment to assure that the business of the Joint Venture is conducted in such a manner as to satisfy the community benefits standard generally required of hospitals under section 501(c)(3) of the Code including in particular: (i) providing healthcare services to all members of the public, (ii) accepting and participating in Medicare/Medicaid and similar publicly funded healthcare programs of federal and Florida governments, (iii) maintaining open emergency rooms at the Joint Venture's general acute care hospitals, (iv) maintaining open medical staffs at the Joint Venture's general acute care hospitals for qualified physicians, subject only to applicable laws, changes mandated by quality assurance activities or managed care contracts or other contracts with third party payers, (v) participating in medical research/teaching/residency programs conducted by institutions of higher education located in the communities in which the Joint Venture does business, (vi) maintaining public health programs of educational benefit to a broad cross section of the communities in which the Joint Venture does business, (vii) generally promoting the health, welfare and wellness of the citizens of the communities in which the Joint Venture conducts business by providing quality healthcare at reasonable cost, and (viii) causing the Hospitals to continue their current practice of accepting all patients in an emergency condition in their respective emergency rooms without regard to the ability of such emergency patients to pay. The Joint Venture shall use all reasonable efforts to operate its business in such a manner so as not to generate unrelated business income to any JHG/UMC Entity.

4.   Capital Contributions, Loans, Capital Accounts

    4.1.   Capital Contributions. Each Joint Venturer has contributed its Capital Contribution to the capital of the Joint Venture.

4.2. <u>Capital Accounts</u>. A Capital Account shall be established for each Joint Venturer. No Joint Venturer shall receive any interest or salary with respect to its Capital Account. No Joint Venturer shall have the right to demand the return of its contribution to the capital of the Joint Venture, except as otherwise provided in this Agreement. Should any Joint Venturer become entitled to receive a return of its contribution to the capital of the Joint Venture, such Joint Venturer shall not have the right to receive property other than cash, except as otherwise provided in this Agreement.

All of the provisions of this Agreement relating to the maintenance of Capital Accounts are intended to comply with Section 1.704-1(b) of the Regulations, and shall be interpreted and applied in a matter consistent with the Regulations.

4.3. <u>Loans</u>.

(a) Any Joint Venturer, with the written consent of the Governing Board, may lend money to the Joint Venture. If any Joint Venturer, with such consent of the Governing Board, makes a loan to the Joint Venture, the amount of any such loan shall not be treated as a contribution to the capital of the Joint Venture but shall be a debt due from the Joint Venture. Any Joint Venturer's loan to the Joint Venture shall be repayable out of the Joint Venture's cash. None of the Joint Venturers shall be obligated to loan money to the Joint Venture. Upon the Approval of the Governing Board, the Joint Venture shall have the right and authority to enter into financing arrangements and use the proceeds thereof for Joint Venture purposes.

(b) UMC is presently the obligor under the UMC Tax Exempt Bonds. The Joint Venturers agree that the UMC Tax Exempt Bonds may be refinanced prior to the Joint Venture Stage II Commencement Date. The Joint Venturers acknowledge that the UMC Tax Exempt Bonds may become taxable and may have to be refinanced prior to the Joint Venture Stage II Commencement Date. To assist UMC in such refinancing, Columbia/Jacksonville shall provide, or, cause Columbia/HCA or a Columbia/HCA Affiliate to provide, a loan facility to UMC of up to Fifty Million Dollars ($50,000,000) (the "Refunding Loan"), which together with the proceeds of a senior loan (the "Senior Loan") shall be used to pay or defease the UMC Tax Exempt Bonds. The Refunding Loan shall be made upon such terms and conditions, and secured by such collateral, as are acceptable to the entity or entities making such loan (the "Lender"). To the extent the Senior Loan is secured by collateral which also secures the Refunding Loan, the lien and security interest of the Lender in such collateral shall be junior and subordinate to the lien and security interest of the maker of the Senior Loan. The terms and conditions of such subordination must be acceptable to Lender in its sole discretion. As interest to the Lender. JHG/UMC shall make payments to the Lender which will have the effect of reducing the Joint Venturer's Sharing Percentage of JHG/UMC in an amount equivalent to two and twenty eight one-hundredths (2.28) percentage points for each Ten Million Dollars ($10.000,000) of principal outstanding, and allocate to the Lender a deemed percentage interest in the Joint Venture in an amount equal to such reduction to

JHG/UMC. The deemed ownership percentage of the Lender related to such interest on the Refunding Loan will be reduced during the first five years of the Refunding Loan on an annual basis to reflect reductions in the outstanding principal amount of the Refunding Loan. To the extent the Refunding Loan has not been fully repaid within five years, the Joint Venturer's Sharing Percentages of each Joint Venturer will be permanently adjusted pursuant to such formula to reflect the then outstanding principal balance of the Refunding Loan, and the Lender shall be admitted to the Joint Venture as an Additional Joint Venturer with a Joint Venturer's Sharing Percentage equal to such reductions, and the balance of the Refunding Loan shall be forgiven; further, no changes shall be made in the composition of the Governing Board as a result thereof.

5.   Allocations

5.1.   Allocations of Profits. After giving effect to the special allocations set forth in Sections 5.3 and 5.4. Profits for each Joint Venture fiscal year shall be allocated to the Joint Venturers in the following order of priority:

(a)   First, 100% to the Joint Venturers in proportion to Losses previously allocated until the cumulative Profits allocated pursuant to this Section 5.1 (a) for the current and all prior fiscal years are equal to the cumulative Losses allocated to the Joint Venturers pursuant to Section 5.2(b); and

(b)   Second, to the Joint Venturers in proportion to each Joint Venturers's Sharing Percentage.

5.2.   Allocations of Losses.

(a)   After giving effect to the special allocations set forth in Sections 5.3 and 5.4, and subject to the limitation in Section 5.2(b) below, Losses for any Joint Venture fiscal year shall be allocated to the Joint Venturers in proportion to each Joint Venturer's Sharing Percentage.

(b)   To the extent Losses allocated to a Joint Venturer pursuant to Section 5.2(a) would create or increase a deficit in the balance of each such Joint Venturer's Adjusted Capital Account, such losses shall be allocated instead to the Joint Venturers with positive Adjusted Account balances.

5.3.   Special Allocations. The following special allocations shall be made in the following order:

(a)   Minimum Gain Chargeback. Notwithstanding any other provision of this Section 5, if there is a net decrease in Joint Venture Minimum Gain during any Joint Venture fiscal year, each Joint Venturer shall be allocated items of Joint Venture income and gain for such year (and, if necessary, subsequent years) in an amount equal to such

Joint Venturer's share of the net decrease in Joint Venture Minimum Gain during such year in the manner and amounts provided in Regulation Sections 1.704-2(f)(6), 1.704-2(g)(2), 1.704-2(j)(2)(i) and 1.704-2(i) or any successor provisions. For purposes of this Section 5.3(a), each Joint Venturer's Adjusted Capital Account balance shall be determined, and the allocation of income or gain required hereunder shall be effected, prior to the application of any other allocations pursuant to this Section 5.3(a) with respect to such fiscal year. This Section 5.3(a) is intended to comply with the minimum gain chargeback requirement in Section 1.704-2(f) of the Regulations and shall be interpreted consistently therewith.

(b)   Joint Venturer Minimum Gain Chargeback. Notwithstanding any other provision of this Section 5, except Section 5.3(a), if there is a net decrease in Joint Venturer Minimum Gain attributable to a Joint Venturer Nonrecourse Debt during any Joint Venture fiscal year, each Joint Venturer who has a share of the Joint Venturer Minimum Gain attributable to such Joint Venturer Nonrecourse Debt shall be allocated items of joint Venture income and gain for such year (and, if necessary, subsequent years) in the manner and amounts provided in Regulations Sections 1.704-2(i)(4) and 1.704-2(j)(2) (ii) or any successor provisions. For purposes of this Section 5.3(b), each Joint Venturer's Adjusted Capital Account balance shall be determined, and the allocation of income or gain required hereunder shall be effected, prior to the application of any other allocations pursuant to this Section 5.3(b) with respect to such fiscal year. This Section 5.3(b) is intended to comply with the minimum gain chargeback requirement in such Sections of the Regulations and shall be interpreted consistently therewith.

(c)   Qualified Income Offset. In the event any Joint Venturer unexpectedly receives any adjustments, allocations, or distributions described in Sections 1.704-1(b)(2)(ii)(d)(4), 1.704-1(b)(2)(ii)(d)(5) or 1.704-1(b)(2)(ii)(d)(6) of the Regulations, items of Joint Venture income and gain shall be specially allocated to each such Joint Venturer in an amount and manner sufficient to eliminate, to the extent required by the Regulations, the deficit balance, if any, in the Adjusted Capital Account created by such adjustments, allocations or distributions as quickly as possible, unless such deficit balance is otherwise eliminated pursuant to Section 5.3(a) or (b).

(d)   Gross Income Allocation. In the event any Joint Venturer has a deficit Capital Account at the end of any Joint Venture fiscal year which is in excess of the sum of (i) the amount such Joint Venturer is obligated to restore pursuant to any provision of this Agreement and (ii) the amount such Joint Venturer is deemed to be obligated to restore under Sections 1.704-2(g) and 1.704-2(i)(5) of the Regulations, each such Joint Venturer shall be allocated items of Joint Venture income and gain in the amount of such excess as quickly as possible, provided that an allocation pursuant to this Section 5.3(d) shall be made only if and to the extent that such Joint Venturer would have a deficit balance in its Adjusted Capital Account in excess of such sum after all other allocations

-18-

provided for in this Section 5 have been made as if this Section 5, were not in this Agreement.

(e)   Nonrecourse Deductions. Any Joint Venturer Nonrecourse Deductions for any fiscal year or other period shall be allocated to the Joint Venturer who bears the Economic Risk of Loss with respect to the Joint Venturer Nonrecourse Debt to which such Joint Venturer Nonrecourse Deductions are attributable in accordance with Section 1.704-2(i) of the Regulations.

(f)   Section 754 Adjustments. To the extent an adjustment to the adjusted tax basis of any Joint Venture asset pursuant to Sections 732, 734(b) or 743(b) of the Code is required, pursuant to Section 1.704-1(b)(2)(iv)(m) of the Regulations, to be taken into account in determining Capital Accounts, the amount of such adjustment to the Capital Accounts shall be treated as an item of gain (if the adjustment increases the basis of the asset) or loss (if the adjustment decreases such basis) and such gain or loss shall be specially allocated to the Joint Venturers in a manner consistent with the manner in which their Capital Accounts are required to be adjusted pursuant to such Section of the Regulations.

5.4.   Curative Allocations.

Notwithstanding any other provision of this Section 5 (other than Section 5.3), the allocations contained in Section 5.3 shall be taken into account in making the allocations contained in Sections 5.1 and 5.2 so that, to the extent possible, the net amount of items of income, gain, loss and deduction allocated to each Joint Venturer under Sections 5.1, and 5.2 and 5.3, together, shall be equal to the net amount of such items that would have been allocated to each Joint Venturer under Sections 5.1 and 5.2 had the allocations under Section 5.3, not otherwise been provided for. The Manager shall have reasonable discretion, with respect to each fiscal year, to apply the provisions of this Section 5.4 and thereby allocate income, gain, loss and deduction in such order and proportion as the Manager deems equitable, practicable and consistent with this Agreement and the applicable Regulations.

5.5.   Tax Allocations.

(a)   Code Section 704(c). If any Joint Venturer contributes any property to the Joint Venture that has a Gross Market Value that is greater than or less than its adjusted basis for federal income tax purposes at the time of such contribution, then all gain, loss and deduction with respect to the contributed property shall, solely for federal income tax purposes, be allocated among the Joint Venturers so as to take account of the variation between the adjusted basis of such property and its initial Gross Market Value as required under Code section 704(c).

(b)   <u>Joint Venture Asset Adjustments</u>. In the event the Gross Market Value of any Joint Venture asset is adjusted pursuant to <u>Section 1.32</u>, subsequent allocations of Joint Venture income, gain, loss and deduction with respect to such asset, as calculated for tax purposes, shall take account of any variation between the adjusted basis of such asset for federal income tax purposes and its Gross Market Value in accordance with the principles of Code Section 704(c), as required pursuant to Regulation Section 1.704-1(b)(4)(i).

(c)   <u>Consistent Allocation</u>. Except as provided above in <u>Sections 5.5(a)</u> and <u>(b)</u>, Joint Venture income, gain, loss, deduction and credit, as calculated for tax purposes, shall be allocated among the Joint Venturers, to the extent possible, in accordance with the allocations of the corresponding Profits, Losses or items thereof pursuant to <u>Sections 5.1</u> through <u>5.3</u>.

(d)   <u>Adjustments by the Joint Venturers</u>. Any elections or other decisions related to Joint Venture tax allocations pursuant to this <u>Section 5.5</u> shall be made by the Manager in any manner that reasonably reflects the purpose and intention of this Agreement. Joint Venture tax allocations pursuant to this <u>Section 5.5</u> are solely for purposes of federal, state and local taxes and shall not affect, or in any way be taken into account in computing, any Joint Venturer's Capital Account or distributive share of the Joint Venture's Profit or Loss (or any item thereof), or Joint Venture distributions to any of the Joint Venturers under this Agreement.

5.6.   <u>Other Allocation Rules</u>.

(a)   In the event that Joint Venturers are admitted to the Joint Venture on different dates during any Joint Venture fiscal year, Joint Venture income or loss allocated to the Joint Venturers for each such fiscal year shall be allocated among the Joint Venturers in proportion to each Joint Venturer's Sharing Percentage from time to time during such fiscal year in accordance with Code section 706, using any convention permitted by law and selected by the Manager.

(b)   For purposes of determining Joint Venture income, gain, losses and deductions allocable to any period, all such Joint Venture items shall be determined on a daily, monthly or other basis, as determined by the Manager using any permissible method under Code section 706 and the Regulations thereunder.

(c)   The Joint Venturers are aware of the income tax consequences of the Joint Venture allocations made under this <u>Section 5</u> and hereby agree to be bound by the provisions of this <u>Section 5</u> in reporting their share of Joint Venture income and loss for federal income tax purposes.

6.   <u>Distributions</u>

6.1. <u>Distributions</u>. Except as may be prohibited or required by applicable law, or unless otherwise agreed by the Governing Board, within one hundred and twenty (120) days after the close of each fiscal year, the Governing Board shall cause to be distributed to the Joint Venturers cash in an amount at least equal to one hundred percent (100%) of the Joint Venture's Excess Cash Flow for such fiscal year. Distributions made under this <u>Section 6.1</u> shall be made in proportion to each Joint Venturer's Sharing Percentage.

6.2. <u>Limit on Distributions</u>. Distributions shall not be made to a Joint Venturer as provided in <u>Section 6.1</u> if the result of such distributions would be to cause such Joint Venturer to have a deficit in its Capital Account.

6.3. <u>Compensation or Reimbursement to a Joint Venturer</u>. Authorized amounts payable as compensation or reimbursement to either a Joint Venturer or to any Person other than in its capacity as a Joint Venturer in the Joint Venture, such as for services rendered, goods purchased or money borrowed, shall not be treated as a distribution for purposes of <u>Section 6.1</u>.

7. <u>Capital Expenditures by Joint Venturers: Expansion Facilities</u>.

7.1. <u>Capital Expenditures</u>. Capital expenditures made by a Joint Venturer at its Facilities shall be made only in accordance with such Facilities' capital budgets. All capital expenditures made in respect of a JHG/UMC Facility shall be funded by JHG/UMC or the JHG/UMC Entity which owns such JHG/UMC Facility, and all capital expenditures made in respect of a Columbia/Jacksonville Related Facility shall be funded by Columbia/Jacksonville or the Columbia/Jacksonville Related Entity owning such Facility. Notwithstanding the foregoing, capital expenditures to acquire major additional facilities or which result in the ability of the Joint Venturer to offer or deliver new services or medical programs (unless, with respect to the JHG/UMC Facilities, prohibited by the UMC Lease) (collectively, "Expansion Expenditures") will be financed jointly by the Joint Venturers in accordance with their respective Joint Venturer's Sharing Percentages, and separate financial information shall be maintained with respect to the operation of such new facilities, services or programs to enable the Partnership to determine EBDITA with respect thereto. All assets associated with such an Expansion Expenditure, including, without limitation, licenses, permits, certificates of need, and the like, will be owned by the Joint Venture or such other jointly owned entity as agreed upon by the Governing Board. Upon dissolution of the Joint Venture, JHG/UMC or one or more of the JHG/UMC Entities designated by JHG/UMC shall be required to acquire title to the assets, including, without limitation, property, plant and equipment, acquired or developed by Expansion Expenditures which are located at or on real property owned or leased by JHG/UMC Entity on or after July 25, 1995 and Columbia/Jacksonville or one of the Columbia/Jacksonville Related Entities designated by Columbia/Jacksonville shall be required to acquire title to the assets, including, without limitation, property, plant and equipment, acquired or developed by Expansion Expenditures which are located on real property owned or leased by a Columbia/Jacksonville Related Entity on or after July 25, 1995 ("On-Campus Expansion Facilities"). In the event On-Campus Expansion Facilities have been in service for less than three (3) years ("Unmatured Expansion Assets"), such acquiring Joint Venturer shall reimburse the other Joint Venturers for their investment in such On-Campus Expansion Facilities, plus an amount equal to ten percent (10%) of such portion for each year since such expenditure was funded. In the event On-Campus Expansion Facilities have been in service for three (3) years or more, such acquiring Joint Venturer shall acquire such On-Campus Expansion Facilities from the Partnership for an amount equal to five (5) times the EBDITA with respect to such On-Campus Expansion Facilities for the trailing twelve (12) full calendar months prior to termination.

7.2.   Expansion Expenditures. Notwithstanding the foregoing, in the event the Governing Board approves an Expansion Expenditure and a Joint Venturer is unwilling or unable to fund its respective portion of such Expenditure, such Joint Venturer may elect not to participate in such funding. To the extent such non-participating Joint Venturer's portion of such Expenditure is funded by the other Joint Venturers, such non-participating Joint Venturer's Sharing Percentage shall be diluted and the Joint Venturer's Sharing Percentage of the other Joint Venturer shall be equitably adjusted. Further, no facilities or services added through an Expansion Expenditure shall be included which, after taking into account any Joint Venturer funding, would have the effect of reducing the Sharing Percentage of Columbia/Jacksonville or the Sharing Percentages of JHG/UMC below twenty percent (20%) or, if such Expansion Expenditure occurs subsequent to the maturity of the Refunding Loan and the Refunding Loan was not fully repaid resulting in a reduction of the JHG/UMC Sharing Percentage, such Expansion Expenditure shall be not be made a part of the Facilities if the effect of such acquisition would be to further reduce the Sharing Percentage of JHG/UMC by more than two (2) percentage points. If as a result of the provisions of the preceding sentence, such proposed Expansion Expenditure is not included in the Joint Venture, the Joint Venturer proposing such Expansion Expenditure may own and operate such facility or provide such service without the restrictions imposed under the terms of the covenant not to compete set forth in Section 24.

8.   Joint Venture Equalizing Payments. To reflect the respective interests of the Joint Venturers in the Joint Venture, annual payments ("Joint Venture Equalizing Payments") will be made between the Joint Venturers with respect to the period commencing on the joint Venture Stage II Commencement Date. In acting for the overall good of the Joint Venture and the community, it is anticipated that a significant degree of consolidation will occur in terms of the operations of participating Facilities. The Joint Venturers have determined that these consolidations are critical to achieve improvements in quality of care and reductions in costs. The Joint Venture Equalizing Payments are intended to ensure that the economic interests of the Joint Venturers are fairly reflected in the overall financial performance of the Joint Venturers as affected by such anticipated consolidations. The inception of Joint Venture Equalizing Payments is contingent upon receipt of either (i) a favorable IRS ruling with respect to the specific items listed above, or (ii) an opinion of counsel to such effect, in form and substance satisfactory to Columbia/Jacksonville and JHG/UMC in their sole discretion.

Joint Venture Equalizing Payments shall be calculated based on the difference between i) each Joint Venturer's Sharing Percentage multiplied by the sum of a) the aggregate EBDITA of the JHG/UMC Facilities and b) the aggregate EBDITA of the Columbia/Jacksonville Related Facilities ("Ratable Share"), and ii) each Joint Venturer's Aggregate EBDITA. To the extent that a Joint Venturer's Aggregate EBDITA is less that its Ratable Share, the other Joint Venturer shall make a Joint Venture Equalizing Payment in the amount of such difference to such Joint Venturer. EBDITA in all cases shall be calculated in accordance with Schedule 1.20, and adjusted to reflect Capital Expenditures and Changes in Working Capital. In calculating EBDITA and Changes in Working Capital, income and expenses and changes in non-cash balance sheet accounts relating to those items set forth in Schedule 8 shall be excluded. Joint Venture Equalizing Payments shall be made in cash within one hundred and twenty (120) days of the end of each calendar year.

"Joint Venturer's Aggregate EBDITA" means the aggregate EBDITA of the JHG/UMC Facilities or the aggregate EBDITA of the Columbia/Jacksonville Related Facilities, as the case may be. "Capital Expenditures" means expenditures made by a Joint Venturer with respect to their respective Facilities, pursuant to capital budgets prepared by the Manager and appropriately approved, and meeting consistently and commonly applied capitalization policies. Capital Expenditures shall be net of cash proceeds from the sale of assets in the case of Capital Expenditures being made to replace such assets being sold. "Changes in Working Capital" means changes in a Joint Venturer's non-cash balance sheet accounts which are components of EBDITA.

For the purpose of determining the amounts of the Joint Venture Equalizing Payments, EBDITA shall be calculated by the Manager based on audited financial statements and using Manager's methods of accounting consistently and commonly applied for all Joint Venturers, and such calculation shall be Approved by the Governing Board. In order to facilitate the foregoing calculations, the JHG/UMC Entities shall, by the Joint Venture Stage II Commencement Date, convert their existing accounting policies and procedures to those used by the Manager, and shall restate their financial statements as of the Joint Venture Stage II Commencement Date using the accounting policies and procedures used by the Manager, but at all times in accordance with GAAP.

9.   Bank Accounts, Books of Account, Tax Compliance and Fiscal Year

    9.1.   Bank Accounts: Investments. The Governing Board or the Manager shall establish one or more bank accounts into which all Joint Venture funds shall be deposited. No other funds shall be deposited into these accounts. Funds deposited in the Joint Venture's bank accounts may be withdrawn only to pay Joint Venture debts or obligations or to be distributed to the Joint Venturers under this Agreement. Joint Venture funds, however, may be invested in such securities and investments as the Governing Board may select (including the centralized cash management system utilized generally by Columbia/HCA Affiliates), until withdrawn for Joint Venture purposes.

    9.2.   Books and Records. The Manager shall be responsible for maintaining or causing to be maintained the books of account and records of the Joint Venture's business. The books shall be prepared in accordance with generally accepted accounting principles using the accrual method of accounting and the Manager's policies and procedures. The accrual method of accounting shall also be used by the Joint Venture for income tax purposes. The Joint Venture's books and records shall at all times be maintained at the principal business office of the Joint Venture or its accountants and shall be available for inspection by the Joint Venturers or their duly authorized representatives during reasonable business hours. The books and records shall be preserved for four (4) years after the term of the Joint Venture ends.

    9.3.   Determination of Profit and Loss; Audited Financial Statements. Except as otherwise provided in Section 12.6 hereof, all items of Joint Venture income, expense, gain, loss, deduction and credit shall be determined with respect to, and allocated in accordance with, this Agreement for each Joint Venturer for each Joint Venture fiscal year. Within one hundred and twenty (120) days after the end of each Joint Venture fiscal year, the Joint Venture shall prepare, at Joint Venture expense, financial statements of the Joint Venture for the preceding fiscal year, including, without limitation, a balance sheet, profit and loss statement, statement of cash flows and statement of the balances in the Joint Venturers' Capital Accounts, prepared in accordance with GAAP with prior periods and audited by a certified public accounting firm selected by the Governing Board. These audited financial statements shall be available for inspection and copying during ordinary business hours at the reasonable request of any Joint Venturer, and will be furnished to any Joint Venturer upon written request therefor. The JHG/UMC Entities may provide copies of such audited financial statements, as well as financial information with respect to the calculation of Joint Venture Equalizing Payments, to the City of Jacksonville, Florida if so requested, and the Joint Venture shall make its auditors available to the City of Jacksonville, Florida to answer any questions the City of Jacksonville, Florida may have with respect thereto.

    9.4.   Tax Returns and Information. The Joint Venturers intend for the Joint Venture to be treated as a partnership for tax purposes. The Joint Venture shall prepare or cause to be prepared all federal, state and local income and other tax returns which the Joint Venture is required to file and shall furnish such returns to the Joint Venturers, together with a copy of each Joint Venturer's Form K-1 and any other information which any Joint Venturer may reasonably request relating to such returns, within such time after end of each Joint Venture fiscal year as is permitted by law, rule or regulation (including any permitted extensions).

    9.5.   Tax Matters General Partner. The Tax Matters General Partner shall be the tax matters partner of the Joint Venture under section 6231(a)(7) of the Code. The Tax Matters General Partner shall inform each of the Joint Venturers of all matters which may come to its attention in its capacity as Tax Matters General Partner by giving the Joint Venturers notice thereof within ten (10) days after becoming so informed. The Tax Matters General Partner shall not take any action contemplated by sections 6222 through 6232 of the Code unless the Tax Matters General Partner has first given each of the Joint Venturers notice of the contemplated action and received the Approval of the Joint Venturers to the contemplated action. This provision is not intended to authorize the Tax Matters General Partner to take any action which is left to the determination of the individual Partner under sections 6222 through 6232 of the Code.

    9.6.   Fiscal Year. The Joint Venture fiscal year shall be the calendar year.

10.   Management of the Joint Venture

     10.1.   Delegation to Governing Board, Reserved Powers. The Columbia/Jacksonville Related Entities will continue to own and operate their respective healthcare facilities. The JHG/UMC Entities will continue to own or lease their respective facilities and the same shall be managed pursuant to the terms and conditions set forth in the Interim Management Services Agreement and the Management Services Agreement; however, subject to the fiduciary obligations and limitations imposed upon them at law, and except as otherwise provided in this Agreement or required under non-waivable provisions of the Act, the Joint Venturers hereby delegate to the Governing Board the specific authority set forth in Section 10.2 with respect to the management and control of the Joint Venture and its business, affairs and policies, and the authority to make all decisions and take all actions as the Governing Board may deem to be necessary or appropriate in connection therewith. Notwithstanding the foregoing, Columbia/Jacksonville will retain the right to veto any action by the Governing Board which, with respect to any of the Columbia/Jacksonville Related Facilities, would be in conflict with or violate (a) licensure requirements, (b) requirements of other regulatory agencies, (c) requirements for JCAHO accreditation, or (d) any covenant under the outstanding debt instruments of any Columbia/Jacksonville Related Entity. JHG/UMC will retain the right to veto any action by the Manager or the Governing Board which, with respect to any of the JHG/UMC Facilities, would be in conflict with or violate (a) license requirements, (b) requirements of other regulatory agencies, (c) requirements for JCAHO accreditation, or (d) any covenant under the outstanding debt instruments of any JHG/UMC Entity. In addition, JHG/UMC will retain the right to veto an action by the Governing Board which would prevent JHG and/or UMC from complying with (w) the UMC Lease, (x) the Indigent Care Contract, (y) the Affiliation Agreement or (z) requirements for the JHG/UMC Entities' exemptions under section 501(c)(3) of the Code as established by the IRS in Revenue Ruling 69-545 or other binding legal precedent which requirements currently include an open medical staff, and an emergency room open to all and other community benefit activities.

     10.2.   Governing Board.

       (a)   General Authority. On the date of this Agreement, the Joint Venturers shall form a governing board of the Joint Venture (the "Governing Board") by appointing thereto the Category A Governors and the Category B Governors, as applicable. From the date of this Agreement until the Joint Venture Stage II Commencement Date, the Governing Board shall be responsible for planning for the full implementation of the Joint Venture contemplated by this Agreement on the Joint Venture Stage II Commencement Date, including but not limited to the development of strategies and goals for the accomplishment of the purposes of the Joint Venture set forth in Section 3.2 and the activities of the Governing Board set forth in this Section 10.2 to accomplish the same; provided, however, the Governing Board shall not have the authority to direct the activities of or bind a Joint Venturer in connection therewith. Commencing on the Joint Venture Stage II Commencement Date, the Governing Board shall be vested with the full, exclusive and complete right, duty and authority specifically delegated to the

Governing Board and the following specific duties (collectively, the "Joint Venture Activities"): (i) changes in vision statements; (ii) approval of the capital budget for each of the Facilities to the extent such budget contemplates expenditures in excess of such Facility's average capital budget for fiscal years 1993, 1994 and 1995, increased annually for inflation by a factor equal to the medical component of the consumer price index ("CPI"); (iii) establishment and maintenance of, and changes to, cultural characteristics; (iv) ratification of Manager's selection of the Chief Executive Officer of the UMC Facilities; (v) approval of any consolidation or movement of programs or services among Facilities; (vi) the incurrence of debt by any of the Columbia/Jacksonville Related Entities or any of the JHG/UMC Entities in respect of any assets to be acquired or developed pursuant to an Expansion Expenditure in excess of ten percent (10%) of the aggregate fair market value of all assets of the Columbia/Jacksonville Related Entities or the JHG/ JMC Entities, as the case may be; (vii) the sale, lease, transfer or other disposition of a Joint Venturer's assets in excess of twenty percent (20%) of the aggregate fair market value of all assets of the Columbia/Jacksonville Related Entities or the JHG/UMC Entities, as the case may be; (viii) release or substantial modification of any contractual obligation between a Joint Venturer and any related Controlled entity; (ix) review of Manager's performance and compliance with provisions of the Management Services Agreements; and (x) selection of a manager upon expiration or early termination of the Interim Management Services Agreement or the Management Services Agreement. Action may be taken by the Governing Board upon Approval of the Governing Board acting at a meeting, or upon written Approval of the Governing Board acting without a meeting.

Neither the structure of the Governing Board (i.e. consisting of Category A Governors and Category B Governors with each such category having an equal number of governors), the manner of acting by the Governing Board, nor what constitutes Approval of the Governing Board shall be modified or affected by any change in the respective Sharing Percentages of the Joint Venturers.

(b)   Selection, Terms, Removal, and Vacancy of Members of Governing Board. Each individual selected to serve on the Governing Board shall serve until his or her successor is elected, or until his or her earlier death, resignation or removal. A member of the Governing Board may be removed, with or without cause, by the Joint Venturer who had the right to vote for his or her initial appointment. Any vacancy occurring in the Category A Governors shall be filled by an appointment by JHG/UMC and any vacancy occurring in the Category B Governors shall be filled by an appointment by Columbia/Jacksonville, with any replacement serving for the unexpired portion of the term of the person replaced. Members of the Governing Board shall be entitled to such compensation and reimbursement of expenses as each of the Joint Venturers may separately prescribe at such Joint Venturer's sole expense, which may differ between the two categories of governors.

10.3. Meetings of Governing Board. The Governing Board shall hold regular meetings on at least a quarterly basis. In addition, each member of the Governing Board shall be available at all reasonable times to consult with other members of the Governing Board on matters relating to the duties of the Governing Board. Meetings of the Governing Board shall be held at the call of any Joint Venturer or the Chairperson of the Governing Board, upon not less than five (5) business days written or telephonic notice to the members of the Governing Board, such notice specifying all matters to come before the Governing Board for action at such meeting. The presence of any member of the Governing Board at a meeting shall constitute a waiver of notice of the meeting with respect to such member. The members of the Governing Board may, at their election, participate in any regular or special meeting by means of conference telephone or similar communications equipment by means of which all persons participating in the meeting can hear each other. A member's participation in a meeting pursuant to the preceding sentence shall constitute presence in person at such meeting for all purposes of this Agreement.

10.4. Committees. In fulfilling its responsibilities, the Governing Board may, pursuant to resolutions duly adopted by the Governing Board, designate one or more committees of the Governing Board. Each such committee shall have and may exercise such powers of the Governing Board in the management of the business and affairs of the Joint Venture as may be provided in such resolution, subject to any limitations set forth therein. The rules to be followed by committees with respect to appointment of committee members, vacancies, call and notice requirements for meetings, quorum and voting procedures, minutes, compensation, reporting and other similar matters shall be set forth in resolutions duly adopted by the Governing Board in establishing such committees. Notwithstanding the foregoing, each committee shall be comprised of an equal number of Category A Governors and Category B Governors unless either Category agrees not to be equally represented thereon.

10.5. Interim Management Services Agreement. Effective as of the date of this Agreement, the JHG/UMC Entities shall engage the Manager to provide interim management services pursuant to the terms of the Interim Management Services Agreement until the Joint Venture Stage II Commencement Date. JHG/UMC hereby delegates, on behalf of itself and the JHG/UMC Entities, to the Manager the right, duty, authority, responsibility and obligation necessary to carry out and provide the services under the Interim Management Services Agreement in a manner not inconsistent with the policies, procedures and guidelines established from time to time by JHG/UMC.

10.6. Management Services Agreement. Effective as of the Joint Venture Stage II Commencement Date, the JHG/UMC Entities shall engage the Manager to provide management services to it pursuant to the terms of the Management Services Agreement. Except as otherwise provided in this Agreement, JHG/UMC, on behalf of itself and the JHG/UMC Entities, hereby delegates to the Manager the right, duty, authority, responsibility and obligation necessary to carry out and provide the services under the Management Services Agreement in a manner consistent with the policies, procedures and guidelines established by the Governing Board.

10.7.   <u>Governing Board Deadlock or Dispute</u>. It is the intention of the Governing Board to make a good faith effort to settle any dispute, controversy, claim or other matters in question arising under or related to the Joint Venture or this Agreement, including all issues of fact and law that constitute a Material Dispute. In settling any Material Dispute, each Category of Governors shall act in accordance with the following procedures:

(a)   First, each Category of Governors shall negotiate in good faith with the other Category of Governors to try to settle each Material Dispute for a period of thirty (30) days.

(b)   In the event by the end of the thirty (30) day period referred to in <u>Section 10.7(a)</u>, the Material Dispute is not settled pursuant to the procedures set forth in <u>Section 10.7(a)</u>, such Material Dispute shall be referred to a committee comprised of one (1) representative designated by a majority of the Category A Governors and one (1) representative designated by a majority of the Category B Governors (the "Deadlock Committee"). The decision of the Deadlock Committee with respect to such Material Dispute shall be deemed Approved by the Governing Board unless within thirty (30) days of the decision of the Deadlock Committee, a majority of either the Category A Governors or the Category B Governors votes to veto such decision. In the event the Deadlock Committee is unable to reach a decision within thirty (30) days of the date the Material Dispute was referred to it for decision, or a majority of either the Category A Governors or the Category B Governors votes to veto such decision, then the Material Dispute shall be resolved in the manner hereinafter set forth.

(c)   In the event the Material Dispute is not settled pursuant to the procedures set forth in <u>Section 10.7(b)</u>, either Category of Governors may invoke the Material Dispute resolution procedures set forth in this <u>Section 10.7(c)</u> by sending written notice to the other invoking the procedures of this <u>Section 10.7(c)</u>. For a period of thirty (30) days after the receipt by the other Category of Governors of such written notice, both Categories of Governors shall then try in good faith to settle the Material Dispute by mutually agreeing on, engaging and meeting with an individual that will serve as a facilitator for the purpose of resolving the Material Dispute. The Joint Venture shall pay the reasonable fees and related expenses of the facilitator.

(d)   In the event that by the end of the thirty (30) day period described in <u>Section 10.7(c)</u> the Material Dispute is not settled pursuant to the procedures set forth in <u>Section 10.7(c)</u>, including as a result of failing to agree upon an individual to serve as a facilitator, both Categories of Governors shall then attempt in good faith to settle the Material Dispute by informal mediation within a period of fifteen (15) days in a manner to be agreed at such date by the Categories of Governors. The Joint Venture shall pay the reasonable fees and related expenses incurred in connection with such mediation.

(e)   In the event that by the end of the fifteen (15) day period described in <u>Section 10.7(d)</u>, the Material Dispute is not settled pursuant to the procedures set forth in

–28–

Section 10.7(d), either Category of Governors may resort to litigation for the purpose of settling the Material Dispute. No action or inaction by either Category of Governors under any of the provisions of this Section 10.7(e) shall constitute any basis for granting or denying any relief sought by either Category of Governors in any such litigation.

(f)   During the pendency of the above litigation, the Joint Venture shall use all reasonable procedures to avoid making a decision or taking action in the area involved in such material dispute. In the event a decision must be made or an action taken during such period, the Joint Venture shall use reasonable efforts to proceed in a manner that will allow the decision or action to be reversed at the end of the litigation, based on the results thereof or to forego taking any such action or making such decision until such litigation is finally concluded, provided no irreparable harm will result therefrom.

10.8.   Officers of the Joint Venture. The sole officer of the Joint Venture shall be the Chairman of the Governing Board, whose sole function and authority shall be to preside over all meetings of the Governing Board. The Category A Governors and the Category B Governors, each voting as a block, shall elect the Chairman annually. The Chairman shall serve for a one (1) year term.

11.   Special Covenants of the Joint Venturers

11.1.   Non-Withdrawal of Joint Venturers. The Joint Venturers have entered into this Agreement based upon their expectations that the Joint Venturers shall continue in that status, with a substantial ownership interest, until the business of the Joint Venture is disposed of in an orderly manner or the Joint Venture otherwise dissolves. Accordingly, each Joint Venturer agrees that, except as otherwise provided herein, it will not voluntarily withdraw as a Joint Venturer in the Joint Venture except with the prior Approval of the Governing Board, or except in respect of a transfer effected under Section 12.7. Each Joint Venturer further agrees that its agreement contained in the immediately preceding sentence may be specifically enforced by the other Joint Venturer.

12.   Transfer of Rights; Substituted and Additional Joint Venturers

12.1.   Transfer by Joint Venturers. Except as provided in Sections 4.3(b) and 12.8, no Joint Venturer may sell, assign, hypothecate or otherwise transfer, voluntarily or by operation of law, all or any part of its interest in the Joint Venture to any Person unless otherwise Approved by the Governing Board.

12.2.   Substituted or Additional Joint Venturer. Except as provided in Sections 4.3(b) and 12.7, no Person taking or acquiring, by whatever means, all or some of the interest of any Joint Venturer in the Joint Venture shall be admitted as a Substituted or Additional Joint Venturer without the consent of the Governing Board (which consent may be unreasonably withheld) and unless such Person:

      (a)   Elects to become a Substituted or Additional Joint Venturer by delivering notice of such election to the Joint Venture;

      (b)   Executes, acknowledges and delivers to the Joint Venture such other instruments as the Governing Board may deem necessary or advisable to effect the admission of such person as a Substituted or Additional Joint Venturer, including, without limitation, the written acceptance and adoption by such Person of the provisions of this Agreement; and

      (c)   Pays a transfer fee to the Joint Venture in an amount sufficient to cover all reasonable expenses connected with the admission of such person or entity as a Substituted or Additional Joint Venturer.

    12.3.   Basis Adjustment. Upon the transfer of all or part of an interest in the Joint Venture, at the request of the transferee of the interest the Manager may, in its sole discretion, cause the Joint Venture to elect, pursuant to section 754 of the Code or the corresponding provisions of subsequent law, to adjust the basis of the Joint Venture properties as provided by sections 754 and 743 of the Code.

    12.4.   Transfer Procedures. The Joint Venture shall establish a transfer procedure consistent with this Section 12 to ensure that all conditions precedent to the admission of a Substituted or Additional Joint Venturer or Additional Joint Venturer have been complied with, and shall execute a certificate that such covenant has been complied with and shall, upon the written request of any Joint Venturer, deliver to such Joint Venturer a copy thereof.

    12.5.   Invalid Transfer. No transfer of an interest in the Joint Venture that is in violation of this Section 12 shall be valid or effective, and the Joint Venture shall not recognize any improper transfer for the purposes of making allocations, payments of profits, return of capital contributions or other distributions with respect to such Joint Venture interest, or part thereof. The Joint Venture may enforce the provisions of this Section 12 either directly or indirectly or through its agents by entering an appropriate stop transfer order on its books or otherwise refusing to register or transfer or permit the registration or transfer on its books of any proposed transfers not in accordance with this Section 12.

    12.6.   Distributions and Allocations in Respect of a Transferred Ownership Interest. If any Joint Venturer sells, assigns or transfers any part of its interest in the Joint Venture during any accounting period in compliance with the provisions of this Section 12, Joint Venture income, gain, deductions and losses attributable to such interest for the respective period shall be divided and allocated between the transferor and the transferee by taking into account their varying interests during the applicable accounting period, using the daily proration method. All Joint Venture distributions or Joint Venture Equalizing Payments on or before the effective date of such transfer shall be made to the transferor, and all such Joint Venture distributions or Joint Venture Equalizing Payments thereafter shall be made to the transferee.

12.7.   Additional Requirements of Admission to Joint Venture. No Person shall be admitted as a Joint Venturer if such admission would have the effect of causing the Joint Venture to be re-classified for federal income tax purposes as an association (taxable as a corporation under the Code), or which would violate any Medicare or other healthcare law, rule or regulation, or which would violate applicable exemptions from securities registration and securities disclosure provisions under federal and state securities laws, or which would (i) adversely affect any JHG/UMC Entity's classification as an organization described in Section 501(c)(3) of the Code, (ii) cause any JHG/UMC Entity to be classified as a private foundation under section 509(a) of the Code, or (iii) result in the share of income of the Joint Venture of JHG/UMC to be unrelated business taxable income.

12.8.   Certain Transfers. Columbia/Jacksonville and any Columbia/HCA Affiliate may transfer all or any part of its interest in the Joint Venture to any Columbia/HCA Affiliate, without obtaining the consent of the Governing Board pursuant to Section 12.1 hereof; provided, however, that none of the interests of such transferee Columbia/HCA Affiliate (other than Columbia/HCA), or any other Columbia/HCA Affiliate then in the Direct Corporate Chain with such transferee (other than Columbia/HCA), shall be owned, directly or indirectly, by (i) a physician having staff privileges at any of the Facilities owned and/or operated by the Joint Venturers or (ii) a management person employed at any of the Facilities owned and/or operated by the Joint Venturers unless JHG/UMC receives, at the sole cost and expense of either the transferor or transferee Columbia/HCA Affiliate (including reasonable attorneys' fees), either an opinion of counsel in a form and from counsel reasonably acceptable to it, or a private letter ruling or a determination letter from the Internal Revenue Service, in any case to the effect that such transfer will not (i) adversely affect any JHG/UMC Entity's classification as an organization described in section 501(c)(3) of the Code, (ii) cause any JHG/UMC Entity to be classified as a private foundation under section 509(a) of the Code or (iii) result in the share of taxable income of the Joint Venture of JHG/UMC to be unrelated business taxable income under section 512 of the Code. In addition to the foregoing, Columbia/Jacksonville and any Columbia/HCA Affiliate may transfer all or any portion of its Sharing Percentages, up to a maximum, in the aggregate, of an amount equal to twenty percent (20%) of its Sharing Percentage, to (i) a physician or physicians having staff privileges at any of the Columbia/Jacksonville Related Facilities, (ii) a management person or persons employed at any of the Columbia/Jacksonville Related Facilities, or (iii) an entity or entities in which some or all of the equity interests, including options to purchase such equity interests, are known by the transferee Joint Venturer to be owned by such a physician or management person, if, but only if, JHG/UMC receives, at the sole cost and expense of either the proposed transferee or the transferor Joint Venturer, including reasonable attorneys' fees, either an opinion of counsel reasonably acceptable to JHG/UMC or a private letter ruling, or a determination letter from the Internal Revenue Service, in any case to the effect that such transfer will not (i) adversely affect JHG/UMC Entity's classification as an organization described in section 501(c)(3) of the Code, (ii) cause any JHG/UMC Entity to be classified as a private foundation under section 509(a) of the Code or (iii) result in the share of taxable income of the Joint Venture of JHG/UMC to be unrelated business taxable income under section 512 of the Code. JHG/UMC or any JHG/UMC Affiliate may transfer all or any part of its interest in the Joint Venture to any other JHG/UMC

-31-

Affiliate, without obtaining the consent of the Joint Venturers pursuant to Section 12.1 hereof. The provisions of this Section 12.1 shall not obviate the need for compliance with Section 12.2 regarding the admission as a transferee as a Substituted or Additional Joint Venturer, other than the requirement therein for the Approval of the Governing Board. The transferee of an interest pursuant to this Section 12.8 shall be required to comply with the provisions of Section 12.2, hereof.

13.   Dissolution

13.1.   Causes. Each Joint Venturer expressly waives any right which such Joint Venturer might otherwise have to dissolve the Joint Venture except as set forth in this Section 13. The Joint Venture shall be dissolved upon the first to occur of the following:

(a)   The Bankruptcy, dissolution, removal or any other occurrence which would legally disqualify a Joint Venturer from acting hereunder;

(b)   The Approval by the Governing Board of an instrument dissolving the Joint Venture;

(c)   Either JHG/UMC or the Manager is in default of its obligations under the Interim Management Services Agreement or the Management Services Agreement and such default has not been cured within the applicable cure period set forth therein or waived by the non-defaulting party, if any;

(d)   the Manager or other entity selected by the Governing Board is not managing all of the Facilities;

(e)   The occurrence of any other circumstance which, by law, requires that the Joint Venture be dissolved;

(f)   The Governing Board in its reasonable discretion determine that a rule, ordinance, regulation. statute or government pronouncement has or may be enacted that would make any material aspect of this Agreement or the activities conducted by the Joint Venture unlawful or eliminate or substantially reduce, either directly or indirectly, the benefits that would accrue to the Joint Venturers with respect to continuing the Joint Venture's business operations; or

(g)   The Internal Revenue Service proposes in writing (i) to revoke the status of any JHG/UMC Entity described in section 501(c)(3) of the Code, (ii) to reclassify any JHG/UMC Entity as a private foundation within the meaning bf section 509(a) of the Code, or (iii) to treat income or distributions from the Joint Venture to JHG/UMC as unrelated business taxable income based on its participation in the Joint Venture, and the circumstances leading to such proposed action by the Internal Revenue Service cannot be addressed through amendments to this Agreement or other actions Approved by the Governing Board.

Nothing contained in this Section 13.1 is intended to grant to any Joint Venturer the right to dissolve the Joint Venture at will (by retirement, resignation, withdrawal or otherwise), or to exonerate any Joint Venturer from liability to the Joint Venture and the remaining Joint Venturers if it dissolves the Joint Venture at will. Any dissolution at will of the Joint Venture shall be in contravention of this Agreement for purposes of the Act. Dissolution of the Joint Venture under Section 13.1(b) shall not constitute a dissolution at will.

13.2.   Reconstitution. If the Joint Venture is dissolved as a result of an event described in Section 13.1 (a) or Section 13.1(b), the Joint Venture may be reconstituted and its business continued if, within ninety (90) days after the date of dissolution, the remaining Joint Venturers who own interests representing at least a majority of the aggregate Joint Venturer's Sharing Percentages of all Joint Venturers affirmatively elect to reconstitute the Joint Venture and execute an instrument confirming such facts. If the Joint Venture is reconstituted, an amendment to this Agreement shall be executed.

13.3.   Interim Manager. If the Joint Venture is dissolved as a result of an event described in Section 13.1(a), the remaining Joint Venturers may appoint an interim manager of the Joint Venture, who shall have and may exercise only the rights, powers and duties of a general partner necessary to preserve the Joint Venture assets, until (a) the Joint Venture is reconstituted; or (b) a Liquidator is appointed under Section 14, if the Joint Venture is not reconstituted. The interim manager shall not be liable as a general partner to the Joint Venturers and shall, while acting in the capacity of interim manager on behalf of the Joint Venture, be entitled to the same indemnification rights as are set forth in Section 26. The interim manager appointed as provided herein shall be entitled to receive such reasonable compensation for its services as may be agreed upon by such interim manager and those remaining Joint Venturers who own interests representing at least a majority of the aggregate Joint Venturer's Sharing Percentage of all Joint Venturers.

14.   Winding Up and Termination

14.1.   General. If the Joint Venture is dissolved and is not reconstituted, a Liquidator or liquidating committee selected by the Governing Board shall commence to wind up the affairs of the Joint Venture and to liquidate and sell the Joint Venture's assets. A Liquidator or a liquidating committee, is herein referred to as the "Liquidator." The Liquidator shall have sufficient business expertise and competence to conduct the winding up and termination of the Joint Venture and, in the course thereof, to cause the Joint Venture to perform any contracts which the Joint Venture has or thereafter enters into. The Liquidator (if other than a Joint Venturer, a Columbia/HCA Affiliate or a JHG/UMC Affiliate) shall have full right and unlimited discretion to determine the time, manner and terms of any sale or sales of Joint Venture property under such liquidation, having due regard for the activity and condition of the relevant market and general financial and economic conditions. The Liquidator (if other than a Joint Venturer, a Columbia/HCA Affiliate or a JHG/UMC Affiliate) appointed as provided herein shall be entitled to receive such reasonable compensation for its services as shall be agreed upon by the

–33–

Liquidator and the Governing Board. If a Joint Venturer, a Columbia/HCA Affiliate or a JHG/UMC Affiliate serves as the Liquidator, it shall not be entitled to receive any fee for carrying out the duties of the Liquidator. The Liquidator may resign at any time by giving fifteen (15) days prior written notice and may be removed at any time, with or without cause, by written notice of the Governing Board. Upon the death, dissolution, removal or resignation of the Liquidator, a successor and substitute Liquidator (who shall have and succeed to all the rights, powers and duties of the original Liquidator) will, within thirty (30) days thereafter, be appointed by the Governing Board, evidenced by written appointment and acceptance. The right to appoint a successor or substitute Liquidator in the manner provided herein shall be recurring and continuing for so long as the functions and services of the Liquidator are authorized to continue under the provisions hereof, and every reference herein to the Liquidator will be deemed to refer also to any such successor or substitute Liquidator appointed in the manner herein provided. The Liquidator shall have and may exercise, without further authorization or consent of any of the parties hereto or their legal representatives or successors in interest, all of the powers necessary or desirable in the good faith judgment of the Liquidator to perform its duties and functions. The Liquidator (if other than a Joint Venturer, a Columbia/HCA Affiliate or a JHG/UMC Affiliate) shall not be liable as a general partner to the Joint Venturers and shall, while acting in such capacity on behalf of the Joint Venture, be entitled to the indemnification rights set forth in Section 26.

14.2. Court Appointment of Liquidator. If, within ninety (90) days following the date of dissolution or other time provided in Section 14.1, a Liquidator or successor Liquidator has not been appointed in the manner provided therein, any interested party shall have the right to make application to any United States Federal District Judge (in his or her individual and not judicial capacity) for the Middle District of Florida for appointment of a Liquidator or successor Liquidator, and the Judge, acting as an individual and not in his or her judicial capacity, shall be fully authorized and empowered to appoint and designate a Liquidator or successor Liquidator who shall have all the powers, duties, rights and authority of the Liquidator herein provided.

14.3. Liquidation. In the course of winding up and terminating the business and affairs of the Joint Venture, the assets of the Joint Venture (other than cash) shall be sold, its liabilities and obligations to creditors, including any Joint Venturers who made loans to the Joint Venture and all expenses incurred in its liquidation shall be paid, and all resulting items of Joint Venture income, gain, loss or deduction shall be credited or charged to the Capital Accounts of the Joint Venturers in accordance with Section 5. Except as otherwise provided in this Agreement, all Joint Venture property shall be sold upon liquidation of the Joint Venture and no Joint Venture property shall be distributed in kind to the Joint Venturers. Thereafter, all Joint Venture assets shall be distributed among the Joint Venturers in the ratio of the then credit balances in their Capital Accounts. Upon the completion of the liquidation of the Joint Venture and the distribution of all the Joint Venture funds, the Joint Venture shall terminate and the Liquidator shall have the authority to execute and record all documents required to effectuate the dissolution and termination of the Joint Venture.

14.4.   Creation of Reserves. After making payment or provision for payment of all debts and liabilities of the Joint Venture and all expenses of liquidation, the Liquidator may set up such cash reserves as the Liquidator may deem reasonably necessary for any contingent or unforeseen liabilities or obligations of the Joint Venture.

14.5.   Final Statement. Within a reasonable time following the completion of the liquidation, the Liquidator shall supply to each of the Joint Venturers a statement which shall set forth the assets and the liabilities of the Joint Venture as of the date of complete liquidation, each Joint Venturer's pro rata portion of distributions under Section 14.3, and the amount retained as reserves by the Liquidator under Section 14.4.

14.6.   Compliance with Timing Requirements of Regulations. In the event the Joint Venture is "liquidated" within the meaning of Regulations Section 1.704-1(b)(2)(ii)(g), distributions shall be made pursuant to this Section 14 to the Joint Venturers who have positive Capital Accounts in compliance with Regulations Section 1.704-1(b)(2)(ii)(b)(2). No Joint Venturer that has a deficit balance in its Capital Account (after giving effect to all contributions, distributions and allocations for all taxable years, including the year during which such liquidation occurs) shall have any obligation to make any contribution to the capital of the Joint Venture to make up any such deficit, and such deficit shall not be considered a debt owed to the Joint Venture or any other Person for any purpose whatsoever. Income and loss allocations in connection with a liquidation of the Joint Venture shall be allocated among the Joint Venturers in the manner set forth in Sections 5.1 and 5.2 hereof. In the discretion of the Liquidator, a pro rata portion of the distributions that would otherwise be made to the Joint Venturers may instead be distributed to a trust established for the benefit of the Joint Venturers for the purposes of liquidating Joint Venture property, collecting amounts owed to the Joint Venture, and paying contingent or unforeseen liabilities or obligations of the Joint Venture or of the Joint Venturers arising out of or in connection with the Joint Venture. The assets of any such trust shall be distributed to the Joint Venturers from time to time, in the reasonable discretion of the Liquidator, in the same proportions as the amount distributed to such trust by the Joint Venture would otherwise have been distributed to the Joint Venturers pursuant to this Agreement.

14.7. Deemed Distribution and Recontribution. Notwithstanding any other provision of this Section 15, in the event the Joint Venture is liquidated within the meaning of Regulations Section 1.704-1(b)(2)(ii)(g) but no event described in Section 13.1 has occurred, the Joint Venture's properties shall not be liquidated, the Joint Venture's liabilities shall not be paid or discharged, and the Joint Venture's affairs shall not be wound up. Instead, the Joint Venture shall be deemed to have distributed the Joint Venture's properties in kind to the Joint Venturers, who shall be deemed to have assumed and taken such assets subject to all Joint Venture liabilities, all in accordance with their respective Capital Accounts. Immediately thereafter, the Joint Venturers shall be deemed to have recontributed the Joint Venture's properties in kind to the Joint Venture, which shall be deemed to have assumed and taken such assets subject to all such liabilities.

14.8.   Terminating Payments. Upon termination or dissolution of the Joint Venture, the Joint Venturers shall be responsible for, or entitled to, terminating payments ("Joint Venture Termination Payments") calculated as follows: The final EBDITA of Columbia/Jacksonville shall be deemed to be the aggregate EBDITA of the Columbia/Jacksonville Related Entities relating to the Columbia/Jacksonville Related Facilities for the "trailing" twelve (12) months prior to the date of termination or dissolution, and the final EBDITA of JHG/UMC shall be the aggregate EBDITA of the JHG/UMC Entities relating to the JHG/UMC Facilities for the trailing twelve (12) months prior to the date of termination or dissolution. Each Joint Venturer's percentage (the "Final Percentage") of the aggregate final EBDITA of Columbia/Jacksonville and JHG/UMC, so determined, (the "Total Final EBDITA") shall then be compared to such Joint Venturer's Sharing Percentage. To the extent such Joint Venturer's Final Percentage is less than its Sharing Percentage, such Joint Venturer shall be entitled to a Termination Payment from the other Joint Venturer whose Final Percentage exceeds its Sharing Percentage equal to the percentage point difference between such Joint Venturer's Final Percentage and Joint Venturer's Sharing Percentage multiplied times an amount equal to five (5) times the Total Final EBDITA. Notwithstanding the foregoing, the EBDITA related to any Unratured Expansion Assets shall not be included in any calculation of any Joint Venture Termination Payment. In calculating EBDITA, income and expenses relating to those items set forth in Schedule 8 shall be excluded.

15.   Affiliation with University of Florida. The Joint Venturers acknowledge the existence of the Affiliation Agreement and recognize the value this academic relationship currently brings to UMC. The Joint Venture endorses and supports an academic tie with the University of Florida. In stating its recognition and support of the academic mission of the University of Florida to the Joint Venture, the Joint Venturers intend to conduct themselves in a way as to not advantage or disadvantage one medical staff of a Facility in relation to the medical staffs of the other Facilities. Moreover, it is anticipated that UMC will continue its fiscal support of the University of Florida's academic programs. It is anticipated that in each of the first three (3) years of the Joint Venture, the continuation of fiscal support of the University of Florida's academic programs will, at a minimum, be derived from the current funding model (presently yields approximately $21,000,000 in annual support). This level of support will be subject to adjustment to reflect material changes in state or federal funding support of medical education. After the third year of the Joint Venture's operations, the level of such funding for the fourth year and beyond will be established by the Governing Board in coordination with the University of Florida. It is anticipated that the Joint Venture will continue to adhere to the principle of commitment to the academic mission throughout its duration.

16.   Representations and Warranties of the JHG/UMC

Except as set forth in the schedules attached hereto, as of the date hereof and as of the Closing Date, JHG/UMC represents and warrants to Columbia/Jacksonville the following:

(a)   Corporate Capacity. Each JHG/UMC Entity is a non-profit corporation and is duly organized, validly existing and in good standing under the laws of the State of Florida. JHG/UMC has the requisite corporate power and authority to enter into this

Agreement, perform its obligations hereunder and to conduct its business as now being conducted.

(b)   Corporate Powers: Consents: Absence of Conflicts With Other Agreements, Etc. The execution, delivery and performance of this Agreement by JHG/UMC and all other agreements referenced herein or ancillary hereto to which any of the JHG/UMC Entities is a party, and the consummation of the transactions contemplated herein and therein:

(i)   are within their respective corporate powers, are not in contravention of law or of the terms of their respective Articles of Incorporation, Code of Regulations or any amendments thereto, and have been duly authorized by all appropriate corporate action;

(ii)   to the best of its knowledge after due inquiry and except as otherwise expressly provided herein, do not require any approval or consent of, or filing with, any governmental agency or authority which is required by law or the regulations of any such agency or authority other than those consents and approvals the respective JHG/UMC Entities will obtain from those governmental agencies and authorities set forth in Schedule 16(b);

(iii)   will neither conflict with nor result in any material breach or contravention of nor permit the acceleration of the maturity of any of their respective indebtedness or other liabilities, or the creation of any lien, charge or encumbrance affecting any of their respective assets;

(iv)   to the best of its knowledge will not violate any statute, law, rule or regulation of any governmental authority to which the JHG/UMC Entities or any of their respective assets may be subject; and

(v)   will not violate any judgment of any court or governmental authority to which the JHG/UMC Entities or any of their respective assets may be subject.

(c)   Binding Agreement. This Agreement and all agreements to which any JHG/UMC Entity will become a party pursuant to this Agreement are and will constitute the valid and legally binding obligations of each such JHG/UMC Entity and are and will be enforceable against them in accordance with their respective terms.

(d)   No Subsidiaries. Schedule 16(d) sets forth each for profit corporation owned in whole or in part by a JHG/UMC Entity and each not-for-profit corporation which has as a member a JHG/UMC Entity. Except as set forth in Schedule 16(d), no JHG/UMC Entity has any subsidiaries or any investment constituting more than ten percent (10%) of the equity interests in any other entity. No JHG/UMC Entity is a member of another not-for-profit corporation providing healthcare services except as set forth in Schedule 16(d), and the only corporate members of the JHG/UMC Entities are listed in Schedule 16(d). No JHG/UMC Entity is a party to any joint venture or other arrangement with physicians on the medical staff of any of the JHG/UMC Facilities, other than as disclosed in Schedule 16(d).

(e)   Financial Statements. Each JHG/UMC Entity has delivered to Columbia/Jacksonville copies of the following statements of financial condition and results from operations (collectively, the "JHG/UMC Entity Financial Statements"), which JHG/UMC Entity Financial Statements are maintained on an accrual basis, copies of which are attached hereto as Schedule 16(e):

(i)   Unaudited Balance Sheets for the seven month period ending as of January 31, 1996 (the "JHG/UMC Entity Balance Sheet Date");

(ii)   Unaudited Income Statements for the seven month period ended on the JHG/UMC Entity Balance Sheet Date; and

(iii)   Audited Balance Sheets, Income Statements and Statements of Cash Flow for the fiscal years ended June 30, 1992, June 30, 1993, June 30, 1994 and June 30, 1995.

Such audited JHG/UMC Entity Financial Statements have been prepared in accordance with GAAP throughout the periods indicated. Subject to year-end adjustments consistent with past practice, such unaudited JHG/UMC Entity Financial Statements materially conform to GAAP, except as set forth in Schedule 16(e). Except as set forth in Schedule 16(e), such Balance Sheets present fairly the financial condition of each JHG/UMC Entity as of the dates indicated thereon, and such Income Statements present fairly the results of operations of each JHG/UMC Entity for the periods indicated thereon. Since the JHG/UMC Entity Balance Sheet Date, there have occurred no material adverse changes in the financial condition or results of operations of any JHG/UMC Entity as reflected in such JHG/UMC Entity Financial Statements.

(f)   Extraordinary Liabilities. Each JHG/UMC Entity has delivered to Columbia/Jacksonville an accurate list (Schedule 16(f)) of all of its liabilities not included in the JHG/UMC Entity Financial Statements which are of the kind and character required in financial statements prepared in accordance with GAAP and which were incurred other than in the ordinary course of business, whether accrued, absolute, contingent or otherwise, together with, in the case of those liabilities as to which the liabilities are not fixed, a reasonable estimate of the maximum amount which may be payable in respect thereof. Except as disclosed in Schedule 16(f) or the JHG/UMC Entity Financial Statements, no JHG/UMC Entity has any liabilities of any nature, whether accrued, absolute, contingent or otherwise. There are no facts in existence on the date hereof known or which should be known to any JHG/UMC Entity which might reasonably serve as the basis for any liability or obligation of any JHG/UMC Entity which is not fully disclosed in Schedule 16(f), or the JHG/UMC Entity Financial Statements.

(g)   Licenses. Each JHG/UMC Facility is duly licensed as a facility to perform the services described on Schedule 16(g)-1. The pharmacies, laboratories and all other ancillary departments owned by the JHG/UMC Entities and located at any of the JHG/UMC Facilities or operated for the benefit of any of the JHG/UMC Facilities which are required to be specially licensed are duly licensed by the Florida Department of Health or other appropriate licensing agency. Each JHG/UMC Entity has all other licenses, permits and approvals which are needed or required by law to operate the business related to or affecting any of the JHG/UMC Facilities. Each JHG/UMC Entity has delivered to Columbia/Jacksonville an accurate list and summary description (Schedule 16(g)-2) of all such licenses and permits owned or held by such JHG/UMC Entity relating to the ownership, development or operation of any of the JHG/UMC Facilities, all of which are now and as of Closing shall be in good standing and not subject to meritorious challenge.

      (h)   Medicare Participation/Accreditation. Each JHG/UMC Facility is qualified for participation in the Medicare and Medicaid programs, has a current and valid provider contract with the Medicare and Medicaid programs, is in compliance with the conditions of participation in such programs and has received all approvals or qualifications necessary for capital reimbursement. Each JHG/UMC Facility is duly accredited, with no contingencies other than as shown on the most recent Joint Commission of Accreditation of Healthcare Organizations ("JCAHO") survey, by the JCAHO for the three (3) year periods ending on the dates specified therefor on Schedule 16(h). Correct and complete copies of the most recent accreditation letters from the JCAHO pertaining to each JHG/UMC Facility have been delivered to Columbia/Jacksonville. Except as set forth on Schedule 16(h), no JHG/UMC Entity has received notice from either the Medicare or Medicaid programs of any pending or threatened investigations or surveys, and no JHG/UMC Entity has reason to believe that any such investigations or surveys are pending, threatened or imminent.

      (i)   Regulatory Compliance. Except as set forth on Schedule 16(i), each JHG/UMC Entity is in compliance in all material respects with all applicable laws, statutes, rules, regulations, ordinances and the requirements of all federal, state and local commissions, boards, bureaus, permits and agencies having jurisdiction over any of the JHG/UMC Facilities or the operations of any of the JHG/UMC Facilities, including, without limitation, the Internal Revenue Service, the Environmental Protection Agency, the Florida Environmental Protection Agency, and the Florida Department of Health, which compliance includes, without limitation, possession by each JHG/UMC Entity of all permits and other governmental authorizations required under all such laws; and each JHG/UMC Entity has timely filed all reports, data and other information required to be filed with such commissions, boards, bureaus and agencies where a failure to file timely would have a material adverse effect on the its assets.

      (j)   Insurance. The JHG/UMC Entities have delivered to Columbia/Jacksonville an accurate schedule (Schedule 16(j))disclosing the insurance policies covering the ownership and operations of the JHG/UMC Facilities, which Schedule reflects the policies' numbers, terms, identity of insurers, amounts, premiums and coverage. All of such policies are now and will be until Closing in full force and effect on a claims-made basis with no premium arrearage. Except as set forth in Schedule 16(j), each JHG/UMC Entity has given in a timely manner to its insurers all notices required to be given under its insurance policies with respect to all of the claims and actions covered by insurance, and no insurer has denied coverage of any such claims or actions or reserved its rights in respect of or rejected any of such claims. No JHG/UMC Entity has (i) received any notice or other communication from any such insurance company canceling or materially amending any of such insurance policies, and no such cancellation or amendment is threatened, or (ii) failed to give any required notice or present any claim which is still outstanding under any of such policies with respect to any of its assets.

(k)   <u>Employee Benefit Plans</u>. All employee pension benefit plans and employee health or welfare benefits plans (as such terms are defined in ERISA) maintained by the JHG/UMC Entities (collectively "the JHG/UMC Entity Benefit Plans") have been administered in accordance with ERISA and the applicable provisions of the Code. There are no "accumulated funding deficiencies" within the meaning of ERISA or the Code or any federal excise tax or liability on account of any deficient fundings in respect of the JHG/UMC Entity Benefit Plans. No reportable event (within the meaning of ERISA) or prohibited transaction (within the meaning of the Code) has occurred in respect of the JHG/UMC Entity Benefit Plans. There are no threatened or pending claims by or on behalf of the JHG/UMC Entity Benefit Plans or by any employee of any JHG/UMC Entity alleging a breach or breaches of fiduciary duties or violations of other applicable state or Federal law which could result in liability on the part of either a JHG/UMC Entity or any of the JHG/UMC Entity Benefit Plans under ERISA or any other law, nor is there any basis for such a claim. The JHG/UMC Entity Benefit Plans do not discriminate in operating in favor of employees who are officers or highly compensated. Except as set forth on <u>Schedule 16(k)</u>, all returns, reports, disclosure statements and premium payments required to be made under ERISA and the Code with respect to the JHG/UMC Entity Benefit Plans have been timely filed or delivered. Except as set forth on <u>Schedule 16(k)</u>,the JHG/UMC Entity Benefit Plans have not been audited or investigated by either the Internal Revenue Service, the Department of Labor or the Pension Benefit Guaranty Corporation within the last five (5) years, and there are no outstanding issues with reference to the JHG/UMC Entity Benefit Plans pending before such governmental agencies.

(l)   <u>Employee Relations</u>. The employee relations of the JHG/UMC Entities are generally good, when considered in the aggregate, pertaining to the JHG/UMC Facilities. There is no pending or threatened employee strike, work stoppage or labor dispute, and no union representation question exists, respecting any employees of the JHG/UMC Entities. Except as disclosed on <u>Schedule 16(l)</u>, no collective bargaining agreement exists or is currently being negotiated by the JHG/UMC Entities, no demand has been made for recognition by a labor organization by or with respect to any employees of the JHG/UMC Entities, no union organizing activities by or with respect to any employees of the JHG/UMC Entities are taking place, and none of the employees of the JHG/UMC Entities is represented by any labor union or organization. There is no unfair practice claim against the JHG/UMC Entities before the National Labor Relations Board, or any strike, dispute, slowdown, or stoppage pending or threatened against or involving any of the JHG/UMC Facilities, and none has occurred. Each JHG/UMC Entity is in compliance with all federal and state laws respecting employment and employment practices, terms and conditions of employment, and wages and hours. No JHG/UMC Entity is engaged in any unfair labor practices. Except as set forth on <u>Schedule 16(l)</u>, there are no pending or threatened EEOC claims, wage and hour claims; unemployment compensation claims, workers' compensation claims or the like.

(m)   Litigation or Proceedings. The JHG/UMC Entities have delivered to Columbia/Jacksonville an accurate list and summary description (Schedule 16(m)) of all litigation or proceedings involving any JHG/UMC Entity with respect to the JHG/UMC Facilities or otherwise. No JHG/UMC Entity is in material default under any law or regulation relating to the operation of any of the JHG/UMC Facilities. No JHG/UMC Entity is in default under any order of any court or federal, state, municipal or other governmental department, commission, board, bureau, agency or instrumentality wherever located. Except to the extent set forth on Schedule 16(m), there are no claims or investigations pending or threatened against or affecting the JHG/UMC Entities with respect to any of the JHG/UMC Facilities, at law or in equity, or before or by any federal, state, municipal or other governmental department, commission, board, bureau, agency or instrumentality wherever located.

(n)   Third Party Payor Cost Reports. Each JHG/UMC Entity has duly filed all required cost reports for all the fiscal years through and including the most recent fiscal year, and such reports have been filed either on a timely basis or prior to the time any penalty could be incurred for failure to file on a timely basis. All of such cost reports accurately reflect the information to be included thereon and do not claim, and neither any JHG/UMC Entity nor any of the JHG/UMC Facilities has received reimbursement in excess of the amount provided by law, except as provided in Schedule 16(n) hereto. Schedule 16(n) hereto indicates which of such cost reports have been audited and finally settled, the status of such cost reports which have not been audited and finally settled and a brief description of any and all notices of program reimbursement, proposed or pending audit adjustments, disallowances, appeals of disallowances and any and all other unresolved claims or disputes in respect of such cost reports. Except as set forth on Schedule 16(n),there are no facts or circumstances which may reasonably be expected to give rise to any material disallowance under any such cost reports.

(o)   Medical Staff Matters. Each JHG/UMC Entity has heretofore provided or made available to Columbia/Jacksonville true, correct, and complete copies of the bylaws and rules and regulations of the medical staffs of each of the JHG/UMC Facilities. With regard to the medical staffs of the JHG/UMC Facilities and except as set forth on Schedule 16(o) hereto, there are no pending or threatened disputes with applicants, staff members or health professional affiliates, and all appeal periods in respect of any medical staff member or applicant against whom an adverse action has been taken have expired. Each JHG/UMC Entity has delivered to Columbia/Jacksonville a written disclosure containing a brief description of all adverse actions taken against medical staff members or applicants which could result in claims or actions against such JHG/UMC Entity and which are not disclosed in the minutes of the meetings of the Medical Executive Committee of the Medical Staff of each of the JHG/UMC Facilities, which have been provided or made available to Columbia/Jacksonville.

(p)   Tax Liabilities.

-41-

(i)   True and correct copies of each JHG/UMC Entity's informational or income tax returns (including Forms 990 and 990T, as appropriate) for the most recent fiscal year, and the two previous fiscal years, of each JHG/UMC Entity have been delivered to Columbia/Jacksonville;

(ii)   All tax returns, including, without limitation, income tax returns, employee payroll tax returns, employee unemployment tax returns and franchise tax returns, for periods prior to and including Closing which are required to be filed by any JHG/UMC Entity (collectively "the JHG/UMC Entity Returns") have been filed or will be filed in the manner provided by law, and all JHG/UMC Entity Returns are or will be true and correct and accurately reflect the tax liabilities of the JHG/UMC Entities;

(iii)   All taxes, penalties, interest and any other statutory additions which have become due by any JHG/UMC Entity pursuant to the JHG/UMC Entity Returns and any assessments received by any JHG/UMC Entity (collectively "the JHG/UMC Entity Payable Tax Items") have been paid or adequately provided for by the reserves shown in the applicable JHG/UMC Entity Balance Sheet as of the applicable JHG/UMC Entity Balance Sheet Date;

(iv)   There are no tax liens on any of the assets of any JHG/UMC Entity except in respect of taxes not yet due and payable; and

(v)   Except as set forth on Schedule-16(p) hereto, there are no audit questions pending nor are there issues relating to, or claims or assessments for, the JHG/UMC Entity Payable Tax Items. Proper and accurate amounts have been withheld by each JHG/UMC Entity from its employees for all periods in full and complete compliance with the tax and other withholding provisions of all applicable laws and all of such amounts have been duly and validly remitted to the proper taxing authority.

(q)   Post-Balance Sheet Results. Except as set forth on Schedule 16(q) hereto, since the applicable Balance Sheet Date, there has not been:

(i)   any material adverse change in the financial position, assets, liabilities (contingent or otherwise), income or business of any JHG/UMC Entity;

(ii)   any damage, destruction or loss (whether or not covered by insurance) materially adversely affecting any JHG/UMC Entity or its assets;

(iii)   any labor dispute, any law or regulation or any event or condition of any character not generally known to the healthcare community materially adversely affecting the business of any JHG/UMC Entity;

(iv)   any sale, assignment, transfer or disposition of any single item of plant, property or equipment having a book value in excess of Ten Thousand Dollars ($10,000) (other than supplies), except in the ordinary course of business with comparable replacement thereof, if required; or

(v)   any transaction by any JHG/UMC Entity outside the ordinary course of business.

(r)   Environmental Claims. Except as disclosed on Schedule 16(r):
(i)   No JHG/UMC Entity has received any communication (written or oral) from any governmental authority, citizen group, employee or otherwise that alleges that any JHG/UMC Entity is not in full compliance with the Environmental Laws (as hereinafter defined), and there are no circumstances that may prevent or interfere with such full compliance in the future. There is no Environmental Claim (as hereinafter defined) pending or threatened against any JHG/UMC Entity.

(ii)   There are no past or present actions, activities, circumstances, conditions, events or incidents, including, without limitation, the generation, handling, transportation, treatment, storage, release, emission, discharge, presence, disposal or arranging for disposal of any Hazardous Substance, that could form the basis of any Environmental Claim against any JHG/UMC Entity under any Environmental Law (as defined below) in effect at any time at or prior to the Closing.

(iii)   Without in any way limiting the generality of the foregoing, (1) all underground storage tanks, and the capacity and contents of such tanks, located on the JHG/UMC Facilities are identified in Schedule 16(r), (2) except as identified in Schedule 16(r), there is no asbestos contained in or forming part of any building, building component, structure or office space owned or leased by any JHG/UMC Entity, and (3) except as identified in Schedule 16(r), no polychlorinated biphenyls (PCBs) are used or stored at any of the JHG/UMC Facilities.

(iv)   There have been no remedial, response or removal actions related in any way to Hazardous Substances located on, in or associated with any real property either currently or previously owned or leased in connection with the operation of the JHG/UMC Facilities, or on which any JHG/UMC Entity either currently has or previously had any operations; and no lien of any type has been attached with respect to any real property either currently or previously owned or leased by any JHG/UMC Entity, or on which any JHG/UMC Entity either currently has or previously had any operations, related to the presence or alleged presence of Hazardous Substances or otherwise pursuant to Environmental Laws.

(s)   No Admission. The inclusion of any item disclosed in Schedule 16(r), or the reference to any matter in any environmental report relating to the JHG/UMC Facilities delivered to Columbia/Jacksonville prior to Closing as contemplated by Section 16(r) (the "Environmental Report"), does not constitute an admission by the JHG/UMC Entity that any matters disclosed in such schedule or Environmental Report constitutes a violation of any Environmental Law.

–43–

(t)   Certain Definitions. The following terms shall have the following meanings:

(i)   "Environmental Claim" means for the purposes of Section 16(r)any claim, action, cause of action, investigation or written notice by any governmental authority or other person alleging potential liability (including, without limitation, potential liability for investigatory costs, cleanup costs, governmental response costs, natural resources damages, property damages, personal injuries or penalties) arising out of, based on or resulting from (a) the presence, or release into the environment, of any Hazardous Substances by the JHG/UMC Entities at any location, whether or not owned or operated by the JHG/UMC Entities in violation of an Environmental Law or (b) circumstances forming the basis of any violation, or alleged violation, of any Environmental Law.

(ii)   "Environmental Laws" means the federal, state (including specifically, but not by way of limitation, the State of Florida), and local environmental, health or safety laws, regulations and ordinances in effect on the date hereof and the Closing Date relating to the environment (including, without limitation, ambient air, surface water, ground water, land surface or subsurface strata) or the regulation or control of Hazardous Substances (as hereinafter below), as the same may be amended or modified to the date hereof and the Closing Date, including, without limitation, the statutes and regulations listed in subsection (iv), below.

(iii)   "Hazardous Substances" means any toxic or hazardous waste, pollutants or substances, explosives, radioactive materials, or Medical Waste (as hereinafter defined), including, without limitation, asbestos, PCBs, petroleum products and byproducts, substances defined or listed as "hazardous substance," "toxic substance," "toxic pollutant," or similarly identified substance or mixture, in or pursuant to any Environmental Law.

(iv)   "Medical Waste" means any substance, pollutant, material, infectious waste or contaminant listed or regulated under the Medical Waste Tracking Act of 1988, 42 U.S.C. § 6992, et seq., 49 C.F.R. § 173, 186, and/or comparable Florida statutory or regulatory provisions.

(u)   Investment Representation. JHG/UMC is acquiring an interest in the Joint Venture for its own account, for investment purposes only and with no present intention of distributing or reselling such interests or any part thereof, other than as provided herein. JHG/UMC acknowledges and understands that such interests will not be registered under the Securities Act of 1933, as amended (the "Act"), or under any other applicable blue sky or state securities law on the grounds that the offering and sale of such interests are exempt from registration pursuant to Section 4(2) of the Act and exempt from registration pursuant to comparable available exemptions in various states, and that the Joint Venture's reliance on such exemption is predicated in part upon the representations and warranties of JHG/UMC set forth in this Section 16(u). JHG/UMC acknowledges and understands that such interests must be held indefinitely unless such interests are subsequently registered under the Act and other applicable blue sky and state securities laws or unless exemption from such registration is available. JHG/UMC (i) has such knowledge and experience in financial and business matters as to be capable of evaluating the merits and risks of the prospective investment in the Joint Venture; (ii) has the ability to bear the economic risk of the investment, including a complete loss of the investment; (iii) is an accredited investor within the definition set forth in Rule 501(a) promulgated under the Act; (iv) has been furnished with and has had access to such information as it has considered necessary to make a determination as to the purchase of interests in the Joint Venture; and (v) has had all questions which have been asked satisfactorily answered by Columbia/Jacksonville.

(v)   Anti-Referral Legislation. No JHG/UMC Entity has committed to any action, entered into any agreement, contract or undertaking or taken or omitted to take any other action of any nature whatsoever that was or is in material violation of Medicare and Medicaid Anti-Fraud and Abuse or Anti-Kickback Amendments to the Social Security Act, the federal "anti-dumping'" law, the so-called "Stark I" federal legislation, the so-called "Stark II" federal legislation or any Florida laws corresponding in substance to any of the foregoing federal laws, and no JHG/UMC Entity has received any notice or inquiry relating to a violation or alleged violation of any of the above.

(w)   Full Disclosure. This Agreement and Schedules hereto and all Closing documents furnished and to be furnished to Columbia/Jacksonville and its representatives by the JHG/UMC Entities pursuant hereto do not and will not include any untrue statement of a material fact or, to the best knowledge of JHG/UMC, omit to state any material fact necessary to make the statements made and to be made not misleading.

(x)   Not Negotiating. No JHG/UMC Entity is bound under, or currently negotiating, any contract or agreement, not previously disclosed to Columbia/Jacksonville, with any third party concerning any matter or activity to be provided for in the Agreement.

17.   Representations and Warranties of Columbia/Jacksonville

Except as set forth in the schedules attached hereto, as of the date hereof, and as of the Closing Date, the Columbia/Jacksonville represents and warrants to JHG/UMC the following:

(a)   Corporate Capacity. Each Columbia/Jacksonville Related Entity is a corporation or a limited partnership and is duly organized, validly existing and in good standing under the laws of the state of its organization. Columbia/Jacksonville has the requisite power and authority to enter into this Agreement, perform its obligations hereunder and to conduct its business as now being conducted.

(b)   Powers; Consents; Absence of Conflicts With Other Agreements, Etc. The execution, delivery and performance of this Agreement by Columbia/Jacksonville and all other agreements referenced herein or ancillary hereto to which any of the Columbia/Jacksonville Related Entities is a party, and the consummation of the transactions contemplated herein and therein:

(i)   are within their respective powers, are not in contravention of law or of the terms of their respective articles of incorporation, bylaws or code of regulations, limited partnership agreement or any amendments thereto, and have been duly authorized by all appropriate action;

(ii)   to the best of its knowledge after due inquiry and except as otherwise expressly provided herein, do not require any approval or consent of, or filing with, any governmental agency or authority bearing on the validity of this Agreement which is required by law or the regulations of any such agency or authority other than those consents and approvals the respective Columbia/Jacksonville Related Entities will obtain from those governmental agencies and authorities set forth in Schedule 17(b);

(iii)   will neither conflict with nor result in any material breach or contravention of nor permit the acceleration of the maturity of any of their respective indebtedness or other liabilities, or the creation of any lien, charge or encumbrance affecting any of their respective assets;

(iv)   to the best of its knowledge will not violate any statute, law, rule or regulation of any governmental authority to which the Columbia/Jacksonville Related Entities or any of their respective assets may be subject; and

(v)   will not violate any judgment of any court or governmental authority to which they or any of their respective assets may be subject.

(c)   Binding Agreement. This Agreement and all agreements to which any Columbia/Jacksonville Related Entity will become a party pursuant to this Agreement are and will constitute the valid and legally binding obligations of each such Columbia/Jacksonville Related Entity and are and will be enforceable against them in accordance with their respective terms.

(d)   No Subsidiaries. Schedule 17(d) sets forth each for profit corporation owned in whole or in part by a Columbia/Jacksonville Related Entity and each not-for-profit corporation which has as a member a Columbia/Jacksonville Related Entity. Except as set forth in Schedule 17(d), no Columbia/Jacksonville Related Entity has any subsidiaries or any investment constituting more than ten percent (10%) of the equity interests in any other entity. No Columbia/Jacksonville Related Entity is a shareholder of another for profit corporation providing healthcare services except as set forth in Schedule 17(d), and the only corporate shareholders of the Columbia/Jacksonville

–46–

Related Entities are listed in Schedule 17(d). No Columbia/Jacksonville Related Entity is a party to any joint venture or other arrangement with physicians on the medical staff of any of the Columbia/Jacksonville Related Entities, other than as disclosed in Schedule 17(d).

         (e)   Financial Statements. Each Columbia/Jacksonville Related Entity has delivered to JHG/UMC copies of the following statements of financial condition and results from operations (collectively, the "Columbia/Jacksonville Related Entity Financial Statements"), which Columbia/Jacksonville Related Entity Financial Statements are maintained on an accrual basis, copies of which are attached hereto as Schedule 17(e):

         (i)   Unaudited Balance Sheets for the one month period ending as of January 31, 1996 (the "Columbia/Jacksonville Related Entity Balance Sheet Date");

         (ii)   Unaudited Income Statements for the one month period ended on the Columbia/Jacksonville Related Entity Balance Sheet Date; and

         (iii)   For GFI, with respect to Orange Park Medical Center, audited Balance Sheets, Income Statements and Statements of Cash Flow for the fiscal years ended December 31, 1992, December 31, 1993 and December 31, 1994, and unaudited Balance Sheets, Income Statements and Statements of Cash Flow for the fiscal year ended December 31, 1995; and

         (iv)   For MHG, with respect to Memorial Hospital of Jacksonville, audited Balance Sheets, Income Statements and Statements of Cash Flow for the fiscal years ended April 30, 1992, April 30, 1993, April 30, 1994 and January 2, 1995, and unaudited Balance Sheets, Income Statements and Statements of Cash Flow for the fiscal year ended December 31, 1995, and with respect to Memorial Specialty Hospital, audited Balance Sheets, Income Statements and Statements of Cash Flow for the fiscal years ended August 31, 1992 (as Jacksonville Medical Center, debtor-in-possession), August 31, 1993, April 30, 1994 and January 2, 1995, and unaudited Balance Sheets, Income Statements and Statements of Cash Flow for the fiscal year ended December 31, 1995.

Such audited Columbia/Jacksonville Related Entity Financial Statements have been prepared in accordance with GAAP throughout the periods indicated. Subject to year-end adjustments consistent with past practice, such unaudited Columbia/Jacksonville Related Entity Financial Statements materially conform to GAAP, except as set forth in Schedule 17(e). Except as set forth in Schedule 17(e), such Balance Sheets present fairly the financial condition of each Columbia/Jacksonville Related Entity as of the dates indicated thereon, and such Income Statements present fairly the results of operations of each Columbia/Jacksonville Related Entity for the periods indicated thereon. Since the Columbia/Jacksonville Related Entity Balance Sheet Date, there have occurred no material adverse changes in the financial condition or results of operations of any Columbia/Jacksonville Related Entity as reflected in such Columbia/Jacksonville Related Entity Financial Statements.

     (f)   Extraordinary Liabilities. Each Columbia/Jacksonville Related Entity has delivered to JHG/UMC an accurate list (Schedule 17(f)) of all of its liabilities not included in the Columbia/Jacksonville Related Entity Financial Statements which are of the kind and character required in financial statements prepared in accordance with GAAP and which were incurred other than in the ordinary course of business, whether accrued, absolute, contingent or otherwise, together with, in the case of those liabilities as to which the liabilities are not fixed, a reasonable estimate of the maximum amount which may be payable in respect thereof. Except as disclosed in Schedule 17(f) or the Columbia/Jacksonville Related Entity Financial Statements, no Columbia/Jacksonville Related Entity has any liabilities of any nature, whether accrued, absolute, contingent or otherwise. There are no facts in existence on the date hereof known or which should be known to any Columbia/Jacksonville Related Entity which might reasonably serve as the basis for any liability or obligation of any Columbia/Jacksonville Related Entity which is not fully disclosed in Schedule 17(f) or the Columbia/Jacksonville Related Entity Financial Statements.

     (g)   Licenses. Each Columbia/Jacksonville Related Facility is duly licensed as a facility to perform the services described on Schedule 17(g)-1. The pharmacies, laboratories and all other ancillary departments owned by the Columbia/Jacksonville Related Entities and located at any of the Columbia/Jacksonville Related Facilities or operated for the benefit of any of the Columbia/Jacksonville Related Facilities which are required to be specially licensed are duly licensed by the Florida Department of Health or other appropriate licensing agency. Each Columbia/Jacksonville Related Entity has all other licenses, permits and approvals which are needed or required by law to operate the business related to or affecting any of the Columbia/Jacksonville Related Facilities. Each Columbia/Jacksonville Related Entity has delivered to JHG/UMC an accurate list and summary description (Schedule 17(g)-2) of all such licenses and permits owned or held by such Columbia/Jacksonville Related Entity relating to the ownership, development or operation of any of the Columbia/Jacksonville Related Facilities, all of which are now and as of Closing shall be in good standing and not subject to meritorious challenge.

     (h)   Medicare Participation/Accreditation. Each Columbia/Jacksonville Related Facility is qualified for participation in the Medicare and Medicaid programs, has a current and valid provider contract with the Medicare and Medicaid programs, is in compliance with the conditions of participation in such programs and has received all approvals or qualifications necessary for capital reimbursement. Each Columbia/Jacksonville Related Facility is duly accredited, with no contingencies other than as shown on the most recent Joint Commission of Accreditation of Healthcare Organizations ("JCAHO") survey, by the JCAHO for the three (3) year periods ending on the dates specified therefor on Schedule 17(h). Correct and complete copies of the most recent accreditation letters from the JCAHO pertaining to each Columbia/Jacksonville

Related Facility have been delivered to JHG/UMC. Except as set forth on Schedule 17(h), no Columbia/Jacksonville Related Entity has received notice from either the Medicare or Medicaid programs of any pending or threatened investigations or surveys, and no Columbia/Jacksonville Related Entity has reason to believe that any such investigations or surveys are pending, threatened or imminent.

(i)   Regulatory Compliance. Except as set forth on Schedule 17(i),each Columbia/Jacksonville Related Entity is in compliance in all material respects with all applicable laws, statutes, rules, regulations, ordinances and the requirements of all federal, state and local commissions, boards, bureaus, permits and agencies having jurisdiction over any of the Columbia/Jacksonville Related Facilities or the operations of any of the Columbia/Jacksonville Related Facilities, including, without limitation, the Internal Revenue Service, the Environmental Protection Agency, the Florida Environmental Protection Agency, and the Florida Department of Health, which compliance includes, without limitation, possession by each Columbia/Jacksonville Related Entity of all permits and other governmental authorizations required under all such laws; and each Columbia/Jacksonville Related Entity has timely filed all reports, data and other information required to be filed with such commissions, boards, bureaus and agencies where a failure to file timely would have a material adverse effect on the its assets.

(j)   Insurance. Columbia/Jacksonville has delivered to JHG/UMC an accurate schedule (Schedule 17(j)) disclosing the insurance policies covering the ownership and operations of the Columbia/Jacksonville Related Facilities, which Schedule reflects the policies' numbers, terms, identity of insurers, amounts, premiums and coverage. All of such policies are now and will be until Closing in full force and effect on a claims-made basis with no premiums, arrearage. Except as set forth in Schedule 17(j), each Columbia/Jacksonville Related Entity has given in a timely manner to its insurers all notices required to be given under its insurance policies with respect to all of the claims and actions covered by insurance, and no insurer has denied coverage of any such claims or actions or reserved its rights in respect of or rejected any of such claims. No Columbia/Jacksonville Related Entity has (i) received any notice or other communication from any such insurance company canceling or materially amending any of such insurance policies, and no such cancellation or amendment is threatened, or (ii) failed to give any required notice or present any claim which is still outstanding under any of such policies with respect to any of its assets.

(k)   Employee Benefit Plans. All employee pension benefit plans and employee health or welfare benefits plans (as such terms are defined in ERISA) maintained by the Columbia/Jacksonville Related Entities (collectively "the Columbia/Jacksonville Related Entity Benefit Plans") have been administered in accordance with ERISA and the applicable provisions of the Code. There are no "accumulated funding deficiencies" within the meaning of ERISA or the Code or any federal excise tax or liability on account of any deficient fundings in respect of the

Columbia/Jacksonville Related Entity Benefit Plans. No reportable event (within the meaning of ERISA) or prohibited transaction (within the meaning of the Code) has occurred in respect of the Columbia/Jacksonville Related Entity Benefit Plans. There are no threatened or pending claims by or on behalf of the Columbia/Jacksonville Related Entity Benefit Plans or by any employee of any Columbia/Jacksonville Related Entity alleging a breach or breaches of fiduciary duties or violations of other applicable state or Federal law which could result in liability on the part of either a Columbia/Jacksonville Related Entity or any of the Columbia/Jacksonville Related Entity Benefit Plans under ERISA or any other law, nor is there any basis for such a claim. The Columbia/Jacksonville Related Entity Benefit Plans do not discriminate in operating in favor of employees who are officers or highly compensated. Except as set forth on Schedule 17(k), all returns, reports, disclosure statements and premium payments required to be made under ERISA and the Code with respect to the Columbia/Jacksonville Related Entity Benefit Plans have been timely filed or delivered. Except as set forth on Schedule 17(k),the Columbia/Jacksonville Related Entity Benefit Plans have not been audited or investigated by either the Internal Revenue Service, the Department of Labor or the Pension Benefit Guaranty Corporation within the last five (5) years, and there are no outstanding issues with reference to the Columbia/Jacksonville Related Entity Benefit Plans pending before such governmental agencies.

(l)   Employee Relations. The employee relations of the Columbia/Jacksonville Related Entities are generally good, when considered in the aggregate, pertaining to the Columbia/Jacksonville Related Facilities. There is no pending or threatened employee strike, work stoppage or labor dispute, and no union representation question exists, respecting any employees of the Columbia/Jacksonville Related Entities. Except as disclosed on Schedule 17(l), no collective bargaining agreement exists or is currently being negotiated by the Columbia/Jacksonville Related Entities, no demand has been made for recognition by a labor organization by or with respect to any employees of the Columbia/Jacksonville Related Entities, no union organizing activities by or with respect to any employees of the Columbia/Jacksonville Related Entities are taking place, and none of the employees of the Columbia/Jacksonville Related Entities is represented by any labor union or organization. There is no unfair practice claim against the Columbia/Jacksonville Related Entities before the National Labor Relations Board, or any strike, dispute, slowdown or stoppage pending or threatened against or involving any of the Columbia/Jacksonville Related Facilities, and none has occurred. Each Columbia/Jacksonville Related Entity is in compliance with all federal and state laws respecting employment and employment practices, terms and conditions of employment, and wages and hours. No Columbia/Jacksonville Related Entity is engaged in any unfair labor practices. Except as set forth on Schedule 17(l) there are no pending or threatened EEOC claims, wage and hour claims, unemployment compensation claims, workers' compensation claims or the like.

(m)   Litigation or Proceedings. The Columbia/Jacksonville Related Entities have delivered to JHG/UMC an accurate list and summary description (Schedule 17(m)) of all litigation or proceedings involving any Columbia/Jacksonville Related Entity with respect to the Columbia/Jacksonville Related Facilities or otherwise. No Columbia/Jacksonville Related Entity is in material default under any law or regulation relating to the operation of any of the Columbia/Jacksonville Related Facilities. No Columbia/Jacksonville Related Entity is in default under any order of any court or federal, state, municipal or other governmental department, commission, board, bureau, agency or instrumentality wherever located. Except to the extent set forth on Schedule 17(m), there are no claims or investigations pending or threatened against or affecting the Columbia/Jacksonville Related Entities with respect to any of the Columbia/Jacksonville Related Facilities, at law or in equity, or before or by any federal, state, municipal or other governmental department, commission, board, bureau, agency or instrumentality wherever located.

(n)   Third Party Payor Cost Reports. Each Columbia/Jacksonville Related Entity has duly filed all required cost reports for all the fiscal years through and including the most recent fiscal year, and such reports have been filed either on a timely basis or prior to the time any penalty could be incurred for failure to file on a timely basis. All of such cost reports accurately reflect the information to be included thereon and do not claim, and neither any Columbia/Jacksonville Related Entity nor any of the Columbia/Jacksonville Related Facilities has received reimbursement in excess of the amount provided by law, except as provided in Schedule 17(n) hereto. Schedule 17(n) hereto indicates which of such cost reports have been audited and finally settled, the status of such cost reports which have not been audited and finally settled and a brief description of any and all notices of program reimbursement, proposed or pending audit adjustments, disallowances, appeals of disallowances and any and all other unresolved claims or disputes in respect of such cost reports. Except as set forth on Schedule 17(n), there are no facts or circumstances which may reasonably be expected to give rise to any material disallowance under any such cost reports.

(o)   Medical Staff Matters. Each Columbia/Jacksonville Related Entity has heretofore provided or made available to JHG/UMC true, correct, and complete copies of the bylaws and rules and regulations of the medical staffs of each of the Columbia/Jacksonville Related Facilities. With regard to the medical staffs of the Columbia/Jacksonville Related Facilities and except as set forth on Schedule 17(o) hereto, there are no pending or threatened disputes with applicants, staff members or health professional affiliates, and all appeal periods in respect of any medical staff member or applicant against whom an adverse action has been taken have expired. Each Columbia/Jacksonville Related Entity has delivered to JHG/UMC a written disclosure containing a brief description of all adverse actions taken against medical staff members or applicants which could result in claims or actions against such Columbia/Jacksonville Related Entity and which are not disclosed in the minutes of the meetings of the Medical

−51−

Executive Committee of the Medical Staff of each of the Columbia/Jacksonville Related Facilities, which have been provided or made available to JHG/UMC.

(p)   Tax Liabilities.

(i)   True and correct copies of each Columbia/Jacksonville Related Entity's informational or income tax returns (including Forms 990, 1065 and/or 1120, as appropriate) for the most recent fiscal year, and the two previous fiscal years, of each Columbia/Jacksonville Related Entity have been made available to JHG/UMC;

(ii)   All tax returns, including, without limitation, income tax returns, employee payroll tax returns, employee unemployment tax returns and franchise tax returns, for periods prior to and including Closing which are required to be filed by any Columbia/Jacksonville Related Entity (collectively "the Columbia/Jacksonville Related Entity Returns") have been filed or will be filed in the manner provided by law, and all Columbia/Jacksonville Related Entity Returns are or will be true and correct and accurately reflect the tax liabilities of the Columbia/Jacksonville Related Entities;

(iii)   All taxes, penalties, interest and any other statutory additions which have become due by any Columbia/Jacksonville Related Entity pursuant to the Columbia/Jacksonville Related Entity Returns and any assessments received by any Columbia/Jacksonville Related Entity (collectively "the Columbia/Jacksonville Related Entity Payable Tax Items") have been paid or adequately provided for by the reserves shown in the applicable Columbia/Jacksonville Related Entity Balance Sheet as of the applicable Columbia/Jacksonville Related Entity Balance Sheet Date;

(iv)   There are no tax liens on any of the assets of any Columbia/Jacksonville Related Entity except in respect of taxes not yet due and payable; and

(v)   Except as set forth on Schedule 17(p) hereto, there are no audit questions pending nor are there issues relating to, or claims or assessments for, the Columbia/Jacksonville Related Entity Payable Tax Items. Proper and accurate amounts have been withheld by each Columbia/Jacksonville Related Entity from its employees for all periods in full and complete compliance with the tax and other withholding provisions of all applicable laws and all of such amounts have been duly and validly remitted to the proper taxing authority.

(q)   Post-Balance Sheet Results. Except as set forth on Schedule 17(q) hereto, since the applicable Balance Sheet Date, there has not been:

(i)   any material adverse change in the financial position, assets, liabilities (contingent or otherwise), income or business of any Columbia/Jacksonville Related Entity;

(ii)   any damage, destruction or loss (whether or not covered by insurance) materially adversely affecting any Columbia/Jacksonville Related Entity or its assets;

(iii)   any labor dispute, any law or regulation or any event or condition of any character not generally known to the healthcare community materially adversely affecting the business of any Columbia/Jacksonville Related Entity;

(iv)   any sale, assignment, transfer or disposition of any single item of plant, property or equipment having a book value in excess of Ten Thousand Dollars ($10,000) (other than supplies), except in the ordinary course of business with comparable replacement thereof, if required; or

(v)   any transaction by any Columbia/Jacksonville Related Entity outside the ordinary course of business.

(r)   <u>Environmental Claims</u>. Except as disclosed on <u>Schedule 17(r)</u>:

(i)   No Columbia/Jacksonville Related Entity has received any communication (written or oral) from any governmental authority, citizen group, employee or otherwise that alleges that any Columbia/Jacksonville Related Entity is not in full compliance with the Environmental Laws, and there are no circumstances that may prevent or interfere with such full compliance in the future. There is no Environmental Claim (as hereinafter defined) pending or threatened against any Columbia/Jacksonville Related Entity.

(ii)   There are no past or present actions, activities, circumstances, conditions, events or incidents, including, without limitation, the generation, handling, transportation, treatment, storage, release, emission, discharge, presence, disposal or arranging for disposal of any Hazardous Substance, that could form the basis of any Environmental Claim against any Columbia/Jacksonville Related Entity under any Environmental Law in effect at any time at or prior to the Closing.

(iii)   Without in any way limiting the generality of the foregoing, (i) all underground storage tanks, and the capacity and contents of such tanks, located on the Columbia/Jacksonville Related Facilities are identified in <u>Schedule 17(r)</u>, (ii) except as identified in <u>Schedule 17(r)</u>, there is no asbestos contained in or forming part of any building, building component, structure or office space owned or leased by any Columbia/Jacksonville Related Entity, and (iii) except as identified in Schedule 17(r), no polychlorinated biphenyls (PCBs) are used or stored at any of the Columbia/Jacksonville Related Facilities.

(iv) There have been no remedial, response or removal actions related in any way to Hazardous Substances located on, in or associated with any real property either currently or previously owned or leased in connection with the operation of the Columbia/Jacksonville Related Facilities, or on which any Columbia/Jacksonville Related Entity either currently has or previously had any operations; and no lien of any type has been attached with respect to any real property either currently or previously owned or leased by any Columbia/Jacksonville Related Entity, or on which any Columbia/Jacksonville Related Entity either currently has or previously had any operations, related to the presence or alleged presence of Hazardous Substances or otherwise pursuant to Environmental Laws.

(s) No Admission. The inclusion of any item disclosed in Schedule 17(r), or the reference to any matter in any environmental report relating to the Columbia/Jacksonville Related Facilities delivered to JHG/UMC prior to Closing as contemplated by Section 17(r) (the "Environmental Report"), does not constitute an admission by the Columbia/Jacksonville Related Entities that any matters disclosed in such schedule or Environmental Report constitutes a violation of any Environmental Law.

(t) Certain Definitions.

"Environmental Claim" means, for the purposes of Section 17(r), above, any claim, action, cause of action, investigation or written notice by any governmental authority or other person alleging potential liability (including, without limitation, potential liability for investigatory costs, cleanup costs, governmental response costs, natural resources damages, property damages, personal injuries or penalties) arising out of, based on or resulting from (a) the presence, or release into the environment, of any Hazardous Substances by the Columbia/Jacksonville Related Entities at any location, whether or not owned or operated by the Columbia/Jacksonville Related Entities in violation of an Environmental Law or (b) circumstances forming the basis of any violation, or alleged violation, of any Environmental Law.

(u) Investment Representation. Columbia/Jacksonville is acquiring interests in the Joint Venture for its own account, for investment purposes only and with no present intention of distributing or reselling such interests or any part thereof, other than as provided herein. Columbia/Jacksonville acknowledges and understands that such interests will not be registered under the Securities Act of 1933, as amended (the "Act"), or under any other applicable blue sky or state securities law on the grounds that the offering and sale of such interests are exempt from registration pursuant to Section 4(2) of the Act and exempt from registration pursuant to comparable available exemptions in various states, and that the Joint Venture's reliance on such exemption is predicated in part upon the representations and warranties of each Columbia/Jacksonville Related Entity set forth in this Section 17(u). Columbia/Jacksonville acknowledges and understands that such interests must be held indefinitely unless such interests are subsequently registered under the Act and other applicable blue sky and state securities laws or unless exemption from such registration is available. Columbia/Jacksonville (i) has such knowledge and experience in financial and business matters as to be capable of evaluating the merits and risks of the prospective investment in the Company; (ii) has the ability to bear the economic risk of the investment, including a complete loss of the investment; (iii) is an accredited investor within the definition set forth in Rule 501(a) promulgated under the Act; (iv) has been furnished with and has had access to such information as it has considered necessary to make a determination as to the purchase of interests in the Joint Venture; and (v) has had all questions which have been asked satisfactorily answered by JHG/UMC.

(v)   Anti-Referral Legislation. No Columbia/Jacksonville Related Entity has committed to any action, entered into any agreement, contract or undertaking or taken or omitted to take any other action of any nature whatsoever that was or is in material violation of Medicare and Medicaid Anti-Fraud and Abuse or Anti-Kickback Amendments to the Social Security Act, the federal "anti-dumping" law, the so-called "Stark I" federal legislation, the so-called "Stark II" federal legislation or any Florida laws corresponding in substance to any of the foregoing federal laws, and no Columbia/Jacksonville Related Entity has received any notice or inquiry relating to a violation or alleged violation of any of the above.

(w)   Full Disclosure. This Agreement and Schedules hereto and all Closing documents furnished and to be furnished to JHG/UMC and their representatives by the Columbia/Jacksonville Related Entities pursuant hereto do not and will not include any untrue statement of a material fact or, to the best knowledge of the Columbia/Jacksonville Related Entities, omit to state any material fact necessary to make the statements made and to be made not misleading.

(x)   Not Negotiating. Neither any Columbia/Jacksonville Related Entity nor any Columbia/HCA Affiliate is bound under, or currently negotiating, any contract or agreement, not previously disclosed to JHG/UMC, with any third party concerning the formation of a joint venture or another transaction in the First Coast Area which, if implemented or consummated, as the case may be, would materially adversely affect the prospects of the Joint Venture.

18.   Closing

18.1. Closing. Subject to the satisfaction or waiver by the appropriate party of all of the conditions precedent to Closing specified in Sections 21, 22 and 23, the consummation of transactions contemplated by and described in this Agreement (the "Closing") shall take place at the offices of Columbia/Jacksonville, 3627 University Boulevard South, Jacksonville, Florida 32218, not later than ten (10) business days (unless waived by the parties) following the satisfaction of all conditions to Closing set forth in Sections 21, 22 and 23 (the "Closing Date"). The Closing shall be effective as of 12:01 a.m. on the next day thereafter (the "Joint Venture Stage II Commencement Date"). Unless waived in writing by all parties, if the conditions to Closing set forth in Sections 21, 22 and 23 have not been satisfied on or before March 31, 1998, then, except with respect to the rights and obligations of the parties set forth in Sections 26 and 27.7, this Agreement shall be null and void. The parties will endeavor to cause the Closing to occur on the last day of a calendar month, and in any event all financial calculations will be made as of 12:01 a.m. on the first day of the calendar month closest to the Closing.

18.2. Action of the Parties. At the Closing, the Joint Venturers shall make the capital contributions to the Joint Venture, if any, and execute and deliver the Management Services Agreements and such other documents, agreements, instruments and certificates as may be necessary or reasonably requested, and to evidence the satisfaction of the conditions precedent to the obligations of the parties hereto, except to the extent waived in writing by the appropriate party. In addition, the parties hereto shall cause the Joint Venture to take all actions contemplated by this Agreement and shall execute and deliver such other documents, agreements, certificates and instruments as the parties hereto shall deem reasonably necessary to consummate the transactions described herein.

19. Covenants of JHG/UMC Prior to the Joint Venture Stage II Commencement Date

Between the date of this Agreement and Joint Venture Stage II Commencement Date:

19.1. Tax Matters Opinion; Private Letter Ruling. JHG/UMC shall promptly engage experienced tax counsel satisfactory to them to render an opinion of counsel with respect to the matters set forth in Section 23(a), or if he is unable to do so, to advise them of the reasons therefor, and, if JHG/UMC deems it reasonable or necessary, to prepare and file, and diligently pursue obtaining, a private letter ruling from the Internal Revenue Service with respect to such matters. JHG/UMC shall keep Columbia/Jacksonville promptly and fully apprised of their actions and any developments or results with respect thereto.

19.2. Information. JHG/UMC shall afford to the officers and authorized representatives and agents of Columbia/Jacksonville (which shall include their accountants, attorneys, bankers and other consultants) at the sole cost of Columbia/Jacksonville, full and complete access to and the right to inspect during normal business hours and upon reasonable prior notice the plants, properties, books and records of the JHG/UMC Entities and the JHG/UMC Facilities and will furnish or make available to Columbia/Jacksonville with such additional financial and operating data and other information as to the business and properties of the JHG/UMC Entities and the

JHG/UMC Facilities as Columbia/Jacksonville may from time to time reasonably request without regard to where such information may be located. Columbia/Jacksonville's right of access and inspection shall be exercised in such a manner as not to interfere unreasonably with the operations of the JHG/UMC Facilities or the JHG/UMC Entities.

19.3. Additional Financial Information. Within twelve (12) days following the end of each calendar month prior to the Joint Venture Stage II Commencement Date. JHG/UMC will deliver to Columbia/Jacksonville true and complete copies of the unaudited balance sheets and the related unaudited statements of income and cash flow of each JHG/UMC Entity and the operations of each of the JHG/UMC Facilities for each month then ended, together with a year-to-date compilation and the notes, if any, related thereto, which presentation shall be true, correct and complete in all material respects, shall have been prepared from and in accordance with the books and records of such JHG/UMC Entity, and which shall fairly present the financial position, results of operations and cash flow of such JHG/UMC Entity and each of the JHG/UMC Facilities, as of the date and for the period indicated, all in accordance with GAAP, subject to year-end adjustment consistent with past practice, except that such financial statements need not include required footnote disclosures.

19.4. Operations. From the date hereof until the Joint Venture Stage II Commencement Date. JHG/UMC shall cause each JHG/UMC Entity to:

(a) carry on its businesses in substantially the same manner as presently conducted and not make any material change in operations, finance, accounting policies or real or personal property which would have a detrimental effect on its financial performance or business prospects;

(b) maintain the JHG/UMC Facilities and all, parts thereof in substantially the same condition as they are now in, ordinary wear and tear and replacements excepted;

(c) perform all of its obligations under agreements relating to or affecting the JHG/UMC Entities or the JHG/UMC Facilities, including without limitation the Interim Management Services Agreement;

(d) continue to make routine capital expenditures to the extent they were planned for and budgeted by such JHG/UMC Entity;

(e) keep in full force and effect present insurance policies or other comparable insurance; and

(f) use its best efforts to maintain and preserve its business organizations intact and maintain its relationships with physicians, customers and others having business relations with the JHG/UMC Entities.

19.5.   Negative Covenants. From the date hereof until the Joint Venture Stage II Commencement Date, JHG/UMC will not permit any JHG/UMC Entity, without the prior written consent of Columbia/Jacksonville, to:

(a)   amend or cause the early termination of any of its contracts, including without limitation the Interim Management Services Agreement, enter into any contract or commitment, or incur or agree to incur any liability, except in the ordinary course of business:

(b)   create, assume or permit to exist any new debt, mortgage, pledge or other lien or encumbrance in excess of $1,000,000 individually and $5,000,000 in the aggregate, upon any of the assets of such JHG/UMC Entity, whether now owned or hereafter acquired, except purchase money liens and encumbrances in the ordinary course of business and consistent with past practice;

(c)   sell, assign, lease or otherwise transfer or dispose of any property, plant or equipment except in the normal course of business with comparable replacement thereof; or

(d)   take any action outside the ordinary course of business.

19.6.   No-Shop Clause. From and after the date of the execution and delivery of this Agreement by JHG/UMC until the Joint Venture Stage II Commencement Date or earlier termination of this Agreement, no JHG/UMC Entity will, without the prior written consent of the Columbia/Jacksonville: (i) offer for sale or lease all or any material portion of the assets of the JHG/UMC Facilities or any membership interests in any JHG/UMC Entity or change the management of any JHG/UMC Entity, (ii) solicit offers to buy all or any material portion of the JHG/UMC Facilities or any membership interests in any JHG/UMC Entity, (iii) hold discussions with any party (other than Columbia/Jacksonville) looking toward such an offer or solicitation or looking toward a merger or consolidation of any JHG/UMC Entity, or (iv) enter into any agreement with any party (other than Columbia/Jacksonville) with respect to the sale or other disposition of the JHG/UMC Facilities (or any material portion thereof) or any ownership interests in any JHG/UMC Entity or with respect to any merger, consolidation, or similar transaction involving any JHG/UMC Entity.

19.7.   Valuation Opinions. JHG, for its sole use, shall promptly engage a third party consultant acceptable to JHG to prepare opinions as to the valuation of the JHG/UMC Related Facilities and the Columbia/Jacksonville Related Facilities, and shall promptly deliver a copy of the same to Columbia/Jacksonville. Columbia/Jacksonville shall reimburse JHG for the lesser of $62,500 (plus one-half (1/2) of such consultant's reasonable out-of-pocket expenses) or one-half (1/2) of the cost of such valuation opinions (including such consultant's professional fees and reasonable out-of-pocket expenses) ("Columbia/Jacksonville's Share") within thirty (30) days of the receipt thereof. If a) JHG elects to terminate this Agreement pursuant to the provisions of Section 1.44(c), or b) Columbia elects to terminate this Agreement as a result of a default on the part of JHG/UMC, including without limitation a failure of JHG/UMC to fulfill its obligations under Sections 19.1 and 19.8, which default is not cured by JHG/UMC within the applicable cure period, if any, JHG/UMC shall refund Columbia/Jacksonville's Share to Columbia/Jacksonville within thirty (30) days of such termination.

19.8.   Required Authorizations. Between the date of this Agreement and the Joint Venture Stage II Commencement Date. JHG/UMC shall use its best efforts to obtain an opinion from the City Attorney for the City of Jacksonville. Florida that the consent and approval of the City of Jacksonville. Florida to the transactions contemplated by this Agreement is not required, or if such consent and approval is required, obtain the consent and approval of the City of Jacksonville. Florida to the transactions contemplated by this Agreement.

19.9.   Approved Capital Projects. Except in the case of any Emergency, in the event that any JHG/UMC Entity desires to commence any non-routine or unbudgeted capital project in respect of any of the JHG/UMC Facilities between the date of this Agreement and the Joint Venture Stage II Commencement Date having a projected cost in excess of $1,000.000, JHG/UMC shall notify Columbia/Jacksonville thereof and prior to commencement deliver to Columbia/Jacksonville a schedule relating to such project which contains (i) a description of such project (including the anticipated benefits to be derived therefrom), (ii) the projected costs of such project, (iii) the anticipated completion date of such project, and (iv) a place for Columbia/Jacksonville to indicate its approval thereof (if and to the extent that Columbia/Jacksonville, in its discretion, determine to approve such project). JHG/UMC shall also furnish to Columbia/Jacksonville any additional information Columbia/Jacksonville might reasonably request concerning such project. "Emergency" shall mean a situation in which, unless the affected JHG/UMC Entity acts within a time frame in which it is not reasonably possible to provide to Columbia/Jacksonville the information described above and obtain their approval, the operation of the affected JHG/UMC Facility would be in violation of any regulatory requirement, seriously impaired or the integrity or condition of the affected JHG/UMC Facility would be seriously jeopardized; provided, however, in the event of an Emergency, JHG/UMC shall notify Columbia/Jacksonville as soon as practicable of the nature of the Emergency and the action it intends to take in response thereto, and shall thereafter keep Columbia/Jacksonville fully apprised of developments and their actions with respect thereto.

20.   Covenants of Columbia/Jacksonville Prior to the Joint Venture Stage II Commencement Date Between the date of this Agreement and the Joint Venture Stage II Commencement Date:

20.1.   Information. Columbia/Jacksonville shall afford to the officers and authorized representatives and agents of JHG/UMC (which shall include their accountants, attorneys, bankers and other consultants) at the sole cost of JHG/UMC, full and complete access to and the right to inspect during normal business hours and upon reasonable prior notice the plants, properties, books and records of the Columbia/Jacksonville Related Entities and the Columbia/HCA Related Facilities and will furnish or make available to JHG/UMC with such additional financial and operating data and other information as to the business and properties of

–59–

the Columbia/Jacksonville Related Entities and the Columbia/HCA Related Facilities as JHG/UMC may from time to time reasonably request without regard to where such information may be located. JHG/UMC's right of access and inspection shall be exercised in such a manner as not to interfere unreasonably with the operations of the Columbia/HCA Related Facilities or the Columbia/Jacksonville Related Entities.

    20.2.   Additional Financial Information. Within twelve (12) days following the end of each calendar month prior to the Joint Venture Stage II Commencement Date, Columbia/Jacksonville will deliver to JHG/UMC true and complete copies of the unaudited balance sheets and the related unaudited statements of income and cash flow of such Columbia/Jacksonville Related Entity and the operations of each of the Columbia/HCA Related Facilities for each month then ended, together with a year-to-date compilation and the notes, if any, related thereto, which presentation shall be true, correct and complete in all material respects, shall have been prepared from and in accordance with the books and records of such Columbia/Jacksonville Related Entity, and which shall fairly present the financial position, results of operations and cash flow of such Columbia/Jacksonville Related Entity and each of the Columbia/HCA Related Facilities, as of the date and for the period indicated, all in accordance with GAAP, subject to year-end adjustment consistent with past practice, except that such financial statements need not include required footnote disclosures.

    20.3.   Operations. From the date hereof until the Joint Venture Stage II Commencement Date. Columbia/Jacksonville shall cause each Columbia/Jacksonville Related Entity to:

        (a)   carry on its businesses in substantially the same manner as presently conducted and not make any material change in personnel, operations, finance, accounting policies, or real or personal property;

        (b)   maintain the Columbia/HCA Related Facilities and all parts thereof in substantially the same condition as they are now in, ordinary wear and tear and replacements excepted;

        (c)   perform all of its obligations under agreements relating to or affecting the Columbia/Jacksonville Related Entities or the Columbia/HCA Related Facilities, including without limitation the Interim Management Services Agreement;

        (d)   continue to make routine capital expenditures to the extent they were planned for and budgeted by such Columbia/Jacksonville Related Entity;

        (e)   keep in full force and effect present insurance policies or other comparable insurance; and

        (f)   use its best efforts to maintain and preserve its business organizations intact, retain substantially all of its present employees at the Columbia/HCA Related

Facilities and maintain its relationships with physicians, suppliers, customers and others having business relations with the Columbia/Jacksonville Related Entities.

20.4. <u>Negative Covenants</u>. From the date hereof until the Joint Venture Stage II Commencement Date, Columbia/Jacksonville will not permit any Columbia/Jacksonville Related Entity, without the prior written consent of JHG/UMC, to:

    (a)   amend or cause the early termination of any of its contracts, including without limitation the Interim Management Services Agreement, enter into any contract or commitment, or incur or agree to incur any liability, except in the ordinary course of business;

    (b)   create, assume or permit to exist any new debt, mortgage, pledge or other lien or encumbrance, in excess of $1,000,000 individually or $5,000,000 in the aggregate, upon any of the assets of such Columbia/Jacksonville Related Entity, whether now owned or hereafter acquired, except purchase money liens and encumbrances in the ordinary course of business and consistent with past practice;

    (c)   sell, assign, lease or otherwise transfer or dispose of any property, plant or equipment except in the normal course of business with comparable replacement thereof; or

    (d)   take any action outside the ordinary course of business.

20.5. <u>No-Shop Clause</u>. From and after the date of the execution and delivery of this Agreement by Columbia/Jacksonville until the Joint Venture Stage II Commencement Date or earlier termination of this Agreement, no Columbia/Jacksonville Related Entity will, without the prior written consent of JHG/UMC: (i) offer for sale or lease all or any material portion of the assets of the Columbia/HCA Related Facilities or any interest in any Columbia/Jacksonville Related Entity or change the management of any Columbia/Jacksonville Related Entity, (ii) solicit offers to buy all or any material portion of the Columbia/HCA Related Facilities or any interests in any Columbia/Jacksonville Related Entity, (iii) hold discussions with any parry (other than JHG/UMC) looking toward such an offer or solicitation or looking toward a merger or consolidation of any Columbia/Jacksonville Related Entity, or (iv) enter into any agreement with any party (other than JHG/UMC) with respect to the sale or other disposition of the Columbia/HCA Related Facilities (or any material portion thereof) or any ownership interests in any Columbia/Jacksonville Related Entity or with respect to any merger, consolidation, or similar transaction involving any Columbia/Jacksonville Related Entity; provided however, nothing herein shall be deemed to prohibit Columbia/HCA from engaging in any of the foregoing described activities with respect to all or substantially all of its assets or stock, or entering in any merger, consolidation or corporate reorganization.

20.6. <u>Approved Capital Projects</u>. Except in the case of any Emergency, in the event that any Columbia/Jacksonville Related Entity desires to commence any non-routine or unbudgeted capital project in respect of any of the Columbia/HCA Related Facilities between the date of this Agreement and the Joint Venture Stage II Commencement Date having a projected cost in excess of $1,000,000, Columbia/Jacksonville shall notify JHG/UMC thereof and prior to commencement deliver to JHG/UMC schedule relating to such project which contains (i) a description of such project (including the anticipated benefits to be derived therefrom), (ii) the projected costs of such project, (iii) the anticipated completion date of such project, and (iv) a place for JHG/UMC to indicate its approval thereof (if and to the extent that JHG/UMC, in its discretion, determines to approve such project). Columbia/Jacksonville shall also furnish to JHG/UMC any additional information JHG/UMC might reasonably request concerning such project. "Emergency" shall mean a situation in which, unless the affected Columbia/Jacksonville Related Entity acts within a time frame in which it is not reasonably possible to provide to JHG/UMC the information described above and obtain its approval, the operation of the affected Columbia/HCA Related Facility would be in violation of any regulatory requirement, seriously impaired or the integrity or condition of the affected Columbia/Jacksonville Related Facility would be seriously jeopardized: provided, however, in the event of an Emergency, Columbia/Jacksonville shall notify JHG/UMC as soon as practicable of the nature of the Emergency and the action it intends to take in response thereto, and shall thereafter keep JHG/UMC fully apprised of developments and their actions with respect thereto.

21.   Conditions Precedent to Obligations of Columbia/Jacksonville

Notwithstanding anything herein to the contrary, the obligations of Columbia/Jacksonville to consummate the transactions described herein are subject to the fulfillment, on or prior to the Closing Date, of the following conditions precedent unless (but only to the extent) waived in writing by such parties at Closing:

21.1. Representations/Warranties. The representations and warranties of JHG/UMC contained in this Agreement shall be true when made and, when read in light of any Schedules which have been updated in accordance with the provisions of Section 27.1 hereof, on and as of the Closing Date as though such representations and warranties had been made on and as of such Closing Date; and each and all of the terms, covenants and conditions of this Agreement to be complied with or performed by JHG/UMC on or before the Closing Date pursuant to the terms hereof shall have been duly complied with and performed.

21.2. Pre-Closing Confirmations. Columbia/Jacksonville shall have obtained documentation or other evidence satisfactory to Columbia/Jacksonville (a) that JHG/UMC has:

(i)   Either received a copy of the opinion of the City Attorney for the City of Jacksonville, Florida that the consent and approvals from the City of Jacksonville with respect to the execution and performance by JHG/UMC of this Agreement and the Management Services Agreement is not required, or if such consent and approval is required, such consent and approval has been obtained;

–62–

(ii)   If not refinanced pursuant to <u>Section 4.3(b)</u>, a) received a favorable ruling or satisfactory opinion to the effect that the execution and performance by JHG/UMC of this Agreement and the Management Services Agreement will not adversely affect the exclusion from gross income of a holder thereof of interest on the JHG/UMC Tax Exempt Bonds for federal income tax purposes, and b) has obtained such consents and approvals in connection with the UMC Tax Exempt Bonds as may be necessary in connection with the execution and performance by JHG/UMC of this Agreement and the Management Services Agreement.

(iii)   Received the approval of all governmental agencies whose approval is required to complete the transactions herein contemplated; and

(iv)   Obtained such other consents and approvals as may be legally or contractually required for the consummation of the transactions described herein; and

(b)   that Columbia/Jacksonville has:

(i)   Received the approval of all governmental agencies whose approval is required to complete the transactions required to complete the transactions herein contemplated; and

(ii)   Obtained such other consents and approvals as may be legally or contractually required for the consummation of the transactions described herein.

21.3.   <u>Action/Proceeding</u>. No action or proceeding before a court or any other governmental agency or body shall have been instituted or threatened to restrain or prohibit the transactions herein contemplated, and no governmental agency or body shall have taken any other action or made any request of any party hereto as a result of which Columbia/Jacksonville reasonably and in good faith deems it inadvisable to proceed with the transactions hereunder.

21.4.   <u>Adverse Change</u>. No material adverse change in the results of operations, financial condition or business of the JHG/UMC Entities or the JHG/UMC Facilities, and JHG/UMC shall not have suffered any material change, loss or damage to the JHG/UMC Facilities, whether or not covered by insurance.

21.5.   <u>Extraordinary Liabilities/Obligations</u>. The JHG/UMC Entities shall not have incurred any liability or obligation outside the ordinary course of business since the date hereof, except as set forth on <u>Schedule 16(f)</u>. No JHG/UMC Entity shall (a) be in receivership or dissolution, (b) have made any assignment for the benefit of creditors, (c) have admitted in writing its inability to pay its debts as they mature, (d) have been adjudicated a bankrupt, (e) have filed a petition in voluntary bankruptcy, a petition or answer seeking reorganization, or an arrangement with creditors under the federal bankruptcy law or any other similar law or statute of the United States or any state, or (f) have had filed against it any petition described in (e) above, without such JHG/UMC Entity having filed a motion to dismiss such petition within thirty (30) days and such motion having been granted within ninety (90) days.

21.6.   Opinion of Counsel to JHG/UMC. Columbia/Jacksonville shall have received an opinion from counsel to JHG/UMC dated as of the Closing Date and addressed to Columbia/Jacksonville in the form of Exhibit D hereto.

22.   Conditions Precedent to Obligations of JHG/UMC

Notwithstanding anything herein to the contrary, the obligations of JHG/UMC to consummate the transactions described herein are subject to the fulfillment, on or prior to the Closing Date, of the following conditions precedent unless (but only to the extent) waived in writing by such party at Closing:

22.1.   Representations/Warranties. The representations and warranties of Columbia/Jacksonville contained in this Agreement shall be true when made and, when read in light of any Schedules which have been updated in accordance with the provisions of Section 27.1 hereof, as of the Closing Date as though such representations and warranties had been made on and as of such Closing Date; and each and all of the terms, covenants and conditions of this Agreement to be complied with or performed by Columbia/Jacksonville on or before the Closing Date pursuant to the terms hereof shall have been duly complied with and performed.

22.2.   Pre-Closing Confirmations. JHG/UMC shall have obtained documentation or other evidence satisfactory to JHG/UMC (a) that JHG/UMC has:

(i)   Either received an opinion of the City Attorney for the City of Jacksonville, Florida that the consent and approval from the City of Jacksonville with respect to the execution and performance by JHG/UMC of this Agreement and the Management Services Agreement, or, if such consent and approval is required, obtained such approval and consent;

(ii)   If not refinanced pursuant to Section 4.3(b), a) received a favorable ruling or satisfactory opinion to the effect that the execution and performance by JHG/UMC of this Agreement and the Management Services Agreement will not adversely affect the exclusion from gross income of a holder thereof of interest on the JHG/UMC Tax Exempt Bonds for federal income tax purposes, and b) has obtained such consents and approvals in connection with the UMC Tax Exempt Bonds as may be necessary in connection with the execution and performance by JHG/UMC of this Agreement and the Management Services Agreement.

(iii)   Received the approval of all governmental agencies whose approval is required to complete the transactions herein contemplated; and

(iv)   Obtained such other consents and approvals as may be legally or contractually required for the consummation of the transactions described herein; and

(b) that Columbia/Jacksonville has:

      (i)   Received the approval of all governmental agencies whose approval is necessary to complete the transaction herein contemplated; and

      (ii)   Obtained such other consents and approvals contractually required for the consummation of the transactions described herein.

      22.3.   Action/Proceeding. No action or proceeding before a court or any other governmental agency or body shall have been instituted or threatened to restrain or prohibit the transaction herein contemplated, and no governmental agency or body shall have taken any other action or made any request of any parry hereto as a result of which JHG/UMC reasonably and in good faith deems it inadvisable to proceed with the transactions hereunder.

      22.4.   Adverse Change. No material adverse change in the results of operations, financial condition or business of the Columbia/Jacksonville Related Entities shall have occurred.

      22.5.   Extraordinary Liabilities/Obligations. The Columbia/Jacksonville Related Entities have not incurred any liability or obligation outside the ordinary course of business since the date hereof, except as set forth in Schedule 17(f). No Columbia/Jacksonville Related Entity shall (a) be in receivership or dissolution, (b) have made any assignment for the benefit of creditors, (c) have admitted in writing its inability to pay its debts as they mature, (d) have been adjudicated a bankrupt, or (e) have filed a petition in voluntary bankruptcy, a petition or answer seeking reorganization, or an arrangement with creditors under the federal bankruptcy law or any other similar law or statute of the United States or any state, or (f) have had filed against it any petition described in (e) above, without such Columbia/Jacksonville Related Entity having filed a motion to dismiss such petition within thirty (30) days and such motion having been granted within ninety (90) days.

      22.6.   Opinion of Counsel to Columbia/Jacksonville Related Entities. JHG/UMC shall have received an opinion from counsel to Columbia/Jacksonville dated as of the Closing Date and addressed to JHG/UMC, in the form of Exhibit E hereto.

23.   Tax Matters Opinions: Termination of Interim Management Services Agreement. The continuing effectiveness of the Joint Venture from and after the Joint Venture Commencement Date is specifically contingent on the receipt by JHG/UMC of a favorable ruling from the Internal Revenue Service or an opinion of counsel as to the specific tax matters set forth below, which opinion must be acceptable to JHG/UMC in its sole discretion:

      (a)   That the Joint Venture as outlined herein will not adversely affect the Section 501(c)(3) or Section 509(a) status of any of the JHG/UMC Entities.

(b)   That payments to JHG/UMC arising from the Joint Venture will not
constitute unrelated business income.

Should it determine to do so, JHG/UMC shall, at its own expense, prepare and submit any ruling
request on an expedited basis.

Upon failure to receive a favorable ruling or satisfactory opinion with respect to Tax
Matters by March 31, 1998, the Interim Management Services Agreement shall terminate and,
except as set forth in Sections 26 and 27.7, the Joint Venturers shall be released from any further
obligations with respect to each other under this Agreement.

24.   Noncompetition

24.1.   Covenant Not to Compete of Columbia/Jacksonville. Columbia/Jacksonville
recognizes that (i) the entry by JHG/UMC into this Agreement is induced primarily because of
the covenants and assurances made by Columbia/Jacksonville hereunder,
(ii) Columbia/Jacksonville's covenant not to compete is necessary to insure the continuation of
the business of the Joint Venture subsequent to Closing and (iii) irreparable harm and damage
will be done to the Joint Venture and the JHG/JMC Entities in the event that any of the
Columbia/Jacksonville Related Entities or any Columbia HCA Affiliate compete with the Joint
Venture within the First Coast Area. Therefore, in consideration of the premises and as an
inducement for JHG/UMC to enter into this Agreement and consummate the transactions
contemplated herein, so long as Columbia/Jacksonville and JHG/UMC are both joint venturers in
the Joint Venture, neither the Columbia/Jacksonville Related Entities nor any Columbia/HCA
Affiliate will (other than through the Joint Venture), directly or indirectly, in any capacity, own,
manage, operate, control, participate in the management or control of, be employed by, consult
with, or maintain or continue any interest whatsoever in any healthcare facility (which shall
include, without limitation, general acute care hospitals, specialty hospitals, nursing homes,
rehabilitation facilities or agencies, ambulatory or other types of surgery centers or similar
enterprise) that is located within the First Coast Area (all of the foregoing are collectively
referred to as a "Competing Business"); provided, however, that the Columbia/Jacksonville
Related Entities and Columbia/HCA Affiliates may acquire, invest in or participate in the
management or control of a Competing Business if the Joint Venture has not affirmatively voted
(through a majority vote of the Governing Board) to pursue an interest in such Competing
Business; provided further that the Joint Venture shall be conclusively deemed to have declined
to pursue such an interest unless within thirty (30) days after a proposal pertaining to such
interest is communicated to the Governing Board they shall vote to pursue such interest as
provided in the immediately preceding proviso and shall have provided a mutually acceptable
reasonably detailed plan for the financing thereof; and provided still further that nothing herein
shall operate or be construed to restrict or prevent any pension plan or employee investment plan
sponsored by any Columbia/HCA Affiliate from owning or acquiring any interest in any
Competing Business which is publicly traded on a national stock market. Columbia/Jacksonville

further agrees that if any restriction contained in this Section is held by an appropriate Court to be unenforceable or unreasonable, a lesser restriction shall be severable therefrom and be enforced in its place, and the remaining restrictions contained herein shall be enforceable independently of each other. In the event of an actual or threatened breach of this covenant by the Columbia/Jacksonville Related Entities or any Columbia/HCA Affiliate, JHG/UMC or the Joint Venture shall be entitled to injunctive relief, without the necessity of posting a bond, cash or otherwise.

 24.2. Covenant Not to Compete of the JHG/UMC Entities. JHG/UMC recognizes that (i) the entry by Columbia/Jacksonville into this Agreement is induced primarily because of the covenants and assurances made by JHG/UMC hereunder, (ii) JHG/UMC's covenant not to compete is necessary to insure the continuation of the business of the Joint Venture subsequent to Closing and (iii) irreparable harm and damage will be done to the Joint Venture and the Columbia/Jacksonville Related Entities in the event that any of the JHG/UMC Entities or any JHG/UMC Affiliate compete with the Joint Venture within the First Coast Area. Therefore, in consideration of the premises and as an inducement for Columbia/Jacksonville to enter into this Agreement and consummate the transactions contemplated herein, so long as Columbia/Jacksonville and JHG/UMC are both joint venturers in the Joint Venture, neither the JHG/UMC Entities nor any JHG/UMC Affiliate will (other than through the Joint Venture), directly or indirectly, in any capacity, own, manage, operate, control, participate in the management or control of, be employed by, consult with, or maintain or continue any interest whatsoever in any healthcare facility (which shall include, without limitation, general acute care hospitals, specialty hospitals, nursing homes, rehabilitation facilities or agencies, ambulatory or other types of surgery centers or similar enterprise) that is located within the First Coast Area (all of the foregoing are collectively referred to as a "Competing Business"); provided, however, that the parties acknowledge that the physicians employed by the State of Florida Board of Regents and assigned to or through the University of Florida are not a JHG/UMC Entity or a JHG/UMC Affiliate; provided further that JHG/UMC Entities- and JHG/UMC Affiliates may acquire, invest in or participate in the management or control of a Competing Business if the Joint Venture has not affirmatively voted (through a majority vote of the Governing Board) to pursue an interest in such Competing Business; provided further that the Joint Venture shall be conclusively deemed to have declined to pursue such an interest unless within thirty (30) days after a proposal pertaining to such interest is communicated to the Governing Board they shall vote to pursue such interest as provided in the immediately preceding proviso and shall have provided a mutually acceptable reasonably detailed plan for the financing thereof; and provided still further that nothing herein shall operate or be construed to restrict or prevent any pension plan or employee investment plan sponsored by any JHG/UMC Affiliate from owning or acquiring any interest in any Competing Business which is publicly traded on a national stock market. JHG/UMC further agrees that if any restriction contained in this Section is held by an appropriate Court to be unenforceable or unreasonable, a lesser restriction shall be severable therefrom and be enforced in its place, and the remaining restrictions contained herein shall be enforceable independently of each other. In the event of an actual or threatened breach of this covenant by the JHG/UMC Entities or any JHG/UMC Affiliate, Columbia/Jacksonville or the

Joint Venture shall be entitled to injunctive relief, without the necessity of posting a bond, cash, or otherwise.

25. Termination Prior to Closing Date. Notwithstanding anything herein to the contrary, this Agreement may be terminated at any time (i) on or prior to the Closing Date by mutual consent of JHG/UMC and Columbia/Jacksonville; (ii) on or prior to the Closing Date by Columbia/Jacksonville if there has been a material and adverse change in the financial condition or prospects for future results of operations of the JHG/UMC Entities or the JHG/UMC Facilities since the date hereof; (iii) on the Closing Date by Columbia/Jacksonville, if any of the conditions specified in Section 21 of this Agreement have not been satisfied and shall not have been waived by the Columbia/Jacksonville Related Entities: (iv) on or prior to the Closing Date by JHG/UMC if there has been a material and adverse change in the financial condition or prospects for future results of operations of the Columbia/Jacksonville Related Entities or the Columbia/HCA Related Facilities since the date hereof: (v) on the Closing Date by JHG/UMC if any of the conditions specified in Section 22 of this Agreement have not been satisfied and shall not have been waived by JHG/UMC; or (vi) by either party if the conditions specified in Section 23 shall not have taken place on or before March 31, 1998 (which date may be extended by mutual agreement of Columbia/Jacksonville and JHG/UMC).

26. Indemnification

26.1. Indemnification by Columbia/Jacksonville. SUBJECT TO THE LIMITATIONS SET FORTH IN SECTION 26.3 HEREOF, COLUMBIA/JACKSONVILLE SHALL DEFEND AND INDEMNIFY JHG/UMC AND HOLD JHG/UMC WHOLLY HARMLESS FROM AND AGAINST ANY AND ALL LOSSES, LIABILITIES, DAMAGES, COSTS (INCLUDING, WITHOUT LIMITATION, COURT COSTS AND COSTS OF APPEAL) AND EXPENSES (INCLUDING, WITHOUT LIMITATION, REASONABLE ATTORNEYS' FEES) THAT JHG/UMC INCURS AS A RESULT OF, OR WITH RESPECT TO: (I) ANY MISREPRESENTATION OR BREACH OF WARRANTY BY COLUMBIA/JACKSONVILLE UNDER THIS AGREEMENT OR IN ANY DOCUMENT OR AGREEMENT CONTEMPLATED HEREBY; AND (II) ANY BREACH BY COLUMBIA/JACKSONVILLE OF, OR ANY FAILURE BY COLUMBIA/JACKSONVILLE TO PERFORM, ANY COVENANT OR AGREEMENT OF, OR REQUIRED TO BE PERFORMED BY, COLUMBIA/JACKSONVILLE UNDER THIS AGREEMENT OR IN ANY DOCUMENT OR AGREEMENT CONTEMPLATED HEREBY.

26.2. Indemnification by JHG/UMC. SUBJECT TO THE LIMITATIONS SET FOURTH IN SECTION 26.3 HEREOF, JHG/UMC SHALL DEFEND AND INDEMNIFY AND HOLD COLUMBIA/JACKSONVILLE WHOLLY HARMLESS FROM AND AGAINST ANY AND ALL LOSSES, LIABILITIES, DAMAGES, COSTS (INCLUDING, WITHOUT LIMITATION, COURT COSTS AND COSTS OF APPEAL) AND EXPENSES (INCLUDING WITHOUT LIMITATION. REASONABLE ATTORNEYS' FEES) THAT

COLUMBIA/JACKSONVILLE INCURS AS A RESULT OF, OR WITH RESPECT TO:
(I) ANY MISREPRESENTATION OR BREACH OF WARRANTY BY THE JHG/UMC
ENTITIES UNDER THIS AGREEMENT OR IN ANY DOCUMENT OR AGREEMENT
CONTEMPLATED HEREBY; (II) ANY BREACH BY JHGIUMC OF, OR ANY FAILURE
BY THE JHG/UMC TO PERFORM, ANY COVENANT OR AGREEMENT OF, OR
REQUIRED TO BE PERFORMED BY, JHG/UMC UNDER THIS AGREEMENT.

26.3. <u>Thresholds with Respect to Breaches of Representations and Warranties</u>. No party
shall be liable for any indemnification pursuant to <u>Section 26.1(I) or 26.2(I)</u> for any claims for
misrepresentations and breaches of warranty which are individually less than $10.000 "Excluded
Claims"). In addition, Columbia/Jacksonville shall be liable under <u>Section 26.1 (I)</u> for any
claims for misrepresentations and breaches of warranty only after total indemnification claims
under <u>Section 26.1(I)</u>, including amounts in respect of Excluded Claims, exceed $100.000.
JHG/UMC shall be liable under <u>Section 26.2(I)</u>, for any claims for misrepresentations and
breaches of warranty only after indemnification claims under <u>Section 26.2(I)</u>, including amounts
in respect of Excluded Claims, exceed $100.000. No party shall be liable for any
indemnification pursuant to <u>Section 26.1(I) or 26.2(I)</u>, as applicable, for any claims for
misrepresentations and breaches of warranty which are the basis upon which any other party
shall have failed to consummate the transactions described herein pursuant to <u>Section 21.1 or
22.1</u>, as applicable, or which are based upon misrepresentations and breaches of warranty which
have been waived in writing pursuant to the initial paragraph of <u>Section 20 or 21</u>, as applicable.

26.4. <u>Notice and Control of Litigation</u>. If any claim or liability is asserted in writing by
a third party against a party entitled to indemnification under this <u>Section 26</u> (the "Indemnified
Party") which would give rise to a claim under this <u>Section 26</u>, the Indemnified Party shall notify
the person giving the indemnity ("Indemnifying Party") in writing of the same within fifteen (15)
days after receipt of such written assertion of a claim or liability. The Indemnifying Party shall
have the right to defend a claim and control the defense, settlement and prosecution of any
litigation. If the indemnifying Party, within twenty (20) days after notice of such claim, fails to
accept and initiate the defense of such claim, the Indemnified Party will (upon further notice to
the Indemnifying Party) have the right to undertake the defense, compromise or settlement of
such claim on behalf of and for the account and at the risk and expense of the Indemnifying
Party. Anything in this <u>Section 26.4</u> notwithstanding, (i) if there is a reasonable probability that
a claim may materially and adversely affect the Indemnified Party other than as a result of
money damages or other money payments, the Indemnified Party shall have the right, at its own
cost and expense, to participate in the defense, compromise and settle such claim, and (ii) the
Indemnifying Party shall not, without the written consent of the Indemnified Party, settle or
compromise any claim or consent to the entry of any judgment which does not include as an
unconditional term thereof the giving by the claimant to the Indemnified Party of a release from
all liability in respect of such claim. All parties agree to cooperate fully as necessary in the
defense of such matters. Should the Indemnified Party fail to notify the Indemnifying Party in
the time required above, the indemnity with respect to the subject matter of the required notice
shall be limited to the damages that would have resulted absent the Indemnified Party's failure to
notify the Indemnifying Party in the time required above after taking into account such actions as

could have been taken by the Indemnifying Party had it received timely notice from the Indemnified Party.

26.5. <u>Notice of Claim</u>. If an Indemnified Party becomes aware of any breach of the representations or warranties of the Indemnifying Party hereunder or any other basis for indemnification under this <u>Section 26</u> (except as otherwise provided for under <u>Section 26.4</u>), the Indemnified Party shall notify the Indemnifying Party in writing of the same within forty-five (45) days after becoming aware of such breach or claim, specifying in detail the circumstances and facts which give rise to a claim under this <u>Section 26</u>. Should the Indemnified Party fail to notify the Indemnifying Party within the time frame required above, the indemnity with respect to the subject matter of the required notice shall be limited to the damages that would have nonetheless resulted absent the Indemnified Party's failure to notify the Indemnifying Party in the time required above after taking into account such actions as could have been taken by the Indemnifying Party had it received timely notice from the Indemnified Party.

27. <u>General</u>

27.1. <u>Schedules and Other Instruments</u>. Each Schedule and Exhibit to this Agreement shall be considered a part hereof as if set forth herein in full.

27.2. <u>Additional Assurances</u>. The provisions of this Agreement shall be self-operative and shall not require further agreement by the parties except as may be herein specifically provided to the contrary; provided, however, at the request of a party, the other party or parties shall execute such additional instruments and take such additional actions as the requesting party may deem necessary to effectuate this Agreement.

27.3. <u>Consents, Approvals and Discretion</u>. Except as herein expressly provided to the contrary, whenever this Agreement requires any consent or approval to be given by a party or a party must or may exercise discretion, the parties agree that such consent or approval shall not be unreasonably withheld or delayed and such discretion shall be reasonably exercised.

27.4. <u>Benefit/Assignment</u>. Subject to provisions herein to the contrary, this Agreement shall inure to the benefit of and be binding upon the parties hereto and their respective legal representatives, successors and assigns; provided, however, that no party may assign this Agreement without the prior written consent of the other party, which consent may be withheld without cause or reason; provided, further, however, that any party may, without the prior written consent of the other party, assign its rights and delegate its duties hereunder to one or more entities controlled by, under common control with or that control the assigning party; provided that neither JHG/UMC nor Columbia/Jacksonville shall be in any circumstances released from any obligations imposed on it under this Agreement. This Agreement is intended solely for the benefit of the parties hereto and is not intended to, and shall not, create any enforceable third party beneficiary rights.

27.5. No Brokerage. The parties hereto represent to each other that no broker has in any way been contacted in connection with the transactions contemplated hereby. Each party agrees to indemnify the other parties from and against all loss, cost, damage or expense arising out of claims for fees or commissions of brokers employed or alleged to have been employed by such indemnifying party.

27.6. Cost of Transaction. Whether or not the transactions contemplated hereby shall be consummated and except as may be provided to the contrary elsewhere herein, the parties will each pay the fees, expenses, and disbursements of their agents, representatives, accountants, and counsel incurred in connection with the subject matter hereof and any amendments hereto.

27.7. Confidentiality: Disclosure. Except as otherwise required by law, the Joint Venturers will keep this Agreement and its contents confidential and not to disclose the same to any third party except attorneys or accountants hired by them and except to the applicable governmental agencies in connection with any required notification or application for approval or exemption therefrom) without the written consent of the other party. It is further understood by the parties hereto that the information, documents and instruments delivered to Columbia/Jacksonville agents and the information, documents and instruments delivered to JHG/UMC by Columbia/Jacksonville or its respective agents are of a confidential and proprietary nature. Each of the parties hereto agrees that both prior and subsequent to the Closing it will maintain the confidentiality of all such confidential information, documents or instruments delivered to it by each of the other parties hereto or their agents in connection with the negotiation of this Agreement or in compliance with the terms, conditions and covenants hereof and will only disclose such information, documents and instruments to its duly authorized officers, partners, directors, representatives and agents, each of whom will agree to keep the information confidential. Each of the parties hereto further agrees that if the transactions contemplated hereby are not consummated, it will return all such documents and instruments and all copies thereof in its possession to the other party to this Agreement and will continue to maintain the same obligation of confidentiality. Each of the parties hereto recognizes that any breach of this Section 27.7 would result in irreparable harm to the other parties to this Agreement and their affiliates and that therefore either JHG/UMC or Columbia/Jacksonville shall be entitled to an injunction to prohibit. any such breach or anticipated breach, without the necessity of posting a bond, cash or otherwise, in addition to all of their other legal and equitable remedies. Nothing in this Section 27.7, however, shall prohibit the use of such confidential information, documents or information for such governmental filings as in the opinion of JHG/UMC's counsel or Columbia/Jacksonville's counsel are required by law or governmental regulations, or which may be required or requested by the City of Jacksonville. Florida in connection with any audit with respect to the UMC Lease or the Indigent Care Contract.

27.8. Public Announcements. The Joint Venturers mutually agree that no party hereto shall release, publish or otherwise make available to the public in any manner whatsoever any information or announcement regarding the transactions herein contemplated without the prior written consent of all the Joint Venturers, except for information and filings reasonably necessary to be directed to governmental agencies to fully and lawfully effect the transactions

–71–

herein contemplated or required in connection with securities and other laws. Nothing herein shall prohibit either parry from responding to questions presented by the press or media without first obtaining prior consent of the other party hereto.

27.9. Waiver of Breach. The waiver by any party of a breach or violation of any provision of this Agreement shall not operate as, or be construed to constitute, a waiver of anv subsequent breach of the same or any other provision hereof.

27.10. Notice. Any notice, demand or communication required, permitted, or desired to be given hereunder shall be deemed effectively given when personally delivered, when received by telegraphic or other electronic means (including telecopy and telex) or overnight courier, or five (5) days after being deposited in the United States mail, with postage prepaid thereon, certified or registered mail, return receipt requested, addressed as follows:

JHG/UMC:

Jacksonville Health Group, Inc.
655 West Eighth Street, 4th Floor
Jacksonville, Florida 32209
Attention: Chairman of the Board

and

University Medical Center, Inc.
655 West Eighth Street, 4th Floor
Jacksonville, Florida 32209
Attention: Chairman of the Board

With a simultaneous
copy to:

William E. Falck, Esq.
653-1 West Eighth Street
Suite 4060
Jacksonville, Florida 32209-6511

Columbia/Jacksonville

Columbia/Jacksonville Healthcare System, Inc.
One Park Plaza
Nashville, Tennessee 37202-0550
Telecopy No. 615/320-2084
Attention: Senior Vice-President - Development

With a simultaneous
copy to:

Columbia/HCA Healthcare Corporation
One Park Plaza
Nashville, Tennessee 37202-0550
Telecopy No. 615/320-2598
Attention: General Counsel

or to such other address, and to the attention of such other person or officer as any party may designate, with copies thereof to the respective counsel thereof as notified by such party.

27.11. <u>Gender, Number and Inferences</u>. Whenever the context of this Agreement requires, the gender of all words herein shall include the masculine, feminine and neuter, and the number of all words herein shall include the singular and plural. Inasmuch as this Agreement is the result of negotiations between sophisticated parties of equal bargaining power represented by counsel, no inference in favor of, or against, any party shall be drawn from the fact that any portion of this Agreement has been drafted by or on behalf of any party hereto.

27.12. <u>Divisions and Headings</u>. The divisions of this Agreement into sections and subsections and the use of captions and headings in connection therewith are solely for convenience and shall have no legal effect in construing the provisions of this Agreement.

27.13. <u>Survival</u>. Except asset forth in the following sentence, all of the representations, warranties, covenants and agreements made by the parties in this Agreement or pursuant hereto in any certificate, instrument or document shall survive the consummation of the transactions described herein, and may be fully and completely relied upon by each party hereto, notwithstanding any investigation heretofore or hereafter made by any of them or on behalf of any of them, and shall not be deemed merged into any instruments or agreements delivered at Closing or thereafter. Any claim based upon a misrepresentation or breach of warranty under <u>Section 16</u> or <u>Section 17</u> hereof must be made, if at all, within three (3) years of the Closing Date.

27.14. <u>Entire Agreement/Amendment</u>. This Agreement supersedes all previous contracts and other agreements, including without limitation that certain letter agreement dated July 25, 1995, and constitutes the entire agreement of whatsoever kind or nature existing between or among the parties respecting the within subject matter and no party shall be entitled to benefits other than those specified herein. As between or among the parties, no oral statements or prior written material not specifically incorporated herein shall be of any force and effect. This Agreement may be executed in two or more counterparts, each and all of which shall be deemed an original and all of which together shall constitute but one and the same instrument.

27.15. <u>Governing Law</u>. This Agreement shall be governed by and construed in accordance with the substantive federal laws of the United States and the laws of the State of Florida, and the courts of competent jurisdiction, federal and state, sitting in such State shall be the exclusive courts of jurisdiction, and more particularly the courts in Duval County, Florida, for venue purposes and for litigation or other proceedings as between the parties that may be brought, or arise out of, or by reason of this Agreement.

27.16. <u>Attorneys' Fees</u>. If any litigation is initiated by the Joint Venture against any Joint Venturer or by any Joint Venturer against another Joint Venturer or the Joint Venture relating to this Agreement or the subject matter hereof, the Person prevailing in such litigation shall be entitled to recover, in addition to all damages allowed by law and other relief, all court costs and reasonable attorneys' fees incurred in connection therewith or, in the event that each party prevails on some of the issues in dispute, such court costs shall be shared equally, and each party shall bear its own cost of attorneys' fees.

27.17. <u>Successors and Assigns</u>. This Agreement shall be binding upon and shall inure to the benefit of the Joint Venturers, and their respective heirs, legal representatives, successors and permitted assigns.

27.18. <u>Construction</u>. Every covenant, term, and provision of this Agreement shall be construed simply according to its fair meaning and not strictly, for or against any Joint Venturer. The failure by any party to specifically enforce any term or provision hereof or any rights of such party hereunder shall not be construed as the waiver by that party of its rights hereunder. The waiver by any party of a breach or violation of any provision of this Agreement shall not operate as, or be construed to be, a waiver of any subsequent breach of the same or other provision hereof.

27.19. <u>Time</u>. Time is of the essence with respect to this Agreement.

27.20. <u>Waiver of Partition</u>. Notwithstanding any statute or principle of law to the contrary, each Joint Venturer hereby agrees that, during the term of the Joint Venture, such Joint Venturer shall have no right (and hereby waives any right that such Joint Venturer might otherwise have had) to cause any Joint Venture property to be partitioned and/or distributed in kind.

27.21. <u>Severability</u>. This Agreement is intended to be performed in accordance with, and only to the extent permitted by, all applicable laws, ordinances, rules and regulations. If any provision of this Agreement or the application thereof to any person or circumstance shall, for any reason and to any extent, be invalid or unenforceable, but the extent of such invalidity or unenforceability does not destroy the basis of the bargain among the Joint Venturers as expressed herein, the remainder of this Agreement and the application of such provision to other persons or circumstances shall not be affected thereby, but rather shall be enforced to the greatest extent permitted by law.

27.22. <u>Counterparts</u>. This Agreement may be executed in counterparts, each of which shall be an original but all of which shall constitute but one document.

27.23. <u>Joint Venturers' Obligations</u>. Each Joint Venturer shall remain fully and solely liable for its respective debts and obligations except as otherwise provided herein. Neither the execution of the Agreement nor the participation of a Joint Venturer in the Joint Venture, shall subject such Joint Venturer to any liability or obligation of another Joint Venturer and each Joint Venturer shall fully indemnify and hold harmless the other Joint Venturers from and against its liabilities and obligations currently in existence and those arising from its participation hereunder.

27.24. <u>Nature of the Joint Venture.</u> No Joint Venturer intends to assume any liability of another Joint Venturer or to be liable for the debts, contracts or other liabilities or obligations of the other Joint Venturers by virtue of the Agreement except to the extent of any joint indebtedness or liability as provided above for Expansion Expenditures. No Joint Venturer shall have the authority to act on behalf of or bind any of the other Joint Venturers by virtue of this Agreement.

IN WITNESS WHEREOF, the Joint Venturers have executed this Agreement on March 26, 1996.

JACKSONVILLE HEALTH GROUP, INC.

By: _____

Its: _____

UNIVERSITY MEDICAL CENTER, INC.

By: _____

Its: _____

COLUMBIA JACKSONVILLE HEALTHCARE SYSTEM, INC.

By: _____

Its: _____

–75–

*

Appendix 2

IRS FORM 1065 WITH SCHEDULE K–1 AND INSTRUCTIONS

Form **1065**	**U.S. Return of Partnership Income**	OMB No. 1545-0099
Department of the Treasury Internal Revenue Service	For calendar year 2003, or tax year beginning ...., 2003, and ending ...., 20..... . ▶ See separate instructions.	2003

A Principal business activity	Use the IRS label. Other- wise, print or type.	Name of partnership	**D** Employer identification number
B Principal product or service		Number, street, and room or suite no. If a P.O. box, see page 14 of the instructions.	**E** Date business started
C Business code number		City or town, state, and ZIP code	**F** Total assets (see page 14 of the instructions) $

G Check applicable boxes: **(1)** ☐ Initial return   **(2)** ☐ Final return   **(3)** ☐ Name change   **(4)** ☐ Address change   **(5)** ☐ Amended return
H Check accounting method: **(1)** ☐ Cash   **(2)** ☐ Accrual   **(3)** ☐ Other (specify) ▶ ....
I Number of Schedules K-1. Attach one for each person who was a partner at any time during the tax year ▶ ....

Caution: *Include only trade or business income and expenses on lines 1a through 22 below. See the instructions for more information.*

Income	**1a** Gross receipts or sales	**1a**		
	b Less returns and allowances	**1b**	**1c**	
	2 Cost of goods sold (Schedule A, line 8)		**2**	
	3 Gross profit. Subtract line 2 from line 1c		**3**	
	4 Ordinary income (loss) from other partnerships, estates, and trusts *(attach schedule)*		**4**	
	5 Net farm profit (loss) *(attach Schedule F (Form 1040))*		**5**	
	6 Net gain (loss) from Form 4797, Part II, line 18		**6**	
	7 Other income (loss) *(attach schedule)*		**7**	
	8 **Total income (loss).** Combine lines 3 through 7		**8**	

Deductions (see page 15 of the instructions for limitations)	**9** Salaries and wages (other than to partners) (less employment credits)		**9**	
	10 Guaranteed payments to partners		**10**	
	11 Repairs and maintenance		**11**	
	12 Bad debts		**12**	
	13 Rent		**13**	
	14 Taxes and licenses		**14**	
	15 Interest		**15**	
	16a Depreciation (if required, attach Form 4562)	**16a**		
	b Less depreciation reported on Schedule A and elsewhere on return	**16b**	**16c**	
	17 Depletion **(Do not deduct oil and gas depletion.)**		**17**	
	18 Retirement plans, etc.		**18**	
	19 Employee benefit programs		**19**	
	20 Other deductions *(attach schedule)*		**20**	
	21 **Total deductions.** Add the amounts shown in the far right column for lines 9 through 20		**21**	

	22 Ordinary income (loss) from trade or business activities. Subtract line 21 from line 8	**22**	

Sign Here

Under penalties of perjury, I declare that I have examined this return, including accompanying schedules and statements, and to the best of my knowledge and belief, it is true, correct, and complete. Declaration of preparer (other than general partner or limited liability company member) is based on all information of which preparer has any knowledge.

May the IRS discuss this return with the preparer shown below (see instructions)? ☐ Yes ☐ No

▶ _____ ▶ _____
Signature of general partner or limited liability company member   Date

Paid Preparer's Use Only	Preparer's signature		Date	Check if self-employed ▶ ☐	Preparer's SSN or PTIN
	Firm's name (or yours if self-employed), address, and ZIP code	▶		EIN ▶	
				Phone no.	( )

For Paperwork Reduction Act Notice, see separate instructions.   Cat. No. 11390Z   Form **1065** (2003)

Form 1065 (2003)   Page **2**

Schedule A   Cost of Goods Sold (see page 18 of the instructions)

1 Inventory at beginning of year	**1**	
2 Purchases less cost of items withdrawn for personal use	**2**	
3 Cost of labor	**3**	
4 Additional section 263A costs (attach schedule)	**4**	
5 Other costs (attach schedule)	**5**	
6 **Total.** Add lines 1 through 5	**6**	
7 Inventory at end of year	**7**	
8 **Cost of goods sold.** Subtract line 7 from line 6. Enter here and on page 1, line 2	**8**	

9a Check all methods used for valuing closing inventory:
- (i) ☐ Cost as described in Regulations section 1.471-3
- (ii) ☐ Lower of cost or market as described in Regulations section 1.471-4
- (iii) ☐ Other (specify method used and attach explanation) ▶ ....
- **b** Check this box if there was a writedown of "subnormal" goods as described in Regulations section 1.471-2(c) . . . . ▶ ☐
- **c** Check this box if the LIFO inventory method was adopted this tax year for any goods (if checked, attach Form 970) . ▶ ☐
- **d** Do the rules of section 263A (for property produced or acquired for resale) apply to the partnership? . . ☐ Yes ☐ No
- **e** Was there any change in determining quantities, cost, or valuations between opening and closing inventory? ☐ Yes ☐ No
  If "Yes," attach explanation.

Schedule B   Other Information

	Yes	No
1 What type of entity is filing this return? Check the applicable box:		
a ☐ Domestic general partnership **b** ☐ Domestic limited partnership		
c ☐ Domestic limited liability company **d** ☐ Domestic limited liability partnership		
e ☐ Foreign partnership **f** ☐ Other ▶		
2 Are any partners in this partnership also partnerships?		
3 During the partnership's tax year, did the partnership own any interest in another partnership or in any foreign entity that was disregarded as an entity separate from its owner under Regulations sections 301.7701-2 and 301.7701-3? If yes, see instructions for required attachment		
4 Is this partnership subject to the consolidated audit procedures of sections 6221 through 6233? If "Yes," see **Designation of Tax Matters Partner** below		
5 Does this partnership meet **all three** of the following requirements?		
a The partnership's total receipts for the tax year were less than $250,000;		
b The partnership's total assets at the end of the tax year were less than $600,000; **and**		
c Schedules K-1 are filed with the return and furnished to the partners on or before the due date (including extensions) for the partnership return.		
If "Yes," the partnership is not required to complete Schedules L, M-1, and M-2; Item F on page 1 of Form 1065; or Item J on Schedule K-1		
6 Does this partnership have any foreign partners? If "Yes," the partnership may have to file Forms 8804, 8805 and 8813. See page 20 of the instructions		
7 Is this partnership a publicly traded partnership as defined in section 469(k)(2)?		
8 Has this partnership filed, or is it required to file, **Form 8264,** Application for Registration of a Tax Shelter? . .		
9 At any time during calendar year 2003, did the partnership have an interest in or a signature or other authority over a financial account in a foreign country (such as a bank account, securities account, or other financial account)? See page 20 of the instructions for exceptions and filing requirements for Form TD F 90-22.1. If "Yes," enter the name of the foreign country. ▶		
10 During the tax year, did the partnership receive a distribution from, or was it the grantor of, or transferor to, a foreign trust? If "Yes," the partnership may have to file Form 3520. See page 20 of the instructions		
11 Was there a distribution of property or a transfer (e.g., by sale or death) of a partnership interest during the tax year? If "Yes," you may elect to adjust the basis of the partnership's assets under section 754 by attaching the statement described under **Elections Made By the Partnership** on page 9 of the instructions		
12 Enter the number of **Forms 8865,** Return of U.S. Persons With Respect to Certain Foreign Partnerships, attached to this return . . . . ▶		

Designation of Tax Matters Partner (see page 20 of the instructions)

Enter below the general partner designated as the tax matters partner (TMP) for the tax year of this return:

Name of designated TMP ▶		Identifying number of TMP ▶	
Address of designated TMP ▶			

Form **1065** (2003)

6511

SCHEDULE K-1
(Form 1065)
Department of the Treasury
Internal Revenue Service

Partner's Share of Income, Credits, Deductions, etc.
► See separate instructions.
For calendar year 2003 or tax year beginning _____ , 2003, and ending _____ , 20 _____

OMB No. 1545-0099

2003

Partner's identifying number ► _____

Partnership's identifying number ► _____

Partner's name, address, and ZIP code

Partnership's name, address, and ZIP code

A This partner is a ☐ general partner ☐ limited partner ☐ limited liability company member

B What type of entity is this partner? ► _____

C Is this partner a ☐ domestic or a ☐ foreign partner?

	(i) Before change or termination	(ii) End of year
D Enter partner's percentage of:		
Profit sharing	_____ %	_____ %
Loss sharing	_____ %	_____ %
Ownership of capital	_____ %	_____ %

E IRS Center where partnership filed return: _____

F Partner's share of liabilities (see instructions):
Nonrecourse . . . . $ _____
Qualified nonrecourse financing . $ _____
Other . . . . $ _____

G Tax shelter registration number . ► _____

H Check here if this partnership is a publicly traded partnership as defined in section 469(k)(2) . . . . . ☐

I Check applicable boxes: **(1)** ☐ Final K-1 **(2)** ☐ Amended K-1

J **Analysis of partner's capital account:**

(a) Capital account at beginning of year	(b) Capital contributed during year	(c) Partner's share of lines 3, 4, and 7, Form 1065, Schedule M-2	(d) Withdrawals and distributions	(e) Capital account at end of year (combine columns (a) through (d))
			( )	

	(a) Distributive share item		(b) Amount	(c) 1040 filers enter the amount in column (b) on:
Income (Loss)	**1** Ordinary income (loss) from trade or business activities . . .	**1**		See page 6 of Partner's Instructions for Schedule K-1 (Form 1065).
	2 Net income (loss) from rental real estate activities	**2**		
	3 Net income (loss) from other rental activities	**3**		
	4 Portfolio income (loss):			
	a Interest income	**4a**		Form 1040, line 8a
	b (1) Qualified dividends	**4b(1)**		Form 1040, line 9b
	(2) Total ordinary dividends	**4b(2)**		Form 1040, line 9a
	c Royalty income	**4c**		Sch. E, Part I, line 4
	d (1) Net short-term capital gain (loss) (post-May 5, 2003) . . .	**4d(1)**		Sch. D, line 5, col. (g)
	(2) Net short-term capital gain (loss) (entire year) . . .	**4d(2)**		Sch. D, line 5, col. (f)
	e (1) Net long-term capital gain (loss) (post-May 5, 2003) . . .	**4e(1)**		Sch. D, line 12, col. (g)
	(2) Net long-term capital gain (loss) (entire year)	**4e(2)**		Sch. D, line 12, col. (f)
	f Other portfolio income (loss) (attach schedule)	**4f**		
	5 Guaranteed payments to partner	**5**		See pages 6 and 7 of Partner's Instructions for Schedule K-1 (Form 1065).
	6a Net section 1231 gain (loss) (post-May 5, 2003)	**6a**		
	b Net section 1231 gain (loss) (entire year)	**6b**		
	7 Other income (loss) (attach schedule)	**7**		
Deductions	**8** Charitable contributions (see instructions) (attach schedule) . .	**8**		Sch. A, line 15 or 16
	9 Section 179 expense deduction	**9**		See page 8 of Partner's Instructions for Schedule K-1 (Form 1065).
	10 Deductions related to portfolio income (attach schedule) . . .	**10**		
	11 Other deductions (attach schedule)	**11**		
Credits	**12a** Low-income housing credit: **(1)** From section 42(j)(5) partnerships	**12a(1)**		Form 8586, line 5
	(2) Other than on line 12a(1)	**12a(2)**		
	b Qualified rehabilitation expenditures related to rental real estate activities	**12b**		See page 9 of Partner's Instructions for Schedule K-1 (Form 1065).
	c Credits (other than credits shown on lines 12a and 12b) related to rental real estate activities.	**12c**		
	d Credits related to other rental activities	**12d**		
	13 Other credits	**13**		

For Paperwork Reduction Act Notice, see Instructions for Form 1065. Cat. No. 11394R **Schedule K-1 (Form 1065) 2003**

6512

Schedule K-1 (Form 1065) 2003 — Page **2**

	(a) Distributive share item		(b) Amount	(c) 1040 filers enter the amount in column (b) on:
Investment Interest	14a	Interest expense on investment debts	14a	Form 4952, line 1
	b	(1) Investment income included on lines 4a, 4b(2), 4c, and 4f .	14b(1)	See page 9 of Partner's Instructions for Schedule K-1 (Form 1065).
		(2) Investment expenses included on line 10	14b(2)	
Self-employment	15a	Net earnings (loss) from self-employment	15a	Sch. SE, Section A or B
	b	Gross farming or fishing income.	15b	See page 9 of Partner's Instructions for Schedule K-1 (Form 1065).
	c	Gross nonfarm income.	15c	
Adjustments and Tax Preference Items	16a	Depreciation adjustment on property placed in service after 1986	16a	
	b	Adjusted gain or loss	16b	See pages 9 and 10 of Partner's Instructions for Schedule K-1 (Form 1065) and Instructions for Form 6251.
	c	Depletion (other than oil and gas)	16c	
	d	(1) Gross income from oil, gas, and geothermal properties .	16d(1)	
		(2) Deductions allocable to oil, gas, and geothermal properties	16d(2)	
	e	Other adjustments and tax preference items (attach schedule)	16e	
Foreign Taxes	17a	Name of foreign country or U.S. possession ▶		
	b	Gross income from all sources	17b	
	c	Gross income sourced at partner level	17c	
	d	Foreign gross income sourced at partnership level:		
		(1) Passive	17d(1)	
		(2) Listed categories (attach schedule)	17d(2)	
		(3) General limitation	17d(3)	
	e	Deductions allocated and apportioned at partner level:		Form 1116, Part I
		(1) Interest expense	17e(1)	
		(2) Other	17e(2)	
	f	Deductions allocated and apportioned at partnership level to foreign source income:		
		(1) Passive	17f(1)	
		(2) Listed categories (attach schedule)	17f(2)	
		(3) General limitation	17f(3)	
	g	Total foreign taxes (check one): ▶ ☐ Paid ☐ Accrued . .	17g	Form 1116, Part II
	h	Reduction in taxes available for credit (attach schedule) . .	17h	Form 1116, line 12
Other	18	Section 59(e)(2) expenditures: a Type ▶		See page 10 of Partner's Instructions for Schedule K-1 (Form 1065).
	b	Amount	18b	
	19	Tax-exempt interest income	19	Form 1040, line 8b
	20	Other tax-exempt income	20	See page 10 of Partner's Instructions for Schedule K-1 (Form 1065).
	21	Nondeductible expenses	21	
	22	Distributions of money (cash and marketable securities) . . .	22	
	23	Distributions of property other than money	23	
	24	Recapture of low-income housing credit:		
	a	From section 42(j)(5) partnerships	24a	Form 8611, line 8
	b	Other than on line 24a.	24b	
Supplemental Information	25	Supplemental information required to be reported separately to each partner (attach additional schedules if more space is needed):		

Schedule K-1 (Form 1065) 2003

Form 1065 (2003)   Page **3**

Schedule K — Partners' Shares of Income, Credits, Deductions, etc.

(a) Distributive share items		(b) Total amount
1 Ordinary income (loss) from trade or business activities (page 1, line 22)	1	
2 Net income (loss) from rental real estate activities *(attach Form 8825)*	2	
3a Gross income from other rental activities	3a	
b Expenses from other rental activities *(attach schedule)*	3b	
c Net income (loss) from other rental activities. Subtract line 3b from line 3a	3c	
4 Portfolio income (loss) *(attach Schedule D (Form 1065) for lines 4d and 4e):*		
a Interest income	4a	
b Dividends: **(1)** Qualified dividends ▶ _____ **(2)** Total ordinary dividends ▶	4b(2)	
c Royalty income	4c	
d Net short-term capital gain (loss): **(1)** post-May 5, 2003 ▶ _____ **(2)** Entire year ▶	4d(2)	
e Net long-term capital gain (loss): **(1)** post-May 5, 2003 ▶ _____ **(2)** Entire year ▶	4e(2)	
f Other portfolio income (loss) *(attach schedule)*	4f	
5 Guaranteed payments to partners	5	
6a Net section 1231 gain (loss) (post-May 5, 2003) *(attach Form 4797)*	6a	
b Net section 1231 gain (loss) (entire year) *(attach Form 4797)*	6b	
7 Other income (loss) *(attach schedule)*	7	
8 Charitable contributions *(attach schedule)*	8	
9 Section 179 expense deduction *(attach Form 4562)*	9	
10 Deductions related to portfolio income (itemize)	10	
11 Other deductions *(attach schedule)*	11	
12a Low-income housing credit: **(1)** From partnerships to which section 42(j)(5) applies	12a(1)	
(2) Other than on line 12a(1)	12a(2)	
b Qualified rehabilitation expenditures related to rental real estate activities *(attach Form 3468)*	12b	
c Credits (other than credits shown on lines 12a and 12b) related to rental real estate activities	12c	
d Credits related to other rental activities	12d	
13 Other credits	13	
14a Interest expense on investment debts	14a	
b (1) Investment income included on lines 4a, 4b(2), 4c, and 4f above	14b(1)	
(2) Investment expenses included on line 10 above	14b(2)	
15a Net earnings (loss) from self-employment	15a	
b Gross farming or fishing income	15b	
c Gross nonfarm income	15c	
16a Depreciation adjustment on property placed in service after 1986	16a	
b Adjusted gain or loss	16b	
c Depletion (other than oil and gas)	16c	
d (1) Gross income from oil, gas, and geothermal properties	16d(1)	
(2) Deductions allocable to oil, gas, and geothermal properties	16d(2)	
e Other adjustments and tax preference items *(attach schedule)*	16e	
17a Name of foreign country or U.S. possession ▶		
b Gross income from all sources	17b	
c Gross income sourced at partner level	17c	
d Foreign gross income sourced at partnership level: **(1)** Passive ▶ _____ **(2)** Listed categories *(attach schedule)* ▶ _____ **(3)** General limitation ▶	17d(3)	
e Deductions allocated and apportioned at partner level: **(1)** Interest expense ▶ _____ **(2)** Other	17e(2)	
f Deductions allocated and apportioned at partnership level to foreign source income: **(1)** Passive ▶ _____ **(2)** Listed categories *(attach schedule)* ▶ _____ **(3)** General limitation ▶	17f(3)	
g Total foreign taxes (check one): ▶ Paid ☐ Accrued ☐	17g	
h Reduction in taxes available for credit *(attach schedule)*	17h	
18 Section 59(e)(2) expenditures: **a** Type ▶ _____ **b** Amount ▶	18b	
19 Tax-exempt interest income	19	
20 Other tax-exempt income	20	
21 Nondeductible expenses	21	
22 Distributions of money (cash and marketable securities)	22	
23 Distributions of property other than money	23	
24 Other items and amounts required to be reported separately to partners *(attach schedule)*		

Form **1065** (2003)

Form 1065 (2003)   Page **4**

Analysis of Net Income (Loss)

1 Net income (loss). Combine Schedule K, lines 1 through 7 in column (b). From the result, subtract the sum of Schedule K, lines 8 through 11, 14a, 17g, and 18b **1**

2 Analysis by partner type:	(i) Corporate	(ii) Individual (active)	(iii) Individual (passive)	(iv) Partnership	(v) Exempt organization	(vi) Nominee/Other
a General partners						
b Limited partners						

Note: Schedules L, M-1 and M-2 are not required if Question 5 of Schedule B is answered "Yes."

Schedule L	Balance Sheets per Books	Beginning of tax year		End of tax year	
	Assets	(a)	(b)	(c)	(d)
1	Cash				
2a	Trade notes and accounts receivable				
b	Less allowance for bad debts				
3	Inventories				
4	U.S. government obligations				
5	Tax-exempt securities				
6	Other current assets (attach schedule) . . .				
7	Mortgage and real estate loans				
8	Other investments (attach schedule)				
9a	Buildings and other depreciable assets . . .				
b	Less accumulated depreciation				
10a	Depletable assets				
b	Less accumulated depletion				
11	Land (net of any amortization)				
12a	Intangible assets (amortizable only).				
b	Less accumulated amortization				
13	Other assets (attach schedule)				
14	**Total** assets				
	Liabilities and Capital				
15	Accounts payable				
16	Mortgages, notes, bonds payable in less than 1 year				
17	Other current liabilities (attach schedule) . . .				
18	All nonrecourse loans				
19	Mortgages, notes, bonds payable in 1 year or more				
20	Other liabilities (attach schedule)				
21	Partners' capital accounts				
22	**Total** liabilities and capital				

Schedule M-1	Reconciliation of Income (Loss) per Books With Income (Loss) per Return	

1 Net income (loss) per books . . . . .

2 Income included on Schedule K, lines 1 through 4, 6b, and 7, not recorded on books this year (itemize): . . . .

3 Guaranteed payments (other than health insurance) . . . .

4 Expenses recorded on books this year not included on Schedule K, lines 1 through 11, 14a, 17g, and 18b (itemize):

a Depreciation $ . . . .

b Travel and entertainment $ . . . .
. . . .

5 Add lines 1 through 4 . . . .

6 Income recorded on books this year not included on Schedule K, lines 1 through 7 (itemize):

a Tax-exempt interest $ . . . .
. . . .

7 Deductions included on Schedule K, lines 1 through 11, 14a, 17g, and 18b, not charged against book income this year (itemize):

a Depreciation $ . . . .
. . . .

8 Add lines 6 and 7 . . . .

9 Income (loss) (Analysis of Net Income (Loss), line 1). Subtract line 8 from line 5 . . . .

Schedule M-2	Analysis of Partners' Capital Accounts	

1 Balance at beginning of year . . . .

2 Capital contributed: **a** Cash . . . . .

　　　　　　　　b Property . . . .

3 Net income (loss) per books . . . . .

4 Other increases (itemize): . . . .
. . . .

5 Add lines 1 through 4 . . . .

6 Distributions: **a** Cash . . . .

　　　　　　　b Property . . . . . .

7 Other decreases (itemize): . . . .
. . . .

8 Add lines 6 and 7 . . . .

9 Balance at end of year. Subtract line 8 from line 5

Form **1065** (2003)

20**03**

Department of the Treasury
Internal Revenue Service

Instructions for Form 1065

(Rev. February 2004)
U.S. Return of Partnership Income
Section references are to the Internal Revenue Code unless otherwise noted.

Changes To Note

• Under the Jobs and Growth Tax Relief Reconciliation Act of 2003, the general tax rates applicable to net capital gains for individuals have been reduced. The new gains rates also apply to qualified dividends under new section 1(h)(11). The new rates apply to capital gains (including installment payments) occurring on or after May 6, 2003, and to all qualified dividends received after December 31, 2002. Schedules K and K-1 have been revised to take into account the partners' shares of these gains and dividends.

• The instructions for line 6 of Form 1065 and line 25 of Schedule K-1 have been revised to change how dispositions of property are reported if the partnership passed through a section 179 expense deduction to any of its partners for the property.

• This version (February 2004) of these instructions was issued to reflect changes to the text for **Qualified dividends** on page 22 that occurred after the original version was sent to print.

Photographs of Missing Children

The Internal Revenue Service is a proud partner with the National Center for Missing and Exploited Children. Photographs of missing children selected by the Center may appear in instructions on pages that would

otherwise be blank. You can help bring these children home by looking at the photographs and calling **1-800-THE-LOST** (1-800-843-5678) if you recognize a child.

Unresolved Tax Issues

If the partnership has attempted to deal with an IRS problem unsuccessfully, it should contact the Taxpayer Advocate. The Taxpayer Advocate independently represents the partnership's interests and concerns within the IRS by protecting its rights and resolving problems that have not been fixed through normal channels.

While the Taxpayer Advocates cannot change the tax law or make a technical tax decision, they can clear up problems that resulted from previous contacts and ensure that the partnership's case is given a complete and impartial review.

The partnership's assigned personal advocate will listen to its point of view and will work with the partnership to address its concerns. The partnership can expect the advocate to provide:

• A "fresh look" at a new or ongoing problem.
• Timely acknowledgement.
• The name and phone number of the individual assigned to its case.
• Updates on progress.
• Timeframes for action.
• Speedy resolution.
• Courteous service.

When contacting the Taxpayer Advocate, the partnership should provide the following information:

• The partnership's name, address, and employer identification number.
• The name and telephone number of an authorized contact person and the hours he or she can be reached.
• The type of tax return and year(s) involved.
• A detailed description of the problem.
• Previous attempts to solve the problem and the office that had been contacted.
• A description of the hardship the partnership is facing (if applicable).

The partnership may contact a Taxpayer Advocate by calling a toll-free number, **1-877-777-4778**. Persons who have access to TTY/TDD equipment may call 1-800-829-4059 and ask for the Taxpayer Advocate. If the partnership prefers, it may call, write, or fax the Taxpayer Advocate office in its area. See **Pub. 1546**, The Taxpayer Advocate Service of the IRS, for a list of addresses and fax numbers.

Cat. No. 11392V

How To Get Forms and Publications

Personal Computer

You can access the IRS website 24 hours a day, 7 days a week at **www.irs.gov** to:
• Order IRS products online.
• Download forms, instructions, and publications.
• See answers to frequently asked tax questions.
• Search publications online by topic or keyword.
• Send us comments or request help by email.
• Sign up to receive local and national tax news by email.

You can also reach us using file transfer protocol at **ftp.irs.gov**.

CD-ROM

Order **Pub. 1796**, 2003 Federal Tax Products CD-ROM, and get:
• Current year forms, instructions, and publications.
• Prior year forms, instructions, and publications.
• Frequently requested tax forms that may be filled in electronically, printed out for submission, and saved for recordkeeping.
• The Internal Revenue Bulletin.

Buy the CD-ROM on the Internet at **www.irs.gov/cdorders** from the National Technical Information Service (NTIS) for $22 (no handling fee), or call **1-877-CDFORMS** (1-877-233-6767) toll free to buy the CD-ROM for $22 (plus a $5 handling fee).

By Phone and In Person

You can order forms and publications 24 hours a day, 7 days a week, by calling **1-800-TAX-FORM** (1-800-829-3676). You can also get most forms and publications at your local IRS office.

General Instructions

Purpose of Form

Form 1065 is an information return used to report the income, deductions, gains, losses, etc., from the operation of a partnership. A partnership does not pay tax on its income but "passes through" any profits or losses to its partners. Partners must include partnership items on their tax returns.

Definitions

Partnership

A partnership is the relationship between two or more persons who join to carry on a trade or business, with each person contributing money, property, labor, or skill and each expecting to share in the profits and losses of the business whether or not a formal partnership agreement is made.

The term "partnership" includes a limited partnership, syndicate, group, pool, joint venture, or other unincorporated organization, through or by which any business, financial operation, or venture is

carried on, that is not, within the meaning of the regulations under section 7701, a corporation, trust, estate, or sole proprietorship.

A joint undertaking merely to share expenses is not a partnership. Mere co-ownership of property that is maintained and leased or rented is not a partnership. However, if the co-owners provide services to the tenants, a partnership exists.

Foreign Partnership

A foreign partnership is a partnership that is not created or organized in the United States or under the law of the United States or of any state.

General Partner

A general partner is a partner who is personally liable for partnership debts.

General Partnership

A general partnership is composed only of general partners.

Limited Partner

A limited partner is a partner in a partnership formed under a state limited partnership law, whose personal liability for partnership debts is limited to the amount of money or other property that the partner contributed or is required to contribute to the partnership. Some members of other entities, such as domestic or foreign business trusts or limited liability companies that are classified as partnerships, may be treated as limited partners for certain purposes. See, for example, Temporary Regulations section 1.469-5T(e)(3), which treats all members with limited liability as limited partners for purposes of section 469(h)(2).

Limited Partnership

A limited partnership is formed under a state limited partnership law and composed of at least one general partner and one or more limited partners.

Limited Liability Partnership

A limited liability partnership (LLP) is formed under a state limited liability partnership law. Generally, a partner in an LLP is not personally liable for the debts of the LLP or any other partner, nor is a partner liable for the acts or omissions of any other partner, solely by reason of being a partner.

Limited Liability Company

A limited liability company (LLC) is an entity formed under state law by filing articles of organization as an LLC. Unlike a partnership, none of the members of an LLC are personally liable for its debts. An LLC may be classified for Federal income tax purposes either as a partnership, a corporation, or an entity disregarded as an entity separate from its owner by applying the rules in Regulations section 301.7701-3. See **Form 8832**, Entity Classification Election, for more details.

Note: *A domestic LLC with at least two members that does not file Form 8832 is classified as a partnership for Federal income tax purposes.*

Nonrecourse Loans

Nonrecourse loans are those liabilities of the partnership for which no partner bears the economic risk of loss.

Who Must File

Domestic Partnerships

Except as provided below, every domestic partnership must file Form 1065, unless it neither receives income nor incurs any expenditures treated as deductions or credits for Federal income tax purposes.

Entities formed as LLCs that are classified as partnerships for Federal income tax purposes must file Form 1065.

A religious or apostolic organization exempt from income tax under section 501(d) must file Form 1065 to report its taxable income, which must be allocated to its members as a dividend, whether distributed or not. Such an organization must figure its taxable income on an attachment to Form 1065 in the same manner as a corporation. The organization may use **Form 1120**, U.S. Corporation Income Tax Return, for this purpose. Enter the organization's taxable income, if any, on line 4b(2) of Schedule K and each member's pro rata share on line 4b(2) of Schedule K-1. Net operating losses are not deductible by the members but may be carried back or forward by the organization under the rules of section 172. The religious or apostolic organization also must make its annual information return available for public inspection. For this purpose, "annual information return" includes an exact copy of Form 1065 and all accompanying schedules and attachments, except Schedules K-1. For more details, see Regulations section 301.6104(d)-1.

A qualifying syndicate, pool, joint venture, or similar organization may elect under section 761(a) not to be treated as a partnership for Federal income tax purposes and will not be required to file Form 1065 except for the year of election. For details, see section 761(a) and Regulations section 1.761-2.

An electing large partnership (as defined in section 775) must file **Form 1065-B**, U.S. Return of Income for Electing Large Partnerships.

Real estate mortgage investment conduits (REMICs) must file **Form 1066**, U.S. Real Estate Mortgage Investment Conduit (REMIC) Income Tax Return.

Certain publicly traded partnerships treated as corporations under section 7704 must file Form 1120.

Foreign Partnerships

Generally, a foreign partnership that has gross income effectively connected with the conduct of a trade or business within the United States or has gross income derived from sources in the United States must file Form 1065, even if its principal place of business is outside the United States or all its members are foreign persons. A foreign partnership required to file a return generally must report all of its foreign and U.S. source income.

A foreign partnership with U.S. source income is not required to file Form 1065 if it qualifies for either of the following two exceptions.

Exception for foreign partnerships with U.S. partners. A return is not required if:
• The partnership had no effectively connected income (ECI) during its tax year,

-2-

Instructions for Form 1065

• The partnership had U.S. source income of $20,000 or less during its tax year,
• Less than 1% of any partnership item of income, gain, loss, deduction, or credit was allocable in the aggregate to direct U.S. partners at any time during its tax year, **and**
• The partnership is not a withholding foreign partnership as defined in Regulations section 1.1441-5(c)(2)(i).

Exception for foreign partnerships with no U.S. partners. A return is not required if:
• The partnership had no ECI during its tax year,
• The partnership had no U.S. partners at any time during its tax year,
• All required Forms 1042 and 1042-S were filed by the partnership or another withholding agent as required by Regulations section 1.1461-1(b) and (c),
• The tax liability of each partner for amounts reportable under Regulations sections 1.1461-1(b) and (c) has been fully satisfied by the withholding of tax at the source, **and**
• The partnership is not a withholding foreign partnership as defined in Regulations section 1.1441-5(c)(2)(i).

A foreign partnership filing Form 1065 solely to make an election (such as an election to amortize organization expenses) need only provide its name, address, and employer identification number (EIN) on page one of the form and attach a statement citing "Regulations section 1.6031(a)-1(b)(5)" and identifying the election being made. A foreign partnership filing Form 1065 solely to make an election must obtain an EIN if it does not already have one.

Termination of the Partnership

A partnership terminates when:
　1. All its operations are discontinued and no part of any business, financial operation, or venture is continued by any of its partners in a partnership **or**
　2. At least 50% of the total interest in partnership capital and profits is sold or exchanged within a 12-month period, including a sale or exchange to another partner. See Regulations section 1.708-1(b)(1) for more details.

The partnership's tax year ends on the date of termination. For purposes of **1** above, the date of termination is the date the partnership winds up its affairs. For purposes of **2** above, the date of termination is the date the partnership interest is sold or exchanged that, of itself or together with other sales or exchanges in the preceding 12 months, transfers an interest of 50% or more in both partnership capital and profits.

Special rules apply in the case of a merger, consolidation, or division of a partnership. See Regulations sections 1.708-1(c) and (d) for details.

Electronic Filing

Certain partnerships with more than 100 partners are required to file Form 1065, Schedules K-1, and related forms and schedules electronically. Other partnerships generally have the option to file electronically. Unless otherwise noted, this requirement or option does not apply to:
• Fiscal year returns with a tax period ending after June 30, 2004. Partnerships

with any other fiscal year returns ending on or before June 30, 2004 (January 2004–June 2004) may voluntarily file their return electronically.

Note: *Fiscal year returns with an extended due date after October 15, 2004, may not file electronically.*
• Returns filed for religious or apostolic organizations under section 501(d) or for organizations electing not to be treated as a partnership under section 761(a).
• Common trust fund returns. Common trust funds using Form 1065 to make a return of income may voluntarily file Form 1065 electronically.
• Returns filed on Form 1065-B.

For more details on electronic filing, see:
• **Pub. 1524,** Procedures for the 1065 e-file Program, U.S. Return of Partnership Income For Tax Year 2003;
• **Pub. 1525,** File Specifications, Validation Criteria and Record Layouts for the 1065 e-file Program, U.S. Return of Partnership Income for Tax Year 2003;
• **Pub. 3416,** 1065 e-file Program, U.S. Return of Partnership Income for Tax Year 2003 (Publication 1525 Supplement);
• **Form 8453-P,** U.S. Partnership Declaration and Signature for Electronic Filing.

For more information on filing electronically:
• **Call** the Electronic Filing Section at the Ogden Service Center at 866-255-0654 or
• **Write** to Internal Revenue Service, Ogden Submission Processing Center, Mail Stop 1057, Ogden, UT 84201.

Electronic Filing Waiver
The IRS may waive the electronic filing rules if the partnership demonstrates that a hardship would result if it were required to file its return electronically. A partnership interested in requesting a waiver of the mandatory electronic filing requirement must file a written request, and request one in the manner prescribed by the Ogden Submission Processing Center (OSPC).
• All written requests for waivers should be mailed to:
Internal Revenue Service
Ogden Submission Processing Center
Mail Stop 1057
Ogden, UT 84201
• Contact OSPC at 866-255-0654 for questions regarding the waiver procedures or process.

When To File
Generally, a domestic partnership must file Form 1065 by the 15th day of the 4th month following the date its tax year ended as shown at the top of Form 1065. For partnerships that keep their records and books of account outside the United States and Puerto Rico, an extension of time to file and pay is granted to the 15th day of the 6th month following the close of the tax year. If the due date falls on a Saturday, Sunday, or legal holiday, file by the next business day.

Private Delivery Services
The partnership can use certain private delivery services designated by the IRS to meet the "timely mailing as timely filing/

paying" rule for Form 1065. The most recent list of designated private delivery services was published by the IRS in September 2002. The list includes only the following:
• Airborne Express (Airborne): Overnight Air Express Service, Next Afternoon Service, Second Day Service.
• DHL Worldwide Express (DHL): DHL "Same Day" Service, DHL USA Overnight.
• Federal Express (FedEx): FedEx Priority Overnight, FedEx Standard Overnight, FedEx 2Day, FedEx International Priority, and FedEx International First.
• United Parcel Service (UPS): UPS Next Day Air, UPS Next Day Air Saver, UPS 2nd Day Air, UPS 2nd Day Air A.M., UPS Worldwide Express Plus, and UPS Worldwide Express.

The private delivery service can tell you how to get written proof of the mailing date.

Extension
If you need more time to file a partnership return, file **Form 8736,** Application for Automatic Extension of Time To File U.S. Return for a Partnership, REMIC, or for Certain Trusts, for an automatic 3-month extension. File Form 8736 by the regular due date of the partnership return. The automatic 3-month extension period includes any 2-month extension granted to partnerships that keep their records and books of account outside the United States and Puerto Rico.

If, after you have filed Form 8736, you still need more time to file the partnership return, file **Form 8800,** Application for Additional Extension of Time To File U.S. Return for a Partnership, REMIC, or for Certain Trusts, for an additional extension of up to 3 months. The partnership must provide a full explanation of the reasons for requesting the extension in order to get this additional extension. Form 8800 must be filed by the extended due date of the partnership return.

Period Covered
Form 1065 is an information return for calendar year 2003 and fiscal years beginning in 2003 and ending in 2004. If the return is for a fiscal year or a short tax year, fill in the tax year space at the top of the form.

The 2003 Form 1065 may also be used if:
　1. The partnership has a tax year of less than 12 months that begins and ends in 2004 and
　2. The 2004 Form 1065 is not available by the time the partnership is required to file its return.

However, the partnership must show its 2004 tax year on the 2003 Form 1065 and incorporate any tax law changes that are effective for tax years beginning after 2003.

Who Must Sign

General Partner or LLC Member
Form 1065 is not considered to be a return unless it is signed. One general partner or LLC member must sign the return. If a receiver, trustee in bankruptcy, or assignee controls the organization's property or business, that person must sign the return.

Paid Preparer's Information

If a partner or an employee of the partnership completes Form 1065, the paid preparer's space should remain blank. In addition, anyone who prepares Form 1065 but does not charge the partnership should not complete this section.

Generally, anyone who is paid to prepare the partnership return **must**:
* Sign the return in the space provided for the preparer's signature.
* Fill in the other blanks in the **Paid Preparer's Use Only** area of the return.
* Give the partnership a copy of the return in addition to the copy to be filed with the IRS.

Paid Preparer Authorization

If the partnership wants to allow the paid preparer to discuss its 2003 Form 1065 with the IRS, check the "Yes" box in the signature area of the return. The authorization applies only to the individual whose signature appears in the "Paid Preparer's Use Only" section of its return. It does not apply to the firm, if any, shown in the section.

If the "Yes" box is checked, the partnership is authorizing the IRS to call the paid preparer to answer any questions that may arise during the processing of its return. The partnership is also authorizing the paid preparer to:
* Give the IRS any information that is missing from its return,
* Call the IRS for information about the processing of its return, and
* Respond to certain IRS notices that the partnership has shared with the preparer about math errors and return preparation. The notices will not be sent to the preparer.

The partnership is not authorizing the paid preparer to bind the partnership to anything or otherwise represent the partnership before the IRS. If the partnership wants to expand the paid preparer's authorization, see **Pub. 947**, Practice Before the IRS and Power of Attorney.

The authorization cannot be revoked. However, the authorization will automatically end no later than the due date (excluding extensions) for filing the 2004 return.

Penalties

Late Filing of Return

A penalty is assessed against the partnership if it is required to file a partnership return and it **(a)** fails to file the return by the due date, including extensions, or **(b)** files a return that fails to show all the information required, unless such failure is due to reasonable cause. If the failure is due to reasonable cause, attach an explanation to the partnership return. The penalty is $50 for each month or part of a month (for a maximum of 5 months) the failure continues, multiplied by the total number of persons who were partners in the partnership during any part of the partnership's tax year for which the return is due. This penalty will not be imposed on partnerships for which the answer to Question 4 on Schedule B of Form 1065 is **No**, provided all partners have timely filed income tax returns fully reporting their shares of the income, deductions, and credits of the partnership. See page 19 of the instructions for further information.

Failure To Furnish Information Timely

For each failure to furnish Schedule K-1 to a partner when due and each failure to include on Schedule K-1 all the information required to be shown (or the inclusion of incorrect information), a $50 penalty may be imposed with respect to each Schedule K-1 for which a failure occurs. The maximum penalty is $100,000 for all such failures during a calendar year. If the requirement to report correct information is intentionally disregarded, each $50 penalty is increased to $100 or, if greater, 10% of the aggregate amount of items required to be reported, and the $100,000 maximum does not apply.

Trust Fund Recovery Penalty

This penalty may apply if certain excise, income, social security, and Medicare taxes that must be collected or withheld are not collected or withheld, or these taxes are not paid. These taxes are generally reported on:
* **Form 720**, Quarterly Federal Excise Tax Return;
* **Form 941**, Employer's Quarterly Federal Tax Return;
* **Form 943**, Employer's Annual Federal Tax Return for Agricultural Employees; or
* **Form 945**, Annual Return of Withheld Federal Income Tax.

The trust fund recovery penalty may be imposed on all persons who are determined by the IRS to have been **responsible** for collecting, accounting for, and paying over these taxes, and who acted willfully in not doing so. The penalty is equal to the unpaid trust fund tax. See the Instructions for Form 720, **Pub. 15**, Circular E, Employer's Tax Guide, or **Pub. 51**, Circular A, Agricultural Employer's Tax Guide, for more details, including the definition of a responsible person.

Accounting Methods

An accounting method is a set of rules used to determine when and how income and expenditures are reported. Figure ordinary income using the method of accounting regularly used in keeping the partnership's books and records. Generally, permissible methods include:
* Cash,
* Accrual, or
* Any other method authorized by the Internal Revenue Code.

In all cases, the method used must clearly reflect income.

Generally, a partnership may not use the cash method of accounting if **(a)** it has at least one corporate partner, average annual gross receipts of more than $5 million, and it is not a farming business or **(b)** it is a tax shelter (as defined in section 448(d)(3)). See section 448 for details.

If inventories are required, the accrual method must be used for sales and purchases of merchandise. However, qualifying taxpayers and eligible businesses of qualifying small business taxpayers are excepted from using the accrual method and may account for inventoriable items as materials and supplies that are not incidental. For more details, see **Schedule A, Cost of Goods Sold**, on page 18.

Accrual method. Under the accrual method, an amount is includible in income when:
* All the events have occurred that fix the right to receive the income which is the earliest of the date: **(a)** the required performance takes place, **(b)** payment is due, or **(c)** payment is received, and
* The amount can be determined with reasonable accuracy.

See Regulations section 1.451-1(a) for details.

Where To File

File Form 1065 at the applicable IRS address listed below.

If the partnership's principal business, office, or agency is located in:	And the total assets at the end of the tax year (Form 1065, page 1, item F) are:	Use the following Internal Revenue Service Center address:
Connecticut, Delaware, District of Columbia, Illinois, Indiana, Kentucky, Maine, Maryland, Massachusetts, Michigan, New Hampshire, New Jersey, New York, North Carolina, Ohio, Pennsylvania, Rhode Island, South Carolina, Vermont, Virginia, West Virginia, Wisconsin	Less than $10 million	Cincinnati, OH 45999-0011
	$10 million or more	Ogden, UT 84201-0011
Alabama, Alaska, Arizona, Arkansas, California, Colorado, Florida, Georgia, Hawaii, Idaho, Iowa, Kansas, Louisiana, Minnesota, Mississippi, Missouri, Montana, Nebraska, Nevada, New Mexico, North Dakota, Oklahoma, Oregon, South Dakota, Tennessee, Texas, Utah, Washington, Wyoming	Any amount	Ogden, UT 84201-0011
A foreign country or U.S. possession	Any amount	Philadelphia, PA 19255-0011

Instructions for Form 1065

Generally, an accrual basis taxpayer can deduct accrued expenses in the tax year in which:
• All events that determine liability have occurred,
• The amount of the liability can be figured with reasonable accuracy, and
• Economic performance takes place with respect to the expense.

There are exceptions to the economic performance rule for certain items, including recurring expenses. See section 461(h) and the related regulations for the rules for determining when economic performance takes place.

Nonaccrual experience method. Accrual method partnerships are not required to accrue certain amounts to be received from the performance of services that, on the basis of their experience, will not be collected, if:
• The services are in the fields of health, law, engineering, architecture, accounting, actuarial science, performing arts, or consulting or
• The partnership's average annual gross receipts for the 3 prior tax years does not exceed $5 million.

This provision does not apply to any amount if interest is required to be paid on the amount or if there is any penalty for failure to timely pay the amount. For information, see section 448(d)(5) and Temporary Regulations section 1.448-2T. For reporting requirements, see the instructions for line 1a on page 14.

Percentage of completion method. Long-term contracts (except for certain real property construction contracts) must generally be accounted for using the percentage of completion method described in section 460. See section 460 and the underlying regulations for rules on long-term contracts.

Mark-to-market accounting method. Dealers in securities must use the mark-to-market accounting method described in section 475. Under this method, any security that is inventory to the dealer must be included in inventory at its fair market value (FMV). Any security that is not inventory and that is held at the close of the tax year is treated as sold at its FMV on the last business day of the tax year, and any gain or loss must be taken into account in determining gross income. The gain or loss taken into account is generally treated as ordinary gain or loss. For details, including exceptions, see section 475, the related regulations, and Rev. Rul. 94-7, 1994-1 C.B. 151.

Dealers in commodities and *traders in securities and commodities* may elect to use the mark-to-market accounting method. To make the election, the partnership must file a statement describing the election, the first tax year the election is to be effective, and, in the case of an election for traders in securities or commodities, the trade or business for which the election is made. Except for new taxpayers, the statement must be filed by the due date (not including extensions) of the income tax return for the tax year immediately **preceding** the election year and attached to that return, or, if

applicable, to a request for an extension of time to file that return. For more details, see Rev. Proc. 99-17, 1999-1 C.B. 503, and sections 475(e) and (f).

Change in accounting method. Generally, the partnership must get IRS consent to change its method of accounting used to report income (for income as a whole or for any material item). To do so, it must file **Form 3115**, Application for Change in Accounting Method. See Form 3115 and **Pub. 538**, Accounting Periods and Methods.

Section 481(a) adjustment. The partnership may have to make an adjustment to prevent amounts of income or expenses from being duplicated. This is called a section 481(a) adjustment. The section 481(a) adjustment period is generally 1 year for a net negative adjustment and 4 years for a net positive adjustment. However, a partnership may elect to use a 1-year adjustment period if the net section 481(a) adjustment for the change is less than $25,000. The partnership must complete the appropriate lines of Form 3115 to make the election.

Include any net positive section 481(a) adjustment on page 1, line 7. If the net section 481(a) adjustment is negative, report it on Form 1065, line 20.

Accounting Periods

A partnership is generally required to have one of the following tax years:
1. The tax year of a majority of its partners (majority tax year).
2. If there is no majority tax year, then the tax year common to all of the partnership's principal partners (partners with an interest of 5% or more in the partnership profits or capital).
3. If there is neither a majority tax year nor a tax year common to all principal partners, then the tax year that results in the least aggregate deferral of income.

Note: *In determining the tax year of a partnership under 1, 2, or 3 above, the tax years of certain tax-exempt and foreign partners are disregarded. See Regulations section 1.706-1(b) for more details.*

4. Some other tax year, if:
• The partnership can establish that there is a business purpose for the tax year (see Pub. 538 for more information); or
• The partnership elects under section 444 to have a tax year other than a required tax year by filing **Form 8716**, Election to Have a Tax Year Other Than a Required Tax Year. For a partnership to have this election in effect, it must make the payments required by section 7519 and file **Form 8752**, Required Payment or Refund Under Section 7519.

A section 444 election ends if a partnership changes its accounting period to its required tax year or some other permitted year or it is penalized for willfully failing to comply with the requirements of section 7519. If the termination results in a short tax year, type or legibly print at the top of the first page of Form 1065 for the short tax year, "SECTION 444 ELECTION TERMINATED."

• The partnership elects to use a 52–53 week tax year that ends with reference to either its required tax year or a tax year elected under section 444 (see Pub. 538 for more information).

To change its tax year or to adopt or retain a tax year other than its required tax year, the partnership must file **Form 1128**, Application To Adopt, Change, or Retain a Tax Year, unless the partnership is making an election under section 444 (see Pub. 538).

If the partnership changes its tax year solely because its current tax year no longer qualifies as a natural business year, its partners may elect to take into account ratably over 4 tax years their distributive share of income attributable to the partnership's short tax year ending on or after May 10, 2002, but before June 1, 2004. See Rev. Proc. 2003-79, 2003-45 I.R.B. 1036, for details. If the partnership changes its tax year and the change falls within the scope of Rev. Proc. 2003-79, the partnership must attach a statement to Schedule K-1 that provides partners with the information they will need to make this election.

Note: *The tax year of a common trust fund must be the calendar year.*

Rounding Off to Whole Dollars

The partnership may round off cents to whole dollars on its return and schedules. If the partnership does round to whole dollars, it must round all amounts. To round, drop amounts under 50 cents and increase amounts from 50 to 99 cents to the next dollar (for example, $1.39 becomes $1 and $2.50 becomes $3).

If two or more amounts must be added to figure the amount to enter on a line, include cents when adding the amounts and round off only the total.

Recordkeeping

The partnership must keep its records as long as they may be needed for the administration of any provision of the Internal Revenue Code. If the consolidated audit procedures of sections 6221 through 6233 apply, the partnership usually must keep records that support an item of income, deduction, or credit on the partnership return for 3 years from the date the return is due or is filed, whichever is later. If the consolidated audit procedures do not apply, these records usually must be kept for 3 years from the date each partner's return is due or is filed, whichever is later. Keep records that verify the partnership's basis in property for as long as they are needed to figure the basis of the original or replacement property.

The partnership should also keep copies of all returns it has filed. They help in preparing future returns and in making computations when filing an amended return.

Amended Return

To correct an error on a Form 1065 already filed, file an amended Form 1065 and check box G(5) on page 1. If the income, deductions, credits, or other information provided to any partner on Schedule K-1 are incorrect, file an amended Schedule K-1 (Form 1065) for that partner with the amended Form 1065. Also give a copy of the amended Schedule K-1 to that partner. Check box I(2) on the Schedule K-1 to indicate that it is an amended Schedule K-1.

Exception: *If you are filing an amended partnership return and you answered* **Yes** *to Question 4 in Schedule B, the tax matters partner must file* **Form 8082,** *Notice of Inconsistent Treatment or Administrative Adjustment Request (AAR).*

A change to the partnership's Federal return may affect its state return. This includes changes made as a result of an examination of the partnership return by the IRS. For more information, contact the state tax agency for the state in which the partnership return is filed.

Other Forms, Returns, And Statements That May Be Required

Form, Return or Statement	Use this to—
W-2 and W-3 — Wage and Tax Statement; and Transmittal of Wage and Tax Statement	Report wages, tips, other compensation, and withheld income, social security and Medicare taxes for employees.
720 — Quarterly Federal Excise Tax Return	Report and pay environmental excise taxes, communications and air transportation taxes, fuel taxes, manufacturers' taxes, ship passenger tax, and certain other excise taxes. Also, see **Trust Fund Recovery Penalty** on page 4.
940 or 940-EZ — Employer's Annual Federal Unemployment (FUTA) Tax Return	Report and pay FUTA tax if the partnership either : 1. Paid wages of $1,500 or more in any calendar quarter during the calendar year (or the preceding calendar year) or 2. Had one or more employees working for the partnership for at least some part of a day in any 20 different weeks during the calendar year (or the preceding calendar year).
941 — Employer's Quarterly Federal Tax Return	Report quarterly income tax withheld on wages and employer and employee social security and Medicare taxes. Also, see **Trust Fund Recovery Penalty** on page 4.
943 — Employer's Annual Federal Tax Return for Agricultural Employees	Report income tax withheld and employer and employee social security and Medicare taxes on farmworkers. Also, see **Trust Fund Recovery Penalty** on page 4.
945 — Annual Return of Withheld Federal Income Tax	Report income tax withheld from nonpayroll payments, including pensions, annuities, individual retirement accounts (IRAs), gambling winnings, and backup withholding. Also, see **Trust Fund Recovery Penalty** on page 4.
1042 and 1042-S — Annual Withholding Tax Return for U. S. Source Income of Foreign Persons; and Foreign Person : U.S. Source Income Subject to Withholding	Report and send withheld tax on payments or distributions made to nonresident alien individuals, foreign partnerships, or foreign corporations to the extent these payments or distributions constitute gross income from sources within the United States that is not effectively connected with a U.S. trade or business. A domestic partnership must also withhold tax on a foreign partner's distributive share of such income, including amounts that are not actually distributed. Withholding on amounts not previously distributed to a foreign partner must be made and paid over by the earlier of * The date on which Schedule K-1 is sent to that partner or * The 15th day of the 3rd month after the end of the partnership's tax year. For more details, see sections 1441 and 1442 and **Pub. 515**, Withholding of Tax on Nonresident Aliens and Foreign Corporations.
1042-T — Annual Summary and Transmittal of Forms 1042-S	Transmit paper Forms 1042-S to the IRS.
1096 — Annual Summary and Transmittal of U.S. Information Returns	Transmit paper Forms 1099, 1098, 5498, and W-2G to the IRS.
1098 — Mortgage Interest Statement	Report the receipt from any individual of $600 or more of mortgage interest and points in the course of the partnership's trade or business.
1099-A, B, C, INT, LTC, MISC, MSA, OID, R, and S	Report the following: * Acquisitions or abandonments of secured property; * Proceeds from broker and barter exchange transactions; * Cancellation of debts; * Interest payments; * Payments of long-term care and accelerated death benefits; * Miscellaneous income payments; * Distributions from an Archer MSA or a Medicare+Choice MSA; * Original issue discount; * Distributions from pensions, annuities, retirement or profit-sharing plans, IRAs, insurance contracts, etc.; * Proceeds from real estate transactions; and * Amounts that were received as a nominee on behalf of another person. For more details, see the Instructions for Forms 1099, 1098, 5498, and W-2G. **Important:** *Every partnership must file Forms 1099-MISC if, in the course of its trade or business, it makes payments of rents, commissions, or other fixed or determinable income (see section 6041) totaling $600 or more to any one person during the calendar year.*

Form, Return or Statement	Use this to —
5471 — Information Return of U.S. Persons With Respect to Certain Foreign Corporations	A partnership may have to file Form 5471 if it: • Controls a foreign corporation; or • Acquires, disposes of, or owns 5% or more in value of the outstanding stock of a foreign corporation; or • Owns stock in a corporation that is a controlled foreign corporation for an uninterrupted period of 30 days or more during any tax year of the foreign corporation, and it owned that stock on the last day of that year.
5713 — International Boycott Report	Report operations in, or related to, a "boycotting" country, company, or national of a country and to figure the loss of certain tax benefits. The partnership must give each partner a copy of the Form 5713 filed by the partnership if there has been participation in, or cooperation with, an international boycott.
8264 — Application for Registration of a Tax Shelter	Get a tax shelter registration number from the IRS.
8271 — Investor Reporting of Tax Shelter Registration Number	Report the tax shelter's registration number for a tax shelter that is required to be registered. Attach Form 8271 to any return on which a deduction, credit, loss, or other tax benefit attributable to a tax shelter is taken or any income attributable to a tax shelter is reported.
8275 — Disclosure Statement	Disclose items or positions, except those contrary to a regulation, that are not otherwise adequately disclosed on a tax return. The disclosure is made to avoid the parts of the accuracy-related penalty imposed for disregard of rules or substantial understatement of tax. Also use Form 8275 for disclosures relating to preparer penalties for understatements due to unrealistic positions or disregard of rules.
8275-R — Regulation Disclosure Statement	Disclose any item on a tax return for which a position has been taken that is contrary to Treasury regulations.
8288 and **8288-A** — U.S. Withholding Tax Return for Dispositions by Foreign Persons of U.S. Real Property Interests; and Statement of Withholding on Dispositions by Foreign Persons of U.S. Real Property Interests	Report and send withheld tax on the sale of U.S. real property by a foreign person. See section 1445 and the related regulations for additional information.
8300 — Report of Cash Payments Over $10,000 Received in a Trade or Business	Report the receipt of more than $10,000 in cash or foreign currency in one transaction or a series of related transactions.
8308 — Report of a Sale or Exchange of Certain Partnership Interests	Report the sale or exchange by a partner of all or part of a partnership interest where any money or other property received in exchange for the interest is attributable to unrealized receivables or inventory items.
8594 — Asset Acquisition Statement Under Section 1060	Report a sale if goodwill or going concern value attaches, or could attach, to such assets. Both the seller and buyer of a group of assets that makes up a trade or business must use this form.
8697 — Interest Computation Under the Look-Back Method for Completed Long-Term Contracts	Figure the interest due or to be refunded under the look-back method of section 460(b)(2) on certain long-term contracts that are accounted for under either the percentage of completion-capitalized cost method or the percentage of completion method. Partnerships that are not closely held use this form. Closely held partnerships should see the instructions on page 29 for line 25, item 11, of Schedule K-1 for details on the Form 8697 information they must provide to their partners.
8804, 8805, and **8813** — Annual Return for Partnership Withholding Tax (Section 1446); Foreign Partner's Information Statement of Section 1446 Withholding Tax; and Partnership Withholding Tax Payment (Section 1446)	Figure and report the withholding tax on the distributive shares of any effectively connected gross income for foreign partners. This is done on Forms 8804 and 8805. Use Form 8813 to send installment payments of withheld tax based on effectively connected taxable income allocable to foreign partners. **Exception:** *Publicly traded partnerships that do not elect to pay tax based on effectively connected taxable income do not file these forms. They must instead withhold tax on distributions to foreign partners and report and send payments using Forms 1042 and 1042-S. See Rev. Proc. 89-31, 1989-1 C.B. 895 and Rev. Proc. 92-66, 1992-2 C.B. 428 for more information.*
8832 — Entity Classification Election	File an election to make a change in classification. Except for a business entity automatically classified as a corporation, a business entity with at least two members may choose to be classified either as a partnership or an association taxable as a corporation. A domestic eligible entity with at least two members that does not file Form 8832 is classified under the default rules as a partnership. However, a foreign eligible entity with at least two members is classified under the default rules as a partnership only if at least one member does not have limited liability. File Form 8832 only if the entity does not want to be classified under these default rules or if it wants to change its classification.

Form, Return or Statement	Use this to —
8865 — Return of U.S. Person With Respect To Certain Foreign Partnerships	Report an interest in a foreign partnership. A domestic partnership may have to File Form 8865 if it: **1.** Controlled a foreign partnership (e.g., it owned more than 50% direct or indirect interest in the partnership). **2.** Owned at least a 10% direct or indirect interest in a foreign partnership while U.S. persons controlled that partnership. **3.** Had an acquisition, disposition, or change in proportional interest of a foreign partnership that: **a.** Increased its direct interest to at least 10% or reduced its direct interest of at least 10% to less than 10%. **b.** Changed its direct interest by at least a 10% interest. **4.** Contributed property to a foreign partnership in exchange for a partnership interest if: **a.** Immediately after the contribution, the partnership owned, directly or indirectly, at least a 10% interest in the foreign partnership; or **b.** The FMV of the property the partnership contributed to the foreign partnership in exchange for a partnership interest exceeds $100,000, when added to other contributions of property made to the foreign partnership during the preceding 12-month period. Also, the domestic partnership may have to file Form 8865 to report certain dispositions by a foreign partnership of property it previously contributed to that foreign partnership if it was a partner at the time of the disposition. For more details, including penalties for failing to file Form 8865, see Form 8865 and its separate instructions.
8866 — Interest Computation Under the Look-Back Method for Property Depreciated Under the Income Forecast Method	Figure the interest due or to be refunded under the look-back method of section 167(g)(2) for certain property placed in service after September 13, 1995, depreciated under the income forecast method. Partnerships that are not closely held use this form. Closely held partnerships should see the instructions on page 30 for line 25, item 23, of Schedule K-1 for details on the Form 8866 information they must provide to their partners.
8876 — Excise Tax on Structured Settlement Factoring Transactions	Report and pay the 40% excise tax imposed under section 5891.
Form 8886 — Reportable Transaction Disclosure Statement	Report disclosure information for each reportable transaction in which the partnership participated. Form 8886 must be filed for each tax year that the Federal income tax liability of the partnership is affected by its participation in the transaction. The following are reportable transactions. **1.** Any transaction that is the same as or substantially similar to tax avoidance transactions identified by the IRS (i.e., a listed transaction). **2.** Any transaction offered under conditions of confidentiality. **3.** Any transaction for which the partnership has contractual protection against disallowance of the tax benefits. **4.** Any transaction resulting in a loss of at least $2 million in any single year or $4 million in any combination of years. However, for partnerships with only corporations (other than S corporations) as partners, loss amounts of at least $10 million in any single year or $20 million in a combination of years are reportable transactions. **5.** Any transaction resulting in a book-tax difference of more than $10 million on a gross basis. **6.** Any transaction resulting in a tax credit of more than $250,000, if the partnership held the asset generating the credit for 45 days or less. See Regulations section 1.6011-4 and the instructions for line 25, Supplemental Information, item 29 for more information.
Statement of section 743(b) basis adjustments	Report the adjustment of bases under section 743(b). If the partnership is required to adjust the bases of partnership properties under section 743(b) because of a section 754 election on the sale or exchange of a partnership interest or on the death of a partner, the partnership must attach a statement to its return for the year of the transfer. The statement must list: **1.** The name and identifying number of the transferee partner, **2.** The computation of the adjustment, and **3.** The partnership properties to which the adjustment has been allocated.

Assembling the Return

When submitting Form 1065, organize the pages of the return in the following order:
* Pages 1–4,
* Schedule F (if required),
* Form 8825 (if required),
* Any other schedules in alphabetical order, and
* Any other forms in numerical order.

Complete every applicable entry space on Form 1065 and Schedule K-1. Do not write "See attached" instead of completing the entry spaces. Penalties may be assessed if the partnership files an incomplete return. If you need more space on the forms or schedules, attach separate sheets and place them at the end of the return using the same size and format as on the printed forms. Show the totals on the printed forms. Also, be sure to put the partnership's name and EIN on each supporting statement or attachment.

Separately Stated Items

Partners must take into account separately (under section 702(a)) their distributive shares of the following items (whether or not they are actually distributed):

1. Ordinary income or loss from trade or business activities.
2. Net income or loss from rental real estate activities.
3. Net income or loss from other rental activities.
4. Gains and losses from sales or exchanges of capital assets.
5. Gains and losses from sales or exchanges of property described in section 1231.
6. Charitable contributions.
7. Dividends (passed through to corporate partners) that qualify for the dividends-received deduction.
8. Taxes described in section 901 paid or accrued to foreign countries and to possessions of the United States.
9. Other items of income, gain, loss, deduction, or credit, to the extent provided by regulations. Examples of such items include nonbusiness expenses, intangible drilling and development costs, amortizable basis of reforestation expenses, and soil and water conservation expenditures.

Elections Made by the Partnership

Generally, the partnership decides how to figure taxable income from its operations. For example, it chooses the accounting method and depreciation methods it will use. The partnership also makes elections under the following sections:

1. Section 179 (election to expense certain property).
2. Section 614 (definition of property—mines, wells, and other natural deposits). This election must be made before the partners figure their individual depletion allowances under section 613A(c)(7)(D).
3. Section 1033 (involuntary conversions).
4. Section 754 (manner of electing optional adjustment to basis of partnership property).

Under section 754, a partnership may elect to adjust the basis of partnership property when property is distributed or

when a partnership interest is transferred. If the election is made with respect to a transfer of a partnership interest (section 743(b)) and the assets of the partnership constitute a trade or business for purposes of section 1060(c), then the value of any goodwill transferred must be determined in the manner provided in Regulations section 1.1060-1. Once an election is made under section 754, it applies both to all distributions and to all transfers made during the tax year and in all subsequent tax years unless the election is revoked. See Regulations section 1.754-1(c).

This election must be made in a statement that is filed with the partnership's timely filed return (including any extension) for the tax year during which the distribution or transfer occurs. The statement must include:
* The name and address of the partnership.
* A declaration that the partnership elects under section 754 to apply the provisions of section 734(b) and section 743(b).
* The signature of the general partner authorized to sign the partnership return.

The partnership can get an automatic 12-month extension to make the section 754 election provided corrective action is taken within 12 months of the original deadline for making the election. For details, see Regulations section 301.9100-2.

See section 754 and the related regulations for more information.

If there is a distribution of property consisting of an interest in another partnership, see section 734(b).

The partnership is required to attach a statement for any section 743(b) basis adjustments. See page 8 for details.

Elections Made by Each Partner

Elections under the following sections are made by each partner separately on the partner's tax return:

1. Section 59(e) (election to deduct ratably certain qualified expenditures such as intangible drilling costs, mining exploration expenses, or research and experimental expenditures).
2. Section 108 (income from discharge of indebtedness).
3. Section 617 (deduction and recapture of certain mining exploration expenditures paid or incurred).
4. Section 901 (foreign tax credit).

Partner's Dealings With Partnership

If a partner engages in a transaction with his or her partnership, other than in his or her capacity as a partner, the partner is treated as not being a member of the partnership for that transaction. Special rules apply to sales or exchanges of property between partnerships and certain persons, as explained in **Pub. 541**, Partnerships.

Contributions to the Partnership

Generally, no gain (loss) is recognized to the partnership or any of the partners when

property is contributed to the partnership in exchange for an interest in the partnership. This rule does not apply to any gain realized on a transfer of property to a partnership that would be treated as an investment company (within the meaning of section 351) if the partnership were incorporated. If, as a result of a transfer of property to a partnership, there is a direct or indirect transfer of money or other property to the transferring partner, the partner may have to recognize gain on the exchange.

The basis to the partnership of property contributed by a partner is the adjusted basis in the hands of the partner at the time it was contributed, plus any gain recognized (under section 721(b)) by the partner at that time. See section 723 for more information.

Dispositions of Contributed Property

If the partnership disposes of property contributed to the partnership by a partner, income, gain, loss, and deductions from that property must be allocated among the partners to take into account the difference between the property's basis and its FMV at the time of the contribution.

For property contributed to the partnership, the contributing partner must recognize gain or loss on a distribution of the property to another partner within 5 years of being contributed. For property contributed after June 8, 1997, the 5-year period is generally extended to 7 years. The gain or loss is equal to the amount that the contributing partner should have recognized if the property had been sold for its FMV when distributed, because of the difference between the property's basis and its FMV at the time of contribution.

See section 704(c) for details and other rules on dispositions of contributed property. See section 724 for the character of any gain or loss recognized on the disposition of unrealized receivables, inventory items, or capital loss property contributed to the partnership by a partner.

Recognition of Precontribution Gain on Certain Partnership Distributions

A partner who contributes appreciated property to the partnership must include in income any precontribution gain to the extent the FMV of other property (other than money) distributed to the partner by the partnership exceeds the adjusted basis of his or her partnership interest just before the distribution. Precontribution gain is the net gain, if any, that would have been recognized under section 704(c)(1)(B) if the partnership had distributed to another partner all the property that had been contributed to the partnership by the distributee partner within 5 years of the distribution and that was held by the partnership just before the distribution. For property contributed after June 8, 1997, the 5-year period is generally extended to 7 years.

Appropriate basis adjustments are to be made to the adjusted basis of the distributee partner's interest in the partnership and the partnership's basis in the contributed property to reflect the gain recognized by the partner.

For more details and exceptions, see Pub. 541.

Unrealized Receivables and Inventory Items

Generally, if a partner sells or exchanges a partnership interest where unrealized receivables or inventory items are involved, the transferor partner must notify the partnership, in writing, within 30 days of the exchange. The partnership must then file **Form 8308**, Report of a Sale or Exchange of Certain Partnership Interests.

If a partnership distributes unrealized receivables or substantially appreciated inventory items in exchange for all or part of a partner's interest in other partnership property (including money), treat the transaction as a sale or exchange between the partner and the partnership. Treat the partnership gain (loss) as ordinary income (loss). The income (loss) is specially allocated only to partners other than the distributee partner.

If a partnership gives other property (including money) for all or part of that partner's interest in the partnership's unrealized receivables or substantially appreciated inventory items, treat the transaction as a sale or exchange of the property.

See Rev. Rul. 84-102, 1984-2 C.B. 119, for information on the tax consequences that result when a new partner joins a partnership that has liabilities and unrealized receivables. Also, see Pub. 541 for more information on unrealized receivables and inventory items.

Passive Activity Limitations

In general, section 469 limits the amount of losses, deductions, and credits that partners may claim from "passive activities." The passive activity limitations do not apply to the partnership. Instead, they apply to each partner's share of any income or loss and credit attributable to a passive activity. Because the treatment of each partner's share of partnership income or loss and credit depends on the nature of the activity that generated it, the partnership must report income or loss and credits separately for each activity.

The following instructions and the instructions for Schedules K and K-1 (pages 20–30) explain the applicable passive activity limitation rules and specify the type of information the partnership must provide to its partners for each activity. If the partnership has more than one activity, it must report information for each activity on an attachment to Schedules K and K-1.

Generally, passive activities include **(a)** activities that involve the conduct of a trade or business if the partner does not materially participate in the activity; and **(b)** all rental activities (defined below), regardless of the partner's participation. For exceptions, see **Activities That Are Not Passive Activities** below. The level of each partner's participation in an activity must be determined by the partner.

The passive activity rules provide that losses and credits from passive activities

can generally be applied only against income and tax from passive activities. Thus, passive losses and credits cannot be applied against income from salaries, wages, professional fees, or a business in which the taxpayer materially participates; against "portfolio income" (defined on page 11); or against the tax related to any of these types of income.

Special provisions apply to certain activities. First, the passive activity limitations must be applied separately with respect to a net loss from passive activities held through a publicly traded partnership. Second, special rules require that net income from certain activities that would otherwise be treated as passive income must be recharacterized as nonpassive income for purposes of the passive activity limitations.

To allow each partner to correctly apply the passive activity limitations, the partnership must report income or loss and credits separately for each of the following types of activities and income: trade or business activities, rental real estate activities, rental activities other than rental real estate, and portfolio income.

Activities That Are Not Passive Activities

The following are **not** passive activities.

1. Trade or business activities in which the partner materially participated for the tax year.

2. Any rental real estate activity in which the partner materially participated if the partner met both of the following conditions for the tax year:

a. More than half of the personal services the partner performed in trades or businesses were performed in real property trades or businesses in which he or she materially participated **and**

b. The partner performed more than 750 hours of services in real property trades or businesses in which he or she materially participated.

Note: *For a partner that is a closely held C corporation (defined in section 465(a)(1)(B)), the above conditions are treated as met if more than 50% of the corporation's gross receipts are from real property trades or businesses in which the corporation materially participated.*

For purposes of this rule, each interest in rental real estate is a separate activity, unless the partner elects to treat all interests in rental real estate as one activity.

If the partner is married filing jointly, either the partner or his or her spouse must separately meet both of the above conditions, without taking into account services performed by the other spouse.

A real property trade or business is any real property development, redevelopment, construction, reconstruction, acquisition, conversion, rental, operation, management, leasing, or brokerage trade or business. Services the partner performed as an employee are not treated as performed in a real property trade or business unless he or she owned more than 5% of the stock (or more than 5% of the capital or profits interest) in the employer.

3. An interest in an oil or gas well drilled or operated under a working interest if at any time during the tax year the partner held

the working interest directly or through an entity that did not limit the partner's liability (for example, an interest as a general partner). This exception applies regardless of whether the partner materially participated for the tax year.

4. The rental of a dwelling unit used by a partner for personal purposes during the year for more than the **greater of** 14 days or 10% of the number of days that the residence was rented at fair rental value.

5. An activity of trading personal property for the account of owners of interests in the activity. For purposes of this rule, personal property means property that is actively traded, such as stocks, bonds, and other securities. See Temporary Regulations section 1.469-1T(e)(6).

Trade or Business Activities

A trade or business activity is an activity (other than a rental activity or an activity treated as incidental to an activity of holding property for investment) that:

1. Involves the conduct of a trade or business (within the meaning of section 162),

2. Is conducted in anticipation of starting a trade or business, or

3. Involves research or experimental expenditures deductible under section 174 (or that would be if you chose to deduct rather than capitalize them).

If the partner does not materially participate in the activity, a trade or business activity held through a partnership is generally a passive activity of the partner.

Each partner must determine if they materially participated in an activity. As a result, while the partnership's overall trade or business income (loss) is reported on page 1 of Form 1065, the specific income and deductions from each separate trade or business activity must be reported on attachments to Form 1065. Similarly, while each partner's allocable share of the partnership's overall trade or business income (loss) is reported on line 1 of Schedule K-1, each partner's allocable share of the income and deductions from each trade or business activity must be reported on attachments to each Schedule K-1. See **Passive Activity Reporting Requirements** on page 13 for more information.

Rental Activities

Generally, except as noted below, if the gross income from an activity consists of amounts paid principally for the use of real or personal tangible property held by the partnership, the activity is a rental activity.

There are several exceptions to this general rule. Under these exceptions, an activity involving the use of real or personal tangible property is not a rental activity if any of the following apply:

• The **average period of customer use** (defined on page 11) for such property is 7 days or less.

• The average period of customer use for such property is 30 days or less and **significant personal services** (defined on page 11) are provided by or on behalf of the partnership.

• **Extraordinary personal services** (defined on page 11) are provided by or on behalf of the partnership.

* The rental of such property is treated as **incidental** to a nonrental activity of the partnership under Temporary Regulations section 1.469-1T(e)(3)(vi) and Regulations section 1.469-1(e)(3)(vi).
* The partnership customarily makes the property available during defined business hours for nonexclusive use by various customers.
* The partnership provides property for use in a nonrental activity of a partnership or joint venture in its capacity as an owner of an interest in such partnership or joint venture. Whether the partnership provides property used in an activity of another partnership or of a joint venture in the partnership's capacity as an owner of an interest in the partnership or joint venture is determined on the basis of all the facts and circumstances.

In addition, a guaranteed payment described in section 707(c) is not income from a rental activity under any circumstances.

Average period of customer use. Figure the average period of customer use for a class of property by dividing the total number of days in all rental periods by the number of rentals during the tax year. If the activity involves renting more than one class of property, multiply the average period of customer use of each class by the ratio of the gross rental income from that class to the activity's total gross rental income. The activity's average period of customer use equals the sum of these class-by-class average periods weighted by gross income. See Regulations section 1.469-1(e)(3)(iii).

Significant personal services. Personal services include only services performed by individuals. To determine if personal services are significant personal services, consider all the relevant facts and circumstances. Relevant facts and circumstances include:
* How often the services are provided,
* The type and amount of labor required to perform the services, and
* The value of the services in relation to the amount charged for use of the property.

The following services are not considered in determining whether personal services are significant:
* Services necessary to permit the lawful use of the rental property.
* Services performed in connection with improvements or repairs to the rental property that extend the useful life of the property substantially beyond the average rental period.
* Services provided in connection with the use of any improved real property that are similar to those commonly provided in connection with long-term rentals of high-grade commercial or residential property. Examples include cleaning and maintenance of common areas, routine repairs, trash collection, elevator service, and security at entrances.

Extraordinary personal services. Services provided in connection with making rental property available for customer use are extraordinary personal services only if the services are performed by individuals and the customers' use of the rental property is incidental to their receipt of the services.

For example, a patient's use of a hospital room generally is incidental to the care

received from the hospital's medical staff. Similarly, a student's use of a dormitory room in a boarding school is incidental to the personal services provided by the school's teaching staff.

Rental activity incidental to a nonrental activity. An activity is not a rental activity if the rental of the property is incidental to a nonrental activity, such as the activity of holding property for investment, a trade or business activity, or the activity of dealing in property.

Rental of property is **incidental** to an **activity of holding property for investment** if both of the following apply:
* The main purpose for holding the property is to realize a gain from the appreciation of the property.
* The gross rental income from such property for the tax year is less than 2% of the smaller of the property's **unadjusted basis** or its FMV.

Rental of property is **incidental** to a **trade or business activity** if all of the following apply:
* The partnership owns an interest in the trade or business at all times during the year.
* The rental property was mainly used in the trade or business activity during the tax year or during at least 2 of the 5 preceding tax years.
* The gross rental income from the property for the tax year is less than 2% of the smaller of the property's **unadjusted basis** or its FMV.

The sale or exchange of property that is both rented and sold or exchanged during the tax year (where the gain or loss is recognized) is treated as incidental to the activity of dealing in property if, at the time of the sale or exchange, the property was held primarily for sale to customers in the ordinary course of the partnership's trade or business.

See Temporary Regulations section 1.469-1T(e)(3) and Regulations section 1.469-1(e)(3) for more information on the definition of rental activities for purposes of the passive activity limitations.

Reporting of rental activities. In reporting the partnership's income or losses and credits from rental activities, the partnership must separately report rental real estate activities and rental activities other than rental real estate activities.

Partners who actively participate in a rental real estate activity may be able to deduct part or all of their rental real estate losses (and the deduction equivalent of rental real estate credits) against income (or tax) from nonpassive activities. The combined amount of rental real estate losses and the deduction equivalent of rental real estate credits from all sources (including rental real estate activities not held through the partnership) that may be claimed is limited to $25,000. This $25,000 amount is generally reduced for high-income partners.

Report rental real estate activity income (loss) on **Form 8825**, Rental Real Estate Income and Expenses of a Partnership or an S Corporation, and line 2 of Schedules K and K-1 rather than on page 1 of Form 1065. Report credits related to rental real estate activities on lines 12b and 12c and low-income housing credits on line 12a of Schedules K and K-1.

Report income (loss) from rental activities other than rental real estate on line 3 and credits related to rental activities other than rental real estate on line 12d of Schedules K and K-1.

Portfolio Income

Generally, portfolio income includes all gross income, other than income derived in the ordinary course of a trade or business, that is attributable to interest; dividends; royalties; income from a real estate investment trust, a regulated investment company, a real estate mortgage investment conduit, a common trust fund, a controlled foreign corporation, a qualified electing fund, or a cooperative; income from the disposition of property that produces income of a type defined as portfolio income; and income from the disposition of property held for investment. See **Self-Charged Interest** below for an exception.

Solely for purposes of the preceding paragraph, gross income derived in the ordinary course of a trade or business includes (and portfolio income, therefore, does not include) only the following types of income:
* Interest income on loans and investments made in the ordinary course of a trade or business of lending money.
* Interest on accounts receivable arising from the performance of services or the sale of property in the ordinary course of a trade or business of performing such services or selling such property, but only if credit is customarily offered to customers of the business.
* Income from investments made in the ordinary course of a trade or business of furnishing insurance or annuity contracts or reinsuring risks underwritten by insurance companies.
* Income or gain derived in the ordinary course of an activity of trading or dealing in any property if such activity constitutes a trade or business (unless the dealer held the property for investment at any time before such income or gain is recognized).
* Royalties derived by the taxpayer in the ordinary course of a trade or business of licensing intangible property.
* Amounts included in the gross income of a patron of a cooperative by reason of any payment or allocation to the patron based on patronage occurring with respect to a trade or business of the patron.
* Other income identified by the IRS as income derived by the taxpayer in the ordinary course of a trade or business.

See Temporary Regulations section 1.469-2T(c)(3) for more information on portfolio income.

Report portfolio income on line 4 of Schedules K and K-1, rather than on page 1 of Form 1065. Report deductions related to portfolio income on line 10 of Schedules K and K-1.

Self-Charged Interest

Certain self-charged interest income and deductions may be treated as passive activity gross income and passive activity deductions if the loan proceeds are used in a passive activity. Generally, self-charged interest income and deductions result from loans to and from the partnership and its partners. It also includes loans between the partnership and another partnership if each owner in the borrowing entity has the same proportional ownership interest in the lending entity. The self-charged interest rules do not apply to a partner's interest in a partnership if the partnership makes an election under Regulations section 1.469-7(g) to avoid the application of these rules. To make the election, the partnership must attach to its original or amended Form 1065, a statement that includes the name, address, and EIN of the partnership and a declaration that the election is being made under Regulations section 1.469-7(g). The election will apply to the tax year in which it was made and all subsequent tax years. Once made, the election may only be revoked with the consent of the IRS.

For more details on the self-charged interest rules, see Regulations section 1.469-7.

Grouping Activities

Generally, one or more trade or business activities or rental activities may be treated as a single activity if the activities make up an appropriate economic unit for the measurement of gain or loss under the passive activity rules. Whether activities make up an appropriate economic unit depends on all the relevant facts and circumstances. The factors given the greatest weight in determining whether activities make up an appropriate economic unit are:
• Similarities and differences in types of trades or businesses.
• The extent of common control.
• The extent of common ownership.
• Geographical location.
• Reliance between or among the activities.

Example. The partnership has a significant ownership interest in a bakery and a movie theater in Baltimore and a bakery and a movie theater in Philadelphia. Depending on the relevant facts and circumstances, there may be more than one reasonable method for grouping the partnership's activities. For instance, the following groupings may or may not be permissible:
• A single activity,
• A movie theater activity and a bakery activity,
• A Baltimore activity and a Philadelphia activity, or
• Four separate activities.

Once the partnership chooses a grouping under these rules, it must continue using that grouping in later tax years unless a material change in the facts and circumstances makes it clearly inappropriate.

The IRS may regroup the partnership's activities if the partnership's grouping fails to reflect one or more appropriate economic units and one of the primary purposes of the grouping is to avoid the passive activity limitations.

Limitation on grouping certain activities. The following activities may **not** be grouped together:

1. A rental activity with a trade or business activity unless the activities being grouped together make up an appropriate economic unit and
   a. The rental activity is insubstantial relative to the trade or business activity or vice versa or
   b. Each owner of the trade or business activity has the same proportionate

ownership interest in the rental activity. If so, the portion of the rental activity involving the rental of property to be used in the trade or business activity may be grouped with the trade or business activity.

2. An activity involving the rental of real property with an activity involving the rental of personal property (except personal property provided in connection with the real property or vice versa).

3. Any activity with another activity in a different type of business and in which the partnership holds an interest as a limited partner or as a limited entrepreneur (as defined in section 464(e)(2)) if that other activity engages in holding, producing, or distributing motion picture films or videotapes; farming; leasing section 1245 property; or exploring for or exploiting oil and gas resources or geothermal deposits.

Activities conducted through other partnerships. Once a partnership determines its activities under these rules, the partnership as a partner may use these rules to group those activities with:
• Each other,
• Activities conducted directly by the partnership, or
• Activities conducted through other partnerships.

A partner may not treat as separate activities those activities grouped together by a partnership.

Recharacterization of Passive Income

Under Temporary Regulations section 1.469-2T(f) and Regulations section 1.469-2(f), net passive income from certain passive activities must be treated as nonpassive income. Net passive income is the excess of an activity's passive activity gross income over its passive activity deductions (current year deductions and prior year unallowed losses).

Income from the following six sources is subject to recharacterization.

Note: *Any net passive income recharacterized as nonpassive income is treated as investment income for purposes of figuring investment interest expense limitations if it is from (a) an activity of renting substantially nondepreciable property from an equity-financed lending activity or (b) an activity related to an interest in a pass-through entity that licenses intangible property.*

1. Significant participation passive activities. A significant participation passive activity is any trade or business activity in which the partner participated for more than 100 hours during the tax year but did not materially participate. Because each partner must determine the partner's level of participation, the partnership will not be able to identify significant participation passive activities.

2. Certain nondepreciable rental property activities. Net passive income from a rental activity is nonpassive income if less than 30% of the unadjusted basis of the property used or held for use by customers in the activity is subject to depreciation under section 167.

3. Passive equity-financed lending activities. If the partnership has net income from a passive equity-financed lending activity, the smaller of the net passive

income or the equity-financed interest income from the activity is nonpassive income.

Note: *The amount of income from the activities in paragraphs 1 through 3 that any partner will be required to recharacterize as nonpassive income may be limited under Temporary Regulations section 1.469-2T(f)(8). Because the partnership will not have information regarding all of a partner's activities, it must identify all partnership activities meeting the definitions in paragraphs 2 and 3 as activities that may be subject to recharacterization.*

4. Rental of property incidental to a development activity. Net rental activity income is the excess of passive activity gross income from renting or disposing of property over passive activity deductions (current year deductions and prior year unallowed losses) that are reasonably allocable to the rented property. Net rental activity income is nonpassive income for a partner if all of the following apply:
• The partnership recognizes gain from the sale, exchange, or other disposition of the rental property during the tax year.
• The use of the item of property in the rental activity started less than 12 months before the date of disposition. The use of an item of rental property begins on the first day that **(a)** the partnership owns an interest in the property; **(b)** substantially all of the property is either rented or held out for rent and ready to be rented; and **(c)** no significant value-enhancing services remain to be performed.
• The partner materially or significantly participated for any tax year in an activity that involved performing services to enhance the value of the property (or any other item of property, if the basis of the property disposed of is determined in whole or in part by reference to the basis of that item of property).

Because the partnership cannot determine a partner's level of participation, the partnership must identify net income from property described above (without regard to the partner's level of participation) as income that may be subject to recharacterization.

5. Rental of property to a nonpassive activity. If a taxpayer rents property to a trade or business activity in which the taxpayer materially participates, the taxpayer's net rental activity income from the property is nonpassive income.

6. Acquisition of an interest in a pass-through entity that licenses intangible property. Generally, net royalty income from intangible property is nonpassive income if the taxpayer acquired an interest in the pass-through entity after the pass-through entity created the intangible property or performed substantial services, or incurred substantial costs in developing or marketing the intangible property. "Net royalty income" means the excess of passive activity gross income from licensing or transferring any right in intangible property over passive activity deductions (current year deductions and prior year unallowed losses) that are reasonably allocable to the intangible property.

See Temporary Regulations section 1.469-2T(f)(7)(iii) for exceptions to this rule.

Passive Activity Reporting Requirements

To allow partners to correctly apply the passive activity loss and credit rules, any partnership that carries on more than one activity must:

1. Provide an attachment for each activity conducted through the partnership that identifies the type of activity conducted (trade or business, rental real estate, rental activity other than rental real estate, or investment).

2. On the attachment for each activity, provide a schedule, using the same line numbers as shown on Schedule K-1, detailing the net income (loss), credits, and all items required to be separately stated under section 702(a) from each trade or business activity, from each rental real estate activity, from each rental activity other than a rental real estate activity, and from investments.

3. Identify the net income (loss) and credits from each oil or gas well drilled or operated under a working interest that any partner (other than a partner whose only interest in the partnership during the year is as a limited partner) holds through the partnership. Further, if any partner had an interest as a general partner in the partnership during less than the entire year, the partnership must identify both the disqualified deductions from each well that the partner must treat as passive activity deductions, and the ratable portion of the gross income from each well that the partner must treat as passive activity gross income.

4. Identify the net income (loss) and the partner's share of partnership interest expense from each activity of renting a dwelling unit that any partner uses for personal purposes during the year for more than the greater of 14 days or 10% of the number of days that the residence is rented at fair rental value.

5. Identify the net income (loss) and the partner's share of partnership interest expense from each activity of trading personal property conducted through the partnership.

6. For any gain (loss) from the disposition of an interest in an activity or of an interest in property used in an activity (including dispositions before 1987 from which gain is being recognized after 1986):

a. Identify the activity in which the property was used at the time of disposition.

b. If the property was used in more than one activity during the 12 months preceding the disposition, identify the activities in which the property was used and the adjusted basis allocated to each activity.

c. For gains only, if the property was substantially appreciated at the time of the disposition and the applicable holding period specified in Regulations section 1.469-2(c)(2)(iii)(A) was not satisfied, identify the amount of the nonpassive gain and indicate whether the gain is investment income under the provisions of Regulations section 1.469-2(c)(2)(iii)(F).

7. Specify the amount of gross portfolio income, the interest expense properly allocable to portfolio income, and expenses other than interest expense that are clearly and directly allocable to portfolio income.

8. Identify separately any of the following types of payments to partners:

a. Payments to a partner for services other than in the partner's capacity as a partner under section 707(a).

b. Guaranteed payments to a partner for services under section 707(c).

c. Guaranteed payments for use of capital.

d. If section 736(a)(2) payments are made for unrealized receivables or for goodwill, the amount of the payments and the activities to which the payments are attributable.

e. If section 736(b) payments are made, the amount of the payments and the activities to which the payments are attributable.

9. Identify the ratable portion of any section 481 adjustment (whether a net positive or a net negative adjustment) allocable to each partnership activity.

10. Identify the amount of gross income from each oil or gas property of the partnership.

11. Identify any gross income from sources that are specifically excluded from passive activity gross income, including:

a. Income from intangible property if the partner is an individual and the partner's personal efforts significantly contributed to the creation of the property.

b. Income from state, local, or foreign income tax refunds.

c. Income from a covenant not to compete (in the case of a partner who is an individual and who contributed the covenant to the partnership).

12. Identify any deductions that are not passive activity deductions.

13. If the partnership makes a full or partial disposition of its interest in another entity, identify the gain (loss) allocable to each activity conducted through the entity, and the gain allocable to a passive activity that would have been recharacterized as nonpassive gain had the partnership disposed of its interest in property used in the activity (because the property was substantially appreciated at the time of the disposition, and the gain represented more than 10% of the partner's total gain from the disposition).

14. Identify the following items from activities that may be subject to the recharacterization rules under Temporary Regulations section 1.469-2T(f) and Regulations section 1.469-2(f):

a. Net income from an activity of renting substantially nondepreciable property.

b. The smaller of equity-financed interest income or net passive income from an equity-financed lending activity.

c. Net rental activity income from property that was developed (by the partner or the partnership), rented, and sold within 12 months after the rental of the property commenced.

d. Net rental activity income from the rental of property by the partnership to a trade or business activity in which the partner had an interest (either directly or indirectly).

e. Net royalty income from intangible property if the partner acquired the partner's interest in the partnership after the partnership created the intangible property or performed substantial services, or incurred substantial costs in developing or marketing the intangible property.

15. Identify separately the credits from each activity conducted by or through the partnership.

16. Identify the partner's distributive share of the partnership's self-charged interest income or expense (see **Self-Charged Interest** on page 11).

a. Loans between a partner and the partnership. Identify the lending or borrowing partner's share of the self-charged interest income or expense. If the partner made the loan to the partnership, also identify the activity in which the loan proceeds were used. If the loan proceeds were used in more than one activity, allocate the interest to each activity based on the amount of the proceeds used in each activity.

b. Loans between the partnership and another partnership or an S corporation. If the partnership's partners have the same proportional ownership interest in the partnership and the other partnership or S corporation, identify each partner's share of the interest income or expense from the loan. If the partnership was the borrower, also identify the activity in which the loan proceeds were used. If the loan proceeds were used in more than one activity, allocate the interest to each activity based on the amount of the proceeds used in each activity.

Extraterritorial Income Exclusion

The partnership may exclude extraterritorial income to the extent of qualifying foreign trade income. For details and to figure the amount of the exclusion, see **Form 8873**, Extraterritorial Income Exclusion, and its separate instructions. The partnership must report the extraterritorial income exclusion on its return as follows:

1. If the partnership met the foreign economic process requirements explained in the Instructions for Form 8873, it may report the exclusion as a nonseparately stated item on whichever of the following lines apply to that activity:
- Form 1065, page 1, line 20;
- Form 8825, line 15; or
- Form 1065, Schedule K, line 3b.

In addition, the partnership must report as an item of information on Schedule K-1, line 25, the partner's distributive share of foreign trading gross receipts from Form 8873, line 15.

2. If the foreign trading gross receipts of the partnership for the tax year are $5 million or less and the partnership did not meet the foreign economic process requirements, it may **not** report the extraterritorial income exclusion as a nonseparately stated item on its return.

Instead, the partnership must report the following separately stated items to the partners on Schedule K-1, line 25:
- The partner's distributive share of foreign trading gross receipts from the partnership's Form 8873, line 15.
- The partner's distributive share of the extraterritorial income exclusion from the partnership's Form 8873, line 52, and identify the activity to which the exclusion relates.

Note: *Upon request of a partner, the partnership should furnish a copy of the partnership's Form 8873 if that partner has a* reduction for international boycott operations, illegal bribes, kickbacks, etc.

Specific Instructions

These instructions follow the line numbers on the first page of Form 1065. The accompanying schedules will be discussed separately. Specific instructions for most of the lines are provided. Lines that are not discussed are self-explanatory.

Fill in all applicable lines and schedules.

Enter any items specially allocated to the partners on the appropriate line of the applicable partner's Schedule K-1. Enter the total amount on the appropriate line of Schedule K. **Do not** enter separately stated amounts on the numbered lines on Form 1065, page 1, or on Schedule A or Schedule D.

File all four pages of Form 1065. However, if the answer to Question 5 of Schedule B is **Yes**, Schedules L, M-1, and M-2 on page 4 are optional. Also attach a Schedule K-1 to Form 1065 for each partner.

File only one Form 1065 for each partnership. Mark "Duplicate Copy" on any copy you give to a partner.

If a syndicate, pool, joint venture, or similar group files Form 1065, it must attach a copy of the agreement and all amendments to the return, unless a copy has previously been filed.

Note: A foreign partnership required to file a return generally must report all of its foreign and U.S. source income. For rules regarding whether a foreign partnership must file Form 1065, see **Who Must File** on page 2.

Name and Address

Use the label that was mailed to the partnership. Cross out any errors and print the correct information on the label.

Name. If the partnership did not receive a label, print or type the legal name of the partnership as it appears in the partnership agreement.

If the partnership has changed its name, check box G(3).

Address. Include the suite, room, or other unit number after the street address. If a preaddressed label is used, include this information on the label.

If the Post Office does not deliver mail to the street address and the partnership has a P.O. box, show the box number instead.

If the partnership's address is outside the United States or its possessions or territories, enter the information on the line for "City or town, state, and ZIP code" in the following order: city, province or state, and the foreign country. Follow the foreign country's practice in placing the postal code in the address. **Do not** abbreviate the country name.

If the partnership has had a change of address, check box G(4).

If the partnership changes its mailing address after filing its return, it can notify the IRS by filing **Form 8822,** Change of Address.

Items A and C

Enter the applicable activity name and the code number from the list beginning on page 32.

For example, if, as its principal business activity, the partnership **(a)** purchases raw materials, **(b)** subcontracts out for labor to make a finished product from the raw materials, and **(c)** retains title to the goods, the partnership is considered to be a manufacturer and must enter "Manufacturer" in item A and enter in item C one of the codes (311110 through 339900) listed under "Manufacturing" beginning on page 32.

Item D. Employer Identification Number (EIN)

Show the correct EIN in item D on page 1 of Form 1065. If the partnership does not have an EIN, it must be applied for:
• Online—Click on the EIN link at **www.irs.gov/businesses/small.** The EIN is issued immediately once the application information is validated.
• By telephone at 1-800-829-4933, from 7:30 a.m. to 5:30 p.m. in the partnership's local time zone.
• By mailing or faxing **Form SS-4,** Application for Employer Identification Number.

A limited liability company must determine which type of federal tax entity it will be (i.e., partnership, corporation, or disregarded entity) before applying for an EIN (see **Form 8832,** Entity Classification Election, for details). If the partnership has not received its EIN by the time the return is due, write "Applied for" in the space for the EIN. For more details, see **Pub. 583,** Starting a Business and Keeping Records.

Note: The online application process is not yet available for the following types of entities: entities with addresses in foreign countries or Puerto Rico, REMICs, state and local governments, Federal government/ military entities, and Indian Tribal Government/Enterprise entities. Please call the toll-free Business and Specialty Tax Line at 1-800-829-4933 for assistance in applying for an EIN.

Do not request a new EIN for a partnership that terminated because of a sale or exchange of at least 50% of the total interests in partnership capital and profits.

Item F. Total Assets

You are not required to complete item F if the answer to Question 5 of Schedule B is **Yes.**

If you are required to complete this item, enter the partnership's total assets at the end of the tax year, as determined by the accounting method regularly used in keeping the partnership's books and records. If there were no assets at the end of the tax year, enter "0."

Item G

Do not check "Final return" (box G(2)) for a partnership that terminated because of a sale or exchange of at least 50% of the total interests in partnership capital and profits. However, be sure to file a return for the short year ending on the date of termination. See **Termination of the Partnership** on page 3.

For information on amended returns, see page 6.

Income

⚠ Report only trade or business activity income on lines 1a through 8. **Do not report rental activity income or portfolio income on these lines.** See the instructions on **Passive Activity Limitations** beginning on page 10 for definitions of rental income and portfolio income. Rental activity income and portfolio income are reported on Schedules K and K-1. Rental real estate activities are also reported on Form 8825.

Tax-exempt income. Do not include any tax-exempt income on lines 1a through 8. A partnership that receives any tax-exempt income other than interest, or holds any property or engages in any activity that produces tax-exempt income reports the amount of this income on line 20 of Schedules K and K-1.

Report tax-exempt interest income, including exempt-interest dividends received as a shareholder in a mutual fund or other regulated investment company, on line 19 of Schedules K and K-1.

See **Deductions** on page 15 for information on how to report expenses related to tax-exempt income.

Cancelled debt exclusion. If the partnership has had debt discharged resulting from a title 11 bankruptcy proceeding or while insolvent, see **Form 982,** Reduction of Tax Attributes Due to Discharge of Indebtedness, and **Pub. 908,** Bankruptcy Tax Guide.

Line 1a. Gross Receipts or Sales

Enter the gross receipts or sales from all trade or business operations except those that must be reported on lines 4 through 7. For example, do not include gross receipts from farming on this line. Instead, show the net profit (loss) from farming on line 5. Also, do not include on line 1a rental activity income or portfolio income.

In general, advance payments are reported in the year of receipt. To report income from long-term contracts, see section 460. For special rules for reporting certain advance payments for goods and long-term contracts, see Regulations section 1.451-5. For permissible methods for reporting advance payments for services by an accrual method partnership, see Rev. Proc. 71-21, 1971-2 C.B. 549.

Installment sales. Generally, the installment method cannot be used for dealer dispositions of property. A "dealer disposition" is any disposition of:

1. Personal property by a person who regularly sells or otherwise disposes of personal property of the same type on the installment plan or
2. Real property held for sale to customers in the ordinary course of the taxpayer's trade or business.

Exception. These restrictions on using the installment method do not apply to dispositions of property used or produced in a farming business or sales of timeshares and residential lots. However, if the partnership elects to report dealer dispositions of timeshares and residential lots on the installment method, each partner's tax liability must be increased by

Instructions for Form 1065

the partner's allocable share of the interest payable under section 453(f)(3).

Enter on line 1a the gross profit on collections from installment sales for any of the following:
• *Dealer dispositions of property before* March 1, 1986.
• Dispositions of property used or produced in the trade or business of farming.
• Certain dispositions of timeshares and residential lots reported under the installment method.

Attach a schedule showing the following information for the current year and the 3 preceding years:
• Gross sales.
• Cost of goods sold.
• Gross profits.
• Percentage of gross profits to gross sales.
• Amount collected.
• Gross profit on amount collected.

Nonaccrual experience method. Partnerships that qualify to use the nonaccrual experience method (described on page 5) should attach a schedule showing total gross receipts, the amount not accrued as a result of the application of section 448(d)(5), and the net amount accrued. Enter the net amount on line 1a.

Line 2. Cost of Goods Sold

See the instructions for Schedule A on page 18.

Line 4. Ordinary Income (Loss) From Other Partnerships, Estates, and Trusts

Enter the ordinary income (loss) shown on Schedule K-1 (Form 1065) or Schedule K-1 (Form 1041), or other ordinary income (loss) from a foreign partnership, estate, or trust. Show the partnership's, estate's, or trust's name, address, and EIN on a separate statement attached to this return. If the amount entered is from more than one source, identify the amount from each source.

Do not include portfolio income or rental activity income (loss) from other partnerships, estates, or trusts on this line. Instead, report these amounts on the applicable lines of Schedules K and K-1, or on line 20a of Form 8825 if the amount is from a rental real estate activity.

Ordinary income or loss from another partnership that is a publicly traded partnership is not reported on this line. Instead, report the amount separately on line 7 of Schedules K and K-1.

Treat shares of other items separately reported on Schedule K-1 issued by the other entity as if the items were realized or incurred by this partnership.

If there is a loss from another partnership, the amount of the loss that may be claimed is subject to the at-risk and basis limitations as appropriate.

If the tax year of your partnership does not coincide with the tax year of the other

partnership, estate, or trust, include the ordinary income (loss) from the other entity in the tax year in which the other entity's tax year ends.

Line 5. Net Farm Profit (Loss)

Enter the partnership's net farm profit (loss) from **Schedule F (Form 1040),** Profit or Loss From Farming. Attach Schedule F (Form 1040) to Form 1065. **Do not** include on this line any farm profit (loss) from other partnerships. Report those amounts on line 4. In figuring the partnership's net farm profit (loss), do not include any section 179 expense deduction; this amount must be separately stated.

Also report the partnership's fishing income on this line.

For a special rule concerning the method of accounting for a farming partnership with a corporate partner and for other tax information on farms, see **Pub. 225,** Farmer's Tax Guide.

Note: *Because the election to deduct the expenses of raising any plant with a preproductive period of more than 2 years is made by the partner and not the partnership, farm partnerships that are not required to use an accrual method should not capitalize such expenses. Instead, state them separately on an attachment to Schedule K, line 24, and on Schedule K-1, line 25, Supplemental Information. See Regulations section 1.263A-4 for more information.*

Line 6. Net Gain (Loss) From Form 4797

 Include only ordinary gains or losses from the sale, exchange, or involuntary conversion of assets used in a trade or business activity. Ordinary gains or losses from the sale, exchange, or involuntary conversion of rental activity assets are reported separately on line 19 of Form 8825 or line 3 of Schedules K and K-1, generally as a part of the net income (loss) from the rental activity.

A partnership that is a partner in another partnership must include on **Form 4797,** Sales of Business Property, its share of ordinary gains (losses) from sales, exchanges, or involuntary conversions (other than casualties or thefts) of the other partnership's trade or business assets.

Partnerships should not use Form 4797 to report the sale or other disposition of property if a section 179 expense deduction was previously passed through to any of its partners for that property. Instead, report it on line 25 of Schedule K-1. See the instructions for item 4 of line 25 for details.

Line 7. Other Income (Loss)

Enter on line 7 trade or business income (loss) that is not included on lines 1a through 6. List the type and amount of income on an attached schedule. Examples of such income include:

1. Interest income derived in the ordinary course of the partnership's trade or business, such as interest charged on receivable balances.
2. Recoveries of bad debts deducted in prior years under the specific charge-off method.
3. Taxable income from insurance proceeds.
4. The amount of credit figured on **Form 6478,** Credit for Alcohol Used as Fuel.
5. All section 481 income adjustments resulting from changes in accounting methods. Show the computation of the section 481 adjustments on an attached schedule.
6. The amount of any deduction previously taken under section 179A that is subject to recapture. See **Pub. 535,** Business Expenses, for details, including how to figure the recapture.
7. The recapture amount for section 280F if the business use of listed property drops to 50% or less. To figure the recapture amount, the partnership must complete Part IV of Form 4797.

Do not include items requiring separate computations that must be reported on Schedules K and K-1. See the instructions for Schedules K and K-1 later in these instructions.

Do not report portfolio or rental activity income (loss) on this line.

Deductions

⚠️ *Report **only** trade or business activity deductions on lines 9 through 21.*

Do not report the following expenses on lines 9 through 21:
• Rental activity expenses. Report these expenses on Form 8825 or line 3b of Schedule K.
• Deductions allocable to portfolio income. Report these deductions on line 10 of Schedules K and K-1.
• Nondeductible expenses (e.g., expenses connected with the production of tax-exempt income). Report nondeductible expenses on line 21 of Schedules K and K-1.
• Qualified expenditures to which an election under section 59(e) may apply. The instructions for lines 18a and 18b of Schedules K and K-1 explain how to report these amounts.
• Items the partnership must state separately that require separate computations by the partners. Examples include expenses incurred for the production of income instead of in a trade or business, charitable contributions, foreign taxes paid, intangible drilling and development costs, soil and water conservation expenditures, amortizable basis of reforestation expenditures, and exploration expenditures. The distributive shares of these expenses are reported separately to each partner on Schedule K-1.

Limitations on Deductions

Section 263A uniform capitalization rules. The uniform capitalization rules of section 263A require partnerships to capitalize or include in inventory costs, certain costs incurred in connection with:
• The production of real and tangible personal property held in inventory or held for sale in the ordinary course of business.
• Real property or personal property (tangible and intangible) acquired for resale.
• The production of real property and tangible personal property by a partnership for use in its trade or business or in an activity engaged in for profit.

The costs required to be capitalized under section 263A are not deductible until the property to which the costs relate is sold, used, or otherwise disposed of by the partnership.

Exceptions: Section 263A **does not** apply to:
• Inventoriable items accounted for in the same manner as materials and supplies that are not incidental. See **Schedule A. Cost of Goods Sold** on page 18 for details.
• Personal property acquired for resale if the partnership's average annual gross receipts for the 3 prior tax years were $10 million or less.
• Timber.
• Most property produced under a long-term contract.
• Certain property produced in a farming business. See the note at the end of the instructions for line 5.

The partnership must report the following costs separately to the partners for purposes of determinations under section 59(e):
• Research and experimental costs under section 174.
• Intangible drilling costs for oil, gas, and geothermal property.
• Mining exploration and development costs.

Tangible personal property produced by a partnership includes a film, sound recording, videotape, book, or similar property.

Indirect costs. Partnerships subject to the rules are required to capitalize not only direct costs but an allocable part of most indirect costs (including taxes) that benefit the assets produced or acquired for resale, or are incurred by reason of the performance of production or resale activities.

For inventory, some of the *indirect costs* that must be capitalized are:
• Administration expenses.
• Taxes.
• Depreciation.
• Insurance.
• Compensation paid to officers attributable to services.
• Rework labor.
• Contributions to pension, stock bonus, and certain profit-sharing, annuity, or deferred compensation plans.

Regulations section 1.263A-1(e)(3) specifies other indirect costs that relate to production or resale activities that must be capitalized and those that may be currently deductible.

Interest expense paid or incurred during the production period of designated property must be capitalized and is governed by special rules. For more details, see Regulations sections 1.263A-8 through 1.263A-15.

For more details on the uniform capitalization rules, see Regulations sections 1.263A-1 through 1.263A-3.

Transactions between related taxpayers. Generally, an accrual basis partnership may deduct business expenses and interest owed to a related party (including any partner) only in the tax year of the partnership that includes the day on which the payment is includible in the income of the related party. See section 267 for details.

Business start-up expenses. Business start-up expenses must be capitalized. An election may be made to amortize them over a period of not less than 60 months. See Pub. 535 and Regulations section 1.195-1.

Organization costs. Amounts paid or incurred to organize a partnership are capital expenditures. They are not deductible as a current expense.

The partnership may elect to amortize organization expenses over a period of 60 or more months, beginning with the month in which the partnership begins business. Include the amortization expense on line 20. On the balance sheet (Schedule L) show the unamortized balance of organization costs. See the instructions for line 10 for the treatment of organization expenses paid to a partner. See Pub. 535 for more information.

Syndication costs. Costs for issuing and marketing interests in the partnership, such as commissions, professional fees, and printing costs, must be capitalized. They cannot be depreciated or amortized. See the instructions for line 10 for the treatment of syndication fees paid to a partner.

Reducing certain expenses for which credits are allowable. For each of the following credits, the partnership must reduce the otherwise allowable deductions for expenses used to figure the credit by the amount of the current year credit:
  1. The work opportunity credit.
  2. The welfare-to-work credit.
  3. The credit for increasing research activities.
  4. The enhanced oil recovery credit.
  5. The disabled access credit.
  6. The empowerment zone and renewal community employment credit.
  7. The Indian employment credit.
  8. The credit for employer social security and Medicare taxes paid on certain employee tips.
  9. The orphan drug credit.
  10. The New York Liberty Zone business employee credit.

If the partnership has any of these credits, figure each current year credit before figuring the deductions for expenses on which the credit is based.

Line 9. Salaries and Wages

Enter on line 9 the salaries and wages paid or incurred for the tax year, reduced by the current year credits claimed on:
• **Form 5884**, Work Opportunity Credit;
• **Form 8844**, Empowerment Zone and Renewal Community Employment Credit;
• **Form 8845**, Indian Employment Credit;
• **Form 8861**, Welfare-to-Work Credit; and
• **Form 8884**, New York Liberty Zone Business Employee Credit.

See the instructions for these forms for more information.

Do not include salaries and wages reported elsewhere on the return, such as amounts included in cost of goods sold, elective contributions to a section 401(k) cash or deferred arrangement, or amounts contributed under a salary reduction SEP agreement or a SIMPLE IRA plan.

Line 10. Guaranteed Payments to Partners

Deduct payments or credits to a partner for services or for the use of capital if the payments or credits are determined without regard to partnership income and are allocable to a trade or business activity. Also include on line 10 amounts paid during the tax year for insurance that constitutes medical care for a partner, a partner's spouse, or a partner's dependents.

Do not include any payments and credits that should be capitalized. For example, although payments or credits to a partner for services rendered in organizing or syndicating a partnership may be guaranteed payments, they are not deductible on line 10. They are capital expenditures. However, they should be separately reported on Schedules K and K-1, line 5.

Do not include distributive shares of partnership profits.

Report the guaranteed payments to the appropriate partners on Schedule K-1, line 5.

Line 11. Repairs and Maintenance

Enter the costs of incidental repairs and maintenance that do not add to the value of the property or appreciably prolong its life, but only to the extent that such costs relate to a trade or business activity and are not claimed elsewhere on the return.

New buildings, machinery, or permanent improvements that increase the value of the property are not deductible. They are chargeable to capital accounts and may be depreciated or amortized.

Line 12. Bad Debts

Enter the total debts that became worthless in whole or in part during the year, but only to the extent such debts relate to a trade or business activity. Report deductible nonbusiness bad debts as a short-term capital loss on Schedule D (Form 1065).

 Cash method partnerships cannot take a bad debt deduction unless the amount was previously included in income.

Line 13. Rent

Enter rent paid on business property used in a trade or business activity. Do not deduct rent for a dwelling unit occupied by any partner for personal use.

If the partnership rented or leased a vehicle, enter the total annual rent or lease expense paid or incurred in the trade or business activities of the partnership. Also complete Part V of **Form 4562**, Depreciation and Amortization. If the partnership leased a vehicle for a term of 30 days or more, the deduction for vehicle lease expense may have to be reduced by an amount called the

-16-

Instructions for Form 1065

inclusion amount. You may have an inclusion amount if:

The lease term began:	And the vehicle's FMV on the first day of the lease exceeded:
After 12/31/02 but before 1/1/04	$18,000
After 12/31/98 but before 1/1/03	$15,500
After 12/31/96 but before 1/1/99	$15,800
After 12/31/94 but before 1/1/97	$15,500

If the lease term began before January 1, 1995, see **Pub. 463**, Travel, Entertainment, Gift, and Car Expenses, to find out if the partnership has an inclusion amount. The inclusion amount for lease terms beginning in 2004 will be published in the Internal Revenue Bulletin in early 2004.

See Pub. 463 for instructions on figuring the inclusion amount.

Line 14. Taxes and Licenses

Enter taxes and licenses paid or incurred in the trade or business activities of the partnership if not reflected in cost of goods sold. Federal import duties and Federal excise and stamp taxes are deductible only if paid or incurred in carrying on the trade or business of the partnership.

Do not deduct the following taxes on line 14:
* Taxes not imposed on the partnership.
* Federal income taxes or taxes reported elsewhere on the return.
* Section 901 foreign taxes. Report these taxes separately on Schedules K and K-1, line 17g.
* Taxes allocable to a rental activity. Taxes allocable to a rental real estate activity are reported on Form 8825. Taxes allocable to a rental activity other than a rental real estate activity are reported on line 3b of Schedule K.
* Taxes allocable to portfolio income. These taxes are reported on line 10 of Schedules K and K-1.
* Taxes paid or incurred for the production or collection of income, or for the management, conservation, or maintenance of property held to produce income. Report these taxes separately on line 11 of Schedules K and K-1.

See section 263A(a) for rules on capitalization of allocable costs (including taxes) for any property.

* Taxes, including state or local sales taxes, that are paid or incurred in connection with an acquisition or disposition of property (these taxes must be treated as a part of the cost of the acquired property or, in the case of a disposition, as a reduction in the amount realized on the disposition).
* Taxes assessed against local benefits that increase the value of the property assessed (such as for paving, etc.).

See section 164(d) for apportionment of taxes on real property between seller and purchaser.

Line 15. Interest

Include only interest incurred in the trade or business activities of the partnership that is not claimed elsewhere on the return.

Do not deduct interest expense on debt required to be allocated to the production of designated property. Designated property includes real property, personal property

that has a class life of 20 years or more, and other tangible property requiring more than 2 years (1 year in the case of property with a cost of more than $1 million) to produce or construct. Interest that is allocable to designated property produced by a partnership for its own use or for sale must be capitalized.

In addition, a partnership must also capitalize any interest on debt that is allocable to an asset used to produce designated property. A partner may be required to capitalize interest that was incurred by the partner for the partnership's production expenditures. Similarly, a partner may have to capitalize interest that was incurred by the partnership for the partner's own production expenditures. The information required by the partner to properly capitalize interest for this purpose must be provided by the partnership on an attachment for line 25 of Schedule K-1. See section 263A(f) and Regulations sections 1.263A-8 through 1.263A-15.

Do not include interest expense on debt used to purchase rental property or debt used in a rental activity. Interest allocable to a rental real estate activity is reported on Form 8825 and is used in arriving at net income (loss) from rental real estate activities on line 2 of Schedules K and K-1. Interest allocable to a rental activity other than a rental real estate activity is included on line 3b of Schedule K and is used in arriving at net income (loss) from a rental activity (other than a rental real estate activity). This net amount is reported on line 3c of Schedule K and line 3 of Schedule K-1.

Do not include interest expense on debt used to buy property held for investment. Do not include interest expense that is clearly and directly allocable to interest, dividend, royalty, or annuity income not derived in the ordinary course of a trade or business. Interest paid or incurred on debt used to purchase or carry investment property is reported on line 14a of Schedules K and K-1. See the instructions for line 14a of Schedules K and K-1 and **Form 4952**, Investment Interest Expense Deduction, for more information on investment property.

Do not include interest on debt proceeds allocated to distributions made to partners during the tax year. Instead, report such interest on line 11 of Schedules K and K-1. To determine the amount to allocate to distributions to partners, see Notice 89-35, 1989-1 C.B. 675.

Temporary Regulations section 1.163-8T gives rules for allocating interest expense among activities so that the limitations on passive activity losses, investment interest, and personal interest can be properly figured. Generally, interest expense is allocated in the same manner that debt is allocated. Debt is allocated by tracing disbursements of the debt proceeds to specific expenditures, as provided in the regulations.

Interest paid by a partnership to a partner for the use of capital should be entered on line 10 as guaranteed payments.

Prepaid interest can only be deducted over the period to which the prepayment applies.

Note: *Additional limitations on interest deductions apply when the partnership is a policyholder or beneficiary with respect to a*

life insurance, endowment, or annuity contract issued after June 8, 1997. For details, see section 264. Attach a statement showing the computation of the deduction disallowed under section 264.

Line 16. Depreciation

On line 16a, enter **only** the depreciation claimed on assets used in a trade or business activity. Enter on line 16b the depreciation reported elsewhere on the return (for example, on Schedule A) that is attributable to assets used in trade or business activities. See the Instructions for Form 4562 or **Pub. 946**, How To Depreciate Property, to figure the amount of depreciation to enter on this line.

Complete and attach Form 4562 only if the partnership placed property in service during the tax year or claims depreciation on any car or other listed property.

Do not include any section 179 expense deduction on this line. This amount is not deducted by the partnership. Instead, it is passed through to the partners on line 9 of Schedule K-1.

Line 17. Depletion

If the partnership claims a deduction for timber depletion, complete and attach **Form T**, Forest Activities Schedule.

Do not deduct depletion for oil and gas properties. Each partner figures depletion on oil and gas properties. See the instructions for Schedule K-1, line 25, item 3, for the information on oil and gas depletion that must be supplied to the partners by the partnership.

Line 18. Retirement Plans, etc.

Do not deduct payments for partners to retirement or deferred compensation plans including IRAs, qualified plans, and simplified employee pension (SEP) and SIMPLE IRA plans on this line. These amounts are reported on Schedule K-1, line 11, and are deducted by the partners on their own returns.

Enter the deductible contributions not claimed elsewhere on the return made by the partnership for its common-law employees under a qualified pension, profit-sharing, annuity, or SEP or SIMPLE IRA plan, and under any other deferred compensation plan.

If the partnership contributes to an individual retirement arrangement (IRA) for employees, include the contribution in salaries and wages on page 1, line 9, or Schedule A, line 3, and not on line 18.

Employers who maintain a pension, profit-sharing, or other funded deferred compensation plan (other than a SEP or SIMPLE IRA), whether or not the plan is qualified under the Internal Revenue Code and whether or not a deduction is claimed for the current year, generally must file the applicable form listed below:
* **Form 5500,** Annual Return/Report of Employee Benefit Plan. File this form for a plan that is not a one-participant plan (see below).
* **Form 5500-EZ,** Annual Return of One-Participant (Owners and Their Spouses) Retirement Plan. File this form for a plan that only covers one or more partners (or partners and their spouses).

There are penalties for not filing these forms on time.

Line 19. Employee Benefit Programs

Enter the partnership's contributions to employee benefit programs not claimed elsewhere on the return (for example, insurance, health, and welfare programs) that are not part of a pension, profit-sharing, etc., plan included on line 18.

Do not include amounts paid during the tax year for insurance that constitutes medical care for a partner, a partner's spouse, or a partner's dependents. Instead, include these amounts on line 10 as guaranteed payments and on Schedule K, line 5, and Schedule K-1, line 5, of each partner on whose behalf the amounts were paid. Also report these amounts on Schedule K, line 11, and Schedule K-1, line 11, of each partner on whose behalf the amounts were paid.

Line 20. Other Deductions

Enter the total allowable trade or business deductions that are **not** deductible elsewhere on page 1 of Form 1065. Attach a schedule listing by type and amount each deduction included on this line. Examples of other deductions include:
• Amortization (except as noted below)— see the Instructions for Form 4562 for more information. Complete and attach Form 4562 if the partnership is claiming amortization of costs that began during the tax year.
• Insurance premiums.
• Legal and professional fees.
• Supplies used and consumed in the business.
• Utilities.
• Part of the cost of qualified clean-fuel vehicle property and qualified clean-fuel vehicle refueling property. For more details, see section 179A.

Also, see **Special Rules** below for limits on certain other deductions.

Do not deduct on line 20:
• Items that must be reported separately on Schedules K and K-1.
• Qualified expenditures to which an election under section 59(e) may apply. See the instructions on page 28 for lines 18a and 18b of Schedule K-1 for details on treatment of these items.
• Amortization of reforestation expenditures under section 194. The partnership can elect to amortize up to $10,000 of qualified reforestation expenditures paid or incurred during the tax year. However, the amortization is not deducted by the partnership but the amortizable basis is instead separately allocated among the partners. See the instructions on page 30 for Schedule K-1, line 25, item 25 and Pub. 535 for more details.
• Fines or penalties paid to a government for violating any law. Report these expenses on Schedule K, line 21.
• Expenses allocable to tax-exempt income. Report these expenses on Schedule K, line 21.
• Net operating losses. Only individuals and corporations may claim a net operating loss deduction.
• Amounts paid or incurred to participate or intervene in any political campaign on behalf of a candidate for public office, or to influence the general public regarding legislative matters, elections, or

referendums. Report these expenses on Schedule K, line 21.
• Expenses paid or incurred to influence Federal or state legislation, or to influence the actions or positions of certain Federal executive branch officials. However, certain in-house lobbying expenditures that do not exceed $2,000 are deductible. See section 162(e) for more details.

Special Rules

Commercial revitalization deduction. If the partnership constructs, purchases, or substantially rehabilitates a qualified building in a renewal community it may qualify for a deduction of either **(a)** 50% of qualified capital expenditures in the year the building is placed in service or **(b)** amortization of 100% of the qualified capital expenditures over a 120-month period beginning with the month the building is placed in service. If the partnership elects to amortize these expenditures, complete and attach Form 4562. To qualify, the building must be nonresidential (as defined in section 168(e)(2)) and placed in service by the partnership. The partnership must be the original user of the building unless it is substantially rehabilitated. The amount of the qualified expenditures cannot exceed the lesser of $10 million or the amount allocated to the building by the commercial revitalization agency of the state in which the building is located. Any remaining expenditures are depreciated over the regular depreciation recovery period. See **Pub. 954,** Tax Incentives for Distressed Communities, and section 1400I for details.

Rental real estate. **Do not** report this deduction on line 20 if the building is placed in service as rental real estate. A commercial revitalization deduction for rental real estate is not deducted by the partnership but is passed through to the partners on line 25 of Schedule K-1.

Travel, meals, and entertainment. Subject to limitations and restrictions discussed below, a partnership can deduct ordinary and necessary travel, meals, and entertainment expenses paid or incurred in its trade or business. Also, special rules apply to deductions for gifts, skybox rentals, luxury water travel, convention expenses, and entertainment tickets. See section 274 and Pub. 463 for more details.

Travel. The partnership cannot deduct travel expenses of any individual accompanying a partner or partnership employee, including a spouse or dependent of the partner or employee, unless:
• That individual is an employee of the partnership and
• His or her travel is for a bona fide business purpose and would otherwise be deductible by that individual.

Meals and entertainment. Generally, the partnership can deduct only 50% of the amount otherwise allowable for meals and entertainment expenses paid or incurred in its trade or business. In addition (subject to exceptions under section 274(k)(2)):
• Meals must not be lavish or extravagant.
• A bona fide business discussion must occur during, immediately before, or immediately after the meal, and
• A partner or employee of the partnership must be present at the meal.

See section 274(n)(3) for a special rule that applies to expenses for meals consumed by individuals subject to the

hours of service limits of the Department of Transportation.

Membership dues. The partnership may deduct amounts paid or incurred for membership dues in civic or public service organizations, professional organizations (such as bar and medical associations), business leagues, trade associations, chambers of commerce, boards of trade, and real estate boards. However, no deduction is allowed if a principal purpose of the organization is to entertain, or provide entertainment facilities for, members or their guests. In addition, the partnership may not deduct membership dues in any club organized for business, pleasure, recreation, or other social purpose. This includes country clubs, golf and athletic clubs, airline and hotel clubs, and clubs operated to provide meals under conditions favorable to business discussion.

Entertainment facilities. The partnership cannot deduct an expense paid or incurred for a facility (such as a yacht or hunting lodge) used for an activity usually considered entertainment, amusement, or recreation.

Note: *The partnership may be able to deduct otherwise nondeductible meals, travel, and entertainment expenses if the amounts are treated as compensation and reported on Form W-2 for an employee or on Form 1099-MISC for an independent contractor.*

Schedule A. Cost of Goods Sold

Cost of Goods Sold

Generally, inventories are required at the beginning and end of each tax year if the production, purchase, or sale of merchandise is an income-producing factor. See Regulations section 1.471-1.

However, if the partnership is a qualifying taxpayer or a qualifying small business taxpayer, it may adopt or change its accounting method to account for inventoriable items in the same manner as materials and supplies that are not incidental (unless its business is a tax shelter (as defined in section 448(d)(3))).

A **qualifying taxpayer** is a taxpayer that, with respect to each prior tax year ending after December 16, 1998, has average annual gross receipts of $1 million or less for the 3-tax-year period ending with that prior tax year. See Rev. Proc. 2001-10, 2001-2 I.R.B. 272 for details.

A **qualifying small business taxpayer** is a taxpayer **(a)** that, with respect to each prior tax year ending on or after December 31, 2000, has average annual gross receipts of $10 million or less for the 3-tax-year period ending with that prior tax year and **(b)** whose principal business activity is not an ineligible activity. See Rev. Proc. 2002-28, 2002-18 I.R.B. 815 for details.

Under this accounting method, inventory costs for raw materials purchased for use in producing finished goods and merchandise purchased for resale are deductible in the year the finished goods or merchandise are sold (but not before the year the partnership paid for the raw materials or merchandise if it is also using the cash method). For additional guidance on this method of accounting for inventoriable items, see Pub. 538.

Enter amounts paid for all raw materials and merchandise during the tax year on line 2. The amount the partnership can deduct for the tax year is figured on line 8.

All filers that have not elected to treat inventoriable items as materials and supplies that are not incidental should see **Section 263A uniform capitalization rules** on page 16 before completing Schedule A.

Line 1. Inventory at Beginning of Year

If the partnership is changing its method of accounting for the current tax year, it must refigure last year's closing inventory using its new method of accounting and enter the result on line 1. If there is a difference between last year's closing inventory and the refigured amount, attach an explanation and take it into account when figuring the partnership's section 481(a) adjustment (explained on page 5).

Line 2. Purchases

Reduce purchases by items withdrawn for personal use. The cost of these items should be shown on line 23 of Schedules K and K-1 as distributions to partners.

Line 4. Additional Section 263A Costs

An entry is required on this line only for partnerships that have elected a simplified method.

For partnerships that have elected the **simplified production method,** additional section 263A costs are generally those costs, other than interest, that were not capitalized under the partnership's method of accounting immediately prior to the effective date of section 263A that are required to be capitalized under section 263A. Interest must be accounted for separately. For new partnerships, additional section 263A costs are the costs, other than interest, that must be capitalized under section 263A, but which the partnership would not have been required to capitalize if it had existed before the effective date of section 263A. For more details, see Regulations section 1.263A-2(b).

For partnerships that have elected the **simplified resale method,** additional section 263A costs are generally those costs incurred with respect to the following categories:
• Off-site storage or warehousing;
• Purchasing;
• Handling, such as processing, assembly, repackaging, and transporting; and
• General and administrative costs (mixed service costs).
For details, see Regulations section 1.263A-3(d).

Enter on line 4 the balance of section 263A costs paid or incurred during the tax year not includable on lines 2, 3, and 5. Attach a schedule listing these costs.

Line 5. Other Costs

Enter on line 5 any other inventoriable costs paid or incurred during the tax year not entered on lines 2 through 4. Attach a schedule.

Instructions for Form 1065

Line 7. Inventory at End of Year

See Regulations sections 1.263A-1 through 1.263A-3 for details on figuring the amount of additional section 263A costs to be included in ending inventory.

If the partnership accounts for inventoriable items in the same manner as materials and supplies that are not incidental, enter on line 7 the portion of its raw materials and merchandise purchased for resale that are included on line 6 and were not sold during the year.

Lines 9a through 9c. Inventory Valuation Methods

Inventories can be valued at:
• Cost,
• Cost or market value (whichever is lower), or
• Any other method approved by the IRS that conforms to the requirements of the applicable regulations cited below.

However, if the partnership is using the cash method of accounting, it is required to use cost.

Partnerships that account for inventoriable items in the same manner as materials and supplies that are not incidental may currently deduct expenditures for direct labor and all indirect costs that would otherwise be included in inventory costs. See Rev. Proc. 2001-10 and Rev. Proc. 2002-28 for more information.

The average cost (rolling average) method of valuing inventories generally does not conform to the requirements of the regulations. See Rev. Rul. 71-234, 1971-1 C.B. 148.

Partnerships that use erroneous valuation methods must change to a method permitted for Federal tax purposes. To make this change, use Form 3115.

On line 9a, check the methods used for valuing inventories. Under lower of cost or market, the term "market" (for normal goods) means the current bid price prevailing on the inventory valuation date for the particular merchandise in the volume usually purchased by the taxpayer. For a manufacturer, market applies to the basic elements of cost—raw materials, labor, and burden. If section 263A applies to the taxpayer, the basic elements of cost must reflect the current bid price of all direct costs and all indirect costs properly allocable to goods on hand at the inventory date.

Inventory may be valued below cost when the merchandise is unsalable at normal prices or unusable in the normal way because the goods are subnormal due to damage, imperfections, shopwear, etc., within the meaning of Regulations section 1.471-2(c). These goods may be valued at the current bona fide selling price, minus the direct cost of disposition (but not less than scrap value) if such a price can be established.

If this is the first year the Last-in First-out (LIFO) inventory method was either adopted or extended to inventory goods not previously valued under the LIFO method, attach **Form 970,** Application To Use LIFO Inventory Method, or a statement with the information required by Form 970. Also check the box on line 9c.

If the partnership has changed or extended its inventory method to LIFO and

-19-

has had to write up its opening inventory to cost in the year of election, report the effect of this write-up as income (line 7, page 1, Form 1065) proportionately over a 3-year period that begins in the tax year of the LIFO election.

For more information on inventory valuation methods, see **Pub. 538,** Accounting Periods and Methods.

Schedule B. Other Information

Question 1
Check box 1(f) for any other type of entity and state the type.

Question 3
The partnership must answer **Yes** to Question 3, if during the tax year, it owned:
• An interest in another partnership (foreign or domestic) or
• A foreign entity that was disregarded as an entity separate from the partnership under Regulations sections 301.7701-2 and 301.7701-3.

If the partnership answered **Yes** to this question, report the following information on an attached schedule:

1. If the partnership owned at least a 10% interest, directly or indirectly, in any other foreign or domestic partnership (other than any partnership for which a Form 8865 is attached to the tax return), show each partnership's name, EIN (if any), and the country under whose laws the partnership was organized.

2. If the partnership owned any entities that have been disregarded as separate from the partnership, show each disregarded entity's name, EIN (if any), and the country under whose laws the entity was organized.

Note: For each entity listed on the attached schedule, clearly indicate whether the entity is a partnership or a disregarded entity.

Question 4. Consolidated Audit Procedures
Generally, the tax treatment of partnership items is determined at the partnership level in a consolidated audit proceeding, rather than in separate proceedings with individual partners.

Answer **Yes** to Question 4 if **any** of the following apply:
• The partnership had more than 10 partners at any one time during the tax year. For purposes of this question, a husband and wife, and their estates, count as one person.
• Any partner was a nonresident alien or was other than an individual, an estate, or a C corporation.
• The partnership is a "small partnership" that has elected to be subject to the rules for consolidated audit proceedings. "Small partnerships" as defined in section 6231(a)(1)(B)(i) are not subject to the rules for consolidated audit proceedings unless an election to be covered by them is made under Regulations section 301.6231(a)(1)-1(b)(2). Once made, the election may not be revoked without IRS consent.

The partnership does not make this election when it answers Yes to Question 4. The election must be made separately.

If a partnership return is filed by an entity for a tax year, but it is determined that the entity is not a partnership for that tax year, the consolidated partnership audit procedures will generally apply to that entity and to persons holding an interest in that entity. See Regulations section 301.6233-1 for details and exceptions.

Question 5

Answer **Yes** to Question 5 if the partnership meets all three of the requirements shown on the form. Total receipts is defined as the sum of gross receipts or sales (page 1, line 1a); all other income (page 1, lines 4 through 7); income reported on Schedule K, lines 3a, 4a, 4b(2), and 4c; income or net gain reported on Schedule K, lines 4d(2), 4e(2), 4f, 6b, and 7; and income or net gain reported on Form 8825, lines 2, 19, and 20a.

Question 6. Foreign Partners

Answer **Yes** to Question 6 if the partnership had any foreign partners (for purposes of section 1446) at any time during the tax year. Otherwise, answer **No**.

If the partnership had gross income effectively connected with a trade or business in the United States **and** foreign partners, it may be required to withhold tax under section 1446 on income allocable to foreign partners (without regard to distributions) and file Forms 8804, 8805, and 8813. See Rev. Proc. 89-31, 1989-1 C.B. 895 and Rev. Proc. 92-66, 1992-2 C.B. 428 for more information.

Question 7

Answer **Yes** to Question 7 if interests in the partnership are traded on an established securities market or are readily tradable on a secondary market (or its substantial equivalent).

Question 8

Organizers of certain tax shelters are required to register the tax shelters by filing **Form 8264**, Application for Registration of a Tax Shelter, no later than the day on which an interest in the shelter is first offered for sale. Organizers filing a properly completed Form 8264 will receive a tax shelter registration number that they must furnish to their investors. See the Instructions for Form 8264 for the definition of a tax shelter and the investments exempted from tax shelter registration.

Question 9. Foreign Accounts

Answer **Yes** to Question 9 if either 1 or 2 below applies to the partnership. Otherwise, check the **No** box.

1. At any time during calendar year 2003, the partnership had an interest in or signature or other authority over a bank account, securities account, or other financial account in a foreign country (see **Form TD F 90-22.1**, Report of Foreign Bank and Financial Accounts); **and**
• The combined value of the accounts was more than $10,000 at any time during the calendar year; **and**
• The accounts were **not** with a U.S. military banking facility operated by a U.S. financial institution.

2. The partnership owns more than 50% of the stock in any corporation that would answer the question **Yes** based on item 1 above.

If the "Yes" box is checked for the question:
• Enter the name of the foreign country or countries. Attach a separate sheet if more space is needed.
• File Form TD F 90-22.1 by June 30, 2004, with the Department of the Treasury at the address shown on the form. Because Form TD F 90-22.1 is not a tax form, do not file it with Form 1065. You can order Form TD F 90-22.1 by calling 1-800-TAX-FORM (1-800-829-3676) or you can download it from the IRS website at **www.irs.gov.**

Question 10

The partnership may be required to file **Form 3520,** Annual Return To Report Transactions With Foreign Trusts and Receipt of Certain Foreign Gifts, if:
• It directly or indirectly transferred property or money to a foreign trust. For this purpose, any U.S. person who created a foreign trust is considered a transferor.
• It is treated as the owner of any part of the assets of a foreign trust under the grantor trust rules.
• It received a distribution from a foreign trust.

For more information, see the Instructions for Form 3520.

Note: *An owner of a foreign trust must ensure that the trust files an annual information return on* **Form 3520-A,** *Annual Information Return of Foreign Trust with a U.S. Owner.*

Designation of Tax Matters Partner (TMP)

If the partnership is subject to the rules for consolidated audit proceedings in sections 6221 through 6233, the partnership may designate a partner as the TMP for the tax year for which the return is filed by completing the **Designation of Tax Matters Partner** section on page 2 of Form 1065. See the instructions for Question 4, consolidated audit procedures, to determine if the partnership is subject to these rules. The designated TMP must be a general partner and, in most cases, must also be a U.S. person. For details, see Regulations section 301.6231(a)(7)-1.

For a limited liability company (LLC), only a member-manager of the LLC is treated as a general partner. A member-manager is any owner of an interest in the LLC who, alone or together with others, has the continuing exclusive authority to make the management decisions necessary to conduct the business for which the LLC was formed. If there are no elected or designated member-managers, each owner is treated as a member-manager. For details, see Regulations section 301.6231(a)(7)-2.

Schedules K and K-1. Partners' Shares of Income, Credits, Deductions, etc.

Purpose of Schedules

Although the partnership is not subject to income tax, the partners are liable for tax on their shares of the partnership income, whether or not distributed, and must include their shares on their tax returns.

Schedule K (page 3 of Form 1065) is a summary schedule of all the partners' shares of the partnership's income, credits, deductions, etc. All partnerships must complete Schedule K. Rental activity income (loss) and portfolio income are not reported on page 1 of Form 1065. These amounts are not combined with trade or business activity income (loss). Schedule K is used to report the totals of these and other amounts.

Schedule K-1 (Form 1065) shows each partner's separate share. Attach a copy of each Schedule K-1 to the Form 1065 filed with the IRS; keep a copy with a copy of the partnership return as a part of the partnership's records; and furnish a copy to each partner. If a partnership interest is held by a nominee on behalf of another person, the partnership may be required to furnish Schedule K-1 to the nominee. See Temporary Regulations sections 1.6031(b)-1T and 1.6031(c)-1T for more information.

Give each partner a copy of either the Partner's Instructions for Schedule K-1 (Form 1065) or specific instructions for each item reported on the partner's Schedule K-1 (Form 1065).

Substitute Forms

The partnership does not need IRS approval to use a substitute Schedule K-1 if it is an exact copy of the IRS schedule, or if it contains only those lines the taxpayer is required to use. The lines must use the same numbers and titles and must be in the same order and format as on the comparable IRS Schedule K-1. The substitute schedule must include the OMB number. The partnership must provide each partner with the Partner's Instructions for Schedule K-1 (Form 1065) or other prepared specific instructions.

The partnership must request IRS approval to use other substitute Schedules K-1. To request approval, write to Internal Revenue Service, Attention: Substitute Forms Program, SE:W:CAR:MP:T:T:SP, 1111 Constitution Avenue, NW, Washington, DC 20224.

Each partner's information must be on a separate sheet of paper. Therefore, separate all continuously printed substitutes before you file them with the IRS.

The partnership may be subject to a penalty if it files Schedules K-1 that do not conform to the specifications of Rev. Proc. 2003-73, 2003-39 I.R.B. 647.

How Income Is Shared Among Partners

Allocate shares of income, gain, loss, deduction, or credit among the partners according to the partnership agreement for sharing income or loss generally. Partners may agree to allocate specific items in a ratio different from the ratio for sharing income or loss. For instance, if the net income exclusive of specially allocated items is divided evenly among three partners but some special items are allocated 50% to one, 30% to another, and 20% to the third partner, report the specially allocated items on the appropriate line of the applicable partner's Schedule K-1 and the total on the appropriate line of Schedule K, instead of on the numbered lines on page 1 of Form 1065 or Schedules A or D.

If a partner's interest changed during the year, see section 706(d) before determining each partner's distributive share of any item of income, gain, loss, deduction, etc. Income (loss) is allocated to a partner only for the part of the year in which that person is a member of the partnership. The partnership will either allocate on a daily basis or divide the partnership year into segments and allocate income, loss, or special items in each segment among the persons who were partners during that segment. Partnerships that report their income on the cash basis must allocate interest expense, taxes, and any payment for services or for the use of property on a daily basis if there is any change in any partner's interest during the year. See Pub. 541 for more details.

Special rules on the allocation of income, gain, loss, and deductions generally apply if a partner contributes property to the partnership and the FMV of that property at the time of contribution differs from the contributing partner's adjusted tax basis. Under these rules, the partnership must use a reasonable method of making allocations of income, gain, loss, and deductions from the property so that the contributing partner receives the tax burdens and benefits of any built-in gain or loss (i.e., precontribution appreciation or diminution of value of the contributed property). See Regulations section 1.704-3 for details on how to make these allocations, including a description of specific allocation methods that are generally reasonable.

See **Dispositions of Contributed Property** on page 9 for special rules on the allocation of income, gain, loss, and deductions on the disposition of property contributed to the partnership by a partner.

If the partnership agreement does not provide for the partner's share of income, gain, loss, deduction, or credit, or if the allocation under the agreement does not have substantial economic effect, the partner's share is determined according to the partner's interest in the partnership. See Regulations section 1.704-1 for more information.

Specific Instructions (Schedule K-1 Only)

General Information

Generally, the partnership is required to prepare and give a Schedule K-1 to each person who was a partner in the partnership at any time during the year. **Schedule K-1 must be provided to each partner on or**

before the day on which the partnership return is required to be filed.

However, if a foreign partnership meets each of the following four requirements, it is not required to file or provide Schedules K-1 for foreign partners (unless the foreign partner is a pass-through entity through which a U.S. person holds an interest in the foreign partnership):
• The partnership had no gross income effectively connected with the conduct of a trade or business within the United States during its tax year.
• All required Forms 1042 and 1042-S were filed by the partnership or another withholding agent as required by Regulations section 1.1461-1(b) and (c).
• The tax liability for each foreign partner for amounts reportable under Regulations sections 1.1461-1(b) and (c) has been fully satisfied by the withholding of tax at the source.
• The partnership is not a withholding foreign partnership as defined in Regulations section 1.1441-5(c)(2)(i).

Generally, any person who holds an interest in a partnership as a nominee for another person must furnish to the partnership the name, address, etc., of the other person.

On each Schedule K-1, enter the names, addresses, and identifying numbers of the partner and partnership and the partner's distributive share of each item.

For an individual partner, enter the partner's social security number (SSN) or individual taxpayer identification number (ITIN). For all other partners, enter the partner's EIN. However, if a partner is an individual retirement arrangement (IRA), enter the identifying number of the custodian of the IRA. Do not enter the SSN of the person for whom the IRA is maintained.

Foreign partners without a U.S. taxpayer identifying number should be notified by the partnership of the necessity of obtaining a U.S. identifying number. Certain aliens who are not eligible to obtain SSNs can apply for an ITIN on **Form W-7,** Application for IRS Individual Taxpayer Identification Number.

If a husband and wife each had an interest in the partnership, prepare a separate Schedule K-1 for each of them. If a husband and wife held an interest together, prepare one Schedule K-1 if the two of them are considered to be one partner.

There is space on line 25 of Schedule K-1 for you to provide information to the partners. This space may be used instead of attachments.

Specific Items and Questions

Question A

Answer Question A on all Schedules K-1. If a partner holds interests as both a general and limited partner, check the first two boxes and attach a schedule for each activity that shows the amounts allocable to the partner's interest as a limited partner.

Question B. What Type of Entity Is This Partner?

State on this line whether the partner is an individual, a corporation, an estate, a trust, a partnership, a limited liability company, an exempt organization, or a nominee (custodian). If the partner is a nominee, use one of the following codes to indicate the

type of entity the nominee represents: I—Individual; C—Corporation; F—Estate or Trust; P—Partnership; LLC—Limited Liability Company; E—Exempt Organization; or IRA—Individual Retirement Arrangement.

Question C. Domestic/Foreign Partner

Check the foreign partner box if the partner is a nonresident alien individual, foreign partnership, foreign corporation, or a foreign estate or trust. Otherwise, check the domestic partner box.

Item D. Partner's Profit, Loss, and Capital Sharing Percentages

Enter in Item D, column (ii), the appropriate percentages as of the end of the year. However, if a partner's interest terminated during the year, enter in column (i) the percentages that existed immediately before the termination. When the profit or loss sharing percentage has changed during the year, show the percentage before the change in column (i) and the end-of-year percentage in column (ii). If there are multiple changes in the profit and loss sharing percentage during the year, attach a statement giving the date and percentage before each change.

"Ownership of capital" means the portion of the capital that the partner would receive if the partnership was liquidated at the end of the year by the distribution of undivided interests in partnership assets and liabilities.

Item F. Partner's Share of Liabilities

Enter each partner's share of nonrecourse liabilities, partnership-level qualified nonrecourse financing, and other liabilities.

"Nonrecourse liabilities" are those liabilities of the partnership for which no partner bears the economic risk of loss. The extent to which a partner bears the economic risk of loss is determined under the rules of Regulations section 1.752-2. Do not include partnership-level qualified nonrecourse financing (defined on page 22) on the line for nonrecourse liabilities.

If the partner terminated his or her interest in the partnership during the year, enter the share that existed immediately before the total disposition. In all other cases, enter it as of the end of the year.

If the partnership is engaged in two or more different types of at-risk activities, or a combination of at-risk activities and any other activity, attach a statement showing the partner's share of nonrecourse liabilities, partnership-level qualified nonrecourse financing, and other liabilities for **each** activity. See **Pub. 925,** Passive Activity and At-Risk Rules, to determine if the partnership is engaged in more than one at-risk activity.

The at-risk rules of section 465 generally apply to any activity carried on by the partnership as a trade or business or for the production of income. These rules generally limit the amount of loss and other deductions a partner can claim from any partnership activity to the amount for which that partner is considered at risk. However, for partners who acquired their partnership interests before 1987, the at-risk rules do not apply to losses from an activity of holding real property the partnership placed in service before 1987. The activity of holding mineral property does not qualify for this exception. Identify on an attachment to Schedule K-1 the amount of any losses that are not subject to the at-risk rules.

If a partnership is engaged in an activity subject to the limitations of section 465(c)(1) (such as, films or videotapes, leasing section 1245 property, farming, or oil and gas property), give each partner his or her share of the total pre-1976 losses from that activity for which there existed a corresponding amount of nonrecourse liability at the end of each year in which the losses occurred. See **Form 6198,** At-Risk Limitations, and related instructions for more information.

Qualified nonrecourse financing secured by real property used in an activity of holding real property that is subject to the at-risk rules is treated as an amount at risk. "Qualified nonrecourse financing" generally includes financing for which no one is personally liable for repayment that is borrowed for use in an activity of holding real property and that is loaned or guaranteed by a Federal, state, or local government or that is borrowed from a "qualified" person. Qualified persons include any person actively and regularly engaged in the business of lending money, such as a bank or savings and loan association. Qualified persons generally do not include related parties (unless the nonrecourse financing is commercially reasonable and on substantially the same terms as loans involving unrelated persons), the seller of the property, or a person who receives a fee for the partnership's investment in the real property. See section 465 for more information on qualified nonrecourse financing.

The partner as well as the partnership must meet the qualified nonrecourse rules. Therefore, the partnership must enter on an attached statement any other information the partner needs to determine if the qualified nonrecourse rules are also met at the partner level.

Item G. Tax Shelter Registration Number

If the partnership is a registration-required tax shelter or has invested in a registration-required tax shelter, it must enter the tax shelter registration number in Item G. Also, a partnership that has invested in a registration-required tax shelter must furnish a copy of its Form 8271 to its partners. See Form 8271 for more details.

Item J. Analysis of Partner's Capital Account

You are not required to complete Item J if the answer to Question 5 of Schedule B is **Yes.** If you are required to complete this item, see the instructions for Schedule M-2 on page 31.

Specific Instructions (Schedules K and K-1, Except as Noted)

Schedules K and K-1 have the same line numbers for lines 1 through 23.

Special Allocations

An item is specially allocated if it is allocated to a partner in a ratio different from the ratio for sharing income or loss generally.

Report specially allocated ordinary gain (loss) on Schedules K and K-1, line 7. Report other specially allocated items on the applicable lines of the partner's Schedule K-1, with the total amount on the applicable line of Schedule K. See **How Income is Shared Among Partners** on page 20.

Example. A partnership has a long-term capital gain that is specially allocated to a partner and a net long-term capital gain reported on line 12, column (f), of Schedule D that must be reported on line 4e(2) of Schedule K. Because specially allocated gains or losses are not reported on Schedule D, the partnership must report both the net long-term capital gain from Schedule D and the specially allocated gain on line 4e(2) of Schedule K. Line 4e(2) of the Schedule K-1 for the partners must include both the specially allocated gain and the partner's distributive share of the net long-term capital gain from Schedule D.

Income (Loss)

Line 1. Ordinary Income (Loss) From Trade or Business Activities

Enter the amount from page 1, line 22. Enter the income (loss) without reference to **(a)** the basis of the partners' interests in the partnership, **(b)** the partners' at-risk limitations, or **(c)** the passive activity limitations. These limitations, if applicable, are determined at the partner level.

If the partnership has more than one trade or business activity, identify on an attachment to Schedule K-1 the amount from each separate activity. See **Passive Activity Reporting Requirements** on page 13.

Line 1 should not include rental activity income (loss) or portfolio income (loss).

Line 2. Net Income (Loss) From Rental Real Estate Activities

Enter the net income (loss) from rental real estate activities of the partnership from Form 8825. Attach this form to Form 1065. If the partnership has more than one rental real estate activity, identify on an attachment to Schedule K-1 the amount attributable to each activity.

Line 3. Net Income (Loss) From Other Rental Activities

On Schedule K, line 3a, enter gross income from rental activities other than those reported on Form 8825. See page 10 of these instructions and Pub. 925 for the definition of rental activities. Include on line 3a, the gain (loss) from line 18 of Form 4797 that is attributable to the sale, exchange, or involuntary conversion of an asset used in a rental activity other than a rental real estate activity.

On line 3b of Schedule K, enter the deductible expenses of the activity. Attach a schedule of these expenses to Form 1065.

Enter the net income (loss) on line 3c of Schedule K. Enter each partner's share on line 3 of Schedule K-1.

If the partnership has more than one rental activity reported on line 3, identify on

an attachment to Schedule K-1 the amount from each activity.

Lines 4a Through 4f. Portfolio Income (Loss)

Enter portfolio income (loss) on lines 4a through 4f.

See page 11 of these instructions for a definition of portfolio income. Do not reduce portfolio income by deductions allocable to it. Report such deductions (other than interest expense) on line 10 of Schedules K and K-1. Interest expense allocable to portfolio income is generally investment interest expense and is reported on line 14a of Schedules K and K-1.

Lines 4a. Enter only taxable interest on this line. Taxable interest is interest from all sources except interest exempt from tax and interest on tax-free covenant bonds.

Lines 4b(1) and 4b(2). Enter only taxable ordinary dividends on these lines. Enter on line 4b(1) all qualified dividends from line 4b(2).

Qualified dividends. Except as provided below, qualified dividends are dividends received after December 31, 2002, from domestic corporations and qualified foreign corporations.

Exceptions. The following dividends are not qualified dividends.
• Dividends the partnership received on any share of stock held for less than 61 days during the 121-day period that began 60 days before the ex-dividend date. When determining the number of days the partnership held the stock, it cannot count certain days during which the partnership's risk of loss was diminished. See Pub. 550 for more details. The ex-dividend date is the first date following the declaration of a dividend on which the purchaser of a stock is not entitled to receive the next dividend payment. When counting the number of days the partnership held the stock, include the day the partnership disposed of the stock but not the day the partnership acquired it.
• Dividends attributable to periods totaling more than 366 days that the partnership received on any share of preferred stock held for less than 91 days during the 181-day period that began 90 days before the ex-dividend date. When determining the number of days the partnership held the stock, do not count certain days during which the partnership's risk of loss was diminished. See Pub. 550 for more details. Preferred dividends attributable to periods totaling less than 367 days are subject to the 61-day holding period rule above.
• Dividends that relate to payments that the partnership is obligated to make with respect to short sales or positions in substantially similar or related property.
• Dividends paid by a regulated investment company that are not treated as qualified dividend income under section 854.
• Dividends paid by a real estate investment trust that are not treated as qualified dividend income under section 857(c).

Qualified foreign corporation. A foreign corporation is a qualified foreign corporation if it is:
1. Incorporated in a possession of the United States or
2. Eligible for benefits of a comprehensive income tax treaty with the

United States that the Secretary determines is satisfactory for this purpose and that includes an exchange of information program. See Notice 2003-69, 2003-42 I.R.B. 851, for details.

If the foreign corporation does not meet either **1** or **2**, then it may be treated as a qualified foreign corporation for any dividend paid by the corporation if the stock associated with the dividend paid is readily tradable on an established securities market in the United States.

However, qualified dividends do not include dividends paid by the following foreign entities in either the tax year of the distribution or the preceding tax year:
• A foreign investment company (section 1246(b)),
• A passive foreign investment company (section 1297), or
• A foreign personal holding company (section 552).

See Notice 2003-79 for more details.

Lines 4d(1) and 4d(2). Enter on line 4d(1) the post-May 5, 2003, gain (loss) from line 5a of Schedule D (Form 1065). Enter on line 4d(2) the gain (loss) for the entire year from line 5b of Schedule D (Form 1065).

Lines 4e(1) and 4e(2). Enter on line 4e(1) the post-May 5, 2003, gain (loss) that is portfolio income (loss) from line 11 of Schedule D (Form 1065) plus any long-term capital gain (loss) that is specially allocated to partners. Enter on line 4e(2) the gain (loss) for the entire year that is portfolio income (loss) from line 12 of Schedule D (Form 1065). See **Special Allocations** on page 22.

⚠ *If any gain or loss from line 5, 11, or 12 of Schedule D is from the* **CAUTION** *disposition of nondepreciable personal property used in a trade or business, it may not be treated as portfolio income. Report such gain or loss on line 7 of Schedules K and K-1.*

Line 4f. Report and identify other portfolio income or loss on an attachment for line 4f.

For example, income reported to the partnership from a real estate mortgage investment conduit (REMIC), in which the partnership is a residual interest holder, would be reported on an attachment for line 4f. If the partnership holds a residual interest in a REMIC, report on the attachment for line 4f the partner's share of the following:
• Taxable income (net loss) from the REMIC (line 1b of Schedules Q (Form 1066)).
• "Excess inclusion" (line 2c of Schedules Q (Form 1066)).
• Section 212 expenses (line 3b of Schedules Q (Form 1066)). Do not report these section 212 expenses on line 10 of Schedules K and K-1.

Because Schedule Q (Form 1066) is a quarterly statement, the partnership must follow the Schedule Q instructions to figure the amounts to report to the partner for the partnership's tax year.

Line 5. Guaranteed Payments to Partners

Guaranteed payments to partners include:
• Payments for salaries, health insurance, and interest deducted by the partnership and reported on Form 1065, page 1, line 10; Form 8825; or on Schedule K, line 3b; and

• Payments the partnership must capitalize. See the Instructions for Form 1065, line 10.

Generally, amounts reported on line 5 are not considered to be related to a passive activity. For example, guaranteed payments for personal services paid to a partner would not be passive activity income. Likewise, interest paid to any partner is not passive activity income.

Line 6. Net Section 1231 Gain (Loss) (Other Than Due to Casualty or Theft)

Enter on line 6a the post-May 5, 2003, net section 1231 gain (loss) from Form 4797, line 7, column (h). Enter on line 6b the net section 1231 gain (loss) for the entire year from Form 4797, line 7, column (g). Do not include specially allocated ordinary gains and losses or net gains or losses from involuntary conversions due to casualties or thefts on this line. Instead, report them on line 7. If the partnership has more than one activity, attach a statement to Schedule K-1 that identifies the activity to which the section 1231 gain (loss) relates.

Line 7. Other Income (Loss)

Use line 7 to report other items of income, gain, or loss not included on lines 1 through 6. If the partnership has more than one activity, identify on an attachment the amount and the activity to which each amount relates.

If the partnership had a gain from the disposition of non-depreciable personal property used in a trade or business and held it more than 5 years, show the total of all such gains on an attachment to Schedule K-1. Indicate on the statement that the partner should include this amount on line 5 of the **Qualified 5-Year Gain Worksheet— Line 35** in the Instructions for Schedule D (Form 1040). If the partnership has more than one activity, identify on an attachment the amount and the activity to which each amount relates. Also identify the amount of post-May 5, 2003, gain or loss.

Include the following items on line 7:
• Gains from the disposition of farm recapture property (see Form 4797) and other items to which section 1252 applies.
• Gains from the disposition of an interest in oil, gas, geothermal, or other mineral properties (section 1254).
• Any net gain or loss from section 1256 contracts from **Form 6781,** Gains and Losses From Section 1256 Contracts and Straddles.
• Recoveries of tax benefit items (section 111).
• Gambling gains and losses subject to the limitations in section 165(d).
• Any income, gain, or loss to the partnership under section 751(b).
• Specially allocated ordinary gain (loss).
• Net gain (loss) from involuntary conversions due to casualty or theft. The amount for this line is shown on **Form 4684,** Casualties and Thefts, line 38a, 38b, or 39.

Each partner's share must be entered on Schedule K-1. Give each partner a schedule that shows the amounts to be reported on the partner's Form 4684, line 34, columns (b)(i), (b)(ii), and (c).

If there was a gain (loss) from a casualty or theft to property not used in a trade or business or for income-producing purposes, notify the partner. The partnership should not complete Form 4684 for this type of

casualty or theft. Instead, each partner will complete his or her own Form 4684.
• Gain from the sale or exchange of qualified small business stock (as defined in the instructions for Schedule D) that is eligible for the 50% section 1202 exclusion. The section 1202 exclusion applies only to qualified small business stock issued after August 10, 1993, and held by the partnership for more than 5 years. Corporate partners are not eligible for the section 1202 exclusion. Additional limitations apply at the partner level. Report each partner's share of section 1202 gain on Schedule K-1. Each partner will determine if he or she qualifies for the section 1202 exclusion. Report on an attachment to Schedule K-1 for each sale or exchange the name of the corporation that issued the stock, the partner's share of the partnership's adjusted basis and sales price of the stock, and the dates the stock was bought and sold.
• Gain eligible for section 1045 rollover (replacement stock purchased by the partnership). Include only gain from the sale or exchange of qualified small business stock (as defined in the instructions for Schedule D) that was deferred by the partnership under section 1045 and reported on Schedule D. See the instructions for Schedule D for more details. Corporate partners are not eligible for the section 1045 rollover. Additional limitations apply at the partner level. Report each partner's share of the gain eligible for section 1045 rollover on Schedule K-1. Each partner will determine if he or she qualifies for the rollover. Report on an attachment to Schedule K-1 for each sale or exchange the name of the corporation that issued the stock, the partner's share of the partnership's adjusted basis and sales price of the stock, and the dates the stock was bought and sold.
• Gain eligible for section 1045 rollover (replacement stock not purchased by the partnership). Include only gain from the sale or exchange of qualified small business stock (as defined in the instructions for Schedule D) the partnership held for more than 6 months but that **was not** deferred by the partnership under section 1045. See the instructions for Schedule D for more details. A partner (other than a corporation) may be eligible to defer his or her distributive share of this gain under section 1045 if he or she purchases other qualified small business stock during the 60-day period that began on the date the stock was sold by the partnership. Additional limitations apply at the partner level. Report on an attachment to Schedule K-1 for each sale or exchange the name of the corporation that issued the stock, the partner's share of the partnership's adjusted basis and sales price of the stock, and the dates the stock was bought and sold.

Deductions

Line 8. Charitable Contributions

Enter on Schedule K the total amount of charitable contributions made by the partnership during its tax year. Enter each partner's distributive share on Schedule K-1. On an attachment to Schedules K and K-1, show separately the dollar amount of contributions subject to each of the 50%, 30%, and 20% adjusted gross income limits. For additional information, see **Pub. 526,** Charitable Contributions.

Generally, no deduction is allowed for any contribution of $250 or more unless the partnership obtains a written acknowledgment from the charitable organization that shows the amount of cash contributed, describes any property contributed, and gives an estimate of the value of any goods or services provided in return for the contribution. The acknowledgment must be obtained by the due date (including extensions) of the partnership return or, if earlier, the date the partnership files its return. Do not attach the acknowledgment to the tax return, but keep it with the partnership's records. These rules apply in addition to the filing requirements for Form 8283 described below.

Certain contributions made to an organization conducting lobbying activities are not deductible. See section 170(f)(9) for more details.

If the deduction claimed for noncash contributions exceeds $500, complete **Form 8283,** Noncash Charitable Contributions, and attach it to Form 1065. The partnership must give a copy of its Form 8283 to every partner if the deduction for an item or group of similar items of contributed property exceeds $5,000. Each partner must be furnished a copy even if the amount allocated to any partner is $5,000 or less.

If the deduction for an item or group of similar items of contributed property is $5,000 or less, the partnership should pass through each partner's share of the amount of noncash contributions so the partners will be able to complete their own Forms 8283. See the Instructions for Form 8283 for additional information.

If the partnership made a qualified conservation contribution, include the FMV of the underlying property before and after the donation and describe the conservation purpose furthered by the donation. Give a copy of this information to each partner.

Line 9. Section 179 Expense Deduction

A partnership may elect to expense part of the cost of certain property the partnership purchased this year for use in its trade or business or certain rental activities. See Pub. 946 for a definition of what kind of property qualifies for the section 179 expense deduction and the Instructions for Form 4562 for limitations on the amount of the section 179 expense deduction.

Complete Part I of Form 4562 to figure the partnership's section 179 expense deduction. The partnership does not claim the deduction itself but instead passes it through to the partners. Attach Form 4562 to Form 1065 and show the total section 179 expense deduction on Schedule K, line 9. Report each partner's allocable share on Schedule K-1, line 9. Do not complete line 9 of Schedule K-1 for any partner that is an estate or trust.

If the partnership is an enterprise zone business, also report on an attachment to Schedules K and K-1 the cost of section 179 property placed in service during the year that is qualified zone property.

See the instructions for line 25 of Schedule K-1, item 5, for any recapture of a section 179 amount.

Line 10. Deductions Related to Portfolio Income

Enter on line 10 and attach an itemized list of the deductions clearly and directly allocable to portfolio income (other than interest expense and section 212 expenses from a REMIC). Interest expense related to portfolio income is investment interest expense and is reported on line 14a of Schedules K and K-1. Section 212 expenses from the partnership's interest in a REMIC are reported on an attachment for line 4f of Schedules K and K-1.

No deduction is allowable under section 212 for expenses allocable to a convention, seminar, or similar meeting.

Line 11. Other Deductions

Use line 11 to report deductions not included on lines 8, 9, 10, 17g, and 18b. On an attachment, identify the deduction and amount and, if the partnership has more than one activity, the activity to which the deduction relates.

Examples of items to be reported on an attachment to line 11 include:
• Amounts paid by the partnership that would be allowed as itemized deductions on any of the partners' income tax returns if they were paid directly by a partner for the same purpose. However, do not enter expenses related to portfolio income or investment interest expense on this line.

If there was a loss from an involuntary conversion due to casualty or theft of income-producing property, include in the total amount for this line the relevant amount from Form 4684, line 32.
• Any penalty on early withdrawal of savings.
• Soil and water conservation expenditures (section 175).
• Expenditures for the removal of architectural and transportation barriers to the elderly and handicapped and which the partnership has elected to treat as a current expense (section 190).
• Contributions to a capital construction fund.
• Any amounts paid during the tax year for health insurance coverage for a partner (including that partner's spouse and dependents). For 2003, a partner may be allowed to deduct up to 100% of such amounts on Form 1040, line 29.
• Payments for a partner to an IRA, qualified plan, or simplified employee pension (SEP) or SIMPLE IRA plan. If a qualified plan is a defined benefit plan, a partner's distributive share of payments is determined in the same manner as his or her distributive share of partnership taxable income. For a defined benefit plan, attach to the Schedule K-1 for each partner a statement showing the amount of benefit accrued for the tax year.
• Interest expense allocated to debt-financed distributions. See Notice 89-35 for more information.
• Interest paid or accrued on debt properly allocable to each general partner's share of a working interest in any oil or gas property (if the partner's liability is not limited). General partners that did not materially participate in the oil or gas activity treat this interest as investment interest; for other general partners, it is trade or business interest.

Credits

Line 12a. Low-Income Housing Credit

Section 42 provides a credit that may be claimed by owners of low-income residential rental buildings. If the partners are eligible to take the low-income housing credit, complete and attach **Form 8586,** Low-Income Housing Credit; **Form 8609,** Low-Income Housing Credit Allocation Certification; and **Schedule A (Form 8609),** Annual Statement, to Form 1065.

Report on line 12a(1) the total low-income housing credit for property with respect to which a partnership is to be treated under section 42(j)(5) as the taxpayer to which the low-income housing credit was allowed. Report any other low-income housing credit on line 12a(2).

If part or all of the credit reported on line 12a(1) or 12a(2) is attributable to additions to qualified basis of property placed in service before 1990, report on an attachment to Schedules K and K-1 the amount of the credit on each line that is attributable to property placed in service **(a)** before 1990 and **(b)** after 1989.

Line 12b. Qualified Rehabilitation Expenditures Related to Rental Real Estate Activities

Enter total qualified rehabilitation expenditures related to rental real estate activities of the partnership. Also complete the applicable lines of **Form 3468,** Investment Credit, that apply to qualified rehabilitation expenditures for property related to rental real estate activities of the partnership for which income or loss is reported on line 2 of Schedule K. See Form 3468 for details on qualified rehabilitation expenditures. Attach Form 3468 to Form 1065.

For line 12b of Schedule K-1, enter each partner's distributive share of the expenditures. On the dotted line to the left of the entry space for line 12b, enter the line number of Form 3468 on which the partner should report the expenditures. If there is more than one type of expenditure, or the expenditures are from more than one rental real estate activity, report this information separately for each expenditure or activity on an attachment to Schedules K and K-1.

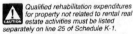 *Qualified rehabilitation expenditures for property not related to rental real estate activities must be listed separately on line 25 of Schedule K-1.*

Line 12c. Credits (Other Than Credits Shown on Lines 12a and 12b) Related to Rental Real Estate Activities

Report any information that the partners need to figure credits related to a rental real estate activity, other than the low-income housing credit and qualified rehabilitation expenditures. On the dotted line to the left of the entry space for line 12c (or in the margin), identify the type of credit. If there is more than one type of credit or the credit is from more than one activity, report this information separately for each credit or activity on an attachment to Schedules K and K-1.

-24-

Instructions for Form 1065

Line 12d. Credits Related to Other Rental Activities

Use this line to report information that the partners need to figure credits related to a rental activity other than a rental real estate activity. On the dotted line to the left of the entry space for line 12d, identify the type of credit. If there is more than one type of credit or the credit is from more than one activity, report this information separately for each credit or activity on an attachment to Schedules K and K-1.

Line 13. Other Credits

Enter on line 13 any other credit, except credits or expenditures shown or listed for lines 12a through 12d of Schedules K and K-1. On the dotted line to the left of the entry space for line 13, identify the type of credit. If there is more than one type of credit or the credit is from more than one activity, report this information separately for each credit or activity on an attachment to Schedules K and K-1. The credits to be reported on line 13 and other required attachments are as follows:

• Credit for backup withholding on dividends, interest, or patronage dividends.
• Nonconventional source fuel credit. The credit is figured at the partnership level and then is apportioned to the partners based on their distributive shares of partnership income attributable to sales of qualified fuels. Attach a separate schedule to the return to show the computation of the credit. See section 29 for more information.
• Qualified electric vehicle credit (Form 8834).
• Unused credits from cooperatives. The unused credits are apportioned to persons who were partners in the partnership on the last day of the partnership's tax year.
• Work opportunity credit (Form 5884). This credit is apportioned among the partners according to their interest in the partnership at the time the wages on which the credit is figured were paid or accrued.
• Welfare-to-work credit (Form 8861). This credit is apportioned in the same manner as the work opportunity credit.
• Credit for alcohol used as fuel (Form 6478). This credit is apportioned to persons who were partners on the last day of the partnership's tax year. The credit must be included in income on page 1, line 7, of Form 1065. See section 40(f) for an election the partnership can make to not have the credit apply. If this credit includes the small ethanol producer credit, identify on a statement attached to each Schedule K-1 **(a)** the amount of the small producer credit included in the total credit allocated to the partner, **(b)** the number of gallons of qualified ethanol fuel production allocated to the partner, and **(c)** the partner's share in gallons of the partnership's productive capacity for alcohol.

• Credit for increasing research activities (Form 6765).
• Enhanced oil recovery credit (Form 8830).
• Disabled access credit (Form 8826).
• Renewable electricity production credit (Form 8835).
• Empowerment zone and renewal community employment credit (Form 8844).
• Indian employment credit (Form 8845).
• Credit for employer social security and Medicare taxes paid on certain employee tips (Form 8846).
• Orphan drug credit (Form 8820).

Instructions for Form 1065

• New markets credit (Form 8874).
• Credit for contributions to selected community development corporations (Form 8847).
• Credit for small employer pension start-up costs (Form 8881).
• Credit for employer-provided child care facilities and services (Form 8882).
• New York Liberty Zone business employee credit (Form 8884).
• General credits from an electing large partnership.

See the instructions for line 25, item 14 of Schedule K-1 to report expenditures qualifying for the **(a)** rehabilitation credit not related to rental real estate activities, **(b)** energy credit, or **(c)** reforestation credit.

Investment Interest

Complete lines 14a through 14b(2) for all partners.

Line 14a. Interest Expense on Investment Debts

Include on this line interest paid or accrued on debt properly allocable to property held for investment. Property held for investment includes property that produces income (unless derived in the ordinary course of a trade or business) from interest, dividends, annuities, or royalties; and gains from the disposition of property that produces those types of income or is held for investment.

Property held for investment also includes each general partner's share of a working interest in any oil or gas property for which the partner's liability is not limited and in which the partner did not materially participate. However, the level of each partner's participation in an activity is determined by the partner and not by the partnership. As a result, interest allocable to a general partner's share of a working interest in any oil or gas property (if the partner's liability is not limited) should not be reported on line 14a. Instead, report this interest on line 11.

Investment interest does not include interest expense allocable to a passive activity.

The amount on line 14a will be deducted (after applying the investment interest expense limitations of section 163(d)) by individual partners on Schedule A (Form 1040), line 13.

For more information, see Form 4952.

Lines 14b(1) and 14b(2). Investment Income and Expenses

Enter on line 14b(1) only the investment income included on lines 4a, 4b(2), 4c, and 4f of Schedules K and K-1. Do not include other portfolio gains or losses on this line.

Enter on line 14b(2) only the investment expense included on line 10 of Schedules K and K-1.

If there are other items of investment income or expense included in the amounts that must be passed through separately to the partner on Schedule K-1 (such as net short-term capital gain or loss, net long-term capital gain or loss, and other portfolio gains or losses) give each partner a schedule identifying these amounts.

Investment income includes gross income from property held for investment, the excess of net gain from the disposition of property held for investment over net capital gain from the disposition of property

held for investment, and any net capital gain from the disposition of property held for investment that each partner elects to include in investment income under section 163(d)(4)(B)(iii). Generally, investment income and investment expenses do not include any income or expenses from a passive activity.

Property subject to a net lease is not treated as investment property because it is subject to the passive loss rules. Do not reduce investment income by losses from passive activities.

Investment expenses are deductible expenses (other than interest) directly connected with the production of investment income. See the Form 4952 instructions for more information on investment income and expenses.

Self-Employment

Note: *If the partnership is an options dealer or a commodities dealer, see section 1402(i) before completing lines 15a, 15b, and 15c, to determine the amount of any adjustment that may have to be made to the amounts shown on the **Worksheet for Figuring Net Earnings (Loss) From Self-Employment** on page 26. If the partnership is engaged solely in the operation of a group investment program, earnings from the operation are not self-employment earnings for either general or limited partners.*

General partners. General partners' net earnings (loss) from self-employment do not include:
• Dividends on any shares of stock and interest on any bonds, debentures, notes, etc., unless the dividends or interest are received in the course of a trade or business, such as a dealer in stocks or securities or interest on notes or accounts receivable.
• Rentals from real estate, except rentals of real estate held for sale to customers in the course of a trade or business as a real estate dealer or payments for rooms or space when significant services are provided.
• Royalty income, except royalty income received in the course of a trade or business.

See the instructions for **Schedule SE (Form 1040)**, Self-Employment Tax, for more information.

Limited partners. Generally, a limited partner's share of partnership income (loss) is not included in net earnings (loss) from self-employment. Limited partners treat as self-employment earnings only guaranteed payments for services they actually rendered to, or on behalf of, the partnership to the extent that those payments are payment for those services.

Line 15a. Net Earnings (Loss) From Self-Employment

Schedule K. Enter on line 15a the amount from line 5 of the worksheet.
Schedule K-1. Do not complete this line for any partner that is an estate, trust, corporation, exempt organization, or individual retirement arrangement (IRA).

Enter on line 15a of Schedule K-1 each individual general partner's share of the amount shown on line 5 of the worksheet and each individual limited partner's share of the amount shown on line 4c of the worksheet.

-25-

Line 15b. Gross Farming or Fishing Income

Enter the partnership's gross farming or fishing income from self-employment. Individual partners need this amount to figure net earnings from self-employment under the farm optional method in Section B, Part II of Schedule SE (Form 1040).

Line 15c. Gross Nonfarm Income

Enter the partnership's gross nonfarm income from self-employment. Individual partners need this amount to figure net earnings from self-employment under the nonfarm optional method in Section B, Part II of Schedule SE (Form 1040).

Worksheet Instructions

Line 1b. Include on line 1b any part of the net income (loss) from rental real estate activities from Schedule K, line 2, that is from:

1. Rentals of real estate held for sale to customers in the course of a trade or business as a real estate dealer or

2. Rentals for which services were rendered to the occupants (other than services usually or customarily rendered for the rental of space for occupancy only). The supplying of maid service is such a service; but the furnishing of heat and light, the cleaning of public entrances, exits, stairways and lobbies, trash collection, etc., are not considered services rendered to the occupants.

Lines 3b and 4b. Allocate the amounts on these lines in the same way Form 1065, page 1, line 22, is allocated to these particular partners.

Line 4a. Include in the amount on line 4a any guaranteed payments to partners reported on Schedules K and K-1, line 5, and derived from a trade or business as defined in section 1402(c). Also include other ordinary income and expense items (other than expense items subject to separate limitations at the partner level, such as the section 179 expense deduction)

reported on Schedules K and K-1 that are used to figure self-employment earnings under section 1402.

Adjustments and Tax Preference Items

Lines 16a through 16e must be completed for all partners except certain small corporations exempt from the alternative minimum tax (AMT) under section 55(e).

Enter items of income and deductions that are adjustments or tax preference items for the AMT. See **Form 6251,** Alternative Minimum Tax— Individuals; **Form 4626,** Alternative Minimum Tax—Corporations; or Schedule I of **Form 1041,** U.S. Income Tax Return for Estates and Trusts, to determine the amounts to enter and for other information.

Do not include as a tax preference item any qualified expenditures to which an election under section 59(e) may apply. Instead, report these expenditures on lines 18a and 18b. Because these expenditures are subject to an election by each partner, the partnership cannot figure the amount of any tax preference related to them.

Line 16a. Depreciation Adjustment on Property Placed in Service After 1986

Figure the adjustment for line 16a based only on tangible property placed in service after 1986 (and tangible property placed in service after July 31, 1986, and before 1987 for which the partnership elected to use the general depreciation system). **Do not** make an adjustment for motion picture films, videotapes, sound recordings, certain public utility property (as defined in section 168(f)(2)), property depreciated under the unit-of-production method (or any other method not expressed in a term of years), qualified Indian reservation property, property eligible for a special depreciation allowance, qualified revitalization expenditures, or the section 179 expense deduction.

For property placed in service **before 1999,** refigure depreciation for the AMT as follows (using the same convention used for the regular tax):
• For section 1250 property (generally, residential rental and nonresidential real property), use the straight line method over 40 years.
• For tangible property (other than section 1250 property) depreciated using the straight line method for the regular tax, use the straight line method over the property's class life. Use 12 years if the property has no class life.
• For any other tangible property, use the 150% declining balance method, switching to the straight line method the first year it gives a larger deduction, over the property's AMT class life. Use 12 years if the property has no class life.

Note: *See Pub. 946 for a table of class lives.*

For property placed in service **after 1998,** refigure depreciation for the AMT **only** for property depreciated for the regular tax using the 200% declining balance method. For the AMT, use the 150% declining balance method, switching to the straight line method the first tax year it gives a larger deduction, and the same convention and recovery period used for the regular tax.

Figure the adjustment by subtracting the AMT deduction for depreciation from the regular tax deduction and enter the result on line 16a. If the AMT deduction is more than the regular tax deduction, enter the difference as a negative amount. Depreciation capitalized to inventory must also be refigured using the AMT rules. Include on this line the current year adjustment to income, if any, resulting from the difference.

Line 16b. Adjusted Gain or Loss

If the partnership disposed of any tangible property placed in service after 1986 (or after July 31, 1986, if an election was made to use the general depreciation system), or if it disposed of a certified pollution control

---

Worksheet for Figuring Net Earnings (Loss) From Self-Employment

1a Ordinary income (loss) (Schedule K, line 1)	**1a**		
b Net income (loss) from **certain** rental real estate activities (see instructions)	**1b**		
c Net income (loss) from other rental activities (Schedule K, line 3c)	**1c**		
d Net loss from Form 4797, Part II, line 18, included on line 1a above. Enter as a positive amount	**1d**		
e Combine lines 1a through 1d	**1e**		
2 Net gain from Form 4797, Part II, line 18, included on line 1a above	**2**		
3a Subtract line 2 from line 1e. If line 1e is a loss, increase the loss on line 1e by the amount on line 2	**3a**		
b Part of line 3a allocated to limited partners, estates, trusts, corporations, exempt organizations, and IRAs	**3b**		
c Subtract line 3b from line 3a. If line 3a is a loss, reduce the loss on line 3a by the amount on line 3b. Include each individual general partner's share on line 15a of Schedule K-1		**3c**	
4a Guaranteed payments to partners (Schedule K, line 5) derived from a trade or business as defined in section 1402(c) (see instructions)	**4a**		
b Part of line 4a allocated to individual limited partners for **other than** services and to estates, trusts, corporations, exempt organizations, and IRAs	**4b**		
c Subtract line 4b from line 4a. Include each individual general partner's share and each individual limited partner's share on line 15a of Schedule K-1		**4c**	
5 Net earnings (loss) from self-employment. Combine lines 3c and 4c. Enter here and on Schedule K, line 15a		**5**	

Instructions for Form 1065

facility placed in service after 1986, refigure the gain or loss from the disposition using the adjusted basis for the AMT. The property's adjusted basis for the AMT is its cost or other basis minus all depreciation or amortization deductions allowed or allowable for the AMT during the current tax year and previous tax years. Enter on this line the difference between the regular tax gain (or loss) and the AMT gain (or loss). If the AMT gain is less than the regular tax gain, **or** the AMT loss is more than the regular tax loss, **or** there is an AMT loss and a regular tax gain, enter the difference as a negative amount.

If any part of the adjustment is allocable to net short-term capital gain (loss), net long-term capital gain (loss), or net section 1231 gain (loss), attach a schedule that identifies the amount of the adjustment allocable to each type of gain or loss. For a net long-term capital gain (loss), also identify the amount of the adjustment that is 28% rate gain (loss). For a net section 1231 gain (loss), also identify the amount of adjustment that is unrecaptured section 1250 gain. Also indicate the amount of any qualified 5-year gain and the portion of that amount that is post-May 5, 2003, gain or loss.

Line 16c. Depletion (Other Than Oil and Gas)

Do not include any depletion on oil and gas wells. The partners must figure their depletion deductions and preference items separately.

Refigure the depletion deduction under section 611 for mines, wells (other than oil and gas wells), and other natural deposits for the AMT. Percentage depletion is limited to 50% of the taxable income from the property as figured under section 613(a), using only income and deductions allowed for the AMT. Also, the deduction is limited to the property's adjusted basis at the end of the year, as refigured for the AMT. Figure this limit separately for each property. When refiguring the property's adjusted basis, take into account any AMT adjustments made this year or in previous years that affect basis (other than the current year's depletion).

Enter the difference between the regular tax and AMT deduction. If the AMT deduction is greater, enter the difference as a negative amount.

Lines 16d(1) and 16d(2)

Enter only the income and deductions for oil, gas, and geothermal properties that are used to figure the partnership's ordinary income or loss (line 22 of Form 1065). If there are items of income or deduction for oil, gas, and geothermal properties included in the amounts required to be passed through separately to the partners on Schedule K-1 (items not reported on line 1 of Schedule K-1), give each partner a schedule identifying these amounts.

Figure the amount for lines 16d(1) and (2) separately for oil and gas properties that are not geothermal deposits and for all properties that are geothermal deposits.

Give each partner a schedule that shows the separate amounts that are included in the computation of the amounts on lines 16d(1) and (2).

Instructions for Form 1065

Line 16d(1). Gross income from oil, gas, and geothermal properties. Enter the aggregate amount of gross income (within the meaning of section 613(a)) from all oil, gas, and geothermal properties that was received or accrued during the tax year and included on page 1, Form 1065.

Line 16d(2). Deductions allocable to oil, gas, and geothermal properties. Enter the amount of any deductions allowed for the AMT that are allocable to oil, gas, and geothermal properties.

Line 16e. Other Adjustments and Tax Preference Items

Attach a schedule that shows each partner's share of other items not shown on lines 16a through 16d(2) that are adjustments or tax preference items or that the partner needs to complete Form 6251, Form 4626, or Schedule I of Form 1041. See these forms and their instructions to determine the amount to enter.

Other adjustments and tax preference items or information the partner needs include the following:
• Accelerated depreciation of real property under pre-1987 rules.
• Accelerated depreciation of leased personal property under pre-1987 rules.
• Long-term contracts entered into after February 28, 1986. Except for certain home construction contracts, the taxable income from these contracts must be figured using the percentage of completion method of accounting for the AMT.
• Losses from tax shelter farm activities. No loss from any tax shelter farm activity is allowed for the AMT.
• Any information needed by certain corporate partners to compute the adjusted current earnings (ACE) adjustment.

Foreign Taxes

Lines 17a through 17h must be completed if the partnership has foreign income, deductions, or losses or has paid or accrued foreign taxes. See **Pub. 514,** Foreign Tax Credit for Individuals, for more information.

Line 17a. Name of Foreign Country or U.S. Possession

Enter the name of the foreign country or U.S. possession from which the partnership had income or to which the partnership paid or accrued taxes. If the partnership had income from, or paid or accrued taxes to, **more than one** foreign country or U.S. possession, enter "See attached" and attach a schedule for each country for lines 17a through 17h.

Line 17b. Gross Income From All Sources

Enter the partnership's gross income from all sources (both U.S. and foreign source).

Line 17c. Gross Income Sourced at Partner Level

Enter the total gross income of the partnership that is required to be sourced at the partner level. This includes income from the sale of most personal property other than inventory, depreciable property, and certain intangible property. See Pub. 514 and section 865 for details. Attach a schedule showing the following information:
• The amount of this gross income (without regard to its source) in each category

identified in the instructions for line 17d, including each of the listed categories.
• Specifically identify gains on the sale of personal property other than inventory, depreciable property, and certain intangible property on which a foreign tax of 10% or more was paid or accrued. Also list losses on the sale of such property if the foreign country would have imposed a 10% or higher tax had the sale resulted in a gain. See **Sales or exchanges of certain personal property** in Pub. 514 and section 865.
• Specify the net foreign source capital gain or loss within each separate limitation category shown below in the instructions for line 17d(2). Also, in the case of noncorporate partners, separately identify the net foreign source gain or loss within each separate limitation category that is 28% rate gain or loss, unrecaptured section 1250 gain, and qualified 5-year gain and indicate the post-May 5, 2003, portion of each.

Line 17d. Foreign Gross Income Sourced at Partnership Level

Separately report gross income from sources outside the United States by category of income as follows. For partnership and corporate partners only, attach a schedule identifying the total amount of foreign gross income in each category of income attributable to foreign branches. See Pub. 514 for information on the categories of income.

Line 17d(1). Passive foreign source income. Enter the partnership's passive foreign source income.

Line 17d(2). Attach a schedule showing the amount of foreign source income included in each of the following listed categories of income:
• Financial services income;
• High withholding tax interest;
• Shipping income;
• Dividends from each noncontrolled section 902 corporation;
• Dividends from a domestic international sales corporation (DISC) or a former DISC;
• Distributions from a foreign sales corporation (FSC) or a former FSC;
• Section 901(j) income; and
• Certain income re-sourced by treaty.

Line 17d(3). General limitation foreign source income (all other foreign source income). Enter the partnership's general limitation foreign source income. Include all foreign income sourced at the partnership level that is not reported on lines 17d(1) and 17d(2).

Line 17e. Deductions Allocated and Apportioned at Partner Level

Enter on line 17e(1) the partnership's total interest expense (including interest equivalents under Temporary Regulations section 1.861-9T(b)). Do not include interest directly allocable under Temporary Regulations section 1.861-10T to income from a specific property. This type of interest is allocated and apportioned at the partnership level and is included on lines 17f(1) through (3). On line 17e(2), enter the total of all other deductions or losses that are required to be allocated at the partner level. For example, include on line 17e(2) research and experimental expenditures (see Regulations section 1.861-17(f)).

Line 17f. Deductions Allocated and Apportioned at Partnership Level to Foreign Source Income

Separately report partnership deductions that are apportioned at the partnership level to (1) passive foreign source income, (2) each of the listed foreign categories of income, and (3) general limitation foreign source income (see the instructions for line 17d). See Pub. 514 for more information.

For partnership and corporate partners only, attach a schedule identifying the total amount of deductions apportioned to each category of income shown in the instructions for line 17d that are attributable to foreign branches.

Line 17g. Total Foreign Taxes

Enter in U.S. dollars the total foreign taxes (described in section 901 or section 903) that were paid or accrued by the partnership (according to its method of accounting for such taxes). Translate these amounts into U.S. dollars by using the applicable exchange rate (see Pub. 514).

Attach a schedule reporting the following information:

1. The total amount of foreign taxes (including foreign taxes on income sourced at the partner level) relating to each category of income (see instructions for line 17d).
2. The dates on which the taxes were paid or accrued, the exchange rates used, and the amounts in both foreign currency and U.S. dollars, for:
   • Taxes withheld at source on interest.
   • Taxes withheld at source on dividends.
   • Taxes withheld at source on rents and royalties.
   • Other foreign taxes paid or accrued.

Line 17h. Reduction in Taxes Available for Credit

Enter the total reductions in taxes available for credit.

Attach a schedule showing the reductions for:
• Taxes on foreign mineral income (section 901(e)).
• Taxes on foreign oil and gas extraction income (section 907(a)).
• Taxes attributable to boycott operations (section 908).
• Failure to timely file (or furnish all of the information required on) Forms 5471 and 8865.
• Any other items (specify).

Other

Lines 18a and 18b

Generally, section 59(e) allows each partner to make an election to deduct the partner's distributive share of the partnership's otherwise deductible qualified expenditures ratably over 10 years (3 years for circulation expenditures), beginning with the tax year in which the expenditures were made (or for intangible drilling and development costs, over the 60-month period beginning with the month in which such costs were paid or incurred). The term "qualified expenditures" includes only the following types of expenditures paid or incurred during the tax year:
• Circulation expenditures.
• Research and experimental expenditures.
• Intangible drilling and development costs.

• Mining exploration and development costs.

If a partner makes this election, these items are not treated as tax preference items.

Because the partners are generally allowed to make this election, the partnership cannot deduct these amounts or include them as adjustments or tax preference items on Schedule K-1. Instead, on lines 18a and 18b of Schedule K-1, the partnership passes through the information the partners need to figure their separate deductions.

On line 18a, enter the type of expenditures claimed on line 18b. Enter on line 18b the qualified expenditures paid or incurred during the tax year to which an election under section 59(e) may apply. Enter this amount for all partners whether or not any partner makes an election under section 59(e). If the expenditures are for intangible drilling and development costs, enter the month in which the expenditures were paid or incurred (after the type of expenditure on line 18a). If there is more than one type of expenditure included in the total shown on line 18b (or intangible drilling and development costs were paid or incurred for more than 1 month), report this information separately for each type of expenditure (or month) on an attachment to Schedules K and K-1.

Line 19. Tax-Exempt Interest Income

Enter on line 19 tax-exempt interest income, including any exempt-interest dividends received from a mutual fund or other regulated investment company. Individual partners must report this information on line 8b of Form 1040. The adjusted basis of the partner's interest is increased by the amount shown on this line under section 705(a)(1)(B).

Line 20. Other Tax-Exempt Income

Enter on line 20 all income of the partnership exempt from tax other than tax-exempt interest (for example, life insurance proceeds). The adjusted basis of the partner's interest is increased by the amount shown on this line under section 705(a)(1)(B).

Line 21. Nondeductible Expenses

Enter on line 21 nondeductible expenses paid or incurred by the partnership. Do not include separately stated deductions shown elsewhere on Schedules K and K-1, capital expenditures, or items the deduction for which is deferred to a later tax year. The adjusted basis of the partner's interest is decreased by the amount shown on this line under section 705(a)(2)(B).

Line 22. Distributions of Money (Cash and Marketable Securities)

Enter on line 22 the total distributions to each partner of cash and marketable securities that are treated as money under section 731(c)(1). Generally, marketable securities are valued at FMV on the date of distribution. However, the value of marketable securities does not include the distributee partner's share of the gain on the securities distributed to that partner. See section 731(c)(3)(B) for details.

If the amount on line 22 includes marketable securities treated as money, state separately on an attachment to

Schedules K and K-1 (a) the partnership's adjusted basis of those securities immediately before the distribution and (b) the FMV of those securities on the date of distribution (excluding the distributee partner's share of the gain on the securities distributed to that partner).

Line 23. Distributions of Property Other Than Money

Enter on line 23 the total distributions to each partner of property not included on line 22. In computing the amount of the distribution, use the adjusted basis of the property to the partnership immediately before the distribution. In addition, attach a statement showing the adjusted basis and FMV of each property distributed.

Line 24 (Schedule K Only)

Attach a statement to report the partnership's total income, expenditures, or other information for the items listed under **Line 25 (Schedule K-1 Only). Supplemental Information** below.

Lines 24a and 24b (Schedule K-1 Only). Recapture of Low-Income Housing Credit

If recapture of part or all of the low-income housing credit is required because (a) prior year qualified basis of a building decreased or (b) the partnership disposed of a building or part of its interest in a building, see **Form 8611**, Recapture of Low-Income Housing Credit. The instructions for Form 8611 indicate when the form is completed by the partnership and what information is provided to partners when recapture is required.

If a partner's ownership interest in a building decreased because of a transaction at the partner level, the partnership must provide the necessary information to the partner to enable the partner to figure the recapture.

Report on line 24a the total low-income housing credit recapture with respect to a partnership treated under section 42(j)(5) as the taxpayer to which the low-income housing credit was allowed. Report any other low-income housing credit recapture on line 24b.

If the partnership filed **Form 8693**, Low-Income Housing Credit Disposition Bond, to avoid recapture of the low-income housing credit, no entry should be made on line 24 of Schedule K-1.

See Form 8586, Form 8611, and section 42 for more information.

Line 25 (Schedule K-1 Only). Supplemental Information

Enter in the line 25 Supplemental Information space of Schedule K-1, or on an attached schedule if more space is needed, each partner's share of any information requested on lines 1 through 24b that must be reported in detail, and the following items 1 through 31. Identify the applicable line number next to the information entered in the Supplemental Information space. Show income or gains as a positive number. Show losses in parentheses.

1. Taxes paid on undistributed capital gains by a regulated investment company or a real estate investment trust (REIT). As a shareholder of a regulated investment company or a REIT, the partnership will receive notice on **Form 2439**, Notice to Shareholder of Undistributed Long-Term

Capital Gains, of the amount of tax paid on undistributed capital gains.

2. The number of gallons of each fuel sold or used during the tax year for a nontaxable use qualifying for the credit for taxes paid on fuels, type of use, and the applicable credit per gallon. See **Form 4136,** Credit for Federal Tax Paid on Fuels, for details.

3. The partner's share of gross income from each property, share of production for the tax year, etc., needed to figure the partner's depletion deduction for oil and gas wells. The partnership should also allocate to each partner a proportionate share of the adjusted basis of each partnership oil or gas property. The allocation of the basis of each property is made as specified in section 613A(c)(7)(D).

The partnership cannot deduct depletion on oil and gas wells. The partner must determine the allowable amount to report on his or her return. See Pub. 535 for more information.

4. Gain or loss on the sale, exchange, or other disposition of property for which a section 179 expense deduction was passed through to partners. The partnership must provide all the following information with respect to a disposition of property for which a section 179 expense deduction was passed through to partners (see the instructions for line 6 on page 15).

a. Description of the property.

b. Date the property was acquired.

c. Date of the sale or other disposition of the property.

d. The partner's distributive share of the gross sales price.

e. The partner's distributive share of the cost or other basis plus the expense of sale (reduced as explained in the instructions for Form 4797, line 21).

f. The partner's distributive share of the depreciation allowed or allowable, determined as described in the instructions for Form 4797, line 22, but excluding the section 179 expense deduction.

g. The partner's distributive share of the section 179 expense deduction (if any) passed through for the property and the partnership's tax year(s) in which the amount was passed through.

h. An indication if the disposition is from a casualty or theft.

i. If this is an installment sale made during the partnership's tax year, any information the partner needs to complete **Form 6252,** Installment Sale Income. The partnership also must separately report the partner's distributive share of all payments received for the property in the following tax years. (Installment payments received for installments made in prior tax years should be reported in the same manner used in prior tax years.)

5. Recapture of section 179 expense deduction if business use of the property dropped to 50 percent or less. If the business use of any property (placed in service after 1986) for which a section 179 expense deduction was passed through to partners dropped to 50% or less (for a reason other than disposition) the partnership must provide all the following information.

a. The partner's distributive share of the original basis and depreciation allowed or allowable (not including the section 179 expense deduction).

b. The partner's distributive share of the section 179 expense deduction (if any) passed through for the property and the partnership's tax year(s) in which the amount was passed through.

6. Recapture of certain mining exploration expenditures (section 617).

7. Any information or statements a partner needs to comply with section 6111 (registration of tax shelters) or section 6662(d)(2)(B)(ii) (regarding adequate disclosure of items that may cause an understatement of income tax).

8. The partner's share of preproductive period farm expenses, if the partnership is not required to use the accrual method of accounting. See Regulations section 1.263A-4.

9. Any information a partner needs to figure the interest due under section 453(l)(3). If the partnership elected to report the disposition of certain timeshares and residential lots on the installment method, each partner's tax liability must be increased by the partner's allocable share of the interest on tax attributable to the installment payments received during the tax year.

10. Any information a partner needs to figure interest due under section 453A(c). If an obligation arising from the disposition of property to which section 453A applies is outstanding at the close of the year, report each partner's allocable share of the outstanding installment obligation to which section 453A(b) applies.

11. For closely held partnerships (as defined in section 460(b)(4)), provide the information a partner needs to figure the partner's allocable share of any interest due or to be refunded under the look-back method of section 460(b)(2) on certain long-term contracts that are accounted for under either the percentage of completion-capitalized cost method or the percentage of completion method. Also attach to Form 1065 the information specified in the Instructions for Form 8697, Part II, lines 1 and 3, for each tax year in which such a long-term contract is completed.

12. Any information a partner needs relating to interest expense that the partner is required to capitalize. A partner may be required to capitalize interest that was incurred by the partner for the partnership's production expenditures. Similarly, a partner may have to capitalize interest that was incurred by the partnership for the partner's own production expenditures. See Regulations sections 1.263A-8 through 1.263A-15 for more information.

13. Any information a partner that is a tax-exempt organization may need to figure its share of unrelated business taxable income under section 512(a)(1) (but excluding any modifications required by paragraphs (8) through (15) of section 512(b)). Partners are required to notify the partnership of their tax-exempt status. See **Form 990-T,** Exempt Organization Business Income Tax Return, for more information.

14. Expenditures qualifying for the **(a)** rehabilitation credit not related to rental real estate activities, **(b)** energy credit, or **(c)** reforestation credit. Complete and attach Form 3468. See Form 3468 and the related instructions for information on eligible property and the lines on Form 3468 to complete. Do not include that part of the cost of the property the partnership has elected to expense under section 179.

Attach to each Schedule K-1 a separate schedule in a format similar to that shown on Form 3468 detailing each partner's share of qualified expenditures. Also indicate the lines of Form 3468 on which the partners should report these amounts.

15. Recapture of investment credit. Complete and attach **Form 4255,** Recapture of Investment Credit, when investment credit property is disposed of, or it no longer qualifies for the credit, before the end of the recapture period or the useful life applicable to the property. State the type of property at the top of Form 4255 and complete lines 2, 4, and 5, whether or not any partner is subject to recapture of the credit. Attach to each Schedule K-1 a separate schedule providing the information the partnership is required to show on Form 4255, but list only the partner's distributive share of the cost of the property subject to recapture. Also indicate the lines of Form 4255 on which the partners should report these amounts.

16. Any information a partner may need to figure the recapture of the qualified electric vehicle credit. See Pub. 535 for more information.

17. Recapture of new markets credit (Form 8874).

18. Any information a partner may need to figure recapture of the Indian employment credit. Generally, if a partnership terminates a qualified employee less than 1 year after the date of initial employment, any Indian employment credit allowed for a prior tax year by reason of wages paid or incurred to that employee must be recaptured. For details, see section 45A(d).

19. Nonqualified withdrawals by the partnership from a capital construction fund.

20. Unrecaptured section 1250 gain. Figure this amount for each section 1250 property in Part III of Form 4797 (except property for which gain is reported using the installment method on Form 6252) for which you had an entry in Part I of Form 4797 by subtracting line 26g of Form 4797 from the **smaller** of line 22 or line 24 of Form 4797. Figure the total of these amounts for all section 1250 properties. Generally, the result is the partnership's unrecaptured section 1250 gain. However, if the partnership is reporting gain on the installment method for a section 1250 property held more than 1 year, see the next paragraph to figure the unrecaptured section 1250 gain on that property. Report each partner's distributive share of the total amount as "Unrecaptured section 1250 gain."

The total unrecaptured section 1250 gain for an installment sale of section 1250 property held more than 1 year is figured for the year of the sale in a manner similar to that used in the preceding paragraph. However, the total unrecaptured section 1250 gain must be allocated to the installment payments received from the sale. To do so, the partnership generally must treat the gain allocable to each installment payment as unrecaptured section 1250 gain until all such gain has been used in full. Figure the unrecaptured section 1250 gain for installment payments received during the tax year as the **smaller** of **(a)** the amount from line 26 or line 37 of Form 6252 (whichever applies) or **(b)** the total unrecaptured section 1250 gain for the sale reduced by all gain reported in prior years (excluding section 1250 ordinary

Instructions for Form 1065

income recapture). However, if the partnership chose not to treat all of the gain from payments received after May 6, 1997, and before August 24, 1999, as unrecaptured section 1250 gain, use only the amount the partnership chose to treat as unrecaptured section 1250 gain for those payments to reduce the total unrecaptured section 1250 gain remaining to be reported for the sale.

If the partnership received a Schedule K-1 or Form 1099-DIV from an estate, a trust, a REIT, or a mutual fund (or other regulated investment company) reporting "unrecaptured section 1250 gain," **do not** add it to the partnership's own unrecaptured section 1250 gain. Instead, report it as a separate amount. For example, if the partnership received a Form 1099-DIV from a REIT with unrecaptured section 1250 gain, report it as "Unrecaptured section 1250 gain from a REIT."

Also report as a separate amount any gain from the sale or exchange of an interest in another partnership attributable to unrecaptured section 1250 gain. See Regulations section 1.1(h)-1 and attach the statement required under Regulations section 1.1(h)-1(e).

21. 28% rate gain (loss). Attach a statement to each Schedule K-1 showing each partner's distributive share of the gain (loss) attributable to collectibles. To figure each partner's distributive share, identify the gains (losses) from collectibles that are included on each of lines 6 through 11 of Schedule D (Form 1065). A **collectibles gain (loss)** is any long-term gain or deductible long-term loss from the sale or exchange of a collectible that is a capital asset.

Collectibles include works of art, rugs, antiques, metal (such as gold, silver, and platinum bullion), gems, stamps, coins, alcoholic beverages, and certain other tangible property.

Also, include gain (but not loss) from the sale or exchange of an interest in a partnership or trust held for more than 1 year and attributable to unrealized appreciation of collectibles. For details, see Regulations section 1.1(h)-1. Also attach the statement required under Regulations section 1.1(h)-1(e).

22. Qualified 5-year gain for dispositions before May 6, 2003. Attach a statement to each Schedule K-1 indicating the net long-term capital gain (not losses) from the disposition of assets (excluding stock that could qualify for section 1202 gain) held more than 5 years that are portfolio income included on line 12 of Schedule D (Form 1065). Also indicate the aggregate amount of all section 1231 gains from property held more than 5 years. Qualified 5-year gains should be reported only for the portion of the tax year before May 6, 2003. Do not include any section 1231 gain attributable to straight-line depreciation from section 1250 property. Indicate on the statement that this amount should be included in the partner's computation of qualified 5-year gain only if the amount on the partner's Form 4797, line 7, column (g), is more than zero, and that none of the gain is unrecaptured section 1250 gain.

23. If the partnership is a closely held partnership (as defined in section 460(b)(4)) and it depreciated certain property placed in service after September 13, 1995, under the

income forecast method, it must attach to Form 1065 the information specified in the instructions for Form 8866, line 2, for the 3rd and 10th tax years beginning after the tax year the property was placed in service. It must also report the line 2 amounts to its partners. See the instructions for Form 8866 for more details.

24. Any information a partner that is a publicly traded partnership may need to determine if it meets the 90% qualifying income test of section 7704(c)(2). Partners are required to notify the partnership of their status as a publicly traded partnership.

25. Amortization of reforestation expenditures. Report the amortizable basis and year in which the amortization began for the current year and the 7 preceding years. For limits that may apply, see section 194 and Pub. 535.

26. Any information needed by a partner to figure the interest due under section 1260(b). If any portion of a constructive ownership transaction was open in any prior year, each partner's tax liability must be increased by the partner's pro rata share of interest due on any deferral of gain recognition. See section 1260(b) for details, including how to figure the interest.

27. Extraterritorial income exclusion. See the instructions on page 13 for information that is required to be reported on line 25.

28. Commercial revitalization deduction from rental real estate activities. If the deduction is for a nonrental building, it is deducted by the partnership on line 20 of Form 1065. See the instructions for line 20 on page 18 for details.

29. If the partnership participates in a transaction that must be disclosed on Form 8886 (see page 8), both the partnership and its partners may be required to file Form 8886. The partnership must determine if any of its partners are required to disclose the transaction and provide those partners with information they will need to file Form 8886. This determination is based on the category(s) under which a transaction qualified for disclosures. See the instructions for Form 8886 for details.

30. Recapture of the credit for employer-provided child care facilities and services (Form 8882).

31. Any other information a partner may need to file his or her return that is not shown anywhere else on Schedule K-1. For example, if one of the partners is a pension plan, that partner may need special information to properly file its tax return.

Analysis of Net Income (Loss)

For each type of partner shown, enter the portion of the amount shown on line 1 that was allocated to that type of partner. Report all amounts for LLC members on the line for limited partners. The sum of the amounts shown on line 2 must equal the amount shown on line 1. In addition, the amount on line 1 must equal the amount on line 9, Schedule M-1 (if the partnership is required to complete Schedule M-1).

In classifying partners who are individuals as "active" or "passive," the partnership should apply the rules below. In applying these rules, a partnership should

classify each partner to the best of its knowledge and belief. It is assumed that in most cases the level of a particular partner's participation in an activity will be apparent.

1. If the partnership's principal activity is a trade or business, classify a general partner as "active" if the partner materially participated in all partnership trade or business activities; otherwise, classify a general partner as "passive."

2. If the partnership's principal activity consists of a working interest in an oil or gas well, classify a general partner as "active."

3. If the partnership's principal activity is a rental real estate activity, classify a general partner as "active" if the partner actively participated in all of the partnership's rental real estate activities; otherwise, classify a general partner as "passive."

4. Classify as "passive" all partners in a partnership whose principal activity is a rental activity other than a rental real estate activity.

5. If the partnership's principal activity is a portfolio activity, classify all partners as "active."

6. Classify as "passive" all limited partners and LLC members in a partnership whose principal activity is a trade or business or rental activity.

7. If the partnership cannot make a reasonable determination whether a partner's participation in a trade or business activity is material or whether a partner's participation in a rental real estate activity is active, classify the partner as "passive."

Schedule L. Balance Sheets per Books

Note: *Schedules L, M-1, and M-2 are not required to be completed if the partnership answered* **Yes** *to Question 5 of Schedule B.*

The balance sheets should agree with the partnership's books and records. Attach a statement explaining any differences.

Partnerships reporting to the Interstate Commerce Commission (ICC) or to any national, state, municipal, or other public officer may send copies of their balance sheets prescribed by the ICC or national, state, or municipal authorities, as of the beginning and end of the tax year, instead of completing Schedule L. However, statements filed under this procedure must contain sufficient information to enable the IRS to reconstruct a balance sheet similar to that contained on Form 1065 without contacting the partnership during processing.

All amounts on the balance sheet should be reported in U.S. dollars. If the partnership's books and records are kept in a foreign currency, the balance sheet should be translated in accordance with U.S. generally accepted accounting principles (GAAP).

Exception. *If the partnership or any qualified business unit of the partnership uses the U.S. dollar approximate separate transactions method, Schedule L should reflect the tax balance sheet prepared and translated into U.S. dollars according to Regulations section 1.985-3(d), and not a U.S. GAAP balance sheet.*

Line 5. Tax-Exempt Securities

Include on this line:

1. State and local government obligations, the interest on which is excludable from gross income under section 103(a) and

2. Stock in a mutual fund or other regulated investment company that distributed exempt-interest dividends during the tax year of the partnership.

Line 18. All Nonrecourse Loans

Nonrecourse loans are those liabilities of the partnership for which no partner bears the economic risk of loss.

Schedule M-1. Reconciliation of Income (Loss) per Books With Income (Loss) per Return

Line 2

Report on this line income included on Schedule K, lines 1, 2, 3c, 4a, 4b(2), 4c, 4d(2), 4e(2), 4f, 6b, and 7 not recorded on the partnership's books this year. Describe each such item of income. Attach a statement if necessary.

Line 3. Guaranteed Payments

Include on this line guaranteed payments shown on Schedule K, line 5 (other than amounts paid for insurance that constitutes medical care for a partner, a partner's spouse, and a partner's dependents).

Line 4b. Travel and Entertainment

Include on this line:

• Meal and entertainment expenses not deductible under section 274(n).

• Expenses for the use of an entertainment facility.

• The part of business gifts over $25.

• Expenses of an individual allocable to conventions on cruise ships over $2,000.

• Employee achievement awards over $400.

• The part of the cost of entertainment tickets that exceeds face value (also subject to 50% limit).

• The part of the cost of skyboxes that exceeds the face value of nonluxury box seat tickets.

• The part of the cost of luxury water travel expenses not deductible under section 274(m).

• Expenses for travel as a form of education.

• Nondeductible club dues.

• Other nondeductible travel and entertainment expenses.

Schedule M-2. Analysis of Partners' Capital Accounts

Show what caused the changes during the tax year in the partners' capital accounts as reflected on the partnership's books and records. The amounts on Schedule M-2 should equal the total of the amounts reported in Item J of all the partners' Schedules K-1.

The partnership may, but is not required to, use the rules in Regulations section 1.704-1(b)(2)(iv) to determine the partners' capital accounts in Schedule M-2 and Item J of the partners' Schedules K-1. If the beginning and ending capital accounts reported under these rules differ from the amounts reported on Schedule L, attach a statement reconciling any differences.

Line 2. Capital Contributed During Year

Include on line 2a the amount of money contributed and on line 2b the amount of property contributed by each partner to the partnership as reflected on the partnership's books and records.

Line 3. Net Income (Loss) per Books

Enter on line 3 the net income (loss) shown on the partnership books from Schedule M-1, line 1.

Line 6. Distributions

Line 6a. Cash. Enter on line 6a the amount of money distributed to each partner by the partnership.

Line 6b. Property. Enter the amount of property distributed to each partner by the partnership as reflected on the partnership's books and records. Include withdrawals from inventory for the personal use of a partner.

Paperwork Reduction Act Notice. We ask for the information on this form to carry out the Internal Revenue laws of the United States. You are required to give us the information. We need it to ensure that you are complying with these laws and to allow us to figure and collect the right amount of tax.

You are not required to provide the information requested on a form that is subject to the Paperwork Reduction Act unless the form displays a valid OMB control number. Books or records relating to a form or its instructions must be retained as long as their contents may become material in the administration of any Internal Revenue law. Generally, tax returns and return information are confidential, as required by section 6103.

The time needed to complete and file this form and related schedules will vary depending on individual circumstances. The estimated average times are:

Form	Recordkeeping	Learning about the law or the form	Preparing the form	Copying, assembling, and sending the form to the IRS
1065	42 hr., 56 min.	25 hr., 33 min.	44 hr., 17 min.	4 hr., 49 min.
Sch. D (Form 1065)	6 hr., 56 min.	2 hr., 17 min.	2 hr., 29 min.	
Sch. K-1 (Form 1065)	28 hr., 42 min.	11 hr., 7 min.	12 hr., 4 min.	
Sch. L (Form 1065)	15 hr., 32 min.	6 min.	21 min.	
Sch. M-1 (Form 1065)	3 hr., 21 min.	12 min.	15 min.	
Sch. M-2 (Form 1065)	3 hr., 6 min.	6 min.	9 min.	

If you have comments concerning the accuracy of these time estimates or suggestions for making these forms simpler, we would be happy to hear from you. You can write to the Tax Products Coordinating Committee, Western Area Distribution Center, Rancho Cordova, CA 95743-0001. **Do not** send the tax form to this address. Instead, see **Where To File** on page 4.

Codes for Principal Business Activity and Principal Product or Service

This list of Principal Business Activities and their associated codes is designed to classify an enterprise by the type of activity in which it is engaged to facilitate the administration of the Internal Revenue Code. These Principal Business Activity Codes are based on the North American Industry Classification System.

Using the list of activities and codes below, determine from which activity the business derives the largest percentage of its "total receipts." Total receipts is defined as the sum of gross receipts or sales (page 1, line 1a); all other income (page 1, lines 4 through 7); income reported on Schedule K, lines 3a, 4a, 4b(2), and 4c; income or net gain reported on Schedule K, lines 4d(2), 4e(2), 4f, 6b, and 7; and income or net gain reported on Form 8825, lines 2, 19, and 20a. If the business purchases raw materials and supplies them to a subcontractor

to produce the finished product, but retains title to the product, the business is considered a manufacturer and must use one of the manufacturing codes (311110 – 339900).

Once the Principal Business Activity is determined, enter the six-digit code from the list below on page 1, item C. Also enter a brief description of the business activity in item A and the principal product or service of the business in item B.

Code		Code		Code		Code	
Agriculture, Forestry, Fishing and Hunting		237310	Highway, Street, & Bridge Construction	321900	Other Wood Product Mfg	333200	Industrial Machinery Mfg
Crop Production		237990	Other Heavy & Civil Engineering Construction	**Paper Manufacturing**		333310	Commercial & Service Industry Machinery Mfg
111100	Oilseed & Grain Farming	**Specialty Trade Contractors**		322100	Pulp, Paper, & Paperboard Mills	333410	Ventilation, Heating, Air-Conditioning, & Commercial Refrigeration Equipment Mfg
111210	Vegetable & Melon Farming (including potatoes & yams)	238100	Foundation, Structure, & Building Exterior Contractors	322200	Converted Paper Product Mfg		
111300	Fruit & Tree Nut Farming		(including framing carpentry, masonry, glass, roofing, & siding)	**Printing and Related Support Activities**		333510	Metalworking Machinery Mfg
111400	Greenhouse, Nursery, & Floriculture Production			323100	Printing & Related Support Activities	333610	Engine, Turbine & Power Transmission Equipment Mfg
111900	Other Crop Farming (including tobacco, cotton, sugarcane, hay, peanut, sugar beet & all other crop farming)	238210	Electrical Contractors	**Petroleum and Coal Products Manufacturing**		333900	Other General Purpose Machinery Mfg
		238220	Plumbing, Heating, & Air-Conditioning Contractors	324110	Petroleum Refineries (including integrated)	**Computer and Electronic Product Manufacturing**	
Animal Production		238290	Other Building Equipment Contractors	324120	Asphalt Paving, Roofing, & Saturated Materials Mfg	334110	Computer & Peripheral Equipment Mfg
112111	Beef Cattle Ranching & Farming	238300	Building Finishing Contractors (including drywall, insulation, painting, wallcovering, flooring, tile, & finish carpentry)	324190	Other Petroleum & Coal Products Mfg	334210	Communications Equipment Mfg
112112	Cattle Feedlots			**Chemical Manufacturing**		334310	Audio & Video Equipment Mfg
112120	Dairy Cattle & Milk Production			325100	Basic Chemical Mfg		
112210	Hog & Pig Farming	238900	Other Specialty Trade Contractors (including site preparation)	325200	Resin, Synthetic Rubber, & Artificial & Synthetic Fibers & Filaments Mfg	334410	Semiconductor & Other Electronic Component Mfg
112300	Poultry & Egg Production					334500	Navigational, Measuring, Electromedical, & Control Instruments Mfg
112400	Sheep & Goat Farming			325300	Pesticide, Fertilizer, & Other Agricultural Chemical Mfg		
112510	Animal Aquaculture (including shellfish & finfish farms & hatcheries)	**Manufacturing**		325410	Pharmaceutical & Medicine Mfg	334610	Manufacturing & Reproducing Magnetic & Optical Media
		Food Manufacturing					
112900	Other Animal Production	311110	Animal Food Mfg	325500	Paint, Coating, & Adhesive Mfg	**Electrical Equipment, Appliance, and Component Manufacturing**	
Forestry and Logging		311200	Grain & Oilseed Milling	325600	Soap, Cleaning Compound, & Toilet Preparation Mfg	335100	Electric Lighting Equipment Mfg
113110	Timber Tract Operations	311300	Sugar & Confectionery Product Mfg				
113210	Forest Nurseries & Gathering of Forest Products	311400	Fruit & Vegetable Preserving & Specialty Food Mfg	325900	Other Chemical Product & Preparation Mfg	335200	Household Appliance Mfg
113310	Logging	311500	Dairy Product Mfg	**Plastics and Rubber Products Manufacturing**		335310	Electrical Equipment Mfg
Fishing, Hunting and Trapping		311610	Animal Slaughtering and Processing	326100	Plastics Product Mfg	335900	Other Electrical Equipment & Component Mfg
114110	Fishing			326200	Rubber Product Mfg	**Transportation Equipment Manufacturing**	
114210	Hunting & Trapping	311710	Seafood Product Preparation & Packaging	**Nonmetallic Mineral Product Manufacturing**		336100	Motor Vehicle Mfg
Support Activities for Agriculture and Forestry		311800	Bakeries & Tortilla Mfg	327100	Clay Product & Refractory Mfg	336210	Motor Vehicle Body & Trailer Mfg
115110	Support Activities for Crop Production (including cotton ginning, soil preparation, planting, & cultivating)	311900	Other Food Mfg (including coffee, tea, flavorings & seasonings)	327210	Glass & Glass Product Mfg	336300	Motor Vehicle Parts Mfg
		Beverage and Tobacco Product Manufacturing		327300	Cement & Concrete Product Mfg	336410	Aerospace Product & Parts Mfg
115210	Support Activities for Animal Production	312110	Soft Drink & Ice Mfg	327400	Lime & Gypsum Product Mfg	336510	Railroad Rolling Stock Mfg
		312120	Breweries	327900	Other Nonmetallic Mineral Product Mfg	336610	Ship & Boat Building
115310	Support Activities For Forestry	312130	Wineries			336990	Other Transportation Equipment Mfg
		312140	Distilleries	**Primary Metal Manufacturing**			
Mining		312200	Tobacco Manufacturing	331110	Iron & Steel Mills & Ferroalloy Mfg	**Furniture and Related Product Manufacturing**	
211110	Oil & Gas Extraction	**Textile Mills and Textile Product Mills**		331200	Steel Product Mfg from Purchased Steel	337000	Furniture & Related Product Manufacturing
212110	Coal Mining	313000	Textile Mills			**Miscellaneous Manufacturing**	
212200	Metal Ore Mining	314000	Textile Product Mills	331310	Alumina & Aluminum Production & Processing	339110	Medical Equipment & Supplies Mfg
212310	Stone Mining & Quarrying	**Apparel Manufacturing**		331400	Nonferrous Metal (except Aluminum) Production & Processing	339900	Other Miscellaneous Manufacturing
212320	Sand, Gravel, Clay, & Ceramic & Refractory Minerals Mining & Quarrying	315100	Apparel Knitting Mills				
		315210	Cut & Sew Apparel Contractors	331500	Foundries		
212390	Other Nonmetallic Mineral Mining & Quarrying	315220	Men's & Boys' Cut & Sew Apparel Mfg	**Fabricated Metal Product Manufacturing**		**Wholesale Trade**	
213110	Support Activities for Mining	315230	Women's & Girls' Cut & Sew Apparel Mfg	332110	Forging & Stamping	**Merchant Wholesalers, Durable Goods**	
				332210	Cutlery & Handtool Mfg	423100	Motor Vehicle & Motor Vehicle Parts & Supplies
Utilities		315290	Other Cut & Sew Apparel Mfg	332300	Architectural & Structural Metals Mfg		
221100	Electric Power Generation, Transmission & Distribution	315990	Apparel Accessories & Other Apparel Mfg	332400	Boiler, Tank, & Shipping Container Mfg	423200	Furniture & Home Furnishings
221210	Natural Gas Distribution	**Leather and Allied Product Manufacturing**		332510	Hardware Mfg	423300	Lumber & Other Construction Materials
221300	Water, Sewage & Other Systems	316110	Leather & Hide Tanning & Finishing	332610	Spring & Wire Product Mfg	423400	Professional & Commercial Equipment & Supplies
		316210	Footwear Mfg (including rubber & plastics)	332700	Machine Shops; Turned Product; & Screw, Nut, & Bolt Mfg	423500	Metal & Mineral (except Petroleum)
Construction							
Construction of Buildings		316990	Other Leather & Allied Product Mfg	332810	Coating, Engraving, Heat Treating, & Allied Activities	423600	Electrical & Electronic Goods
236110	Residential Building Construction	**Wood Product Manufacturing**		332900	Other Fabricated Metal Product Mfg	423700	Hardware, & Plumbing & Heating Equipment & Supplies
236200	Nonresidential Building Construction	321110	Sawmills & Wood Preservation	**Machinery Manufacturing**			
Heavy and Civil Engineering Construction		321210	Veneer, Plywood, & Engineered Wood Product Mfg	333100	Agriculture, Construction, & Mining Machinery Mfg		
237100	Utility System Construction						
237210	Land Subdivision						

Codes for Principal Business Activity and Principal Product or Service *(continued)*

Code	
423800	Machinery, Equipment, & Supplies
423910	Sporting & Recreational Goods & Supplies
423920	Toy & Hobby Goods & Supplies
423930	Recyclable Materials
423940	Jewelry, Watch, Precious Stone, & Precious Metals
423990	Other Miscellaneous Durable Goods

Merchant Wholesalers, Nondurable Goods

Code	
424100	Paper & Paper Products
424210	Drugs & Druggists' Sundries
424300	Apparel, Piece Goods, & Notions
424400	Grocery & Related Products
424500	Farm Product Raw Materials
424600	Chemical & Allied Products
424700	Petroleum & Petroleum Products
424800	Beer, Wine, & Distilled Alcoholic Beverages
424910	Farm Supplies
424920	Book, Periodical, & Newspapers
424930	Flower, Nursery Stock, & Florists' Supplies
424940	Tobacco & Tobacco Products
424950	Paint, Varnish, & Supplies
424990	Other Miscellaneous Nondurable Goods

Wholesale Electronic Markets and Agents and Brokers

Code	
425110	Business to Business Electronic Markets
425120	Wholesale Trade Agents & Brokers

Retail Trade

Motor Vehicle and Parts Dealers

Code	
441110	New Car Dealers
441120	Used Car Dealers
441210	Recreational Vehicle Dealers
441221	Motorcycle Dealers
441222	Boat Dealers
441229	All Other Motor Vehicle Dealers
441300	Automotive Parts, Accessories, & Tire Stores

Furniture and Home Furnishings Stores

Code	
442110	Furniture Stores
442210	Floor Covering Stores
442291	Window Treatment Stores
442299	All Other Home Furnishings Stores

Electronics and Appliance Stores

Code	
443111	Household Appliance Stores
443112	Radio, Television, & Other Electronics Stores
443120	Computer & Software Stores
443130	Camera & Photographic Supplies Stores

Building Material and Garden Equipment and Supplies Dealers

Code	
444110	Home Centers
444120	Paint & Wallpaper Stores
444130	Hardware Stores
444190	Other Building Material Dealers
444200	Lawn & Garden Equipment & Supplies Stores

Food and Beverage Stores

Code	
445110	Supermarkets and Other Grocery (except Convenience) Stores
445120	Convenience Stores
445210	Meat Markets
445220	Fish & Seafood Markets
445230	Fruit & Vegetable Markets
445291	Baked Goods Stores
445292	Confectionery & Nut Stores
445299	All Other Specialty Food Stores
445310	Beer, Wine, & Liquor Stores

Health and Personal Care Stores

Code	
446110	Pharmacies & Drug Stores
446120	Cosmetics, Beauty Supplies, & Perfume Stores
446130	Optical Goods Stores
446190	Other Health & Personal Care Stores

Gasoline Stations

Code	
447100	Gasoline Stations (including convenience stores with gas)

Clothing and Clothing Accessories Stores

Code	
448110	Men's Clothing Stores
448120	Women's Clothing Stores
448130	Children's & Infants' Clothing Stores
448140	Family Clothing Stores
448150	Clothing Accessories Stores
448190	Other Clothing Stores
448210	Shoe Stores
448310	Jewelry Stores
448320	Luggage & Leather Goods Stores

Sporting Goods, Hobby, Book, and Music Stores

Code	
451110	Sporting Goods Stores
451120	Hobby, Toy, & Game Stores
451130	Sewing, Needlework, & Piece Goods Stores
451140	Musical Instrument & Supplies Stores
451211	Book Stores
451212	News Dealers & Newsstands
451220	Prerecorded Tape, Compact Disc, & Record Stores

General Merchandise Stores

Code	
452110	Department Stores
452900	Other General Merchandise Stores

Miscellaneous Store Retailers

Code	
453110	Florists
453210	Office Supplies & Stationery Stores
453220	Gift, Novelty, & Souvenir Stores
453310	Used Merchandise Stores
453910	Pet & Pet Supplies Stores
453920	Art Dealers
453930	Manufactured (Mobile) Home Dealers
453990	All Other Miscellaneous Store Retailers (including tobacco, candle, & trophy shops)

Nonstore Retailers

Code	
454110	Electronic Shopping & Mail-Order Houses
454210	Vending Machine Operators
454311	Heating Oil Dealers
454312	Liquefied Petroleum Gas (Bottled Gas) Dealers
454319	Other Fuel Dealers
454390	Other Direct Selling Establishments (including door-to-door retailing, frozen food plan providers, party plan merchandisers, & coffee-break service providers)

Transportation and Warehousing

Air, Rail, and Water Transportation

Code	
481000	Air Transportation
482110	Rail Transportation
483000	Water Transportation

Truck Transportation

Code	
484110	General Freight Trucking, Local
484120	General Freight Trucking, Long-distance
484200	Specialized Freight Trucking

Transit and Ground Passenger Transportation

Code	
485110	Urban Transit Systems
485210	Interurban & Rural Bus Transportation
485310	Taxi Service

Code	
485320	Limousine Service
485410	School & Employee Bus Transportation
485510	Charter Bus Industry
485990	Other Transit & Ground Passenger Transportation

Pipeline Transportation

Code	
486000	Pipeline Transportation

Scenic & Sightseeing Transportation

Code	
487000	Scenic & Sightseeing Transportation

Support Activities for Transportation

Code	
488100	Support Activities for Air Transportation
488210	Support Activities for Rail Transportation
488300	Support Activities for Water Transportation
488410	Motor Vehicle Towing
488490	Other Support Activities for Road Transportation
488510	Freight Transportation Arrangement
488990	Other Support Activities for Transportation

Couriers and Messengers

Code	
492110	Couriers
492210	Local Messengers & Local Delivery

Warehousing and Storage

Code	
493100	Warehousing & Storage (except lessors of miniwarehouses & self-storage units)

Information

Publishing Industries (except Internet)

Code	
511110	Newspaper Publishers
511120	Periodical Publishers
511130	Book Publishers
511140	Directory & Mailing List Publishers
511190	Other Publishers
511210	Software Publishers

Motion Picture and Sound Recording Industries

Code	
512100	Motion Picture & Video Industries (except video rental)
512200	Sound Recording Industries

Broadcasting (except Internet)

Code	
515100	Radio & Television Broadcasting
515210	Cable & Other Subscription Programming

Internet Publishing and Broadcasting

Code	
516110	Internet Publishing & Broadcasting

Telecommunications

Code	
517000	Telecommunications (including paging, cellular, satellite, cable & other program distribution, resellers, & other telecommunications)

Internet Service Providers, Web Search Portals, and Data Processing Services

Code	
518111	Internet Service Providers
518112	Web Search Portals
518210	Data Processing, Hosting, & Related Services

Other Information Services

Code	
519100	Other Information Services (including news syndicates & libraries)

Finance and Insurance

Depository Credit Intermediation

Code	
522110	Commercial Banking
522120	Savings Institutions
522130	Credit Unions
522190	Other Depository Credit Intermediation

Nondepository Credit Intermediation

Code	
522210	Credit Card Issuing
522220	Sales Financing
522291	Consumer Lending
522292	Real Estate Credit (including mortgage bankers & originators)
522293	International Trade Financing
522294	Secondary Market Financing
522298	All Other Nondepository Credit Intermediation

Activities Related to Credit Intermediation

Code	
522300	Activities Related to Credit Intermediation (including loan brokers, check clearing, & money transmitting)

Securities, Commodity Contracts, and Other Financial Investments and Related Activities

Code	
523110	Investment Banking & Securities Dealing
523120	Securities Brokerage
523130	Commodity Contracts Dealing
523140	Commodity Contracts Brokerage
523210	Securities & Commodity Exchanges
523900	Other Financial Investment Activities (including portfolio management & investment advice)

Insurance Carriers and Related Activities

Code	
524140	Direct Life, Health, & Medical Insurance & Reinsurance Carriers
524150	Direct Insurance & Reinsurance (except Life, Health & Medical) Carriers
524210	Insurance Agencies & Brokerages
524290	Other Insurance Related Activities (including third-party administration of insurance and pension funds)

Funds, Trusts, and Other Financial Vehicles

Code	
525100	Insurance & Employee Benefit Funds
525910	Open-End Investment Funds (Form 1120-RIC)
525920	Trusts, Estates, & Agency Accounts
525930	Real Estate Investment Trusts (Form 1120-REIT)
525990	Other Financial Vehicles (including closed-end investment funds)

"Offices of Bank Holding Companies" and "Offices of Other Holding Companies" are located under **Management of Companies (Holding Companies)** on page 34.

Real Estate and Rental and Leasing

Real Estate

Code	
531110	Lessors of Residential Buildings & Dwellings
531114	Cooperative Housing
531120	Lessors of Nonresidential Buildings (except Miniwarehouses)
531130	Lessors of Miniwarehouses & Self-Storage Units
531190	Lessors of Other Real Estate Property
531210	Offices of Real Estate Agents & Brokers
531310	Real Estate Property Managers
531320	Offices of Real Estate Appraisers
531390	Other Activities Related to Real Estate

Rental and Leasing Services

Code	
532100	Automotive Equipment Rental & Leasing

Codes for Principal Business Activity and Principal Product or Service *(continued)*

Code		Code		Code		Code	
532210	Consumer Electronics & Appliances Rental	**Management of Companies (Holding Companies)**		621399	Offices of All Other Miscellaneous Health Practitioners	721120	Casino Hotels
532220	Formal Wear & Costume Rental	551111	Offices of Bank Holding Companies	**Outpatient Care Centers**		721191	Bed & Breakfast Inns
532230	Video Tape & Disc Rental	551112	Offices of Other Holding Companies	621410	Family Planning Centers	721199	All Other Traveler Accommodation
532290	Other Consumer Goods Rental			621420	Outpatient Mental Health & Substance Abuse Centers	721210	RV (Recreational Vehicle) Parks & Recreational Camps
532310	General Rental Centers	**Administrative and Support and Waste Management and Remediation Services**		621491	HMO Medical Centers	721310	Rooming & Boarding Houses
532400	Commercial & Industrial Machinery & Equipment Rental & Leasing	**Administrative and Support Services**		621492	Kidney Dialysis Centers	**Food Services and Drinking Places**	
Lessors of Nonfinancial Intangible Assets (except copyrighted works)		561110	Office Administrative Services	621493	Freestanding Ambulatory Surgical & Emergency Centers	722110	Full-Service Restaurants
533110	Lessors of Nonfinancial Intangible Assets (except copyrighted works)	561210	Facilities Support Services	621498	All Other Outpatient Care Centers	722210	Limited-Service Eating Places
		561300	Employment Services	**Medical and Diagnostic Laboratories**		722300	Special Food Services (including food service contractors & caterers)
Professional, Scientific, and Technical Services		561410	Document Preparation Services	621510	Medical & Diagnostic Laboratories	722410	Drinking Places (Alcoholic Beverages)
Legal Services		561420	Telephone Call Centers	**Home Health Care Services**		**Other Services**	
541110	Offices of Lawyers	561430	Business Service Centers (including private mail centers & copy shops)	621610	Home Health Care Services	**Repair and Maintenance**	
541190	Other Legal Services			**Other Ambulatory Health Care Services**		811110	Automotive Mechanical & Electrical Repair & Maintenance
Accounting, Tax Preparation, Bookkeeping, and Payroll Services		561440	Collection Agencies	621900	Other Ambulatory Health Care Services (including ambulance services & blood & organ banks)	811120	Automotive Body, Paint, Interior, & Glass Repair
541211	Offices of Certified Public Accountants	561450	Credit Bureaus			811190	Other Automotive Repair & Maintenance (including oil change & lubrication shops & car washes)
541213	Tax Preparation Services	561490	Other Business Support Services (including repossession services, court reporting, & stenotype services)	**Hospitals**			
541214	Payroll Services			622000	Hospitals	811210	Electronic & Precision Equipment Repair & Maintenance
541219	Other Accounting Services			**Nursing and Residential Care Facilities**			
Architectural, Engineering, and Related Services		561500	Travel Arrangement & Reservation Services	623000	Nursing & Residential Care Facilities	811310	Commercial & Industrial Machinery & Equipment (except Automotive & Electronic) Repair & Maintenance
541310	Architectural Services	561600	Investigation & Security Services	**Social Assistance**			
541320	Landscape Architecture Services	561710	Exterminating & Pest Control Services	624100	Individual & Family Services	811410	Home & Garden Equipment & Appliance Repair & Maintenance
541330	Engineering Services	561720	Janitorial Services	624200	Community Food & Housing, & Emergency & Other Relief Services	811420	Reupholstery & Furniture Repair
541340	Drafting Services	561730	Landscaping Services				
541350	Building Inspection Services	561740	Carpet & Upholstery Cleaning Services	624310	Vocational Rehabilitation Services	811430	Footwear & Leather Goods Repair
541360	Geophysical Surveying & Mapping Services	561790	Other Services to Buildings & Dwellings	624410	Child Day Care Services	811490	Other Personal & Household Goods Repair & Maintenance
541370	Surveying & Mapping (except Geophysical) Services	561900	Other Support Services (including packaging & labeling services, & convention & trade show organizers)	**Arts, Entertainment, and Recreation**		**Personal and Laundry Services**	
541380	Testing Laboratories			**Performing Arts, Spectator Sports, and Related Industries**		812111	Barber Shops
Specialized Design Services		**Waste Management and Remediation Services**		711100	Performing Arts Companies	812112	Beauty Salon's
541400	Specialized Design Services (including interior, industrial, graphic, & fashion design)	562000	Waste Management & Remediation Services	711210	Spectator Sports (including sports clubs & racetracks)	812113	Nail Salons
Computer Systems Design and Related Services				711300	Promoters of Performing Arts, Sports, & Similar Events	812190	Other Personal Care Services (including diet & weight reducing centers)
541511	Custom Computer Programming Services	**Educational Services**		711410	Agents & Managers for Artists, Athletes, Entertainers, & Other Public Figures	812210	Funeral Homes & Funeral Services
541512	Computer Systems Design Services	611000	Educational Services (including schools, colleges, & universities)	711510	Independent Artists, Writers, & Performers	812220	Cemeteries & Crematories
541513	Computer Facilities Management Services			**Museums, Historical Sites, and Similar Institutions**		812310	Coin-Operated Laundries & Drycleaners
541519	Other Computer Related Services	**Health Care and Social Assistance**		712100	Museums, Historical Sites, & Similar Institutions	812320	Drycleaning & Laundry Services (except Coin-Operated)
Other Professional, Scientific, and Technical Services		**Offices of Physicians and Dentists**		**Amusement, Gambling, and Recreation Industries**		812330	Linen & Uniform Supply
541600	Management, Scientific, & Technical Consulting Services	621111	Offices of Physicians (except mental health specialists)	713100	Amusement Parks & Arcades	812910	Pet Care (except Veterinary) Services
541700	Scientific Research & Development Services	621112	Offices of Physicians, Mental Health Specialists	713200	Gambling Industries Code	812920	Photofinishing
541800	Advertising & Related Services	621210	Offices of Dentists	713900	Other Amusement & Recreation Industries (including golf courses, skiing facilities, marinas, fitness centers, & bowling centers)	812930	Parking Lots & Garages
541910	Marketing Research & Public Opinion Polling	**Offices of Other Health Practitioners**				812990	All Other Personal Services
541920	Photographic Services	621310	Offices of Chiropractors			**Religious, Grantmaking, Civic, Professional, and Similar Organizations**	
541930	Translation & Interpretation Services	621320	Offices of Optometrists	**Accommodation and Food Services**		813000	Religious, Grantmaking, Civic, Professional, & Similar Organizations (including condominium and homeowners associations)
541930	Translation & Interpretation Services	621330	Offices of Mental Health Practitioners (except Physicians)	**Accommodation**			
541940	Veterinary Services	621340	Offices of Physical, Occupational & Speech Therapists, & Audiologists	721110	Hotels (except Casino Hotels) & Motels		
541990	All Other Professional, Scientific, & Technical Services	621391	Offices of Podiatrists				

Index

20**03**

Department of the Treasury
Internal Revenue Service

Partner's Instructions for Schedule K-1 (Form 1065)

Partner's Share of Income, Credits, Deductions, etc. (For Partner's Use Only)

Section references are to the Internal Revenue Code unless otherwise noted.

Changes To Note

• Under the Jobs and Growth Tax Relief Reconciliation Act of 2003, the general tax rates applicable to net capital gain for individuals have been reduced. The new gains rates also apply to qualified dividend income under new section 1(h)(11). The new rates apply to sales, other dispositions, and installment payments received after May 5, 2003. Schedule K-1 has been revised to take into account the partner's shares of these gains and dividends.

• The instructions for line 25 of Schedule K-1 have been revised to change how dispositions of property are reported if the partnership previously passed through a section 179 expense deduction to any of its partners for the property.

• On page 12, under **Supplemental Information, Line 25,** we added item 21 for collectibles gain (loss), and item 22 for qualified 5-year gain. These items were added due to the deletion of these specific line items from Schedule K-1.

General Instructions

Purpose of Schedule K-1

The partnership uses Schedule K-1 to report your share of the partnership's income, credits, deductions, etc. **Keep it for your records. Do not file it with your tax return.** The partnership has filed a copy with the IRS.

Although the partnership generally is not subject to income tax, you are liable for tax on your share of the partnership income, whether or not distributed. Include your share on your tax return if a return is required. Use these instructions to help you report the items shown on Schedule K-1 on your tax return.

The amount of loss and deduction that you may claim on your tax return may be less than the amount reported on Schedule K-1. **It is the partner's responsibility to consider and apply any applicable limitations.** See **Limitations on Losses, Deductions, and Credits** beginning on page 2 for more information.

Where "attach schedule" appears beside a line item on Schedule K-1, see

either the schedule that the partnership has attached for that line or line 25 of Schedule K-1.

Inconsistent Treatment of Items

Generally, you must report partnership items shown on your Schedule K-1 (and any attached schedules) the same way that the partnership treated the items on its return. This rule does not apply if your partnership is within the "small partnership exception" and does not elect to have the tax treatment of partnership items determined at the partnership level.

If the treatment on your original or amended return is inconsistent with the partnership's treatment, or if the partnership was required to but has not filed a return, you must file **Form 8082,** Notice of Inconsistent Treatment or Administrative Adjustment Request (AAR), with your original or amended return to identify and explain any inconsistency (or to note that a partnership return has not been filed).

If you are required to file Form 8082 but fail to do so, you may be subject to the accuracy-related penalty. This penalty is in addition to any tax that results from making your amount or treatment of the item consistent with that shown on the partnership's return. Any deficiency that results from making the amounts consistent may be assessed immediately.

Errors

If you believe the partnership has made an error on your Schedule K-1, notify the partnership and ask for a corrected Schedule K-1. **Do not** change any items on your copy of Schedule K-1. Be sure that the partnership sends a copy of the corrected Schedule K-1 to the IRS. If you are a partner in a partnership that does not meet the small partnership exception and you report any partnership item on your return in a manner different from the way the partnership reported it, you must file Form 8082.

Sale or Exchange of Partnership Interest

Generally, a partner who sells or exchanges a partnership interest in a

section 751(a) exchange must notify the partnership, in writing, within 30 days of the exchange (or, if earlier, by January 15 of the calendar year following the calendar year in which the exchange occurred). A "section 751(a) exchange" is any sale or exchange of a partnership interest in which any money or other property received by the partner in exchange for that partner's interest is attributable to unrealized receivables (as defined in section 751(c)) or inventory items (as defined in section 751(d)).

The written notice to the partnership must include the names and addresses of both parties to the exchange, the identifying numbers of the transferor and (if known) of the transferee, and the exchange date.

An exception to this rule is made for sales or exchanges of publicly traded partnership interests for which a broker is required to file **Form 1099-B,** Proceeds From Broker and Barter Exchange Transactions.

If a partner is required to notify the partnership of a section 751(a) exchange but fails to do so, a $50 penalty may be imposed for each such failure. However, no penalty will be imposed if the partner can show that the failure was due to reasonable cause and not willful neglect.

Nominee Reporting

Any person who holds, directly or indirectly, an interest in a partnership as a nominee for another person must furnish a written statement to the partnership by the last day of the month following the end of the partnership's tax year. This statement must include the name, address, and identifying number of the nominee and such other person, description of the partnership interest held as nominee for that person, and other information required by Temporary Regulations section 1.6031(c)-1T. A nominee that fails to furnish this statement must furnish to the person for whom the nominee holds the partnership interest a copy of Schedule K-1 and related information within 30 days of receiving it from the partnership.

A nominee who fails to furnish when due all the information required by Temporary Regulations section

Cat. No. 11396N

1.6031(c)-1T, or who furnishes incorrect information, is subject to a $50 penalty for each statement for which a failure occurs. The maximum penalty is $100,000 for all such failures during a calendar year. If the nominee intentionally disregards the requirement to report correct information, each $50 penalty increases to $100 or, if greater, 10% of the aggregate amount of items required to be reported, and the $100,000 maximum does not apply.

International Boycotts

Every partnership that had operations in, or related to, a boycotting country, company, or a national of a country must file **Form 5713,** International Boycott Report.

If the partnership cooperated with an international boycott, it must give you a copy of its Form 5713. You must file your own Form 5713 to report the partnership's activities and any other boycott operations that you may have. You may lose certain tax benefits if the partnership participated in, or cooperated with, an international boycott. See Form 5713 and the instructions for more information.

Definitions

General Partner

A general partner is a partner who is personally liable for partnership debts.

Limited Partner

A limited partner is a partner in a partnership formed under a state limited partnership law, whose personal liability for partnership debts is limited to the amount of money or other property that the partner contributed or is required to contribute to the partnership. Some members of other entities, such as domestic or foreign business trusts or limited liability companies that are classified as partnerships, may be treated as limited partners for certain purposes. See, e.g., Temporary Regulations section 1.469-5T(e)(3), which treats all members with limited liability as limited partners for purposes of section 469(h)(2).

Nonrecourse Loans

Nonrecourse loans are those liabilities of the partnership for which no partner bears the economic risk of loss.

Elections

Generally, the partnership decides how to figure taxable income from its operations. However, certain elections are made by you separately on your income tax return and not by the partnership. These elections are made under the following code sections:
• Section 59(e) (deduction of certain qualified expenditures ratably over the period of time specified in that section). For more information, see the instructions for lines 18a and 18b of Schedule K-1 on page 10.
• Section 108(b)(5) (income from discharge of indebtedness).

• Section 617 (deduction and recapture of certain mining exploration expenditures).
• Section 901 (foreign tax credit).
If the partnership attaches a statement to Schedule K-1 indicating that it has changed its tax year and that you may elect to report your distributive share of the income attributable to that change ratably over 4 tax years, see Rev. Proc. 2003-79, 2003-45 I.R.B. 1036, for details on making the election. To make the election, you must file **Form 8082,** Notice of Inconsistent Treatment or Administrative Adjustment Request, with your income tax return for each of the 4 tax years. File Form 8082 for this purpose in accordance with Rev. Proc. 2003-79 instead of the Form 8082 instructions.

Additional Information

For more information on the treatment of partnership income, credits, deductions, etc., see **Pub. 541,** Partnerships, and **Pub. 535,** Business Expenses.

To get forms and publications, see the instructions for your tax return.

Limitations on Losses, Deductions, and Credits

There are three separate potential limitations on the amount of partnership losses that you may deduct on your return. These limitations and the order in which you must apply them are as follows: the basis rules, the at-risk limitations, and the passive activity limitations. Each of these limitations is discussed separately below.

Other limitations may apply to specific deductions (e.g., the section 179 expense deduction). Generally, these limitations apply before the basis, at-risk, and passive loss limitations.

Basis Rules

Generally, you may **not** claim your share of a partnership loss (including a capital loss) to the extent that it is greater than the adjusted basis of your partnership interest at the end of the partnership's tax year.

The partnership is not responsible for keeping the information needed to figure the basis of your partnership interest. Although the partnership does provide an analysis of the changes to your capital account in Item J of Schedule K-1, that information is based on the partnership's books and records and cannot be used to figure your basis.

You can figure the adjusted basis of your partnership interest by adding items that increase your basis and then subtracting items that decrease your basis.

Items that **increase** your basis are:
• Money and your adjusted basis in property contributed to the partnership.
• Your share of the increase in the partnership's liabilities (or your individual liabilities caused by your assumption of partnership liabilities).

• Your share of the partnership's income (including tax-exempt income).
• Your share of the excess of the deductions for depletion over the basis of the property subject to depletion.
Items that **decrease** your basis (but not below zero) are:
• Money and the adjusted basis of property distributed to you.
• Your share of the decrease in the partnership's liabilities (or your individual liabilities assumed by the partnership).
• Your share of the partnership's losses (including capital losses).
• Your share of the partnership's section 179 expense deduction (even if you cannot deduct all of it).
• Your share of the partnership's nondeductible expenses.
• The amount of your deduction for depletion of any partnership oil and gas property (not to exceed your allocable share of the adjusted basis of that property).
For more details on the basis rules, see Pub. 541.

At-Risk Limitations

Generally, if you have **(a)** a loss or other deduction from any activity carried on as a trade or business or for the production of income by the partnership and **(b)** amounts in the activity for which you are not at risk, you will have to complete **Form 6198,** At-Risk Limitations, to figure your allowable loss.

The at-risk rules generally limit the amount of loss and other deductions that you can claim to the amount you could actually lose in the activity. These losses and deductions include a loss on the disposition of assets and the section 179 expense deduction. However, if you acquired your partnership interest before 1987, the at-risk rules do not apply to losses from an activity of holding real property placed in service before 1987 by the partnership. The activity of holding mineral property does not qualify for this exception. The partnership should identify on an attachment to Schedule K-1 the amount of any losses that are not subject to the at-risk limitations.

Generally, you are not at risk for amounts such as the following:
• Nonrecourse loans used to finance the activity, to acquire property used in the activity, or to acquire your interest in the activity, that are not secured by your own property (other than the property used in the activity). See the instructions for Item F on page 5 for the exception for qualified nonrecourse financing secured by real property.
• Cash, property, or borrowed amounts used in the activity (or contributed to the activity, or used to acquire your interest in the activity) that are protected against loss by a guarantee, stop-loss agreement, or other similar arrangement (excluding casualty insurance and insurance against tort liability).
• Amounts borrowed for use in the activity from a person who has an interest

in the activity, other than as a creditor, or who is related, under section 465(b)(3), to a person (other than you) having such an interest.

To help you complete Form 6198, the partnership should specify on an attachment to Schedule K-1 your share of the total pre-1976 losses from a section 465(c)(1) activity for which there existed a corresponding amount of nonrecourse liability at the end of the year in which the losses occurred. Also, you should get a separate statement of income, expenses, etc., for each activity from the partnership.

Passive Activity Limitations

Section 469 provides rules that limit the deduction of certain losses and credits. These rules apply to partners who:
• Are individuals, estates, trusts, closely held corporations, or personal service corporations and
• Have a passive activity loss or credit for the tax year.

Generally, passive activities include:

1. Trade or business activities in which you **did not** materially participate and

2. Activities that meet the definition of rental activities under Temporary Regulations section 1.469-1T(e)(3) and Regulations section 1.469-1(e)(3).

Passive activities **do not** include:

1. Trade or business activities in which you materially participated.

2. Rental real estate activities in which you materially participated if you were a "real estate professional" for the tax year. You were a **real estate professional** only if you met both of the following conditions:

a. More than half of the personal services you performed in trades or businesses were performed in real property trades or businesses in which you materially participated **and**

b. You performed more than 750 hours of services in real property trades or businesses in which you materially participated.

Note: *For a closely held C corporation (defined in section 465(a)(1)(B)), the above conditions are treated as met if more than 50% of the corporation's gross receipts were from real property trades or businesses in which the corporation materially participated.*

For purposes of this rule, each interest in rental real estate is a separate activity, unless you elect to treat all interests in rental real estate as one activity. For details on making this election, see the Instructions for Schedule E (Form 1040).

If you are married filing jointly, either you or your spouse must separately meet both of the above conditions, without taking into account services performed by the other spouse.

A real property trade or business is any real property development, redevelopment, construction, reconstruction, acquisition, conversion, rental, operation, management, leasing, or brokerage trade or business. Services

you performed as an employee are not treated as performed in a real property trade or business unless you owned more than 5% of the stock (or more than 5% of the capital or profits interest) in the employer.

3. Working interests in oil or gas wells if you were a general partner.

4. The rental of a dwelling unit any partner used for personal purposes during the year for more than the **greater of** 14 days or 10% of the number of days that the residence was rented at fair rental value.

5. Activities of trading personal property for the account of owners of interests in the activities.

If you are an individual, an estate, or a trust, and you have a passive activity loss or credit, use **Form 8582**, Passive Activity Loss Limitations, to figure your allowable passive losses and **Form 8582-CR**, Passive Activity Credit Limitations, to figure your allowable passive credits. For a corporation, use **Form 8810**, Corporate Passive Activity Loss and Credit Limitations. See the instructions for these forms for more information.

If the partnership had more than one activity, it will attach a statement to your Schedule K-1 that identifies each activity (trade or business activity, rental real estate activity, rental activity other than rental real estate, etc.) and specifies the income (loss), deductions, and credits from each activity.

Material participation. You must determine if you materially participated **(a)** in each trade or business activity held through the partnership and **(b)** if you were a real estate professional (defined above), in each rental real estate activity held through the partnership. **All determinations of material participation are made based on your participation during the partnership's tax year.**

Material participation standards for partners who are individuals are listed below. Special rules apply to certain retired or disabled farmers and to the surviving spouses of farmers. See the Instructions for Form 8582 for details.

Corporations should refer to the Instructions for Form 8810 for the material participation standards that apply to them.

Individuals (other than limited partners). If you are an individual (either a general partner or a limited partner who owned a general partnership interest at all times during the tax year), you materially participated in an activity only if one or more of the following apply:

1. You participated in the activity for more than 500 hours during the tax year.

2. Your participation in the activity for the tax year constituted substantially all the participation in the activity of all individuals (including individuals who are not owners of interests in the activity).

3. You participated in the activity for more than 100 hours during the tax year, and your participation in the activity for

the tax year was not less than the participation in the activity of any other individual (including individuals who were not owners of interests in the activity) for the tax year.

4. The activity was a significant participation activity for the tax year, and you participated in all significant participation activities (including activities outside the partnership) during the year for more than 500 hours. A **significant participation activity** is any trade or business activity in which you participated for more than 100 hours during the year and in which you did not materially participate under any of the material participation tests (other than this test 4).

5. You materially participated in the activity for any 5 tax years (whether or not consecutive) during the 10 tax years that immediately precede the tax year.

6. The activity was a personal service activity and you materially participated in the activity for any 3 tax years (whether or not consecutive) preceding the tax year. A **personal service activity** involves the performance of personal services in the fields of health, law, engineering, architecture, accounting, actuarial science, performing arts, consulting, or any other trade or business in which capital is not a material income-producing factor.

7. Based on all the facts and circumstances, you participated in the activity on a regular, continuous, and substantial basis during the tax year.

Limited partners. If you are a limited partner, you do not materially participate in an activity unless you meet one of the tests in paragraphs 1, 5, or 6 above.

Work counted toward material participation. Generally, any work that you or your spouse does in connection with an activity held through a partnership (where you own your partnership interest at the time the work is done) is counted toward material participation. However, work in connection with the activity is not counted toward material participation if either of the following applies.

1. The work is not the type of work that owners of the activity would usually do and one of the principal purposes of the work that you or your spouse does is to avoid the passive loss or credit limitations.

2. You do the work in your capacity as an investor and you are not directly involved in the day-to-day operations of the activity. Examples of work done as an investor that would not count toward material participation include:

a. Studying and reviewing financial statements or reports on operations of the activity.

b. Preparing or compiling summaries or analyses of the finances or operations of the activity for your own use.

c. Monitoring the finances or operations of the activity in a nonmanagerial capacity.

Effect of determination. If you determine that you materially participated in **(a)** a trade or business activity of the partnership or **(b)** if you were a real estate professional (defined above) in a rental real estate activity of the partnership, report the income (loss), deductions, and credits from that activity as indicated in either column (c) of Schedule K-1 or the instructions for each line.

If you determine that you did not materially participate in a trade or business activity of the partnership or if you have income (loss), deductions, or credits from a rental activity of the partnership (other than a rental real estate activity in which you materially participated as a real estate professional), the amounts from that activity are passive. Report passive income (losses), deductions, and credits as follows:

1. If you have an overall gain (the excess of income over deductions and losses, including any prior year unallowed loss) from a passive activity, report the income, deductions, and losses from the activity as indicated on Schedule K-1 or in these instructions.

2. If you have an overall loss (the excess of deductions and losses, including any prior year unallowed loss, over income) or credits from a passive activity, report the income, deductions, losses, and credits from **all** passive activities using the Instructions for Form 8582 or Form 8582-CR (or Form 8810), to see if your deductions, losses, and credits are limited under the passive activity rules.

Publicly traded partnerships. The passive activity limitations are applied separately for items (other than the low-income housing credit and the rehabilitation credit) from each publicly traded partnership (PTP). Thus, a net passive loss from a PTP may not be deducted from other passive income. Instead, a passive loss from a PTP is suspended and carried forward to be applied against passive income from the same PTP in later years. If the partner's entire interest in the PTP is completely disposed of, any unused losses are allowed in full in the year of disposition.

If you have an overall gain from a PTP, the net gain is nonpassive income. In addition, the nonpassive income is included in investment income to figure your investment interest expense deduction.

Do not report passive income, gains, or losses from a PTP on Form 8582. Instead, use the following rules to figure and report on the proper form or schedule your income, gains, and losses from passive activities that you held through each PTP you owned during the tax year.

1. Combine any current year income, gains and losses, and any prior year unallowed losses to see if you have an overall gain or loss from the PTP. Include only the same types of income and losses you would include in your net income or

loss from a non-PTP passive activity. See **Pub. 925,** Passive Activity and At-Risk Rules, for more details.

2. If you have an overall gain, the net gain portion (total gain minus total losses) is nonpassive income. On the form or schedule you normally use, report the net gain portion as nonpassive income and the remaining income and the total losses as passive income and loss. To the left of the entry space, write **"From PTP."** It is important to identify the nonpassive income because the nonpassive portion is included in modified adjusted gross income for purposes of figuring on Form 8582 the "special allowance" for active participation in a non-PTP rental real estate activity. In addition, the nonpassive income is included in investment income when figuring your investment interest expense deduction on Form 4952.

Example. If you have Schedule E income of $8,000, and a Form 4797 prior year unallowed loss of $3,500 from the passive activities of a particular PTP, you have a $4,500 overall gain ($8,000 – $3,500). On Schedule E, Part II, report the $4,500 net gain as nonpassive income in column (j). In column (g), report the remaining Schedule E gain of $3,500 ($8,000 – $4,500). On the appropriate line of Form 4797, report the prior year unallowed loss of $3,500. Be sure to write "From PTP" to the left of each entry space.

3. If you have an overall loss (but did not dispose of your entire interest in the PTP to an unrelated person in a fully taxable transaction during the year), the losses are allowed to the extent of the income, and the excess loss is carried forward to use in a future year when you have income to offset it. Report as a passive loss on the schedule or form you normally use the portion of the loss equal to the income. Report the income as passive income on the form or schedule you normally use.

Example. You have a Schedule E loss of $12,000 (current year losses plus prior year unallowed losses) and a Form 4797 gain of $7,200. Report the $7,200 gain on the appropriate line of Form 4797. On Schedule E, Part II, report $7,200 of the losses as a passive loss in column (f). Carry forward to 2004 the unallowed loss of $4,800 ($12,000 – $7,200).

If you have unallowed losses from more than one activity of the PTP or from the same activity of the PTP that must be reported on different forms, you must allocate the unallowed losses on a pro rata basis to figure the amount allowed from each activity or on each form.

Tax tip. To allocate and keep a record of the unallowed losses, use Worksheets 5, 6, and 7 of Form 8582. List each activity of the PTP in Worksheet 5. Enter the overall loss from each activity in column (a). Complete column (b) of Worksheet 5 according to its instructions. Multiply the total unallowed loss from the PTP by each ratio in column (b) and enter the result in column (c) of Worksheet 5.

Then, complete Worksheet 6 if all the loss from the same activity is to be reported on one form or schedule. Use Worksheet 7 instead of Worksheet 6 if you have more than one loss to be reported on different forms or schedules for the same activity. Enter the net loss plus any prior year unallowed losses in column (a) of Worksheet 6 (or Worksheet 7 if applicable). The losses in column (c) of Worksheet 6 (column (e) of Worksheet 7) are the allowed losses to report on the forms or schedules. Report both these losses and any income from the PTP on the forms and schedules you normally use.

4. If you have an overall loss and you disposed of your entire interest in the PTP to an unrelated person in a fully taxable transaction during the year, your losses (including prior year unallowed losses) allocable to the activity for the year are not limited by the passive loss rules. A fully taxable transaction is one in which you recognize all your realized gain or loss. Report the income and losses on the forms and schedules you normally use.

Note: For rules on the disposition of an entire interest reported using the installment method, see the Instructions for Form 8582.

Special allowance for a rental real estate activity. If you **actively participated** in a rental real estate activity, you may be able to deduct up to $25,000 of the loss from the activity from nonpassive income. This "special allowance" is an exception to the general rule disallowing losses in excess of income from passive activities. The special allowance is not available if you were married, file a separate return for the year, and did not live apart from your spouse at all times during the year.

Only individuals and qualifying estates can actively participate in a rental real estate activity. Estates (other than qualifying estates), trusts, and corporations cannot actively participate. Limited partners cannot actively participate unless future regulations provide an exception.

You are not considered to actively participate in a rental real estate activity if at any time during the tax year your interest (including your spouse's interest) in the activity was less than 10% (by value) of all interests in the activity.

Active participation is a less stringent requirement than material participation. You may be treated as actively participating if you participated, for example, in making management decisions or arranging for others to provide services (such as repairs) in a significant and bona fide sense. Management decisions that can count as active participation include approving new tenants, deciding rental terms, approving capital or repair expenditures, and other similar decisions.

An estate is a qualifying estate if the decedent would have satisfied the active participation requirement for the activity for the tax year the decedent died. A qualifying estate is treated as actively participating for tax years ending less than 2 years after the date of the decedent's death.

Modified adjusted gross income limitation. The maximum special allowance that single individuals and married individuals filing a joint return can qualify for is $25,000. The maximum is $12,500 for married individuals who file separate returns and who lived apart all times during the year. The maximum special allowance for which an estate can qualify is $25,000 reduced by the special allowance for which the surviving spouse qualifies.

If your modified adjusted gross income (defined below) is $100,000 or less ($50,000 or less if married filing separately), your loss is deductible up to the amount of the maximum special allowance referred to in the preceding paragraph. If your modified adjusted gross income is more than $100,000 (more than $50,000 if married filing separately), the special allowance is limited to 50% of the difference between $150,000 ($75,000 if married filing separately) and your modified adjusted gross income. When modified adjusted gross income is $150,000 or more ($75,000 or more if married filing separately), there is no special allowance.

Modified adjusted gross income is your adjusted gross income figured without taking into account:
• Any passive activity loss.
• Any rental real estate loss allowed under section 469(c)(7) to real estate professionals (as defined on page 3).
• Any taxable social security or equivalent railroad retirement benefits.
• Any deductible contributions to an IRA or certain other qualified retirement plans under section 219.
• The student loan interest deduction.
• The tuition and fees deduction.
• The deduction for one-half of self-employment taxes.
• The exclusion from income of interest from Series EE or I U.S. Savings Bonds used to pay higher education expenses.
• The exclusion of amounts received under an employer's adoption assistance program.

Commercial revitalization deduction. The special $25,000 allowance for the commercial revitalization deduction from rental real estate activities is not subject to the active participation rules or modified adjusted gross income limits discussed on page 4. See item 28 of the supplemental information instructions on page 12.

Special rules for certain other activities. If you have net income (loss), deductions, or credits from any activity to which special rules apply, the partnership will identify the activity and all amounts relating to it on Schedule K-1 or on an attachment.

If you have net income subject to recharacterization under Temporary Regulations section 1.469-2T(f) and Regulations section 1.469-2(f), report such amounts according to the Instructions for Form 8582 (or Form 8810).

If you have net income (loss), deductions, or credits from any of the following activities, treat such amounts as nonpassive and report them as instructed in column (c) of Schedule K-1 or in these instructions:
1. Working interests in oil and gas wells if you are a general partner.
2. The rental of a dwelling unit any partner used for personal purposes during the year for more than the greater of 14 days or 10% of the number of days that the residence was rented at fair rental value.
3. Trading personal property for the account of owners of interests in the activity.

Self-charged interest. The partnership will report any "self-charged" interest income or expense that resulted from loans between you and the partnership (or between the partnership and another partnership or S corporation if both entities have the same owners with the same proportional ownership interest in each entity). If there was more than one activity, the partnership will provide a statement allocating the interest income or expense with respect to each activity. The self-charged interest rules do not apply to your partnership interest if the partnership made an election under Regulations section 1.469-7(g) to avoid the application of these rules. See the Instructions for Form 8582 for more information.

Specific Instructions

General Information and Questions

Item F

Item F should show your share of the partnership's nonrecourse liabilities, partnership-level qualified nonrecourse financing, and other liabilities as of the end of the partnership's tax year. If you terminated your interest in the partnership during the tax year, Item F should show the share that existed immediately before the total disposition. A partner's "other liability" is any partnership liability for which a partner is personally liable.

Use the total of the three amounts for computing the adjusted basis of your partnership interest.

Generally, you may use only the amounts shown next to "Qualified nonrecourse financing" and "Other" to compute your amount at risk. **Do not** include any amounts that are not at risk if

such amounts are included in either of these categories.

If your partnership is engaged in two or more different types of activities subject to the at-risk provisions, or a combination of at-risk activities and any other activity, the partnership should give you a statement showing your share of nonrecourse liabilities, partnership-level qualified nonrecourse financing, and other liabilities for each activity.

Qualified nonrecourse financing secured by real property used in an activity of holding real property that is subject to the at-risk rules is treated as an amount at risk. **Qualified nonrecourse financing** generally includes financing for which no one is personally liable for repayment that is borrowed for use in an activity of holding real property and that is loaned or guaranteed by a Federal, state, or local government or borrowed from a "qualified" person.

Qualified persons include any persons actively and regularly engaged in the business of lending money, such as a bank or savings and loan association. Qualified persons generally **do not** include related parties (unless the nonrecourse financing is commercially reasonable and on substantially the same terms as loans involving unrelated persons), the seller of the property, or a person who receives a fee for the partnership's investment in the real property.

See Pub. 925 for more information on qualified nonrecourse financing.

Both the partnership and you must meet the qualified nonrecourse rules on this debt before you can include the amount shown next to "Qualified nonrecourse financing" in your at-risk computation.

See **Limitations on Losses, Deductions, and Credits** beginning on page 2 for more information on the at-risk limitations.

Item G

If the partnership is a registration-required tax shelter or has invested in a registration-required tax shelter, it should have completed Item G. If you claim or report any income, loss, deduction, or credit from a tax shelter, you must attach **Form 8271**, Investor Reporting of Tax Shelter Registration Number, to your tax return. If the partnership has invested in a tax shelter, it must give you a copy of its Form 8271 with your Schedule K-1. Use this information to complete your Form 8271.

If the partnership itself is a registration-required tax shelter, use the information on Schedule K-1 (name of the partnership, partnership identifying number, and tax shelter registration number) to complete your Form 8271.

Item H

If the box in Item H is checked, you are a partner in a publicly traded partnership and must follow the rules discussed on page 4 under **Publicly traded partnerships.**

Lines 1 Through 25

The amounts shown on lines 1 through 25 reflect your share of income, loss, credits, deductions, etc., from partnership business or rental activities without reference to limitations on losses or adjustments that may be required of you because of:

   1. The adjusted basis of your partnership interest,

   2. The amount for which you are at risk, or

   3. The passive activity limitations.

   For information on these provisions, see **Limitations on Losses, Deductions, and Credits** beginning on page 2.

   If you are an individual and the passive activity rules do not apply to the amounts shown on your Schedule K-1, take the amounts shown in column (b) and enter them on the lines on your tax return as indicated in column (c). If the passive activity rules do apply, report the amounts shown in column (b) as indicated in the line instructions.

   If you are not an individual, report the amounts in column (b) as instructed on your tax return.

   The line numbers in column (c) are references to forms in use for calendar year 2003. If you file your tax return on a calendar year basis, but your partnership files a return for a fiscal year, enter the amounts shown in column (b) on your tax return for the year in which the partnership's fiscal year ends. For example, if the partnership's tax year ends in February 2004, report the amounts in column (b) on your 2004 tax return.

   If you have losses, deductions, or credits from a prior year that were not deductible or usable because of certain limitations, such as the basis rules or the at-risk limitations, take them into account in determining your net income, loss, or credits for this year. However, except for passive activity losses and credits, **do not combine** the prior-year amounts with any amounts shown on this Schedule K-1 to get a net figure to report on any supporting schedules, statements, or forms attached to your return. Instead, report the amounts on the attached schedule, statement, or form on a year-by-year basis.

⚠️ **CAUTION** *If you have amounts other than those shown on Schedule K-1 to report on Schedule E (Form 1040), enter each item on a separate line of Part II of Schedule E.*

Income (Loss)

Line 1. Ordinary Income (Loss) From Trade or Business Activities

The amount reported for line 1 is your share of the ordinary income (loss) from the trade or business activities of the partnership. Generally, where you report this amount on Form 1040 depends on whether the amount is from an activity that is a passive activity to you. If you are an individual partner filing your 2003 Form 1040, find your situation below and report your line 1 income (loss) as instructed, after applying the basis and at-risk limitations on losses:

   1. Report line 1 income (loss) from partnership trade or business activities in which you materially participated on Schedule E (Form 1040), Part II, column (h) or (j).

   2. Report line 1 income (loss) from partnership trade or business activities in which you did not materially participate, as follows:

   a. If income is reported on line 1, report the income on Schedule E, Part II, column (g). However, if the box in Item H is checked, report the income following the rules for **Publicly traded partnerships** on page 4.

   b. If a loss is reported on line 1, follow the Instructions for Form 8582, to figure how much of the loss can be reported on Schedule E, Part II, column (f). However, if the box in Item H is checked, report the loss following the rules for **Publicly traded partnerships** on page 4.

Line 2. Net Income (Loss) From Rental Real Estate Activities

Generally, the income (loss) reported on line 2 is a passive activity amount for all partners. However, the income (loss) on line 2 is not from a passive activity if you were a real estate professional (defined on page 3) and you materially participated in the activity.

   If you are filing a 2003 Form 1040, use the following instructions to determine where to enter a line 2 amount:

   1. If you have a loss from a passive activity on line 2 and you meet **all** of the following conditions, enter the loss on Schedule E (Form 1040), Part II, column (f).

   a. You actively participated in the partnership rental real estate activities. See **Special allowance for a rental real estate activity** on page 4.

   b. Rental real estate activities with active participation were your only passive activities.

   c. You have no prior year unallowed losses from these activities.

   d. Your total loss from the rental real estate activities was not more than $25,000 (not more than $12,500 if married filing separately and you lived apart from your spouse all year).

   e. If you are a married person filing separately, you lived apart from your spouse all year.

   f. You have no current or prior year unallowed credits from a passive activity.

   g. Your modified adjusted gross income was not more than $100,000 (not more than $50,000 if married filing separately and you lived apart from your spouse all year).

   h. Your interest in the rental real estate activity was **not** held as a limited partner.

   2. If you have a loss from a passive activity on line 2 and you **do not** meet all the conditions in **1** above, report the loss following the Instructions for Form 8582 to figure how much of the loss you can report on Schedule E (Form 1040), Part II, column (f). However, if the box in Item H is checked, report the loss following the rules for **Publicly traded partnerships** on page 4.

   3. If you were a real estate professional and you materially participated in the activity, report line 2 income (loss) on Schedule E (Form 1040), Part II, column (h) or (j).

   4. If you have income from a passive activity on line 2, enter the income on Schedule E, Part II, column (g). However, if the box in Item H is checked, report the income following the rules for **Publicly traded partnerships** on page 4.

Line 3. Net Income (Loss) From Other Rental Activities

The amount on line 3 is a passive activity amount for all partners. Report the income or loss as follows:

   1. If line 3 is a loss, report the loss following the Instructions for Form 8582. However, if the box in Item H is checked, report the loss following the rules for **Publicly traded partnerships** on page 4.

   2. If income is reported on line 3, report the income on Schedule E (Form 1040), Part II, column (g). However, if the box in Item H is checked, report the income following the rules for **Publicly traded partnerships** on page 4.

Lines 4a Through 4f. Portfolio Income (Loss)

Portfolio income or loss is not subject to the passive activity limitations. Portfolio income includes income not derived in the ordinary course of a trade or business from interest, ordinary dividends, annuities, or royalties and gain or loss on the sale of property that produces such income or is held for investment.

   Column (c) of Schedule K-1 tells individual partners where to report this income on Form 1040.

Qualified dividends. Report any qualified dividends on line 9b of Form 1040.

Note: *Qualified dividends are excluded from investment income, but you may elect to include part or all of these amounts in investment income. See the instructions for line 4g of **Form 4952**,*

Investment Interest Expense Deduction, for important information on making this election.

Other portfolio income. The partnership uses line 4f to report portfolio income other than interest, ordinary dividend, royalty, and capital gain (loss) income. It will attach a statement to tell you what kind of portfolio income is reported on line 4f.

If the partnership has a residual interest in a real estate mortgage investment conduit (REMIC), it will report on the statement your share of REMIC taxable income (net loss) that you report on Schedule E (Form 1040), Part IV, column (d). The statement will also report your share of any "excess inclusion" that you report on Schedule E, Part IV, column (c), and your share of section 212 expenses that you report on Schedule E, Part IV, column (e). If you itemize your deductions on Schedule A (Form 1040), you may also deduct these section 212 expenses as a miscellaneous deduction subject to the 2% limit on Schedule A, line 22.

Line 5. Guaranteed Payments to Partners

Generally, amounts on this line are not passive income, and you should report them on Schedule E (Form 1040), Part II, column (j) (for example, guaranteed payments for personal services).

Lines 6a and 6b. Net Section 1231 Gain (Loss) (Other Than Due to Casualty or Theft)

If an amount on line 6a or 6b is from a rental activity, the section 1231 gain (loss) is generally a passive activity amount. Likewise, if the amount is from a trade or business activity and you did not materially participate in the activity, the section 1231 gain (loss) is a passive activity amount.

However, an amount on line 6a or 6b from a rental real estate activity is not from a passive activity if you were a real estate professional (defined on page 3) and you materially participated in the activity.

If the amount on line 6b is either **(a)** a loss that is **not** from a passive activity or **(b)** a gain, report it on line 2, column (g), of **Form 4797**, Sales of Business Property. If any portion of the net section 1231 gain (loss) was generated after May 5, 2003, it will be reported on line 6a. Report this amount on line 2, column (h), of Form 4797. **Do not** complete columns (b) through (f) on line 2. Instead, write "From Schedule K-1 (Form 1065)" across these columns.

If either of the amounts on lines 6a or 6b is a loss from a passive activity, see **Passive loss limitations** in the Instructions for Form 4797. You will need to report the loss following the Instructions for Form 8582 to figure how much of the loss is allowed on Form 4797. However, if the box in Item H is

checked, report the loss following the rules for **Publicly traded partnerships** on page 4.

Any amount of gain from section 1231 property held more than 5 years and sold or otherwise disposed of before May 6, 2003, will be indicated on an attachment to Schedule K-1. Include this amount in your computation of qualified 5-year gain **only** if the amount on your Form 4797, line 7, is more than zero. Report this amount on line 5 of the **Qualified 5-Year Gain Worksheet** in the Schedule D (Form 1040) instructions.

Line 7. Other Income (Loss)

Amounts on this line are other items of income, gain, or loss not included on lines 1 through 6. The partnership should give you a description and the amount of your share for each of these items.

Report loss items that are passive activity amounts to you following the Instructions for Form 8582. However, if the box in Item H is checked, report the loss following the rules for **Publicly traded partnerships** on page 4.

Report income or gain items that are passive activity amounts to you as instructed below. The instructions given below tell you where to report line 7 items if such items are **not** passive activity amounts. Line 7 items may include the following:

• Partnership gains from the disposition of farm recapture property (see Form 4797) and other items to which section 1252 applies.
• Income from recoveries of tax benefit items. A tax benefit item is an amount you deducted in a prior tax year that reduced your income tax. Report this amount on line 21 of Form 1040 to the extent it reduced your tax.
• Gambling gains and losses.

    1. If the partnership was **not** engaged in the trade or business of gambling, **(a)** report gambling winnings on Form 1040, line 21 and **(b)** deduct gambling losses to the extent of winnings on Schedule A, line 27.

    2. If the partnership was engaged in the trade or business of gambling, **(a)** report gambling winnings in Part II of Schedule E and **(b)** deduct gambling losses to the extent of winnings in Part II of Schedule E.

• Any income, gain, or loss to the partnership under section 751(b). Report this amount on Form 4797, line 10.
• Specially allocated ordinary gain (loss). Report this amount on Form 4797, line 10.
• Net gain (loss) from involuntary conversions due to casualty or theft. The partnership will give you a schedule that shows the amounts to be entered on **Form 4684**, Casualties and Thefts, line 34, columns (b)(i), (b)(ii), and (c).
• Net short-term capital gain or loss and net long-term capital gain or loss from Schedule D (Form 1065) that is **not** portfolio income. An example is gain or loss from the disposition of

nondepreciable personal property used in a trade or business activity of the partnership. Report total net short-term gain or loss on Schedule D (Form 1040), line 5, column (f), and the post-May 5, 2003, net short-term gain or loss on Schedule D (Form 1040), line 5, column (g). Report the total net long-term gain or loss on Schedule D (Form 1040), line 12, column (f), and the post-May 5, 2003, net long-term gain or loss on Schedule D (Form 1040), line 12, column (g).

Any amount of long-term capital gain from such property held more than 5 years and sold or otherwise disposed of before May 6, 2003, will be indicated on an attachment to Schedule K-1. Include this amount on line 5 of the worksheet for line 35 of Schedule D (Form 1040).

Any amount of 28% rate gain or loss from collectibles will be indicated on an attachment to Schedule K-1. Include this amount on line 4 of the worksheet for line 20 of Schedule D (Form 1040).

• Any net gain or loss from section 1256 contracts. Report this amount on line 1 of **Form 6781**, Gains and Losses From Section 1256 Contracts and Straddles.
• Gain from the sale or exchange of qualified small business stock (as defined in the Instructions for Schedule D) that is eligible for the partial section 1202 exclusion. The partnership should also give you the name of the corporation that issued the stock, your share of the partnership's adjusted basis and sales price of the stock, and the dates the stock was bought and sold. Corporate partners are not eligible for the section 1202 exclusion. The following additional limitations apply at the partner level:

    1. You must have held an interest in the partnership when the partnership acquired the qualified small business stock and at all times thereafter until the partnership disposed of the qualified small business stock.

    2. Your distributive share of the eligible section 1202 gain cannot exceed the amount that would have been allocated to you based on your interest in the partnership at the time the stock was acquired.

See the Instructions for Schedule D (Form 1040) for details on how to report the gain and the amount of the allowable exclusion.

• Gain eligible for section 1045 rollover (replacement stock purchased by the partnership). The partnership should also give you the name of the corporation that issued the stock, your share of the partnership's adjusted basis and sales price of the stock, and the dates the stock was bought and sold. Corporate partners are not eligible for the section 1045 rollover. To qualify for the section 1045 rollover:

    1. You must have held an interest in the partnership during the entire period in which the partnership held the qualified small business stock (more than 6 months prior to the sale) and

2. Your distributive share of the gain eligible for the section 1045 rollover cannot exceed the amount that would have been allocated to you based on your interest in the partnership at the time the stock was acquired.

See the Instructions for Schedule D (Form 1040) for details on how to report the gain and the amount of the allowable postponed gain.

• Gain eligible for section 1045 rollover (replacement stock not purchased by the partnership). The partnership should also give you the name of the corporation that issued the stock, your share of the partnership's adjusted basis and sales price of the stock, and the dates the stock was bought and sold. Corporate partners are not eligible for the section 1045 rollover. To qualify for the section 1045 rollover:

1. You must have held an interest in the partnership during the entire period in which the partnership held the qualified small business stock (more than 6 months prior to the sale),

2. Your distributive share of the gain eligible for the section 1045 rollover cannot exceed the amount that would have been allocated to you based on your interest in the partnership at the time the stock was acquired, and

3. You must purchase other qualified small business stock (as defined in the Instructions for Schedule D (Form 1040)) during the 60-day period that began on the date the stock was sold by the partnership.

See the Instructions for Schedule D (Form 1040) for details on how to report the gain and the amount of the allowable postponed gain.

Deductions

Line 8. Charitable Contributions

The partnership will give you a schedule that shows the amount of contributions subject to the 50%, 30%, and 20% limitations. For more details, see the Instructions for Schedule A (Form 1040).

If property other than cash is contributed and if the claimed deduction for one item or group of similar items of property exceeds $5,000, the partnership must give you a copy of **Form 8283,** Noncash Charitable Contributions, to attach to your tax return. **Do not** deduct the amount shown on this form. It is the partnership's contribution. Instead, deduct the amount shown on line 8 of your Schedule K-1 (Form 1065).

If the partnership provides you with information that the contribution was property other than cash and does not give you a Form 8283, see the Instructions for Form 8283 for filing requirements. Do not file Form 8283 unless the total claimed deduction for all contributed items of property exceeds $500.

Charitable contribution deductions are not taken into account in figuring your

passive activity loss for the year. Do not enter them on Form 8582.

Line 9. Section 179 Expense Deduction

Use this amount, along with the total cost of section 179 property placed in service during the year from other sources, to complete Part I of **Form 4562,** Depreciation and Amortization. Use Part I of Form 4562 to figure your allowable section 179 expense deduction from all sources. Report the amount on line 12 of Form 4562 allocable to a passive activity from the partnership using the Instructions for Form 8582. However, if the box in Item H is checked, report this amount following the rules for **Publicly traded partnerships** on page 4. If the amount is not a passive activity deduction, report it on Schedule E (Form 1040), Part II, column (i).

Line 10. Deductions Related to Portfolio Income

Amounts entered on this line are deductions that are clearly and directly allocable to portfolio income (other than investment interest expense and section 212 expenses from a REMIC). Generally, you should enter line 10 amounts on Schedule A (Form 1040), line 22. See the Instructions for Schedule A, lines 22 and 27, for more information. However, enter deductions allocable to royalties on Schedule E (Form 1040), line 18. For the type of expense, write "From Schedule K-1 (Form 1065)."

These deductions are not taken into account in figuring your passive activity loss for the year. Do not enter them on Form 8582.

Line 11. Other Deductions

Amounts on this line are deductions not included on lines 8, 9, 10, 17g, and 18b, such as:

• Itemized deductions (Form 1040 filers enter on Schedule A (Form 1040)).

Note: *If there was a gain (loss) from a casualty or theft to property not used in a trade or business or for income-producing purposes, the partnership will notify you. You will have to complete your own Form 4684.*

• Any penalty on early withdrawal of savings.

• Soil and water conservation expenditures. See section 175 for limitations on the amount you are allowed to deduct.

• Expenditures for the removal of architectural and transportation barriers to the elderly and disabled that the partnership elected to treat as a current expense. The deductions are limited by section 190(c) to $15,000 per year from all sources.

• Any amounts paid during the tax year for insurance that constitutes medical care for you, your spouse, and your dependents. On line 29 of Form 1040, you may be allowed to deduct such

amounts, even if you do not itemize deductions. If you do itemize deductions, enter on line 1 of Schedule A (Form 1040) any amounts not deducted on line 29 of Form 1040.

• Payments made on your behalf to an IRA, qualified plan, simplified employee pension (SEP), or a SIMPLE IRA plan. See Form 1040 instructions for line 24 to figure your IRA deduction. Enter payments made to a qualified plan, SEP, or SIMPLE IRA plan on Form 1040, line 30. If the payments to a qualified plan were to a defined benefit plan, the partnership should give you a statement showing the amount of the benefit accrued for the current tax year.

• Interest expense allocated to debt-financed distributions. The manner in which you report such interest expense depends on your use of the distributed debt proceeds. See Notice 89-35, 1989-1 C.B. 675, for details.

• Interest paid or accrued on debt properly allocable to your share of a working interest in any oil or gas property (if your liability is not limited). If you did not materially participate in the oil or gas activity, this interest is investment interest reportable as described on page 9; otherwise, it is trade or business interest.

• Contributions to a capital construction fund (CCF). The deduction for a CCF investment is not taken on Schedule E (Form 1040). Instead, you subtract the deduction from the amount that would normally be entered as taxable income on line 40 (Form 1040). In the margin to the left of line 40, write "CCF" and the amount of the deduction.

The partnership should give you a description and the amount of your share for each of these items.

Credits

If you have credits that are passive activity credits to you, you must complete Form 8582-CR (or Form 8810 for corporations) in addition to the credit forms identified below. See the Instructions for Form 8582-CR (or Form 8810) for more information.

Also, if you are entitled to claim more than one listed general business credit (investment credit, work opportunity credit, welfare-to-work credit, credit for alcohol used as fuel, research credit, low-income housing credit, enhanced oil recovery credit, disabled access credit, renewable electricity production credit, Indian employment credit, credit for employer social security and Medicare taxes paid on certain employee tips, orphan drug credit, and credit for contributions to selected community development corporations), you must complete **Form 3800,** General Business Credit, in addition to the credit forms identified below. If you have more than one credit, see the Instructions for Form 3800.

Line 12a. Low-Income Housing Credit

Your share of the partnership's low-income housing credit is shown on line 12a. Any allowable credit is entered on **Form 8586**, Low-Income Housing Credit.

The partnership will report separately on line 12a(1) that portion of the low-income housing credit to which section 42(j)(5) applies. All other low-income housing credits will be reported on line 12a(2).

If part or all of the credit reported on line 12a(1) or 12a(2) is attributable to additions to qualified basis of property placed in service before 1990, the partnership will attach a statement to tell you the amount of the credit on each line that is attributable to property placed in service **(a)** before 1990 and **(b)** after 1989.

Keep a separate record of the amount of low-income housing credit from each of these sources so that you can correctly compute any recapture of low-income housing credit that may result from the disposition of all or part of your partnership interest. For more information, see the instructions for Form 8586.

Line 12b. Qualified Rehabilitation Expenditures Related to Rental Real Estate Activities

The partnership should identify your share of the partnership's rehabilitation expenditures from each rental real estate activity. Enter the expenditures on the appropriate line of **Form 3468**, Investment Credit, to figure your allowable credit.

Line 12c. Credits (Other Than Credits Shown on Lines 12a and 12b) Related to Rental Real Estate Activities

The partnership will identify the type of credit and any other information you need to compute credits from rental real estate activities (other than the low-income housing credit and qualified rehabilitation expenditures).

Line 12d. Credits Related to Other Rental Activities

The partnership will identify the type of credit and any other information you need to compute credits from rental activities other than rental real estate activities.

Line 13. Other Credits

The partnership will identify the type of credit and any other information you need to compute credits other than on lines 12a through 12d. Expenditures qualifying for the **(a)** rehabilitation credit from other than rental real estate activities, **(b)** energy credit, or **(c)** reforestation credit will be reported to you on line 25.

Credits that may be reported on line 12c, 12d, or 13 (depending on the type of activity they relate to) include the following:
- Credit for backup withholding on dividends, interest income, and other types of income. Include the amount the partnership reports to you in the total that you enter on Form 1040, line 61.
- Nonconventional source fuel credit. Enter this credit on a schedule you prepare yourself to determine the allowed credit to take on your tax return. See section 29 for rules on how to figure the credit.
- Qualified electric vehicle credit (Form 8834).
- Unused credits from cooperatives.
- Work opportunity credit (Form 5884).
- Welfare-to-work credit (Form 8861).
- Credit for alcohol used as fuel (Form 6478).
- Credit for increasing research activities (Form 6765).
- Enhanced oil recovery credit (Form 8830).
- Disabled access credit (Form 8826).
- Renewable electricity production credit (Form 8835).
- Empowerment zone and renewal community employment credit (Form 8844).
- Indian employment credit (Form 8845).
- Credit for employer social security and Medicare taxes paid on certain employee tips (Form 8846).
- Orphan drug credit (Form 8820).
- New markets credit (Form 8874).
- Credit for small employer pension plan startup costs (Form 8881).
- Credit for employer-provided child care facilities and services (Form 8882).
- New York Liberty Zone business employee credit (Form 8884).
- Credit for contributions to selected community development corporations (Form 8847).
- General credits from an electing large partnership. Report these credits on Form 3800, line 1r.
- Qualified zone academy bond credit (Form 8860).

Investment Interest

If the partnership paid or accrued interest on debts properly allocable to investment property, the amount of interest you are allowed to deduct may be limited.

For more information and the special provisions that apply to investment interest expense, see **Form 4952**, Investment Interest Expense Deduction, and **Pub. 550**, Investment Income and Expenses.

Line 14a. Interest Expense on Investment Debts

Enter this amount on Form 4952, line 1, along with your investment interest expense from Schedule K-1, line 11, if any, and from other sources to figure how much of your total investment interest is deductible.

Lines 14b(1) and 14b(2). Investment Income and Investment Expenses

Use the amounts on these lines to figure the amounts to enter in Part II of Form 4952.

⚠️ *The amounts shown on lines 14b(1) and 14b(2) include only investment income and expenses included on lines 4a, 4b(2), 4c, 4f, and 10 of this Schedule K-1. The partnership should attach a schedule that shows the amount of any investment income and expenses included on any other lines of this Schedule K-1. Be sure to take these amounts into account, along with the amounts on lines 14b(1) and 14b(2) and your investment income and expenses from other sources, when figuring the amounts to enter in Part II of Form 4952.*

Self-Employment

If you and your spouse are both partners, each of you must complete and file your own **Schedule SE (Form 1040)**, Self-Employment Tax, to report your partnership net earnings (loss) from self-employment.

Line 15a. Net Earnings (Loss) From Self-Employment

If you are a general partner, reduce this amount before entering it on Schedule SE (Form 1040) by any section 179 expense deduction claimed, unreimbursed partnership expenses claimed, and depletion claimed on oil and gas properties. **Do not** reduce net earnings from self-employment by any separately stated deduction for health insurance expenses.

If the amount on this line is a loss, enter only the deductible amount on Schedule SE (Form 1040). See **Limitations on Losses, Deductions, and Credits** beginning on page 2.

If your partnership is an options dealer or a commodities dealer, see section 1402(i).

If your partnership is an investment club, see Rev. Rul. 75-525, 1975-2 C.B. 350.

Line 15b. Gross Farming or Fishing Income

If you are an individual partner, enter the amount from this line, as an item of information, on Schedule E (Form 1040), Part V, line 42. Also use this amount to figure net earnings from self-employment under the farm optional method on Schedule SE (Form 1040), Section B, Part II.

Line 15c. Gross Nonfarm Income

If you are an individual partner, use this amount to figure net earnings from self-employment under the nonfarm optional method on Schedule SE (Form 1040), Section B, Part II.

Adjustments and Tax Preference Items

Use the information reported on lines 16a through 16e (as well as your adjustments and tax preference items from other sources) to prepare your **Form 6251**, Alternative Minimum Tax—Individuals; **Form 4626**, Alternative Minimum Tax—Corporations; or Schedule I of **Form 1041**, U.S. Income Tax Return for Estates and Trusts.

Note: *A partner that is a corporation subject to alternative minimum tax must notify the partnership of its status.*

Lines 16d(1) and 16d(2). Gross Income From, and Deductions Allocable to, Oil, Gas, and Geothermal Properties

The amounts reported on these lines include only the gross income from, and deductions allocable to, oil, gas, and geothermal properties that are included on line 1 of Schedule K-1. The partnership should have attached a schedule that shows any income from or deductions allocable to such properties that are included on lines 2 through 11 and line 25 of Schedule K-1. Use the amounts reported on lines 16d(1) and 16d(2) and the amounts on the attached schedule to help you figure the net amount to enter on line 25 of Form 6251 (line 22 of Schedule I, Form 1041; line 2n of Form 4626).

Line 16e. Other Adjustments and Tax Preference Items

Enter the information on the schedule attached by the partnership for line 16e on the applicable lines of Form 6251, Form 4626, or Schedule I of Form 1041.

Foreign Taxes

Use the information on lines 17a through 17h and attached schedules to figure your foreign tax credit. For more information, see **Form 1116**, Foreign Tax Credit (Individual, Estate, Trust, or Nonresident Alien Individual), and its instructions; **Form 1118**, Foreign Tax Credit—Corporations, and its instructions; and **Pub. 514**, Foreign Tax Credit for Individuals.

Other

Lines 18a and 18b. Section 59(e)(2) Expenditures

The partnership will show on line 18a the type of qualified expenditures to which an election under section 59(e) may apply. It will identify the amount of the expenditure on line 18b. If there is more than one type of expenditure, the amount of each type will be listed on an attachment.

Generally, section 59(e) allows each partner to elect to deduct certain expenses ratably over the number of years in the applicable period rather than deduct the full amount in the current year. Under the election, you may deduct

circulation expenditures ratably over a 3-year period. Research and experimental expenditures and mining exploration and development costs qualify for a writeoff period of 10 years. Intangible drilling and development costs may be deducted over a 60-month period, beginning with the month in which such costs were paid or incurred.

If you make this election, these items are not treated as adjustments or tax preference items for purposes of the alternative minimum tax. Make the election on Form 4562.

Because each partner decides whether to make the election under section 59(e), the partnership cannot provide you with the amount of the adjustment or tax preference item related to the expenses listed on line 18b. You must decide both how to claim the expenses on your return and compute the resulting adjustment or tax preference item.

Line 19. Tax-Exempt Interest Income

You must report on your return, as an item of information, your share of the tax-exempt interest received or accrued by the partnership during the year. Individual partners must include this amount on Form 1040, line 8b. Increase the adjusted basis of your interest in the partnership by this amount.

Line 20. Other Tax-Exempt Income

Increase the adjusted basis of your interest in the partnership by the amount shown on line 20, but do not include it in income on your tax return.

Line 21. Nondeductible Expenses

The nondeductible expenses paid or incurred by the partnership are not deductible on your tax return. Decrease the adjusted basis of your interest in the partnership by this amount.

Line 22. Distributions of Money (Cash and Marketable Securities)

Line 22 shows the distributions the partnership made to you of cash and certain marketable securities. The marketable securities are included at their fair market value (FMV) on the date of distribution (minus your share of the partnership's gain on the securities distributed to you). If the amount shown on line 22 exceeds the adjusted basis of your partnership interest immediately before the distribution, the excess is treated as gain from the sale or exchange of your partnership interest. Generally, this gain is treated as gain from the sale of a capital asset and should be reported on the Schedule D for your return. However, the gain may be ordinary income. For details, see Pub. 541.

The partnership will separately identify both of the following:

• The FMV of the marketable securities when distributed (minus your share of the gain on the securities distributed to you).
• The partnership's adjusted basis of those securities immediately before the distribution.

Decrease the adjusted basis of your interest in the partnership (but not below zero) by the amount of cash distributed to you and the partnership's adjusted basis of the distributed securities. Advances or drawings of money or property against your distributive share are treated as current distributions made on the last day of the partnership's tax year.

Your basis in the distributed marketable securities (other than in liquidation of your interest) is the **smaller** of:
• The partnership's adjusted basis in the securities immediately before the distribution increased by any gain recognized on the distribution of the securities or
• The adjusted basis of your partnership interest reduced by any cash distributed in the same transaction and increased by any gain recognized on the distribution of the securities.

If you received the securities in liquidation of your partnership interest, your basis in the marketable securities is equal to the adjusted basis of your partnership interest reduced by any cash distributed in the same transaction and increased by any gain recognized on the distribution of the securities.

If, within 5 years of a distribution to you of marketable securities, you contributed appreciated property (other than those securities) to the partnership and the FMV of those securities exceeded the adjusted basis of your partnership interest immediately before the distribution (reduced by any cash received in the distribution), you may have to recognize gain on the appreciated property. For property contributed after June 8, 1997, the 5-year period is generally extended to 7 years. See section 737 for details.

Line 23. Distributions of Property Other Than Money

Line 23 shows the partnership's adjusted basis of property other than money immediately before the property was distributed to you. In addition, the partnership should report the adjusted basis and FMV of each property distributed. Decrease the adjusted basis of your interest in the partnership by the amount of your basis in the distributed property. Your basis in the distributed property (other than in liquidation of your interest) is the **smaller** of:
• The partnership's adjusted basis immediately before the distribution or
• The adjusted basis of your partnership interest reduced by any cash distributed in the same transaction.

If you received the property in liquidation of your interest, your basis in the distributed property is equal to the adjusted basis of your partnership interest

     Partner's Instructions for Schedule K-1 (Form 1065)

reduced by any cash distributed in the same transaction.

If you contributed appreciated property to the partnership within 5 years of a distribution of other property to you, and the FMV of the other property exceeded the adjusted basis of your partnership interest immediately before the distribution (reduced by any cash received in the distribution), you may have to recognize gain on the appreciated property. For property contributed after June 8, 1997, the 5-year period is generally extended to 7 years. See section 737 for details.

Lines 24a and 24b. Recapture of Low-Income Housing Credit

A section 42(j)(5) partnership will report recapture of a low-income housing credit on line 24a. All other partnerships will report recapture of a low-income housing credit on line 24b. Keep a separate record of recapture from each of these sources so that you will be able to correctly compute any recapture of low-income housing credit that may result from the disposition of all or part of your partnership interest. For more information, see **Form 8611**, Recapture of Low-Income Housing Credit.

Supplemental Information

Line 25

Amounts shown on line 25 include:

1. Taxes paid on undistributed capital gains by a regulated investment company or real estate investment trust. Form 1040 filers enter your share of these taxes on line 67, check the box for Form 2439, and add the words "Form 1065."

2. Number of gallons of each fuel sold or used during the tax year for a nontaxable use qualifying for the credit for taxes paid on fuels, type of use, and the applicable credit per gallon. Use this information to complete **Form 4136**, Credit for Federal Tax Paid on Fuels.

3. Your share of gross income from the property, share of production for the tax year, etc., needed to figure your depletion deduction for oil and gas wells. The partnership should also allocate to you a share of the adjusted basis of each partnership oil or gas property. See Pub. 535 for how to figure your depletion deduction.

4. Your distributive share of gain or loss on the sale, exchange, or other disposition of property for which a section 179 expense deduction was passed through to partners. If the partnership passed through a section 179 expense deduction to its partners for the property, you must report the gain or loss and any recapture of the section 179 expense deduction for the property on your income tax return (see the instructions for Form 4797 for details). The partnership must provide all the following information with respect to a disposition of property for which a section 179 expense deduction was passed through to partners.

a. Description of the property.
b. Date the property was acquired.
c. Date of the sale or other disposition of the property.
d. Your distributive share of the gross sales price.
e. Your distributive share of the cost or other basis plus the expense of sale (reduced as explained in the instructions for Form 4797, line 21).
f. Your distributive share of the depreciation allowed or allowable, determined as described in the instructions or Form 4797, line 22, but excluding the section 179 expense deduction.
g. Your distributive share of the section 179 expense deduction passed through for the property and the partnership's tax year(s) in which the amount was passed through. To compute the amount of depreciation allowed or allowable for Form 4797, line 22, add to the amount from item **f** above the amount of your distributive share of the section 179 expense deduction, reduced by any unused carryover of the deduction for this property. This amount may be different than the amount of section 179 expense you deducted for the property if your interest in the partnership has changed.
h. An indication if the disposition is from a casualty or theft (see **Form 4684**, Casualty and Theft, for more information).
i. If this is an installment sale, any information you need to complete **Form 6252**, Installment Sale Income.

5. Recapture of section 179 expense deduction if business use of any property for which the section 179 expense deduction was passed through to partners dropped to 50 percent or less. If business use of the property dropped to 50 percent or less, the partnership must provide all the following information.

a. Your distributive share of the depreciation allowed or allowable (not including the section 179 expense deduction).
b. Your distributive share of the section 179 expense deduction (if any) passed through for the property and the partnership's tax year(s) in which the amount was passed through. Reduce this amount by the portion, if any, of your unused (carryover) section 179 expense deduction for this property.

6. Recapture of certain mining exploration expenditures (section 617).

7. Any information or statements you need to comply with section 6111 (regarding tax shelters) or section 6662(d)(2)(B)(ii) (regarding adequate disclosure of items that may cause an understatement of income tax on your return).

8. Preproductive period farm expenses. You may be eligible to elect to deduct these expenses currently or capitalize them under section 263A. See **Pub. 225**, Farmer's Tax Guide, and Regulations section 1.263A-4.

9. Any information you need to figure the interest due under section 453(l)(3)

with respect to the disposition of certain timeshares and residential lots on the installment method. If you are an individual, report the interest on Form 1040, line 60. Write "453(l)(3)" and the amount of the interest on the dotted line to the left of line 60.

10. Any information you need to figure the interest due under section 453A(c) with respect to certain installment sales. If you are an individual, report the interest on Form 1040, line 60. Write "453A(c)" and the amount of the interest on the dotted line to the left of line 60.

11. Any information you need to figure the interest due or to be refunded under the look-back method of section 460(b)(2) on certain long-term contracts. Use **Form 8697**, Interest Computation Under the Look-Back Method for Completed Long-Term Contracts, to report any such interest.

12. Any information you need relating to interest expense that you are required to capitalize under section 263A for production expenditures. See Regulations sections 1.263A-8 through 1.263A-15 for more information.

13. Any information you need to figure unrelated business taxable income under section 512(a)(1) (but excluding any modifications required by paragraphs (8) through (15) of section 512(b)) for a partner that is a tax-exempt organization.

Reminder: *A partner is required to notify the partnership of its tax-exempt status.*

14. Your share of expenditures qualifying for the **(a)** rehabilitation credit from other than rental real estate activities, **(b)** energy credit, or **(c)** reforestation credit. Enter the expenditures on the appropriate line of Form 3468 to figure your allowable credit.

15. Any information you need to figure your recapture tax on **Form 4255**, Recapture of Investment Credit. See the Form 3468 on which you took the original credit for other information you need to complete Form 4255.

You may also need Form 4255 if you disposed of more than one-third of your interest in a partnership.

16. Any information you need to figure your recapture of the qualified electric vehicle credit. See Pub. 535 for details, including how to figure the recapture.

17. Recapture of new markets credit (see Form 8874).

18. Any information you need to figure your recapture of the Indian employment credit. Generally, if the partnership terminated a qualified employee less than 1 year after the date of initial employment, any Indian employment credit allowed for a prior tax year by reason of wages paid or incurred to that employee must be recaptured. For details, see section 45A(d).

19. Nonqualified withdrawals by the partnership from a CCF. These withdrawals are taxed separately from your other gross income at the highest marginal ordinary income or capital gain tax rate. Attach a statement to your

Federal income tax return to show your computation of both the tax and interest for a nonqualified withdrawal. Include the tax and interest on Form 1040, line 60. To the left of line 60, write the amount of tax and interest and "CCF."

20. Unrecaptured section 1250 gain. Generally, report this amount on line 5 of the **Unrecaptured Section 1250 Gain Worksheet** in the Schedule D (Form 1040) instructions. However, for an amount passed through from an estate, trust, real estate investment trust, or regulated investment company, report it on line 11 of that worksheet. Report on line 10 of that worksheet any gain from the partnership's sale or exchange of an interest in another partnership that is attributable to unrecaptured section 1250 gain.

21. Your share of any collectibles gain or loss. Include this amount on line 4 of the worksheet for Schedule D (Form 1040), line 20.

22. Any information you need to figure qualified 5-year gain. Include on line 5 of the worksheet for Schedule D (Form 1040), line 35, qualified 5-year gain from portfolio income. Take into account any qualified 5-year gain from section 1231 property when completing line 2 of that worksheet, as if it were included in Part I of Form 4797 (but only if line 7, column (g), of your Form 4797 is greater than zero).

23. Any information you need to figure the interest due or to be refunded under the look-back method of section 167(g)(2) for certain property placed in service after September 13, 1995, and depreciated under the income forecast method. Use **Form 8866,** Interest Computation Under the Look-Back Method for Property Depreciated Under the Income Forecast Method, to report any such interest.

24. Any information a publicly traded partnership needs to determine whether it meets the 90% qualifying income test of section 7704(c)(2).

Reminder: *A partner is required to notify the partnership of its status as a publicly traded partnership.*

25. Amortizable basis of reforestation expenses and the year paid or incurred. To figure your allowable amortization, including limits that may apply, see section 194 and Pub. 535. Follow the Instructions for Form 8582 to report amortization allocable to a passive activity. However, if the box in Item H is checked, report the amortization following the rules for **Publicly traded partnerships** on page 4. Report amortization from a trade or business activity in which you materially participated on a separate line in Part II, column (h), of Schedule E (Form 1040).

26. Any information you need to figure the interest due under section 1260(b). If the partnership had gain from certain constructive ownership transactions, your tax liability must be increased by the interest charge on any deferral of gain recognition under section 1260(b). Report the interest on Form 1040, line 60. Write "1260(b)" and the amount of the interest on the dotted line to the left of line 60. See section 1260(b) for details, including how to figure the interest.

27. Extraterritorial income exclusion:

a. *Partnership did not claim the exclusion.* If the partnership reports your distributive share of foreign trading gross receipts and the extraterritorial income exclusion, the partnership was not entitled to claim the exclusion because it did not meet the foreign economic process requirements. You may qualify for your distributive share of this exclusion because the partnership's foreign trading gross receipts for the tax year were $5 million or less. To qualify for this exclusion, your foreign trading gross receipts from all sources for the tax year also must have been $5 million or less. See **Form 8873,** Extraterritorial Income Exclusion, for more information. If you qualify for the exclusion, report the exclusion amount in accordance with the instructions for **Income (Loss)** on page 6 for line 1, 2, or 3, whichever applies.

b. *Partnership claimed the exclusion.* If the partnership reports your distributive

share of foreign trading gross receipts but not the amount of the extraterritorial income exclusion, the partnership met the foreign economic process requirements and claimed the exclusion when figuring your distributive share of partnership income. You also may need to know the amount of your distributive share of foreign trading gross receipts from this partnership to determine if you met the $5 million or less exception discussed above for purposes of qualifying for an extraterritorial income exclusion from other sources.

Note: *Upon request, the partnership should furnish you a copy of the partnership's Form 8873 if there is a reduction for international boycott operations, illegal bribes, kickbacks, etc.*

28. Commercial revitalization deduction from rental real estate activities. Follow the instructions on Form 8582 for commercial revitalization deductions from rental real estate activities to figure how much of the deduction can be reported on Schedule E, Part II, column (f).

29. Any information you need to disclose certain reportable transactions in which the partnership participates. If the partnership participates in a transaction that must be disclosed on **Form 8886,** Reportable Transaction Disclosure Statement, both the partnership and its partners may be required to file Form 8886 for the transaction. The determination of whether you are required to disclose a partnership transaction is based on the category(s) under which the transaction qualified for disclosure. See the Instructions for Form 8886 for details.

30. Recapture of the credit for employer-provided child care facilities and services (Form 8882).

31. Any other information you may need to file your return not shown elsewhere on Schedule K-1.

The partnership should give you a description and the amount of your share for each of these items.

Index

†